INTERNATIONAL LAW IN
DOMESTIC LEGAL ORDERS

Series Editors

ANDRÉ NOLLKAEMPER

Professor of Public International Law at the University of Amsterdam

AUGUST REINISCH

Professor of International and European Law at the University of Vienna

The Engagement of Domestic Courts with International Law

INTERNATIONAL LAW IN DOMESTIC LEGAL ORDERS

The topic of international law in domestic legal orders has risen in prominence since the end of the Cold War. Recent decades have witnessed a tremendous increase in international agreements on various subjects, impacting on domestic law and proving to be relevant to domestic litigation. These changes mean that domestic courts have the potential to make a greater contribution to the application and development of international law. This series analyses and examines these trends, looking at questions of international law in domestic legal orders from a variety of perspectives.

OTHER BOOKS PUBLISHED IN THIS SERIES

Justice and Memory after Dictatorship
Latin America, Central Eastern Europe, and the Fragmentation of International Criminal Law
Raluca Grosescu

The UN Convention on the Rights of Persons with Disabilities in Practice
A Comparative Analysis of the Role of Courts
Edited by Lisa Waddington and Anna Lawson

Legal Monism
Law, Philosophy, and Politics
Paul Gragl

The Interpretation of International Law by Domestic Courts
Uniformity, Diversity, Convergence
Edited by Helmut Philipp Aust and Georg Nolte

Domestic Application of the ECHR
Courts as Faithful Trustees
Eirik Bjorge

The Role of National Courts in Applying International Humanitarian Law
Sharon Weill
The Privileges and Immunities of International

Organizations in Domestic Courts
Edited by August Reinisch

The Engagement of Domestic Courts with International Law

Comparative Perspectives

Edited by

ANDRÉ NOLLKAEMPER, YUVAL SHANY, AND
ANTONIOS TZANAKOPOULOS

Assistant Editor
ELENI METHYMAKI

OXFORD
UNIVERSITY PRESS

OXFORD
UNIVERSITY PRESS

Great Clarendon Street, Oxford, OX2 6DP,
United Kingdom

Oxford University Press is a department of the University of Oxford.
It furthers the University's objective of excellence in research, scholarship,
and education by publishing worldwide. Oxford is a registered trade mark of
Oxford University Press in the UK and in certain other countries

Published in the United States of America by Oxford University Press
198 Madison Avenue, New York, NY 10016, United States of America

British Library Cataloguing in Publication Data

Data available

Library of Congress Control Number: 2023948543

ISBN 978–0–19–286418–5

DOI: 10.1093/law/9780192864185.001.0001

Printed and bound by
CPI Group (UK) Ltd, Croydon, CR0 4YY

Preface

Against the background of an already sizeable body of literature on the role of domestic courts in the international legal order, the present volume seeks to break new ground by advancing and developing a new paradigm for describing, assessing, and understanding this role of domestic courts. This new paradigm is one of pragmatic engagement, replacing the older, binary, and doctrinal paradigms of monism and dualism.

The volume is driven by two parallel trends that can be witnessed across the world. On the one hand, the traditional dividing lines between national and international law norms and institutions have blurred to a considerable extent. On the other hand, the practice of domestic courts that operate in this new context can less and less be understood by reference to a formal approach that dictates how national legal orders receive international law.

The solutions that courts reach are often based on a variety of other considerations that are not captured by the classical formal models. The aim of the volume is to bring together the wide variety of types of engagement, as an important step towards a better understanding of what courts do and, eventually, to a normative exercise of articulating principles or guidelines for the engagement of domestic courts with international law.

To bring together the pragmatic approaches of domestic courts, between 2011 and 2016 a Study Group of the International Law Association (*Study Group on Principles on the Engagement of Domestic Courts with International Law*) engaged in studies of and discussions with experts from a large variety of different jurisdictions. It laid down the results of this work in its 2016 Final Report, *Mapping the Engagement of Domestic Courts with International Law*. On the basis of the final Report, the editors of the present volume continued to work with experts from different jurisdictions to collect and analyse different pragmatic forms of engagement by domestic courts. This volume contains the outcome of this process.

The volume starts with the chapter *Engagement of Domestic Courts with International Law: Principled or Unprincipled?* that brings together and develops the main outcomes of the work of the ILA Study Group. The full Final ILA Report is annexed to the present volume for further reference. This chapter presents the analytical typology that is used to uncover and discuss the practice of courts in individual jurisdictions in Parts A and B.

Part A contains thirteen case-studies, spanning all continents. While these thirteen studies of course represent only part of the practice of domestic courts across the world, they have been selected based on a diversity of formal constructions of the relationship between international and national law, and provide a richness of different practices of engagement.

Part B contains four chapters discussing the engagement of domestic courts in different thematic fields. This practice is not limited to the jurisdictions discussed in Part A, and thus presents a wider picture of relevant domestic practices.

This volume is to be seen as one further building block in a continuous process in which the practice of domestic courts across the world evolves, and at the same time, our understanding of what these practices are and how they should be assessed evolves. In this respect, the volume calls for further studies—both of an empirical nature to advance our understanding of what courts actually do and what impact different forms of engagement make, and of a normative nature, by articulating principle or guidelines that articulate what courts should do.

We thank all the experts who, as authors of studies prepared for the ILA Study Group, or as participants in meetings organized by the Study Group have contributed to the final result. In particular, we thank Eleni Methymaki and Tal Gross for their editorial work on the volume, and the ILA for lending its support to the research.

André Nollkaemper
Yuval Shany
Antonios Tzanakopoulos

Contents

Table of Cases xi
List of Abbreviations xxxv
List of Contributors xxxix

PART 1: INTRODUCTION

1. Engagement of Domestic Courts with International Law: Principled or Unprincipled? 3
André Nollkaemper, Yuval Shany, and Antonios Tzanakopoulos
A. Introduction 3
B. The Premise of the ILA Study 6
C. The Legal Context for Engagement 9
D. The Main Patterns of Engagement 12
E. Concluding Remarks 15

PART 2: NATIONAL AND REGIONAL THEMES

2. Engagement of Domestic Courts with International Law in Anglophone Africa 19
Magnus Killander
A. Introduction 19
B. Ratified Treaties 20
C. Unratified Treaties, Comparative Case Law, and Soft Law 30
D. Customary International Law 32
E. Hierarchy 33
F. Conclusion 35

3. Engagement of South African Domestic Courts with International Law 37
Hannah Woolaver
A. Introduction 37
B. Relevant Constitutional Provisions 38
C. Techniques of Alignment 40
D. Techniques of Avoidance 49
E. Conclusion 55

4. Engagement of Chinese Courts with International Law 57
Dai Ruijun
A. Introduction 57
B. The Status of International Treaties in the Chinese Legal System 57
C. The Practice of Chinese Courts 62
D. Conclusion 77

5. Engagement of Israel's Supreme Court with International Law 79
Osnat Grady Schwartz
A. The Status of International Law in the Israeli Legal System 79
B. What Determines the Engagement of the Israeli Supreme Court with International Law? 80
C. The Practice of the Israeli Supreme Court 82
D. Conclusion 95

6. Engagement of Sri Lanka's Supreme Court with International Law in its Fundamental Rights Jurisdiction 97
Dakshinie Ruwanthika Gunaratne
A. Introduction 97
B. The Status of International Law in the Sri Lankan Legal System 98
C. Engagement with International Law 106
D. Conclusion 115

7. Engagement of Argentina's Supreme Court with International Law 117
Mónica Pinto and Nahuel Maisley
A. Introduction 117
B. The Era of Affirmative Avoidance (1853–1992) 118
C. The Era of Transition (1992–1994) 120
D. The Era of Overriding Alignment (1994–2017) 121
E. A New Era, or Simply a Pause? (2017) 133
F. Conclusion 140

8. Engagement of Canadian Courts with International Law 143
Gib van Ert
A. Introduction 143
B. The Status of International Law in the Canadian Legal System 144
C. Engagement with International Law in Canadian Practice 151
D. Conclusion 163

9. Engagement of United States Courts with International Law 165
David Sloss
A. Introduction 165
B. International Law in the United States Legal System 165
C. Practice of United States Courts 170
D. Conclusion 184

10. Engagement of Albanian Courts with International Law 187
Gentian Zyberi and Semir Sali
A. Introduction 187
B. The Status of International Law in the Albanian Legal System 189
C. The Practice of Albanian Courts 191
D. Conclusion 206

11. Engagement of Belgian Courts with International Law 209
Frédéric Dopagne
A. General Features of the Constitutional Framework in Belgium 209
B. Alignment Techniques 212
C. Avoidance Techniques 219
D. Contestation Techniques 223
E. Conclusion 225

12. Engagement of English Courts with International Law 227
Shaheed Fatima KC
A. Increasing Engagement of English Courts with International Law 227
B. Practice of English Courts 230
C. Blunting/Moderating Techniques and Foreign Relations 243
D. Conclusion 244

13. Engagement of Kosovo's Domestic (Internationalized) Courts with International Law 245
Zane Ratniece
A. Introduction 245
B. Internationalization of Kosovo Domestic Courts 246
C. Practice of Kosovo Domestic Courts 251
D. Conclusion 267

14. Engagement of Swiss Courts with International Law 271
Eva Maria Belser and Rekha Oleschak-Pillai
A. Introduction 271
B. The Status of International Law in the Swiss Legal Order 273
C. Avoiding Engagement of Courts with International Law 277
D. Aligning Statutory Law with International Law—or Refusing to Do So 280
E. Muddling through the Jungle of Non-Aligned Constitutional Law 285
F. Conclusion 288

PART 3: CROSS-CUTTING THEMES

15. Engagement of Domestic Courts with the Findings of United Nations Human Rights Treaty Monitoring Bodies 293
Machiko Kanetake
A. Introduction 293

B. The Practice of Domestic Courts 294
C. Bindingness as Normative Basis for Judicial Engagement 301
D. Persuasiveness as Normative Basis for Judicial Engagement 304
E. Conclusion 308

16. A Paradoxical Engagement: International Investment Law and Arbitration before Domestic Courts 311
Andreas Kulick and Joel Dahlquist
A. Introduction: Two Paradoxes 311
B. Instruments of Alignment: Enforcement and Beyond 315
C. Instruments of Contestation: Challenge and Beyond 316
D. European Union Law and International Investment Law before Domestic and EU Courts 321
E. International Investment Arbitration, Domestic Courts, and General International Law—Towards the Second Paradox 324
F. Conclusion 328

17. Engagement of Domestic Courts with International Humanitarian Law 333
Sharon Weill
A. Introduction 333
B. Misuse of the Law—the Apologist Role of Courts 334
C. The Use of Avoidance Doctrines 337
D. Deference to the Executive 340
E. Normative Application of the Law: Alignment with International Humanitarian Law 343
F. Activism in Domestic Courts 345
G. Conclusion 347

18. 'Amp Up and Amplify: Defy!': Engagement of Domestic Courts with International Sanctions 349
Eleni Methymaki and Antonios Tzanakopoulos
A. Introduction 349
B. Terminological Clarifications and Legal Framework 351
C. Alignment(-*cum*-Contestation) 354
D. Contestation(-*cum*-Alignment) 362
E. Conclusion 367

Annex 371
International Law Association Johannesburg Conference (2016): (Study Group on) Principles on the Engagement of Domestic Courts with International Law 371
Index 403

Table of Cases

INTERNATIONAL COURTS & TRIBUNALS

European Court of Human Rights

Al-Dulimi and Montana Management Inc v Switzerland (GC), App no 5809/08, 21 June 2016 .... 357–58, 367–68, 393–94
Ashingdane v the United Kingdom, App no 8225/78, 28 May 1985 200–1
Barberà, Messegué and Jabardo v Spain, App no 10590/83, 6 December 1988 193
Belilos v Switzerland, App no 10328/83, 29 April 1988 277–78
Bosphorus Hava Yolları Turizm ve Ticaret Anonim Şirketi v Ireland (GC), App no 45036/98, 30 June 2005 363–64
Burghartz v Switzerland, App no 16213/90, 22 February 1994 281
Cudak v Lithuania, App no 15869/02, 23 March 2010 201–2
Grori v Albania, App no 25336/04, 7 July 2009 197–99
Hertel v Switzerland, App no 59/1997/843/1049, 25 August 1998 281–82
Jelić v Croatia, App no 57856/11, 12 June 2014 266
Losonci Rose et Rose c Suisse, App no 664/06, 9 November 2010 281
Lyons and Others v United Kingdom, App no 15227/03, 8 July 2003 (Decision on Admissibility) 195
M and Others v Croatia, App no 50175/12, 2 May 2017 266
Nada v Switzerland (GC), App no 10593/08, 12 September 2012 365
Sabeh El Leil v France, App no 34869/05, 29 June 2011 201–2
Van Marle v Netherlands, App nos 8543/79, 8674/79, 8675/79, 8685/79, 26 June 1986 87–88
Van Mechelen and Others v The Netherlands, App nos 55/1996/674/861-864, 23 April 1997 193
Verein gegen Tierfabriken v Switzerland, App no 24699/94, 28 June 2001 281–82
Verein Gegen Tierfabriken Schweiz v Switzerland, App no 32772/02, 30 June 2009 281–82
Waite and Kennedy v Germany, App nos 26083/94 and 28934/95, 18 February 1999 223–24
Wallishauser v Austria, App no 156/04, 19 November 2012 201–2
Xheraj v Albania, App no 37959/02, 29 July 2008 .... 193–95, 206–7

European Union courts

Court of Justice of the European Union

C-284/16 Slovak Republic v Achmea BV [2018] ECLI:EU:C:2018:158 and Opinion of Advocate General Wathelet [2017] ECLI:EU:C:2017:699 321–22
C-457/09 Claude Chartry v Belgian State [2011] ECR I-00819 220
C-264/09 Commission v Slovak Republic [2011] ECR I-08065 321
C-205/06 Commission v Republic of Austria [2009] ECR I-01301 321
C-249/06 Commission v Kingdom of Sweden [2009] ECR I-01335 321
C-402/05P and C-415/05P Yassin Abdullah Kadi and Al Barakaat International Foundation v Council of the European Union and Commission of the European Communities [2008] ECLI: EU:2008:461 234

Advisory Opinions

Opinion 2/15 (2017) ECLI:EU:C:2017:376 322
Opinion 2/13 (2014) ECLI:EU:C:2014:2454 321–22

General Court

T-315/01 Yassin Abdullah Kadi v Council of the European Union and Commission of the European Communities [2005] ECLI:EU:T:2005:332 365

International Court of Justice

Accordance with International Law of the Unilateral Declaration of Independence in respect of Kosovo (Advisory Opinion) [2010] ICJ Rep 403 245
Ahmadou Sadio Diallo (Republic of Guinea v Democratic Republic of the Congo) (Merits) [2010] ICJ Rep 639 . . . . 23, 308–9
Alleged Violations of the 1955 Treaty of Amity, Economic Relations, and Consular Rights (Iran v USA) (Preliminary Objections) [2021] ICJ Rep 9 . . . . 213–14, 349–50
Appeal relating to the Jurisdiction of the ICAO Council under Article 8, Section 2, of the 1944 International Air Services Transit Agreement (Bahrain, Egypt, and UAE v Qatar) (Judgment) [2020] ICJ Rep 172 349–50
Appeal relating to the Jurisdiction of the ICAO Council under Article 84 of the Convention on International Civil Aviation (Bahrain, Egypt, Saudi Arabia and UAE v Qatar) (Judgment) [2020] ICJ Rep 81 349–50
Arrest Warrant of 11 April 2000 (Democratic Republic of the Congo v. Belgium) (Judgment) [2002] ICJ Rep 3 213–14
Avena and Other Mexican Nationals (Mexico v United States of America) (Judgment) [2004] ICJ Rep 12 180–83
Certain Iranian Assets (Iran v USA) (Judgment) [2023] ICJ Rep 349–50
Land and Maritime Boundary between Cameroon and Nigeria (Cameroon v Nigeria: Equatorial Guinea intervening) (Judgment) [2002] ICJ Rep 303 31
Legal Consequences of the Construction of a Wall in the Occupied Palestinian Territory (Advisory Opinion) [2004] ICJ Rep 136 84–85

Inter-American Court of Human Rights

Barrios Altos v Peru (Merits) IACtHR Series C No 75 (14 March 2001) 131, 345–46
Bueno-Alves v Argentina (Merits, Reparations and Costs) IACtHR Series C No 164 (11 May 2007) 132
Bulacio v Argentina (Merits, Reparations and Costs) IACtHR Series C No 100 (18 September 2003) 131
Caballero-Delgado and Santana v Colombia (Merits) IACtHR Series C No 22 (8 December 1995) 133
Cantos v Argentina (Merits, Reparations and Costs) IACtHR Series C No 97 (28 November 2002) 130–31
Case of the Constitutional Court v Peru (Competence) IACtHR Series C No 55 (24 September 1999) 135–36
Cesti-Hurtado v Peru (Merits) IACtHR Series C No 56 (29 September 1999) 133
Fontevecchia and D'Amico v Argentina (Supervisión de Cumplimiento de Sentencia) IACtHR (18 October 2017) 134–38, 139, 140–41
Fontevecchia and D'Amico v Argentina (Merits, Reparations and Costs) IACtHR Series C No 238 (29 November 2011) 134–38
'Masacre de Mapiripán' v Colombia (Merits) IACtHR Series C No 134 (15 September 2005) 345–46
Matter of Milagro Sala regarding Argentina (Provisional Measures) IACtHR (23 November 2017) 137

International Criminal Tribunal for the Former Yugoslavia

Prosecutor v Dusko Tadić a/k/a "Dule" (Interlocutory Appeal on Jurisdiction) ICTY-94-I (2 October 1995) 258–59

International Criminal Tribunal for Rwanda

Prosecutor v Akayesu Case No. ICTR-96-4-A (Appeals Chamber), 1 June 2001 156

Investor-State Arbitrations

ADF Group Incorporated v United States of America, ICSID Case No ARB(AF)/00/1, Award (6 January 2003) 318–19
ATA Construction, Industrial and Trading Company v Hashemite Kingdom of Jordan, ICSID Case No ARB/08/2, Award (18 May 2010) 312
BG Group PLC v Argentine Republic, UNICTRAL, Final Award (24 December 2007) 319–20, 324, 326–27
Cargill, Inc v United Mexican States, ICISD Case No ARB(AF)/05/02, Award (18 September 2009) 318–19
Chevron Corporation (USA) and Texaco Petroleum Company (USA) v Republic of Ecuador, UNCITRAL, PCA Case No 34877, Award (31 August 2011) 317, 320
CMS Gas Transmission Company v Argentine Republic, ICSID Case No ARB/01/8, Award (12 May 2005) 315
Eureko BV v Slovak Republic, UNCITRAL, PCA Case No 2008-13, Award on Jurisdiction, Arbitrability and Suspension (26 October 2010) 321–22
European Media Ventures SA v The Czech Republic, UNCITRAL, Award on Jurisdiction (15 May 2007) 319–20
Frontier Petroleum Services Ltd v Czech Republic, UNCITRAL, Final Award (12 November 2010) 312
GEA Group Aktiengesellschaft v Ukraine, ICSID Case No ARB/08/16, Award (21 March 2011) 312
Hulley Enterprises Limited (Cyprus) v Russian Federation, UNCITRAL, PCA Case No AA226, Interim Award (30 November 2009) and Final Award (18 July 2016) 313–14
Metalclad Corporation v United Mexican States, ICSID Case No ARB(AF)/97/1, Award (30 August 2000) 318–19, 329
Mondev International Limited v United States of America, ICSID Case No ARB(AF)/99/2, Award (11 October 2002) 318–19
Saipem SpA v Bangladesh, ICSID Case No ARB/05/07, Decision on Jurisdiction and Recommendation on Provisional Measures (21 March 2007) and Award (30 June 2009) 312
Sanum Investments Limited v Lao People's Democratic Republic, UNCITRAL, PCA Case No. 2013-13, Award on Jurisdiction (13 December 2013) 324–25
Veteran Petroleum Limited (Cyprus) v Russian Federation, UNCITRAL, PCA Case No AA228, Interim Award (30 November 2009) and Final Award (18 July 2016) 313–14
White Industries Australia Limited v India, UNCITRAL, Final Award (31 November 2011) 312
Yukos Universal Limited (Isle of Man) v Russian Federation, UNCITRAL, PCA Case No AA227, Interim Award (30 November 2009) and Final Award (18 July 2016) 313–14

Kosovo Specialist Chambers

Appeals Against 'Decision on Motions Challenging the Jurisdiction of the Specialist Chambers', KSC-BC-2020-06/IA009/F00030, Decision of 23 December 2021 (Panel of the Court of Appeals Chamber) 262

Motions Challenging the Jurisdiction of the Specialist Chambers, KSC-BC-2020-06/F00412, Decision of 22 July 2021 (Pre-Trial Judge) 262
Referral of the Rules of Procedure and Evidence adopted by Plenary on 17 March 2017 to the Specialist Chamber of the Constitutional Court pursuant to Article 19(5) of Law no 05/L-053 on Specialist Chambers and Specialist Prosecutor's Office, KSC–CC-PR-2017-01, Judgment of 26 April 2017 251

Permanent Court of International Justice

Case concerning the Factory at Chorzów (Merits) [1928] PCIJ Ser A No 17 361
Jurisdiction of the Courts of Danzig (Advisory Opinion) [1928] PCIJ Ser B No 15 211–12

Southern Africa Development Community Tribunal

Mike Campbell (Pvt) Ltd and ors v Republic of Zimbabwe (2/2007) [2008] SADCT 2 (28 November 2008) 45–46

OTHER INTERNATIONAL BODIES

Committee on Economic, Social and Cultural Rights

CESCR 'Consideration of Reports submitted by States Parties under Articles 16 and 17 of the Covenant: Concluding Observations of the Committee on Economic, Social and Cultural Rights: Switzerland' (26 November 2010) UN Doc E/C.12/CHE/CO/2-3 279
CESCR 'Implementation of the International Covenant on Economic, Social and Cultural Rights, List of Issues: Switzerland' (4 December 2009) UN Doc E/C.12/CHE/Q/2-3 279

Committee on the Rights of the Child

CRC 'Concluding Observations: Argentina' (21 June 2010) UN Doc CRC/C/ARG/CO/3-4 297
CRC 'Concluding Observations: Canada' (27 October 2003) UN Doc CRC/C/15/Add.215 300

Committee against Torture

CAT 'Conclusions and Recommendations: Canada' (7 July 2005) UN Doc CAT/C/CR/34/CAN 299–300
CAT 'Concluding Observations: Canada' (25 June 2012) UN Doc CAT/C/CAN/CO/6 299–300

Human Rights Committee

CONCLUDING OBSERVATIONS
Human Rights Committee 'Concluding Observations: Peru' (15 November 2000) UN Doc CCPR/CO/70/PER 297
Human Rights Committee 'Concluding Observations: The Gambia' (12 August 2004) UN Doc CCPR/CO/75/GMB 297
Human Rights Committee 'Concluding Observations: Argentina' (31 March 2010) UN Doc CCPR /C/ARG/CO/4 297

Individual Communications
Human Rights Committee 'Views: Communication No 2844/2016' (25 August 2021) UN Doc CCPR/C/132/D/2844/2016 345–46
Human Rights Committee 'Views: Communication No. 1608/2007' (28 April 2011) UN Doc CCPR/C/101/D/1608/2007 297–98

Inter-American Commission of Human Rights

Jorge Luis Bronstein and others v Argentina, Case Nos 11/205 et al, IACommHR, Report No 2/97 (11 March 1997) OEA/Ser.L/V/II.95 Doc 7 rev 138
Juan Carlos Abella v Argentina, Case No 11/137, IACommHR, Report No 55/97 (18 November 1997) OEA/Ser.L/V/II.98 Doc 6 rev 128–29

NATIONAL COURTS

Albania

Constitutional Court
Constitutional Court, Judgment on Admissibility No 242/16, 21 December 2016 204
Constitutional Court, Judgment No 18/16, 16 March 2016 204
Constitutional Court, Judgment No 20/11, 1 June 2011 195
Constitutional Court, Judgment No 15/10, 15 April 2010 204–5
Constitutional Court, Decision on Inadmissibility No 22/10, 9 March 2010 194
Constitutional Court, Judgment No 13/04, 12 July 2004 197–98
Constitutional Court, Judgment No 186/02, 23 September 2002 196–97
Constitutional Court, Judgment No 65/99, 10 December 1999 191–93

Supreme Court
Supreme Court, Civil Bench, Judgment No 00-2016-2159 (228), 29 June 2016 204
Supreme Court, Civil Bench, Judgment No 00-2015-1245(187), 8 April 2015 204
Supreme Court, Civil Bench, Judgment No 00-2013-2586(679), 19 December 2013 203–4
Supreme Court, Criminal Bench, Judgment No 52102-01226-00-2011, 7 March 2012 196
Supreme Court, Civil Bench, Judgment No 00-2011-2304(569), 13 December 2011 203–4
Supreme Court, Joint Benches, Unifying Civil Judgment No 8, 10 June 2011 200
Supreme Court, Joint Benches, Unifying Criminal Judgment No 1, 30 January 2003 197–98

Other Courts
Sky Petroleum, Inc v Republic of Albania (UNCITRAL), Case No 32/1010, Decision of 1 March 2012 (Tirana Court of Appeal) 316

Argentina

Supreme Court
Acosta, Claudia Beatriz 321:3555 (1998) 122, 129, 130–31
Alonso, Gregorio v Haras 'Los Cardos' S.A. 211:161 (1940) 118–19
APSAI v Autopistas del Sol S.A. 344:233 (2021) 137–38, 140–41
Aquino, Isacio v Cargo Servicios Industriales SA 327:3753 (2004) 127–28
Arancibia Clavel, Enrique Lautar 327:3312 (2004) 124–25, 131
Astiz, Alfredo Ignacio 326:4797 (2003) 131

ATE v Ministerio de Trabajo 331:2499 (2008) 127–28
Batalla, Rufino 341:1768 (2018) 139–41
Becker, Juan 208:39 (1947) 118–19
Bramajo, Hernán Javier 319:1840 (1996) 127–28
Cabrera, Washington Julio Efrain v Comision Tecnica 305:2150 (1983) 118–19
Cafés La Virginia 317:1282 (1994) 120–21
Campodónico de Beviacqua, Ana Carina v Ministerio de Salud y Acción Social - Secretaría de Programas de Salud y Banco de Drogas Neoplásicas 323:3229 (2000) 127–28
Carranza Latrubesse, Gustavo v Estado Nacional 336:1024 (2013) 132–33
Carro Evangelista, Delia 327:352 (2004) 131
Chantrain, Alfonso 208:84 (1947) 118–19
Costa, Héctor Rubén v Municipalidad de la Ciudad de Buenos Aires 310:508 (1987) 118–19
Dag, Eric Th. 201:477 (1945) 119
Derecho, René Jesús 334:1504 (2011) 132
Derecho, René Jesús, 330:3074 (2007) 132
Deutsche Rückversicherun 342:1524 (2019) 140–41
Díaz, Paulo Vicente v Cervecería y Maltería Quilmes SA 336:593 (2013) 122
Ekmekdjian, Miguel Angel v Neustadt, Bernardo 311:2497 (1988) 118–19, 120
Ekmekdjian, Miguel Angel v Sofovich, Gerardo 315:1492 (1992) 120, 121
Espósito, Miguel Ángel 327:5668 (2004) 131–32
Esso SA v Gobierno Nacional 271:7 (1968) 118–19
F.A.L. 335:197 (2012) 127–28
Felicetti, Roberto 323:4130 (2000) 129–30
Festram 343:1389 (2020) 137–38
Fibraca Constructora SCA v Comisión Técnica 316:1669 (1993) 120–21
Giroldi, Horacio David 318:514 (1995) 122, 127
La Pilcomayo 43:321 (1891) 119
Maldonado, Daniel Enrique 328:4343 (2005) 127–28
Martín & Cía Ltda v Nación 257:199 (1963) 118–19
Mazzeo, Julio Lilo 330:3248 (2007) 125
Merck Química Argentina v Nación Argentina, 211:162 (1948) 118–19
Milagro 340:1775 (2017) 137
Milantic Trans S.A. c Ministerio de la Producción 344:1857 (2021) 140–41
Ministerio de Relaciones Exteriores y Culto ('Fontevecchia y D'Amico vs Argentina') 340:47 (2017) 134–35
Molinos Río de la Plata S.A. c Dirección General Impositiva, 344:2175 (2021) 140–41
Monges, Analía v UBA 319:3148 (1996) 122–23
Muiña, Luis 340:549 (2017) 138–41
Nardelli, Pietro Antonio 319:2557 (1996) 127–28
Priebke, Erich 318:2148 (1995) 123–25
Sánchez Abelenda, Raúl v Ediciones de la Urraca SA 311:2553 (1988) 118–19
Schiffrin, Leopoldo Héctor 340:257 (2017) 140–41
Simón, Julio Héctor 328:2056 (2005) 125
Urteaga, Facundo Raúl v Estado Nacional 321:2767 (1998) 127–28

Other courts

Cámara Criminal y Correccional Federal, Sala I, CFP 8419/2019 "Burmese Rohingya Organisation s/ legajo de apelación" (26 November 2021) (Federal Court of Appeals) 126–27
Juzgado Nacional Criminal y Correccional Federal 1, CFP 4591/2010 'N.N. s/ genocidio', Decision, 18 September 2013 (Federal Court) 126, 129–30
Cámara Criminal y Correccional Federal, Sala I, C/N° 44.196 "Luo Gan s/archivo" (21 December 2010) (Federal Court of Appeals) 126

Australia

Minister for Immigration and Ethnic Affairs v Teoh (1995) 183 CLR 273 (HC) 158–59, 240–41, 382–83

Bangladesh

Bangladesh Legal Aid and Services Trust and ors v Government of Bangladesh, Writ Petition Nos 5863 of 2009, 754 of 2010, 4275 of 2010, Judgment of 8 July 2010 (Supreme Court of Bangladesh, High Court Division) 296–97

Belize

Aurelio Cal and ors v Attorney-General of Belize, Claims Nos 171 and 172 of 2007, Judgment of 18 October 2007, (2007) 71 WIR 110 (SC) 297
British Caribbean Bank Limited v The Attorney General of Belize, Civil Appeal No 6 of 2011, Judgment of 3 August 2012 (CA) 316

Belgium

Constitutional Court

Judgment No 162/2015 (19 November 2015) 216
Judgment No 32/2015 (12 March 2015) 216
Judgment No 147/2004 (15 September 2004) 214–15
Judgment No 106/2003 (22 July 2003) 216
Judgment No 12/94 (3 February 1994) 214–15

Court of Cassation

Bindels v Administration des Finances (16 June 1947) Pasicrisie I 1947 221
Case No C.98.0477.F (14 January 2000) 217
Case No P.98.0974.N (17 August 1998) 218
Case No P.94.1005.N (23 August 1994) 218
Case No 19900410.6 (10 April 1990) 218
Compagnie Osram (8 January 1925) Pasicrisie I 1925 212–13
Ertl (16 February 1970) Pasicrisie 1970(I) 218
État belge v CPAS de Wavre (27 June 2008) Pasicrisie 2008(6-8) 217
État belge v FJML, Case No C.02.0570.F (28 September 2006) 217
Fromagerie Franco-Suisse "Le Ski" (27 May 1971) Pasicrisie I 1971(4) 211–12
Garage Herbosch-La Louvière, Case No C.06.0457.F (21 December 2007) 217
HSA and others v SA and YA, Case No P.02.1139.F/2 (12 February 2003) 212–13
J-P A v Royaume des Pays-Bas and De Nederlandsche Bank, Case No C.14.0322.F (23 October 2015) 221–22
Leroy (25 November 1955) Pasicrisie I 1955 210
Ligue des États arabes v TM, Case No S.99.0103.F/1 (12 March 2001) 210–11
NS, Case No P.01.1765.F (13 March 2002) 218
ONSS v LH and DP (25 October 2004) Pasicrisie 2004 217
Pittacos, 26 May 1966, Pasicrisie I 1966(3) 212, 213–14
République d'Argentine v NMC Capital Ltd, Case No C.11.0688.F/1 (22 November 2012) 221–22
Secrétariat du Groupe ACP v BD, Case No C.07.0407.F (21 December 2009) 223–24
Secrétariat du Groupe ACP v Lutchmaya (L M-A), Case No C.03.0328.F (21 December 2009) 223–24
Touax, Touax Rom v État belge, Case No C.13.0528.F (9 February 2017) 217–19
ÜG, Case No P.08.0070.N (17 June 2008) 214
Union de l'Europe occidentale v Siedler (SM), Case No S.04.0129.F (21 December 2009) 223–24

Vulstoffen Exploitatie, Case No C.07.0073.N (5 June 2008) 217
Yahoo! Inc, Case No P.13.2082.N (1 December 2015) 224–25, 395

Council of State
ASBL Pétitions patrimoine, Judgment No 192.641 (23 April 2009) 216
ASBL Mouvement contre le racisme, l'antisémitisme et la xénophobie,
Judgment No 83.584 (23 November 1999) 212–13
Corveleyn v Etat belge, ministre de la Justice (7 October 1968) 216
Orde van Vlaamse Balies, Judgment No 206.397 (2 July 2010) 220
SA Mobistar, Judgment No 214.183 (27 June 2011) 216
Ville d'Andenne, Judgment No 216.815 (12 December 2011) 216
XXX, Judgment No 196.388 (25 September 2009) 216
XXX, Judgment No 73.027 (9 April 1998) 219

Other courts
Aartsbisdom Mechelen en Godfried Danneels, Case No 4970
(22 December 2010) (CA Chamber of Indictments) (unreported) 216

Botswana

Attorney-General v Dow (1992) BLR 119 (CA) 28
Clover Petrus v The State [1984] BLR 14 (CA) 33
Good v The Attorney-General No 2 (2005) 2 BLR 337 (CA) 29
Republic of Angola v Springbok Investments (Pty) Ltd [2005] 2 BLR 159 (HC) 32

Canada

Supreme Court
Baker v Canada (Minister of Citizenship and Immigration) [1999] 2 SCR 817 . . . . . 145–46, 154, 158–59
B010 v Canada (Citizenship and Immigration) 2015 SCC 58, [2015] 3 SCR 704 . . . 144–45, 153, 162–63, 381–82
Canada Labour Code, Re [1992] 2 SCR 50 152
Canada (Justice) v Khadr 2008 SCC 28, [2008] 2 SCR 125 340–41
Canada (Minister of Citizenship and Immigration) v Vavilov 2019 SCC 65 154
Canada (Prime Minister) v Khadr 2010 SCC 3, [2010] 1 SCR 44 145
Canadian Foundation for Children, Youth and the Law v Canada
(Attorney General) 2004 SCC 4, [2004] 1 SCR 76 . . . . 154, 300
Crown Forest Industries Ltd. v Canada [1995] 2 SCR 802 162–63
Divito v Canada (Public Safety and Emergency Preparedness) 2013 SCC 47,
[2013] 3 SCR 157 161
Ezokola v Canada (Citizenship and Immigration) 2013 SCC 40, [2013]
2 SCR 678 . . . . 144–45, 157
Francis v The Queen [1956] SCR 618 145–46
Gouvernement de la République démocratique du Congo v Venne [1971] SCR 997 . . . 152
GreCon Dimter inc v J R Normand inc 2005 SCC 46, [2005] 2 SCR 401 . . . . . . 144–45, 154
Health Services and Support—Facilities Subsector Bargaining Assn v
British Columbia 2007 SCC 27, [2007] 2 SCR 391 . . . . 144–45, 161
India v Badesha 2017 SCC 44, [2017] 2 SCR 127 161
Kazemi Estate v Islamic Republic of Iran 2014 SCC 62, [2014]
3 SCR 176 . . . . 144–45, 149, 161
Ktunaxa Nation v British Columbia (Forests, Lands and Natural
Resource Operations) 2017 SCC 54, [2017] 2 SCR 386 161

Mugesera v Canada (Minister of Citizenship and Immigration) 2005 SCC 40, [2005] 2 SCR 100 155–56
National Corn Growers v Canadian Import Tribunal [1990] 2 SCR 1324 162–63
Németh v Canada (Justice) 2010 SCC 56, [2010] 3 SCR 281 144–45
Nevsun Resources Ltd. v Araya 2020 SCC 5 . . . . . 144–45, 148, 149–50, 160
Office of the Children's Lawyer v Balev 2018 SCC 16, [2018] 1 SCR 398 158
Ontario (Attorney General) v Fraser 2011 SCC 20, [2011] 2 SCR 3 144–45
Operation Dismantle v The Queen [1985] 1 SCR 441 145
Ordon Estate v Grail [1998] 3 SCR 437 154
Public Service Employee Relations Act (Alberta), Re [1987] 1 SCR 313 160–61
R v Appulonappa 2015 SCC 59, [2015] 3 SCR 754 144–45
R v Finta [1994] 1 SCR 701 155–56
R v Hape 2007 SCC 26, [2007] 2 SCR 292 . . . . . 144–45, 381–82
Reference re Newfoundland Continental Shelf [1984] 1 SCR 86 152
Reference as to Powers to Levy Rates on Foreign Legations and High Commissioners' Residences [1943] SCR 208 148
Reference re Secession of Quebec [1998] 2 SCR 217 152
Reference as to Whether Members of the Military or Naval Forces of the United States of America are Exempt from Criminal Proceedings in Canadian Criminal Courts [1943] SCR 483 148
Quebec (Attorney General) v 9147-0732 Québec inc. 2020 SCC 32 161–62
Saint John (Municipality of) v Fraser-Brace Overseas Corp. [1958] SCR 263 148
Saskatchewan Federation of Labour v Saskatchewan 2015 SCC 4, [2015] 1 SCR 245 . . . 161
The Ship "North" v The King (1906) 37 SCR 385 . . . . . 144–45, 148
Suresh v Canada (Minister of Citizenship and Immigration) 2002 SCC 1, [2002] 1 SCR 3 . . . . . 152, 162, 295–96
Thibodeau v Air Canada 2014 SCC 67, [2014] 3 SCR 340 . . . . . 144–45, 155
USA and Canada (Minister of Justice) v Anekwu 2009 SCC 41, [2009] 3 SCR 3 154–55
World Bank Group v Wallace 2016 SCC 15, [2016] 1 SCR 207 144–45

FEDERAL COURT OF APPEAL

Abdelrazik v Canada (Minister of Foreign Affairs) 2009 FC 580, [2010] 1 FCR 267 . . . . . 358–61, 362, 367, 392, 399–400
Apotex Inc v Astrazeneca Canada Inc 2012 FC 559 (CanLII) 162–63
Canada (Attorney General) v SD Myers Inc 2004 FC 38 (CanLII); [2004] 3 FCR 368 318–20
Canada v Seaboard Lumber Sales Co. [1995] 3 FC 113, (1995) CanLII 3604 162–63
Friends of the Earth v Canada (Governor in Council) 2009 FCA 297 (CanLII) 159–60
Gitxaala Nation v Canada 2015 FCA 73 (CanLII) 162–63
Ramirez v Canada (Minister of Employment and Immigration) [1992] 2 FC 306, (1992) CanLII 8540 157
Tapambwa v Canada (Citizenship and Immigration) 2019 FCA 34 162–63

OTHER COURTS

Bayview Irrigation District No 11 and Others v United Mexican States (ICSID(AF)) (2008) CanLII 22120 (ON SC) 317, 318–19
Black v Canada (Prime Minister) (2001) CanLII 8537 (ON CA) 145
Bouzari v Islamic Republic of Iran (2004) CanLII 871 (ON CA) 148, 299
Bouzari v Islamic Republic of Iran [2002] OJ No 1624, Ontario Superior Court of Justice (1 May 2002) 299–300
Canadian Foundation for Children, Youth and the Law v Canada (Attorney-General) (2002) 57 OR (3d) 511; 207 DLR (4th) 632 (ON CA) 300

Canadian Foundation for Children, Youth and the Law v Canada (Attorney General) (2000) CanLII 22397 (ON SC) 300, 303
Council of Canadians et al v Canada (Attorney General) (2006) CanLII 40222 (ON CA) 320, 321–22
Mack v Canada (Attorney General) (2002) CanLII 45062 (ON CA) 148
Regina and Palacios, Re (1984) CanLII 1870 (ON CA) 152
Sistem Mühendislik İnşaat Sanayi Ve Ticaret Anonim Sirketi v Kyrgyz Republic and Kyrgyzaltyn JSC (ICSID) (2012) ONSC 4351, Order of 25 July 2012 (Ontario Superior Court of Justice) 315
Strugarova v Air France (2009) CanLII 40552 (ON SC) 158
United Mexican States v Cargill Inc (ICSID (AF)) (2011) ONCA 622 318–19
United Mexican States v Feldman Karpa (2005) CanLII 249 (ON CA) 317, 318–19
Victoria (City) v Adams (2008) BCSC 1363 (SC British Columbia) 296
United Mexican States v Metalclad Corporation (ICSID(AF)) (2001) BCSC 664 (CanLII) (SC British Columbia) 318–19, 329

Cayman Islands

Palladyne International Asset Management BV v Upper Brook (A) Ltd and others, CICA Appeal No 5 of 2019, Judgment of 18 November 2019 355

China *see* **People's Republic of China (PRC)**

Colombia

Colombian Constitutional Court, Sentencia T-077/13, 14 February 2013 298
Colombian Constitutional Court, Sentencia T-025/04, 22 January 2004 304

Denmark

Republic of Latvia v SwemBalt Aktiebolag, Maritime and Commercial Court of Copenhagen, Case No S-22-01, Decision of 7 January 2003 324

Ecuador

Constitutional Court, Dictamen No 027-10-DTI-CC, 17 August 2010 320

Eswatini

Swaziland National Ex-mine Workers Association v The Minister of Education and Others (2/10) [2010] SZSC 35 (28 May 2010) 22

France

Energoalians SARL (Komstroy) v Moldova, Cour de Cassation, Chambre civile 1, Case No 16-16568, Judgment of 28 March 2018 319–20
Czech Republic v Mr Pren Nreka, Paris Court of Appeal, Record No 07/04675, Judgment of 25 September 2008 . . . . 319–20, 324
Kyrgyz Republic v Valerie Belokon, Paris Court of Appeal, Record No 15/01650, Judgment of 21 February 2017 319–20
Moldova v Energoalians, Paris Court of Appeal, Record No 13/22531, Judgment of 12 April 2016 319–20
Ukraine v Tatneft, Paris Court of Appeal, 14/17964, 29 November 2016 319–20

Germany

Federal Constitutional Court

B and others v Federal Republic of Germany, Judgment of 13 October 2016, 2 BvR 1368/16 and others ... 320
BVerfG, Order of the First Senate of 8 May 2013, 1 BvL 1/08 ... 296
Mr Franz Sedelmayer v Russian Federation (SCC), Order of 4 September 2008, 2 BvR 2162/07 and 2 BvR 227 ... 315
BVerfG, Order of the Third Chamber of the Second Senate of 24 January 1991, 2 BvR 1704/90 ... 297–98

Federal Supreme Court

Mr Franz Sedelmayer v Russian Federation (SCC), Decision of 1 October 2009, BGH VII ZB 37/08 ... 315
Slovak Republic v Achmea BV, Decision of 31 October 2018, BGH I ZB 2/15 ... 322–23
Werner Schneider, acting in his capacity as insolvency administrator of Walter Bau AG (In Liquidation) v Kingdom of Thailand (formerly Walter Bau AG (In Liquidation) v Kingdom of Thailand) (UNCITRAL), Decision of 30 January 2013, BGH III ZB 40/12 ... 315

Other courts

Achmea (Eureko), Frankfurt Higher Regional Court, Case No 26 Sch 3/13, Decision of 18 December 2014 ... 321–22
Slovak Republic v Eureko BV (UNCITRAL), Frankfurt Higher Regional Court, Case No 26 SchH 11/10, Decision of 10 May 2012 ... 321–22

The Gambia

Matty Faye v Dawda Jawara; Karla Keita v Mustapha Dampha, HC/427/11/MF/059/F1 (HC) ... 25

Ghana

Ahumah Ocansey v The Electoral Commission and Centre for Human Rights and Civil Liberties (CHURCIL) v Attorney-General [2010] SCGLR 575 (SC) ... 31
Banful and Another v Attorney General and Another (J1 7 of 2016) [2017] GHASC 21 (22 June 2017) (SC) ... 31
Ghana Lotto Operators Association and Others v National Lottery Authority [2007-8] SCGLR 1088 (SC) ... 34
Mensah v Mensah (J4 20 of 2011) [2012] GHASC 8 (22 February 2012) (SC) ... 23
New Patriotic Party v Attorney-General [1996-97] SCGLR 729 (SC) ... 28
New Patriotic Party v Inspector-General of Police [1993-94] 2 SCGLR 459 SC (SC) ... 28
Republic v High Court (Commercial Division) Accra, ex parte Attorney General and NML Capital Ltd, Civil Motion No J5/10/2013, 20 June 2013 (SC) (unreported) ... 32

Hong Kong

R v Sin Yau-ming (1991) 1 HKPLR 88 (Hong Kong, Court of Appeal) ... 303

India

Laxmi Mandal v Deen Dayal Harinagar Hospital and ors, WP(C) Nos 8853/2008, and 10700/2009, Judgment of 4 June 2010 (High Court of Delhi) ... 296

Ireland

Bosphorus Hava v Minister for Transport [1994] 2 ILRM 551 (HC) 363–64

Israel

Supreme Court

HCJ 9353/08 Abu-Dahim v Rear Area Headquarters Commander, Nevo)15 Jan 2009(.......... 95
HCJ 9060/08 Abdullah v Minister of Defence (2011) 93
HCJ 8276/05 Adalah – The Legal Center for Arab Minority Rights in Israel v Minister of Security (2005) 93–94
HCJ 3799/02 Adalah – The Legal Center for Arab Minority Rights in Israel et al v GOC Central Command IDF (2005) 60(3) PD 67 84–85
HCJ 7146/12 Adam v The Knesset (2013) 60(1) PD 717 88
HCJ 785/87 Affu v The IDF Commander in the West Bank (1989) 42(2) PD 79, 91
HCJ 7015/02 Ajuri v IDF Commander in the West Bank (2002) 56(6) PD 352 .... 84–85, 92, 397–98
HCJ 3451/02 Almadani et al v Minister of Security (2002) 56(3) PD 30 85–86
HCJ 852/86 Aloni et al v Minister of Justice (1987) 41(1) PD 1 92
HCJ 9132/07 Al-Basiuni v The Prime Minister (2008) 84–85
HCJ 8887/06 Al-Nabut v Minister of Defence (2011) 93
HCJ 581/06 Amona, Agricultural Cooperative Association for Communal Settlement LTD. v Minister of Defence (2006) 93
HCJ 4481/91 Bargil, CEO of the "Peace Now" Movement v The Government of Israel (1993) 47(4) PD 210 .... 93, 340
HCJ 2587/04 Buchris v Hadera Assessor (2005) 91
HCJ 302/72 Chilu v The Government of Israel (1973) 27(2) PD 169 92
CA 22/55 The Conservator of Absentees' Property v Samara (1956) 10 PD 80
HCJ 390/79 Dawiqat v The Government of Israel (1979) 34(1) PD 1 .... 92, 93
HCJ 124/09 Dawi'at v Minister of Defence, Nevo (18 Mar 2009) 95
HCJ 5026/04 Design 22 - Shark Deluxe Furniture LTS v Head of Sabbath work permits department, Ministry of Labor and Welfare (2004) 60(1) PD 38 89–90
CrimA 336/61 Eichmann v Attorney General (1962) 16 PD 2033 79
HCJ 256/72 Electricity Company for Jerusalem District v Minister of Defense (1972) 27(1) PD 124 335–36
CrA 11196/02 Frudenthal v State of Israel (2003) 57(6) PD 40 89–90
HCJ 1661/05 Gaza Shore Regional Council v Knesset (2005) 59(2) PD 481 .... 87–88, 91
HCJ 10687/02 Handyman Do It Yourself LTD v The State of Israel (2003) 57(3) PD 1 89–90
HCJ 10662/04 Hassan v The Social Security Institute (2012) 65(1) PD 782 88
HCJ 3125/98 Iad v IDF Commander in Judea and Samaria (1988) 55(1) PD 913 .... 84–85, 93
HCJ 1715/97 Israel Investment Managers Association v Minister of Treasury (1997) 51(4) PD 367 87–88
HCJ 393/82 Jam'iat Iscan Al-Ma'almoun Al-Tha'auniya Al-Mahduda Al-Mauliya v Commander of the IDF Forces in the Area of Judea and Samaria (1983) 37(3) PD 785 .... 92, 94–95
HCJ 4542/02 Kav LaOved – Worker's Hotline Association v The Government of Israel (2006) 61(1) PD 346 89–90
HCJ 5872/01 Knesset Member Muhammad Bara'ke v Prime Minister, Ariel Sharon (2002) 56(3) PD 1 81–82
HCJ 73/53 Kol Ha'am Corporation v Minister of Interior (1953) 7(2) PD 871 87
HCJ 8276/05 Legal Centre for Arab Minority Rights in Israel v Minister of Defence, Nevo (12 Dec 2006) 86

HCJ 3239/02 Marab et al v The IDF Commander in the Area of Judah and Samaria (2003) 57(2) PD 349 . . . . 84–85, 86–87
HCJ 7957/04 Mara'abe et al v The Prime Minister of Israel et al (2005) 60(2) PD 477 84–86
HCJ 8111/96 The New General Federation of Labor v Israel Aerospace Industries Ltd. (2004) 58(6) PD 481 88–89
HCJ 606/78 Oyeb v Minister of Defence (1978) 33(2) PD 610 93
HCJ 201/09 Physicians for Human Rights v IDF Commander in Prime Minister of Israel (2009) 2009(1) Tak-El 565 85–86
HCJ 4764/04 Physicians for Human Rights v IDF Commander in Gaza (2004) 58(5) PD 385 85–86
HCJ 4363/00 Poria Ilit Board v Minister of Education (2002) 56(4) PD 203 89–90
CrimHR 8823/07 Ploni v The State of Israel (2010) 63(3) PD 500 87–88
CrimA 6659/06 Ploni v The State of Israel (2008) 64(2) PD 329 . . . . 86–88, 91
CrimFH 7048/97 Plonim v Minister of Defence (2000) 54(1) PD 721 . . . . 84, 91
HCJ 769/02 The Public Committee against Torture in Israel et al v Israel Government (2006) 2006(4) Tak-El 3958 . . . . 84–85, 339
HCJ 256/01 Rabach v Local Matters Court in Jerusalem (2002) 56(2) PD 930 91
HCJ 253/88 Sagedia v Minister of Security (1988) 42(2) PD 301 91–92
CrimA 174/54 Schtamper v Attorney General (1956) 10(5) PD 1825 79
HCJ 1308/17 Silwad Municipality v The Knesset, Nevo (19 June 2020) 86
HCJ 3648/97 Stamka v Minister of the Interior (1999) 53(2) PD 728 . . . . 81–82, 89–90
HCJ 6504/95 Wadjia v The State of Israel, Nevo (1 Nov 1995) 91–92
HCJ 8414/05 Yasin v The Government of Israel (2007) 62(2) PD 822 93
HCJ 2599/00 Yated – The Association of Parents of Down Syndrome Children v Ministry of Education, (2002) 56(5) PD 834 89–90
HCJ 2690/09 Yesh Din v IDF Commander in the West Bank, Nevo (28 Mar 2010) 91–92, 94
HCJ 2164/09 Yesh Din v IDF West Bank Command, Nevo (26 Dec 2011) 84–85, 91–92
CrimA 5121/98 Yissacharov v Chief Military Prosecutor (2006) 60(1) PD 461 88–89

Italy

Italian Constitutional Court, Judgment No 113/2011, 4 April 2011 196

Lesotho

Molefi Ts'epe v Independent Electoral Commission and Others (11/05 CC:135/05) [2005] LSCA 14 (CA) 30, 295–96

Kenya

African Development Bank v Acholla (Civil Appeal 135 of 2002) [2015] eKLR (CA) 32–33
Attorney General v Mohamud Mohammed Hashi & 8 Others (Civil Appeal 113 of 2011) [2012] eKLR (CA) 32–33
Charles Gitau Mande v Embassy of the Kingdom of Belgium in Nairobi (Cause 416 of 2016) [2017] eKLR (Employment and Labour Relations Court) 32–33
Eric Gitari v Non-Governmental Organisations Co-ordination Board and Attorney General (Petition 440 of 2013) [2015] eKLR (HC) 31
Mitu-Bell Welfare Society v Kenya Airports Authority & 2 Others; Initiative for Strategic Litigation in Africa (Amicus Curiae) (Petition 3 of 2018) [2021] KESC 34 (KLR) (11 January 2021) (SC) 21–22
Mukazitoni Josephine v Attorney General Republic of Kenya (Criminal Appeal 128 of 2009) [p2015] eKLR (CA) 32–33
RM v Attorney-General (2006) AHRLR 256 (HC) 295–96

Kosovo

Constitutional Court

Constitutional Review of Judgments [A.A.U.ZH. No. 20/2019 of 30 October 2019 and A.A.U.ZH. No. 21/2019, of 5 November 2019] of the Supreme Court of the Republic of Kosovo, Case No KI 207/19, Judgment of 10 December 2020 (published 5 January 2021) ... 268–69
Constitutional Review of Decree No 24/2020 of the President of the Republic of Kosovo of 30 April 2020, Case No KO 72/20, Judgment of 28 May 2020 ... 250
Constitutional Review of Decision Pml. No 313/2018 of the Supreme Court of 10 December 2018, Case No KI 12/19, Resolution on inadmissibility of 10 April 2019 ... 268–69
Amendment to the Constitution proposed by the Government and referred by the President of the Assembly on 9 March 2015, by Letter No 05-433/DO-318, Case No KO 26/15, Judgment of 14 April 2015 ... 263, 265, 266–67
Constitutional Review of the Law No 04/L-199, on Ratification of the First International Agreement of Principles Governing the Normalization of Relations between the Republic of Kosovo and the Republic of Serbia and the Implementation Plan of this Agreement (Visar Ymeri and others), Case No KO 95/13, Judgment of 2 September 2013 ... 268–69
Gezim and Makfire Kastrati against Municipal Court in Prishtina and Kosovo Judicial Council, Case No KI 41/12, Judgment of 25 January 2012 ... 268–69
Constitutional Review of the Decision of the Special Chamber of the Supreme Court of Kosovo, ASC-09-089, dated 4 February 2010, Case No KI 25/10, Judgment of 30 March 2011 ... 249–50
Ćemailj Kurtiši and the Municipal Assembly of Prizren, Case No KO 01/09, Judgment of 30 November 2009 (published 18 March 2010) ... 268–69

Supreme Court

Gashi et al, Plm KZZ 18/2016, Judgment of 13 May 2016 ... 261–62
Gashi et al, AP-KZ No 89/2010, Decision of 26 January 2011 ... 261–62
Gashi et al, AP-KZ No 139/2004, Decision of 21 July 2005 ... 260
Case No ASC-09-089, Appellate Decision of 4 February 2010 (Special Chamber of the Supreme Court) ... 249–50, 253
SOE v AA, Appeal No SCA-09-0042, Decision of 29 November 2012 (Special Chamber of the Supreme Court of Kosovo) ... 254–55, 267–68

Other courts

Gashi et al, PAKR 440/13, Judgment of 11 August 2015 (Court of Appeals) ... 261–62
Gashi et al, P No 448/2012, Decision of 7 June 2013 (Basic Court of Pristina) ... 261–62
Gashi et al, Case No 526/2005, Decision of 2 October 2009 (District Court of Pristina) ... 261
Prosecutor v Latif Gashi et al (Llapi), Case No 425/2001, Judgment of 16 July 2003 (District Court of Pristina) ... 257

Malawi

The Adoption of Children Act CAP 26:01; CJ A Female Infant of C/o P.O.Box 30871, Chichiri, Blantyre 3 [2009] MWSC 1 (11 June 2009) (SCA) ... 31, 35
Kalinda v Libme Leaf Tobacco Ltd [2003] MWHC 79 (21 November 2003) (HC) ... 22
Malawi Telecommunications Limited v Makande and Omar, Civil Appeal No 2/2006, Judgment of 7 May 2007 (SCA) ... 22
Okeke v Minister of Home Affairs [2001] MWHC 36 (8 July 2001) (HC) ... 31

Namibia

Alexander v Minister of Justice and Others [2010] NASC 2 (9 April 2010) (SC) 31
Kauesa v Minister of Home Affairs [1994] NR 102 (HC) 27
S v Mushwena and Others [2004] NASC 2 (SC) 20–21
Thudinyane v Edward [2012] NASC 22 (SC) 20–21

Nepal

Sunil Babu Pant and others v Nepal Government and others (2007) 138 ILR 500 (unofficial English translation prepared by the Supreme Court of Nepal) (Supreme Court, 21 December 2007) 297–98

Netherlands

Appellante v de Raad van Bestuur van de Sociale Verzekeringsbank, Central Appeals Tribunal, 21 July 2006, LJN: AY5560 305–6
Republic of Ecuador v Chevron Corporation (USA) and Texaco Petroleum Company (USA) (UNCITRAL), The Hague District Court, Cases Nos 386934/HA ZA 11-402 and 408948/HA ZA 11-2813, Judgment of 2 May 2012 . . . . 317, 320
Russia Federation v Veteran Petroleum Ltd, Russian Federation v Yukos Universal Ltd, Russian Federation v Hulley Enterprises Ltd, The Hague District Court, Joint Cases C/09/477160/HA ZA 15-1, C/09/477162/ HA ZA 15-2, C/09/481619/HA ZA 15-112, Judgment of 20 April 2016 313–14
Test Trial Fund Clara Wichmann (Stichting Proefprocessenfonds Clara Wichmann) and ors v Netherlands, District Court, Judgment of 7 September 2005, (2005) HA ZA 03/3395, LJN: AU2088, ILDC 221 (NL 2005) 304
Judgment of 26 September 2014, Hoge Raad, ECLI:NL:HR:2014:2837 317

New Zealand

Mansouri-Rad v Department of Labour, Refugee Status Appeals Authority (2004) Refugee Appeal No 74665/03, (2005) NZAR 60 . . . . 306–7, 308
R v Goodwin (No 2) [1993] 2 NZLR 390 305–6
Tavita v Minister of Immigration [1994] 2 NZLR 257 158–59

Nigeria

General Sanni Abacha v Chief Gani Fawehinmi (SC 45/1997) [2000] 4 NJSC 400 (SC) 28

Norway

Federation of Offshore Workers Trade Unions (Oljearbeidernes Fellessammenslutning, OFS), Supreme Court of Norway, Rt 1997-580 297–98

Pakistan

Societe Generale de Surveillance (SGS) SA v Pakistan, Supreme Court, Civil Appeal Nos 459/2002 and 460/2002, Judgment of 3 July 2002 316

Peru

Cuzco Bar Association and ors v Congress of the Republic, Case Nos 050-2004-A1/TC, 051-2004A1/TC, 004-2005-P1/TC, 007-2005-P1/TC, 009-2005-P1/TC, Judgment of 3 June 2005, ILDC 679 (PE 2005) 296

The Philippines

Minors Oposa v Secretary of the Department of Environmental and Natural Resources, Supreme
Court of Philippines, Judgment of 30 July 1993 [1994] 33 ILM 173 373

People's Republic of China

Local People's Courts

High People's Courts

Abdul Wahid v China Eastern Airlines Co., Ltd. [2005] Pu Min Yi Min Chu Zi No 12164 (Civil Judgment) People's Court of Pudong District of Shanghai Municipality (21 December 2005) 63–64, 66–67
Contira Company v State Intellectual Property Office of China [2005] Administration Final No 369 of Beijing High People's Court 69
Crown Company v Tiger Co. Ltd [2012] Gao Xing Zhong Zi No 1255 (Administrative Judgment) Higher People's Court of Beijing Municipality (17 December 2012) 62–63
Geng Qunying vs Elborsh Company [2010] Ji Min San Zhong Zi No 59 (Civil Judgment) Higher People's Court of Hebei Province (15 December 2010) . . . 67
Hucheng v the Ministry of Foreign Affairts (MFA) [2015] Gao Xing Zhong Zi No 03490 (Administrative Ruling) Higher People's Court of Beijing Municipality (15 December 2015) 74–75
Inmobiliaria Palacio Oriental SA v Anhui Foreign Economic Construction (Group) Co., Ltd., [2014] Wan Min Er Zhong Zi No 00389 (Civil Judgment) Higher People's Court of Anhui Province (19 March 2015) 71
Intentional killing by Yang and Ma [2017] Yue 0115 Xing Chu No 255 (Criminal Judgement) People's Court of Nansha District, Guangzhou city, Guangdong Province (30 June 2017) 68
National Air Cargo Group, Inc v Aerospace Science and Technology Export and Import Company Ltd [2019] Jing Min Xia Zhong No 258 (Civil Ruling) Higher People's Court of Beijing Municipality (27 December 2019) 76–77

Intermediate People's Courts

Zhang Yubai v Jinniu District People's Hospital of Chengdu City [2016] 01 Min Zhong Zi No 11274 (Civil Judgment) Intermediate People's Court of Chengdu city of Sichuan Province (15 December 2016) 75
Chen Ying v Luo Ronggeng [2015] Hu Yi Zhong Shao Min Zhong Zi No 56 (Civil Judgment) First Intermediate People's Court of Shanghai Municipality (17 June 2016) 77
Abdul Wahid v China Eastern Airlines Co., Ltd [2006] Hu Yi Zhong Min Yi Min Zhong Zi No 609 (Civil Judgment) First Intermediate People's Court of Shanghai Municipality (24 February 2006) 63–64, 66–67
Anhui Foreign Economic Construction (Group) Co., Ltd. v Inmobiliaria Palacio Oriental SA [2012] He Min Si Chu Zi No 00005 (Civil Judgment) Intermediate People's Court of Hefei City of Anhui Province (9 April 2014) 71
Contira Company v State Intellectual Property Office of China [2005] Civil First No 378 of Beijing First Intermediate People's Court 69
Han and others smuggled, trafficked and transported drugs [2007] Kun Xing San Chu Zi No 8 (Criminal Judgment) Kunming Intermediate People's Court of Yunnan Province (22 November 2007) 64
Hucheng v the Ministry of Foreign Affairts (MFA) [2015] San Zhong Xing Chu Zi No 00658 (Administrative Ruling) Third Intermediate People's Court of Beijing Municipality (10 August 2015) 74–75

Supreme People's Court

Archangelos Gabriel [2016] Zui Gao Fa Min Zai No 61 (Civil Judgment) Supreme People's Court (7 July 2016) 70
China Biodiversity Conservation and Green Development Foundation v Ningxia Ruitai Science and Technology Co., Ltd. [2016] Zui Gao Fa Min Zai No 47 (Civil Judgment) Supreme People's Court (28 January 2016) 68
Crown Company v Tiger Co. Ltd [2013] Zhi Xing Zi No 81 (Administrative Ruling) Supreme People's Court (26 November 2013) 63
Dalian City Oceanic and Fishery Administration v Ondimar Transportes Maritimos Ltda and another [2015] Min Shen Zi No 1637 (Civil Ruling) Supreme People's Court (29 December 2015) 67
ELBORSH v Geng Qunying and Saide Company [2012] Min Shen Zi No 1402 (Civil Ruling) Supreme People's Court (24 December 2012) 67
Inmobiliaria Palacio Oriental SA v AFECG [2017] Zui Gao Fa Min Zai No 134 (Civil Judgment) Supreme People's Court (14 December 2017) 72
International (Overseas) Pte Ltd v ThyssenKrupp Metallurgical Products GmbH [2013] Min Si Zhong Zi No 35 (Civil Judgment) Supreme People's Court (30 June 2014) 64–65
Jinyingang Company v Sanxia Senlin Company and another [2013] Min Shen Zi No 869 (Civil Ruling) Supreme People's Court (30 September 2013) 75–76
Lianzhong Company (Hong Kong) v Xiamen International Trade Group [2016] Zui Gao Fa Min Zai No 373 (Civil Judgment) Supreme People's Court (13 March 2017) 70
Luoyang Runyuan Trade Company Ltd v the Ministry of Commerce [2018] Zui Gao Fa Xing Shen No 5686 (Administrative Ruling) Supreme People's Court (2 January 2019) 74
Maersk China Ltd v Yinghai Company [2010] Min Ti Zi No 213 (Civil Judgment) Supreme People's Court (28 June 2011) 76

Seychelles

Mohamed Hassan Ali v R [2014] SCCA 34 . . . . . 32–33, 88

Singapore

Government of the Lao People's Democratic Republic v Sanum Investments [2015] SGHC 15 . . . . . 319–20, 324–26
Sanum Investments Ltd v Government of the Lao People's Democratic Republic [2016] SGCA 57 326

South Africa

Constitutional Court

Carmichele v Minister of Safety and Security [2001] ZACC 22; (2001) (4) SA 938 43–44
De Vos NO and Others v Minister of Justice and Constitutional Development [2015] ZACC 21, (2015) (2) SA 217 46–47
Florence v Government of the Republic of South Africa [2014] ZACC 22, (2014) (6) SA 456 43
Law Society of South Africa v President of the Republic of South Africa [2018] ZACC 51, (2019) (3) SA 30 56
Glenister v President of the Republic of South Africa and Others [2011] ZACC 6, (2011) (3) SA 347 . . . . . 41–42, 43, 44–45, 46, 55
Government of the Republic of South Africa v Grootboom [2000] ZACC 19, (2001) (1) SA 46 43–44

Government of the Republic of Zimbabwe v Fick [2013] ZACC 22, (2013) (5) SA 325 .... 43, 45–46, 47, 48
Legal Aid South Africa v Magidiwana [2015] ZACC 28, (2015) (6) SA 494 44
National Commissioner of the South African Police Service v Southern African Human Rights Litigation Centre [2014] ZACC 30, (2015) (1) SA 315 42–43
Koyabe v Minister for Home Affairs [2009] ZACC 23, (2010) (4) SA 327 52
Shoprite Checkers v Member of the Executive Council for Economic Development, Environmental Affairs and Tourism [2016] ZACC 23, (2015) (6) SA 125 44
S v Basson [2005] ZACC 10, (2007) (3) SA 582 52
S v Makwanyane [1995] ZACC 3, (1995) (3) SA 391 .... 43–44, 52
S v Williams [1995] ZACC 5, (1995) (3) SA 632 .... 44, 52, 53

Supreme Court of Appeal

Minister of Justice and Constitutional Development v South Africa Litigation Centre [2016] ZASCA 15, (2016) (3) SA 317 47–48
Nduli v Minister of Justice 1978 (1) SA 893 (A) 39, 50–51
Progress Office Machines CC v South African Revenue Services and Others [2007] ZASCA 118, (2008) (2) SA 13 .... 41, 42
Richtersveld Community v Alexkor Ltd [2003] ZASCA 14 52
S v Petane 1988 (3) SA 51 50–51

High Court

Residents of Bon Vista Mansions v. Southern Metropolitan Local Council (2002) 6 BCLR 625 (High Court Witwatersrand, Local Division) 305–6

Spain

Spanish Constitutional Court, Judgment 245/1991, 16 December 1991, BOE (Official State Gazette) No 13 of 15 January 1992, 39 193
Asociación Solcom para la solidaridad comunitaria de las personas con diversidad funcional y la inclusión social and Asociación Asistencia para a vida independente v Conselleria de Traballo e Benestar, Judgment of 26 October 2011, No 1090/2011, ILDC 1899 (ES 2011) 300–1

Sri Lanka

Supreme Court

Abasin Banda v SI Gunaratne [1995] 1 Sri LR 244 110–11
Ambasevana v Ajith, Police Constable, Police Station, Dummalasuriya SC (FR) Case No 555/2009 .... 101–2, 113–14
Bulankulama v Secretary, Ministry of Industrial Development [2000] 3 Sri LR 243 .... 101, 104–5, 110–11
Centre for Policy Alternatives v Dayanada Dissanyake, Commissioner of Elections [2003] 1 Sri LR 273 .... 107, 109–10
Ediriweera Arukpatabandige Sugath Rohan Jayasuriya v Police Constable, Manikkaratnam SC (FR) Case No 43/2008 113–14
FJC de Mel and Thelma de Mel, Re [1975] 78 NLR 65 .... 101, 106
Hewa Maddumage Karunapala v Jayantha Prema Kumara Siriwardhana SC (FR) Case No 97/2017 .... 101–2, 110
Hikkadu Koralalage Don Chandrasoma v Mawai S Senathirajah SC SPL No 03/2014 101–2
Hunter and Company Ltd v The Minister of Labor and Vocational Training [1997] 1 Sri LR 337 101
Kaviratne v Commissioner General of Examinations [2012] SC 29 101

Lama Hewage Lal (Deceased) v Officer-in-Charge Minor Offences, Seeduwa Police Station [2005] 1 Sri LR 40 .... 101–2, 109
Mallawarachchi v Seneviratne, Officer in Charge, Police Station Kollupitiya [1992] 1 Sri LR 181 100
MAM Sarjun v Kamaldeen (Reserve PC) 39753 SC (FR) Case No 559/2003 112
Mediwake v Dayananda Dissanayake, Commissioner of Elections [2001] 1 Sri LR 177 .... 107, 109–10
Nallaratnam Singarasa v Attorney General (2006) SC SpL (LA) 182/99 98–99
Palle Kankanamge Sunil Shantha v Sub-Inspector Seneviratne SC (FR) Case No 479/2009 108–9
Rajavarothiam Sampananthan v Kabir Hashim SC (FR) Case No 351/ 2018 .... 99–100, 113–14
Ramuppillai v Festus Perera, Minister of Public Administration, Provincial Councils and Home Affairs [1991] 1 Sri LR 11 101
Ratnasingham v Tikiribanda Dassanaike [1998] 1 Sri LR 8 .... 101–2, 107
Ravindra Gunawardena Kariyawasam v Central Environment Authority SC (FR) Case No 141/2015 105
Romesh Cooray v Jayalath, Sub Inspector General of Police [2008] 2 Sri LR 43 107
Sanjeewa, Attorney-at-Law (on behalf of Gerald Mervin Perera) v Suraweera, OIC, Police Station, Wattala [2003] 1 Sri LR 317 109–10
Seneviratne v University Grants Commission [1978-79-80] 1 Sri LR 170 .... 100, 106
Sepala Ekanayake v Attorney General [1987] 1 Sri LR 107 .... 102, 107, 111
Sriyani Silva v Iddamalgoda, OIC, Police Station, Paiyagala [2003] 2 Sri LR 63 107–8
Watte Gedera Wijebanda v Conserver General of Forests [2009] 1 Sri RL 337 105
Weerawansa v Attorney General [2000] 1 Sri LR 387 .... 100, 103, 106, 107, 108–9
Wijekoon Herath Mudiyanselage Nimal Bandara v National Gem and Jewellery Authority SC (FR) Case No 118/2013 101
WMN Kumarihami v Galagamage Indrawansa Kumarasiri SC TAB Appeal No 02/201 101–2
Sunila Abeysekera v Ariya Rubasinghe [2000] 1 Sri LR 314 112
Wijebahu v Sumanasekara [1998] 3 Sri LR 355 .... 101–2, 106
Sirisena v Earnest Perera [1991] 2 Sri LR 97 101
Rubberite Company Ltd v Labour Officer, Negambo [1990] 2 Sri LR 42 101
Velmurugu v Attorney General [1981] 1 Sri LR 406 101–2
Walker Sons and Co (UK) Ltd v Gunatilake [1978-1979] 1 Sri LR 231 .... 97–98, 99–100, 103
WMK de Silva v Chairman, Ceylon Fertilizer Corporation [1989] 2 Sri LR 393 .... 100–1, 108–9, 110–11, 112

Sweden

Cem Uzan v Turkey, Case No T 6582-16, Svea Court of Appeal, Judgment of 26 February 2018 319–20
Czech Republic v CME, Case No T 8735-01, Svea Court of Appeal, Judgment of 15 May 2003 317
Kyrgyz Republic v Petrobart, Case No T-5208-05, Svea Court of Appeal, Judgment of 19 January 2007 324
Republic of Kazakhstan v Ascom Stati et al, Case No T 2675-14, Svea Court of Appeal, Judgment of 9 December 2016 .... 319–20, 324
Russian Federation v ALOS 34 et al, Case No T 9294-12, Svea Court of Appeal, Judgment of 7 June 2018 319–20
Spain v Novenergia II Energy & Environment (SCA), Case No T 4658-18, Svea Court of Appeal, Judgment of 16 May 2018 323

Switzerland

Federal Supreme Court

Arrêt, Case No 6B_894/2021, 28 March 2022 281
Hungary v EDF, Case No 4A_34/2015, 6 October 2015 324
RECOFI SA v Vietnam, Case No 4A_616/2015, 20 September 2016 . . . . 317, 319–20
Saluka v Czech Republic, Case No 4P_114/2006, 7 September 2006 . . . . 319–20, 324
Yousef Nada v State Secretariat for Economic Affairs and Federal Department of Economic Affairs, Case No 1A_45/2007, Judgment of 14 November 2007 . . . . 360, 392
BGE 146 V 87 (2020) 285
BGE 144 IV 332 (2018) 286
BGE 143 I 129 (2016) 275
BGE 142 II 35 (2015) 286–87
BGE 139 I 330 (2013) 283
BGE 139 I 306 (2013) 281–82
BGE 139 I 16 (2012) 284, 285–86
BGE 138 II 42 (2012) 278–79
BGE 138 I 246 (2012) 283
BGE 138 I 131 (2011) 275
BGE 137 I 305 (2011) 283
BGE 136 I 290 (2010) 279
BGE 126 IV 236 (2010) 280
BGI 134 II 120 (2008) 281–82
BGE 133 V 367 (2007) 286–87
BGE 133 I 286 (2007) 277–78
BGE 130 I 113 (2003) 279
BGE 126 I 240 (2000) 279
BGE 125 III 185 (1999) 281–82
BGE 122 I 109 (1996) 295–96
BGE 120 Ia 1 (1994) 279
BGE 125 II 417 (1991) 284–85
BGE 109 Ib 183 (1983) 283
BGE 106 Ib 182 (1980) 278–79
BGE 94 I 669 (1968) 280
BGE 26 I 444 (1900) 273

Tanzania

East African Development Bank v Blueline Enterprises Ltd, Civil Appeal 110 of 2009 (22 December 2011) (CA) 32–33

Uganda

Center for Health, Human Rights and Development (CEHURD) and Others v Attorney General, Constitutional Petition No 16 of 2011, 19 August 2020 (CC) 27
Uganda Law Society v Attorney General [2009] UGCC 1 (CC) 23

United Kingdom

Supreme Court

Ahmed v HM Treasury [2010] UKSC 2 . . . . 356–58, 364–65, 366–67, 381, 395–96, 397
Al-Malki v Reyes [2017] UKSC 61, [2019] AC 735 . . . . 231–32, 243

A v Secretary of State for the Home Department (No 1) [2004] UKHL 56, [2005] 2 AC 68 238
BelHaj v Straw [2017] UKSC 3, [2017] 2 WLR 456 243–44
Benkharbouche v Embassy of the Republic of Sudan [2017] UKSC 62, [2019] AC 777 .... 239–40, 242
British Airways v Laker Airways [1984] UKHL 7, [1985] AC 58 230–31
Council of Civil Service Unions v Minister for the Civil Service [1985] AC 374 230
Fothergill v Monarch Airlines [1980] UKHL 6, [1981] AC 251 231–32
General Dynamics United Kingdom Ltd v State of Libya [2021] UKSC 22, [2022] AC 318 242
JH Rayner (Mincing Lane) v Department of Trade and Industry [1990] 2 AC 418 230
Jones v Saudi Arabia [2006] UKHL 26, [2007] 1 AC 270 299–300
Konecny v District Court in Brno-Venkov, Czech Republic [2019] UKSC 8, [2019] 1 WLR 1586 236
MacDonald v Advocate General for Scotland [2003] UKHL 34, [2003] ICR 937 236
Maduro Board of the Central Bank of Venezuela v Guaido Board of the Central Bank of Venezuela [2021] UKSC 57, [2022] 2 WLR 167 243–44
McKerr, Re [2004] UKHL 12, [2004] 1 WLR 807 237
R (Cornerhouse) v Director of Serious Fraud Office [2008] UKHL 60, [2009] 1 AC 756 .... 230–31, 239–40
R (Friends of the Earth) v Secretary of State for Transport [2020] UKSC 52, [2021] PPTSR 190 .... 159–60, 230, 240
R v G [2003] UKHL 50, [2004] 1 AC 1034 236–37
R (Jackson) v Attorney General [2005] UKHL 56, [2006] 1 AC 262 229–30
R v Jones [2006] UKHL 16, [2007] 1 AC 136 .... 149, 241
R (Keyu) v Secretary of State for Foreign and Commonwealth Affairs [2015] UKSC 69, [2016] AC 1355 243
R (Miller) v Prime Minister [2019] UKSC 41, [2020] AC 373 227–29
R (Miller) v Secretary of State for Exiting the European Union [2017] UKSC 5, [2017] 2 WLR 583 .... 227–28, 229, 230
R (SC) v Secretary of State for Work and Pensions [2021] UKSC 26, [2022] AC 223 228–29
R (Serdar Mohammed) v Ministry of Defence [2017] UKSC 2, [2017] 2 WLR 327 234
R (Yam) v Central Criminal Court [2015] UKSC 76, [2016] AC 771 .... 228–29, 238–39
Shergill v Khaira [2014] UKSC 33, [2015] AC 359 243–44
ZH Tanzania v Secretary of State for the Home Department [2011] UKSC 4, [2011] 2 AC 166 238
R (Al-Jedda) v Secretary of State for Defence [2007] UKHL 58 .... 234, 366–67
R v Caldwell [1982] AC 341 236–37
R v Jones [2006] UKHL 16, [2007] 1 AC 136 .... 149, 241
R (European Roma Rights Centre) v Immigration Officer at Prague Airport [2004] UKHL 55, [2005] 2 AC 1 .... 231–32, 237–38, 240–41
R v Lyons [2002] UHL 44, [2003] 1 AC 976 .... 232, 236–37, 393–94
R v Secretary of State for the Home Department, ex p Brind [1991] UKHL 4, [1991] AC 696 .... 236, 238–39
R v Secretary of State for the Home Department, ex p Launder [1997] UKHL 20, [1997] 1 WLR 839 239–40
R v Secretary of State for the Home Department ex p Pierson [1997] UKHL 37, [1998] AC 539 237–38
R v Secretary of State for the Home Department, ex p Simms [1999] UKHL 33, [2000] 2 AC 115 237–38

R v Secretary of State for the Home Department, ex p Venables [1997] UKHL 25, [1998] AC 407 238–39

Privy Council

Attorney-General for Canada v Attorney-General for Ontario ('Labour Conventions') [1937] UKPC 6, [1937] AC 326 (PC) 347 145
Higgs and David Mitchell v The Minister of National Security (Bahamas) [1999] UKPC 55 19
Lewis v Attorney General of Jamaica [2000] UKPC 35, [2001] 2 AC 50 230
McIntosh v Lord Advocate [2001] UKPC D1, [2003] 1 AC 1078 . . . . . 238, 383
Tangiora v Wellington District Legal Services Committee [1999] UKPC 42 (NZ) . . . 307–8
Thomas v Baptiste [1999] UKPC 13, [2000] 2 AC 1 (PC) 158–59

Court of Appeal

Al-Malki v Reyes [2015] EWCA Civ 32, [2015] ICR 931 . . . . . 231–32, 243
Behluli v Secretary of State for the Home Department [1998] EWCA Civ 788, [1998] Imm AR 407 240–41
Libyan Investment Authority v Maud [2016] EWCA Civ 788 355–56
R (Abbasi) v Secretary of State for Foreign and Commonwealth Affairs [2002] EWCA Civ 1598 341–43
R (Al-Saadoon) v Secretary of State for Defence [2016] EWCA Civ 811 . . . . . 230, 234, 237–38, 243
R (EOT and KTT) v Secretary of State for the Home Department [2022] EWCA Civ 307 238–39
R (European Roma Rights Centre) v Immigration Officer [2003] EWCA Civ 666, [2004] QB 811 240–41
R (Freedom and Justice Party) v Secretary of State for the Foreign and Commonwealth Affairs [2018] EWCA Civ 1719 242
R (Gulf Centre for Human Rights) v Prime Minster [2018] EWCA Civ 1855 229
R v Kelly [2000] QB 198 (CA) 236
Republic of Ecuador v Occidental Exploration Production Co [2007] EWCA Civ 656 319–20
R v Secretary of State for the Home Department, ex p Ahmed [1999] Imm LR 22 (CA) 240–41
Salomon v Commissioners of Customs and Excise [1967] 2 QB 116 (CA) 162–63, 234–35, 237
Trendtex Trading Corp v Central Bank of Nigeria [1977] 1 QB 529 (CA) 148–49, 241

High Court

AIG Capital Partners Inc and CJSC Tema Real Estate Company v Republic of Kazakhstan (ICSID) [2005] EWHC 2239 (Comm) 315
Badea v Romanian Judicial Authority [2022] EWHC 1025 (Admin) 236
Chief Constable of Sussex v Secretary of State for Transport [2016] EWHC 2280 (QB) 232
Chundawadra v IAT [1988] Imm AR 161 240–41
Crown Prosecution Service v Beaumont [2022] EWHC 849 (Admin) 238
Czech Republic v European Media Ventures SA [2007] EWHC 2851 (Comm) 319–20
GPF GP Sàrl v The Republic of Poland [2018] EWHC 409 (Comm) 319–20
Ibrahimi and Abasi v Secretary of State for the Home Department [2016] EWHC 2049 (Admin) 234
Micula and ors v Romania [2017] EWHC 31 (Comm) 395
R (Akarcay) v Chief Constable of the West Yorkshire Police [2017] EWHC 159 (Admin) 243

R (Al-Saadoon) v Secretary of State for Defence [2015] EWHC 715 (Admin), [2015] 3 WLR 503 . . . . . . 230, 243
R (Campaign for Nuclear Disarmament) v Prime Minister [2002] EWHC 2777 (Admin) 230–31
R (Friends of the Earth) v (1) Secretary of State for International Trade (2) Chancellor of the Exchequer [2022] EWHC 568 (Admin) 240
R (Hany Youssef) v Secretary of State for Foreign, Commonwealth and Development Affairs [2021] EWHC 3188 (Admin) 356–58, 366–67, 368–69
R (KTT) v Secretary of State for the Home Department [2021] EWHC 2722 (Admin) 238–39
R (Freedom and Justice Party) v Secretary of State for the Foreign and Commonwealth Office [2016] EWHC 2010 (Admin) 242
R (Gulf Centre for Human Rights) v Prime Minster [2016] EWHC 1323 (Admin) 229
R (ICO Satellite) v The Office of Communications [2010] EWHC 2010 (Admin) 239–40
R v Keyn (1876) 2 Ex D 63 (Ct Crim Cas Res) 149, 399–400
R (Othman) v Secretary of State for Work and Pensions [2001] EWHC 1022 361–62
R v Secretary of State for the Home Department, ex p Ahmed [1999] Imm AR 22 . . . . . . 158–59, 240–41
R v Uxbridge Magistrates' Court, ex p Adimi [1999] EWHC 765 (Admin), [2001] QB 667 240–41
R (Western Sahara Campaign UK) v HMRC [2015] EWHC 2989 (Admin) 234

United States

Supreme Court

BG Group PLC v Argentine Republic 134 S Ct 1198 (2014) 319–20, 324, 326–27
Bolivarian Republic of Venezuela v Helmerich & Payne Intern Drilling Co 137 S Ct 1312 (2017) 173
Bond v United States 134 S Ct 2077 (2014) 169–70
Breard v Greene 523 US 371 (1998) 181–83, 184–85
Chew Heong v United States 112 US 536 (1884) 177–78
Cook v United States 288 US 102 (1933) 176–77
Hamdan v Rumsfeld 548 US 557 (2006) 340–41, 343–44
Lawrence v Texas 539 US 558 (2003) 167
Loving v Virginia 388 US 1 (1967) 174–75
Medellín v Texas 552 US 491 (2008) 166–67, 182–85, 381, 386–87, 393–94, 396–97
Murray v The Charming Betsey 6 US 64 (1804) 167, 381–82
OBB Personenverkehr AG v Carol P Sachs 577 US 27, 136 S Ct 390 (2015) 170–71
Ex Parte Quirin 317 US 1 (1942) 343–44
Republic of Argentina v NML Capital, Ltd 573 US 134, 134 S Ct 2250 (2014) 170–71, 221–22
Robinson v California 370 US 660 (1962) 174
Roper v Simmons 543 US 551 (2005) 167, 178–79, 383
Samantar v Yousuf 560 US 305 (2010) 170–71
Sanchez-Llamas v Oregon 548 US 331 (2006) 180–83, 397
The Scotia 81 US 14 Wall 170 (1871) 144–45
Stanford v Kentucky 492 US 361 (1989) 178–79
Thompson v Oklahoma 487 US 815 (1988) 171, 172
United States v Alvarez-Machain 504 US 655 (1992) 180, 181

Circuit Courts
Al-Bahlul v the US 792 F 3d 1 (DC Cir 2015) 343–44
Baah v Virgin Atlantic Airways, Ltd 473 F Supp 2d 591 (SDNY 2007) 173
Blue Ridge Investments LLC v Argentine Republic (ICSID) 902 F Supp 2d 367 (SDNY 2012) 315
Cohen v Cohen 858 F 3rd 1150 (8th Cir 2017) 173
Continental Casualty Company v Argentine Republic (ICSID) 893 F Supp 2d 747 (ED Va 2012) 315
Hamdan v United States 696 F 3d 1238 (DC Cir 2012) 340–41, 343–44
Matar v Dichter 563 F 3d 9 (2nd Cir 2009) 168–69
Owens v Republic of Sudan 864 F 3d 751 (DC Cir 2017) 183–84
Republic of Marshall Islands v United States 865 F 3d 1187 (9th Cir 2017) 171–72, 185
Thunderbird v Mexico, International Thunderbird Gaming Operations v United Mexican States 473 F Supp 2d 80 (DDC 2007) 316–17
Yousuf v Samantar, 699 F 3d 763 (4th Cir 2012) 184–85
Zuza v Office of the High Representative 857 F 3d 935 (DC Cir 2017) 179

District Courts
Al-Aulaqi v Obama, 727 F Supp 2d 1 (DDC 2010) 338–39
Sky Petroleum, Inc v Republic of Albania (UNCITRAL), Case No A-12–CA-023-SS (District Court, WD Texas, Austin Div), Order and Preliminary Injunction of 20 January 2012 316
Zuza v Office of High Representative 107 F Supp 3d 90 (DDC 2015) 179

Immigration
In Re Fauziya Kasinga 21 I&N Dec 357 (BIA 1996) 176

Zambia

Mwanza & Another v Attorney General (Appeal 153 of 2016) [2019] ZMSC 33 (9 December 2019) (SC) 24, 27, 31, 34

Zimbabwe

Supreme Court
Kachingwe and Others v Minister of Home Affairs NO and Another (17/03) [2005] ZWSC 134 (17 July 2005) 22–23
Mildred Mapingure v Minister of Home Affairs and Others (SC 406/12) [2014] ZWSC 22 (24 March 2014) 29–30
Simbi (Steelmakers) (Pvt) Ltd. v Shamu & Others (SC 71 of 2015, Civil Appeal SC 479 of 2014) [2015] ZWSC 71 (20 November 2015) (SC) 31

Other courts
Gramara (Private) Limited and Colin Bailie Cloete v Government of the Republic of Zimbabwe and Attorney-General of Zimbabwe and Normal Kapanga (Intervener), Opposed Application, HC 33/09, Harare High Court (24 November 2009 and 26 January 2010) 33–34
Shumba & 2 Others v Minister of Justice, Legal and& Parliamentary Affairs & 5 Others (CCZ 4 of 2018, CCZ 3 of 2018) [2018] ZWCC 4 (30 May 2018) (CC) 22–23

List of Abbreviations

ACC	Albanian Constitutional Court
ACHR	American Convention on Human Rights
AEDPA (US)	Antiterrorism and Effective Death Penalty Act (US)
AFMP (EU-Switzerland)	Agreement on Free Movement of Persons (EU-Switzerland)
AJIL	American Journal of International Law
ANC	African National Congress
ASC	Albanian Supreme Court
ATCA (US)	Alien Tort Claims Act (US)
BYIL	British Yearbook of International Law
CAT	Committee against Torture
CCJ	Caribbean Court of Justice
CCP	Code of Criminal Procedure (Albania)
CED	Committee on Enforced Disappearances
CEDAW	Committee on the Elimination of Discrimination against Women
CERD	Committee on the Elimination of Racial Discrimination
CESCR	Committee on Economic, Social and Cultural Rights
CETA	EU-Canada Comprehensive Economic and Trade Agreement
ChiJIL	Chinese Journal of International Law
CIL	Customary International Law
CISG	United Nations Convention on the International Sale of Goods
CISG	Vienna Convention on the International Sale of Goods
CMW	Committee on Migrant Workers
CNASL	Convention on the Non-Applicability of Statutory Limitations to War Crimes and Crimes Against Humanity
CoE	Council of Europe
CRC	Committee on the Rights of the Child
CRPD	Committee on the Rights of Persons with Disabilities
CWC Act	Chemical Weapons Convention Implementation Act (US)
DEA	Drug Enforcement Administration (US)
DPSP	Directive Principles of State Policy
EAC	East African Community
EACJ	East African Court of Justice
EC	European Community

ECHR	European Convention for the Protection of Human Rights and Fundamental Freedoms
ECJ	European Court of Justice
ECtHR	European Court of Human Rights
EJIL	European Journal of International Law
ETC	Energy Treaty Charter
EU	European Union
EULEX	European Union Mission in Kosovo
FCN Treaties	Friendship, Commerce and Navigation (FCN) Treaties
FSC	Federal Supreme Court
FSIA	Foreign Sovereign Immunities Act (US)
FTAA	Financial and Technical Assistance Agreement
GATT	General Agreement on Tariffs and Trade
GLJ	German Law Journal
HCJ	High Court of Justice (Israel)
HRA	Human Rights Act 1998 (UK)
HRC	Human Rights Committee
IACommHR	Inter-American Commission on Human Rights
IACtHR	Inter-American Court of Human Rights
ICC	International Chamber of Commerce
ICCPR	International Covenant on Civil and Political Rights
ICESCR	International Covenant on Economic, Social and Cultural Rights
ICJ	International Court of Justice
ICLQ	International and Comparative Law Quarterly
ICR	International Civilian Representative (Kosovo)
ICSID Convention	Convention on the Settlement of Investment Disputes between States and Nationals of Other States
IDF	Israel Defence Forces
IHL	International Humanitarian Law
IHRL	International Human Rights Law
IIA	International Investment Agreements
IIL	International Investment Law
ILA	International Law Association
ILC	International Law Commission
ILDC	International Law in Domestic Courts
ILM	International Legal Materials
ILO	International Labour Organization
ILR	International Law Reports
Int J Hum Rights	International Journal of Human Rights
JICJ	Journal of International Criminal Justice
KLA	Kosovo Liberation Army
KTA	Kosovo Trust Agency

LAP	Libyan Africa Investment Portfolio
LFB	Libyan Foreign Bank
LIA	Libyan Investment Authority
LII	Legal Information Institute
MFN	Most Favoured Nation
MPEPIL	Max Planck Encyclopedia of Public International Law
NAFTA	North America Free Trade Agreement
NILR	Netherlands International Law Review
NIOC	National Iranian Oil Company
NPC	National People's Congress
NPT	Treaty on the Non-Proliferation of Nuclear Weapons
NSE	Non-Self-Executing
NYU	New York University
OPT	Occupied Palestinian Territories
PACE	Parliamentary Assembly of the Council of Europe
PAK	Privatisation Agency of Kosovo
PCT	Patent Cooperation Treaty
POC	Presumption of Compatibility
POL	Principle of Legality
POW	Prisoner of War
PRC	People's Republic of China
SA ICC Act	Implementation of the Rome Statute Act (South Africa)
SADC	Southern African Development Community
SAR	Special Administrative Region
SCA	Supreme Court of Appeal (South Africa)
SCC	Stockholm Chamber of Commerce
SFC	Swiss Federal Supreme Court
SPC	Supreme People's Court (China)
SPT	Subcommittee on Prevention of Torture
SRSG	Special Representative of the Secretary-General of the United Nations
TRIPS	Agreement on Trade-Related Aspects of Intellectual Property Rights
TVPA	Torture Victim Protection Act (US)
UDHR	Universal Declaration of Human Rights
UN	United Nations
UNCITRAL	United Nations Commission on International Trade Law
UNCJISP	United Nations Convention on Jurisdictional Immunities of States and Their Property
UNCLOS	United Nations Convention on the Law of the Sea
UNMIK	United Nations Interim Administration in Kosovo
UNSC	United Nations Security Council
US	United States

USAID	United States Agency for International Development
USMCA	United States-Mexico-Canada Agreement
VaJIL	Virginia Journal of International Law
VCCR	Vienna Convention on Consular Relations
VCDR	Vienna Convention on Diplomatic Relations
VCLT	Vienna Convention on the Law of Treaties
ZaöRV	Zeitschrift für ausländisches öffentliches Recht und Völkerrecht

List of Contributors

Eva Maria Belser is Professor of Law at the University of Fribourg, where she holds a Chair for Constitutional and Administrative Law and a UNESCO Chair in Human Rights and Democracy. She is Co-Director of the Institute of Federalism heading its international centre, and is a member of the Board of Advisers of the International Institute for Democracy and Electoral Assistance (International IDEA).

Joel Dahlquist (PhD) acts as an Advisor in international arbitrations arising under investment treaties and contracts at Arnold & Porter (London office). In particular, he has experience representing sovereign states in investor-state arbitrations. Before joining the firm, Dahlquist worked as secretary to arbitral tribunals in more than twenty large-scale international arbitrations, governed by the ICSID, SCC, UNCITRAL, and ICC rules, as well as *ad hoc*. Before that, he worked as a full-time academic for six years, teaching public and private international law, as well as international commercial and investment arbitration, to both undergraduate and postgraduate students. Dahlquist maintains a keen interest in academia, and currently teaches international arbitration at the London School of Economics and Uppsala University, from where he also received his doctorate in public international law in 2019.

Frédéric Dopagne is Professor of Public International Law at the University of Louvain (UCL, Belgium), where he mainly teaches diplomatic law and the law of State immunity. He is also currently a Guest Professor in EU Law at Sciences Po Lille and in International Institutional Law at the University of Liège (Belgium). As a member of the Brussels Bar, he has advised and represented foreign States as well as international organizations on a wide range of international law issues. A former Secretary-General of the Belgian Society of International Law, he is now on the Board of the French Society for International Law, and the respective boards of editors of the *Belgian Review of International Law* and *Oxford International Organizations*.

Gib van Ert practises civil litigation and public law with Olthuis van Ert in Ottawa and Vancouver. He is the President of the Canadian Council on International Law. From 2015 to 2018, he was the Executive Legal Officer to two successive chief justices of Canada, the Rt Hon Beverley McLachlin PC and the Rt Hon Richard Wagner PC. The Executive Legal Officer is the chief justice's principal advisor in matters concerning the administration of the Supreme Court of Canada, the Canadian Judicial Council, and the National Judicial Institute. Van Ert is the author of *Using International Law in Canadian Courts* and other works on the reception of international law in Canada. He is an annual contributor to the *Canadian Yearbook of International Law*. He served as a law clerk to Justices Charles Gonthier and Morris Fish of the Supreme Court of Canada and Madam Justice Joanne Prowse of the Court of Appeal for British Columbia. Van

Ert has a BA (Hons) from McGill, an MA in law from the University of Cambridge, and an LLM from the University of Toronto.

Shaheed Fatima KC is an award-winning Barrister practising from Blackstone Chambers, London. She specializes in international law, public law, and commercial law. Her practice extends beyond English courts and includes the European Court of Human Rights, UN treaty bodies, arbitral tribunals, and the EU courts. She is identified as a leading silk in the latest editions of both Chambers UK and Legal 500 for her expertise in Public International Law, Civil Liberties and Human Rights, Administrative and Public Law, and Commercial Litigation/Dispute Resolution. Before being appointed King's Counsel in 2016, Fatima was a member of the Attorney General's Public International Law 'A' Panel (2014–2016) and the Attorney General's 'A' Panel (2011–2016), having previously been on the 'B' Panel (2009–2011). She is the lead author of *Protecting Children in Armed Conflict* (2019, for which she received the #WritetheWrong award from Theirworld). She is working on the second edition of her book, *International Law and Foreign Affairs in English Courts* (forthcoming 2024) and is a Founding Editor of the transatlantic national security blog, *Just Security*. She has taught law at Pembroke College/University of Oxford, Harvard Law School, NYU School of Law, and the Graduate Institute in Geneva.

Dakshinie Ruwanthika Gunaratne is a Sri Lankan Lawyer specializing in international law, international humanitarian law, and international human rights law, focusing on armed groups, protection of civilians, sexual violence, and sanctions. Previously, she served as the Coordinator and the Armed Groups Expert (2019–2022) and International Humanitarian Law Expert (2014–2018) to the United Nations Security Council Panels of Experts concerning Yemen and Sudan. Before joining the United Nations, she worked with the International Committee of the Red Cross, Colombo, as Head of Communications and Implementation and Promotion of Law, and as a Legal Officer for the Ministry of Foreign Affairs, Sri Lanka. She was a Practitioner-in-Residence at the Human Rights Institute, Columbia University, New York. Gunaratne has an LLM from the University of Cambridge and an MSt in International Human Rights Law from the University of Oxford. She has lectured in various academic institutions in Sri Lanka and the United States and has published on international law and sanctions. She is an Attorney at Law, enrolled in the Supreme Court of Sri Lanka since 2005. Gunaratne currently serves as the Regional Coordinator for the Prevention of Sexual Misconduct to the World Health Organization in the Western Pacific Region and is a non-resident fellow at the Middle East Institute.

Machiko Kanetake is an Associate Professor of Public International Law at Utrecht University and the Director of the master's programme in Public International Law. She was previously a Postdoctoral Researcher at the University of Amsterdam and has held visiting appointments at New York University School of Law, Harvard Law School, and King's College London. She is an Editor of the *Leiden Journal of International Law*. She is also a member of the Management Board of the Utrecht Centre for Regulation and Enforcement in Europe.

Magnus Killander is a Professor of Human Rights Law at the Centre for Human Rights, Faculty of Law, University of Pretoria. He is the Academic Coordinator of the master's programme in Human Rights Democratisation in Africa (Global Campus Africa) and the Executive Secretary of the Association of Human Rights Institutes (AHRI).

Andreas Kulick (Privatdozent and Dr. iur., Eberhard Karls University Tübingen) is currently a Visiting Professor at the Albert Ludwigs University Freiburg, Germany. His main areas of interest pertain to general international law, international adjudication, international investment law, and international and regional human rights law. Kulick is the author, editor, and co-editor of seven books with Cambridge University Press, Oxford University Press, and Mohr Siebeck. He has published over 50 contributions in international peer-reviewed journals and edited collections. Kulick is an active member of the International Law Association and currently serves on its Committee on 'Submarine Cables and Pipelines under International Law'. Moreover, Kulick has extensive experience representing sovereign and non-sovereign clients before international courts and tribunals and advising states on all aspects of international law.

Nahuel Maisley is an Associate Professor of International Law at the University of Buenos Aires (UBA) and a Global Associate Professor of Law at New York University (NYU). He is an Associate Researcher at the Argentinean National Council for Scientific and Technical Research, based at UBA's Instituto Gioja. Maisley holds a Law Degree and a Doctorate in Law from UBA, and an LLM in International Legal Studies from NYU. He has received several scholarships and awards, including the Hauser Global Scholarship, the Jerome Lipper Award in International Legal Studies, the Thomas Franck Scholarship in International Law, the Lloyd N. Cutler Fellowship in International Law, and UBACyT and DeCyT scholarships. His work, which usually combines legal and political theory with international law, has been published in various outlets, including the *European Journal of International Law*, the *NYU Law Review*, the *Annual Review of Law and Social Science*, and *Jurisprudence*. In the past, Maisley has been a visiting scholar at the Universitat Pompeu Fabra (Barcelona) and the Max Planck Institute for Comparative Public Law and International Law (Heidelberg).

Eleni Methymaki is a Departmental Lecturer in Public International Law at the University of Oxford, where she is also finalizing her DPhil thesis on the role of domestic law in international adjudication. She was previously a Research Associate in International Law at the University of Glasgow and Leuphana University Lüneburg. Methymaki has lectured on international law topics at Queen Mary University of London, the University of Tartu, and the University of World Economy and Diplomacy of the Ministry of Foreign Affairs of Uzbekistan. She has published on a range of international law topics, including international inspections, international dispute settlement, and the relationship between international and domestic law. Beyond academia, she has experience in advising states, international organizations, and private parties on international law matters and dispute resolution.

Andre Nollkaemper is a University Professor of International Law and Sustainability at the University of Amsterdam (UvA). He was previously a Professor of Public International

Law and Dean at the Faculty of Law of the UvA. He is a member of the Institut de Droit International and former president of the European Society for International Law. He is the Editor-in-Chief of *International Law and Domestic Courts* (OUP) and has published extensively on the relationship between the international and the national legal order, including the book *National Courts and the International Rule of Law* (OUP 2011).

Rekha Oleschak-Pillai studied law at the Universities of Kerala, Aberdeen, St. Gallen and Bern. She is a Senior Research Fellow at the Institute of Federalism, University of Fribourg. Her research interests lie in the areas of comparative constitutional law, public international law, migration, and development.

Mónica Pinto is Professor *Emerita* at the Universidad de Buenos Aires Law School, where she taught International Law and International Human Rights Law and served as Dean (2010–2018). She is a member of the *Institut de Droit International* and of the Committee of Experts on the Application of ILO Conventions and Recommendations (2017–2026). Pinto has acted as counsel and advisor in international law cases, and as arbitrator and member of *ad hoc* committees in foreign investment cases. She has professional experience with universal and regional human rights instances, arbitral tribunals, and the International Court of Justice. She has been an *ad hoc* Judge in a case at the International Court of Justice (since 2021). Pinto is a member of the Permanent Court of Arbitration (since 2022) and of the Permanent Tribunal of Revision of Mercosur (since 2021). She has taught at The Hague Academy of International Law and CLS, Paris I & II, Rouen. She held several UN human rights mandates. She sat as Judge and President of the Administrative Tribunals of the World Bank and the IADB. She was Vice-President of the Advisory Committee for Nominations for the ICC (2013–2018) and a member of the Independent Expert Review (2020). In Argentina, Pinto headed the area of Human Rights at the Ministry of Foreign Affairs and of International Affairs at the Ministry of Justice. She was awarded the Chevalier de l'Ordre National du Mérite, France (2006); the Goler T. Butcher Medal (2009), and the Honorary Membership Award (2019), both with the American Society of International Law. Pinto published five books and several articles in periodical publications in the United States and Europe.

Zane Ratniece is a Judicial Cooperation Officer at the European Union Agency for Criminal Justice Cooperation (Eurojust), working in the area of core international crimes. Previously, she worked as a Legal Advisor at various international judicial institutions, including the European Court of Human Rights and the internationalized courts in Kosovo. Ratniece has also practised law for several years with a law firm in Riga. She has guest lectured at various universities in Europe, published on issues of public international and human rights law, and provided legal advice in proceedings before the European Court of Human Rights.

Dai Ruijun got her Master's and PhD in International Law from the Graduate School of the Chinese Academy of Social Sciences (CASS). She is a Professor of International Law at the University of CASS. She also serves as the Director of the Department of International Human Rights Law of the International Law Institute of CASS. Ruijun has published on a range of international law topics, including the law of treaties, international human rights law, and gender and human rights. Her books include *International Treaties in*

China's Legal System (China Social Sciences Press 2020) and *Domestic Implementation of International Human Rights Treaties: Worldwide Perspective* (Social Sciences Academic Press (China) 2013). She has also translated *The UN Convention on the Elimination of All Forms of Discrimination against Women* (OUP 2013, paperback) into Chinese, which was published by the Social Sciences Academic Press in 2020.

Semir Sali is an International Law Consultant. His background includes experience as both a generalist international lawyer (at the United Nations Secretariat and NATO) and as an international criminal lawyer (at the Kosovo Specialist Chambers and International Criminal Tribunal for the former Yugoslavia). He specializes in appellate and constitutional cases concerning complex domestic legal matters. During his tenure as Legal Advisor at the Supreme Court of the Republic of Albania, he provided legal opinions on hundreds of appeals and drafted several judgments, including three judgments issued by the Joint Benches of the Supreme Court. He is a Doctoral candidate in the law of international organizations at the University of Helsinki. In 2017, he spent time at the Max Planck Institute in Luxembourg as a Visiting Research Fellow. Sali is a Licensed Attorney with the Tirana Bar Association. He holds advanced degrees in Law from the University of Turin, as well as an LLM from Leiden University.

Osnat Grady Schwartz has a PhD in Law from the Hebrew University of Jerusalem, studying the engagement of national courts with international law and the mutual empowerment of national and international courts. She was previously a Postdoctoral Researcher and Research Fellow at UC Berkeley as a Fulbright scholar. Schwartz worked as a Legal Adviser to the Turkel Commission for the investigation of the Mavi Marmara incident. She also participated in several international law study groups and worked as a teaching fellow at Hebrew University from 2014 to 2019, following which she retired from the academy and embarked on a new chapter in life, studying music composition and performance at the Ono Academic College School of Music.

Yuval Shany is the Hersch Lauterpacht Chair in International Law and former Dean of the Law Faculty of the Hebrew University of Jerusalem. He was a member of the United Nations Human Rights Committee from 2013 to 2020 and served as Chair of the Committee in 2018–2019. He currently serves as a Senior Research Fellow at the Israel Democracy Institute, as the Head of the Cyber Law programme of the Hebrew University Cyber Security Research Centre, and as a Visiting Fellow at the Ethics in AI Institute of the University of Oxford. Shany is also currently directing an ERC research project on the development of digital human rights.

David Sloss is John A. and Elizabeth H. Sutro Professor of Law at Santa Clara University School of Law and an internationally renowned scholar who has published five books and several dozen book chapters and law review articles. His books have won prestigious awards from the American Bar Association, the American Society of International Law, and the Alpha Sigma Nu Jesuit Honor Society. His scholarship covers a broad range of areas, including international law, constitutional law, and international affairs. Sloss is informed by a decade of experience in the federal government, where he helped draft and negotiate several major international treaties. He is currently writing a book about how the US Supreme Court is subverting American democracy. Sloss is a member of the bar of the US Supreme Court, a member of the American Law Institute, and a Counsellor to the American Society of International Law.

Antonios Tzanakopoulos is a Professor of Public International Law at the University of Oxford and a Fellow of St Anne's College, Oxford. He advises states and other actors in matters of public international law, including before international and domestic courts and tribunals from Three Stone Chambers in Lincoln's Inn.

Sharon Weill is an Associate Professor of International Law at the American University of Paris and a Senior Lecturer at Sciences Po Paris. In 2022, she was nominated as a Research Associate with the Centre for Comparative Law & the Internationalization of Law at Sorbonne University. She holds a PhD in Law from the University of Geneva (2012). Weill previously served as an expert member of the French National Consultative Commission for Human Rights (2018–2020) and as a UNHCR Asylum Judge in France (2019–2022). Her research focuses on the connections between law, armed conflict, terrorism, and the role of courts, using socio-legal approaches, including trial ethnography. Since 2017, she has been part of a multidisciplinary research group examining the role of French judges as transnational actors in the 'fight against terrorism' and the transformation of legal systems in response to transnational jihadism. Her postdoctoral research conducted at the University of California, Berkeley, focused on the Guantanamo Bay trials and Israeli military tribunals in the occupied territories. Weill currently co-directs an ethnographic research project within the French Asylum Court. She is the author of the book *The Role of National Courts in Applying International Humanitarian Law* (OUP 2014), co-editor of *The President on Trial: Prosecuting Hissène Habré* (OUP 2020), and her work *Terror on Trial: An Ethnography of French Courts* is forthcoming with Cambridge University Press.

Hannah Woolaver is an Associate Professor of Public International Law in the Law Faculty of the University of Cape Town. Her research and teaching interests lie in public international law, especially the relationship between international law and domestic law, the law on the use of force, and international criminal law. Woolaver earned her LLB from Durham University, BCL at the University of Oxford, and PhD at the University of Cambridge. She has held visiting positions at the University of New South Wales, Australia, the University of Toronto, and the University of Cambridge.

Gentian Zyberi is a Professor of International Law and Human Rights at the Norwegian Centre for Human Rights, Faculty of Law, University of Oslo. Zyberi was previously a member of the United Nations Human Rights Committee (2019–2022) and is a member of the Permanent Court of Arbitration (2016–2028). He is a member of the Scientific Committee of the EU Fundamental Rights Agency for the period 2023–2028. Over the last two decades, Zyberi has done research, published, and taught in the areas of international human rights law, international humanitarian law, international criminal law, and public international law at various universities in the Netherlands, Albania, China, the United States, Kosovo, North Macedonia, and Norway. His research interests include the role of international courts and international and regional judicial and quasi-judicial human rights mechanisms in developing international law, the protection of community interests through international law, and transitional justice processes, especially in the Balkans.

PART 1
INTRODUCTION

1

Engagement of Domestic Courts with International Law

Principled or Unprincipled?

André Nollkaemper, Yuval Shany, and Antonios Tzanakopoulos

A. Introduction

The proposition that the 'future of international law is domestic'[1] may be somewhat of an overstatement, but it does convey the significance of domestic institutions in interpreting and applying international law. Given the institutional limits of international bodies—whose powers are often legally circumscribed, and under-utilized for lack of material capacity or political will—right holders and other interested natural and legal persons increasingly rely on national institutions, in particular domestic courts, to give effect to international law norms.

The dependence on national institutions for 'giving teeth' to international law norms is, however, not a new state of affairs. Already in the 1930s, Georges Scelle developed the theory of *dédoublement fonctionnel* to describe the dual role of national institutions as organs of the national and international legal system, exercising powers of legislation, adjudication, and law-application on behalf of the international community.[2] Customary international law doctrines, such as universal jurisdiction, and treaties containing specific obligations to transpose international obligations into domestic law and to exercise national jurisdiction in response to violation of international norms,[3] reflect the insight of international law-makers that national institutions play a key role in giving actual content and real effect to international law norms.

[1] See William Burke-White and Anne-Marie Slaughter, 'The Future of International Law is Domestic (or, The European Way of Life)' (2006) 47 Harvard Journal of International 327.

[2] See Georges Scelle, *Précis de droit des gens: Principes et systématique* (première partie, Recueil Sirey 1932) 43, 54–56, 217; Georges Scelle, *Précis de droit des gens: Principes et systématique* (seconde partie, Recueil Sirey 1934) 10, 91–202, 319, 450.

[3] See, eg, Convention against Torture and Other Cruel, Inhuman or Degrading Treatment of Punishment (adopted 10 December 1984, entered into force 26 June 1987) 1465 UNTS 85 art 4:

At a conceptual level, there is no reason to consider the task of national institutions as fundamentally different from that of international institutions that are also entrusted with giving content and real effect to international law norms. Respect for the rule of law as a basic principle of governance, which encompasses within its scope all valid legal norms, including international law norms, generates normative expectations that both national and international institutions will uphold the rules of international law binding on them. This applies, in particular, to national courts, whose main task is to interpret and apply valid legal norms. Furthermore, the more the contents of national and international law norms come to resemble one another—especially, in areas such as international human rights law, whose provisions often mirror domestic constitutional law provisions,[4] and international criminal law, which often overlaps procedurally and substantively with domestic criminal law[5]—the greater the epistemic ease with which domestic courts are expected to approach the interpretation and application of international law norms.

There is no need to overestimate, in this regard, the disruption created by the 'background noise' of domestic law, against which domestic courts engage in the interpretation and application of international law norms. Although there may be cases in which provisions of domestic law constrain domestic courts' ability to give full effect to applicable international law norms, such a challenge also confronts international courts since they are often constrained by virtue of the jurisdictional and applicable law provisions found in their constitutive instruments from giving full effect to all the international law norms binding on the parties before them.[6] As a result, both national and international courts

1. Each State Party shall ensure that all acts of torture are offences under its criminal law. The same shall apply to an attempt to commit torture and to an act by any person which constitutes complicity or participation in torture.
2. Each State Party shall make these offences punishable by appropriate penalties which take into account their grave nature.

[4] For a discussion of the overlap between international human rights law and domestic constitutional law, see Stephen Gardbaum, 'Human Rights as International Constitutional Rights' (2008) 19 EJIL 749.

[5] For a discussion of the interplay between domestic and international criminal law, see Jonathan Charney, 'International Criminal Law and the Role of Domestic Court' (2001) 95 AJIL 120.

[6] See, eg, *Application of the Convention on the Prevention and Punishment of the Crime of Genocide (Bosnia and Herzegovina v Serbia and Montenegro)* (Merits) [2007] ICJ Rep 43, 220–21 [429]:

> The decision of the Court does not, in this case, purport to establish a general jurisprudence applicable to all cases where a treaty instrument, or other binding legal norm, includes an obligation for States to prevent certain acts. Still less does the decision of the Court purport to find whether, apart from the texts applicable to specific fields, there is a general obligation on States to prevent the commission by other persons or entities of acts contrary to certain norms of general international law. The Court will therefore confine itself to determining the specific scope of the duty to prevent in the Genocide Convention, and to the extent that such a determination is necessary to the decision to be given on the dispute before it. This

apply at times only a truncated version of international law in a manner that is partial and mediated through other applicable norms. Indeed, it has been asserted in the past by one of us that national courts can be regarded as performing a comparable task to that of 'special regime' courts;[7] only that, unlike international specialized courts whose special regime is an international regime typically limited in the scope of its subject matter, domestic courts operate within a 'special regime' that is the national legal system in which they are embedded, and which governs their ability to apply all bodies of law, including international law.

At the end of the day, the main differences between domestic court judges and international court judges appear to be sociological and political—in that they involve different levels of familiarity with international law and different outlooks on the political desirability of giving effect to its contents.[8] Judges of domestic courts form part of a social group that speaks the language of domestic law, not international law,[9] whose principal loyalty is to the sources of authority producing domestic law, not international law, and who view the community of States and actors comprising the international legal order as an outsider group, a group whose prescriptions should not always command deference and support.[10] International judges, even those serving on special regime courts, such as the European Court of Human Rights (ECtHR) or the World Trade Organization Appellate Body, are expected to be better versed in the language of general international law, to respect the authority of the international legal process, which is the same process that generated their specialized legal sources, and view from their perspective national legal communities as the outsider group.

But if indeed the difference between positions of judges of domestic and international courts vis-à-vis the status and authority of international law is

will, of course, not absolve it of the need to refer, if need be, to the rules of law whose scope extends beyond the specific field covered by the Convention.

[7] Yuval Shany, 'National Courts as International Actors: Jurisdictional Implications' (2009) Federalismi.it No 15/2009, available at <https://federalismi.it/ApplOpenFilePDF.cfm?artid=13810&dpath=document&dfile=29072009111203.pdf&content=National%2Bcourts%2Bas%2Binternational%2Bactors%3A%2Bjurisdictional%2Bimplications%2B%2D%2Bdottrina%2B%2D%2Bdottrina%2B%2D%2B>.

[8] See Lisa Conant, 'Whose Agents? The Interpretation of International Law in National Courts' in Jeffrey L Dunoff and Mark A Pollack (eds), *Interdisciplinary Perspectives on International Law and International Relations: The State of the Art* (CUP 2013) 402–13.

[9] See Francesco Francioni, 'International Law as a Common Language for National Courts' (2001) 36 Texas International Law Journal 587.

[10] See, eg, Sheldon Bernard Lyke, 'Making Strange Laws' (2014) 35 University of Pennsylvania Journal of International Law 675, 730.

mostly sociological and political rather than legal or structural, then great variations are expected to be found in the approach of different domestic courts (and other national institutions) towards international law, across time and space and variations in composition. In fact, different judges on the same bench may adopt a different outlook towards international law depending on their familiarity with the language of international law, and their nationalistic or cosmopolitan leanings.

Against this background where formal legal structures have little explanatory value for how particular domestic courts, and individual domestic judges, go about in interpreting and applying international law, and where the actual engagement of courts and judges with international norms is determined by a much wider set of considerations, the present volume sets itself the task to identify and articulate the principles that underlie such engagement.

It is clear from the outset that the variations in approach towards international law render the task of articulating 'principles of engagement' a complicated one. Above all, it requires us to infer such principles from actual practice. If engagement is a matter of degree, influenced by a host of 'soft' factors, such as education, lived experience, and ideology, which change from country to country, from court to court, and from judge to judge, then 'hard' legal doctrine such as monism or dualism has little if any value in explaining or predicting practices of engagement. Instead of focusing on deductive principles, emanating from traditional theoretical constructs of the relationship between the national and international legal orders, this volume seeks to identify and offer a typology of patterns of engagement on the basis of practical experience of engagement in the life of international law.[11] In so doing, the volume constitutes part of a shift in the research from top-down doctrinal analysis to ground-up conceptualization of practice.

B. The Premise of the ILA Study

The present volume builds on the Final Report of the International Law Association (ILA) Study Group on Principles on the Engagement of Domestic Courts with International Law, 'Mapping the Engagement of Domestic Courts with International Law', published in 2016.[12] This report was premised on two

[11] cf Oliver Wendell Holmes, Jr, *The Common Law* (first published 1881, Mark Howe ed, 1963) 5.

[12] ILA Study Group on Principles on the Engagement of Domestic Courts with International Law, 'Final Report: Mapping the Engagement of Domestic Courts with International Law' (Johannesburg, 2016) (ILA Final Report).

key and interrelated insights that also underlie this volume: The first is that the traditional dividing lines between national and international law norms and institutions have blurred to a considerable extent. The second is that domestic courts tend to engage or not engage with international law norms regardless of the formal approach prescribed by the legal doctrines and traditions relating to the interplay between national and international law that they (are expected to) follow. The combined effect of these developments appears to invite a new theoretical paradigm to describe, analyse, and evaluate the relations between domestic courts and international law—a nuanced paradigm of pragmatic engagement—replacing the older, binary, doctrinal paradigms of acceptance (monism) or rejection (dualism).[13] At the heart of this new paradigm is the insight that although the old doctrinal commitments are still formally applicable, their impact on the actual practice of domestic courts is quite limited, and courts committed to widely different doctrines and theories of interplay between national and international law nonetheless reach similar results, giving effect or denying effect to relevant international law norms. In the same vein, courts committed to similar doctrines and theories often obtain very different results.

The transition towards a more pragmatic approach to engagement is supported by the growing relevance of what the ILA Final Report refers to as 'inward-looking' international law obligations.[14] Such norms regulate issues typically also governed by the domestic legal order of the State, and consequently feature multiple contact points with domestic law. The growing prevalence of inward-looking international law norms coincides with a tendency by domestic law to develop 'outward-looking' norms, covering situations and transactions occurring partly or fully outside the territory of the State, like extraterritorial crimes or torts or contracts with domestic antitrust implications.[15]

In addition to the combination of inward- and outward-looking norms, the transition towards a more pragmatic approach to engagement is explained by a variety of push (by States) and pull (by international law norms and institutions) factors. On the push side, one can note the increased interest of States in influencing the content of international norms and in partaking in their development. While the decisions of domestic courts have long been considered in

[13] On the traditional distinction between monism and dualism (or pluralism), see Hans Kelsen, *Principles of International Law* (Rinehart & Co 1952; 1959 reprint) 40e *et seq.*

[14] ILA Final Report (n 12) para 12.

[15] See Yuval Shany, *Regulating Jurisdictional Relations Between National and International Courts* (OUP 2007) 9–14.

the literature a subsidiary means for the determination of rules of international law pursuant to Article 38(1)(d) of the Statute of the International Court of Justice,[16] as well as a source for state practice and *opinio juris*, actual reliance on them was limited given their limited engagement with international law, its sources, and its methods of interpretation.[17] The growing interaction between national and international legal proceedings in fields such as human rights law, investment law, and criminal law, however, has rendered domestic courts more adept in the language of international law than before.

In some cases, the structure of the interaction between domestic and international courts has created incentives for the former to adopt the decision-making pattern of the latter, and to engage in the application of the same norms as a way to establish their own authority and preserve a space for domestic decisions. Examples include the ECtHR's willingness to confer a broader margin of appreciation to domestic courts that follow its proportionality analysis,[18] and the International Criminal Court's embrace of the 'same person/same conduct' test when deciding whether or not to extend complementarity to domestic courts over comparable criminal charges.[19] In other cases, domestic courts have developed an interest in influencing the content of international law norms in fields such as counter-terrorism law and immigration law, thereby infusing relevant international law norms with the perspectives and interests of the society they serve and the legal tradition they follow.[20] Such moves potentially allow domestic courts to contest (to some extent) the interpretive dominance of international bodies, such as international courts, in steering the direction of the development of international law.

On the pull side, norms of international law increasingly penetrate into the national legal realm, by requiring States to give effect within their domestic legal systems to international norms, and to provide effective remedies for breaches of international norms.[21] Once international norms are incorporated

[16] But see Alain Pellet and Daniel Müller, 'Article 38' in Andreas Zimmermann and Christian J Tams (eds), *The Statute of the International Court of Justice: A Commentary* (3rd edn, OUP 2019) 819.

[17] For a discussion, see Aldo Zammit Borda, 'A Formal Approach to Article 38(1)(d) of the ICJ Statute from the Perspective of the International Criminal Courts and Tribunals' (2013) 24 EJIL 649.

[18] See, eg, *Von Hannover v Germany (No 2)*, App Nos 40660/08 and 60641/08 (ECtHR, 7 February 2012, GC) paras 124–26.

[19] *Prosecutor v Katanga* (Decision of Pre-Trial Chamber on Evidence and Information on Arrest Warrant) ICC-01/04-01/07-4 (7 July 2007) para 20.

[20] For a discussion, see Eyal Benvenisti and George W Downs, 'National Courts, Domestic Democracy, and the Evolution of International Law' (2009) 20 EJIL 59.

[21] See, eg, International Covenant on Civil and Political Rights (adopted 16 December 1966, entered into force 23 March 1976) 999 UNTS 171 art 2(3), as interpreted in Human Rights Committee, 'General Comment No 31: The Nature of the General Legal Obligation Imposed on States Parties to the Covenant' (26 May 2004) UN Doc CCPR/C/21/Rev.1/Add. 13 paras 15–17.

into domestic law, pursuant to international criminal law or human rights treaties, for example, the traditional distinction between monist and dualist States is rendered largely obsolete. Moreover, the duty to afford an effective remedy encourages domestic court litigation over issues covered by the relevant international norms. This results almost always in some form of engagement of the domestic court with the content of such international norms.

C. The Legal Context for Engagement

The ILA Final Report and the chapters in this book confirm the limited relevance of the traditional distinction between monism and dualism in explaining and predicting patterns of engagement of domestic courts with international law. This does not mean, however, that the legal context in which domestic courts operate is irrelevant for their engagement with international law norms. Engagement is not only a matter of sociological and political factors.

The first insight which the ILA Final Report provides is that national patterns of engagement tend to be **source-specific**. Many States have developed different constitutional rules and practices for international treaties, customary international law, and other sources of international law.[22] A notable example in this regard is the distinction between the direct applicability of custom and the need for legislative incorporation of international treaties, which has been developed in the UK, and has been subsequently adopted by other common law jurisdictions.[23] However, the ILA Final Report suggests that source-specificity exists in other contexts as well. In some States the constitutional rule is clear with regard to one set of international law sources, and unclear with respect to the others; and in other States a specific status attaches to specific treaties only—for example, to human rights or investment treaties.[24]

Source-specificity has significant consequences for the engagement of domestic courts with international law. In particular, it requires courts to develop a level of familiarity with the language and method of international law. The very need to categorize international norms as applicable or not applicable by virtue of their source requires an engagement with the content and legal status of those norms. Moreover, given the considerable cross-over between different legal sources (as evident in treaty norms reflecting customary international

[22] ILA Final Report (n 12) para 18.
[23] See, eg, James Crawford, *Brownlie's Principles of Public International Law* (9th edn, OUP 2019) 45ff.
[24] ILA Final Report (n 12) para 18.

law, whether through codification, crystallization, or subsequent development), even engagement with only one source of international law may introduce to the domestic sphere significant parts of international law.

The second insight of the ILA Final Report is that the engagement of domestic courts with international law is mediated through the diverse approaches to **legal hierarchy and interpretation** featured in the relations between applicable national and international law norms.[25] Hence, even if international law is part of the law of the land, the manner in which it will fall to be applied may vary radically pursuant to nationally accepted rules on conflict of norms and canons of interpretation. Hence, a treaty norm may be applicable but be pushed aside by a higher-ranking rule of (eg, constitutional) law, or, to the contrary, it may disapply a conflicting primary or secondary piece of domestic legislation in those legal systems where (part of) international law is the supreme law of the land or at least enjoys higher hierarchical standing.

Different sources of international law may obtain different status in the domestic legal hierarchy (eg, European Union law or the European Convention on Human Rights may have an elevated legal status in certain European legal systems compared to other legal sources).[26] The variations are even greater when the role of legal interpretation is factored in. In some national legal systems, unincorporated international law norms can nonetheless be relied upon when interpreting domestic law (or incorporated international law), including domestic constitutional law.[27] The results of this latter legal move could be significant, as they may result in the disapplication of domestic legislation by virtue of a constitutional norm whose contents have been significantly shaped by a nominally inapplicable international law norm.[28] In other legal systems, different canons of interpretation apply, which may marginalize or render uncertain the use of international law standards, including customary international law.[29]

The upshot of these contextual elements is that there are many doctrinal variations for explaining the legal status of international law in domestic legal orders and for predicting its application. Furthermore, the application of the doctrinal rules under the existing complex doctrinal structures invites considerable judicial discretion in categorizing international sources, determining

[25] ibid para 19.
[26] ibid paras 18–19.
[27] ibid fn 51.
[28] See, eg, Yuval Shany, 'Israel' in Fulvio Palombino (ed), *Duelling for Supremacy: International Law vs National Fundamental Principles* (CUP 2019) 167
[29] See, eg, Curtis A Bradley, *International Law in the US Legal System* (3rd edn, OUP 2021) 170–74.

their specific content, and interpreting domestic laws in light of them. The large number of variables affecting the end result—the specific terms of engagement—renders crude doctrinal distinctions, such as the traditional dichotomy between monist and dualist legal systems, even more useless.

The gap between doctrine and actual practice of engagement is explained in the ILA Final Report through the notion of *blunting moves* or *moderating techniques*—a combination of avoidance strategies, interpretative tools, and reactive application of conflicting or overlapping (or *consubstantial*) domestic norms.[30] These moves or techniques allow domestic courts considerable latitude to either embrace or reject specific international law norms across a spectrum ranging between automatic incorporation (monism) and legal transformation (dualism). It is against this backdrop that the ILA Final Report focused its attention on actual patterns of engagement developed by domestic courts, concentrating on the impact had by, or effect given to, international law norms in the domestic legal system, regardless of any doctrinal reasons provided for the manner in which international law norms were invoked and applied.

Given the wide variety of relevant factors, this volume, and the ILA Final Report on which it builds, are premised on the position that it is less useful, and indeed less feasible, to evaluate and classify decisions of domestic courts based on an assessment as to whether they align with or breach international obligations.[31] Although for many purposes such outcomes obviously are very important, we are of the view that it is incredibly difficult to deduce from them stable patterns of engagement, as the choice of outcome is often the product of a set of decisions made by domestic courts which can be explained by reference to a multiplicity of factors other than legal doctrine, including considerations deriving from sociology, ideology, and attachment to specific policy preferences. Note that in this area of judicial activity, the room for judicial discretion is exceptionally wide, since domestic courts have to interpret the less-than-clearly established content of domestic law, international law, and the rules governing their interaction. Hence, it is hard to identify the pattern of engagement adopted vis-à-vis international law independently of the different variables affecting the entire judicial decision-making process.

Moreover, if domestic courts are motivated by an interest in influencing the content of international law norms, as we suspect they often are, they may strategically opt for aligning their decisions with a particular interpretation

[30] ILA Final Report (n 12) paras 27–30.
[31] ibid paras 31–33.

of international law that many observers would consider a breach, although, if other States follow suit, it could become the new norm.[32] The ambiguity, or even indeterminacy, attaching to the content of international law at any given moment in time, and the dynamism characterizing such content over time, render it exceptionally difficult to assess on the basis of outcomes alone whether domestic courts are actually engaged in alignment or breach. This is why the ILA Study Group ultimately focused its attention on processes of engagement reflected in specific strategies or postures.

D. The Main Patterns of Engagement

The ILA Final Report identifies three main strategies or postures of engagement: avoidance, contestation, and alignment. It draws an analogy between these three forms and Albert Hirschman's organizational sociology matrix of exit, voice, and loyalty.[33] Indeed, one can perhaps associate practices of disengagement with exit and engagement with either voice or loyalty—including practices seeking to influence the content of the relevant international law norm (voice), and practices seeking to influence the content of relevant domestic law by resorting to international law (loyalty). As can be imagined, in practice, the lines separating the different strategies or postures tend to become blurred, and sometimes the strategies or postures blend into one another.

To some extent, domestic courts have a choice as to which of the three strategies to pursue. Often, however, they may be constrained in their choice, since domestic law may limit their ability to invoke international law as a binding source of law or even as a source for interpretation. They may also be constrained in more subtle ways—for example, when international sources of authority lack domestic legitimacy or when domestic judges lack information, training, or even the confidence to properly apply international law.

On one side of the spectrum of practices of engagement we find practice where courts seek *not* to engage with international law, for instance by resorting to avoidance techniques. Whatever the reasons that may explain such lack of engagement by domestic courts with international law, the outcome will always be to blunt the impact of international law on domestic law. The actual extent of blunting may depend on the precise avoidance strategy or posture

[32] See ibid para 31.

[33] Albert O Hirschman, *Exit, Voice and Loyalty: Responses to Decline in Firms, Organizations and States* (Harvard UP 1970)

which has been adopted by the domestic court. Invocation of formal obstacles to engagement (such as non-justiciability or dualism) may simply pass the buck to another branch of government—the executive or legislative branch—who can still take action to give effect to the relevant international norms.[34] But if the avoidance is the product of interpretation of international law as irrelevant or merely repetitive of domestic law, or of the application of domestic constitutional law to block the application of international law, a more permanent obstacle might be placed in the path of engagement. On the other end of the spectrum, engagement could lead to more or less meaningful forms of alignment, varying between almost meaningless 'fair weather' alignment to 'overriding' alignment, resulting in the displacement of a rule of domestic law by a rule of international law.[35]

The upshot of this is that strategies or postures provide us with tools to identify attitudinal markers towards international law. However, and as ever, appearances can be deceiving, and distinct approaches may generate widely different outcomes in terms of actual engagement and giving effect to international law within the domestic legal system. Add to that the aforementioned confusion that often surrounds the content of international law, and the result will be uncertainty as to whether international law was actually aligned with or not. Such uncertainty may lead to alignment with a norm of international law not binding on the relevant State or one that most authorities on the topic do not deem to even exist, resulting in what the ILA Final Report refers to as 'hyper-alignment'.[36]

The discussion on engagement is further complicated by the prevalence of consubstantial norms—defined in the ILA Final Report as 'norms which happen to exist both at the international and at the domestic level, and provide for the same substantive regulation'.[37] Once a State is applying such a norm, it is—nominally—applying a norm of domestic law, and the fact that it reflects also international law may be irrelevant to the judicial decision-maker. At the same time, the very act of transformation to domestic law may derive from a deliberate choice by the legislature to give effect to international law. It is sometimes difficult to identify whether the contents of the domestic norm were influenced by the international norm or *vice versa*. It is therefore difficult to identify the mode of engagement intended by the domestic court in question and resorted to in practice.

[34] ibid para 41.
[35] ibid paras 43–48.
[36] ibid para 55.
[37] ibid para 30. See also ibid paras 49–54.

Specific attention was given in the ILA Final Report to practices of contestation—that is, the deliberate use of a domestic or international law norm to challenge the traditionally accepted content of another international law norm.[38] Such a strategy or posture of engagement can derive from an interest in influencing the content of international law, or in avoiding the application of a specific international law norm, or both. By contesting the substantive content of an international law norm—because it conflicts, in the judgment of the court, with other principles of law or justice reflected in a competing legal norm—domestic or international—domestic courts encourage a revaluation of existing international law norms and the traditional way in which they are interpreted, and may serve as catalysts for legal reform, and for inducing reactions by other domestic courts, international courts, or other international law-makers, predominantly States, and norm-entrepreneurs. In any event, this form of engagement accentuates the potential role of domestic courts as normative actors in and under international law.[39]

Finally, the ILA Final Report discusses some of the policies underlying the various engagement practices.[40] Here too, much variety and uncertainty exists. For instance, is reliance on domestic law to bar the application of international law an indication of lack of ability or lack of will? And does any such lack of will derive from concerns about the content of international law, or concerns about the division of power between the different branches of government within the domestic system? What is clear is that motivations for engagement are not directly correlated with specific engagement practices. Still, the ILA Final Report identifies some salient variables—the constitutional framework for the application of international law, the relative position of the State in question in the international community, or its traditional approach to international law and the nature of the international law norms whose implementation is at stake, the propensity of lawyers and judges to raise international law issues, judicial independence from the executive, and the 'shadow' of monitoring mechanisms—which can affect the choice of an engagement strategy or posture. The distinction between inward- and outward-looking norms may be also particularly significant in this regard.

[38] ibid paras 57–65.

[39] For a comparable discussion, see Joanne Scott and Susan Sturm, 'Courts as Catalysts: Re-Thinking The Judicial Role in New Governance' (2007) 13 Columbia Journal of European Law 565.

[40] ILA Final Report (n 12) paras 71–79.

E. Concluding Remarks

Describing the different forms of engagement of domestic courts with international law represents a particularly difficult challenge given the loose connection between doctrine and practice in this field, the multiplicity of forms of engagement and their intertwined nature, which allows different observers to characterize differently the same engagements, and the gap between what courts do and what they say (or think) they do. The practice of domestic courts also varies over time, and often depends on the specific judicial philosophy, sensibility, or ideology of specific judges. The main usefulness of the ILA Final Report, and the underlying research papers, reproduced in this volume, is to offer a typology of engagement, and to introduce criteria that allow evaluating the results of the engagement process. Monitoring by other courts—domestic and international—as well as by States, plays an important role in placing in check engagement practices with a view to ensuring that they are channelled towards developing, not corroding international law.[41] Though the question remains: what constitutes development, as opposed to corrosion, of international law? But that is a question beyond the remit of this work.

[41] ibid paras 69–70.

PART 2
NATIONAL AND REGIONAL THEMES

2

Engagement of Domestic Courts with International Law in Anglophone Africa

Magnus Killander

A. Introduction

This chapter discusses the engagement of domestic courts with international law in 18 Anglophone African states: Botswana, Eswatini (Swaziland), The Gambia, Ghana, Kenya, Lesotho, Liberia, Malawi, Mauritius, Namibia, Nigeria, Seychelles, Sierra Leone, South Sudan, Tanzania, Uganda, Zambia, and Zimbabwe. These include all African states, except South Africa,[1] with English as the language of record in the highest court in the state.

With independence, these states inherited a political system largely based on the British model, though with written constitutions.[2] Over the years the political systems of many of these states have changed. Prime ministers were replaced by presidents to distance themselves from the former colonial master; multiparty democracy made way for one party states and then back to multiparty democracy; constitutional supremacy replaced parliamentary sovereignty. However, with regard to the relationship between international and domestic law, African Anglophone constitutions were for long quiet, while judicial practice, in the few cases the issue arose, applied the English approach of dualism with regard to treaties and monism in relation to customary international law.[3]

[1] On South Africa see the chapter by Hannah Woolaver in this volume.

[2] These states with the exception of Liberia are former colonies, protectorates, or trusteeships of the United Kingdom.

[3] cf with regard to treaties: *Higgs and David Mitchell v The Minister of National Security and Others (Bahamas)* [1999] UKPC 55 [12]: '[U]nincorporated treaties cannot change the law of the land'; cf the analysis in Ernest Yaw Ako and Richard Frimpong Oppong, 'Foreign Relations Law in the Constitutions and Courts of Commonwealth African Countries' in Curtis A Bradley (ed), *The Oxford Handbook of Comparative Foreign Relations Law* (OUP 2019) 587–89.

This chapter maps the engagement of courts in Anglophone African states with international law issues. It sets out the constitutional or legislative framework dealing with the role of international law, where such exists, and provides examples of judicial practice. It should be noted that judicial practice in most states is limited, and that with regard to some states it is difficult to access judgments.[4] Space constraints are also a limitation given the number of states covered in this chapter.

The chapter is structured according to the type of international law obligation under consideration. Thus, the first section of the chapter deals with ratified treaties, the second section with unratified treaties and soft law, and the third section with customary international law. The fourth and last section deals with the place of international law in the hierarchy of the domestic legal order.

B. Ratified Treaties

This section discusses the constitutional framework, where such exists, in relation to the application or use of ratified treaties and judicial practice of engagement with such treaties, including their use as interpretive tools by courts. As will be shown, there is great variance in approaches, with some Anglophone African states providing for the potential application of all ratified treaties, some providing for application of treaties ratified before the adoption of the constitution, and some not allowing for any direct applicability. However, even in the absence of direct applicability treaties may play a role in statutory and constitutional interpretation.

First, some Anglophone African states have, in revising their constitutions, left the traditional dualist approach behind for a monist approach to treaties. The first constitution in Anglophone Africa which provided for a monist approach to international treaties was the independence Constitution of Namibia adopted in 1990. Article 144 provides that '[u]nless otherwise provided by this Constitution or Act of Parliament … international agreements binding upon Namibia under this Constitutional shall form part of the law of Namibia'.[5] In

[4] Most Anglophone African states have Legal Information Institutes (LIIs) which provide free access to legislation and judgments on their own website and also via the African LII, available at <www.africanlii.org> accessed 21 July 2023. The most incomplete LIIs are in relation to Liberian and Nigerian case law. South Sudan does not have a LII.

[5] Namibian Constitution 1990 (as amended) art 144. For a recent discussion see Ndjodi Ndeunyema, 'The Namibian Constitution, International Law and the Courts: A Critique' (2020) 9 Global Journal of Comparative Law 271.

Namibia, the Supreme Court has thus held that the International Covenant on Civil and Political Rights (ICCPR),[6] the United Nations (UN) Convention and Protocol on the Status of Refugees,[7] and the UN Convention on the Rights of the Child[8] form part of the law of Namibia.[9] However, in practice these treaties have been used only to support the court's finding as national legislation provided for the same outcome in the case.[10]

For its part, Article 2(6) of the Kenyan 2010 Constitution provides, that '[a]ny treaty or convention ratified by Kenya shall form part of the law of Kenya under this Constitution'.[11] This does not mean that there is no need for implementing legislation. Indeed, with regard to human rights, the Constitution provides that '[t]he State shall enact and implement legislation to fulfil its international obligations in respect of human rights and fundamental freedoms'.[12] In the Kenyan legal order, the Constitution is supreme.[13] Already during the last years of the previous constitution, Kenyan courts had taken an international law friendly approach.[14] This engagement of domestic courts with international law, including the direct application of international human rights treaties, has increased under the 2010 Constitution.[15] The Supreme Court in its January 2021 judgment in *Mitu-Bell Society* provided that relevant ratified treaties should be applied by Kenyan courts as long as they are 'not in conflict with, the Constitution, local statutes, or a final judicial pronouncement'.[16] A court may further refer to a treaty norm 'as an aid in interpreting or

[6] (adopted 16 December 1966, entered into force 23 March 1976) 999 UNTS 171.

[7] (adopted 28 July 1951, entered into force 22 April 1954) 189 UNTS 137; (adopted 31 January 1967, entered into force 4 October 1967) 606 UNTS 267.

[8] (adopted 20 November 1989, entered into force 2 September 1990) 1577 UNTS 3.

[9] *S v Mushwena and others* [2004] NASC 2 (Supreme Court of Namibia); *Thudinyane v Edward* [2012] NASC 22 [18] (Supreme Court of Namibia).

[10] ibid. This evinces the adoption of a strategy of simple or fair weather alignment by the Supreme Court. See ILA Study Group on Principles on the Engagement of Domestic Courts with International Law, 'Final Report: Mapping the Engagement of Domestic Courts with International Law' (Johannesburg, 2016) (ILA Final Report) para 44.

[11] Prior to the 2010 Constitution (The Constitution of Kenya 2010), the Kenyan Constitution did not deal with the relationship between international law and domestic law, but courts increasingly took notice of international law norms. See, eg, Nicholas Wasonga Orago 'The 2010 Kenyan Constitution and the Hierarchical Place of International Law in the Kenyan Domestic Legal System: A Comparative Perspective' (2013) 13 African Human Rights Law Journal 415, 416–18.

[12] Constitution of Kenya (n 11) art 21(4). See also ibid art 51(3)(b) with regard to the enactment of legislation related to the rights of detained persons.

[13] ibid art 2.

[14] John Osogo Ambani 'Navigating Past the "Dualist Doctrine": The Case for Progressive Jurisprudence on the Application of International Human Rights Norms in Kenya' in Magnus Killander (ed), *International Law and Domestic Human Rights Litigation in Africa* (Pretoria UP 2010).

[15] Orago (n 11).

[16] *Mitu-Bell Welfare Society v Kenya Airports Authority & 2 Others; Initiative for Strategic Litigation in Africa (Amicus Curiae)* (Petition 3 of 2018) [2021] KESC 34 (KLR) (11 January 2021) [132] (Supreme Court of Kenya).

clarifying a Constitutional provision'.[17] Prior to this judgment the approach as to how to interpret Article 2(6) had been inconsistent.

The Malawian Constitution provides that treaties ratified after the entry into force of the Constitution (18 May 1995) 'shall form part of the law of the Republic if so provided for in the Act of Parliament ratifying the agreement'.[18] However, '[i]nternational agreements entered into before the commencement of this Constitution and binding on the Republic shall form part of the law of the Republic, unless Parliament subsequently provides otherwise or the agreement otherwise lapse'.[19] Thus, the Supreme Court of Appeal held in *Malawi Telecommunications Limited v Makande and Omar* that the 1982 ILO Convention on Termination of Employment, which was ratified by Malawi in 1986, was part of Malawian law.[20]

Similar to the South African Constitution, the Constitution of Eswatini (Swaziland) provides that '[u]nless it is self-executing, an international agreement becomes law in Swaziland only when enacted into law by Parliament'.[21] In *Swaziland National Ex-mine Workers Association v The Minister of Education and Others*,[22] the Supreme Court missed an opportunity to engage with the relationship between international law and domestic law, and the provision on self-executing treaty provisions in particular. The respondent argued that the provision of free primary education was not a self-executing norm, but the Court did not engage with this argument in dismissing the appeal.[23] This is an example of evasive avoidance, as discussed in the ILA Final Report.[24]

The 2013 Zimbabwean Constitution provides that an international treaty 'does not form part of the law of Zimbabwe unless it has been incorporated into the law through an Act of Parliament'.[25] However, the Constitution also provides that '[t]he state must ensure that all international conventions, treaties and agreements to which Zimbabwe is a party are incorporated into domestic law'.[26] This ambivalent approach towards ratified treaties is reflective of Zimbabwean

[17] ibid.

[18] Constitution of the Republic of Malawi 1994 (as amended), s 211(1).

[19] ibid s 211(2).

[20] Convention (No 158) concerning Termination of Employment at the Initiative of the Employer (adopted 22 June 1982, entered into force 23 November 1985) 1412 UNTS 3. See *Malawi Telecommunications Limited v Makande and Omar*, Civil Appeal No 2/2006, Judgment of 7 May 2007 (Malawi Supreme Court of Appeal). See also *Kalinda v Libme Leaf Tobacco Ltd* [2003] MWHC 79 (21 November 2003) (Malawi High Court).

[21] The Constitution of the Kingdom of Swaziland Act 2005, s 238(4).

[22] (2/10) [2010] SZSC 35 (28 May 2010).

[23] ibid [9].

[24] ILA Final Report (n 10) paras 39–40.

[25] Constitution of Zimbabwe Amendment (No 20) Act 2013, s 327(2)(b).

[26] ibid s 34.

constitutional history. In the 2005 case of *Kachingwe and Another v Minister of Home Affairs and Others*, the Supreme Court of Zimbabwe held that a 1993 constitutional amendment amended the then Constitution so that treaties ratified before 1 November 1993 formed part of the law of Zimbabwe,[27] similar to the position in Malawi. However, case law under the new Constitution makes it clear that treaties must be incorporated to be applied.[28]

The Constitutional Court of Uganda in *Uganda Law Society v Attorney General* held that Article 287 (now 286) of the Constitution incorporates treaties into domestic law, with one judge going as far as to find that the African Charter on Human and Peoples' Rights was 'part and parcel' of the Constitution.[29]

Another provision of the Ugandan Constitution referred to by the Constitutional Court in *Uganda Law Society* was Article 45, which provides that '[t]he rights, duties, declarations and guarantees relating to the fundamental and other human rights and freedoms specifically mentioned in this chapter shall not be regarded as excluding others not specifically mentioned'. The Court noted that the fair trial rights provided in the Ugandan Bill of Rights were not exhaustive but that the issues before the Court were covered by the constitutional provisions.

Article 33(5) of the Constitution of Ghana,[30] which is similarly worded to Article 45 of the Ugandan Constitution, has been used by Ghanaian courts to rely on human rights treaties in expanding the protection under the Bill of Rights.[31] Interpretation by human rights treaty bodies is not generally accepted as binding on states,[32] and, where such pronouncements determine the outcome of a case before domestic courts, it could be viewed as hyper-alignment.[33] This will be discussed further in Section C in relation to unratified treaties and soft law.

[27] *Kachingwe and others v Minister of Home Affairs NO and another* (17/03) [2005] ZWSC 134 (17 July 2005) (Zimbabwe Supreme Court).

[28] *Shumba and 2 others v Minister of Justice, Legal and Parliamentary Affairs and 5 others* (CCZ 4 of 2018, CCZ 3 of 2018) [2018] ZWCC 4 (30 May 2018) (Zimbabwe Constitutional Court).

[29] *Uganda Law Society v Attorney General* [2009] UGCC 1 (Uganda Constitutional Court). Constitution of Uganda of 1995 with amendments through 2017, available at <https://www.constituteproject.org/constitution/Uganda_2017.pdf?lang = en> accessed 21 July 2023. See, for a discussion of the case, Henry Onoria, 'Uganda' in Dinah Shelton (ed), *International Law and Domestic Legal Systems* (OUP 2011) 606–7. To my knowledge, there has been no judicial pronouncement on the similar treaty saving provision in art 95(b) of the Liberian Constitution.

[30] Constitution of the Republic of Ghana 1992 (as amended), art 33(5).

[31] See *Mensah v Mensah* (J4 20 of 2011) [2012] GHASC 8 (22 February 2012) (Ghana Supreme Court).

[32] *Ahmadou Sadio Diallo (Republic of Guinea v Democratic Republic of the Congo)* (Merits) [2010] ICJ Rep 639, 663–64 [66]. But see the discussion in Machiko Kanetake in this volume.

[33] See ILA Final Report (n 10) para 55.

The Constitution of South Sudan provides that '[a]ll rights and freedoms enshrined in international human rights treaties, covenants and instruments ratified or acceded to by the Republic of South Sudan shall be an integral part of this Bill'.[34] South Sudan has been ravaged by conflict and to my knowledge courts have not engaged with the issue of the role of international law in the domestic legal order.

There is no provision in the Tanzanian Constitution allowing Tanzanian courts to apply ratified but unincorporated international treaties. However, as noted by Kazoba and Mmbando, international law can still play an important role before domestic courts: 'It all depends on the presiding judge as to whether he or she will accept the legal persuasion to lead him to a conclusion which aligns itself to international law or not'.[35] This approach can also be seen in a recent case decided by the Supreme Court of Zambia where it read in a right to food for prisoners in the right to life and the prohibition of inhuman or degrading treatment in the bill of rights. The Zambian Constitution does not have justiciable socio-economic rights and does not include any provision on the relationship between international and domestic law.[36] The Court in referring to treaties, soft law, and comparative case law noted that 'directly applying international human rights instruments and standards is a growing practice in domestic courts in different parts of the world'.[37]

As can be seen from above, it is only Kenya and Namibia that provide for the incorporation of all ratified treaties into domestic law, both with the caveat that treaties are inferior to domestic legislation. Malawi, Eswatini (Swaziland), Uganda, and Ghana provide for automatic incorporation of some treaties or treaty provisions, but with regard to other treaty provisions there is a need for incorporating legislation to make them directly applicable in the domestic legal order/before domestic courts. In some states this need for domestication is provided for explicitly in the constitution.[38]

Pre-emptive consubstantial alignment is not common in Anglophone Africa.[39] Thus, studies to ensure that legislation is in line with treaties, before or

[34] The Transitional Constitution of the Republic of South Sudan 2011 (as amended), s 9(3).
[35] Grace Kamugisha Kazoba and Charles Mmbando, 'The Impact of the African Charter and the Maputo Protocol in Tanzania' in Victor Oluwasina Ayeni (ed), *The Impact of the African Charter and the Maputo Protocol in Selected African States* (Pretoria UP 2016) 252. See also Chacha Bhoke Murungu 'The Place of International Law in Human Rights Litigation in Tanzania' in Killander (n 14) 57–69. See for this point ILA Final Report (n 10) para 78.
[36] *Mwanza and another v Attorney General* (Appeal 153 of 2016) [2019] ZMSC 33 (9 December 2019) (Zambia Supreme Court).
[37] ibid [13.9].
[38] See, eg, Constitution of the Federal Republic of Nigeria 1999 (as amended), s 12.
[39] ILA Final Report (n 10) para 49.

after ratification, are quite rare. An example of such a study is the gender audit of Gambian legislation which in line with a provision of the Women's Act 2010, the implementing Act for the Convention on the Elimination of All Forms of Discrimination Against Women (CEDAW),[40] and the Protocol on the Rights of Women in Africa (Maputo Protocol),[41] made recommendations for review of legislation and policies.[42]

This notwithstanding, Anglophone African states have incorporated numerous treaties through domestic legislation.[43] In some instances, such as with the Nigerian African Charter on Human and Peoples' Rights Act, treaties are incorporated verbatim.[44] Other statutes are hybrid in that they set out that they aim to incorporate one or more treaties through their provisions. However, substantive provisions in these hybrid statutes may differ from the treaty, despite the stated objective to incorporate the treaty.[45] For example, the aforementioned Gambian Women's Act 2010 was adopted to incorporate the CEDAW and the Maputo Protocol, even though there are many provisions of these treaties not covered in the Act. The impact of the Maputo Protocol can be seen in two recent Gambian High Court judgments dealing with equitable share of the joint property at divorce in accordance with section 43 of the Women's Act, which replicates Article 7 of the Maputo Protocol.[46] This is an example of consubstantial alignment in that the Court would reach the same result whether it applied the Act or the treaty.[47]

Where treaties have been incorporated into domestic law, practice varies as to whether a domestic court would refer to the incorporating Act or the underlying treaty. For example, the East African Community (EAC) Treaty[48] was

[40] (adopted 18 December 1979, entered into force 3 September 1981) 1249 UNTS 1.

[41] Protocol to the African Charter on Human and Peoples' Rights on the Rights of Women in Africa (adopted 1 July 2003, entered into force 25 November 2005) OAU Doc CAB/LEG/66.6.

[42] Satang Nabaneh, 'The Impact of the African Charter and the Maputo Protocol in the Gambia' in Ayeni (n 35). See Women's Act 2010, Act No 12/2010, available at <http://www.ilo.org/dyn/natlex/natlex4.detail?p_lang=en&p_isn=90619> accessed 21 July 2023.

[43] Bugalo Maripe 'Giving Effect to International Human Rights Law in the Domestic Context of Botswana: Dissonance and Incongruity in Judicial Interpretation' (2014) 14 Oxford University Commonwealth Law Journal 251, 257; Onoria (n 29) 595–96, 607; Babafemi Akinrinade, 'Nigeria' in Shelton (n 29) 458.

[44] See African Charter on Human and Peoples' Rights (Ratification and Enforcement) Act, Cap 10 LFN 1990, No 2 of 1983 (Nigeria), with the text of the African Charter on Human and Peoples' Rights annexed as a Schedule to the Act.

[45] This has the potential of leading to cases of evasive avoidance as discussed in the ILA Final Report (n 10) para 40.

[46] *Matty Faye v Dawda Jawara* and *Karla Keita v Mustapha Dampha*, as discussed in The Republic of The Gambia, 'National Review Report on The Beijing Declaration and Platform for Action- Beijing Plus 20' (June 2014) s 5.9.17.2, available at <https://archive.uneca.org/sites/default/files/uploaded-documents/Beijing20/NationalReviews/gambia_beijing_review_report.pdf> accessed 21 July 2023.

[47] See ILA Final Report (n 10) paras 49, 51.

[48] Treaty for the Establishment of the East African Community (adopted 30 November 1999, entered into force 7 July 2000) 2144 UNTS 255.

incorporated in Uganda through the East African Community Act 2002.[49] When hearing a case alleging a violation of the EAC Treaty, the Constitutional Court of Uganda, dealing with a matter similar in substance to one that had previously been addressed by the East African Court of Justice (EACJ), applied the EAC Treaty and not the Act and deferred to the judgment of the EACJ.[50]

Incorporating statutes rarely contain any provisions on what sources should be used for their interpretation, as for example does the UK Human Rights Act 1998 which obligates domestic courts to take the case law of the European Court of Human Rights into consideration.[51] While not an incorporating statute as such, the Constitution of Seychelles provides in relation to the interpretation of the Bill of Rights:[52]

> This Chapter shall be interpreted in such a way so as not to be inconsistent with any international obligations of Seychelles relating to human rights and freedoms and a court shall, when interpreting the provision of this Chapter, take judicial notice of—
> a. the international instruments containing these obligations;
> b. the reports and expression of views of bodies administering or enforcing these instruments;
> c. the reports, decisions or opinions of international and regional institutions administering or enforcing Conventions on human rights and freedoms;
> d. the Constitutions of other democratic States or nations and decisions of the courts of the States or nations in respect of their Constitutions.

With regard to Nigeria, Akinrinade notes that '[c]ourts generally apply international rules of treaty interpretation'.[53] For their part, some Ugandan statutes implicitly provide that courts should defer to the executive's interpretation of the underlying treaty provisions,[54] which might lead to cases of affirmative contestation.[55]

[49] East African Community Act 2002, Act 13 of 2002, Uganda Gazette No 27 (10 May 2002).
[50] Onoria (n 29) 604–5; Henry Onoria 'Botched-Up Elections, Treaty Amendments and Judicial Independence in the East African Community' (2010) 54 Journal of African Law 74, 79.
[51] See Human Rights Act 1998, s 4.
[52] Constitution of the Republic of Seychelles 1993 (as amended), Act 2 of 1992, s 48.
[53] Akinrinade (n 43) 459.
[54] Onoria (n 29).
[55] See ILA Final Report (n 10) para 58.

As noted in the ILA Final Report, consistent interpretation may lead to consubstantial alignment.[56] The Malawian Constitution provides that courts should in interpreting the Constitution 'where applicable, have regard to current norms of public international law and comparative foreign law'.[57] The Zimbabwean Constitution is closer to the South African Bill of Rights interpretation provision[58] in providing that 'a court, tribunal, forum or body' in interpreting the Bill of Rights 'must take into account international law and all treaties and conventions to which Zimbabwe is a party'.[59] It further provides that in interpreting legislation, courts must 'adopt any reasonable interpretation' that is consistent with Zimbabwe's international law obligations 'in preference to an alternative interpretation inconsistent with' such obligations, an example of constitutionally enshrined consistent interpretation.[60] The Interpretation Act of Botswana provides that in interpreting a piece of legislation a court may consider 'any relevant international treaty, agreement or convention'.[61] Provisions such as these do not give any indication as to whether the interpretive guidance is limited to the treaty text and customary international law, or extend to authoritative interpretation by international courts, tribunals, and treaty monitoring bodies. However, they all point towards a preference for consistent interpretation, based on interpretive guidance from various international bodies, which in many cases leads to consubstantial alignment.[62]

The absence of legislative provisions on international law as a tool for interpretation has been highlighted as one of the reasons for the relative paucity of international law references in the case law in other jurisdictions discussed in this chapter. Thus, with regard to Uganda, Onoria has noted that '[t]he absence of a provision expressly requiring the courts to consider international law when interpreting the Constitution has resulted in international law being completely ignored or referred to cursorily'.[63] However, in the last decade there has been an increasing interpretive reliance on treaties and soft law in Uganda, at least in human rights cases.[64]

56 ILA Final Report (n 10) para 46.

57 Constitution of Malawi (n 18) s 11(2)(c). In Namibia, the application of the principle of consistent interpretation to the Constitution has been confirmed by courts. See *Kauesa v Minister of Home Affairs* [1994] NR 102 (HC) (Namibia High Court), and Ndeunyema (n 5) 286–88 for a discussion.

58 See Hannah Woolaver in this volume, s A(2).

59 Constitution of Zimbabwe (n 25) s 46(1)(c).

60 ibid s 326(2) (customary international law), s 327(6) (treaties). cf the Constitution of the Republic of South Africa 1996 (as amended), s 233. See also ILA Final Report (n 10) paras 23–24.

61 Interpretation Act, Act 20 of 1984, s 24(1).

62 See, eg, *Mwanza* (n 36); *Center for Health, Human Rights and Development (CEHURD) and Others v Attorney General*, Constitutional Petition No 16 of 2011, 19 August 2020 (Constitutional Court of Uganda).

63 Onoria (n 29) 611.

64 ibid 612–18. See, eg, *CEHURD* (n 62).

Ratified treaties which have not been incorporated are still relevant as a tool of interpretation. Thus, the Supreme Court of Nigeria noted in *Abacha v Fawehinmi*:[65]

> [T]he provisions of an [unincorporated] treaty might have indirect effect upon the construction of statutes or might give rise to a legitimate expectation by citizens that the government, in its acts affecting them, would observe the terms of the treaty.

Similarly, the Supreme Court of Ghana held in *NPP v Inspector General of Police* that courts can rely on the African Charter on Human and Peoples' Rights, even though it has not been incorporated into domestic law:[66]

> Ghana is a signatory to this African Charter and member states of the OAU and parties to the Charter are expected to recognise the rights, duties and freedoms enshrined in the Charter and to undertake to adopt legislative and other measures to give effect to the rights and duties. I do not think the fact that Ghana has not passed specific legislation to give effect to the Charter means that the Charter cannot be relied upon. On the contrary, article 21 of our Constitution, 1992 has recognised the right of assembly mentioned in article 11 of the African charter.

In *Dow*, Justice Amissah of the Botswana Court of Appeal noted:[67]

> Even if it is accepted that those treaties and conventions do not confer enforceable rights on individuals within the State until Parliament has legislated its provisions into the law of the land, in so far as such relevant international treaties and conventions may be referred to as an aid to construction of enactments, including the Constitution, I find myself at a loss to understand the complaint made against their use in that manner in the interpretation of what no doubt are some difficult provisions of the Constitution.

[65] *General Sanni Abacha v Chief Gani Fawehinmi* (SC 45/1997) [2000] 4 NJSC 400, 466 as quoted in Akinrinade (n 43) 456.

[66] *New Patriotic Party v Inspector-General of Police* [1993–94] 2 SCGLR 459 SC, 466. The willingness of the Supreme Court to apply unincorporated international human rights law in this case has been attributed to the fact that 'the instruments did not alter but reinforced the domestic law position on the rights involved', and to the fact that the domestic and the international rights in question were consubstantial (as defined in the ILA Final Report (n 8) para 30). See Dominic Dagbanja, 'New Patriotic Party v Inspector-General of Police, Original Jurisdiction, ILDC 2548 (GH 1993), [1993-94] 2 GLR 459 SC, 30th November 1993, Ghana; Supreme Court' in ILDC (OUP), A2.

[67] *Attorney-General v Dow* (1992) BLR 119 (CA), 153.

Commenting on the *Dow* judgment, Maripe notes that the Court of Appeal held that there was a role for ratified but unincorporated treaties in the interpretation of national legislation

> not only in cases where there is some ambiguity in the legislation whose provisions are under construction. The only time they will not be used is when, by very clear and unambiguous language, the state has, by legislation, clearly signified its intention to depart from its international obligations[.][68]

This is in line with a strong presumption of consistency in the use of the principle of consistent interpretation.[69]

However, in later case law, the Botswana Court of Appeal has clearly taken a contestation approach noting that '[t]he rule of law is ... the cornerstone of the domestic law of the country and its application is not dependent upon some concept of a quality of law inherent in the articles of international treaties or conventions which were not in existence when the Botswana Constitution was framed'.[70] The Court here adopted a strategy of negatory local contestation.[71] Maripe calls the Court's reasoning 'the worst manifestation of a cop-out position adopted by the highest court of the land', arguing that if it wanted to avoid reference to international treaties, the Court could instead have held that the relevant provisions of the Immigration Act were sufficiently clear so as not require interpretation in light of international obligations,[72] and (in the terms of the ILA Final Report) choose avoidance over contestation.

However, courts in most Anglophone African states remain open to the use of treaties in the interpretation of domestic law provisions, including how such treaties have been interpreted by international courts, tribunals, and treaty monitoring bodies. For example in *Mapingure*, the Supreme Court of Zimbabwe held:[73]

> In strict constitutional terms, the prescriptions of [international law] instruments cannot operate to override or modify domestic law unless and until they are internalised and transformed into rules of domestic law. ... Nevertheless,

[68] Maripe (n 43) 263.
[69] See ILA Final Report (n 10) paras 23–24 for a discussion and, for what this might mean in terms of domestic court engagement, see ibid para 46.
[70] *Good v The Attorney-General* (2) (2005) 2 BLR 337 (CA).
[71] ILA Final Report (n 10) para 61.
[72] Maripe (n 43) 266.
[73] *Mildred Mapingure v Minister of Home Affairs and Others* (SC 406/12) [2014] ZWSC 22 (24 March 2014) (*Mapingure*) 14.

> it is proper and necessary for national courts, as part of the judicial process, to have regard to the country's international obligations, whether or not they have been incorporated into domestic law. By the same token, it is perfectly proper in the construction of municipal statutes to take into account the prevailing international human rights jurisprudence.

Finally, the relevance of ratified treaties is recognized even in states with no provisions in their constitutions explicitly referring to international law. Thus, the Court of Appeal of Lesotho has noted that 'where there is uncertainty as regards the terms of domestic legislation, a treaty becomes relevant, because there is a *prima facie* presumption that the legislature does not intend to act in breach of international law, including treaty obligations'.[74] This presumption seemingly only applies in relation to ambiguous text, and is thus a call for consistent interpretation rather than overriding alignment.[75]

C. Unratified Treaties, Comparative Case Law, and Soft Law

As noted by the Zimbabwean Supreme Court in *Mapingure*, 'it is perfectly proper' for courts to take into consideration international human rights jurisprudence in statutory interpretation.[76] This is in line with what the International Court of Justice (ICJ) said in *Diallo* with reference to the interpretation of the ICCPR by the UN Human Rights Committee:[77]

> Although the Court is in no way obliged, in the exercise of its judicial functions, to model its own interpretation of the Covenant on that of the Committee, it believes that it should ascribe great weight to the interpretation adopted by this independent body that was established specifically to supervise the application of that treaty. The point here is to achieve the necessary clarity and the essential consistency of international law, as well as legal security, to which both the individuals with guaranteed rights and the States obliged to comply with treaty obligations are entitled.

[74] *Molefi Ts'epe v Independent Electoral Commission and Others* (11/05 CC:135/05) [2005] LSCA 14 [16].
[75] ILA Final Report (n 10) para 46.
[76] *Mapingure* (n 73) 14.
[77] *Diallo* (n 32).

Similarly, there is a role in interpretation for unratified treaties and soft law that elucidate the content of international norms binding on the state. Thus, in interpreting domestic legislation, in particular domestic bills of rights, courts in many Anglophone African states make reference to various soft law instruments and treaties which the state has not ratified, resolutions by international organizations, and interpretations by expert bodies.[78] The use of such persuasive authority, which is often cited together with case law from foreign and, sometimes, international courts, is rarely underpinned by a theoretical approach as to how it should be used. Such jurisprudence is a clear example of hyper-alignment, as discussed in the ILA Final Report.[79]

In some instances soft law and unratified treaties are raised as relevant by counsel but the court chooses to ignore them without providing any reasons. Formal rejection to consider such sources is rare. An example of rejection is the Supreme Court of Appeal of Malawi which held in one case that 'Mr. Msisha drew our attention to two Conventions not yet ratified by Malawi which we do not think we need to consider as Mr. Msisha himself has doubts on whether these have crystalized into norms of customary international law'.[80]

International case law has also been rejected in rare cases such as when the Supreme Court of Ghana rejected the statement by the ICJ 'that there is no general legal obligation for States to keep themselves informed of the legislative and constitutional developments in other States'.[81] The Supreme Court held that 'this position is untenable in the context of the modern dispensation of international relations, which is characterized by, and operates within an environment of, democracy and written constitutions'.[82]

[78] See, eg, Maripe (n 43) 276; *Ahumah Ocansey v The Electoral Commission and Centre for Human Rights and Civil Liberties (CHURCIL) v Attorney-General* [2010] SCGLR 575 (Ghana Supreme Court); *Eric Gitari v Non-Governmental Organisations Co-ordination Board and Attorney General* (Petition 440 of 2013) [2015] eKLR (Kenya High Court); *Mitu-Bell Society* (n 16); *Okeke v Minister of Home Affairs* [2001] MWHC 36 (8 July 2001) (Malawi High Court); *Alexander v Minister of Justice and Others* [2010] NASC 2 (9 April 2010) (Namibia Supreme Court); *CEHURD* (n 62); *Mwanza* (n 36). See also Machiko Kanetake in this volume at x.

[79] ILA Final Report (n 10) para 5].

[80] *The Adoption of Children Act CAP 26:01; CJ A Female Infant of C/o PO Box 30871, Chichiri, Blantyre 3* [2009] MWSC 1 (11 June 2009). See also *Simbi (Steelmakers) (Pvt) Ltd. v Shamu and others* (SC 71 of 2015, Civil Appeal SC 479 of 2014) [2015] ZWSC 71 (20 November 2015) (Zimbabwe Supreme Court).

[81] *Banful and another v Attorney General and another* (J1 7 of 2016) [2017] GHASC 21 (22 June 2017) citing *Land and Maritime Boundary between Cameroon and Nigeria (Cameroon v Nigeria: Equatorial Guinea intervening)* (Judgment) [2002] ICJ Rep 303, 430 [266].

[82] This attitude of the Supreme Court could be characterized as negatory contestation, perhaps internationally minded, see ILA Final Report (n 10) paras 61, 65.

D. Customary International Law

This section discusses the approach of courts in Anglophone Africa to customary international law. Even in the absence of constitutional or legislative provisions on customary international law states tend to follow the approach under common law that customary international law forms part of the law of the land.

The Malawi Constitution provides that '[c]ustomary international law, unless inconsistent with this Constitution or an Act of Parliament, shall have continued application.'[83] Similarly, the Zimbabwean Constitution provides that '[c]ustomary international law is part of the law of Zimbabwe, unless it is inconsistent with this Constitution or an Act of Parliament.'[84] In other states, judicial practice has confirmed the legal status of customary international law.[85] The Botswana High Court, for example, has subjected the application of customary international law not only to domestic legislation but also to the common law.[86] This is an example of affirmative avoidance, where the court explicitly rejects reliance on customary international law when it is contrary to domestic law.[87]

The Namibian Constitution does not refer to customary international law but to 'the general rules of public international law' which shall form part of the law of Namibia '[u]nless otherwise provided by this Constitution or Act of Parliament.'[88] Similarly, the Kenyan Constitution of 2010 in Article 2(5) provides: 'The general rules of international law shall form part of the law of Kenya.' The latter provision does not provide for where in the legal hierarchy 'the general rules of international law' fall. In *Mitu-Bell Society*, the Supreme Court of Kenya held that, similar to ratified treaties, customary international law is applicable law in Kenya and should be applied by the courts as long as it is 'not in conflict with, the Constitution, local statutes, or a final judicial pronouncement.'[89]

Case law on customary international law in Anglophone African states is rare. Cases have included issues of state immunity,[90] immunity of international

[83] Constitution of Malawi (n 18) s 211(3).
[84] ibid s 326(1).
[85] See, eg, *Republic v High Court (Commercial Division) Accra, ex parte Attorney General and NML Capital Ltd*, Civil Motion No J5/10/2013, 20 June 2013 (Supreme Court of Ghana) (unreported).
[86] *Republic of Angola v Springbok Investments (Pty) Ltd* [2005] 2 BLR 159 (Botswana High Court).
[87] See ILA Final Report (n 10) para 41.
[88] Namibian Constitution (n 5) art 144. For a discussion see Onkemetse Tshosa, 'The Status of International Law in Namibian National Law: A Critical Appraisal of the Constitutional Strategy' (2010) 2 Namibia Law Journal 3, 12–15 and generally; Ndeunyema (n 5) 279–83.
[89] *Mitu-Bell Society* (16) [132].
[90] *Charles Gitau Mande v Embassy of the Kingdom of Belgium in Nairobi* (Cause 416 of 2016) [2017] eKLR (Employment and Labour Relations Court at Nairobi); *Springbok Investments* (n 86).

organizations (including disputes over employment conditions of staff),[91] and universal criminal jurisdiction (piracy).[92] In these cases the courts' approach has generally been one of alignment. Some cases have gone into detailed discussion to determine the current status of customary international law.[93] Other cases have made sweeping findings of dubious merit. For example, in relation to criminal jurisdiction, one of the judges of the Kenyan Court of Appeal wrote that 'customary international law gives universal jurisdiction to all countries to deal with crimes committed outside the territorial jurisdiction'.[94] While the statement is probably correct with regard to piracy, which was the crime considered in the case at hand, there is clearly no acceptance in the international community in relation to universal jurisdiction for all crimes.

E. Hierarchy

Most Anglophone African states provide for constitutional supremacy and stipulate that any law that is inconsistent with the Constitution is void.[95] In some (older) Constitutions, constitutional supremacy is not explicitly provided for in the constitution itself but has been confirmed by case law.[96] International human rights treaties have influenced many of the provisions in constitutional bills of rights. Particularly in the area of human rights law, there is thus much prospect for consubstantial alignment.

The constitutional supremacy clause sometimes has a bearing on how domestic courts deal with international obligations. Thus, in *Gramara*, the High Court of Zimbabwe refused to enforce a judgment by the Tribunal of the Southern African Development Community (SADC), as it would breach explicit provisions of the Constitution of Zimbabwe.[97] This is a clear example of

[91] *African Development Bank v Acholla* (Civil Appeal 135 of 2002) [2015] eKLR (Kenyan Court of Appeal); *East African Development Bank v Blueline Enterprises* Ltd, Civil Appeal 110 of 2009 (22 December 2011) (Tanzania Court of Appeal)

[92] *Attorney General v Mohamud Mohammed Hashi and 8 others* (Civil Appeal 113 of 2011) [2012] eKLR (Kenyan Court of Appeal); *Mohamed Hassan Ali v R* [2014] SCCA 34 (Seychelles Court of Appeal).

[93] See, eg, the discussion in *Mukazitoni Josephine v Attorney General Republic of Kenya* (Criminal Appeal 128 of 2009) [2015] eKLR (Kenyan Court of Appeal) on whether UN Security Council resolutions constitute customary international law.

[94] *Hashi* (n 92) Koome JA [13].

[95] eg, Constitution of The Second Republic of The Gambia 1996 (as amended) s 4; Constitution of Ghana (n 30) art 1(2); Constitution of Mauritius s 2; Namibian Constitution (n 5) s 1(6); Constitution of Uganda s 2; Constitution of Zimbabwe (n 25) s 3.

[96] See, eg, *Clover Petrus v The State* [1984] BLR 14 (Botswana Court of Appeal).

[97] *Gramara (Private) Limited and Colin Bailie Cloete v Government of the Republic of Zimbabwe and Attorney-General of Zimbabwe and Normal Kapanga (Intervener)*, Opposed Application, HC 33/09, Harare High Court (24 November 2009 and 26 January 2010) 17–18.

negatory contestation, as the SADC Tribunal Protocol clearly provides for the enforcement of the Tribunal's judgments.[98]

A number of Anglophone African constitutions contain directive principles of state policy which include respect for international law.[99] For example, section 219(c) and (d) of Chapter XX on Directive Principles of State Principles in the Gambian Constitution provides:[100]

> The State shall endeavour to ensure that in international relations it ... fosters respect for international law, treaty obligations ... and ... is guided by the principles and goals of international and regional organizations of which The Gambia is a signatory.

According to the Constitution, however, the directive principles 'shall not confer legal rights or be enforceable in any court'.[101] Similarly, the directive principles in the Constitutions of Namibia, Nigeria, and Eswatini (Swaziland) are not directly enforceable by courts.[102] This constitutionally imposed non-justiciability may, in turn, foster affirmative avoidance by domestic courts.[103]

The Directive Principles in the Constitutions of Ghana, Sierra Leone, South Sudan, and Zimbabwe include similar provisions in relation to respect for international law, but do not provide that the Directive Principles are not justiciable.[104] The Supreme Court of Ghana has held that the Directive Principles can be enforced by the courts.[105]

In Malawi, it is clear that an incorporated treaty norm is inferior to domestic legislation. The Supreme Court of Appeal has held that courts

[98] Protocol on Tribunal in the Southern African Development Community (adopted 7 August 2000, entered into force 14 August 2001) art 32, available at <https://www.sadc.int/sites/default/files/2021-08/Protocol_on_the_Tribunal_and_Rules_thereof2000.pdf> accessed 21 July 2023.

[99] See, for other examples, Ako and Oppong (n 3) 585–87.

[100] Constitution of The Gambia (n 95) s 219(c). See also Namibian Constitution (n 5) s 96; Constitution of Nigeria (n 38) s 19; Constitution of Swaziland (n 21) s 61 (see also ibid s 236 which is not covered by the provision providing that the issues may not be submitted to the courts).

[101] Constitution of The Gambia (n 95) s 211.

[102] Namibia (n 5) s 101; Constitution of Nigeria (n 38) s 6(6)(c); Constitution of Swaziland (n 21) s 56(3).

[103] See discussion in ILA Final Report (n 10) paras 21, 41. cf *Mwanza* (n 36).

[104] Constitution of Ghana (n 30) s 40; The Constitution of Sierra Leone 1991, Act No 6 of 1991 (as amended), s 10; Constitution of South Sudan (n 34) s 43; Constitution of Uganda s XXVIII; Constitution of Zimbabwe (n 25) s 12. See also Constitution of Sierra Leone, ibid, s 40(3) providing that the President shall 'ensure the respect for treaties and international agreements'.

[105] *Ghana Lotto Operators Association and Others v National Lottery Authority*, Ref J6/1/2008, judgment, 23 July 2008.

> will have to look at our Constitution and our statutes and see if the international agreement in question or the customary international law in question is consistent or in harmony with the law of the land and the Constitution. In doing so the courts will try as much as possible to avoid a clash between what our laws say on the subject and what the international agreements or conventions are saying on the subject, but where this is not possible, the provisions of our Constitution and the laws made under it will carry the day.[106]

In Kenya, the Supreme Court in 2021 clarified that international norms incorporated through the 2010 Constitution are inferior to domestic legislation.[107]

F. Conclusion

Generally, there is little evidence in Anglophone African states of evasive avoidance, where domestic courts would avoid considering international law even if its relevance is clear to everyone involved in the case.

Fair weather alignment is very common, in particular in human rights cases. Thus, international human rights treaties are often cited in support of similar constitutional provisions. Overriding alignment, in the sense that international law would be applied instead of conflicting domestic law, is not reflected in the case law I have reviewed for this chapter. Most common is the practice of domestic courts trying to reconcile domestic and international law through consistent interpretation. There is generally no pre-emptive consubstantial alignment in Anglophone African states. Instead, consubstantial alignment and consistent interpretation is used by domestic courts. Hyper-alignment, where the court goes beyond what is generally accepted as binding international law, is relatively common among activist judges. In such cases, courts enter controversial territory as they essentially take up functions of the legislature in addition to their role as adjudicators.

What an analysis of Anglophone African case law illustrates is that in the absence of a clear constitutional framework, the individual judge is the most important determinant in how international law is used, and that how litigators present their cases is also crucial.[108] Most judges would rarely resort to international law. The main exceptions are Kenya, Uganda and Zimbabwe where

106 *Adoption of Children Act* (n 80).
107 *Mitu-Bell Society* (n 16).
108 As discussed more generally in ILA Final Report (n 10) para 78.

international law is increasingly being used mainly as a result of an international law friendly constitutional framework. The Zimbabwean 2013 Constitution is interesting in this regard as it provides that '[m]embers of the judiciary must take reasonable steps to maintain and enhance their professional knowledge, skills and personal qualities, and in particular must keep themselves abreast of developments in domestic and *international law*'.[109] That said, a clear constitutional framework does not guarantee extensive engagement with international law in all cases, as illustrated by judicial practice in Namibia, where references to international law are relatively rare despite a clearly 'monist' Constitution both with regard to treaties and customary international law.[110]

[109] Constitution of Zimbabwe (n 25) s 165(7) (emphasis added).
[110] See also Tshosa (n 88) 29–30; Ndeunyema (n 5).

3

Engagement of South African Domestic Courts with International Law

Hannah Woolaver

A. Introduction

The new Final South African Constitution[1] (Final Constitution) came into force in 1997, supplanting the apartheid-era Constitution and the transitional Interim Constitution of 1993,[2] after a lengthy constitution-making process involving widespread domestic and international consultation. Appropriately, given the role played by international law and international institutions in inducing strong international opposition to the apartheid regime, the Final Constitution gives international law a prominent role in the domestic law of South Africa.[3] Customary international law and some treaties are made directly enforceable in domestic law without the need for transformation by the legislature, and international law can significantly influence the content of domestic law indirectly through various interpretative obligations imposed on the courts to interpret and develop domestic law compatibly with South Africa's international legal obligations. The Constitution, therefore, seeks to align domestic law with international law wherever possible. As such, the possible avoidance of international law by domestic South African courts is greatly restricted under the new constitutional framework.

Substantial consequences have flowed from the prominent place given to international law in the South African Constitution. Courts, and especially the Constitutional Court, have widely invoked, relied on, and applied international law in the South African domestic legal system. Nonetheless, the enthusiastic application of international law has not been without controversy. In particular, it has been argued that the constitutionally mandated relationship

[1] Constitution of the Republic of South Africa Act 108 of 1996 (FC).
[2] Constitution of the Republic of South Africa Act 200 of 1993 (IC).
[3] See John Dugard, 'International Law and the South African Constitution' (1997) 1 EJIL 77.

between domestic law and international law has been neglected, leading to the direct application of international law without the consent of the legislature. In addition, at times South African courts have claimed to be aligning domestic law with rules of international law that are of questionable legal status, occasionally in fact leading to unintended violations of international law. Finally, in contrast, South African domestic courts have at times sought to avoid the application of international law even when it seemed that the Constitution mandated such application. The South African experience therefore provides rich ground for exploration of domestic judicial engagement with international law.

This chapter will proceed in three parts. First, a brief overview of the relevant constitutional provisions will be provided, setting out the constitutionally mandated methods of engagement with international law. Second, the techniques that have been used by South African domestic courts to align domestic law with international law will be set out, showing that the technique of 'consistent interpretation' has been particularly significant in the South African context. Another technique of alignment used by the courts, which I term the 'moral imperative' technique, has had a mixed record in successfully bringing South African law into compliance with international law. Third, the strategies of avoidance of international law used by the South African courts will be described, indicating three such strategies that have been employed, namely: rejecting the customary international law status of rules pleaded before domestic courts, distinguishing the domestic from the international context, and the denial of self-execution of treaties. From this discussion, I conclude that South African courts since 1994, and especially the Constitutional Court, have adopted an overall posture of alignment with international law rather than one that seeks to avoid the application of or contest the content of rules of international law.

B. Relevant Constitutional Provisions

1. Directly Enforceable International Law

a. Treaties

Section 231 of the Constitution[4] governs the relationship between domestic law and South Africa's treaty obligations. Treaty-making is the responsibility

[4] This section builds on the discussion in Hannah Woolaver, 'South Africa' in Fulvio M Palombino (ed), *Duelling for Supremacy: International Law vs. National Fundamental Principles* (CUP 2019).

of the executive,[5] and most treaties require Parliamentary approval before ratification.[6] However, treaties signed by the executive of a 'technical, administrative or executive nature', as well as treaties that do not require ratification or accession, need not receive Parliamentary approval.[7] The executive is only obliged to publish the text of such treaties within a 'reasonable time'.

A largely dualist approach is taken to the relationship between domestic law and international treaties. In order for treaties binding on South Africa in the international sphere to be directly enforceable in domestic law, most treaties must be transformed by national legislation.[8] The treaty rule then has the same status as the type of national legislation by which it was transformed, whether, for example, an Act of Parliament or subsidiary legislation.

The requirement of transformation is, however, subject to the exception of self-executing treaties, which are directly enforceable in domestic law without enactment of domestic legislation, as long as the provisions are not contrary to an Act of Parliament or the Constitution.[9] The concept of self-executing treaties was introduced into the South African legal system for the first time in the new Constitution, having been borrowed from United States constitutional law. As will be discussed in Section D below, this transplant has not been wholly successful.

b. Customary international law

The Final Constitution establishes a largely monist approach to customary international law. Under Section 232 of the Constitution, 'customary international law is law in the Republic unless it is inconsistent with the Constitution or an Act of Parliament'. This provision continued the rule of automatic incorporation from the pre-1994 constitutional regime,[10] but also elevated the status of customary international law from its place under the previous constitutional regime. Prior to the Final Constitution, customary international law had the status of rules of common law, and was therefore superseded not only by contrary rules of Acts of Parliament and the Constitution, but also by subsidiary legislation.[11]

As discussed in Section D, one of the key techniques of avoidance used in the past by South African courts was to deny the customary status of international

[5] FC (n 1) s 231(1).
[6] ibid s 231(2).
[7] ibid s 231(3).
[8] ibid s 231(4).
[9] ibid.
[10] *Nduli v Minister of Justice* 1978 (1) SA 893 (A) (SCA).
[11] ibid 906.

law rules pleaded before them—a technique which has fallen out of favour in the new constitutional era.

2. Indirect Effect of International Law

The place of international law in the domestic law of South Africa is perhaps most prominent in relation to the interpretative obligations imposed on domestic courts. Three key constitutional obligations of varying strengths require domestic law to be interpreted compatibly with international law. First, Section 233 of the Constitution imposes the strongest interpretative obligation on domestic courts, mandating that when interpreting *any* legislation, courts must adopt an interpretation of the legislation that is consistent with international law over any inconsistent interpretation, as long as the interpretation is a 'reasonable' one. Second, under Section 39(1)(b), courts are subject to a weaker obligation to 'consider' international law when interpreting the Bill of Rights. Finally, Section 39(2) requires courts to promote the 'spirit, purport, and object' of the Bill of Rights when interpreting any legislation or developing the common law. Though this provision does not mention international law expressly, it has been held that determining the 'spirit' of the Bill of Rights will often require consideration of international law, as many of the rights in the Bill were intentionally drawn from various international human rights instruments—that is, the rights in the Bill of Rights are 'consubstantial' with those in international human rights law.[12] As will be discussed in Section C below, these interpretative obligations have been used extensively by South African courts to give effect in domestic law even to untransformed treaty obligations and to provisions of international law that are not binding on South Africa.

C. Techniques of Alignment

In this section, the techniques used by South African courts to bring domestic law into alignment with international law are set out and discussed. Two such techniques are addressed—that of consistent interpretation and the 'moral

[12] See ILA Study Group on Principles on the Engagement of Domestic Courts with International Law, 'Final Report: Mapping the Engagement of Domestic Courts with International Law' (Johannesburg, 2016) (ILA Final Report) para 30.

imperative' technique. Both have had a significant impact on the judicial application of international law in South Africa, enabling international law to shape the content of domestic law even more widely than might have been anticipated from the already generous provisions of the Constitution.

1. Consistent Interpretation

The South African Constitution contains three provisions mandating, to varying degrees, that courts adopt interpretations of domestic law that are consistent with international law. These interpretative obligations represent perhaps the most significant role given to international law in the Constitution, enabling all South African domestic law to be shaped by international law.[13] This part will set out how this technique of alignment has been used to great effect by domestic courts, and particularly the Constitutional Court, in relation to the interpretation of legislation in general, and in relation to the Bill of Rights in particular.

a. Legislative Interpretation

Section 233 of the Constitution obliges courts to adopt any reasonable interpretation of legislation that is consistent with international law over any alternative interpretation that is inconsistent with international law. In relation to this section, courts have interpreted 'international law' to mean all international law that is *binding* on South Africa[14]—including, therefore, both transformed and untransformed treaties to which South Africa is a party, and customary international law.

The wording of this provision makes clear that this is a strong obligation on the courts. As put by Moseneke DCJ and Cameron J in the *Glenister* case, Section 233 '*demands* any reasonable interpretation that is consistent with international law when legislation is interpreted'.[15] In addition, contrary to several other jurisdictions, this provision indicates that no ambiguity in the legislative text is required to activate the obligation of consistent interpretation. Indeed, by requiring a 'reasonable' interpretation consistent with international

[13] See *Glenister v President of the Republic of South Africa and Others* [2011] ZACC 6, (2011) (3) SA347 (CC), Diss Op [97] (Ngcobo CJ).

[14] See eg *Progress Office Machines CC v South African Revenue Services and Others* [2007] ZASCA 118, (2008) (2) SA 13 (SCA) [6].

[15] *Glenister* (n 13) [202] (Moseneke DCJ and Cameron J) (emphasis added). The *Glenister* decision is discussed further in Section C(1)(b).

law to be preferred over *any alternative interpretation*, it is clear that even if the most natural interpretation of the legislation would be contrary to international law, the court must adopt a reasonable but less natural interpretation of the legislation consistent with international law.[16]

This has proven to be a powerful tool of alignment of domestic law with international law for South African courts. In particular, it has been used to, in effect, circumvent the requirement of transformation of treaties binding on South Africa to be given direct effect under domestic law. This has been possible because of the above-noted definition given to 'international law', as meaning all international law that is binding on South Africa in the international sphere.

This is demonstrated in the *Progress Office Machines* case.[17] Here, the Supreme Court of Appeal (SCA) relied on South Africa's international obligations under the General Agreement on Tariffs and Trade (GATT) to interpret subordinate legislation imposing anti-dumping duties to be subject to a sunset clause that was not provided for in the text of the legislation. The SCA emphasized that limitless anti-dumping duties were contrary to binding international obligations under the GATT.[18] The SCA acknowledged that South Africa had not enacted the relevant international obligations into domestic law, and that 'no rights are therefore derived from the international agreements themselves'.[19] Nonetheless, the SCA held that given the interpretative mandate in Section 233, an interpretation of the subordinate legislation allowing an anti-dumping duty without time limit would be unreasonable, requiring the time limit to be read into the legislation.[20]

Section 233 has also been used to interpret treaties domesticated in legislation in an expansive manner, to read provisions into the domesticated treaty that are held to accord with other binding rules of international law. For example, in the *South African Litigation Centre (SALC)* decision, the Constitutional Court held that the Implementation of the Rome Statute Act ('SA ICC Act'),[21] which domesticated the Rome Statute into South African law, must be interpreted using Section 233 to impose an obligation on South African authorities to investigate international crimes committed outside of South Africa. This was held to be the result of an international obligation on

[16] In such cases, it is likely that the use of the principle of consistent interpretation may lead to overriding alignment. See ILA Final Report (n 12) para 46.
[17] *Progress Office Machines* (n 14).
[18] ibid [6], [11].
[19] ibid [6].
[20] ibid [11].
[21] Implementation of the Rome Statute of the International Criminal Court Act 27 of 2002.

South Africa to exercise universal jurisdiction, which the Court claimed to be derived from the Rome Statute, other international treaties to which South Africa was a party, and also the 'international nature' of the crimes.[22]

These cases illustrate the significant use of binding international law to shape domestic legislation through the obligation of consistent interpretation, including by reading in obligations that were not included in the legislation, and giving direct effect to provisions of untransformed treaties. Similar results were also reached in the *Glenister* and *Fick* cases, which are discussed below.[23]

Nonetheless, the Constitutional Court has indicated that there are limits to the powers of Section 233 in this regard. In the recent *Florence* decision, the Court rejected an argument that domestic land restitution legislation should be interpreted to provide for the remedies recognized under customary international law in the case of unlawful expropriation of property by a foreign State. The Court held that these remedies were incompatible with the legislative scheme, and therefore could not be incorporated through interpretation:[24] 'Our duty to interpret our law consistent with international law arises only when international law is not irreconcilable with our own explicit law.'[25] Therefore, an interpretation that aligns with international law only by running contrary to the text of the legislation appears not to be a 'reasonable' one, as required by Section 233.

b. Bill of Rights interpretation

Two provisions of the Bill of Rights have been used by courts to enable alignment with international law. Section 39(1)(b) of the Constitution explicitly obliges 'consideration' of international law when interpreting the Bill of Rights. In addition, Section 39(2), according to the case law, implicitly allows consideration of international law when promoting the 'spirit, purport, and object' of the Bill of Rights in interpreting legislation or developing the common law. Under both provisions, courts have considered binding and 'non-binding'—the latter meaning both treaties to which South Africa is not a party and 'soft law'—international law to be relevant and therefore warranting of consideration.[26]

[22] *National Commissioner of the South African Police Service v Southern African Human Rights Litigation Centre* [2014] ZACC 30, (2015) (1) SA 315 (CC) (*SALC*) [40]. As discussed below, such an international obligation to prosecute international crimes is difficult to substantiate.

[23] See Section C(1)(b), since these cases focus on Bill of Rights interpretation.

[24] *Florence v Government of the Republic of South Africa* [2014] ZACC 22, (2014) (6) SA 456 (CC) [143]–[144].

[25] ibid [144].

[26] See *S v Makwanyane* [1995] ZACC 3, (1995) 3 SA 391 (CC) [36] (interpreting the IC (n 2)); see also *Carmichele v Minister of Safety and Security* [2001] ZACC 22; (2001) (4) SA 938 (CC); *Government of the Republic of South Africa v Grootboom* [2000] ZACC 19, (2001) (1) SA 46 (CC). See John Dugard, *International Law: A South African Perspective* (4th edn, Juta 2011) ch 4. And see for a discussion Dire

These provisions of the Constitution, therefore, have been interpreted to allow norms of international law to which the State has not consented, as well as untransformed treaty provisions, to have significant domestic legal effect, raising separation of powers concerns, as discussed below.

The early case law of the Constitutional Court emphasized that the interpretative obligations in the Bill of Rights did not require adherence to international law. As put by Chaskalson P in the *Makwanyane* judgment, '[w]e can derive assistance from public international law and foreign case law, but we are in no way bound to follow it'.[27] In its early cases international law was largely used as a comparative example from which 'lessons' could be drawn, but ultimately played a minor role in the decision made by the Court.[28]

More recently, however, provisions of international law, and particularly untransformed treaty provisions, have had a major influence on the interpretation of the Bill of Rights and development of the common law. Two recent decisions illustrate this. First, in the *Glenister* decision, the Constitutional Court reviewed the constitutionality of a newly established anti-corruption investigatory unit, known as the 'Hawks'. The Constitutional Court, by majority, held that the Hawks were insufficiently independent from the executive to meet the requirements of the Bill of Rights.

The use of international law was crucial to the finding of unconstitutionality in the *Glenister* case. The majority decision of Moseneke DCJ and Cameron J held that Section 7(2) of the Bill of Rights required the State to take 'reasonable and effective' positive steps to protect the rights in the Bill of Rights, including the establishment of an independent anti-corruption agency, because corruption poses a threat to the realization of the rights in the Constitution.[29] Using Section 39(1)(b) to interpret the requisite standard of independence, the Court relied on binding but untransformed treaties, including the United Nations (UN) Convention Against Corruption, the UN Convention against Transnational Organised Crime, the African Union Convention on Preventing and Combating Corruption, and the Southern African Development Community (SADC) Protocol against Corruption. The standards in these

Tladi, 'The Interpretation and Identification of International Law in South African Courts' (2018) 135 South African Law Journal 708, 715ff.

[27] *Makwanyane* (n 26) [39]. See also *S v Williams* [1995] ZACC 5, (1995) (3) SA 632 (CC) [23] (Langa J).

[28] See *Legal Aid South Africa v Magidiwana* [2015] ZACC 28, (2015) (6) SA 494 (CC) [111]; *Shoprite Checkers v Member of the Executive Council for Economic Development, Environmental Affairs and Tourism* [2016] ZACC 23, (2015) (6) SA 125 (CC) [109] for recent examples of this type of use of non-binding sources of international law.

[29] *Glenister* (n 13) [189] (Moseneke DCJ and Cameron J).

treaties were relied on as being determinative of the required standard of independence—as being of the 'foremost interpretive significance'—and it was found that the legislative scheme fell short of these standards. The Court held therefore that as the legislation establishing the Hawks did not satisfy South Africa's binding treaty obligations to establish an independent anti-corruption unit, 'to create an anti-corruption unit that is not adequately independent would not constitute a reasonable step' to satisfy Section 7(2).[30]

Perhaps unsurprisingly, a dissenting opinion argued strongly that this amounted to enforcing unincorporated treaties 'by the back door', contrary to the constitutionally mandated relationship between domestic and international law. The dissenting opinion of Ngcobo CJ emphasized the constitutional requirement of transformation of treaties, and argued that the majority had overstepped the boundary between interpretation of the Bill of Rights with 'consideration' of international law, and giving direct effect to untransformed treaties.[31] The majority held, however, that their decision did not create new constitutional obligations out of the State's international obligations, but rather merely gave international law the interpretive role that the Constitution mandated.[32]

It can be seen, therefore, that by using untransformed treaties as an interpretive tool, these treaties had substantial influence on the content of the State's constitutional obligations. Whether this went beyond constitutional 'interpretation', the treaty provisions in effect became directly enforceable by the domestic courts.

Second, similarly powerful effect was given to another untransformed treaty in the decisions of the SCA and the Constitutional Court in the *Fick* case, here through development of the common law under Section 39(2). This case concerned the domestic enforceability of decisions of the SADC Tribunal according to the terms of the Protocol of the SADC Tribunal, which was binding on South Africa by way of the SADC Treaty. Two Zimbabwean farmers whose farms had been expropriated without compensation by the Zimbabwean government had brought a complaint against Zimbabwe to the SADC Tribunal.[33]

[30] ibid [194] (Moseneke DCJ and Cameron J).

[31] ibid Diss Op Ngcobo CJ [108]–[112].

[32] ibid [195] (Moseneke DCJ and Cameron J).

[33] The Southern African Development Community (SADC) Tribunal became operational in 2005, and was vested with authority to hear complaints by individuals against SADC Member States. One of the first cases brought to the Tribunal was the *Mike Campbell v Republic of Zimbabwe* (2/2007) [2008] SADCT 2 (28 November 2008), which was one of the cases that was the subject of appeal in *Government of the Republic of Zimbabwe v Fick* [2013] ZACC 22, (2013) (5) SA 325 (CC). After the Tribunal gave judgment in favour of Campbell against the government of Zimbabwe, the Tribunal's jurisdiction was amended by SADC Member States to restrict it to hearing cases brought by States.

The Tribunal held in the farmers' favour, holding that this expropriation was contrary to the SADC Treaty, and ordered compensation to be given to them.[34] After persistent non-compliance by Zimbabwe, including with a subsequent costs order issued by the Tribunal,[35] the farmers launched an action in South African courts for the enforcement of the costs order via execution against Zimbabwean government-owned property located in South Africa. Both the SCA and the Constitutional Court held that the order was enforceable in South Africa, and upheld the execution against the Zimbabwean property.[36]

As with the *Glenister* case, provisions of the unincorporated treaty were essential to the outcome of the case. Both the SCA and the Constitutional Court held that Section 39(2) of the Bill of Rights required South African courts to develop the common law on the enforcement of foreign judgments to include the enforcement of all decisions of the SADC Tribunal, even those to which South Africa was not a party (as was the case here, where Zimbabwe was the only State party to the relevant Tribunal judgments). The fact that the SADC Treaty was binding on South Africa, when considered in light of the constitutional right of access to court,[37] was crucial to the Constitutional Court's decision that the spirit, purport, and object of the Bill of Rights required the common law to be developed in this manner.[38] As such, decisions of the regional international tribunal that were not binding on South Africa[39] were rendered directly enforceable in South African domestic courts. Thus, as tools of interpretation, the untransformed treaty provisions, along with non-binding decisions of an international tribunal, were given direct effect.

The Constitutional Court has seemingly acknowledged the augmented role it has lately given to international law, recently holding that 'Section 39(1)(b) *requires* courts to interpret the Bill of Rights and our law in a way that complies with international law'.[40] This is difficult to reconcile with the text of

[34] *Campbell* (n 33).
[35] *Fick* (n 33) [3].
[36] This was arguably contrary to Zimbabwe's immunity from execution under customary international law, as discussed in Section C(2).
[37] FC (n 1) s 34.
[38] *Fick* (n 33) [57].
[39] *Pace* the finding of the Court, South Africa was not a party to the relevant decisions of the Tribunal, and therefore, under the Protocol on Tribunal in the Southern African Development Community (adopted 7 August 2000) (SADCT Protocol) art 32(3), these decisions were not binding on South Africa. Zimbabwe was therefore the only Member State bound by the decisions. See *Fick* (n 33) [59], for the Court's reasoning on why it held South Africa to be bound to enforce the Tribunal decision domestically. For further analysis, see Hannah Woolaver, 'Domestic Enforcement of International Judicial Decisions against Foreign States in South Africa: Government of the Republic v Fick' (2015) 6 Constitutional Court Review VI 217.
[40] *De Vos NO and Others v Minister of Justice and Constitutional Development* [2015] ZACC 21, (2015) (2) SA 217 (CC) [29] [emphasis added].

Section 39(1)(b), which only requires *consideration* of international law when interpreting the Bill of Rights, and the earlier judgments of the Constitutional Court noted above that emphasized the freedom to depart from international law under this provision. The technique of consistent interpretation has therefore clearly grown in impact and importance over the course of the Constitutional Court's judgments.

2. The 'Moral Imperative' Technique

Another technique that has recently been used by South African courts to justify alignment with international law can be described as the 'moral imperative' technique. By this, I mean that courts have invoked universal moral principles and South Africa's role in their enforcement for the benefit of the international community to justify alignment of domestic law with international law, as a supplement to or even in place of constitutionally authorized techniques. Such invocations of moral necessity have been used in particular to justify the domestic enforcement of international judicial decisions and international criminal proceedings. Perhaps ironically, in all instances in which this technique has been used, it has resulted in 'alignment' with rules of international law that are of questionable status, and/or the violation of established rules of customary international law of immunity.[41]

This technique is primarily evident in the decisions of the Constitutional Court in the *Fick* and *SALC* cases, discussed above, and of the SCA in the *Bashir* decision. In the *Bashir* decision, the SCA upheld South Africa's international obligation under the Rome Statute to arrest President Bashir of Sudan, who was the subject of two outstanding ICC arrest warrants, holding that the Executive's failure to fulfil this obligation violated the State's duties under international law, the SA ICC Act, and the South African Constitution. The decision therefore sought to vindicate South Africa's compliance with its international obligations.

However, in doing so, the SCA controversially held that the SA ICC Act intentionally did away with all forms of immunity concerning the prosecution of international crimes under the Act, even eliminating the *ratione personae* immunity of sitting senior foreign State officials from prosecution for

[41] And thus facilitating affirmative contestation. See ILA Final Report (n 12) para 59.

international crimes before the domestic courts of South Africa.[42] This was justified, not entirely convincingly, on the basis of South Africa's international legal and moral duty to fight impunity for human rights violations and international crimes. Wallis J expressly recognized that this was a violation of customary international law on immunity *ratione personae*, codified in another piece of domestic legislation. However, he justified this interpretation of the SA ICC Act as a 'departure [from customary international law] in a progressive direction'.[43]

Thus, South Africa's role as an enforcer of universal moral principles was invoked to justify a judicial decision at odds with binding rules of international law, but intended to effectuate compliance with South Africa's international obligation to co-operate with the ICC.

This type of reasoning is also evident in the *Fick* and *SALC* cases. In both cases, this technique led to 'overreach' by the Court, requiring the alignment of South African law with claimed international obligations that are of questionable status. In *Fick*, for instance, the Constitutional Court stated that it intended to combat the perception that Africa is 'a continent which has little regard for human rights, the rule of law and good governance'.[44] The Court justified its development of the common law to enforce SADC Tribunal decisions domestically in part by invoking South Africa's role in the protection of human rights and the fight against impunity in the Continent. It was emphasized that South Africa was the only possible forum for the enforcement of the international order against Zimbabwe. This resort to the moral necessity of finding in favour of the farmers resulted in 'alignment' of the common law with a specious international obligation: as noted above, the decision of the Tribunal was not binding on South Africa, and South Africa bore no clear international legal obligation to enforce the decision under the relevant provisions of the SADC Treaty.[45] In addition, by doing so, the Court overrode the Zimbabwean government's right to immunity from enforcement and execution, recognized in customary international law as well as South African domestic legislation, without convincingly illustrating that one of the recognized exceptions to immunity applied in the circumstances.[46]

[42] *Minister of Justice and Constitutional Development v South Africa Litigation Centre* [2016] ZASCA 15, (2016) (3) SA 317 (SAC) (*Bashir*) [103]. See, for a discussion of the judgment generally, Tladi (n 26) 727ff.

[43] Diplomatic Immunities and Protections Amendment Act 35 of 2008, s 4. This is an example of consubstantial contestation as discussed in the ILA Final Report (n 12) para 63.

[44] *Fick* (n 33) [1].

[45] See SADCT Protocol (n 39) art 32(3), imposing a duty only on States parties to a dispute before the SADC Tribunal to enforce its decisions in that case domestically.

[46] See Woolaver (n 39).

Similarly, in the *SALC* case, the Constitutional Court referred to former President Mandela's foreign policy that

> human rights should be the core concern of international relations, and we are ready to play a role in fostering peace and prosperity in the world we share with the community of nations. . . . The time has come for South Africa to take up its rightful and responsible place in the community of nations.[47]

This role of post-apartheid South Africa as a responsible member of the international community, and the fact that impunity would persist if South Africa did not pursue investigations of international crimes in this case, was referenced in the reasoning holding that South Africa bore an international legal obligation to exercise universal jurisdiction over crimes against humanity committed by non-nationals abroad.[48] The Court held that this obligation existed in part 'as [the alleged crimes] offend against the human conscience'. This reliance on South Africa's moral duty to fight impunity was therefore clearly influential in the court's determination that South Africa was bound by international law to exercise universal jurisdiction over extra-territorial international crimes by non-nationals. Arguably, however, this technique again led to an overreach, as this asserted international obligation cannot be found either in the Rome Statute or customary international law.[49] In these cases, the claimed alignment in fact undermined the very international rule of law that the judgments sought to support.

D. Techniques of Avoidance

I will now turn to the techniques used by South African courts to avoid the application of international law in domestic law. Three such methods can be distilled: the rejection of the customary international law status of rules; distinguishing the domestic and the international law context; and, also, the denial of the self-executing effect of treaties binding on the State. As will be shown below, these techniques have had a far more limited impact on the South African jurisprudence than the techniques of alignment described above.

[47] *SALC* (n 22) [1].
[48] *SALC* (n 22) [37].
[49] See Woolaver (n 39).

1. Rejection of Customary International Law Status of Rules Pleaded before South African Courts

While South African courts have, since 1994, become receptive to international law, this was not the case during the apartheid era. Given the international condemnation of the policies of the apartheid State, the eventual determination of apartheid as a crime against humanity,[50] and the suspension of South Africa's right to sit in the UN General Assembly, it is unsurprising that domestic courts during this time were not enthusiastic about international law. As a result, courts often sought to avoid the application of international law rules that were pleaded before them. The fact that the apartheid government declined to become a party to almost all international treaties reinforced this attitude.

Interestingly, the refusal by South African courts to apply international law often was achieved through the rejection of the customary international law status of the rules relied on by parties to the cases before them. This was done by applying a very stringent threshold for the proof of sufficient State practice and *opinio juris* to establish a customary rule.

The key case in which this approach was laid out was *Nduli v Minister of Justice*. Here, the Appeals Court confirmed that customary international law was automatically incorporated into South African domestic law, emphasizing the Roman-Dutch origins of this principle.[51] However, the judgment of Rumpff CJ then insisted that 'universal acceptance' was required in order to prove the existence of a rule of custom.[52] It can be seen that by requiring such a high level of proof for the recognition of a rule of customary international law, domestic courts are able to avoid the application of rules of international law that would likely be considered to be binding rules of custom if the 'widespread acceptance' threshold was applied.

This technique of avoidance, however, has since been abandoned by South African courts, as clearly held in *S v Petane*, concerning terrorist charges laid against a member of the military arm of the African National Congress (ANC). The defendant argued against the court's jurisdiction on the basis that

[50] International Convention on the Suppression and Punishment of the Crime of Apartheid (adopted 30 November 1973, entered into force 18 July 1976) 1015 UNTS 243.

[51] *Nduli* (n 9) 906(B).

[52] ibid 906(D). See Dugard (n 26) 28; and Dermott J Devine, 'Some Reflections on the Contribution of the Appellate Division to the Development of International Law within the South African Legal System' in Ellison Kahn (ed), *The Quest for Justice: Essays in Honour of Michael McGregor Corbett Chief Justice of the Supreme Court of South Africa* (Juta 1995) 166. This attitude may also be considered as indicative of affirmative contestation to the extent that the decision relied on a test for the identification of custom that is 'different from that which is generally accepted' in international law, including in the practice of international courts and tribunals. See ILA Final Report (n 12) para 58.

the situation in South Africa amounted to a conflict of national liberation, and therefore an international armed conflict under the definition of Additional Protocol I to the Geneva Conventions (API),[53] and as such was entitled to prisoner of war status. Conradie J explicitly rejected the standard put forward by the *Nduli* decision, holding that South Africa accepts that customary international law is established on the basis of practice that is 'widely accepted'.[54] The court therefore aligned the South African standard for proof of custom to that in international law itself.

However, even after this statement, indications of an exceptionally rigid interpretation of the requirements of State practice and *opinio juris* for the establishment of custom can be seen in the judgment. The court rejected the argument that the defendant was entitled to prisoner of war (POW) status, holding that the definition of international armed conflict in API did not reflect customary international law. In coming to this conclusion, the court made several statements indicating a restrictive approach to the establishment of custom: first, that UN General Assembly resolutions cannot constitute State practice capable of giving rise to a new rule of customary international law; second, that if a State verbally supports the existence of customary rule, but acts in a manner contrary to that rule, this negates the value of the statement as *opinio juris*; and, finally, that there would have to be near universal ratification for a treaty such as the API to influence the formation of custom.[55]

Throughout the judgment, South Africa's pariah status seemed to weigh heavily on the judicial reasoning:

> [T]he practice of condemnation of South Africa is evidence only of a general dislike of its internal policies. There is nothing in the condemnation from which the content of a rule of customary international law may be derived. I fail completely to appreciate how the condemnation of South Africa, or even the labeling of apartheid as a crime against humanity, leads to the inference that Protocol I has been accepted as part of customary international law by those States uttering those condemnations. ... United Nations resolutions cannot be said to be evidence of State practice if they relate, not to what the resolving States take it upon themselves to do, but to what they

[53] Protocol Additional to the Geneva Conventions of 12 August 1949, and relating to the Protection of Victims of International Armed Conflicts (adopted 8 June 1977, entered into force 7 December 1978) 1125 UNTS 3 art 1(4).
[54] *S v Petane* 1988 (3) SA 51 (C), at 57[f].
[55] ibid 58–65.

> prescribe for others. Customary international law is founded on practice, not on preaching.[56]

Evidently, therefore, that international condemnation of South Africa influenced the adoption of the unduly strict approach to the elements of customary international law.[57]

After the establishment of democratic government in the 1990s and the new constitutional era, South Africa's restoration to good standing in the international community has been accompanied by a new receptiveness to international law. This has extended to a less stringent approach to the assessment of State practice and *opinio juris* for the acceptance of the customary status of rules of international law. Indeed, in many contemporary cases in which customary international law is invoked, very little proof is provided to substantiate the customary status of the claimed rule.[58]

2. Distinguishing the Domestic and International Context

Despite their general enthusiasm for the application of international law, there have been some instances in which South African courts have resisted the application of international law under the new constitutional framework. This was seen particularly in the early case law of the Constitutional Court.

In cases such as *Makwanyane* and *Williams*, discussed above, the Court articulated the need to consider the specific domestic context when interpreting the South African Constitution, and also to be careful to appreciate the differences in the drafting of constitutional provisions from potentially relevant international legal provisions. In *Makwanyane*, Chaskalson P stated:

> [W]e must bear in mind that we are required to construe the South African Constitution, and not an international instrument or the constitution of some foreign country, and that this has to be done with due regard to our legal system, our history and circumstances, and the structure and language of our own Constitution.[59]

[56] ibid 59[a].
[57] See also the discussion in ILA Final Report (n 12) paras 74–79.
[58] See *Koyabe v Minister for Home Affairs* [2009] ZACC 23, (2010) (4) SA 327 (CC) [41], [45]; *Richtersveld Community v Alexkor Ltd* [2003] ZASCA 14 (SCA) [46]; *S v Basson* [2005] ZACC 10, (2007) (3) SA 582 (CC) [177].
[59] *Makwanyane* (n 26) [39].

The Court therefore held that the right to life in the South African Bill of Rights did not allow for the death penalty, declining to follow the corresponding provisions in the International Covenant on Civil and Political Rights (ICCPR), which expressly provides for the legality of the death penalty. In the *Williams* case, the judgment of Langa J qualified corporal punishment against juvenile offenders as cruel, inhuman, and degrading treatment, despite the fact that it had not been defined as such by various international tribunals, emphasizing the distinct South African context and history of violence when interpreting this provision.[60] Thus, both differences in drafting and differences in the domestic context have been relied on in part to justify the adoption of a distinct South African approach to the interpretation of particular rights in the Bill of Rights.

It should be noted, however, that this technique was not used to avoid engagement with international law binding on the State. In these cases, the Court distinguished the South African position from that in international treaties to which South Africa was not a party, and which were being invoked by virtue of the Section 39 interpretation mechanism. Furthermore, given that the relevant treaties provide for minimum standards, allowing States to provide fuller protection, these judgments would not have constituted violations of the relevant international obligations. Finally, as set out in Section C, in the time since these earlier decisions, the Court has augmented its reliance on even non-binding sources of international law.

3. Denial of Self-Execution of Treaties

As set out in Section B, the Final Constitution introduces the concept of self-executing treaties into South African law. This concept, which has been debated in United States courts for decades, is proving to be difficult and controversial for South African courts as well. Indeed, South African courts seem to be reluctant to define the concept or to decide on whether particular treaties are self-executing. This of course may result in the avoidance of the application of treaty rules that should be directly applied by virtue of their self-executing status.[61]

[60] *Williams* (n 27) [51]–[52].

[61] As discussed in the ILA Final Report (n 12) para 21, declaring a treaty as non-self-executing (or, in the South African context, refusing to recognize it as self-executing) is one of the blunting or moderating techniques that may well lead to affirmative avoidance.

This difficulty is best illustrated in the *Quagliani* case, a Constitutional Court decision in a joint appeal of two High Court decisions concerning the status of the US-South African Extradition Agreement. This Agreement had not been transformed into domestic law, and several individuals had relied on this lack of transformation to challenge the legality under South African domestic law of their extradition to the USA. The State, however, argued that the extradition treaty was self-executing, since national legislation, the Extradition Act (which preceded the Agreement), established all necessary structures to implement the Agreement with the USA. Three courts heard legal argument to this effect, and each court reached a different conclusion on the self-executing status of the extradition treaty. The High Court in the first case held that the Agreement was not enacted into domestic law, and was therefore not in force domestically. In contrast, in the second case that was joined in the *Quagliani* appeal, the High Court held that the Agreement was self-executing, and was therefore directly enforceable in South African law. The Constitutional Court, in a judgment by Sachs J, declined to decide on the issue of self-execution, arguing that it was not necessary to the decision.

The refusal of the Constitutional Court to address the issue of self-execution was unfortunate, given the confusion surrounding the concept. However, it did not result in the non-application of the international treaty in question. The Court held that the Extradition Agreement was enforceable in South African law, either because it had been transformed into domestic law by the earlier legislation of the Extradition Act, or because it was self-executing. Sachs J held that since either option would lead to the enforceability of the Act, it was not necessary to declare which option was in fact legally correct.[62] Thus, despite the refusal to determine the self-executing character of the treaty, the relevant international law was applied.

Nonetheless, the absence of clear guidance from the Constitutional Court on the meaning of self-executing treaties in the South African Constitution creates the potential for the emergence of a new method of avoidance. While this was not in fact the result in this particular case, the *Quagliani* decision underscores the reluctance of South African courts to declare treaty provisions to be directly applicable without legislative transformation. As such, courts may in the future rely on the absence of guidance from the Constitutional Court as to what constitutes a self-executing treaty to justify their refusal to apply

[62] This is a questionable conclusion. The South African Constitution does not provide for transformation of treaties into domestic law by pre-existing legislation. Therefore, it is only if the Extradition Agreement can be said to be self-executing that it could be given direct effect in domestic law.

international law stemming from untransformed treaties, when these treaties should be enforceable by virtue of the constitutional mandate in Section 231 of the Constitution. This reluctance sits uncomfortably with the enthusiastic application of untransformed treaties through the obligations of consistent interpretation discussed in the previous section.

E. Conclusion

South African courts have become remarkably receptive to international law since the adoption of the new Constitution, and the latest judgments of the Constitutional Court illustrate perhaps the highest watermark in this regard thus far. In particular, the obligation of consistent interpretation has been used to give wide-ranging effect to international law when courts undertake the interpretation and development of domestic law. It is submitted that the courts' interpretations of Sections 233, 39(1)(b), and 39(2) of the Constitution have rendered this effect even more significant than the strongly worded interpretative mandates might have been anticipated to produce. The wide interpretation of what constitutes 'international law' according to these sections of the Constitution have enabled untransformed treaty obligations, and even provisions of international law that are not binding on South Africa, to have substantial influence on the content of domestic law. Such judicial interpretations, therefore, have augmented the already strong constitutional obligation to apply international law, and therefore reduced the possibility of the development of avoidance techniques.

Nonetheless, the controversy surrounding the heavy use of international law by domestic courts, particularly in the most recent judgments of the Constitutional Court, must not be ignored. The strongly worded dissent in the *Glenister* case, and political unhappiness with the Court's execution against foreign government property, could indicate the beginning of a turning point. It is possible, perhaps, that the 'overreach' and the negation of criminal and civil immunity in the cases employing the 'moral imperative' technique have already begun to bite. The announcement of South Africa's attempted (and now withdrawn) withdrawal from the ICC, a month before the Constitutional Court appeal in the *Bashir* case addressed above, may well have been a reaction, at least in part, to the controversial judgment of the SCA in that case.[63]

[63] For discussion, see Hannah Woolaver, 'Domestic and International Limitations on Treaty Withdrawal: Lessons from South Africa's Attempted Departure from the International Criminal Court' (2017) 111 AJIL Unbound 450.

South African courts must be mindful, therefore, of the constitutional limitations of the use of international law, as well as their responsibility to accurately assess the status of rules of international law with which they seek to align.[64] Failure to do so may increase the risk of resort to the ultimate 'avoidance technique' of treaty withdrawal by the Executive, or even the re-emergence of a general approach of isolationism as seen in the pre-democratic history of South Africa.

[64] See for similar points the discussion of *Law Society of South Africa v President of the Republic of South Africa* [2018] ZACC 51, (2019) (3) SA 30 (CC) in Sanya Samtani, 'International Law, Access to Courts and Non-Retrogression: *Law Society v President of the Republic of South Africa*' (2020) 10 Constitutional Court Review 197.

4

Engagement of Chinese Courts with International Law

Dai Ruijun

A. Introduction

China has been involved in international affairs extensively by means of concluding international treaties and participating in international law formation more generally. As of 2019, China has concluded more than 500 multilateral treaties and more than 27,000 bilateral treaties.[1] Bound by the customary rule *pacta sunt servanda*, China reaffirmed recently that States 'have the obligation to comply with international law in good faith and in a coherent and consistent manner'.[2] This general attitude towards international law and international obligations is partly reflected in China's Constitution and legislation, and partly in the judicial practice of Chinese courts.[3]

B. The Status of International Treaties in the Chinese Legal System

Unlike many other countries, the constitutional set-up of the relationship between international and domestic law in the current Constitution of China is to some extent obscure. There is no quick constitutional answer to the question

[1] Data from Jia Guide, 'New China and International Law: Practice and Contribution in 70 Years' (2019) 18 ChiJIL 727, 728.

[2] The Declaration of the People's Republic of China and the Russian Federation on the Promotion of International Law (People's Republic of China-Russian Federation) (Beijing, 25 June 2016) para 2, <https://www.fmprc.gov.cn/eng/wjdt_665385/2649_665393/201608/t20160801_679466.html> accessed 22 July 2023.

[3] This chapter focuses on courts' practice in mainland China. The relevant practice of the courts in the Hong Kong Special Administrative Region (SAR), the Macao SAR, and Taiwan are not covered here. Data used in this chapter has been updated up to 1 May 2021.

of what is the status of international treaties in the Chinese legal system.[4] As to international law-related issues, the Constitution merely refers to and allocates treaty-making power: the State Council, the Central People's Government, is responsible for concluding treaties and agreements (Article 89(9)); the Standing Committee of the National People's Congress (NPC)—the highest organ of State power—makes the decision on ratification or abrogation of treaties and important agreements concluded with foreign States (Article 67(15)); and the President of the People's Republic of China (PRC) ratifies or abrogates treaties and important agreements concluded with foreign countries in accordance with the decisions of the NPC Standing Committee (Article 81).[5]

Since there is no constitutional provision on the hierarchical position of international treaties in the Chinese legal system, nor any mention of the way international treaties could be used domestically, it is arguable that China's Constitution is of little relevance to Chinese courts' engagement with international law.[6] This constitutional silence has arguably led to 'fragmentation and unpredictability' in international treaty application by domestic courts.[7]

Nevertheless, after comparing the treaty-making process with the law enacting procedure, as outlined in the Constitution, Wang Tieya presumed that since it is the NPC Standing Committee which has the power to enact laws and to decide on the ratification of treaties, and both laws and treaties are to be promulgated by the President, 'therefore, laws and treaties appear to have equal legal force'.[8] Furthermore, he asserted that 'as a general rule, there is no need of legislative enactment for the implementation of treaties', and 'the internal effect of the treaties comes immediately upon promulgation of the President of the PRC'.[9] However, no authority was provided to support this assertion.

If the above statement was true, domestic laws and treaties concluded by China would possess the same hierarchical status within the Chinese legal order. This might lead to the deduction that international obligations assumed

[4] On this silence of China's Constitution towards international law, see Cai Congyan, 'International Law in Chinese Courts during the Rise of China' (2016) 110 AJIL 269, 272–73. This possibility of constitutional silence was not explicitly considered by the ILA Study Group on Principles on the Engagement of Domestic Courts with International Law, 'Final Report: Mapping the Engagement of Domestic Courts with International Law' (Johannesburg, 2016) (ILA Final Report) (see paras 16–18).

[5] Constitution of the People's Republic of China (1982). See Xue Hanqin and Jin Qian, 'International Treaties in the Chinese Domestic Legal System' (2009) 8 ChiJIL 299.

[6] See Xue and Jin (n 5) 300, '[s]trictly speaking, international treaties, even after ratification, accession or approval, do not automatically become part of national law and consequently do not automatically have domestic legal effect'.

[7] Cai (n 4) 272.

[8] Wang Tieya, 'International Law in China: Historical and Contemporary Perspectives' (1990) 221 Recueil des Cours 328. Compare, also, Xue and Jin (n 5) 301–2.

[9] ibid 329.

by China in treaties could be overthrown by domestic laws subsequently enacted, since in that case the rule *lex posterior derogat legi priori* would apply. However, this is not the case in reality. On the one hand, a number of Chinese laws expressly give superiority to international treaties over domestic law where there is potential conflict or where the treaty stipulates differently.[10] On the other, no court has ever refused the application of an international treaty due to a conflict with domestic legislation, irrespectively of whether the latter was enacted before or after the assumed international obligation.

Despite the existence of no constitutional prescription on the status of international law in the domestic legal order, 54 out of the 287 current Chinese laws[11] stipulate to varying degrees the possibility of applying international treaties domestically, in the following ways: First, international treaties concluded or acceded to by China can be applied directly in certain international affairs, such as in its military relations with other States,[12] in international cooperation for drugs control,[13] anti-terrorism,[14] anti-money laundering,[15] extradition,[16] etc, or in dealing with foreign related legal relationships.[17] Second, according to the Criminal Law, China may exercise criminal jurisdiction over crimes stipulated in international treaties.[18] Third, in some areas, such as consular and diplomatic privileges and immunities, marine environmental protection, tax collection and civil relations, international treaties prevail when they contain provisions that diverge from relevant domestic law.[19] Furthermore, according

[10] Eg, Meteorology Law of People's Republic of China (Order No 23 [1999] of President) art 44 stipulates that '[w]here differences in provisions are found between an international treaty on meteorological activities concluded or acceded to by the People's Republic of China and this law, the provisions contained in the international treaty shall prevail, with the exception of the clauses on which the People's Republic of China has expressed reservations'. See also Xue and Jin (n 5) 303.

[11] 'Law' here refers in particular to laws enacted by the NPC and the NPC Standing Committee. Statistics of the number of laws (as of 1 May 2021) comes from the National Laws and Regulations Database (GUO JIA FA LV FA GUI SHU JU KU) operated by the NPC Standing Committee.

[12] The Law of the People's Republic of China on National Defence (Order No 84 [1997] of President) art 70.

[13] Narcotics Control Law of the People's Republic of China (Order No79 [2007] of President) art 53.

[14] Counterterrorism Law of the People's Republic of China (Order No 36 [2015] of President) art 68.

[15] Anti-Money Laundering Law of the People's Republic of China (Order No 56 [2007] of President) art 68.

[16] Extradition Law of the People's Republic of China (Order No 42 [2000] of President) arts 4, 16, 49, 54.

[17] On the meaning of 'Foreign Related Legal Relationship', cf Interpretations of the Supreme People's Court on Several Issues Concerning Application of the Law of the People's Republic of China on Choice of Law for Foreign-Related Civil Relationship (I) (Interpretation No 24 [2012] of the Supreme People's Court) art 1.

[18] See Criminal Law of the People's Republic of China (Order No 83 [1997] of President) art 9; Counter-Terrorism Law of the People's Republic of China (Order No 23 [2015] of President) art 11.

[19] Eg, art 96 of the Marine Environment Protection Law of the People's Republic of China (Order No [9] 1983 of President, revised in 1999, as amended) provides: 'Where an international treaty regarding marine environment protection concluded or acceded to by the People's Republic of China contains provisions differing from those contained in this law, the provisions of the international treaty shall

to Chinese intellectual property laws, nationals and enterprises may seek to obtain trademark registration, patent, and copyright protection on the basis of international treaties to which China is a party.[20]

China is not a caselaw country, law is made by the legislature. In judicial practice, past judgments are not binding precedent; courts rely almost exclusively on statutory law.[21] Therefore, laws which expressly refer to international treaties without doubt provide a strong basis upon which courts may engage with international law. In the past few years, Chinese law has witnessed some retrogression in the application of treaty provisions. A typical example is the repeal of Article 72, the 'treaty superiority clause',[22] in the Administrative Procedure Law (APL). Some observers held that the main consideration for the repeal might have been to 'shield China's executive authority from potentially increasing judicial challenges', especially 'by applying international law'.[23] However, it is a little hasty to reach this conclusion. First, the APL is a procedural law, and Article 72 only gave superiority to treaty provisions which may diverge from the domestic *procedural* rules. For regulating the administrative act, what really matters is substantive administrative law. In this regard, at least 12 administrative laws stipulate that relevant administrative activities can be undertaken in accordance with treaties concluded by China.[24] These administrative laws are the basis for courts to carry out trial activities, and the applicable treaty provisions place the administrative acts under potential review by the courts in accordance with international treaties.

The Supreme People's Court (SPC) is China's highest judicial organ. Besides hearing cases assigned by laws and decrees to its jurisdiction, the SPC has the authority to give interpretations on questions concerning the specific application of laws and decrees in judicial proceedings,[25] including provisions which

apply; however the provisions about which the People's Republic of China has made reservations shall be excepted.'

[20] See Trademark Law of the People's Republic of China (Order No 10 [1982] of the Fifth Standing Committee of the NPC, as amended) arts 17, 21; Patent Law of the People's Republic of China (Order No 11 [1984] of President, as amended), arts 17, 19; Copyright Law of the People's Republic of China (Order No 31 [1990] of President, as amended) art 2.

[21] See Organic Law of the People's Courts of the People's Republic of China (Order No 3 [1979] of Chairman of the NPC Standing Committee, as revised in 1983, as amended) art 4.

[22] See Art 72 of Administrative Procedure Law (Order No 16 [1989] of President) (APL), which gave superiority to international treaties concluded by China over provisions of the APL. But this provision was repealed by a 2014 amendment (Order No 15 [2014] of President).

[23] See Cai (n 4) 275.

[24] These 12 administrative laws are the Education Law, the Law on Physical Culture and Sports, the Surveying and Mapping Law, the Customs Law, the Notary Law, the Law on Diplomatic Personnel Stationed Abroad, the Narcotics Control Law, the Marine Environment Protection Law, the Frontier Health and Quarantine Law, the Counterterrorism Law, the Biosecurity Law, and Meteorology Law.

[25] Organic Law (n 22) art 18.

explicitly refer to international treaties. The power to issue judicial interpretations was first vested in the SPC by the NPC Standing Committee,[26] then confirmed in the Organic Law of the People's Court of China.[27] Judicial interpretations are legally binding,[28] and provide courts with concrete guidance in their engagement with international law, and to some extent guarantee consistency of their practice.[29]

A notable judicial interpretation which plays the role of a general principle in dealing with cases including foreign elements is Provisions on Several Issues concerning the Handling of Foreign Related Cases.[30] In this document, the SPC jointly with other authorities[31] stated that in dealing with cases with foreign elements, competent authorities, including the courts, shall strictly fulfil China's international treaty obligations on the basis of the principle of reciprocity. When domestic law conflicts with international treaty obligations assumed by China, the relevant treaty provisions shall prevail. The competent authorities shall not refuse to comply with international treaty obligations on grounds of domestic law or internal regulations.[32] Accordingly, Chinese courts have to, first, 'give effect to treaty obligations as provided by relevant legislation' and, second, 'in interpreting and applying domestic laws, the courts should give due regard to China's international obligations and construe domestic laws in a way that does not conflict with those obligations'.[33]

Guided by the above statutory laws and judicial interpretations, the practice of Chinese courts appears mostly to be one of alignment with or, at worst, avoidance of international law; cases of contestation are quite rare.

[26] See NPC Standing Committee, Resolution Providing an Improved Interpretation of the Law (10 June 1981) CLI.1.1006(EN).

[27] Organic Law (n 22).

[28] See Provisions of the Supreme People's Court on the Judicial Interpretation Work (No 12 [2007] of SPC) art 5.

[29] See also Xue and Jin (n 5) 314. The SPC has issued a few judicial interpretations concerning the application of international treaties by Chinese courts. See ibid 314ff.

[30] See Provisions of the Ministry of Foreign Affairs, the Supreme People's Court, the Supreme People's Procuratorate, the Ministry of Public Security, the Ministry of Security and the Ministry of Justice on Several Issues Concerning the Handling of Foreign Related Cases (No 17 [1995] of Foreign Affairs) (Provisions Concerning the Handling of Foreign Related Cases) (author's translation).

[31] Apart from issuing its own judicial interpretations, the SPC may also issue such interpretations 'jointly with the competent authorities of governmental departments to provide guidance for lower courts on treaty implementation'. See Xue and Jin (n 5) 315.

[32] Provisions Concerning the Handling of Foreign Related Cases (n 30) art 1(3).

[33] Xue and Jin (n 5) 316.

C. The Practice of Chinese Courts

1. Alignment Postures of Chinese Courts

Generally speaking, Chinese courts tend to engage with international treaties concluded by China where domestic legislation explicitly provides the basis to use international treaties. References to such international treaties in Chinese courts' judgments reflect to varying degrees alignment with international law, in the sense identified in the International Law Association (ILA) Final Report.[34] With regard to international trade administrative cases,[35] where there is more than one reasonable interpretation of the law applied by the court, the interpretation consistent with the international treaties concluded or acceded to by China should apply.[36] This explicit authorization for the use of the principle of consistent interpretation indicates a strategy of overriding alignment.[37] This section demonstrates that this alignment happens primarily (but not exclusively) in cases where private relations are involved, often of a cross-border character, and not so much where politically problematic or charged rules of international law are concerned.[38]

a. Fair weather alignment

It is difficult to give a typical example of this ordinary alignment with international law which has no 'special' characteristics.[39] That said, international treaties have been expressly invoked in several cases to support the application of a specific domestic law in a particular case.

A pertinent example here is the trademark dispute *Crown Company v Tiger Co Ltd* (*Tiger*), where a court of second instance initiatively invoked the Berne Convention for the Protection of Literary and Artistic Works (Berne Convention),[40] to support its judgment on Tiger's copyright over the tiger

[34] ILA Final Report (n 4) paras 43–56.

[35] The following cases are the international trade administrative cases: administrative cases relating to international goods trade, relating to international service trade, intellectual property administrative cases relating to international trade, and other international trade administrative cases. See Provisions on Several Issues Concerning the Hearing of International Trade Administrative Cases (Interpretation No 27 [2002] of SPC) art 1.

[36] See Provisions on Several Issues Concerning the Hearing of International Trade Administrative Cases (n 35) art 9.

[37] The practice of explicit authorization by judicial interpretation for the use of the principle of consistent interpretation is not very usual in state practice, as the principle in many other states has mostly been developed through judicial practice. See the discussion in ILA Final Report (n 4) para 23.

[38] ILA Final Report (n 4) paras 44, 76, 77.

[39] ibid para 44.

[40] (amended 28 September 1979, entered into force 19 November 1984) WIPO Lex No TRT/BERNE/001.

logo.[41] Crown Company—the claimant—challenged this decision, initiating retrial proceedings before the SPC, where it argued that the court of second instance abused its discretion and the power of interpretation since neither of the parties had mentioned the Berne Convention in their arguments.

Tiger Co Ltd was a company registered and located in Japan where it had obtained protection for its copyright. Since both China and Japan are parties to the Berne Convention, according to the Copyright Law of China, 'any work of a foreigner or stateless person which enjoys copyright under an agreement concluded between the country to which the author belongs to or in which the author permanently resides and China, or under an international treaty to which both countries are parties', shall be protected by Chinese law.[42] The SPC stated that 'the court of the second instance cited the Berne Convention in the part of setting forth reasons for its judgment, in order to prove that the artwork of the Tiger Co. Ltd. should be protected by the copyright law of China'.[43] Immediately following this, the SPC distinguished between the 'reasons' for the judgment and the 'direct legal basis' of the judgment. The SPC continued:

> [T]he legal basis of its judgment quoted by the court of second instance is not the Berne Convention but the stipulation of China's Copyright Law. Therefore, the accused abuse of discretion and abuse of interpretation power of the Court can not be the grounds for retrial.[44]

In light of this, the *Tiger* case could be read as both Chinese law and international treaties supporting Tiger's copyright over the artworks, or, in other words, as a case where the contents of international law and domestic law 'converge',[45] since the Copyright Law of China safeguards copyrights obtained under international treaties to which China is a party.

Additionally, this case raised the question of to what extent an international treaty may be used in such cases. Pursuant to the SPC ruling, the usage of the Berne Convention was limited to the court's reasoning, and the Convention was not part of the direct legal basis of the judgment. The court of second instance ostensibly based its decision on the Berne Convention but this was in

[41] [2012] Gao Xing Zhong Zi No 1255 (Administrative Judgment) Higher People's Court of Beijing Municipality (17 December 2012).

[42] Copyright Law of the People's Republic of China (Order No 31 [1990] of President, as amended) art 2(2).

[43] [2013] Zhi Xing Zi No 81 (Administrative Ruling) Supreme People's Court (26 November 2013) [6] (author's translation).

[44] ibid.

[45] ILA Final Report (n 4) para 44.

fact due to a *renvoi* (reference) in the Chinese Copyright Law. It is possible then that if the Convention had been used directly as the legal basis of the judgment, the decision would have been overthrown by the SPC for incorrect application of the law. It seems that according to the collegiate panel (He Yi Ting) of this case, international treaties, even if domestic law refers to them, still may not be used as direct legal basis for a court's judgment. Nevertheless, SPC verdicts do not establish binding rules and principles for lower courts or in the adjudication of other cases. In fact, several cases can be found, in which courts have cited international treaties directly as the legal basis of their judgments.[46]

Some other cases, where international treaties have been cited through a reference in domestic law, also constitute examples of fair weather alignment. In the case of *Han and others smuggled, trafficked and transported drugs*, one of the defendants was neither a Chinese national, nor did his trafficking and transporting act take place in China. Still, the court established its criminal jurisdiction over his act through the provision of the Criminal Law of China, which 'is applicable to the crimes specified in the international treaties concluded or acceded to by the People's Republic of China and over which the People's Republic of China exercises criminal jurisdiction within its obligations in accordance with the treaties'.[47] The Court asserted that trafficking and transporting drugs are crimes explicitly stipulated in international treaties to which China is a party, and over which parties to the 'Convention'[48] should exercise universal jurisdiction, and therefore it had criminal jurisdiction over the defendant's behaviour. In this case, the court was authorized by international treaties to exercise jurisdiction, and there was no obvious reason to prevent it from doing so. As has been observed, Chinese courts are 'becoming more willing' to exercise such criminal jurisdiction.[49]

Finally, in the case *Sinochem International (Overseas) Pte Ltd v ThyssenKrupp Metallurgical Products GmbH*, which concerned the international sale of goods, the judges elucidated the reason why the United Nations Convention on the Contracts for the International Sale of Goods (UNCISC)[50] should be

[46] For example, in *Abdul Wahid v China Eastern Airlines Co, Ltd*, besides domestic law, the Court invoked the Convention for the Unification of Certain Rules relating to International Carriage by Air (n 59) and the Convention, Supplementary to the Warsaw Convention, for the Unification of Certain Rules relations to International Carriage by Air Performed by a Person Other Than the Contracting Carrier (n 60) as legal basis for the judgment. See [2006] Hu Yi Zhong Min Yi Min Zhong Zi No 609 (Civil Judgment) First Intermediate People's Court of Shanghai Municipality (24 February 2006).

[47] Criminal Law (n 19) art 9 (author's translation).

[48] It is disappointing that the Court did not specify in the judgment which 'Convention' its jurisdiction was based on. See [2007] Kun Xing San Chu Zi No 8 (Criminal Judgment) Kunming Intermediate People's Court of Yunnan Province (22 November 2007).

[49] Cai (n 4) 286.

[50] United Nations Convention on Contracts for the International Sale of Goods (adopted 11 April 1980, entered into force 1 January 1988) 1489 UNTS 1.

used as applicable law. As both parties involved were foreign companies, that was a case with foreign-related elements. The court of final instance resorted to China's conflict laws,[51] according to which the law agreed upon by the parties should be used. Since in the proceedings before the first instance court, both parties had unanimously chosen the UNCISC as the applicable law, the court consequently concluded that the Convention should be applied.[52] In this case, the application of the international treaty resulted from the prior application of Chinese (conflict) law; therefore the application of the treaty was the result of applying Chinese law. It is worth noting that in this case, the UNCISC formed both the direct legal basis of the judgment and part of the court's reasoning, an approach which deviated from the one followed in the aforementioned *Tiger* case.

b. Overriding alignment

Several domestic laws explicitly provide that international treaties to which China is party may 'override' Chinese law, where the treaty contains provisions 'differing from'[53] those in domestic law, or when there are 'other provisions'[54] in the treaty, except where China has made reservations on such provisions. Thirteen laws, which cover the areas of consular and diplomatic privileges and immunities, management of international or border river or lakes, maritime law, negotiable instrument (Piao Ju), health and quarantine, animal and plant quarantine, civil aviation, civil procedure law, maritime procedure law, meteorology, marine environment protection, tax collection, as well as enterprise income tax, make such stipulations. Despite the existence of these laws which grant superiority to the provisions of international treaties over those of domestic laws, it cannot be deduced that as a general principle international treaties prevail over Chinese law.[55] The 13 laws mentioned above are all ordinary laws and not constitutional rules,[56] and 'are specific in nature and are related only to those specific matters which the laws concerned regulate'.[57] Nevertheless, by virtue of such provisions Chinese courts may apply

[51] Namely, the Law of the People's Republic of China on the Laws Applicable to Foreign-Related Civil Relations (Order No 36 [2010] of President), and relevant provisions of the General Principles of Civil Law of the People's Republic of China (Order No 37 [1986] of President, invalidated by Civil Code of PRC effective on 1 Jan 2021).

[52] See [2013] Min Si Zhong Zi No 35 (Civil Judgment) Supreme People's Court (30 June 2014).

[53] See General Principles of the Civil Law (n 51) art 142(2).

[54] See Regulations of the People's Republic of China Concerning Diplomatic Privileges and Immunities (Order No 44 [1986] of President) art 27(1).

[55] See also Xue and Jin (n 5) 304.

[56] Tieya (n 8) 332.

[57] ibid 331.

international treaties when a matter is not regulated by domestic law or even where there is a conflict with domestic law. It is worth noting that these types of 'conflict' provisions whereby international treaties prevail over conflicting domestic law are found not only in legislation concerned with civil and commercial matters, but also administrative matters or ever foreign affairs, and are applied not only in legal relation with foreign elements, but also legal relations without foreign elements, such as marine environmental protection, meteorology, and tax collection.

A representative instance for this is the case of *Abdul Wahid v China Eastern Airlines Co, Ltd*. The plaintiff was a national of Pakistan who purchased an air ticket from Shanghai to Karachi, but missed the connecting flight because of a delay in his first flight. The plaintiff believed that the flight delay of China Eastern Airlines and its refusal to reschedule the flight had caused him economic losses, so he filed the lawsuit to People's Court of Pudong District of Shanghai Municipality, and demanded that the airline be ordered to compensate for the airfare and luggage ticket. In this case, the court of first instance went straight to Article 142 of the General Principles of Civil Law which regulates civil relations with foreign-related factors.[58] In accordance with this provision, international treaties apply when they prescribe differently from Chinese civil law. On this basis, the court relied exclusively on the Convention for the Unification of Certain Rules relating to International Carriage by Air (Warsaw Convention, as amended in 1955)[59] and the Convention, Supplementary to the Warsaw Convention, for the Unification of Certain Rules relating to International Carriage by Air Performed by a Person Other Than the Contracting Carrier (Guadalajara Convention)[60] to which both Pakistan and China are parties. In line with these two Conventions, the court established its jurisdiction, determined the rights and obligations of the litigants, and made a judgment requiring China Eastern Airlines to compensate the plaintiff for the loss.[61] The defendant, China Eastern Airlines, refused to accept the judgment and appealed. The court of the second instance delivered the final judgment,[62] which upheld the original one. Although 142 was invoked in the judgments, neither court indicated how Chinese law differed from international law in this

[58] General Principles of Civil Law (n 51) art 142.

[59] (adopted 12 October 1929, entered into force 13 February 1933) 137 UNTS 11, with Protocol to Amend the Convention for the Unification of Certain Rules relating to International Carriage by Air (adopted 28 September 1955, entered into force 1 August 1963) 478 UNTS 371.

[60] (adopted 18 September 1961, entered into force 1 May 1964) 500 UNTS 31.

[61] [2005] Pu Min Yi Min Chu Zi No 12164 (Civil Judgment) People's Court of Pudong District of Shanghai Municipality (21 December 2005).

[62] See *Abdul Wahid* (n 46).

particular case, or whether there was a lacuna in Chinese law. This is a typical example of a Chinese court judgment which is quite brief, without in-depth clarification of the reasons why the court could apply international treaties. Further explanation could have made the court's engagement with international law a more convincing case of overriding alignment.

Similarly, in *Dalian City Oceanic and Fishery Administration v Ondimar Transportes Maritimos Ltda and another*, the court resorted to the International Convention on Civil Liability for Oil Pollution Damage (Oil Pollution Convention)[63] through a reference in Article 268(1) of the Maritime Law of China. The court held that as regards applicable law, the Oil Pollution Convention should be given priority over domestic law.[64] In this case again, the court did not provide details on why international law prevailed, but logically that could be either due to a conflict between Chinese domestic law and the Convention, or due to the existence of no corresponding content in Chinese law.

The case of *ELBORSH v Geng Qunying and Saide Company* involved a contract for the international sale of goods between an Egyptian company (ELBORSH) and a Chinese company. ELBORSH challenged before the SPC the law applied by the court of second instance,[65] which had resorted to Chinese law in accordance with the most significant relationship doctrine. During the retrial, and as regards the issue of applicable law, the SPC clarified that whereas the buyer and the seller had not agreed in the invoice or otherwise to choose the applicable law, and 'given that both China and Egypt are parties to the [UNCISC], the Convention shall be applied in this case to determine the rights and obligations of the buyer and the seller'.[66] The SPC bluntly pointed out that it was wrong for the court of second instance to take Chinese law as the applicable law. In this case, the SPC applied an international treaty over the respective Chinese law, adopting a strategy of overriding alignment with international law. However, the SPC still did not explain why the treaty and not the Chinese law should be applied in the case at hand.

[63] (adopted 29 November 1969, entered into force 19 June 1975) 973 UNTS 3.

[64] [2015] Min Shen Zi No 1637 (Civil Ruling Supreme People's Court (29 December 2015).

[65] *Geng Qunying vs Elborsh Company* [2010] Ji Min San Zhong Zi No 59 (Civil Judgment) Higher People's Court of Hebei Province (15 December 2010).

[66] [2012] Min Shen Zi No 1402 (Civil Ruling) Supreme People's Court (24 December 2012) [5] (author's translation).

c. Consubstantial alignment

Some Chinese courts prefer to invoke international treaties where they happen to contain consubstantial norms with domestic law. In other circumstances, Chinese courts also have tried to harmonize domestic law with China's international obligations, by 'clearly indicat[ing] that applicable international norms will be taken into consideration in the construction of the consubstantial domestic norms'.[67]

In the case of *Intentional killing by Yang and Ma*, both domestic law (Criminal Law and the Law on Protection of Minors) and international law (Convention on the Rights of the Child or 'CRC')[68] were invoked by the court of trial, in order to emphasize that the victim's right to life was safeguarded by international law, as well as Chinese law.[69] Here, penalizing and prosecuting the offence of intentional killing as prescribed by the Criminal Law constituted a remedy for the infringement of the right to life, as required under the CRC. Therefore, the relevant provisions of domestic law and the Convention could be deemed as 'consubstantial norms', as defined in the ILA Final Report.[70] However, the court referred to the Convention generally, without specifying the provisions that were relevant in that case.

In addition to invoking consubstantial norms, Chinese courts also take into consideration international conventions when they interpret the meaning of domestic law.[71] For example, in the retrial case upon application by the China Biodiversity Conservation and Green Development Foundation, the SPC resorted to the Convention on Biological Diversity[72] to interpret the term 'biological diversity' enshrined in the Environmental Protection Law of China.[73] In accordance with the Convention, the court asserted that 'biodiversity protection is an important content of environmental protection and also an essential component of safeguarding the environment public interest'.[74] Consequently the China Biodiversity Conservation and Green Development Foundation, the plaintiff in that case, was found to be a competent person to launch environmental public interest litigation.[75]

67 See ILA Final Report (n 4) para 54.

68 (adopted 20 November 1989, entered into force 2 September 1990) 1577 UNTS 3.

69 [2017] Yue 0115 Xing Chu No 255 (Criminal Judgement) People's Court of Nansha District, Guangzhou city, Guangdong Province (30 June 2017).

70 ILA Final Report (n 4) paras 29–30.

71 ILA Final Report (n 4) para 26.

72 (adopted 5 June1992, entered into force 29 December 1993) 1760 UNTS 79.

73 Environmental Protection Law of the People's Republic of China (Order No 9 [1989] of President, as revised in 2014).

74 *China Biodiversity Conservation and Green Development Foundation v Ningxia Ruitai Science and Technology Co Ltd* [2016] Zui Gao Fa Min Zai No 47 (Civil Judgment) Supreme People's Court (28 January 2016).

75 ibid.

Beyond using international law to 'understand' Chinese law, in *Contira Company v State Intellectual Property Office of China* (*Contira*), where the plaintiff alleged that Chinese law breached international treaty provisions, the courts of trial insisted on a consistent interpretation. The plaintiff argued that the Rules for Implementation of the Patent Law of China were in conflict with the Patent Cooperation Treaty (PCT),[76] the Regulations under the PCT,[77] the Agreement on Trade-Related Aspects of Intellectual Property Rights (TRIPS Agreement),[78] and the Paris Convention for the Protection of Industrial Property,[79] and therefore should not be applied in the dispute at hand. The court of first instance examined the impugned provisions of Chinese law article by article, and concluded that they were all in line with the relevant international treaties, but for one on which China had made a reservation as expressly allowed under the respective treaty. During the appeal, Contira put forward different arguments: first, the applicable domestic law was in conflict with another provision of the PCT (different from the one targeted at first instance); and, second, the court should directly rely on the relevant international treaties instead of the provisions of domestic law. As to the first issue, the court of second instance held that the domestic law provisions under consideration and the PCT regulated different matters, and thus they were not comparable. On the second issue, the court relied on Article 99(2) of the Rules for Implementation of the Patent Law of China, which prescribed that 'where any international application filed under the Patent Cooperation Treaty designating China enters the Chinese national phase, the requirements and procedures prescribed in this Chapter shall apply'. Therefore, the court concluded that the Patent Law and its Rules for Implementation applied in this case, and that the 'argument of the appellant has no legal basis, and will not be supported by this Court'.[80]

In the *Contira* case, the Chinese courts were determined to prove the consistency of Chinese law with the relevant international treaties, demonstrating thus consubstantial alignment with international law. Meanwhile, the practice of the appeal court illustrated that the engagement of Chinese courts with international law is subject to explicit provisions of domestic law; without statutory authorization, the court was inclined to refrain from using international law, as there would be 'no legal basis' to do so.

[76] (as modified 3 October 2001, entered into force 1 April 2002) WIPO Lex TRT/PCT/001.
[77] (adopted 9 October 2019, entered into force 1 July 2020) WIPO Lex TRT/PCT/016.
[78] (adopted 15 April 1994, entered into force 1 January 1995) 1869 UNTS 299.
[79] (adopted 20 March 1883, entered into force 7 July 1884) WIPO Lex TRT/PARIS/008.
[80] *Contira Company v State Intellectual Property Office of China*, [2005] Civil First No 378 of Beijing First Intermediate People's Court; [2005] Administration Final No 369 of Beijing High People's Court.

Finally, in the influential *Archangelos Gabriel* case retried by the SPC in 2016, as in some other cases, despite the fact that the law expressly applied was Chinese law, as agreed upon by the parties, the SPC affirmed in definitive terms that compliance with the International Convention on Salvage,[81] to which China is party, should be observed.[82] According to the SPC:

> China has acceded to the Salvage Convention. The purpose of the Convention, that is encouraging timely and effective relief of ships and other property in danger as well as those that pose a threat to environmental security, and at the same time ensuring adequate encouragement be given to the personnel performing salvage operations, should be followed in this case.[83]

To conclude that the respective provisions of Chinese law were consubstantial with the Salvage Convention, the SPC asserted that substantive contents of the Salvage Convention had been emulated by China's Maritime Law in its chapter on 'Salvage'.[84]

d. Hyper-alignment

Even international treaties to which China is not a party have found a place in the judicial practice of Chinese courts. The *Lianzhong Company (Hong Kong) v Xiamen International Trade Group* case occurred in the early 1990s when Hong Kong had not yet been returned to China. The courts of first and second instance reached their judgments directly on the basis of the UNCISC, because the parties involved had agreed to apply the UNCISC in that case. Several years later, Lianzhong Company appealed the judgment before the SPC requesting a retrial. During the retrial, the SPC reviewed and overturned the application of the UNCISC as the legal basis of the judgment, since Hong Kong was not a party to the Convention at the time when the dispute had occurred. But the SPC further clarified that, since the UNCISC had been selected by the parties as applicable law, its provisions had become part of the content of the contract between the parties.[85]

[81] (adopted 28 April 1989, entered into force 14 July 1996) 1953 UNTS 3.

[82] This is exactly the situation that the ILA Final Report described: 'domestic courts will often give preference to "consubstantial" domestic law over applicable international law, but will clearly indicate that applicable international norms will be taken into consideration in the construction of the consubstantial domestic norms'. See ILA Final Report (n 4) para 54.

[83] *Archangelos Gabriel* [2016] Zui Gao Fa Min Zai No 61 (Civil Judgment) Supreme People's Court (7 July 2016) [66].

[84] See ibid [73].

[85] [2016] Zui Gao Fa Min Zai No 373 (Civil Judgment) Supreme People's Court (13 March 2017).

The SPC's approach in this case suggested that an international treaty could be applied only if it had been acceded to or ratified by all the countries to which the litigants belonged. And the parties' choice of an international treaty as applicable law could only make the treaty part of their contract, but not the direct legal basis upon which a court makes its judgment. This approach has been developed to some extent in the Interpretation of the SPC on Several Issues concerning the Application of the Law of the People's Republic of China on the Law of the Application of Law for Foreign-Related Civil Relations (Interpretation)[86] promulgated by the SPC in 2012. Accordingly,

> [w]here the parties invoke any international treaty not yet binding upon the People's Republic of China in the contract, the people's court may determine the rights and obligations between the parties in accordance with the content of such international treaty, provided that such international treaty is not in violation of the social public interests or mandatory provisions in the laws and regulations of the People's Republic of China.[87]

The Interpretation expressly allows Chinese courts to use international treaties not yet acceded to by China if the parties involved have agreed to select a treaty as applicable law. It is still unclear, however, whether in such cases the treaty could function as the legal basis of the court's judgment or just as a reference in the reasoning. The following case reflects the varying understandings of the Interpretation by different courts.

In *Inmobiliaria Palacio Oriental SA v AFECG*, the courts of first and second instance referred to the UN Convention on Independent Guarantees and Stand-by Letters of Credit[88] to identify guarantee fraud, since neither the applicable law chosen by the parties nor Chinese law regulated the issue under consideration. While China is not a party to this Convention, the court of second instance clarified that the UN Convention

> embodies the general rules governing the operation of independent guarantee and stand-by letters of credit. These rules have been universally recognized by the international community. Even if China is not a party to the Convention, guidance provided by its rules to parties of independent guarantee can not be neglected.[89]

[86] [2012] Interpretation No 24 of SPC. The Interpretation took effect on 7 January 2013.
[87] Interpretation (n 86) art 9 (translation from pkulaw.cn, CLI.3.192329 (EN)).
[88] (adopted 11 December 1995, entered into force 1 January 2000) 2169 UNTS 163.
[89] See *Anhui Foreign Economic Construction (Group) Co, Ltd v Inmobiliaria Palacio Oriental SA* [2012] He Min Si Chu Zi No 00005 (Civil Judgment) Intermediate People's Court of Hefei City of Anhui

However, the final judgment upholding the original one was overturned by the SPC in retrial on the basis that the applicable law had been misused. According to the SPC, neither China had acceded to the Convention, nor did the parties in this case agreed to apply the Convention or to incorporate its content into the letter of guarantee as a rule for their transaction. Therefore, according to the principle of autonomy of will, the Convention should not have been applied.[90] Taking into account the Interpretation, the decisive reason why the Convention could not be applied in that case seemed to be that the parties had not selected it as applicable law to their transaction and the Convention was also not binding on China. If the parties had selected the Convention as applicable law, the court could have resorted to it, even if China was not party to it.

These cases demonstrate to an extent an approach of hyper-alignment of domestic courts with international law, where unratified treaties are applied by Chinese courts,[91] although the application of treaties not binding on China tends to be the result of the choice of the parties in each specific case.

2. Avoidance Strategies of Chinese Courts

Although Chinese courts are inclined to align their pronouncements with international law where there is a definite legal basis for doing so, they also occasionally practice international law avoidance for various reasons or even without any justification.

a. Evasive avoidance

Evasive avoidance is the posture Chinese courts regularly adopt in cases involving international human rights treaties. China has ratified six UN core human rights conventions, namely the Convention on the Elimination of All Forms of Discrimination Against Women, the International Convention on the Elimination of All Forms of Racial Discrimination, the CRC, the Convention Against Torture, the International Covenant on Economic, Social and Cultural Rights, and the Convention on the Rights of Persons with Disabilities.[92] Since

Province (9 April 2014); *Inmobiliaria Palacio Oriental SA v Anhui Foreign Economic Construction (Group) Co Ltd* [2014] Wan Min Er Zhong Zi No 00389 (Civil Judgment) Higher People's Court of Anhui Province (19 March 2015).

[90] [2017] Zui Gao Fa Min Zai No 134 (Civil Judgment) Supreme People's Court (14 December 2017).

[91] ILA Final Report (n 4) paras 55–56.

[92] (adopted 18 December 1979, entered into force 3 September 1981) 1249 UNTS 13; (adopted 21 December 1965, entered into force 4 January 1969) 660 UNTS 195; CRC (n 68); (adopted 10 December

there is no constitutional or equivalent legal basis to guide the judicial application of international human rights treaties in China, Chinese courts are to a considerable degree constrained in applying human rights treaties directly.[93] Additionally, as already alluded to above, because in China judges are expected to use for their decisions express stipulations in legislation, the Chinese legal order allows very little room for judge-made law.

According to research on the judicial application of international human rights law in China, as of 22 November 2018, among the cases published on the website 'China Judgments Online' from 2012 to 2018, 57 explicitly referred to international human rights instruments. In more than 80 per cent of these 57 cases, the application of international human rights law was requested by the parties. In most cases, however, the courts took the attitude of avoidance or neglect, neither referring to nor responding to the parties' invocation of international human rights treaties during the process of ascertaining the merits or in the judgment.[94] In these cases, the courts 'simply remain[ed] silent' and no discussion or argument was offered on why they did not apply the relevant international law.[95] Such cases of evasive avoidance fit well into the paradigm described by the ILA Final Report, which asserted that even with respect to 'inward-looking norms', which international human rights treaties produce, postures of avoidance (or even contestation) by domestic courts may be frequent depending on the interests at stake and how politically charged certain fields may be.[96]

b. Affirmative or professed avoidance

In a number of cases, Chinese courts seem to have taken into account the applicability of international treaties but explicitly rejected their application in light of different reasons.

1984, entered into force 26 June 1987) 1465 UNTS 85; (adopted 16 December 1966, entered into force 3 January 1976) 993 UNTS 3; (adopted 13 December 2006, entered into force 3 May 2008) 2515 UNTS 3.

[93] Some Chinese scholars hold that human rights treaties to be applied in China they have to be transformed by domestic legislation. See Zhao Jianwen, 'The Status of International Treaties in China's Legal System' (2010) 6 ChiJIL 190, 198. Indeed, many rights enshrined in human rights treaties have been stipulated in China's Constitution and in domestic legislation enacted by the NPC and its standing committee. The courts provide judicial remedies for rights by applying these domestic laws.

[94] Dai Ruijun, 'Judicial Application of International Human Rights Treaties in China' (2020) 19 Journal of Human Rights 93, 97–99, 103.

[95] ILA Final Report (n 4) para 40.

[96] ILA Final Report (n 4) paras 76–77.

i. Action in foreign affairs

As the ILA Final Report recounted, 'domestic courts would also traditionally avoid pronouncing on the conduct of international relations or foreign affairs of their own state'.[97] This is true for Chinese courts too. According to the APL, litigation against 'actions taken by the state in national defense and foreign affairs' is inadmissible.[98] In accordance with the Interpretation made by SPC on the application of the APL,[99] 'action taken by the state' means 'an action which the State Council, the Central Military Commission, the Ministry of National Defense, or the Ministry of Foreign Affairs, as authorized by the Constitution or the law, takes in relation to national defense or diplomatic affairs in the name of the state, or an action that a state organ declares a state of emergency as authorized by the Constitution or the Law'.[100] This Interpretation provides a guide for the courts to understand what constitutes 'action take by the state', including action in foreign affairs.

In some cases concerning the implementation of international treaties, the courts rejected the suits on the ground that the acts in question were diplomatic acts. For instance, in *Hucheng v the Ministry of Foreign Affairs (MFA)*, the plaintiff had asked MFA to make known to the public its reports and comments submitted to UN bodies in accordance with international human rights conventions. However, the MFA refused to disclose the relevant information on the grounds that it qualified as a diplomatic act and did not fall within the scope of the duty to disclose government information. Not satisfied with the response, the plaintiff filed an administrative lawsuit, requesting the court to confirm that the reply of the MFA had violated the Regulation of Government Information Disclosure, and request the MFA grant a new reply. The court held, however, that the actions of the MFA concerned in this case should be deemed as action pertaining to foreign affairs, and as such it did not fall within the scope of administrative cases that could be admissible in the people's court

[97] ILA Final Report (n 4) para 9.

[98] APL (n 22) art 13(1). See for a more recent application of this provision *Luoyang Runyuan Trade Company Ltd v the Ministry of Commerce* [2018] Zui Gao Fa Xing Shen No 5686 (Administrative Ruling) Supreme People's Court (2 January 2019), which affirmed that the lower courts had not erred in rejecting the applicant's request for disclosure of a communication between the British Embassy and the Ministry of Commerce for the purposes of civil litigation, as it constituted a diplomatic act. For a summary, see Wu Xiaohui, 'Chronology of Practice: Chinese Practice in Public International Law in 2019' (2020) 19 ChiJIL 717, 801–2.

[99] Interpretation on Application of the Administrative Procedure Law of the People's Republic of China (Interpretation No 1 [2018] by SPC). The Interpretation came into force on 8 February 2018.

[100] ibid art 2(1) (translation by pkulaw.cn, CLI.3.309904 (EN)).

under Article 13(1) of the APL. Therefore the court ruled to not register the case.[101] The court of second instance upheld the original ruling.[102]

ii. Non-justiciability

In China, it is still debated whether basic rights enshrined in the Constitution are justiciable,[103] let alone human rights stipulated in international treaties. A recent judgment clearly demonstrated this point. In this case, the plaintiff alleged that a hospital, against the wishes of the patient and his family, refused to transfer a patient out of the ICU, violating thus their human rights as guaranteed by the Universal Declaration of Human Rights (UDHR),[104] the Constitution, and medical ethics, and requested compensation on this basis. However, the court dismissed their claims on the grounds that the human rights guaranteed by the Constitution and the UDHR are merely declaratory and not equivalent to civil rights as stipulated in substantive civil law provisions. As the rights that formed the subject of the claim could not be directly protected by the judiciary, the claim was inadmissible.[105]

iii. Non-self-execution

Self-executive and non-self-executive treaties are not concepts regularly used by or even familiar to Chinese courts. But, in practice, there are indeed some cases in which application of international treaties was precluded on the basis that the relevant treaty was not directly applicable. In *Jinyingang Company v Sanxia Senlin Company and another*, Jinyingang Company alleged before the SPC that several compulsory provisions in an international convention (which were not expressly mentioned) had been violated, and that the courts of first and second instance had not taken into consideration the applicable international law. The SPC, however, refuted the claim, stating that 'international

[101] [2015] San Zhong Xing Chu Zi No 00658 (Administrative Ruling) Third Intermediate People's Court of Beijing Municipality (10 August 2015).

[102] [2015] Gao Xing Zhong Zi No 03490 (Administrative Ruling) Higher People's Court of Beijing Municipality (15 December 2015).

[103] According to the SPC Interpretation No 25 [2001], a violation of the right to education guaranteed by the Constitution would trigger civil liability. However, this interpretation was later annulled by the SPC on 28 January 2008 without giving reasons, which in turn resulted to further complications and confusion as regards whether courts may directly invoke constitutional provisions on fundamental rights in adjudication. See Zhiwei Tong, 'A Comment on the Rise and Fall of the Supreme People's Court's Reply to Qi Yuling's Case' (2010) 43 Suffolk University Law Review 669, for some observations.

[104] Universal Declaration of Human Rights, UNGA Res 217A (10 December 1948) A/RES/217(III) (A).

[105] *Zhang Yubai v Jinniu District People's Hospital of Chengdu City* [2016] 01 Min Zhong Zi No 11274 (Civil Judgment) Intermediate People's Court of Chengdu city of Sichuan Province (15 December 2016).

conventions are advocacy norms which are not directly applicable without the explicit stipulations of national legislature'.[106]

The SPC in that case made a general statement that, until they are transformed into domestic law, international treaties could not be directly applied by the judiciary. Despite its general character, this statement can still be seen as merely the understanding of the collegiate panel of this case, and need not be taken as a declaration of a general principle. In any event, the judgment is only binding on the parties to that case.

iv. Subject not regulated by the pertinent international law provisions

In *Maersk China Ltd v Yinghai Company*, a court of second instance and the SPC were divided on whether the Convention on a Code of Conduct for Liner Conferences (Liner Conferences Convention)[107] should be applied. According to the court of second instance, Maersk China as an international liner company registered in China, should be bound by the Liner Conferences Convention to which China is a party, and therefore the rule that 'various methods of liner conferences shall not discriminate against any country's shipowners, shippers, or foreign trade' applied to its conduct. However, the SPC held that the non-discrimination obligation was directed against the conduct of liner conferences and not liner companies; Maersk being a liner company rather than a conference, the Convention did not apply to its conduct.[108]

In that case, the SPC denied the application of the treaty on the ground that the dispute under consideration did not fall within the subject regulated by the treaty, and hence the treaty was not applicable.

The case *National Air Cargo Group, Inc v Aerospace Science and Technology Export and Import Company Ltd*[109] is another case in which the courts of both first and second instance discussed the applicability of an international treaty, namely the Convention for the Unification of Certain Rules for International Carriage by Air (Montreal Convention).[110] Whereas both courts confirmed in this case that provisions of the Convention should prevail over Chinese law in determining their jurisdiction, they found further that the dispute under consideration was a contractual one rather than a dispute about compensation

[106] [2013] Min Shen Zi No 869 (Civil Ruling) Supreme People's Court (30 September 2013) [6] (author's translation).

[107] (adopted 6 April 1974, entered into force 6 October 1983) 1334 UNTS 15.

[108] [2010] Min Ti Zi No 213 (Civil Judgment) Supreme People's Court (28 June 2011).

[109] [2019] Jing Min Xia Zhong No 258 (Civil Ruling) Higher People's Court of Beijing Municipality (27 December 2019).

[110] (adopted 28 May 1999, entered into force 4 November 2003) 2242 UNTS 309.

for damages as set out in Article 33 of the Montreal Convention. As such, both courts concluded that the Convention was not applicable.[111]

D. Conclusion

Absent constitutional authorization, statutory law plays a significant role or, arguably, has even become the decisive factor, in Chinese courts' engagement with international law. In most circumstances, the use of international treaties by Chinese courts, either as a supportive argument for their reasoning or as a direct legal basis of their judgments, depends on the existence of an express legislative basis or judicial interpretation, granting the judiciary the power to do so.

Chinese courts seldom resort to international law when there is no explicit legislative foundation. Very limited breakthrough has happened where international human rights treaties are concerned. In a few cases, courts resorted to the CRC directly, merely with the justification that since China is a party to the CRC, provisions and principles enshrined therein should consequently be embodied in Chinese legislation and adjudicative pronouncements.[112] This is obviously an ideal way to implement treaty obligations, and perhaps preferable from an international law perspective. The 'inward-looking'[113] character of international human rights law may also provide more opportunities for domestic courts to pronounce on how treaties should be applied to protect individual rights. However, it might be challenged from the standpoint of domestic law, since courts in China are expected to adjudicate in accordance with the 'law', a narrowly defined concept limited to domestic law enacted by the Chinese legislature, not extending to international treaties which have not yet been received into the legal system of China.[114] Hence, there is some logical fault in light of the habitual judicial practice of China; this gap should be filled either through the enactment of a clear reception provision in the Constitution or a specific law.

[111] For a summary of the case, see Wu Xiaohui (n 98) 800–1.

[112] Eg, a court of trial in a guardianship dispute made this statement while invoking the CRC in its reasoning. *Chen Ying v Luo Ronggeng* [2015] Hu Yi Zhong Shao Min Zhong Zi No 56 (Civil judgment) First Intermediate People's Court of Shanghai Municipality (17 June 2016).

[113] ILA Final Report (n 4) para 12.

[114] There is no mention of international treaties in the Whiter Paper which declared that 'we had put in place a socialist system of laws with Chinese characteristics'. See Information Office of the State Council, *The Socialist System of Laws with Chinese Characteristics* (White Paper, October 2011), available at <http://english.www.gov.cn/archive/white_paper/2014/09/09/content_281474986284659.htm> last accessed 22 July 2022.

Although constrained from the need for an explicit legislative basis, the posture or strategy courts have followed in their engagement with international law still varied. Different positions exist not only among different courts when the same international treaty is concerned, but also within the same court towards different treaties. For some courts, even if authorized by domestic legislation, international treaties could only be used to support reasoning and not as the direct legal basis of a judgment; for others, however, treaties have also functioned as the latter. Some courts have the courage to invoke international law to strengthen their own standpoint even without direct statutory authorization, while others hesitate to do so holding that international treaties are not applicable unless transformed into domestic law. Because, in most cases, courts do not expand on their reasoning and decisions at length, with some judgments being in fact quite brief, it is difficult to analyse the reasons behind specific choices.

Compared to the huge number of treaties concluded by China, the number of cases in which courts have engaged with international law is quite small, and the number of treaties involved is limited, by and large confined to politically unproblematic situations. While there might be linguistic barriers and knowledge limitations, the first and foremost constraint is the absence of a clear constitutional foundation for such engagement.[115] Before more definite and broader engagement of Chinese courts with international law can take place, a series of questions have to be answered by the Constitution: are international treaties concluded by China an inherent part of the Chinese legal system? Do they have direct legally binding force on state organs, and individuals? Which one prevails when an international treaty conflicts with domestic law?

[115] See also Cai (n 19) 240–48.

5

Engagement of Israel's Supreme Court with International Law

Osnat Grady Schwartz

A. The Status of International Law in the Israeli Legal System

Israel does not have a comprehensive constitution, and does not have any specific constitutional arrangements defining the relationship between Israeli law and international law.[1] The relationship between the two systems of law has been crafted by Supreme Court decisions over the years. In the State's formative years, the Court followed the common law tradition, adopting a monist approach towards customary international law, which is automatically incorporated into 'the law of the land'.[2] In case of a conflict between Israeli law and international custom, Israeli law prevails.[3] However, if the potentially inconsistent law can be reasonably interpreted in a manner that aligns it with international law, the Court must employ a presumption of compatibility between Israeli law and international law, and interpret Israeli law accordingly.[4]

[1] Israel's 1948 Declaration of Independence determined that a constitution would be formed within a few months by a democratically elected constitutional assembly. See Declaration of the Establishment of the State of Israel (1948) 1 LSI 3, 4. However, the independence war that broke the day after the declaration, and profound disagreements between the founding political parties, thwarted any attempts to do so. In 1950, the Knesset (namely, Israel's legislative branch) had finally reached a compromise (the 'Harari Resolution'), according to which it would enact separate Basic Laws on matters that can be agreed upon, and those Basic Laws would eventually be combined into one constitutional document. Examples of Basic Laws are: The Knesset (1958) 244 LSI 69; Basic Law: The Government (1968) 540 LSI 226; Basic Law: The Army (1976) 806 LSI 154; and in 1992 the following Basic Laws that deal with human rights: Basic Law: Human Dignity and Liberty (1992) LSI 150; and Basic Law: Freedom of Occupation (1992) LSI 114. For more details on the enactment of the 1992 Basic Laws, and the constitutional revolution that ensued, see Gideon Sapir, 'Constitutional Revolution: Israel as a Case Study' (2009) 4 International Journal of Law in Context 355.

[2] CrimA 174/54 *Schtamper v Attorney General* (1956) 10(5) PD [15].

[3] HCJ 785/87 *Affu v The IDF Commander in the West Bank* (1989) 42(2) PD [4].

[4] CrimA 336/61 *Eichmann v Attorney General* (1962) 16 PD [2033].

As for treaties, the Court has adopted a dualist approach, requiring them to be transformed via legislation to become Israeli law, enforceable in Israeli courts.[5] In a conflict between Israeli law and a legally transformed treaty, neither has automatic supremacy. Rather, the conflict is to be resolved by the regular rules of interpretation of competing and conflicting laws (for example, specific legislation overrides general legislation, later legislation supersedes earlier one, etc).[6]

Gradually, and especially during the era of President Barak at the helm of the Supreme Court (1995-2006), the Court has shown greater openness towards international law, with judges liberally applying alignment techniques both in order to give effect to 'international obligations' (including treaties that were not transformed into Israeli law) and to avoid overriding incorporated international law where it would conflict with domestic legislation. These developments are discussed below.

B. What Determines the Engagement of the Israeli Supreme Court with International Law?

The engagement of the Supreme Court with international law is not so much influenced by the latter's nature as customary or treaty law, but is mostly determined by other factors. It seems that a combination of what branch of international law is at stake in a given case and the judge's individual preferences dictate the latter's strategic choice between engaging with (through alignment or contestation) or avoiding international law. Depending on the particular features of a case (subject matter, conflicting interests, the panel, etc), the same judge can make different strategic choices and engage with international law in various, sometimes contradictory, ways.

1. The Different Branches of International Law at Stake

Israel's geopolitical reality (lack of a constitution, continuous emergency situation, prolonged occupation of the West Bank and other territories makes the fields of international human rights law (IHRL) and international humanitarian

[5] CA 22/55 *The Conservator of Absentees' Property v Samara* (1956) 10 PD [1825].

[6] Ruth Lapidoth, 'The Place of Public International Law in Israeli Law' (1990) 19 Mishpatim 807 (in Hebrew); Ruth Lapidoth, 'International Law within the Israel Legal System' (1990) 24 Israel Law Review 451.

law (IHL) more relevant to it, when compared to other States. These fields share significant features that sometimes make the Supreme Court's engagement with them controversial, thus meriting special discussion.[7]

First, both IHL and IHRL establish the State's humanistic and humanitarian duties and responsibilities vis-à-vis individuals. This grants affected people, at least conceptually, substantial *locus standi* (as distinct from the procedural right of standing that may not exist with regard to non-transformed treaties). In Israel, claims of rights' violations against the State generally fall under the umbrella of administrative law, and all acts and policies by State agencies are, in principle, subject to judicial review by the Supreme Court, sitting as the High Court of Justice (HCJ). Second, these fields contain important 'consubstantial norms', that is basic norms that are shared by IHL, IHRL, and Israeli constitutional and administrative law, in the sense discussed in the International Law Association (ILA) Study Group Final Report,[8] with human dignity being of primary importance. This has allowed the Supreme Court to utilize IHRL both to reinforce judgments on constitutional rights in the absence of a constitution, and to substantiate some tough and unpopular IHL cases. Third, these fields of international law are 'value heavy' and thus have a relatively high political profile. This makes them: (a) harder to transform via legislation in a rifted society like the Israeli society (though many of the relevant international rules are customary and thus do not need legislative transformation), which then creates a 'legislative vacuum' that leaves much room for judicial discretion in engaging with them;[9] and (b) more susceptible to individual judges' tendencies, as discussed in the next section.

2. Individual Preferences and Conceptions of Judges

Individual preferences include the values held by judges, their perception of their role (role-perception), their internationalist inclination, and more. Judges vary in their 'internationalist inclination', namely in their degree of openness towards international law and in their inclination to give it full effect in their decisions. They also vary in their role-perception vis-à-vis the other

[7] See also the discussion in Sharon Weill in this volume.

[8] ILA Study Group on Principles on the Engagement of Domestic Courts with International Law, 'Final Report: Mapping the Engagement of Domestic Courts with International Law' (Johannesburg, 2016) (ILA Final Report) para 30.

[9] As observed in the ILA Final Report (ibid para 76) engagement of domestic courts with international law may differ depending on how 'politically or otherwise problematic the international rule [in question] and compliance with is'.

branches of government, that is in their willingness to intervene in the operations of the political branches on the basis of law in general, and international law in particular.[10] Other individual differences can also influence judges' strategic choices in adopting particular postures towards international law and in employing particular methods in their engagement with its rules. 'Security-minded' judges will tend to defer to the executive when questions of IHL may seem to conflict with national security interests.[11] The very same judges may demonstrate a stronger internationalist sentiment when utilizing IHRL to substantiate domestic constitutional rights and influence other public interests.[12]

Given these considerations, in mapping the Israeli Supreme Court's engagement with international law, the discussion will sometimes refer to specific judges, too, if only to allow the theoretical analysis to be more comprehensive and refined.

C. The Practice of the Israeli Supreme Court

This section maps the judicial techniques employed by the Supreme Court vis-à-vis international law. The general trend is that of alignment (at least, alleged alignment). However, there are still cases and situations of contestation and avoidance. This part looks into these strategies of engagement with international law, and the methods employed in their fulfilment, in the following order: First, it discusses cases where the Court has applied international law, leading to either alignment or contestation of its rules. For alignment, various techniques are identified. For contestation, cases of both affirmative and negatory contestation have been identified. Then, the discussion turns to cases and situations where the Court has engaged in international law avoidance, and analyses both cases of affirmative and evasive avoidance. In cases of evasive avoidance, the Court seems to have ignored or completely disregarded the relevant rules of international law.

Due to significant differences between the treatment of IHL and IHRL in the Israeli context, some of these postures of engagement are more relevant to one

[10] These variables often correlate so the broader the judge's role-perception, the higher her internationalist inclination. See Osnat Grady Schwartz, 'International Law in Domestic Judges' Decisions: The Relationship Between Broad Role-Perception and a Strong Internationalist Inclination' (2011) 34 Tel-Aviv University Law Review 475 (in Hebrew).

[11] See also from a different perspective the discussion in Sharon Weill in this volume.

[12] E g see and compare Cheshin J's methods of alignment with/avoidance of IHRL in HCJ 3648/97 *Stamka v Minister of the Interior* (1999) 53(2) PD [728] (see also n 48 below) and with IHL in HCJ 5872/01 *Knesset Member Muhammad Bara'ke v Prime Minister, Ariel Sharon* (2002) 56 (3) PD [1] (see below n 79), accordingly. See also ILA Final Report (n 8) para 76.

legal regime than to the other, and therefore the discussion will unfold accordingly. The Supreme Court's engagement with IHRL norms and IHL norms, respectively, can be distinguished on the following grounds. First, IHL normally functions as the primary normative framework of HCJ decisions, typically in the context of the Israeli-Palestinian conflict (occupation and active armed conflict situations), whereas IHRL is usually used as an 'auxiliary mechanism' (for example, as an interpretive presumption or a framework for comparative law). Second, engagement with IHL happens within a context of clear international relevance (being therefore more controversial in the Israeli context), whereas the use of IHRL is more frequent in decisions that are domestic in essence. Third, IHRL is usually (though not always) used to influence the content of Israeli law and align it with international law (enforcing 'consubstantial norms'), whereas engagement with IHL is normally independent of domestic law. An exception to this are IHL norms that impact Israeli administrative law applicable to all State agents, including those operating in the Occupied Territories. Engagement with international law in this context may also occur in order to influence the content of international law itself, leading to affirmative contestation.

Given these differences, a discussion of 'reluctance' or 'avoidance' is more relevant to rules of international law that the court has to apply as the primary normative framework for a case (which is the case for IHL). It is less relevant to rules that the court may opt to apply (which is the case for IHRL), given the existence of 'consubstantial norms' in domestic law. Similarly, the strategy of 'contestation' seems more relevant in situations where the court is somewhat 'forced' to apply international law (which is the case for IHL), than in situations where it may altogether ignore potentially contradicting international law rules (which is the case for IHRL). The posture of 'alignment', however, is equally visible in the Court's voluntary (or discretionary) engagement with IHRL,[13] and in its increasing engagement with IHL (the latter can be seen as the reverse side of the posture of 'diminishing avoidance' discussed below). For these reasons, while following the structure sketched out at the start of this section, some of the following sub-sections only refer to one legal regime (IHL or IHRL), while others address both.

[13] 'Voluntary application is the application of IL that could have been avoided or disregarded as the court had done before.' See discussion and references in Osnat Grady Schwartz, 'International Law and National Courts: Between Mutual Empowerment and Mutual Weakening' (2015) 23 Cardozo Journal of International and Comparative Law 587, 590.

1. Engagement with International Law through Alignment and Contestation

a. Postures of alignment

i. International humanitarian law

When it comes to IHL, during the last fifteen years or so the Court has increasingly engaged with this branch of international law. The Court's (or at least the majority of Justices, led by Barak P) acceptance of IHL as dictating 'the rules of the game' in many national security and Occupied Territories cases has arisen since the bargaining chips case in 2000:[14] In a procedure of 'further hearing', Barak P reversed his previous decision to allow the incarceration of Hezbollah fighters-members in order to use them as 'bargaining chips' for the return of Israeli prisoners of war (POWs) and absentees. Whereas in the first round Barak J (Kedmi J concurring, Dorner J dissenting) had deemed international law as irrelevant in the face of existing Israeli law that was anyway superior,[15] in the second round, Barak J reconsidered his position and applied the presumption of compatibility in order to align Israeli security legislation with IHL (in particular, the Geneva Convention IV and the Hostages Convention 1979),[16] which prohibited the incarceration of individuals who do not pose a security risk. The majority of the Court concurred, but Kedmi J and Cheshin J expressed their reservations about relying on international law in that case, and concluded that the incarceration was legal, as discussed further below.

The Court's acceptance of IHL as the primary normative framework has been even more common during the first decade of the 21st century, with the Court providing some of its most important decisions on national security. These cases include: the security barrier case in 2005,[17] in which the Court legitimized the construction of the barrier, while accepting—at least nominally—the legal analysis found in the ICJ's advisory opinion[18] as the normative outline for the decision (Cheshin J resented this methodology, as discussed below); the

[14] CrimFH 7048/97 *Plonim v Minister of Defence* (2000) 54(1) PD [721].

[15] ibid (Barak) [15].

[16] In particular, the Geneva Convention Relative to the Protection of Civilian Persons in Times of War (adopted 12 August 1949, entered into force 21 October 1950) 75 UNTS 287 (Geneva Convention IV), and the International Convention against the Taking of Hostages (adopted 17 December 1979, entered into force 3 June 1983) 1316 UNTS 205. With this, the court produced consubstantial alignment between domestic and international law. See ILA Final Report (n 8) para 46. It is interesting, however, to note in this regard that Israel signed but never ratified the Hostages Convention. Alignment with it can thus be regarded as a manifestation of 'hyper-alignment' (ibid para 55).

[17] HCJ 7957/04 *Mara'abe et al v The Prime Minister of Israel et al* (2005) 60(2) PD [477].

[18] *Legal Consequences of the Construction of a Wall in Occupied Palestinian Territory* (Advisory Opinion) [2004] ICJ Rep 136.

2005 early warning case, in which the Court applied the principle of distinction to declare illegal the Israel Defence Forces' (IDF) practice of using during West Bank raids a neighbouring civilian to persuade a wanted person to step outside of their hiding place (Cheshin J concurred, with reservations);[19] the assigned residence case in 2002, in which the Court examined under Article 78 of the Geneva Convention Relative to the Protection of Civilian Persons in Times of War (Geneva Convention IV) what was argued to be a deportation of three Palestinians from the West Bank to Gaza, upholding two out of the three orders;[20] the targeted killing case in 2006,[21] in which the Court delineated the conditions for legality of operations for targeted killing of terrorists within the prescriptions of Article 51(3) of the First Additional Protocol to the Geneva Conventions;[22] the 2003 special orders case, in which the Court invalidated under the Geneva Convention IV 'Special Order 1500' issued by the IDF Commander in the West Bank during Operation Defensive Shield to allow the detention of thousands of persons suspected of terrorism for up to 18 (later reduced to 12) days prior to judicial review;[23] and the electricity to Gaza (*Al-Basiuni*) case in 2008,[24] where the Court relied on IHL principles to determine that Gaza ceased to be occupied after the 2005 disengagement (a legal position that remains contested among international experts), but that Israel still bears humanitarian responsibilities towards the area's population.[25] While these cases demonstrate a high level of engagement with international law, it is worth mentioning that the outcome in some of them deviated from mainstream interpretations of IHL,[26] and so they can also be considered as instances of affirmative contestation.[27]

The strength of the Court's acceptance of IHL as the normative guideline in all armed conflict situations found its strongest expression in its employment

[19] HCJ 3799/02 *Adalah – The Legal Center for Arab Minority Rights in Israel et al v GOC Central Command IDF* (2005) 60(3) PD [67].
[20] HCJ 7015/02 *Ajuri v IDF Commander in the West Bank* (2002) 56(6) PD [352].
[21] HCJ 769/02 *The Public Committee against Torture in Israel et al v Israel Government* (2006) 2006(4) Tak-El 3958 (*Targeted Killing* case). See for a discussion Sharon Weill in this volume.
[22] Additional Protocol to the Geneva Conventions of 12 August 1949, and relating to the Protection of Victims of International Armed Conflict (Protocol I) (adopted 8 June 1977, entered into force 7 December 1979) 1125 UNTS 3. Israel is not a party to the Additional Protocol, but the Court accepted that its provisions relevant to the case were customary in nature.
[23] HCJ 3239/02 *Marab et al v The IDF Commander in the Area of Judah and Samaria* (2003) 57(2) PD [349].
[24] HCJ 9132/07 *Al-Basiuni v The Prime Minister* (2008).
[25] Many of the decisions, which are of clear interest to the international community, were translated in English and published in the Supreme Court's website: http://elyon1.court.gov.il/VerdictsSearch/EnglishStaticVerdicts.html. For another review of Supreme Court cases, see: http://www.geneva-academy.ch/RULAC/print_state.php?page=9&id_state=113.
[26] See, eg, HCJ 2164/09 *Yesh Din v IDF West Bank Command*, Nevo (26 Dec 2011).
[27] ILA Final Report (n 8) para 58.

of IHL to review IDF's actions 'in real time', while military operations were being carried out, such as during the 2002 Operation Defensive Shield in Bethlehem,[28] the 2004 Operation Rainbow in Rafah,[29] and Operation Cast Lead (the Gaza War), taking place in 2008–2009.[30]

Another area of strong alignment involves review of the constitutionality of legislation in light of IHL norms, where the Court has effectively used a presumption of compatibility with international law. In *Adala* in 2006, the Court, led by Barak P (Ret), found disproportional, and thus unconstitutional, section 5C of the Torts (State Liability) Law (Amendment No 7) 5765-2005, which exempted the State from tort liability for any damage caused by security forces in conflict zones.[31] The Court stressed that the legal frame was domestic, but that domestic law had to be consistent with Israel's duties as an occupier under IHL. And, in 2020, the Court (8 out 9 judges; Solberg J dissenting) struck down the Regularizing Judea and Samaria Settlements Law 5777-2017 (Regularization Law), considering that it disproportionally harmed property rights of Palestinians which are protected under IHL.[32]

The 2008 *Ploni* case[33] was a special case, with the presumption of compatibility integrated into the 'purpose clause' of the law (Incarceration of Unlawful Combatants Law 5762-2002), according to which '[t]his Law is intended to regulate the incarceration of unlawful combatants not entitled to prisoner-of-war status, in a manner conforming with the obligations of the State of Israel under the provisions of international humanitarian law' (Article 1). The Court applied this presumption to reach the conclusion that the law is constitutional only if interpreted narrowly (for example, the law would only apply to foreign elements jeopardizing national security). At the same time, however, the Court stated that existing international law is not suited for the changing reality of terror challenges, and thus a dynamic interpretation of its norms is needed, aiming thus at impacting the content of both Israeli law and international law.[34] It should be noted that in some of these cases the Court engaged with both IHL

[28] See, eg, HCJ 3451/02 *Almadani et al v Minister of Security* (2002) 56(3) PD [30].
[29] See, eg, HCJ 4764/04 *Physicians for Human Rights v IDF Commander in Gaza* (2004) 58(5) PD [385].
[30] See, eg, HCJ 201/09 *Physicians for Human Rights v IDF Commander in Prime Minister of Israel* (2009) 2009(1) Tak-El 565.
[31] HCJ 8276/05 *Legal Centre for Arab Minority Rights in Israel v Minister of Defence*, Nevo (12 December 2006).
[32] HCJ 1308/17 *Silwad Municipality v The Knesset*, Nevo (19 June 2020).
[33] CrimA 6659/06 *Ploni v The State of Israel*, 64(2) PD 329 (2008).
[34] In this sense, then, the court engaged in negatory local contestation. See ILA Final Report (n 8) paras 61–62, 65.

and IHRL, acknowledging their simultaneous application and IHRL's potential to fill lacunas in IHL.[35] This is discussed in the following section.

ii. International human rights law

Turning to engagement with IHRL, Israel is a party to the principal human rights conventions, although it never transformed them into domestic law via legislation. However, many IHRL norms are customary in nature, and are thus automatically incorporated into Israeli law. Also, the content of many of these norms is considered to be part of Israeli constitutional and administrative law by virtue of the State's democratic nature.[36] Thus, while the core of IHRL is both relevant to and applicable in Israeli courts, the latter do not necessarily need to invoke or refer to IHRL in order to protect human rights (and, essentially, align Israeli law with IHRL requirements). Nonetheless, IHRL norms and sources have often found their way into judicial decisions on human rights in one of two forms (which are sometimes hard to distinguish): through the presumption of compatibility, and as part of comparative law. In most cases, however, the reference to IHRL was not essential for the decision.

In certain constitutional cases that struck down primary legislation, international law was invoked as comparative law to support the Court's decisions. For example, in *Investment Managers Association* (1997), Barak P cited a decision of the European Court of Human Rights (ECtHR) on the freedom to enter a profession and property rights to support striking down a law that introduced examination requirements for people who had already worked for years as investment managers.[37] In the 2005 *Gaza Shore Regional Council* case, the Court (10 out of 11 Justices; Levi J dissenting) declared unconstitutional and void four sections of the Disengagement Plan Law 5765-2005, which set compensation arrangements for residents of evacuated settlements: two of the four sections revoked were analysed, amongst others, through ECtHR decisions on property rights.[38] In the *Ploni* case in 2010, Rivlin J, writing the leading opinion, declared unconstitutional and void Article 5 of the Criminal Procedure Law (Enforcement Powers—Detention) (Detainees Suspected of Security Offense) (Temporary Order) 5766-2006, which allowed courts to

[35] See, eg, the *Targeted Killing* case (n 21) [18]; *Marab* (n 23) [19], [27], [41]; the incarceration of unlawful combatants case, *Ploni* (n 33) [20], [9].

[36] The State's democratic nature has been the Court's basis for human rights decisions since HCJ 73/53 *Kol Ha'am corporation v Minister of Interior* (1953) 7(2) PD [871].

[37] HCJ 1715/97 *Israel Investment Managers Association v Minister of Treasury* (1997) 51(4) PD [367], citing ECtHR, *Van Marle v Netherlands* App Nos 8543/79, 8674/79, 8675/79, 8685/79 (Judgment of 26 June 1986) ([53] of Barak's decision).

[38] HCJ 1661/05 *Gaza Shore Regional Council v Knesset* 59(2) PD 481 (2005) [234], [238].

carry out detention hearings for security offenses suspects *in abstentia*, referring to an ECtHR decision on Article 5(4) of the European Convention on Human Rights (ECHR).[39]

In yet other cases, a constitutional presumption of compatibility appears to have been resorted to. For instance, in the 2012 *Hassan* case, the Court, led by Beinisch P, struck down Article 9A(b) of the Income Support Law 5741-1980 that withheld income support (poverty assistance) from people owning or regularly using a private car.[40] Beinisch conducted an extensive discussion on the status of social and economic rights vis-à-vis civil and political rights to reach a conclusion that there is no inherent hierarchy between the two types of rights. The discussion heavily relied on IHRL (specifically the 1966 International Covenant on Civil and Political Rights (ICCPR) and on Economic, Social and Cultural Rights (ICESCR),[41] related literature, and the decisions of treaty monitoring bodies) presuming compatibility and consistency between Israeli (constitutional) law and international law. In *Adam*, in 2013, the Court unanimously revoked section 30A of the Prevention of Infiltration Law (Crimes and Judging) (Third Amendment and temporary provision) 5772-2012, which allowed the detention of 'infiltrators' (their status as asylum seekers or labour immigrants not having been determined) for up to three years, even when the State does not act to deport them.[42] The decision strongly relied on various instruments of IHRL, most notably the Convention relating to the Status of Refugees,[43] but also on other conventions and decisions by United Nations (UN) bodies, rejecting the State's objection to not subject the question of constitutionality of legislation to the presumption of compatibility with international law.

Still, the vast majority of cases with human rights aspects before the Supreme Court did not actually involve striking down laws, but rather reviewing administrative acts and policies. In those cases that involved judicial review of legislation, the Court usually opted to uphold the law, but interpreted it in a manner that promoted or alleged to promote alignment with human rights norms, as these were developed in the Court's own precedents, by other States'

[39] CrimHR 8823/07 *Ploni v The State of Israel* 63(3) PD 500 (2010).

[40] HCJ 10662/04 *Hassan v The Social Security Institute*, 65(1) PD 782 (2012) [26]–[29] of Beinisch' decision.

[41] International Covenant on Civil and Political Rights (adopted 16 December 1966, entered into force 23 March 1976) 999 UNTS 171; International Covenant on Economic, Social and Cultural Rights (adopted 16 December 1966, entered into force 3 January 1976) 993 UNTS 3.

[42] HCJ 7146/12 *Adam v The Knesset* 60(1) PD 717 (2013).

[43] Convention relating to the Status of Refugees (adopted 28 July 1951, entered into force 22 April 1954) 189 UNTS 137.

jurisprudence, and by IHRL. Generally, reference to IHRL in these situations took the form of comparative law.[44]

In some cases of statutory interpretation IHRL had a greater impact, with the Court employing the presumption of compatibility between international law and Israeli law, and in particular administrative acts. For example, in the *Frudenthal* case in 2003,[45] Justice Beinisch (Grunis J and Hayut J concurring) relied on the said presumption to extend the scope of the criminal offense of trafficking in persons so as to align it with IHRL, and more specifically the UN Convention against Transnational Organized Crime and its Protocol on Prevention, Elimination and Punishment of Trafficking in Persons.[46] This interpretation was adopted notwithstanding the principle *nullum crimen sine lege* and the principle *poenlia restraingenda sunt* (restrictive interpretation of penal law),[47] and disregarding the fact that the Protocol had not entered into force at the time, and Israel had not even ratified it.[48] In the 2002 *Yated* case, Dorner J construed the Special Education Law 5748-1988 in light of the UN Convention on the Rights of the Child (CRC),[49] so that the provisions of the law requiring budgetary allocation for special education apply also to children with special needs who have been integrated into mainstream schools.[50] In *Stamka* in 1999, Cheshin J applied several IHRL instruments (including the ICCPR, ICESCR, ECHR, ECtHR cases, the Universal Declaration of Human Rights,[51] and the Convention on the Nationality of Married Women[52]) as constituting the guiding principles for the Minister of Interior's discretion in ordering non-national spouses to leave the country until authenticity of the

[44] See, eg, CrimA 5121/98 *Yissacharov v Chief Military Prosecutor* (2006) 60(1) PD [461]: The Court, led by Beinisch J, established (a somewhat softened version of) the fruit of poisonous tree evidentiary doctrine, based, among others, on several universal and European instruments of IHRL. See also HCJ 8111/96 *The New General Federation of Labor v Israel Aerospace Industries Ltd.* (2004) 58(6) PD 481: Orr decision, utilizing European law sources to establish that that employees should give their consent to a change of employer during privatization of the privatized business.

[45] CrA 11196/02 *Frudenthal v State of Israel* (2003) 57(6) PD [40].

[46] United Nations Convention against Transnational Organized Crime (adopted 15 November 2000, entered into force 29 September 2003) 2225 UNTS 209; Protocol to Prevent, Suppress and Punish Trafficking in Persons, Especially Women and Children, Supplementing the United Nations Convention Against Transnational Organized Crime (adopted 15 November 2000, entered into force 25 December 2003) 2237 UNTS 319.

[47] Boaz Sanjero, 'Broad Interpretation in Criminal Law?' (2003) 3 Aley Mishpat 165 (in Hebrew).

[48] *Frudenthal* (n 45) [5]. This was then an instance of hyper-alignment with international law. See ILA Final Report (n 8) para 55.

[49] Convention on the Rights of the Child (adopted 20 November 1989, entered into force 2 September 1990) 1577 UNTS 3.

[50] HCJ 2599/00 *Yated – The Association of Parents of Down Syndrome Children v Ministry of Education* (2002) 56(5) PD [834].

[51] Universal Declaration of Human Rights, UNGA Res 217 (A) (10 December 1948) UN Doc A/RES/217(III)(A).

[52] Convention on the Nationality of Married Women (adopted 20 February 1957, entered into force 21 August 1958) 309 UNTS 65.

marriage is established.[53] In *Poria Ilit Board* in 2002, Procacia J interpreted the Compulsory Education Law 5709-1949 in light of several IHRL sources (the ICESCR, CRC, ECHR, and the Universal Declaration) in order to minimize mandatory fees in public schools.[54] In the 2003 *Handyman Do It Yourself LTD* case,[55] Dorner J rejected an argument against the constitutionality of Work and Rest Hours Law 5711-1951, reasoning that the law adheres to specific sections of the International Labour Organization Weekly Rest (Commerce and Offices) Convention.[56] In *Kav LaOved—Worker's Hotline Association*, Levi J supported his decision that a Ministerial policy that binds alien workers to specific employers was unconstitutional with several IHRL instruments (including the ICCPR, ICESCR, the Universal Declaration, and an ILO convention).[57]

b. Postures of contestation

Contestation can take the form of a declaration of supremacy of domestic law over conflicting international law. As outlined in the ILA Final Report, it can also be formulated as an express defiance or criticism of international law's substantial elements or procedures.[58] In Israel's domestic context, confrontation with international law usually takes place with a view to subjecting the latter to domestic norms and national interests. In that sense, the Supreme Court engages in local contestation as explained in the ILA Final Report.[59]

A clear case of negatory contestation was Cheshin J's opinion in the Separation Barrier case (*Mara'abe*),[60] where he refused to follow, and thus legitimize, the ICJ's legal analysis in the *Wall* advisory opinion.[61] Cheshin J stressed that the ICJ's decision was coloured with a clear political hue, and therefore concluded: 'I am sorry, but the decision of the ICJ cannot light my path. Its light is too dim for me to guide myself by it to law, truth, and justice in the way a judge does.'[62]

[53] *Stamka* (n 12) 728.

[54] HCJ 4363/00 *Poria Ilit Board v Minister of Education* (2002) 56(4) PD [203].

[55] HCJ 10687/02 *Handyman Do It Yourself LTD v The State of Israel* (2003) 57(3) PD [1].

[56] Convention concerning Weekly Rest in Commerce and Offices (adopted 26 June 1957, entered into force 4 March 1959) 325 UNTS 279.The same convention was later cited by Barak P in a very similar case, this time functioning as 'comparative law'. See HCJ 5026/04 *Design 22 – Shark Deluxe Furniture LTS v Head of Sabbath work permits department, Ministry of Labor and Welfare* (2004) 60(1) PD [38].

[57] HCJ 4542/02 *Kav LaOved – Worker's Hotline Association v The Government of Israel*, 61(1) PD 346 (2006).

[58] See ILA Final Report (n 8) paras 57 et seq.

[59] ibid para 65.

[60] *Mara'abe* (n 17) 477.

[61] *Wall* Advisory Opinion (n 18).

[62] *Mara'abe* (n 17) (Cheshin J) [4].

An earlier situation in which Cheshin J had also expressed his scepticism towards international law was the bargaining chips case,[63] where he joined Kedmi J in rejecting the majority's reliance on international law. Kedmi J pronounced this reluctance by stating:

> [I]n the special circumstances of the case we are not obliged to implement treaty law in the face of the disgraceful and inhuman behaviour of the terror organizations that hold the solution to the question of the 'disappearance' of Ron Arad [captive Israeli pilot. O.G.S.]. These organizations and their members […] crudely trampled on basic human rules of behaviour, and this is enough to deny their members – the petitioners – the option of arguing against the legality of their arrest.[64]

Other situations of contestation can be grouped under the category 'declaration of Israeli law supremacy', although these may vary: a) in some cases, the Court may engage in international law interpretation and conclude that the State does not violate international law, but nonetheless find it important to stress that even if international law were to be understood differently, Israeli law would prevail;[65] b) in some other cases, the Court may choose to avoid examining international law's content due to the fact that it has not been transformed into Israeli law, but 'overcome' the possibility that there would be a violation by stating that Israeli law would prevail anyway;[66] c) finally, the court may acknowledge an actual contradiction between the domestic law and international law, but nonetheless determine the supremacy of the former, giving its imprimatur to the State for its violation of international law.

Cases of this last category are rare to non-existent in current Israeli jurisprudence. However, remnants of past decisions still echo in contemporary decisions of the Court. One example is *Yesh Din* in 2010, in which the petitioners challenged the legality of incarceration of residents of the Occupied Territories ('protected persons' in the terminology of Geneva Convention IV) outside the West Bank and Gaza Strip, in Israeli territory.[67] Beinisch P (Rivlin VP and Procacia J concurring) rejected the petition based on past decisions of the HCJ (the 1988 *Sagedia* decision,[68] and the 1995 *Wadjia* decision),[69]

[63] *Plonim* (n 14) (Cheshin J) [15]–[16].
[64] ibid (Kedmi J) [4].
[65] See, Shamgar P's methodology in *Affu* (n 2); *Ploni* (n 33) (Beinisch P) [9]; *Gaza Shore Regional Council* (n 24) [55]; HCJ 256/01 *Rabach v Local Matters Court in Jerusalem* (2002) 56(2) PD 930 [6].
[66] HCJ 2587/04 *Buchris v Hadera assessor* (2005) [14]–[15] of Barak P's decision.
[67] HCJ 2690/09 *Yesh Din v IDF Commander in the West Bank*, Nevo (28 Mar 2010).
[68] HCJ 253/88 *Sagedia v Minister of Security* (1988) 42(2) PD 301.
[69] HCJ 6504/95 *Wadjia v The State of Israel*, Nevo (1 Nov 1995).

which acknowledged the contradiction with some provisions of the Geneva Convention IV, but nonetheless approved the incarceration based on Israeli law (emergency regulations) supremacy. The Court recalled the rule of supremacy and rejected the argument that the decisions from 1988 and 1995 should be revised due to the change of times, and in light of the developments in the Court's own approach towards the Geneva Convention IV.[70]

2. International Law Avoidance

a. (Diminishing) affirmative avoidance

From the 1980s onwards, the power of procedural barriers in Israel significantly declined, as the HCJ showed greater willingness to engage in judicial review of almost the entire spectrum of administrative (and later on, legislative) actions.[71] In the last two decades this trend has been specifically evident in IHL cases, although in some situations specific judges expressed their reluctance to review security measures and general policies allegedly in breach of IHL, invoking the doctrine of non-justiciability, a commonly used avoidance technique.[72]

Shortly after the occupation of 1967, the HCJ started hearing petitions from residents of the Occupied Territories based on IHL, and in particular the Hague Regulations and the Geneva Convention IV. With the State's initial consent,[73] the Court determined that IHL's customary rules are enforceable in Israeli courts, and established a broad right of standing for individual petitioners, presuming that IHL conferred enforceable individual rights.[74] This allowed the Court to declare as illegal the confiscation of privately owned land for the purpose of establishing new settlements in the West Bank, which were not required for military needs.[75]

[70] Note, however, that the Court also followed the humanitarian prescription of the early decisions, restating the State's duty to comply with the humanitarian requirements of the Convention inside the incarceration facilities.

[71] One of the first cases that established the right of standing of a public petitioner was an extradition case in which the Court had to decide between keeping the State in line with its international obligations under an extradition treaty and protecting the extradited person's life by not extraditing him. See HCJ 852/86 *Aloni et al v Minister of Justice* (1987) 41(1) PD 1.

[72] On that, see ILA Final Report (n 8) para 41.

[73] Later, the Court clarified that it has jurisdiction and that customary IHL applies regardless of the State's consent. See HCJ 302/72 *Chilu v The Government of Israel* (1973) 27(2) PD 169; HCJ 393/82 HCJ 393/82 *Jam'iat Iscan Al-Ma'almoun Al-Tha'auniya Al-Mahduda Al-Mauliya v Commander of the IDF Forces in the Area of Judea and Samaria* (1983) 37(3) PD 785.

[74] This judicial choice is not obvious – see Nollkaemper's interpretation of the HCJ's decision in *Ajuri* (n 20) in this context. André Nollkaemper, *National Courts and the International Rule of Law* (OUP 2011) 111.

[75] HCJ 390/79 *Dawiqat v The Government of Israel* (1979) 34(1) PD 1.

Despite the Court's previous decisions on the Israeli settlements, and although the Court had already established the 'public petitioner' doctrine, in 1993 the Court dismissed a general petition seeking to declare the Israeli settlements in the Occupied Territories illegal under IHL, specifically under Article 49 of the Geneva Convention IV.[76] Shamgar P and Orr J found the petition to be both substantively and institutionally non-justiciable. They also decided that the petitioners did not have a right of standing, as they were not individuals whose private lands had been confiscated for purposes other than military needs.[77] Goldberg J found the petition to be substantively justiciable (that is that it could be decided by applying the law), and that the petitioners did have a right of standing. However, he, too, dismissed the case based on institutional non-justiciability, namely finding that the court was not the appropriate institution to deal with this 'loaded' question. The Court (Matza J, Cheshin J, and Schtrasberg-Cohen J) reaffirmed the non-justiciability of the question in the 2001 *I'ad* case.[78] That said, it is noteworthy that, although the 1993 *Bargil* holding still stands, since then the Court has declared some parts of settlements to be illegal in specific contexts, such as when building beyond the legal borders of the Separation Barrier (as approved by the Supreme Court),[79] when building on Palestinian private property,[80] and when building without building permits.[81]

A more recent case that was dismissed as non-justiciable was Knesset Member Bara'ke's petition against the legality of targeted killings. The petition was dismissed in 2002 by Matza J, Cheshin J, and Edmond Levi J, who declared that 'the choice of means of warfare, which are used by the [state] in order to thwart murderous terrorist attacks, is not of the matters that this court would see fit to interfere with'.[82] However, in a strong demonstration of the

[76] HCJ 4481/91 *Bargil, CEO of the 'Peace Now' Movement v The Government of Israel* (1993) 47(4) PD 210.

[77] In HCJ 606/78 *Oyeb v Minister of Defence* (1978) 33(2) PD 610, and *Dawiqat* (n 75), the HCJ decided that the establishment of settlements in the Occupied Territories required for military needs can justify land confiscation, provided that the land owner is compensated. Since then, Israel has concentrated its efforts to build new settlements on what it considered to be non-private land, so as to prevent similar petitions and judicial review.

[78] HCJ 3125/98 *Iad v IDF Commander in Judea and Samaria* (1988) 55(1) PD 913.

[79] HCJ 8414/05 *Yasin v The Government of Israel* (2007) 62(2) PD 822.

[80] Eg, HCJ 9060/08 *Abdullah v Minister of Defence* (2011) http://elyon2.court.gov.il/files/08/600/090/N20/08090600.N20.htm; decision of 2012 http://elyon2.court.gov.il/files/08/600/090/S22/08090600.S22.pdf] (*Givat Haulpena*); HCJ 8887/06 *Al-Nabut v Minister of Defence* (2011) (*Migron*).

[81] Eg, HCJ 581/06 *Amona, Agricultural Cooperative Association for Communal Settlement Ltd v Minister of Defence* (2006).

[82] *Bara'ke* (n 12) [1]. This approach continues Cheshin J's line of deliberation in *Sabich* (1996) on the anomaly of the Court's review of 'acts of state' (and more specifically, 'acts of war') such as house demolition in response to suicide bombings. See, HCJ 1730/96 *Sabich v IDF Commander, General Ilan Biran* http://www.nevo.co.il/psika_html/elyon/PADI-P-1-353-L.htm (specifically [5], [8], [10] of Cheshin J's opinion). Although the act of State doctrine has significantly weakened during the years, Grunis J in

Court's diminishing reluctance to conduct IHL-based judicial review, in 2006, Barak P (Ret), Beinisch P, and Rivlin VP, decided an identical petition to the one rejected four years earlier in the *Bara'ke* case. This different panel examined the merits (establishing the legality of targeted killing under specific conditions following Article 51(3) of the First Additional Protocol to the Geneva Conventions), while rejecting the argument of non-justiciability:

> [T]he types of questions examined by this Court have also been decided by international courts. ... These courts have examined the legal aspects of the conduct of armies. Why can't an Israeli court perform that same examination? Why do those questions, which are justiciable in international courts, cease to be justiciable in national tribunals?[83]

The Court's recent disinclination to dodge IHL questions found another expression in the Quarries case in 2011.[84] Beinisch P (Naor J and Chayut J concurring) could have dismissed the petition based on avoidance techniques similar to non-justiciability (that is, as a political question, and a generalizing and sweeping petition), and for substantial delay. The Court, indeed, examined these doctrines, found them applicable, and stressed that the petition could actually be dismissed on these bases. Nevertheless, it still engaged with IHL, interpreting and applying Article 55 of the Hague Regulations (in a rather controversial manner), on the basis of which it denied the petition on the merits.

b. Evasive avoidance

Evasive avoidance is encountered in the HCJ's jurisprudence relating to the Occupied Territories, where the Court has preferred to adjudicate the petitions of protected persons based on the laws applicable in the area, including the British Mandate law (and to some extent the Jordanian law in the West Bank, too), the military commanders' orders, and Israeli administrative law, and not on the basis of international law. Formally, this methodology is compatible with Article 43 of the Hague Regulations ('respecting, unless absolutely

2006 thought it right to clarify that it was still part of Israeli law and may be applied in the context of tort claims against the State in some security situations. Note, however, that the State's attempt to invoke this doctrine in that particular case was rejected (including by Grunis J himself) with the Court deciding that not all 'acts of the security forces' should exempt the State from tort liability, but only 'acts of war'. See, HCJ 8276/05 *Adalah – The Legal Center for Arab Minority Rights in Israel v Minister of Security* (2005) (declaring void an article in the Civil Tort Law (State Liability) (seventh amendment) exempting the State from liability to damages caused by the security forces in a conflict zone).

[83] *Targeted Killing* case (Barak) (n 21) [53].
[84] Yesh Din (n 26).

prevented, the laws in force in the country'),[85] however, it opens the door for decisions that do not necessarily adhere to IHL.

The clearest case on this issue is the Court's examination of house demolitions in the Occupied Territories as a security measure under Article 19 of the Defense (Emergency) Regulations 1945 (enacted by the British Mandatory Power and still in force in the area). Generally speaking, the Court limited itself to examining the case under Article 19, disregarding Article 53 of Geneva Convention IV, which strictly limits the occupier's power to destroy private property, and Article 33, which prohibits collective punishment, both of which clearly apply to the situation. It should be noted that the Court's continued choice to ignore IHL in this context[86] seems inconsistent with its demonstrated openness towards IHL in recent years with regard to other highly controversial matters as previously discussed in this chapter.

D. Conclusion

Through a long period of time, Israel's Supreme Court has demonstrated a shift in its attitude towards international law. From a hesitant and reluctant sentiment, it moved to an accepting and promoting approach, which gained a clear expression in the court's decisions. With that, some expressions of the old sentiment still exist, most evident in the postures of contestation and evasive avoidance encountered in certain types of cases. This chapter endeavoured to map this development, covering the spectrum of attitudes towards international law that have been demonstrated in the court's decisions. The focus of the chapter has been the fields of IHRL and IHL. These two fields of international law, given both their interconnectedness and their politically charged status in Israel's domestic context, offered a rich platform on which to appreciate the Supreme Court's engagement with international law.

[85] Hague Convention (IV) respecting the Laws and Customs of War on Land and its Annex: Regulations concerning the Laws and Customs of War on Land (adopted 18 October 1907, entered into force 16 January 1910) 205 CTS 277 art 43. Article 43 was discussed in *Jam'iat Iscan* (n 73), specifying the normative framework applicable to the Occupied Territories, putting the Hague Regulations at the top of the norms' pyramid.

[86] See HCJ 124/09 *Dawi'at v Minister of Defence,* Nevo (18 March 2009); and HCJ 9353/08 *Abu-Dahim v Rear Area Headquarters Commander,* Nevo)15 January 2009(, approving the reinitiating of House Demolition after four years it has not been employed.

6

Engagement of Sri Lanka's Supreme Court with International Law in its Fundamental Rights Jurisdiction

Dakshinie Ruwanthika Gunaratne

A. Introduction

The Supreme Court of Sri Lanka is the final appellate court vested with original jurisdiction to determine matters relating to fundamental rights enshrined in Chapter III of the Constitution of the Democratic Socialist Republic of Sri Lanka.[1] These fundamental rights reflect rights contained in the International Covenant for Civil and Political Rights (ICCPR), to which Sri Lanka is a party.[2] The Court's engagement with international law has been most prominent in its fundamental rights jurisdiction. In the cases examined, the Court's predominant mode of engagement has been alignment of domestic law with international law,[3] including often consubstantial alignment of the two sets of laws. The Court has also, on rare occasion, engaged in affirmative avoidance techniques where 'the court consider[ed] the application of international law but explicitly reject[ed] it, as this is, in the court's view, the appropriate position under domestic law'.[4]

The doctrine of judicial precedent applicable in Sri Lanka ensures that the *reasoning* of Supreme Court decisions is binding on lower courts, and on the

[1] The Constitution of the Democratic Socialist Republic of Sri Lanka 1978 (as amended until 29 October 2020), arts 118 and 126(1) (Constitution). This chapter derives material from the law reports (until 2022), judgments available on the Supreme Court's website and on the internet, and unreported cases printed in the Bar Association of Sri Lanka Journal (until 2012).

[2] International Covenant on Civil and Political Rights (adopted 16 December 1966, entered into force 23 March 1976) 999 UNTS 171 (ICCPR).

[3] See Section C(1).

[4] ILA Study Group on Principles on the Engagement of Domestic Courts with International Law, 'Final Report: Mapping the Engagement of Domestic Courts with International Law' (Johannesburg, 2016) (ILA Final Report) para 41. See Section C(2).

Supreme Court itself when the Bench comprises a smaller number of judges.[5] This also enables the Court's decisions that incorporate international law principles to become part and parcel of the domestic legal system, unless (and until) they are overturned by subsequent legislation.[6] These judgments also contribute to the implementation and enforcement of international law, because they compel relevant State institutions and agents of the State to behave in a manner consistent with international law.[7] The Court's engagement with international law is particularly relevant given that the Constitution and domestic statutory law deal sparingly with international law—the Constitution, for example, has only six substantive provisions relating to international law.[8] Thus, the role of the judiciary in engaging with international law has been vital for the implementation and enforcement of international law in the domestic legal order.

Section B of this chapter will provide an overview of the domestic legal system and outline the modes of reception of international law in the domestic legal order both through the Constitution and as judge-made law. Section C will map the engagement of the Supreme Court with international law, with caselaw demonstrating both alignment and avoidance strategies. The chapter will conclude (Section D) that the Court's engagement with international law has become one of the main methods of transforming treaty, customary and soft law provisions into Sri Lankan domestic law.

B. The Status of International Law in the Sri Lankan Legal System

1. Overview

Article 4 of the Constitution identifies a clear separation of powers between the executive, legislature, and the judiciary: this has repercussions on the reception of international law and norms into the domestic legal system. According to the Constitution, the executive enters into international treaties that bind Sri Lanka.[9] The Parliament 'transforms' these treaties either by enacting enabling

[5] *Walker Sons and Co (UK) Ltd v Gunatilake* [1978–1979] 1 Sri LR 231, 243 and 244.
[6] ibid.
[7] See Section B(2)(b).
[8] See Section B(2)(a).
[9] Constitution (n 1) art 33(h). See also *Nallaratnam Singarasa v Attorney General* (2006) SC SpL (LA) 182/99.

legislation[10] or, in the case of certain economic and investment-related treaties as specified under Article 157 of the Constitution, they come into force with Parliament's approval by a two third majority. The judiciary—primarily the Supreme Court—in the exercise of their judicial functions introduces international law principles, including customary and soft law principles, into the *ratio decidendi* of their decisions. These, then, become part of the domestic legal system, facilitated by the doctrine of judicial precedent.[11]

Even though there are limited provisions in the Constitution explicitly addressing the relationship between domestic and international law 'there seems to be a firm recognition by the judiciary and the political system that the (…) legal system was, and continues to be, dualist in nature'.[12] The application of dualism is supported by two factors. First, international law can only be enforced under domestic law when it has been transformed to domestic law, either by the legislature[13] or through the practice of the higher courts.[14] Second, the Constitution stipulates a hierarchy, in which domestic law is recognized as superior vis-à-vis international treaties. The executive, legislature, and the judiciary cannot act in a manner inconsistent with the Constitution and statutes, including in its engagement with international law.[15] For example, the Constitution, and judgements of the Supreme Court, state that the executive cannot enter into international treaties, and the legislature cannot enact enabling legislation for those treaties, when their provisions are contrary to domestic law.[16] It is only those treaties entered into by the executive 'as permitted by and consistent with the Constitution and written law would bind the Republic qua State'.[17] The Supreme Court also can introduce international norms through its judgements only in so far as it is consistent with the Constitution and statutes.[18] Thus, in the event of a clear conflict between

[10] Constitution (n 1) arts 75 and 154G (11).

[11] See Section B(2)(b).

[12] Deepika Udagama, 'The Politics of Domestic Implementation of International Human Rights Law: *A Case Study of Sri Lanka*' (2015) 16 Asia-Pacific Journal on Human Rights and the Law 104, 108.

[13] The Supreme Court in *Singarasa* (n 9) has also held that international treaties 'have to be implemented by statute enacted under the constitution to have internal effect'. It is likely that the Court was not referring to treaties transformed under art 157 of the Constitution, as those will have internal effect through other means.

[14] See Section B(2)(b).

[15] Constitution (n 1) arts 4, 33 (h), 121, 122, 123, and 126.

[16] The judiciary may also undertake a pre-enactment review of any legislation, including of laws drafted to implement an international treaty, to assess its conformity with the Constitution. It may also review the acts of the executive, including when it enters international treaties, to ensure its conformity with domestic law. See also *Singarasa* (n 9) and *Rajavarothiam Sampananthan v Kabir Hashim* SC (FR) Case No 351/ 2018.

[17] *Singarasa* (n 9)

[18] *Walker Sons* (n 5)

domestic and international law, and where a consistent interpretation is not possible, judges give the domestic law precedence.

Primarily, the Supreme Court introduces international law norms into the domestic legal system in the exercise of its human rights jurisdiction. Judges have mainly referred to, relied on, or contested provisions of international law under Chapters III and VI of the Constitution. Chapter III sets out fundamental rights, permissible restrictions for those rights, and remedies for violations. These rights largely follow the provisions of the International Covenant on Civil and Political Rights (ICCPR).[19] Chapter VI on the Directive Principles of State Policy (DPSP) sets out the broad policy objectives of the government of Sri Lanka, including its policy position on international law.[20] These policies reflect rights found in the International Covenant for Economic, Social and Cultural Rights (ICESCR).[21] According to the Constitution, the DPSP are non-justiciable.[22] Yet, the Court has held that it can legitimately take the directive principles into consideration.[23] It has held that the DPSP 'are in the nature of an instrument of instructions which both the legislature and the executive must respect and follow... the courts must take due recognition of them and make proper allowance for their operation and function'.[24] The Court gives meaning to the DPSP using its fundamental rights jurisdiction.[25]

The Supreme Court has absolute discretion to independently determine the extent of its engagement with different sources of international law. Neither the Constitution nor domestic statutes provide a clarification as to the hierarchy of the various sources within the domestic system. An examination of the caselaw demonstrates the Court's inclination to engage with treaty-based norms more frequently as compared to other sources. If an international obligation is both treaty and customary law based, the Court almost always refers exclusively to the treaty and to other instruments codifying customary law.[26] The Court has also considered treaties that are not binding on Sri Lanka, for example the European or American Convention on Human Rights.[27]

[19] (adopted 16 December 1966, entered into force 23 March 1976) 999 UNTS 171.
[20] See Section B(2)(a).
[21] (adopted 16 December 1966, entered into force 3 January 1976) 993 UNTS 3 (ICESCR).
[22] Constitution (n 1) art 29.
[23] *Seneviratne v University Grants Commission* [1978-79-80] 1 Sri LR 170.
[24] ibid.
[25] Mario Gomez et al, 'Constitutionalizing Economic and Social Rights in Sri Lanka' (2016) CPA Working Papers on Constitutional Reform No 7, available at <https://www.cpalanka.org/wp-content/uploads/2016/09/Working-Paper-7.pdf> last accessed 24 July 2023. See Section C(1)(a).
[26] Eg, see *Weerawansa v Attorney General* [2000] 1 Sri LR 387; *WMK de Silva v Chairman, Ceylon Fertilizer Corporation* [1989] 2 Sri LR 393. See also Udagama (n 12) 113.
[27] Eg, see *Mallawarachchi v Seneviratne, Officer in Charge, Police Station Kollupitiya* [1992] 1 Sri LR 181; de Silva (n 26).

A shortcoming of the Court's consideration of international law is that it does not generally seek to identify customary law through an examination of State practice or general principles of law.[28] When the Court refers to customary law, it almost exclusively refers to codified law. It has, thus, referred, amongst others, to the Universal Declaration of Human Rights (UDHR),[29] the United Nations (UN) Standard Minimum Rules on the Treatment of Prisoners (the Nelson Mandela Rules),[30] and UN General Assembly Resolutions.[31] It rarely uses the terminology 'customary international law' or 'general principles of international law'.[32] Instead, it describes such norms as those that are 'consistent with the accepted standards in other national and regional jurisdictions',[33] or as 'universally recognized set of norms and principles',[34] or states that the 'law of nations is progressing towards a general recognition as a basic right',[35] often without examining the conduct of multiple relevant States. Additionally, the Court rarely moves beyond a finding of the international law nature of a right to identify the scope and breadth of such right under customary law, general principles of law, or soft law.[36] Gomez and others criticize the Court for not undertaking such a similar substantive assessment even for its consideration of pure domestic law rights.[37]

Finally, the Supreme Court rarely engages extensively with the jurisprudence of international or regional courts or tribunals.[38] Instead, it refers to domestic

[28] See Section C(1)(d).

[29] Eg, see *Re FJC de Mel and Thelma de Mel* [1975] 78 NLR 65, where the Court held that the *ex post facto* criminal legislation was contrary to the Universal Declaration of Human Rights, UNGA Res 217(A) (10 December 1948) UN Doc A/RES/217(III)(A) (UDHR) art 11(2); *Kaviratne v Commissioner General of Examinations* [2012] SC 29 (*Z-Score*), where reference was made to the UDHR in respect of the right to higher education; *Wijekoon Herath Mudiyanselage Nimal Bandara v National Gem and Jewellery Authority* SC (FR) Case No 118/2013 referred to art 23 (1) of the UDHR, together with art 14(1)(g) of the Constitution to support the right to engage in a lawful trade.

[30] In *Lama Hewage Lal (Deceased) v Officer-in-Charge Minor Offences, Seeduwa Police Station* [2005] 1 Sri LR 40, the Court held that prison officers are expected to treat prisoners with kindness and humanity on the basis of the UN Standard Minimum Rules for the Treatment of Prisoners (the Nelson Mandela Rules), UNGA Res 70/175 (17 December 2015) Annex.

[31] Eg, see *de Silva* (n 26); *Lama Hewage Lal* (n 30).

[32] In the research for this chapter, two specific references to 'general principles of international law' were found: (1) in relation to retroactive legislation—see below n 42 and (2) as relating to the doctrine of respect for 'acquired rights', see *Hunter and Company Ltd v The Minister of Labor and Vocational Training* [1997] 1 Sri LR 337; *Wijebahu v Sumanasekara* [1998] 3 Sri LR 355.

[33] In *Rubberite Company Ltd v Labour Officer, Negambo* [1990] 2 Sri LR 42 the Supreme Court upheld the right of workmen to strike relying on the ICESCR.

[34] *Ramuppillai v Festus Perera, Minister of Public Administration, Provincial Councils and Home Affairs* [1991] 1 Sri LR 11.

[35] *Sirisena v Earnest Perera* [1991] 2 Sri LR 97.

[36] As an exception, see *Hunter and Company Ltd* (n 32); de Silva (n 26) and the *Bulankulama* case in Section 2(b).

[37] Gomez et al (n 25) 21.

[38] As an exception, see *Velmurugu v Attorney General* [1981] 1 Sri LR 406. See also *Hikkadu Koralalage Don Chandrasoma v Mawai S Senathirajah* SC SPL No 03/2014 where the Court referred to the jurisprudence of the International Court of Justice, in the context of self-determination and secession; and

caselaw from selected jurisdictions, including their interpretations of international law, to interpret domestic statutes, and aid its decisions.[39] It also refers to the views of UN treaty bodies, including the Human Rights Committee[40] or the Committee on the Rights of the Child[41] to support its conclusions.

2. Reception of International Law in the Domestic Legal Order

a. International law in the Constitution

There are only six substantive articles that refer to international law in the Constitution of Sri Lanka. The first is Article 13(6) that sets out the fundamental right of a person not to be subjected to *ex post facto* criminal legislation. The proviso of Article 13(6), following Article 15(2) of the ICCPR, states that '[n]othing in this Article shall prejudice the trial and punishment of any person for any act or omission which, at the time when it was committed, was criminal according to the general principles of law recognized by the community of nations.' There is some debate whether this provision relates to customary law or general principles of international law, although it is more likely that is reflects the latter.[42]

The second reference is found in Article 33(h), which holds that the President has to 'do all such acts and things, not being inconsistent with the provisions of the Constitution or written law, as by international law, custom or usage he is required or authorized to do'. Article 33(h) is the closest provision that can be found in statutory law referring to the reception of international customary law into the domestic system.

The third, Article 27(15), contained in Chapter VI of the Constitution on the DPSP, states that, '[t]he State... shall endeavour to foster respect for international law and treaty obligations in dealings among nations'. A plain reading

WMN Kumarihami v Galagamage Indrawansa Kumarasiri SC TAB Appeal No 02/201, where the Court referred to judgements of the International Criminal Tribunal for Former Yugoslavia.

[39] Eg, Wijebahu (n 32) refers to Australian jurisprudence; Ratnasingham v Tikiribanda Dassanaike [1998] 1 Sri LR 8 relied on findings in the English and French jurisprudence relating to international law.

[40] See, eg, Lama Hewage Lal (n 30); *Ambasevana v Ajith, Police Constable, Police Station, Dummalasuriya* SC (FR) Case No 555/2009.

[41] See, *Hewa Maddumage Karunapala v Jayantha Prema Kumara Siriwardhana* SC (FR) Case No 97/2017.

[42] David Averbuck, *Sepala Ekanayake and Ex Post Facto Legislation: Sri Lankan Domestic Law Incorporates International Law* (Marga Institute 1988) 22–30. On the conflation of customary international law with general principles when discussing retroactive legislation see Valentina Spiga, 'Non-Retroactivity of Criminal Law: A New Chapter in the Hissène Habré Saga' (2011) 9 JICJ 5.

of Article 27(15) indicates that the State's duty in respect of international law under this provision is merely to 'endeavour' to respect it in its international relations. Article 29 of the Constitution further weakens the obligatory nature of the provision by making Article 27(15), as discussed above, non-justiciable. Yet, the Supreme Court has determined that

> Article 27(15) … implies that the State must likewise respect international law and treaty obligations in its dealings with its own citizens, particularly when their liberty is involved. The State must afford to them the benefit of the safeguards which international law recognizes.[43]

Supreme Court judges have used this provision as the constitutional gateway to engage with international law principles, including to introduce rights which were not explicitly provided for in domestic legislation.[44]

The other three provisions are Articles 154(G) and 157, which refers to the Parliament's prerogative to give internal effect to international treaties (see section B(1)). In the Schedule to the Constitution 'international crimes' are included in a list of offences to be investigated by the national police.

b. The doctrine of judicial precedent and its impact on the incorporation of international law

The Supreme Court plays a significant role in the reception of international law in the domestic legal order because of the doctrine of judicial precedent. The principle of *stare decisis* or judicial precedent ensures that the *reasoning* of a Supreme Court decision is binding on lower courts, a bench of the Supreme Court consisting of a smaller number of judges, and on government authorities.[45] The Court has clarified this concept as follows:

> The moment we concede the binding force of precedent we are conceding that the *ratio decidendi* of a case has the force of law. This cannot be so in respect of the decisions of every Court but only in respect of the decisions of the highest Court (…) Once the highest Court of the land has interpreted the law it becomes part and parcel of the law in force.[46]

[43] *Weerawansa* (n 26).
[44] Section C(1)(a).
[45] *Walker Sons* (n 5).
[46] ibid.

In the seminal *Bulankulama* case the Court adopted soft law environmental principles into its reasoning and explicitly stated that through its consideration these principles were now part and parcel of the domestic legal system through the doctrine of judicial precedent.[47] In that case, the Government sought to enter into a mineral investment agreement with a multinational company in respect of a deposit of phosphate rock. The Court, discussing the Rio Declaration on Environment and Development[48] and the Stockholm Declaration on the Human Environment[49], held that

> [a]dmittedly, the principles set out in the Stockholm and Rio De Janeiro Declarations are not legally binding in the way in which an Act of our Parliament would be. It may be regarded merely as "soft law". Nevertheless, as a Member of the United Nations they could hardly be ignored by Sri Lanka. Moreover, they would, in my view, be binding if they have been either expressly enacted or become a part of the domestic law by adoption by the superior Courts of record and by the Supreme Court in particular, in their decisions.[50]

In light of this, the Court ordered the Central Environment Authority to give effect to the environment principles contained in the Rio and Stockholm Declarations when giving approval for projects.[51]

The *Bulankulama* case is also an example of a situation where the Court sought to remedy a lacuna in domestic law through engagement with international law. The principles laid down in the Rio and Stockholm Declarations were far more progressive than those found in domestic law, including on precautionary measures and on the 'polluter pays' principle. One can reasonably argue that through this decision and order, these progressive principles will gradually find their way into domestic law through continuous and consistent interpretation, and government institutions are bound to adopt these principles in future assessments of development projects to avoid litigation. Once a judgment is adopted by the Supreme Court, its reasoning is subject to change only through a subsequent legislative enactment and it is binding on all lower

[47] *Bulankulama v Secretary, Ministry of Industrial Development* [2000] 3 Sri LR 243.

[48] UNGA, 'Report of the UN Conference on Environment and Development: Rio Declaration on Environment and Development' Annex I (12 August 1992) UN Doc A/Conf.151/26 (Vol I).

[49] UNGA, 'Report of the UN Conference on the Human Environment: Declaration of the UN Conference on the Human Environment' UN Doc A/Conf.48/14/Rev.1 (Stockholm, 5–16 June 1972).

[50] *Bulankulama* (n 47).

[51] ibid.

courts as well as a bench of the Supreme Court with a lower composition of judges.

This case can be viewed either as an attempt by the judiciary to maintain the dynamic nature of the legal system or as an endeavour to usurp the power of the legislature by introducing binding legal principles through caselaw,[52] and demonstrates that 'transforming international law into domestic law is not the exclusive preserve of the legislature'[53]. The fact that the legislature has the power to reverse the judicial precedent by passing legislation, yet it did not seek to do so in this case, appears indicative of legislative acquiescence to this decision and its consequences. While this can be understood as hyper-alignment in the terms of the ILA Final Report,[54] it can also be viewed as an instance of progressive development of domestic law and as a domestic court's contribution towards the progressive codification of specific soft law principles into customary international law, given that the Supreme Court, as the highest court of the land, reflects *opinio juris* and State practice.[55] In subsequent cases, the Court revisited its decision in the *Bulankulama* case,[56] and justified the Court's continued reliance on these soft law principles because 'they constitute an important part of the environmental protection regime... the importance and relevance of which must be recognized when reviewing executive action vis-a-vis the environment'.[57]

It is important to note that the Supreme Court faces certain limitations in incorporating norms of international law in its caselaw: First, the Court can only interpret, expand or limit international rights of individuals and obligations of the State in relation to a particular dispute before it. Secondly, a litigant cannot bring a case before the Supreme Court solely based on a violation of international law. To ensure justiciability of their claims, they must frame the case in terms of a violation of their rights derived from domestic law, for example, fundamental rights. Thirdly, it cannot incorporate international law norms that conflict with the Constitution. Yet, despite these limitations, the Supreme Court has engaged positively with international law as discussed below.

[52] See on this more generally Muthucumaraswamy Sornarajah, 'The Reception of International Law in the Domestic Law of Sri Lanka in the Context of the Global Experience' (2016–2017) 25 Sri Lanka Journal of International Law 3, 25–27.

[53] Udagama (n 12) 135.

[54] ILA Final Report (n 4) para 55.

[55] Section C(1)(b).

[56] *Watte Gedera Wijebanda v Conserver General of Forests* [2009] 1 Sri RL 337.

[57] ibid. See also *Ravindra Gunawardena Kariyawasam v Central Environment Authority* SC (FR) Application No 141/2015 where the Court said it continued to be 'guided by the Principles of the Rio Declaration'.

C. Engagement with International Law

1. Strategies of Alignment

The Supreme Court's approach to international law, generally, reflects a preference for harmonization, and results in alignment between domestic and international law norms. This section identifies three stated, and sometimes overlapping, purposes for which the Court engages with international law in its fundamental rights jurisdiction.

a. To ensure domestic law's consistency with the state's international law obligations

The Supreme Court follows the presumption that the Parliament did not intend to legislate in a manner inconsistent with its international obligations.[58] For example, in *Weerawansa v Attorney General*, it held that

> it would be wrong to attribute to Parliament an intention to disregard those (ICCPR) safeguards. The PTA (Prevention of Terrorism Act) cannot be interpreted as dispensing, by implication or inference, with the safeguard of prompt production before a judicial officer under … Article 13(2) (of the Constitution).[59]

Arguably this presumption stems from Article 27(15) of the Constitution, which calls for the State to endeavour to respect its international obligations.[60] In respect of fundamental rights, the Court has held that Article 27(15) obliges the State to 'afford to them [ie individuals] the benefit of the safeguards which international law recognises',[61] thus requiring a consistent interpretation of statutes with international law.

Article 27(15) was also relied by the Supreme Court in *Rathnayake Tharanga Lakmali v Niroshan Abeykoon*, to find that the police violated the right to life after a suspect died in custody. It held that even though the right to life is not expressly recognized as a fundamental right in domestic law,

[58] In *Re FJC de Mel* (n 29) the Court held that 'one may presume, in the absence of anything suggestive of the contrary, that our legislature ordinarily desires to act in accordance with, rather than contrary to, the Declaration (UDHR)'. See also *Wijebahu* (n 32).

[59] *Weerawansa* (n 26).

[60] ibid; *Seneviratne* (n 22).

[61] *Weerawansa* (n 26).

> the conclusion that the right to life is implicitly recognized in Chapter III of the Constitution is reinforced by International Conventions ratified by Sri Lanka. Article 27(2) (15) of the Directive Principles of State Policy mandates the State to *foster respect for international law and treaty obligations in dealings amongst nations*. Interpretation of fundamental rights enshrined in our constitution in light of Sri Lanka's treaty obligations would thus be in furtherance of the aforementioned objective.[62]

Thus, the Court concluded that Chapter III of the Constitution, particularly Articles 11 and 13(4), affirms the right to life, when read considering Article 3 of the UDHR, Article 6 of the ICCPR, Article 11 of the International Convention on the Protection of All Migrant Workers and Members of their Families,[63] Article 10 on the Convention on the Rights of Persons with Disabilities,[64] and the Convention on the Rights of the Child (CRC).[65]

To ensure that domestic law is consistent with international law, the Court has adopted the following guidelines. Firstly, the Court has held that there is no justification to depart from the plain meaning of a statute when the plain meaning is consistent with international law.[66] Secondly, the Court has held that when a domestic law is ambiguous, it must, unless there are other indications to the contrary, favour a construction that is consistent with the State's international obligations.[67] This is particularly relevant when there is clear evidence that an enactment is the offspring of an international convention.[68]

For example, in the 2003 *Sriyani Iddamalgoda* case, the Supreme Court held that Sri Lanka's ratification of the Convention Against Torture and other Cruel, Inhuman, or Degrading Treatment or Punishment (UNCAT) meant that the next of kin of an individual who died as a result of torture could benefit from compensation.[69] The Constitution, on the other hand, only provided for compensation for victims.[70] The Court reiterated that the interpretation which brings domestic law in conformity with the State's international obligations must be preferred, effectively adopting a strategy of overriding alignment.[71] In

[62] SC (FR) Application No 577/2010
[63] (adopted 18 December 1990, entered into force 1 July 2003) 2220 UNTS 3.
[64] (adopted 13 December 2006, entered into force 3 May 2008) 2515 UNTS 3.
[65] (adopted 20 November 1989, entered into force 2 September 1990) 1577 UNTS 3.
[66] *Ratnasingham* (n 39).
[67] *Sepala Ekanayake v Attorney General* [1987] 1 Sri LR 107; *Mediwake v Dayananda Dissanayake, Commissioner of Elections* [2001] 1 Sri LR 177; *Weerawansa* (n 26).
[68] See Sepala Ekanayake (n 67); and Romesh Cooray v Jayalath, Sub Inspector General of Police [2008] 2 Sri LR 43.
[69] *Sriyani Silva v Iddamalgoda, OIC, Police Station, Paiyagala* [2003] 2 Sri LR 63.
[70] ibid.
[71] See ILA Final Report (n 4) para 46.

determining so, the Court overturned a previous judgment according to which the next of kin was not entitled to compensation under the Constitution, on the basis that the Constitution, enacted in 1978, could not possibly have foreseen Sri Lanka's subsequent obligations under the UNCAT.[72]

In ensuring consistency, the Court has also sought to prevent the State from limiting individual rights derived from international law. In *PS Manohari Pelaketiya v HM Gunasekera, Secretary, Ministry of Education*[73] a female worker was sexually harassed in her working place at a State institution. The employer argued that there was no violation of her fundamental rights as she had contravened the Establishment Code—internal regulations governing her service—by subsequently giving an interview to the media. The Court held that under Article 12(2) no citizen shall be discriminated on the grounds of sex and that, in this case, sexual harassment complained of had violated the fundamental rights of the female worker. The Court added that Sri Lanka has undertaken international obligations to eliminate all forms of discrimination against women by acceding to the Convention on the Elimination of All Forms of Discrimination Against Women.[74] It concluded that this 'regime of affirmative rights . . . cannot be restricted or limited by the provisions of Establishment Code'[75] likely alluding to the fact that in this case both domestic and international law operated as affirmative rights to ensure that the worker could benefit from her fundamental rights, despite contravening internal regulations.

b. To understand the scope of domestic rights and support their expansion

In a second set of cases, the Court has engaged with international law to determine the nature, scope, and extent of fundamental rights in Chapter III of the Constitution. For example, in *WMK De Silva v Ceylon Fertilizer Corporation*,[76] the Supreme Court was, for the first time, confronted with a claim of torture that did not involve physical violence, but mental harm. Justice Amerasinghe held that 'this is a novel claim of relief, and it may raise a presumption against its validity. . . yet this court undoubtedly as power to recognize a novel claim if justice so requires . . . to advance fundamental rights as we are required to do so by Article 4(d) of the Constitution'.[77] He concluded that Article 11 of

[72] *Sriyani Silva* (n 69).

[73] SC (FR) Case No 76/2012 (*Pelaketiya*).

[74] (adopted 18 December 1979, entered into force 3 September 1981) 1249 UNTS 1.

[75] *Pelaketiya* (n 73) 16.

[76] SC (FR) Application No 7/88.

[77] Article 4(d) of the Constitution provides 'the fundamental rights which are by the Constitution declared and recognized shall be respected, secured and advanced by all the organs of government and shall not be abridged, restricted or denied, save in the manner and to the extent hereinafter provided.'

the Constitution includes both physical violence and mental aggression and held that 'the fact that mental aggression should be looked upon in the same manner as we contemplate physical attack is supported by' the Declaration on the Protection of All Persons from Being Subjected to Torture and Other Cruel, Inhuman or Degrading Treatment or Punishment.[78] Following this landmark judgment, it is widely recognized that under Article 11 and domestic law, torture includes both mental and physical aggression.[79]

In the *Lama Hewage Lal* case, the Court referring to the views of the Human Rights Committee (HRC), which had held that denial of medical treatment constituted degrading treatment contrary to Articles 7 and 10 of the ICCPR, found a violation of Article 11 of the Constitution that prohibited torture and degrading treatment.[80] In that same case, it also referred to the Nelson Mandela Rules to determine the scope of humane treatment. In these cases, international law 'provide[d] a set of definitions which help the domestic court to *understand* domestic legislation rather than *override* it', as discussed in the ILA Final Report.[81]

Judges have also justified the expansion of domestic rights based on international law. For example, in the *Mediwaka* case,[82] the Court was confronted with the question whether the right to freedom of expression under Article 14(2) of the Constitution, was sufficient to find a violation of an individual's right to vote when they had voted, but others were prevented from voting. The Court found that the more expansive Article 25 of the ICCPR that guarantees for 'every citizen (...) the right to "take part" in public affairs, through representatives *freely chosen* by him, at *a genuine* election, by universal and equal suffrage, held by *secret ballot*, ensuring the *free expression* of the will of the electorate', were essential components of Article 14(2).[83] The Court has also relied on Article 25 of the ICCPR to expand the right to vote to include the right to be represented by qualified persons who have been elected by the people.[84] In another case, where the Court ordered reimbursement for expenses accrued at a private hospital following a finding of torture, it simply referred to Article

[78] UNGA Res 3452 (XXX) (9 December 1975) annex.

[79] See also Weerawansa (n 26); *Palle Kankanamge Sunil Shantha v Sub-Inspector Seneviratne*, SC (FR) Application No 479/2009, 20.

[80] Lama Hewage Lal (n 30).

[81] ILA Final Report (n 4) para 26 (emphasis in original).

[82] *Mediwake* (n 67).

[83] ibid (emphasis in original).

[84] *Centre for Policy Alternatives v Dayanada Dissanyake, Commissioner of Elections* [2003] 1 Sri LR 273. The petitioner alleged that a person who was not in the electoral nomination paper was appointed to an elected post.

12 of the ICESCR[85] to find the right to health included the right to choose a medical care provider.[86]

In two cases related to the rights of the child, the Supreme Court has depended rather extensively on international law to clarify the scope of domestic law and to expand the rights of children under domestic law. In in *Landage Ishara Anjani (Minor) v Waruni Bohahawatte*,[87] the Court used the CRC and the UN Rules for the Protection of Juveniles Deprived of their liberty[88] to flesh out the State's obligations relating to children who have been deprived of liberty and held that 'officials... should not flout these (international law) safeguards as they please'.[89] The Court has also held while Article 13(2) of the Constitution does not draw a distinction between the types of persons held in custody, even a child whose liberty is deprived is allowed to claim rights contained in Article 13(2) because of Articles 37(d) of the UNCRC and 9(4) of the ICCPR. It has also depended on the UNCAT, ICCPR, and UNCRC to uphold a child's right to freedom from torture and to be treated with dignity in a manner which considers the needs of child's age. In *Hewa Maddumage Karunapala v Jayantha Prema Kumara Siriwardhana*[90] the Court, discussed extensively the CRC and the findings of the Committee on the Rights of the Child to find incompatibility of corporal punishment with domestic statutes.

c. To fill a lacuna in domestic law

Finally, the Court relies on international law to identify and introduce State obligations within the realm of its fundamental rights jurisdiction where none had previously existed. In some cases the Court justified this reliance on international law as giving effect to Sri Lanka's international obligations as envisaged by the Constitution, in particular Article 27(15) of the Constitution,[91] and in others because the Court is bound by Article 4(d) of the Constitution to advance and to give full effect to fundamental rights.[92] The cases where the Court filled a lacunae includes the *Bulankulama* case, where it relied on soft law to introduce environmental obligations;[93] the *De Silva* case, where it introduced

[85] ICESCR (n 18) art 12 'recognizes the right of everyone to the enjoyment of the highest attainable standard of physical and mental health'.

[86] *Sanjeewa, Attorney-at-Law (on behalf of Gerald Mervin Perera) v Suraweera, OIC, Police Station, Wattala* [2003] 1 Sri LR 317.

[87] SC (FR) Application No 677/2012.

[88] United Nations Rules for the Protection of Juveniles Deprived of Their Liberty, UNGA Res 45/113 (2 April 1991) UN Doc A/RES/45/113.

[89] ibid 13.

[90] SC (FR) Case No 97/2017.

[91] Section C(1)(a).

[92] *Sunil Shantha* (n 79).

[93] See n 47 above.

mental aggression as an element of torture[94] and the *Absan Banda* case, where the Court relied on Articles 10 to 13 of the UNCAT to outline educational and procedural measures relevant to ensuring 'a meaningful course of action to minimize violations of Article 11 (...) of the Constitution' on freedom of torture.[95]

The Court has also relied on customary law, in the absence of treaty law, to fill domestic law deficits. For example, as noted above, in 1988, it relied on the UN Declaration on the Protection of All Persons from Being Subjected to Torture and Other Cruel, Inhuman or Degrading Treatment or Punishment to introduce a definition of 'torture' in the absence of such under domestic law.[96]

d. Other considerations

There have been situations where, in an attempt to harmonize or align domestic law with international law, the Court has incorporated international law in its analysis with inadequate reasoning. For example, in 1982, the Supreme Court upheld the constitutionality of *ex post facto* legislation—the Offences against Aircraft Act (No 24) of 1982,[97] which had transformed into domestic law international conventions relating to offences against aircraft—relying on Article 13(6) of the Constitution. The Court, without any stated reasoning, held that the offenses referred to in the Act were all criminal according to the general principles of law recognized by the community of nations.[98] This unreasoned determination was particularly problematic given that, at the time, there was confusion as to whether the crime of hijacking had the necessary level of acceptance to make it an offence according to the general principles of law.[99]

[94] See n 75 above.

[95] *Abasin Banda v SI Gunaratne* [1995] 1 Sri LR 244.

[96] *de Silva* (n 26).

[97] In the Supreme Court Determination on the Constitutionality of 'The Offences against Aircraft Bill', SD No 2 (1982).

[98] ibid. In this case, Sepala Ekanayake, a Sri Lankan, hijacked an aircraft from an Italian carrier. At the time of hijacking, Sri Lanka was party to three international conventions on anti-hijacking, but these had not been transformed into domestic law.

[99] Averbuck cites a parliamentary debate where one parliamentarian doubted if the crime had attained the necessary level of acceptance. He states that 115 countries had become signatories to the three Anti-Hijacking Conventions and only half of those had enacted domestic legislation prior to July 1982. Averbuck (n 39) 27–28. This is compounded by a subsequent Court of Appeal statement that '[t]hough this (hijacking) is not an international crime as in the case of genocide, there was an obligation on the part of Sri Lanka as a contracting party (to the Hague Convention on Hijacking) to make such an act a crime according to our law and hence the Offences Against the Aircraft Act has been enacted' (emphasis added). It is not clear whether the Court meant that hijacking was not an international crime or that it was not a crime as serious as genocide. It is assumed that the Court meant the latter; because, if not, the phrase in italics would not, in itself, give the State the basis to enact retroactive legislation.

There have been other situations where the Court sought to expand domestic rights in face of what it viewed as more limiting international legislation, displaying a posture of hyper-alignment.[100] For example, in *Sarjun v Kamaldeen*, it held that the definition of torture under Article 11 of the Constitution is not limited by the three purposes set out in the UNCAT, and that infliction of severe bodily harm because of a refusal to pay a bribe constituted torture.[101] This decision was contrary to previous purpose-based constructions of the definition of torture adopted by the Court.[102]

In this same context, it is relevant to note that in the *Sunil Shantha* case,[103] the Court held that 'Article 11 specifies no limitation with regard to "a narrow definition of 'torture' on a '*purpose related basis*' should not be applied to restrict the sweep of the absolute prohibition declared by Article 11. In my view, that narrow definition is relevant only to define criminal liability as set out in Section 12 of the Act, which is based on the aforesaid (UNCAT) Convention'.[104] This then creates a duality as to the extent that a claimant can the benefit from a wider range of acts constituting torture, and a perpetrator will only be penalized on a narrow set of purpose-based acts. This finding of the Court that the Act should be 'purposed based' like the UNCAT is consistent with its previous jurisprudence where the Court will attempt to strictly align domestic and international norms in interpreting enabling legislation.[105]

There have also been instances where the Court has cautioned against complete harmonization. In *Sunila Abeysekera v Ariya Rubasinghe*, the Court highlighted the need to preserve domestic values while aiming to achieve universality of human rights.[106]

2. Strategies of Avoidance

Generally, it is difficult to identify the use of evasive avoidance strategies by the Court, when '[t]he court simply remains silent where the application of international law is plainly called for'.[107] The Court's use of affirmative avoidance,

[100] ILA Final Report (n 4) para 55. This can also be understood as a case of affirmative contestation. See ILA Final Report (n 4) para 58.
[101] *MAM Sarjun v Kamaldeen (Reserve PC) 39753* SC (FR) Case No 559/2003.
[102] *Cooray* (n 60); *de Silva* (n 26).
[103] *Sunil Shantha* (n 79).
[104] (Emphasis in original.)
[105] See Section C(1)(b).
[106] *Sunila Abeysekera v Ariya Rubasinghe* [2000] 1 Sri LR 314.
[107] ILA Final Report (n 4) para 40.

where the Court 'explicitly rejects' the application of international law,[108] was rarer in the cases examined, than those of alignment, but was exemplified in the *Singarasa* case.[109] In that case, the Supreme Court 'took an extremely restrictive approach in giving effect to Sri Lanka's treaty obligations'.[110]

In 2006, Singarasa sought to enforce the views of the Human Rights Committee in a case relating to a conviction under the Prevention of Terrorism Act (No 48) of 1979. The Supreme Court found (1) that the implementation of the alternative remedies suggested by the Human Rights Committee, which included release or retrial and compensation, was procedurally incompatible with fundamental principles of domestic law;[111] (2) that it could not set aside or vary its order based on the findings of the Human Rights Committee, as the latter was not vested with judicial power under the Constitution; (3) that there was no basis for an argument of legitimate expectations to have the findings of the Human Rights Committee enforced in Sri Lanka; and (4) that the accession to the Optional Protocol to the ICCPR was a violation of Article 33(f) of the Constitution, and the President acted *ultra vires* when acceding to the Protocol,[112] the latter having no legal effect within Sri Lanka. Consequently, according to the Court, it would be unconstitutional to give effect to the views of the Human Rights Committee in Sri Lanka.

In the *Singarasa* case, the Court rejected the 'judicial' nature of the Human Rights Committee's statements, despite the fact that its views were recommendations. This questionable rationale[113] then formed the basis of its ensuing decision, including that the Optional Protocol had no legal effect in Sri Lanka, and that the latter was not bound by it.[114] Subsequently, this decision created tensions within the State regarding its international obligations vis-à-vis the Protocol, as the executive refused to withdraw from the treaty and,

[108] ibid para 56.

[109] *Sinharasa* (n 9).

[110] Amrith Rohan Perera, 'Sri Lanka' in Simon Chesterman et al (eds), *The Oxford Handbook of International Law in Asia and the Pacific* (OUP 2019) 670.

[111] The Court held that release and compensation was possible under Sri Lankan law only if there was a baseless bad faith prosecution, and retrial could be ordered when there is sufficient evidence that the conviction was flawed by a serious procedural illegality.

[112] The Court held that the President by acceding to the Optional Protocol and through the Declaration of Accession conferred public law rights in what was a 'purported exercise of legislative power which comes within the realm of Parliament and the people at a referendum'. According to the Court, a recognition of the power of the HRC to receive and consider a communication of alleged violation of rights under the ICCPR was a purported conferment of judicial power on the HRC 'to vindicate a Public Law right of an individual within the Republic in respect of acts that take place within the Republic'.

[113] See also Sornarajah (n 48) 30–31.

[114] See also the discussion in Udagama (n 12) 116–17.

simultaneously, the government refused to engage with the Human Rights Committee on individual complaints or to take cognisance of the Committee's views domestically as a direct result of this judgment. In September 2016, the Sri Lankan Bar Association expressed its intention to request the Supreme Court to revise its judgment,[115] yet as of date this judgment has not been overturned.[116] However, in a subsequent judgement Court subsequently referred to Human Rights Committee Communications as 'international case law' when the Court, using findings in these communications, concluded that the evidence to adduce an act of torture fell below the standard expected by the Court in the specific case before the Supreme Court.[117]

Another aspect of the *Singarasa* judgment that may also represent affirmative avoidance was when the Court held that the ICCPR rights had not been given effect in domestic law.[118] This view cannot be supported because fundamental rights under the Constitution closely emulate ICCPR rights, and previous, and subsequent, Supreme Court decisions had taken cognizance of ICCPR rights.[119] In any case, subsequently, the Parliament enacted the International Covenant on Civil and Political Rights Act (No 56) of 2007 (ICCPR Act 2007), which contained some ICCPR rights that were not previously explicitly mentioned in the Constitution and statutes.[120] The Court, in a subsequent determination, also held that statutes and decisions of the courts of Sri Lanka gave adequate recognition to ICCPR rights, and that individuals in Sri Lanka derived the benefit and guarantee of these rights.[121]

[115] 'BASL seeks revision of "Singarasa case" Judgment' *The Sunday Times* (11 September 2016), <http://www.sundaytimes.lk/160911/news/basl-to-seek-revision-of-singarasa-case-judgment-208421.html> last accessed 24 July 2023.

[116] In 2018, this was again considered in *Rajavarothiam Sampananthan* (n 17) in the context of the executive's powers.

[117] See *Ambasevana v Ajith, Police Constable, Police Station, Dummalasuriya* SC (FR) Case No 555/2009, decided in 2014. See also *Ediriweera Arukpatabandige Sugath Rohan Jayasuriya v Police Constable, Manikkaratnam* SC (FR) Case No 43/2008, decided in 2013.

[118] The Court argued that remedies are available only where there are rights. The Optional Protocol was acceded purporting to give a remedy in respect of the violation of ICCPR rights, but the Court held in a very controversial statement that the legislature had not taken measures to give domestic effect to ICCPR rights. Therefore, no remedy was conceivable in the domestic forum without a corresponding domestic law based right.

[119] See also Udagama (n 12) 117; Sornarajah (n 48) 31–32.

[120] Udagama (n 12) 123–25, including a discussion of some considerations that led to the adoption of the ICCPR Act 2007.

[121] Supreme Court Determination on the International Civil and Political Rights Covenant Act, In the matter of a Reference under Article 129(1) of the Constitution, SC Ref No 01/2008.

D. Conclusion

This chapter examined the engagement of Sri Lanka's Supreme Court with international law through the exercise of its fundamental rights jurisdiction. In doing so, it analysed the Constitution and Supreme Court jurisprudence to demonstrate that the Court's engagement with international law has become one of the main methods of incorporating treaty, customary, and soft law provisions into domestic law. The chapter identified that, while the Court endeavours to align domestic with international norms, in certain instances it had also sought to avoid the application of international law in the domestic system.

Generally, the Court's engagement with international law is limited. On one hand, the number of judgments with references to international law, when compared to the Court's overall number of judgments, is dismal, even within the realm of fundamental rights jurisprudence. Even in those instances when the Court engages with international law, its engagement has mostly been limited to mere comparisons between international law treaty provisions and fundamental rights provisions. It rarely seeks to elicit different components of a right, or examine whether a particular norm has attained customary law status by reference to State practice and opinion juris. These quantitative and qualitative references to international law are determined by a set of variables that include judicial comprehension of international law, 'judicial personalities; judicial independence; receptivity to international law in the interpretation of domestic law; judicial perceptions of the "significance" of the issue; judicial comprehension of the scope of a given fundamental right; and civil society activism' amongst others.[122]

Yet, one cannot quantify the reception of international law based on the number of references in caselaw. In most situations, once the Court expands or clarifies a fundamental right referring to a corresponding international norm, judges would not find it necessary to invoke international law in subsequent decisions. Rather, once a right is expanded or clarified based on international law, it becomes part and parcel of domestic law because of the doctrine of judicial precedent. Thus, subsequent judgments may only refer to the domestic law or previous judgements. Therefore, while a strategy of alignment is adopted explicitly in the first judgment, subsequently, in practice, this alignment continues without explicit reference to international law in the many judgments that follow.

[122] Gomez et al (n 22) 18–19; see also ILA Final Report (n 4) paras 77–78 discussing some of these variables.

In conclusion, that should the judiciary endeavour to engage more substantively with international law in its fundamental rights jurisprudence, as envisaged by Article 4(d) of the Constitution, the Court would likely be able to further advance and to give full effect to fundamental rights. At the same time, in its engagement with international law, judges of the Supreme Court have moved beyond the limited wording of the Constitution and statutes, to ensure that international law norms become part and parcel of domestic law.

Acknowledgement

The author acknowledges the assistance provided by Justice Priyasath Dep, Shavindra Fernando, and research assistance provided by Rakitha Rajapakshe, Ruwanthi Amerasinghe, and Wishka Tilakaratne. The views expressed are those of the author alone.

7

Engagement of Argentina's Supreme Court with International Law

Mónica Pinto and Nahuel Maisley

A. Introduction

As part of the International Law Association (ILA) Study Group's work, this chapter aims to map the engagement of Argentinean domestic courts with international law.[1] The focus will be mostly set upon the Supreme Court, and not lower tribunals, given that they usually follow the Court's precedents in their reasonings, rarely making autonomous contributions to these discussions. The chapter will divide the Court's caselaw into three different eras. First, what we will call an 'era of affirmative avoidance', which lasted from 1853 to 1992, and during which the Supreme Court adopted in most cases a restrictive approach, blunting the incorporation of international law into the domestic legal order. Second, an 'era of transition', in which the Court radically modified its previous posture and lifted many of the restrictions it had placed upon the incorporation of international law. This new approach was soon endorsed by a constitutional reform, making the domestic legal order explicitly receptive of international law. And, third, an 'era of overriding alignment', in which the Court, despite some initial contradictions and dubitative rulings, has considered that not only international law, but also the decisions of international courts and tribunals, and even the recommendations of other international organs, must be taken into account when deciding domestic cases. After presenting these three eras, we will comment on a series of fairly recent decisions

[1] ILA Study Group on Principles on the Engagement of Domestic Courts with International Law, 'Final Report: Mapping the Engagement of Domestic Courts with International Law' (Johannesburg, 2016) (ILA Final Report). Provisions of the Argentinean Constitution quoted here in English are from the English version found on the website of the Argentinean Congress unless stated otherwise, available at <https://www.congreso.gob.ar/nationalConstitution.php> last accessed 24 July 2021. All direct quotes from the text of judgment and decisions of the Argentinean Supreme Court, unless stated otherwise, are the authors' translation.

in which the Court has begun hinting towards a 'reactive turn to domestic law'.[2] Although it is still too early to call, these decisions may either constitute a new, contestatory era, or simply a temporary pause in the Court's strong alignment with the international legal order. In the concluding section, we offer some thoughts on these developments and on the legacy of the Argentinean Supreme Court in relation to international law.

B. The Era of Affirmative Avoidance (1853–1992)

Argentina's first Constitution of 1853 included three main references to the reception of international treaties into the domestic legal order. First, Article 27 mandated the Federal Government to 'strengthen its relationships of peace and trade with foreign powers, by means of treaties in accordance with the principles of public law laid down by this Constitution'. Second, Article 31 established that the 'Constitution, the laws of the Nation enacted by Congress in pursuance thereof, and treaties with foreign powers, are the supreme law of the Nation'. And third, Article 67(19) empowered Congress to 'approve or dismiss treaties with other nations and concordats with the Apostolic Seat'.

Despite the seemingly monist wording of these provisions, the Supreme Court originally interpreted them as corresponding with a 'dualist' doctrine regarding the reception of international law in the domestic sphere.[3] Notwithstanding its own language, however, what the Court deployed during this era was a set of 'moderating techniques',[4] limiting the effect of the incorporation of international law into the Argentinean legal order. Three of these techniques are particularly salient. First, the Court considered that international treaties were non self-executing in the Argentinean legal order.[5] The Court understood, for example, that the rights established in International Labour Organization (ILO) Conventions only entailed a commitment to modify domestic legislation, which would eventually be the one granting said rights to workers.[6] Second, for the Court, the Constitution remained in all

[2] See ibid para 22.

[3] See *Merck Química Argentina v Nación Argentina* 211:162 (1948), 205. For a critique of the concept of 'dualism', see Carlos Santiago Nino, *Derecho, Moral Y Política. Una Revisión de La Teoría General Del Derecho* (Siglo XXI 2014) 64–66.

[4] As per the ILA Final Report (n 1) para 21.

[5] ibid. See also, Alejandro Chehtman, 'Constitutions and International Law' in Conrado Hübner Mendes et al (eds), *The Oxford Handbook of Constitutional Law in Latin America* (OUP 2022) 3–4.

[6] *Alonso, Gregorio v Haras 'Los Cardos' SA* 211:161 (1940). See also *Costa, Héctor Rubén v Municipalidad de la Ciudad de Buenos Aires* 310:508 (1987); *Sánchez Abelenda, Raúl v Ediciones de la Urraca SA* 311:2553 (1988); *Ekmekdjian, Miguel Angel v Neustadt, Bernardo* 311:2497 (1988).

cases hierarchically superior to international treaties.[7] As stated by the Court in 1947, 'according to article 31 of the Constitution, international treaties must respect the commands of the Constitution, whose supremacy over all rules of positive law is assured by said precept'.[8] And third, the Court considered that international treaties had the same hierarchical status as domestic laws,[9] their relationship being governed by principles such as *lex specialis* and *lex posterior*.[10] In sum, the Supreme Court considered that its role was to adjudicate on the basis of domestic law, and thus, that it could only take into consideration international rules when the Constitution so provided.[11] The potential responsibility of the State for the violation of international law was not an institutional concern of the Court, which understood itself only bound by domestic rules.[12]

Despite this posture of avoidance with respect to international treaties, the Court adopted during this period, somewhat paradoxically, a more receptive approach regarding international custom.[13] Most of the invocations of 'the law of nations', which local authors traditionally related to customary international law (CIL),[14] occurred in cases dealing with jurisdictional immunities of foreign officials, as a result of the Court's original jurisdiction to hear those cases.[15] However, custom was also used by the Court to interpret the President's war powers,[16] to deny a foreigner a permit to exit the country during a time of war,[17] and to grant asylum to foreign prisoners.[18] In none of these cases did the Court provide a clear constitutional foundation for its reference to CIL.

[7] *Becker, Juan* 208:39 (1947); *Chantrain, Alfonso* 208:84 (1947); *Cabrera, Washington Julio Efrain v Comision Tecnica* 305:2150 (1983). See also Luis Alberto Podestá Costa and José María Ruda, *Derecho Internacional Público* (Tipográfica Editora Argentina 1979) 43; Guillermo Moncayo et al, *Derecho Internacional Público* (Zavalía 1990) 60.

[8] *Chantrain, Alfonso*, 208:84 (1947).

[9] According to a 1963 ruling of the Court, 'neither article 31 nor article 100 of the Constitution give priority or superiority to treaties with foreign powers with respect to laws validly enacted by the National Congress. Both – laws and treaties – are equally deemed "supreme law of the land", and there is no normative foundation to give priority of rank to neither of them' (*Martín & Cía Ltda v Nación* 257:199 (1963) [6]). See also *Esso SA v Gobierno Nacional* 271:7 (1968).

[10] *Martín & Cía* (n 9) [8]. See also *Esso* (n 9).

[11] See Moncayo et al (n 7) 63.

[12] As the Court expressed in *Martín & Cía* (n 9) [9], 'the possible question of international order is foreign, in principle, to the jurisdiction of domestic tribunals. It depends on circumstances which relate to the conduct of the foreign affairs of the Nation, which can eventually be subject to claims between the High Contracting Parties, to which respect this Court cannot make a judgment'.

[13] This illustrates the point made in the ILA Final Report (n 1) para 18, that a domestic legal order's treatment of international law may differ for different sources of international law.

[14] Moncayo et al (n 7) 68; Damián González-Salzberg, 'The Implementation of Decisions from the Inter-American Court of Human Rights in Argentina: An Analysis of the Jurisprudential Swings of the Supreme Court' (2011) 8 International Journal of Human Rights 113, 116; Mónica Pinto, *Temas de Derechos Humanos* (Editores del Puerto 2009) 80.

[15] Moncayo et al (n 7) 68.

[16] *Merck Química Argentina* (n 3).

[17] *Dag, Eric Th.* 201:477 (1945).

[18] *La Pilcomayo* 43:321 (1891).

C. The Era of Transition (1992–1994)

The Supreme Court's own understanding of its institutional role regarding international law radically changed in its 1992 landmark decision in *Ekmekdjian v Sofovich*. In that case, the Court strongly stated that it was bound to accept the primacy of international treaties over domestic rules. The Court provided two reasons for this revision of its position. First, it held that treaties were 'organically federal acts', meaning that their ratification required the participation of both the executive and the legislative branch. Thus, 'the derogation of an international treaty by an act of Congress', ie the nullification of the content of a treaty through the enactment of subsequent domestic laws with contrary provisions, 'would breach the distribution of competences among powers'.[19] Second, after the entry into force of the Vienna Convention on the Law of Treaties (VCLT),[20] and in light of Article 27, a 'priority of rank [to international law was] now fully incorporated into the Argentinean legal system'.[21] The Court further noted that this new approach granting primacy to international treaties extended not only to a potential conflict between a treaty and an act of Congress, but also to Congress' omission to enact legislation required by a treaty, explicitly acknowledging the operative nature of international treaties.[22] Finally, the Court considered that its new position with respect to international law 'prevent[ed] the possible responsibility of the State for the actions of its internal organs, a matter which is not alien to this Court, as long as it can constitutionally avoid it'.[23]

This new approach towards international law was affirmed by the Court in the subsequent *Fibraca*[24] and *Cafés La Virginia*[25] cases. In the latter case, for instance, it stated that 'the legislator has no attribution to modify a treaty through an act of Congress',[26] and that any provision of such legislation which would be incompatible with a treaty 'would constitute a transgression of the principle of legal hierarchy (article 31 of the Constitution), and thus, a constitutionally invalid act'.[27] However, in both decisions, the Court also softened its position,

[19] *Ekmekdjian, Miguel Angel v Sofovich, Gerardo* 315:1492 (1992) (*Ekmekdjian*) [17].
[20] Vienna Convention on the Law of Treaties (adopted 23 May 1969, entered into forcé 27 January 1980) 1155 UNTS 331.
[21] *Ekmekdjian* (n 19) [18]. See also [19].
[22] ibid [19]–[20].
[23] *Fibraca Constructora SCA v Comisión Técnica* 316:1669 (1993) [3]; *Cafés La Virginia* 317:1282 (1994) [9].
[24] *Fibraca* (n 23).
[25] *Cafés La Virginia* (n 23).
[26] ibid [10].
[27] ibid.

holding that the obligation to give primacy to international law was applicable 'once respect for the principles of constitutional public law was secured'.[28]

Partly because of this shift in the Court's caselaw,[29] but also as a consequence of the pressure of human rights activists, the provisions governing the reception of international treaties were substantially modified in the constitutional reform of 1994.[30] Article 67(19) was replaced by Article 75(22), which now states, first, that 'treaties and concordats have a higher hierarchy than laws', and second, that nine human rights treaties and two human rights declarations, 'in the conditions of their validity, have constitutional hierarchy, do no[t] repeal any section of the First Part of this Constitution and are to be understood as complementing the rights and guarantees recognized herein'.[31]

As of 1994, then, all international treaties which have been ratified by Argentina and are currently in force are hierarchically superior to domestic laws. However, the Constitution still retains its primacy over most international conventions, while it shares its hierarchical status with a series of human rights treaties which are, to a great degree, 'consubstantial' to the rules established in the Constitution itself.[32]

D. The Era of Overriding Alignment (1994–2017)

The constitutional reform of 1994 paved the way for the Court's new era of 'overriding alignment'[33] with international law. In the years after the reform, first, the Court held, with only minor exceptions, that international treaties override domestic law. Second, the Court also confirmed its traditional position regarding CIL, now providing it with constitutional foundations. And finally, it expanded its deference to international law by, not without some hesitations, giving unprecedented consideration to the decisions of international courts and tribunals, and even to those of other international organs.

[28] ibid; *Fibraca* (n 23).

[29] Most commentators attribute the new wording of the Constitution to the leading *Ekmekdjian* case (n 18) case. See, eg, Zlata Drnas de Clement, *La Aplicación Del Derecho Internacional En Los Fallos de La Corte Suprema de Justicia de La Nación Argentina* (Lerner 2010) 23; Pinto (n 14) 78.

[30] Constitution of the Argentine Nation of 1853, reinstated in 1983, as amended 1994.

[31] (Authors' translation) The same provision also established a procedure to grant constitutional hierarchy to other human rights treaties, through which three other treaties have gained constitutional status to date.

[32] See ILA Final Report (n 1) para 30.

[33] See ibid para 45.

1. International Treaties Overriding Domestic Law

After the 1994 reform, the Court adopted the position that the Constitution fully incorporated international law into domestic law.[34] This was done through two different strategies. First, a strategy of 'fair weather alignment',[35] stating that there had been 'an express will of the constituents to provide constitutional hierarchy [to certain international treaties]'.[36] As a result of this will, not only the Court, but 'any judge, with any hierarchical rank, and in any jurisdiction'[37] represented 'the national sovereignty, and thus, [was] bound to safeguard the good faith that should guide the conduct of the State in the international sphere, faithfully complying with the obligations emanating from treaties and other sources of international law'.[38] In this context, the judiciary was bound to ensure that the State did not breach its obligations 'neither by acts nor by omissions of its internal organs'.[39] The Court first adopted this reasoning with respect to those human rights instruments that were expressly granted constitutional status, but it later extended it to cover other treaties, which according to the Constitution enjoyed hierarchy over domestic laws.[40]

The second strategy adopted by the Court was one of harmonization of international and domestic rules through 'consistent interpretation'.[41] The reformed Article 75 of the Constitution stated that those international treaties that were granted constitutional standing 'do not repeal any section of the First Part of this Constitution and are to be understood as complementing the rights and guarantees recognized herein'.[42] Early on, the Court had to decide on the meaning of this clause, when an apparent contradiction between the International Covenant on Economic, Social and Cultural Rights (ICESCR)[43] and the first part of the Constitution arose. It then stated that 'the constituents have already performed a judgment of verification, in which they have compared the treaties with the articles of the constitution, and they have confirmed that there is no derogation whatsoever (. . .). Thus, the harmony between these

[34] This attitude of the Court transformed it into an important 'compliance partner' of the Inter-American Court of Human Rights (IACtHR). See Raffaela Kunz, 'Judging International Judgments Anew? The Human Rights Courts before Domestic Courts' (2020) 30 EJIL 1129, 1139–41.
[35] See ILA Final Report (n 1) para 44.
[36] *Giroldi, Horacio David* 318:514 (1995) [11].
[37] *Acosta, Claudia Beatriz* 321:3555 (1998) [16].
[38] ibid [15].
[39] ibid.
[40] See, eg, *Díaz, Paulo Vicente v Cervecería y Maltería Quilmes SA* 336:593 (2013) [11]–[12].
[41] See ILA Final Report (n 1) para 46.
[42] Constitution (n 30) art 75(22).
[43] (adopted 16 December 1966, entered into force 3 January 1976) 993 UNTS 3.

treaties and the Constitution is a constitutional judgment',[44] and no contradiction can possibly arise. Harmonization was, for the Court, a constitutional imperative.

Somewhat paradoxically, this reasoning was used by the Court on at least one occasion to perform what has been described as a 'bastard application of international law',[45] or what we can call an instance of 'affirmative contestation'.[46] In a 1996 case regarding social security, the Court interpreted Article 14bis of the Constitution, which granted such benefits, under the light of Article 26 of the American Convention on Human Rights (ACHR), which limits this type of obligations, in its Spanish version, 'to the extent allowed by the available resources'.[47] In other words, the Court applied an international human rights treaty against its own spirit, using it to restrict the enjoyment of a right recognized in Argentinean domestic law, something explicitly prohibited by Article 29 of the ACHR.[48] The harmonization strategy, in this case, was used to avoid compliance with obligations the State had assumed both domestically and internationally.

2. A Constitutional Foundation for the Incorporation of Customary International Law

A second feature of this new era of overriding alignment with respect to international law was the receptive position adopted by the Supreme Court regarding international custom. Not only did the Court continue to consider 'the law of nations' as part of the Argentinean legal system, as it had done in its previous caselaw, but it also devised a somewhat rare constitutional foundation for this established practice.

The first step in this direction was taken in the 1995 *Priebke* case. In 1944, Erich Priebke, a German SS captain, had supervised the killing of 335 civilians in Rome, in what became known as the Massacre of the Ardeatine. After the

[44] *Monges, Analía v UBA* 319:3148 (1996) [20]–[21].

[45] Martín Abregú, 'La Aplicación Del Derecho Internacional de Los Derechos Humanos Por Los Tribunales Locales: Una Introducción' in Martín Abregú and Christian Courtis (eds), *La aplicación de los tratados sobre derechos humanos por los tribunales locales* (Editores del Puerto 1997).

[46] See ILA Final Report (n 1) para 58.

[47] See American Convention on Human Rights (Pact of San José, Costa Rica) (adopted 22 November 1969, entered into force 18 July 1978) 1144 UNTS 123 (ACHR) art 26: '... en la medida de los recursos disponibles...' (Spanish text).

[48] ibid art 29 reads: 'No provision of this Convention shall be interpreted as: (...) b. restricting the enjoyment or exercise of any right or freedom recognized by virtue of the laws of any State Party or by virtue of another convention to which one of the said States is a party...'.

end of the war, he fled to Argentina on a Vatican passport, where he lived in the Patagonian city of Bariloche for over fifty years. In 1994, however, after a journalist found and exposed him, the Italian authorities requested his extradition to be put on trial in Rome. The case eventually arrived at the Supreme Court, which had to decide on the appropriateness of the extradition, considering that the crime of murder is subject to a statute of limitations of ten years under Argentine law. To decide the case, the Court referred, among other arguments, to Article 118 of the Constitution, which regulates the location of criminal trials. This article states that when crimes are 'committed outside the territory of the Nation, *against the law of nations*, the trial shall be held at such place as Congress may determine by a special law'.[49] In this case, the Court found not only that the crimes committed were against the law of nations, but that they also constituted the crime of genocide.[50] As such, according to the Court, Priebke's actions were in breach of *jus cogens* rules incorporated into Argentinean law, and therefore exempt from the statute of limitations. Thus, the Court ruled in favour of Italy's request, allowing the extradition of Priebke, who was later tried and convicted in Rome.

In 2004, the *Priebke* precedent became relevant to a case of a different nature. Between 1974 and 1978, the Chilean intelligence officer Enrique Arancibia Clavel supervised a task force that carried out illegal operations in Buenos Aires, including committing the murder of General Carlos Prats, the former Head of the Chilean Army under President Salvador Allende. When he was finally prosecuted, Arancibia Clavel invoked the statute of limitations and claimed that the case had to be dismissed. When the case reached the Supreme Court, the latter was faced with a dilemma: on the one hand, the Convention on the Non-Applicability of Statutory Limitations to War Crimes and Crimes Against Humanity (CNASL),[51] which had been incorporated into the Constitution in 2003, mandated that the prosecution continued despite any statutory limitation; on the other, the principle of legality in Article 18 of the Constitution protected Arancibia Clavel from the retroactive application of the Convention, which was ratified by Argentina in 1995, twenty years after he committed his crimes. The solution found by the Court was to hold that the Convention codified customary rules, and that these customary rules already existed in the 1970s. Thus, 'the prohibition of retroactivity of criminal legislation is not violated, but instead, a principle established by customary

[49] Constitution (n 30) art 118 (emphasis added) (authors' translation).
[50] *Priebke, Erich* 318:2148 (1995) [2].
[51] (adopted 16 November 1968, entered into force 11 November 1970) 754 UNTS 73.

international law is reaffirmed, one that was already binding at the time the crimes were committed'.[52]

For this solution to be acceptable, the Court had to justify the direct applicability of CIL to domestic criminal affairs. For this purpose, the majority held that the non-applicability of statutory limitations for war crimes and crimes against humanity was not only an international custom in the 1970s, but also one of *jus cogens* nature. Thus, the Argentinean State was already bound to accept it, even without its express consent.[53] Further, two judges also opined that custom was directly binding in the Argentinean legal system, as a result of Article 118 of the Constitution.[54] Judge Maqueda stated that with this article, the Constitution 'recognized the supremacy of the law of nations, and thus directly incorporated it'.[55] Three dissenting judges challenged these two assertions.[56]

The *Arancibia Clavel* precedent was fundamental for the resolution of one of the most important cases in the history of the Supreme Court, the 2005 *Simón* case.[57] During the military dictatorship that ruled the country between 1976 and 1983, Julio Simón had been in charge of a clandestine detention centre, where people who had been forcefully disappeared were held, tortured, and often murdered. After the dictatorship ended, two laws limited the scope of the prosecution of the crimes committed by military officials,[58] and Simón was never brought to trial. However, these laws were 'annulled' by Congress in 2003, and Simón was indicted with a series of charges. As in the case of *Arancibia Clavel*, Simón claimed that he was protected by statutory limitations. And, as in *Arancibia Clavel*, the Court faced the problem of the retroactive application of the CNASL. Not surprisingly, the Court resorted to similar arguments to solve the case. However, this time, four judges,[59] out of the eight that voted, considered that CIL had been fully incorporated into the Argentinean legal system via Article 118 of the Constitution.[60]

[52] *Arancibia Clavel, Enrique Lautar*, 327: 3312 (2004) [28].
[53] ibid [28]–[33].
[54] ibid Sep Op Boggiano [40]; Sep Op Maqueda [10] and [57].
[55] ibid, Sep Op Maqueda [22].
[56] ibid, Diss Op Belluscio [16]; Diss Op Fayt [43]; Diss Op Vázquez [24].
[57] *Simón, Julio Héctor* 328:2056 (2005). See, generally, Christine Bakker, 'A Full Stop to Amnesty in Argentina: The Simon Case' (2005) 3 JICJ 1106.
[58] On the history of these two laws, see Ricardo Gil Lavedra, 'The Possibility of Criminal Justice: The Argentinean Experience' in Carlos Espósito and Jessica Almqvist (eds), *The Role of Courts in Transitional Justice: Voices from Latin America and Spain* (Routledge 2012) 56–70; Carlos Santiago Nino, *Radical Evil on Trial* (Yale University Press 1997).
[59] *Simón* (n 57) Sep Op Boggiano [28] and [49]; Sep Op Maqueda [60] and [83]; Sep Op Highton [31]; Sep Op Lorenzetti [19].
[60] In the 2007 *Mazzeo* case, again four judges used the argument of the incorporation of custom via Constitution (n 30) art 118. This time, however, they constituted the majority out of the six judges that voted in the case. *Mazzeo, Julio Lilo* 330:3248 (2007). See also Kunz (n 34) 1146 for a comment.

Soon after, this line of reasoning by the Supreme Court led lower tribunals to accept the principle of universal jurisdiction in relation to crimes committed 'against the law of nations'.[61] In 2009, a federal judge ordered the arrest of China's former President Jiang Zemin and his former security chief Luo Gan for crimes against humanity in the alleged persecution of the Falun Gong spiritual movement.[62] In its consideration of the matter, the Federal Court of Appeals of the city of Buenos Aires agreed with the judge on the existence of an 'exception to the principle of territoriality, motivated by the presence of crimes committed outside the limits of the Nation that would affect the law of nations (art. 118 CN)'.[63] Three years later, in 2013, a federal judge accepted to hear a case concerning crimes against humanity committed during the 1936–1977 dictatorship of Francisco Franco, in Spain. In her decision, she also acknowledged that the Argentinean Criminal Code restricted its application to crimes committed in the territory of the country, or by Argentinean authorities abroad.[64] However, after recalling both Article 118 and the many international instruments binding upon Argentina which require the prosecution of crimes against humanity, she explained that:

> [T]he Criminal Code and the other special criminal laws cannot validly circumscribe or limit the jurisdictional extension attributed by the Constitution or the treaties to which the Nation is a party, to crimes under international law. The opposite would imply an evident undermining of the National Constitution and the international agreements that the Republic has committed to fulfill and respect.[65]

Based on these precedents, claimants have resorted to Argentinean courts to litigate crimes committed in Paraguay by the Stroessner regime and alleged crimes by Israeli officials against Palestinians in Gaza.[66] Recently, the Federal Court of Appeals has accepted an important case with allegations of genocide and crimes against humanity against the Rohingyia minority in Myanmar.[67]

[61] See, eg, Máximo Langer and Mackenzie Eason. 'The quiet expansion of universal jurisdiction' (2019) 30 EJIL 779, 800–3.

[62] LA Henao, 'Argentina Judge Asks China Arrests over Falun Gong' (Reuters, 22 December 2009), available at www.reuters.com/article/us-argentina-china-falungong-idUSTRE5BM02B20091223 last accessed 24 July 2023.

[63] Cámara Criminal y Correccional Federal, Sala I, C/N° 44.196 'Luo Gan s/archivo' (21 December 2010), 9.

[64] See Criminal Code art 1.

[65] Juzgado Nacional Criminal y Correccional Federal 1, CFP 4591/2010 'N.N. s/ genocidio', Decision, 18 September 2013, p 149.

[66] See Langer and Eason, 'The quiet expansion of universal jurisdiction' (n 61) p 803.

[67] Cámara Criminal y Correccional Federal, Sala I, CFP 8419/2019 'Burmese Rohingya Organisation s/ legajo de apelación' (26 November 2021), 9.

So far, none of these cases has actually led to arrests, given the refusals of other nations to extradite those being prosecuted.[68]

3. Growing Deference to International Courts and Tribunals

The third and final feature of the era of overriding alignment is a growing, albeit sinuous, deference of the Supreme Court to international courts and tribunals, and even towards other international organs.

The first precedent in this matter was set in 1993, during the 'era of transition'. In the *La Nación* case, the Supreme Court used an Advisory Opinion of the Inter-American Court of Human Rights (IACtHR) and a case at the European Court of Human Rights (ECtHR) to confirm its own views on the validity of restrictions to the freedom of the press. In that occasion, the Court did not explain the specific authority it derived from those precedents, nor did it ground its reference to them on any particular constitutional provision.

However, after the constitutional reform, the Court considered that it had the means to provide legal grounding to the practice of referring to international organs. In the 1995 *Giroldi* case, it recalled that the new Article 75(22) of the Constitution incorporated international human rights treaties 'in the conditions of their validity', meaning that their application should 'particularly consider their effective application by the international tribunals which are competent for their interpretation and application'.[69] In that particular case, the Court made reference to the caselaw of the IACtHR and interpreted Article 8(2)(h) of the ACHR as mandating the establishment of an Appeals Tribunal for criminal cases.

The following year, the Supreme Court expanded its interpretation of the wording of Article 75(22) to include not only the IACtHR, but also the Inter-American Commission on Human Rights (IACommHR) as an official interpreter of the Convention.[70] According to the Court, 'the opinion of the IACommHR must serve as a guide for the interpretation of conventional precepts since Argentina recognized its competence to hear all those cases relative

[68] See Langer and Eason, 'The quiet expansion of universal jurisdiction' (n 61).

[69] *Giroldi* (n 36) [11]. See also González-Salzberg (n 14) 119.

[70] *Bramajo, Hernán Javier* 319:1840 (1996) [8]. It is worth noting that the Court decided to consider the IACommHR's decision in a case in which the Commission had agreed with Argentina regarding its non-violation of the ACHR. In other words, the Court used the reference to the Inter-American system to justify a restricted interpretation of the right, and not otherwise. See Mónica Pinto, 'El Valor Jurídico de Las Decisiones de Los Órganos de Control En Materia de Derechos Humanos En La Jurisprudencia de La Corte Suprema de Justicia' in Víctor Abramovich et al (eds), *La aplicación de los tratados sobre derechos humanos en el ámbito local. La experiencia de una década* (Editores del Puerto 2007) 131.

to the interpretation and application of the ACHR'.[71] A few months later, the Court also considered the Human Rights Committee (HRC) as a valid interpretive reference, this time with regard to the International Covenant on Civil and Political Rights (ICCPR),[72] also incorporated into the Constitution. And two years after that, the Court granted an *habeas data* writ basing its decision on 'guidelines formulated by the UN, the OAS, the Council of Europe, and even the case-law of the ECtHR'.[73] A few years later, the Court also acknowledged the Committee on Economic, Social and Cultural Rights as the 'authorized interpreter' of the ICESCR,[74] and the Committee on the Rights of the Child as the interpreter of the Convention on the Rights of the Child.[75] The Court has also recently referred to the work of various ILO Committees to interpret ILO Conventions.[76] To the extent that some of these outputs are not directly binding on Argentina or constitute soft law, this attitude of the Supreme Court can be considered as 'hyper-alignment' in the terms of the ILA Final Report.[77]

In 1998, the Supreme Court had to decide for the first time on a situation involving a report by a treaty organ referring to Argentina.[78] In 1989, a group of militants of the 'Todos por la Patria Movement' had attempted to take by force the military garrison of La Tablada, in the province of Buenos Aires. The attack was brutally repressed: some of the militants were tortured, others were forcefully disappeared, and a number were executed. After the events, the twenty militants that survived were tried and convicted for breaching the Law for the Defense of Democracy,[79] and were given prison terms that ranged from 10 years to life. Their appeals were in turn successively dismissed, and they decided to take the case to the Inter-American system. In 1998, the IACommHR found that the State was internationally responsible, and recommended that Argentina 'identif[ied] and punish[ed] all the persons who may be responsible for the human rights violations', make 'fully effective, in the future, the judicial

[71] *Bramajo* (n 70) [8].

[72] (adopted 16 December 1966, entered into force 23 March 1976) 999 UNTS 171. See *Nardelli, Pietro Antonio* 319:2557 (1996); also *F.A.L.* 335:197 (2012) [6] and [12].

[73] *Urteaga, Facundo Raúl v Estado Nacional* 321:2767 (1998) [11].

[74] *Campodónico de Beviacqua, Ana Carina v Ministerio de Salud y Acción Social—Secretaría de Programas de Salud y Banco de Drogas Neoplásicas* 323:3229 (2000). *Aquino, Isacio v Cargo Servicios Industriales SA* 327:3753 (2004) [9].

[75] (adopted 20 November 1989, entered into force 2 September 1990) 1577 UNTS 3. See *Maldonado, Daniel Enrique* 328:4343 (2005); also *FAL* (n 72) [6] and [13].

[76] *ATE v Ministerio de Trabajo* 331:2499 (2008).

[77] ILA Final Report (n 1) paras 55–56.

[78] *Juan Carlos Abella v Argentina*, Case No 11/137, IACommHR, Report No 55/97 (18 November 1997) OEA/Ser.L/V/II.98 doc 6 rev.

[79] Ley de defensa de la democracia, Ley No 23.077 (9 August 1984).

guarantee of the right to appeal for persons tried under' the Law for Defense of Democracy, and 'repair[ed] the harm suffered' by the claimants.[80]

After the IACommHR's decision, the claimants took the case back to the Argentinean system, requesting a writ of *habeas corpus*, which was denied, but an appeal to the Supreme Court was granted. In that 1998 *Acosta* decision, the Court adopted the first of a series of rulings in which it followed a strategy of 'affirmative avoidance',[81] finding different arguments to circumvent the rulings of international organs with respect to the Argentinean state. In this case, the Court began its decision by reiterating its position as to the guiding nature of the decisions of treaty organs, but stating that 'from the text of the Convention it appears that the decision to which the states consider themselves bound is that of the Court',[82] and not of the Commission. It then conclusively held that:

> even if according to the principle of good faith (…) the state must make its best efforts to give a favourable answer to the recommendations made by the Commission, that does not amount to consecrating a duty for judges to comply with their content, since they are not binding for the Judicial Branch. International case-law, in spite of its novelty and pertinence, cannot constitute a reason for revision of domestic judicial decisions –comparable to the writ of appeal–, since that would affect the stability of judicial decisions, which, being an inescapable requirement for legal certainty, is thus demanded by public order and therefore has a constitutional rank.[83]

Despite this decision, the claimants decided once again to question the outcome of the proceedings, this time not through an *habeas corpus* writ, but by appealing the original decision that had convicted them. The Court denied this request, and this time it was the executive branch that decided to appeal the denial, claiming that it was its task to prevent the State from engaging in international responsibility. When the case again reached the Supreme Court, the latter dismissed it, holding that the Executive had no standing to bring the case. However, the Court decided to make a statement on the merits, 'with the purpose of establishing that it does not confine itself to formal arguments and that it is not insensitive regarding the concern for the fulfilment of international commitments that the Executive has shown by attempting to intervene in the case'.[84] Substantively, the Court recalled that the IACommHR's

[80] *Abella v Argentina* (n 78) [438].
[81] ILA Final Report (n 1) para 41.
[82] *Acosta* (n 37) [9].
[83] ibid [13].
[84] *Felicetti, Roberto* 323:4130 (2000) [3].

recommendation with regard to the violation of the right of appeal—the one that was under discussion in these proceedings—mentioned that it should be made fully effective 'in the future'. Thus, according to the Supreme Court, by not granting this right in this case, the Argentinean State would not be committing an internationally wrongful act.[85] This decision, while still in tension with the workings of the Inter-American system, marked a slight shift in the sensitivity of the Supreme Court, moving from an openly 'negatory contestation'[86] of the value of the IACommHR's recommendations to opening an international legal debate with it, in what could be called 'affirmative contestation'.[87]

In 2003, the Court had to decide for the first time on the implementation of a decision made not by the IACommHR, but by the IACtHR with respect to Argentina.[88] The case involved complex judicial proceedings in which José María Cantos, a businessman from the province of Santiago del Estero, was denied the right of access to court as a result of, first, the imposition of excessive filing fees, and, second, the ruling of excessive honoraria to different lawyers intervening in the process. Surprisingly—considering its dictum in the *Acosta* case, negating the value of the IACommHR's decisions, but acknowledging that of the IACtHR's judgments—the implementation of the IACtHR's judgment was denied by the Supreme Court, with two different arguments. First, Judges Fayt, Moliné O'Connor, and Vázquez held that accepting the IACtHR's decision would imply 'the obvious infringement of clauses of unequivocal constitutional nature which protect the rights of the different professionals that have intervened in the case'.[89] Since these professionals had not participated in the proceedings at the Inter-American level, overturning the domestic ruling on the basis of the IACtHR's judgment would breach their right to a fair trial. In turn, this would amount to a 'patent and deliberate abdication of [the Court's] highest and most transcendent function, for which it has been instituted as the head of the Judicial Power, which is to be the guardian and final interpreter of the Constitution'.[90] Second, Judges Petracchi and López held that the Court 'lack[ed] the capacity to modify judicial decisions which are protected by *res judicata*' and that the executive power 'should adopt the measures it sees fit,

[85] ibid [7].
[86] ILA Final Report (n 1) para 61.
[87] ibid para 58.
[88] *Cantos v Argentina* (Merits, Reparations and Costs) IACtHR Series C No 97 (28 November 2002).
[89] *Cantos, José María*, Resolución 1404/2003 [3]–[4]. See, generally, Mónica Pinto, 'National and International Courts: Disdain or Deference?' (2008) 30 Loyola LA International and Comparative Law Review 247, 250–52.
[90] *Cantos* (n 89) [3].

within its capacity, or—in any event—take the initiative contemplated by article 77 of the Constitution', and propose a bill to Congress to resolve the situation.[91]

Despite these harsh statements indicating a posture of local negatory contestation,[92] this doctrine did not last very long. The Court's position with respect to international courts and tribunals began to shift again in 2003, when some changes in the composition of the Court occurred. That year, an *obiter dictum* written by Judges Zaffaroni and Maqueda held that, according to the caselaw of the IACtHR, the laws that restricted the prosecution of the crimes committed during the 1976–1983 dictatorship were invalid.[93] In 2004, the Court once again held that the IACommHR's reports were important for the interpretation of legal provisions of the ACHR,[94] and that the reports rendered with regard to Argentina were 'an interpretive guide for the Court'.[95] That same year, the Court decided the *Arancibia Clavel* case, and in 2005, it made its ruling in the *Simón* case.[96] In both occasions, one of the judges' most prominent arguments, besides that of CIL, was the fact that the caselaw of the IACtHR considered that amnesties granted for crimes against humanity were invalid under the ACHR.[97]

The confirmation of this renewed posture of alignment came in the 2004 *Espósito* case.[98] In that occasion, the Supreme Court had to deal with the implementation of the decision made by the IACtHR in the *Bulacio* case,[99] in which the Court had found that Argentina had breached a series of human rights of a young man killed by the police, and of his family. In the domestic case, Miguel Ángel Espósito, the superintendent in charge of the police station where Walter Bulacio was murdered, had been able to avoid a conviction after a series of judicial delays, as a result of a statute of limitations. In its 2004 decision, the Supreme Court held that although it would have regularly dismissed the case, 'since the IACtHR's decision under scrutiny is mandatory for the Argentinean state (art. 68.1 ACHR), this Court is also bound, in principle, to subordinate the content of its decisions to those of that international tribunal'.[100] Thus, the Court decided in favour of Bulacio's family.

91 ibid, Sep Op Petracchi and López [1].
92 See ILA Final Report (n 1) paras 61 et seq, 65.
93 *Astiz, Alfredo Ignacio* 326:4797 (2003), Sep Op Zaffaroni and Maqueda [6].
94 *Carro Evangelista, Delia* 327:352 (2004).
95 ibid.
96 See Section C(2).
97 *Barrios Altos v Peru* (Merits) IACtHR Series C No 75 (14 March 2001).
98 *Espósito, Miguel Ángel* 327:5668 (2004).
99 *Bulacio v Argentina* (Merits, Reparations and Costs) IACtHR Series C No 100 (18 September 2003).
100 ibid para 6.

Seven years later, in the 2011 *Derecho* case, the Supreme Court explicitly confirmed its adherence to the doctrine established in *Espósito*, despite some previous dubitative decisions.[101] In 1988, Juan Francisco Bueno Alves had been detained and tortured alongside his lawyer, Carlos Pérez Galindo, in the context of a fraud case. After a few years, one of the policemen indicted for the torments, René Jesús Derecho, was set free on the basis of a statute of limitations. Pérez Galindo appealed this decision, and reached the Supreme Court. Simultaneously, the case was taken to the Inter-American system, reaching eventually the IACtHR, where Argentina accepted its international responsibility.[102] The Supreme Court's first decision in that case was issued in 2007, two months after the IACtHR ruling, and, surprisingly, made no reference to it. The Court considered that torture did not constitute a crime against humanity, and, thus, that the statute of limitations was indeed applicable to Derecho.[103]

The claimants then presented a writ of certiorari, requesting the Court to explain 'the authentic jurisdictional reach of [its] decision under the light of the IACtHR's decision in the 'Bueno Alves v. Argentina' case'.[104] Interestingly, the Supreme Court noted that the IACtHR's judgment was officially notified to the Argentinean Supreme Court only in September 2007,[105] namely four months after it was rendered, and two months after the Court had decided the case. Now that the IACtHR's decision had been notified, the Court recalled the *Espósito* doctrine and 'corrected' its own previous decision to comply with the IACtHR ruling.[106]

The final step in this growing deference to international organs came in the 2013 *Carranza Latrubesse* case—perhaps the clearest example of what the ILA Final Report calls 'hyper-alignment'.[107] Gustavo Carranza Latrubesse was a first instance judge from the province of Chubut who had been removed from his position by the military government in 1976. After the dictatorship, he requested to be reinstated and compensated, but his request was denied by a provincial tribunal. When the Supreme Court dismissed his appeal, he took the case to the IACommHR, which in 1997 issued a report in his favour. Carranza Latrubesse then presented a declarative action which eventually reached the Supreme Court, after years of litigation.

[101] *Derecho, René Jesús* 334:1504 (2011).

[102] *Bueno-Alves v Argentina* (Merits, Reparations and Costs) IACtHR Series C No 164 (11 May 2007).

[103] *Derecho, René Jesús*, 330:3074 (2007). See also for a comment on both the *Bulacio* and *Derecho* decisions of the Supreme Court, Kunz (n 34) 1147–48.

[104] *Derecho* (n 101) [2].

[105] ibid [5].

[106] ibid [4]–[5].

[107] *Carranza Latrubesse, Gustavo v Estado Nacional* 336:1024 (2013). See ILA Final Report (n 1) para 55.

The Court was faced with a situation in which it was asked to reverse its own decision, but this time not on the basis of an IACtHR judgment, but on the basis of a recommendation of the IACommHR. It understood that its task consisted in interpreting 'whether the "recommendations" that are formulated by the IACommHR under article 51.2 of the ACHR are of an obligatory nature for the state or not'.[108] To answer this question, the Court presented a detailed explanation of the functioning of the Inter-American system, and a general understanding of the obligations established by the ACHR in accordance with the rules of treaty interpretation of the VCLT. After dismissing the IACtHR's interpretation of the term 'recommendations' (which had held that the ordinary meaning of the term should take precedence, and that they were thus non-binding)[109] for constituting merely an *obiter dictum*,[110] the Supreme Court recalled another decision of the IACtHR, in which it had considered that states have 'the obligation to make every effort to apply the recommendations of a protective organ such as the Inter-American Commission'.[111] The Supreme Court considered that this obligation, read in the light of general principles such as those of good faith, *pro homine*, and *effet utile*, led it to 'acknowledge the obligatory nature of the recommendations rendered under article 51.2 of the ACHR'.[112] Thus, it considered itself obliged to accept the IACommHR report, and decided in favour of Carranza Latrubesse.

E. A New Era, or Simply a Pause? (2017)

A change in the composition of the Supreme Court, in 2016, prompted a new reversal in the Court's engagement with international law.[113] In 2017, the Court rendered two decisions engaging in 'affirmative contestation',[114] whose long-term impact upon the Argentinean legal order is still unclear.[115]

[108] *Carranza Latrubesse* (n 107) [4].
[109] *Caballero-Delgado and Santana v Colombia* (Merits) IACtHR Series C No 22 (8 December 1995).
[110] *Carranza Latrubesse* (n 107) [14].
[111] *Cesti-Hurtado v Peru* (Merits) IACtHR Series C No 56 (29 September 1999) [186].
[112] *Carranza Latrubesse* (n 107) [18].
[113] Following the proposal of the President, and after approval by the Senate, two new judges were sworn to the Court: Horacio Rosatti and Carlos Rosenkrantz. The three remaining judges were Chief Justice Ricardo Lorenzetti, Justices Juan Carlos Maqueda, and Elena Highton de Nolasco (who retired in 2021).
[114] See ILA Final Report (n 1) para 58.
[115] This turn is surprising in that the Argentinian Supreme Court has been 'long considered to be one of the strongest allies of the IACtHR and defender of neo-constitutionalism in Latin America', see Kunz (n 34) 1130, and 1151.

1. The *Fontevecchia* Decision

The first case concerned the implementation of the *Fontevecchia* decision of the IACtHR, regarding the appropriate balance between freedom of expression and the right to privacy. The IACtHR found that the Argentinean Supreme Court had erred in its appreciation of a certain publication as libellous. As a result, among other reparations, it ordered the State to 'set aside the civil sentence imposed on Mr. Jorge Fontevecchia and Mr. Hector D'Amico [the editors of the magazine in question], as well as all of its consequences'.[116]

In its 2017 decision, the Supreme Court refused to comply with this specific remedy ordered by the IACtHR (though accepting the others).[117] It began by clarifying that 'it is beyond discussion that the decisions of the Inter-American Court, dictated in contentious proceedings against the Argentinean state are, in principle, binding for the state (art. 68.1, ACHR)'.[118] However, such obligatory nature 'only characterizes those decisions dictated by the international tribunal within the framework of its remedial powers'.[119] In this case, according to the Supreme Court, these remedial powers were exceeded, for three reasons. The first had to do with the institutional structure of the system. Since the IACtHR does not constitute a 'fourth instance', said the Court, it cannot revise or annul domestic judicial decisions.[120] The second had to do with the text of the ACHR: according to the Court's reading, 'the literal text of the rule [article 68.1 ACHR] does not contemplate the possibility that the Inter-American Court may decide to remove the effects of a decision of a national tribunal'.[121] The third and final reason was to be found in the Argentinean Constitution itself. '[T]he constituents have consecrated in article 27 a sphere of sovereign reserve', said the Court, 'delimited by the principles of public law established in the National Constitution, to which the international treaties must be adjusted, and which must be in accordance to them'.[122] Specifically, 'within these immovable principles is, without any doubt, the character of this [Supreme] Court as a supreme organ, and the head of the Judiciary'.[123] Thus, 'to revoke a decision dictated by this tribunal implies depriving it of its character as a supreme organ

[116] *Fontevecchia and D'Amico v Argentina* (Merits, Reparations and Costs) IACtHR Series C No 238 (29 November 2011) [137(2)].

[117] *Ministerio de Relaciones Exteriores y Culto ('Fontevecchia y D'Amico vs Argentina')* 340:47 (2017).

[118] ibid [6].

[119] ibid.

[120] ibid [8]. On why this argument is problematic, see Pinto (n 89) 251.

[121] *Fontevecchia* (n 117) [13].

[122] ibid [16].

[123] ibid [17].

of the Argentinean judiciary, and substituting it with an international tribunal, in clear transgression of articles 27 and 108 of the National Constitution'.[124]

These arguments clearly reflect a shift in the attitude of the Supreme Court towards international tribunals.[125] However, the Court took pains in trying to fit this reasoning within the structure of its previous jurisprudence. This is clear from the final paragraph of the decision. There, it is stated that

> [w]hat has been said up to this moment does not imply denying an obligatory nature to the decisions of the Inter-American Court, but rather merely understanding that the binding force that emanates from article 68.1 ACHR must be circumscribed to those matters over which the international tribunal has competence.[126]

In other words, the Court still sees international law as authoritative, but now it underlines that it, and not international tribunals, must be the last interpreter of international treaties binding upon Argentina. Thus, it engages in 'affirmative contestation', 'accepting the validity or applicability of the international law norm but giving it a meaning different from that which is generally accepted'.[127]

This new position of the Argentinean Supreme Court is problematic, to say the least.[128] First, it challenges the general rules of international law on competence, according to which the IACtHR is the judge of its own faculties—a principle known as *competence-competence*.[129] Second, regardless of such rules, it challenges the very foundations of the Inter-American system: allowing domestic courts to decide whether an international tribunal has acted within its

[124] ibid.

[125] See for a comment, Alejandro Chehtman, 'The Relationship between Domestic and International Courts: The Need to Incorporate Judicial Politics into the Analysis' (EJIL:*Talk!*, 8 June 2020), available at <https://www.ejiltalk.org/the-relationship-between-domestic-and-international-courts-the-need-to-incorporate-judicial-politics-into-the-analysis/> last accessed 24 July 2023; cf the discussion in Jorge Contesse, 'Judicial Interactions and Human Rights Contestations in Latin America' (2021) 12 JIDS 271, 282–84, 288–89.

[126] *Fontevecchia* (n 117) [20].

[127] ILA Final Report (n 1) para 58.

[128] For similar commentaries, see, eg, Víctor Abramovich, 'Comentarios sobre "Fontevecchia", la autoridad de las sentencias de la Corte Interamericana y los principios de derecho público argentino' (2017) 5 Pensar en Derecho 10, 9; Lautaro Furfaro, 'Las ataduras de Ulises se aflojan: el pronunciamiento de la CSJN frente al caso "Fontevecchia" de la Corte IDH' (2017) 5 Pensar en Derecho 10, 37; Isaías Losada Revol, 'The Ministry of Foreign Affairs Case: A Ruling with Unforeseen Consequences in the Enforcement of Human Rights in Argentina' (2017) 49 Georgetown Journal of International Law 461; Agostina Cichero and Marcos Kotlik, 'La CSJN y el empleo de la Convención de Viena sobre el Derecho de los Tratados en el caso Fontevecchia: falencias en la interpretación y retrocesos en materia de derechos humanos' (2017) 98 Lecciones y Ensayos 305.

[129] See *Case of the Constitutional Court v Peru* (Competence) IACtHR Series C No 55 (24 September 1999) [31]–[33].

competence or not would destroy the *raison d'être* of international tribunals in the field of human rights. Third, the argument that the IACtHR should not order the revision of domestic sentences is incompatible with the requirement of exhaustion of local remedies:[130] 'it would be absurd that the Convention demanded that the victims exhausted domestic legal processes before accessing the international system, and then barred the organs of the system from revising those judicial decisions'.[131] And finally, fourth, the Court's identification of 'a sphere of sovereign reserve delimited by the principles of public law established in the National Constitution to which the international treaties must be adjusted'[132] is openly incompatible with the text of Article 75(22), which grants constitutional hierarchy to international human rights instruments (including those provisions accepting the jurisdiction of international tribunals). If anything, those 'principles of public law' mentioned by Article 27 must include – and not be subjugated to– the principles acknowledged in these international human rights instruments.

Despite the seemingly irreconcilable positions evinced in the original decisions, the clash between the IACtHR and the Argentinean Supreme Court in *Fontevecchia* was resolved in a low-key manner. In its 2017 decision monitoring compliance, the IACtHR explained that its original order of 'set[ting] aside the civil sentence (. . .) as well as all of its consequences'[133] did not necessarily mean 'revoking' the previous decision by the Supreme Court:

> Given that it is a civil sentence which does not leave criminal records, the state could have adopted any other kind of legal act, different from revising the sentence, to comply with the reparation ordered by the Court: for instance, it could have deleted the publication of the sentence from the websites of the Supreme Court and the Centre for Judicial Information, or it could have maintained the publication, adding some sort of annotation indicating that the sentence was found to be in violation of the American Convention by the Inter-American Court'.[134]

The Argentinean Supreme Court took up this invitation of the IACtHR to put the episode behind, saving face for both tribunals. In December 2017, it

[130] See ACHR (n 47) art 46.
[131] Abramovich (n 128) 14.
[132] *Fontevecchia* (n 107) [16].
[133] *Fontevecchia and D'Amico v Argentina* (n 106) [137(2)].
[134] *Fontevecchia and D'Amico v Argentina* (Supervisión de Cumplimiento de Sentencia) IACtHR (18 October 2017) [21].

considered that 'the annotation suggested by the Inter-American Court does not impinge upon the principles of public law established in the National Constitution (Article 27)' and that it was therefore 'appropriate to accede to what ha[d] been suggested'.[135] As of then, the Supreme Court's website includes a resolution with the following legend alongside the original decision: 'This sentence was considered incompatible with the American Convention on Human Rights by the Inter-American Court (sentence of 29 November 2011)'.[136]

In subsequent cases, the Supreme Court took a less contestatory position towards international law and international tribunals. In 2017, only months after the Supreme Court's challenge in the *Fontevecchia* case, the IACtHR ordered provisional measures in the *Milagro Sala* case, dealing with the detention of an activist for a series of alleged crimes (including corruption charges) in the Argentinean province of Jujuy. The Inter-American Court requested that Argentina adopted 'those protection measures which are necessary and effective to guarantee the life, personal integrity, and health of Ms. Milagro Sala', specifically substituting 'her pre-trial detention for house arrest'.[137] In response, the Supreme Court quoted a 2007 case stating that, when facing provisional measures by the IACtHR, the Supreme Court is 'under an obligation to adopt those measures which, without affecting the attributions of other powers, tend to maintain the observance of the National Constitution'.[138] Thus, it ordered the judicial authorities in charge of Sala's case to 'urgently adopt the measures at bar to comply with what was ordered by the IACtHR'.[139]

In 2020 and 2021, the Court took a position of 'hyper-alignment'[140] towards international law in two cases related to workers' freedom of association. In both cases, the Court endorsed the opinion of the Advocate General, who granted constitutional hierarchy to ILO Convention No 87 on Freedom of Association and Protection of the Right to Organise Convention, despite not being listed in Article 75(22) of the Constitution. To do so, he argued that the Convention's provisions were 'included' in Articles 8(3) of the ICESCR and 22(3) of the ICCPR—both of which have, indeed, constitutional hierarchy, according to Article 75(22) of the Constitution.[141] These articles, which have the

135 Resolution N° 4015/17, File 6439/12 (5 December 2017) [4].

136 ibid decision.

137 *Matter of Milagro Sala regarding Argentina* (Provisional Measures) IACtHR (23 November 2017) 19.

138 *Sala, Milagro* 340:1775 (2017) [11], citing *Lavado, Diego Jorge c Mendoza* L 733. XLII (2006) [8].

139 *Sala* (n 138). Two of the five judges dissented with the wording of this specific paragraph, distinguishing this case from *Fontevecchia* and granting the measures.

140 ILA Final Report (n 1) para 55.

141 *Festram*,343:1389 (2020), Opinion of the Advocate General, 5; *APSAI v Autopistas del Sol SA* 344:233 (2021), Opinion of the Advocate General, 3.

same wording, establish that neither the ICESCR nor the ICCPR authorize states to take measures which would prejudice the guarantees provided for in ILO Convention No 87. In the 2021 case, *APSAI*, the Advocate General and the Court also paid special attention to a series of reports by the ILO Committee of Experts on the Application of Conventions and Recommendations (CEACR) dealing with the specific Argentinean labour law being considered in the case.[142]

2. The *Muiña* Decision

The second suggestion of a new era in the relationship of the Supreme Court with international law came in the 2017 *Muiña* decision.[143] The case concerned the application of Law 24.390, which had been in place between 1994 and 2001.[144] This statute mandated that after the first two years of pre-trial detention in criminal proceedings, each day was to be counted twice for the purposes of complying with the ultimate sentence decided in trial. Law 24.390 was adopted in the context of more than twenty cases dealt with by the IACommHR, in which people were held in pre-trial detention for ordinary crimes.[145] Back then, crimes against humanity committed during the 1976-1983 military dictatorship were not being prosecuted due to a series of amnesties and pardons, and due to the operation of statutes of limitations.

In 2012, Luis Muiña was convicted for crimes against humanity. During the military dictatorship, he had been in charge of a clandestine detention centre located inside a hospital, where people were kidnapped, tortured, and murdered. When he was sentenced, Muiña, demanded the application of Law 24.390 to the calculation of his jail time. Muiña, however, had not been in pre-trial detention before 2001, when the law in question was repealed—he was only detained in 2007. Thus, he invoked the application of this bill by reference to the principle of the most favourable criminal law, acknowledged in Article 2 of the Argentinean Criminal Code, and understood to be derived from the principle of legality.

The majority of the Court ruled in favour of Muiña, on two main grounds: first, a literal interpretation of Article 2 of the Criminal Code,[146] and

142 *APSAI* (n 141) Opinion of the Advocate General 8–9.
143 *Muiña, Luis* 340:549 (2017).
144 Law 24.390 (1994) on Pre-Trial Detention Periods.
145 *Jorge Luis Bronstein and others v Argentina*, Cases 11.205 et al, IACommHR, Report No 2/97 (11 March 1997) OEA/Ser.L/V/II.95 Doc 7 rev.
146 *Muiña* (n 143) [7].

second, the principle of *in dubio pro reo*.[147] However, the judges once again took pains (although with a quite superficial and brief reasoning) in trying to square their decision with the Court's caselaw concerning the relationship between domestic and international law. First, the Court stated that the IACtHR had not yet ruled on the application of the principle of the most favourable criminal law to continuing crimes, such as this one.[148] Second, it held that the fact that the crime in question was a crime against humanity did not exempt it from the application of this principle.[149] And, third, it grounded the principle in international law itself, making a reference to Article 24(2) of the Rome Statute,[150] and to the caselaw of the International Criminal Tribunal for the Former Yugoslavia.[151] The two dissenting judges also made important references to international law, basing their arguments to reject Muiña's claim on the state's obligation to prosecute and punish these crimes, and on 'the prohibition of sanctioning those responsible for crimes against humanity in an inadequate manner'.[152] Interestingly, instead of attempting an 'evasive avoidance'[153] of the application of international law (basing its claim on the domestic principle of legality), the Court engaged again in 'affirmative contestation', explicitly referring to international law, albeit with a controversial reading of its provisions.[154]

Although the more technical decision in the *Fontevecchia* case resonated most prominently only amongst those following the Court's practice, the *Muiña* decision created huge public outrage. A week after it was issued, tens of thousands populated the streets of Buenos Aires and other cities protesting the decision, and Congress passed an almost unanimous 'interpretive' law, stating that Law 24,390 was not applicable to crimes against humanity (Law 27,362).[155] In the following days, lower courts throughout the country refused to apply the *Muiña* precedent to other cases concerning crimes against humanity, invoking this new law, but also dissenting with the interpretation provided by the Supreme Court.

In 2018, the Court itself aligned with the 'interpretive' law, reversing the position it had taken in *Muiña*.[156] To justify this reversal, it incurred in a long

[147] ibid [9].
[148] ibid [13].
[149] ibid [15].
[150] Rome Statute of the International Criminal Court (17 July 1998, 1 July 2002) 2187 UNTS 3, art 24(2).
[151] *Muiña* (n 143) [16].
[152] ibid, Diss Op Lorenzetti [19]; Diss Op Maqueda [12].
[153] ILA Final Report (n 1) para 40.
[154] ibid para 58.
[155] Law 27.362 (on crimes against humanity, genocide, or war crimes).
[156] *Batalla, Rufino* 341:1768 (2018).

exploration of the role of legislatures and courts in a constitutional democracy, concluding that Congress holds the power of rendering 'authentic' interpretations of the laws, which courts must usually follow.[157] But the Court also referred to the substance of the interpretation, and used international law to argue that

> it is not unreasonable to agree with the legislator-interpreter on the point that the seriousness of the criminal behaviour classified as 'crimes against humanity, genocide or war crimes, according to domestic or international law' (…) constitutes sufficient grounds to sustain the impossibility of applying to its authors the ultraactivity of the '2x1' benefit in the requested computation.[158]

Based on these reasons, the Court decided that the benefits of Law 24,390 were not applicable to those responsible of crimes against humanity, coinciding with the interpretation made by Congress in Law 27,362.

F. Conclusion

It is hard to predict how much will the decisions in *Fontevecchia* and *Muiña* impact the relationship between the Argentinean legal order and international law, in the long term. On the one hand, it is clear that the Court has hinted towards a new, contestatory position towards international law, and the IACtHR specifically, reviving problematic *res judicata* and domestic supremacy arguments.[159] The Court had been building up an important caselaw on how international law, and especially international human rights law, is relevant in the domestic legal order to interpret and apply the rights afforded to individuals. This new attitude does not support, for instance, decisions like *Simón*,[160] where the Court validated the decision to resume judicial proceedings in cases dealing with crimes against humanity. This is problematic, as it is misaligned with the constitutional hierarchy established in Article 75(22) and, more broadly, with

[157] ibid [8]–[9].
[158] ibid [16].
[159] See Pinto (n 89) 251; cf Kunz (n 34) 1161; Chehtman (n 4) 18–19, for comments. Commenting on three other recent cases from Latin American states, Huneeus and Urueña observed that domestic courts have the potential to 'act as gatekeepers that blunt or entirely deflect the domestic impact of international law' and that high courts in the region have assumed a strong role in that respect. See Alexandra Huneeus and René Urueña, 'Treaty Exit and Latin America's Constitutional Courts' (2017) 111 AJIL Unbound 456.
[160] Simón (n 57); Bakker (n 57).

the constitutional mandate of acknowledging an international system for the protection of human rights. However, these hints from the Court may have been temporary and exceptional, as proven by later cases such as *Sala*, *APSAI*, or *Batalla*.[161] Tellingly, in none of the six cases in which the *Fontevecchia* sentence was so far cited did the majority of the Court recall the controversial holding of the decision.[162]

On the other hand, it is true that the Court has attempted to justify these restrictive arguments not only based on domestic provisions, but also on the need for deference to international law itself. In both *Fontevecchia* and *Muiña*, the Court attempted to provide alternative (even if problematic) interpretations of international law, rather than shunning its application altogether. Thus, if these decisions do foreshadow the dawn of a new contestatory era, it will be one different from that which existed between 1853 and 1992—one in which international law, and the decisions of international bodies, are not openly negated, but in any event acknowledged and contested. In other words, it seems like the incorporation of international law into the Argentinean legal order is sufficiently solidified in the minds of Argentinean lawyers and judges, and that the only alternative for the sceptics is to challenge every specific application of international law with proper international legal arguments.

In any event, what is certain is that, after the *Muiña* decision, judges will be under more intense public scrutiny, and that every decision related to international law will probably be hotly debated beyond the walls of the Palace of Justice. Hopefully, the important legacy of the Argentinean Supreme Court as a trailblazer in the protection of human rights will not be lost, and the Court will find the way to stand up to its institutional role and engage in a constructive, rather than destructive, dialogue with its international counterparts concerning the best way of assuring the protection of human rights in the region.

[161] See *Sala* (n 138); *APSAI* (n 142); *Batalla* (n 156).

[162] See *Sala* (n 138); *Schiffrin, Leopoldo Héctor* 340:257 (2017) [14]; *Milantic Trans SA c Ministerio de la Producción* 344:1857 (2021) [11]. The holding of the case was indeed cited in dissenting opinions: see *Molinos Río de la Plata SA c Dirección General Impositiva*, 344:2175 (2021), Dis Op Judge Rosenkrantz [19]; *Deutsche Rückversicherun* 342:1524 (2019), Dis Op Judge Rosatti [11]; Judge Maqueda cited his dissenting opinion in the *Fontevecchia* case in *Schiffrin, Leopoldo Héctor* 340:257 (2017), Sep Op Judge Maqueda [42]; *Romero Feris, Raúl Rolando*,CSJ 1260/2017/CS1 (2021), Sep Op Judge Maqueda [4].

8

Engagement of Canadian Courts with International Law

Gib van Ert

A. Introduction

There is, in broad terms, an attitude of openness to international law in Canadian legal doctrine. The constitutional and interpretive rules governing the reception of international law into the Canadian legal system tend to favour, and even promote, the alignment of Canada's domestic laws with its international obligations. The supposedly dualist arrangement of Canada's constitution in respect of international law is important in theory but does not usually pose much of an obstacle to the alignment of Canadian and international law in practice. The International Law Association (ILA) Study Group Final Report's observation[1] that the distinction between monism and dualism can be unhelpful, and that both approaches may be adopted within a given legal system, is pertinent in Canada's case. The main obstacle to greater coordination between Canada's domestic laws and its international obligations may not be the country's reception system but the unfamiliarity and inexperience of most Canadian lawyers and judges with the principles of international law and its domestic reception.[2] International law is not a required course in most law schools and only rarely features in Canadian litigation except in specialist areas, such as refugee law and constitutional challenges to legislation or executive action under the Canadian Charter of Rights and Freedoms.[3] Canadian judicial decisions that run afoul of international requirements can often be explained as a failure by counsel to brief the issue properly, and thus assist the

[1] ILA Study Group on Principles on the Engagement of Domestic Courts with International Law, 'Final Report: Mapping the Engagement of Domestic Courts with International Law' (Johannesburg, 2016) (ILA Final Report) para 18.
[2] See also ibid para 78.
[3] Enacted as Part I of Schedule B to the Canada Act 1982 (UK).

judge to reach an internationally-compliant result, rather than by any systemic obstacle to compliance or hostility to the principle of compliance itself.

Four features of the Canadian legal system govern domestic engagement with international law: the principle of judicial notice; the treaty implementation requirement; the incorporation of customary international law by Canadian common law; and the interpretive presumption of conformity with international law. The latter is, practically speaking, the most important. But an appreciation of all four is needed to understand the Canadian reception system and the engagement of Canadian courts with international law.

B. The Status of International Law in the Canadian Legal System

1. Judicial Notice of International Law

Canadian courts have regard to, or at least make reference to, relevant rules of international law with some frequency. Resort to international legal norms is more common in the Supreme Court of Canada and the federal courts than in superior courts, but all Canadian courts are called upon to consider matters touching upon international law occasionally, and they usually do so without hesitating about the propriety of this exercise. The conduct of Canadian courts in this regard is generally consistent with the common law evidentiary rule, affirmed by commentators but rarely stated in judicial decisions,[4] that courts take judicial notice of international law.[5] In particular, Canadian courts will have regard to Canadian treaty obligations for the purpose of interpreting domestic law, without requiring that the treaties themselves be proven in evidence or be made the subject of expert opinion evidence.[6] Lower court practice

[4] But now see *Nevsun Resources Ltd v Araya* 2020 SCC 5 [97]–[99].

[5] Eg, *The Scotia* 81 US (14 Wall) 170 (1871), 188; *The Ship 'North' v The King* (1906) 37 SCR 385 (Ca); *Halsbury's Laws of England* (4th edn, Butterworths 1973–2008) vol 17 [100], vol 18 [1403]; *Restatement (Third) of the Foreign Relations Law of the United States (Revised)* (American Law Institute 1987) s 113 comment b; Hersch Lauterpacht, 'Is International Law a Part of the Law of England' (1939) 25 Transactions of the Grotius Society 51, 59n(i); Ronald St John Macdonald et al (eds), *Canadian Perspectives on International Law and Organizations* (Toronto UP 1974) 113; Francis Bennion, *Statutory Interpretation: A Code* (4th edn, Butterworths 2002) s 270.

[6] Eg, *World Bank Group v Wallace* 2016 SCC 15, [2016] 1 SCR 207; *R v Appulonappa* 2015 SCC 59, [2015] 3 SCR 754; *B010 v Canada (Citizenship and Immigration)* 2015 SCC 58, [2015] 3 SCR 704 (*B010 v Canada*); *Thibodeau v Air Canada* 2014 SCC 67, [2014] 3 SCR 340; *Kazemi Estate v Islamic Republic of Iran* 2014 SCC 62, [2014] 3 SCR 176 (*Kazemi*); *Ezokola v Canada (Citizenship and Immigration)* 2013 SCC 40, [2013] 2 SCR 678 (*Ezokola*); *Ontario (Attorney General) v Fraser* 2011 SCC 20, [2011] 2 SCR 3; *Németh v Canada (Justice)* 2010 SCC 56, [2010] 3 SCR 281 (*Németh*); *Health Services and Support—Facilities Subsector Bargaining Assn v British Columbia* 2007 SCC 27, [2007] 2 SCR 391; *R v Hape* 2007

in recent years has sometimes seen litigants attempting to 'prove' controversial aspects of international law through expert opinions.[7] This practice in individual cases, however, has seemingly not affected the willingness of Canadian judges to resort to international law themselves, unassisted by experts or sometimes even by counsel, where necessary.

2. The Treaty Implementation Requirement

In Canadian practice, following the Westminster model, treaty-making is a prerogative of the Crown while law-making is the exclusive preserve of the federal and provincial legislatures.[8] It follows that a treaty to which Canada is party does not, itself, have direct force of law, but must be given such force through legislative enactment.[9] In principle, this rule is admirable as a democratic constraint on what has (in the past at least) been regarded by the courts as a largely unreviewable power of the executive to conduct foreign affairs.[10]

The implementation requirement can be harsh in cases where a treaty accords a right that domestic legislation does not. In *Francis v The Queen*,[11] an indigenous man imported goods from the United States without paying duty. He sought to rely on Article III of the 1794 US-UK Jay Treaty, which permitted indigenous persons to pass and repass into the territories of the parties 'with their own proper Goods and Effects of whatever nature' without paying duty.[12] The Jay Treaty's provisions had been implemented in Canadian law until the War of 1812 but had subsequently been repealed without re-enactment. In the absence of current implementing legislation, whatever right Francis may have had under the treaty was legally unenforceable. This is a striking example of

SCC 26, [2007] 2 SCR 292 (*Hape*); *GreCon Dimter inc v J R Normand inc* 2005 SCC 46, [2005] 2 SCR 401 (*GreCon Dimter*).

[7] See also Gib van Ert, *Using International Law in Canadian Courts* (2nd edn, Irwin Law 2008) 44–56.

[8] Charles-Emmanuel Côté, 'Federalism and Foreign Affairs in Canada' in Curtis A Bradley (ed), *The Oxford Handbook of Comparative Foreign Relations Law* (OUP 2019) 279–80.

[9] *Attorney-General for Canada v Attorney-General for Ontario ('Labour Conventions')* [1937] UKPC 6, [1937] AC 326 (PC) 347; *Kazemi* (n 6) [149]; see also Côté (n 8) 280–82.

[10] But see today *Canada (Prime Minister) v Khadr* 2010 SCC 3, [2010] 1 SCR 44; *Black v Canada (Prime Minister)* (2001) CanLII 8537 (ON CA); *Operation Dismantle v The Queen* [1985] 1 SCR 441. See also for a discussion Joanna Harrington, 'Scrutiny and Approval: The Role for Westminster-Style Parliaments in Treaty-Making' (2006) 55 ICLQ 121; Côté (n 8) 291–93.

[11] [1956] SCR 618, cited with approval in *Baker v Canada (Minister of Citizenship and Immigration)* [1999] 2 SCR 817 (*Baker*) [69].

[12] Treaty of Amity, Commerce and Navigation between Great Britain and the United States 8 Stat 116, (1841) I BSP 984.

how Canada's treaty dualism can result in what the ILA Final Report describes as affirmative avoidance.[13]

Canadian legislatures are free to give domestic legal effect to treaty obligations in any form they see fit.[14] The simplest way is to declare the treaty, or parts of it, as having force of law, in which case the treaty is almost always included in the enactment as a schedule.[15] Frequently, however, the treaty to be implemented is given force by restatement in Canadian legal terminology,[16] a sort of paraphrasing which may give rise to questions as to what extent the legislature intended to conform to the underlying treaty. When this mode of implementation is employed, the legislature will frequently signal its intention to implement the treaty in the name of the enactment[17] or its preamble.[18] But there is no such requirement, and at times Canadian legislatures will choose not to do so.[19] In such cases, resort to records of parliamentary proceedings (Hansard) or even government press releases may reveal what the legislation itself does not, namely that it was enacted to fulfil a Canadian treaty obligation. Additionally, while treaties are most often implemented by primary legislation, the legislature is free to delegate the power to implement treaties to a minister by means of secondary legislation, and this is sometimes done, particularly at the federal level.[20] In short, there is no required form of words, nor even a single fixed practice, governing how treaties are implemented by federal or provincial legislation.

There is, however, a rather strict rule about which legislative body—the federal Parliament or the provincial legislatures—is competent to implement a given treaty. While treaty-making is, in practice,[21] an exclusive power of the

[13] ILA Final Report (n 1) para 41.

[14] ibid para 51.

[15] Eg, Canada-Namibia Tax Convention Act 2013 SC 2013 c 27 s 2.

[16] Eg, Crimes Against Humanity and War Crimes Act SC 2000 c 24.

[17] Eg, ibid, the full title of which is 'An Act respecting genocide, crimes against humanity and war crimes and to implement the Rome Statute of the International Criminal Court, and to make consequential amendments to other Acts'.

[18] Eg, Quebec's Act respecting the civil aspects of international and interprovincial child abduction RSQ c A-23.01.

[19] Eg, s 269.1 of the (federal) Criminal Code RSC 1985 c C-46, which criminalizes the infliction of torture by officials as required by the Convention against Torture and Other Cruel, Inhuman or Degrading Treatment or Punishment (adopted 10 December 1984, entered into force 26 June 1987) 1465 UNTS 85.

[20] Eg, Canada Shipping Act 2001 SC 2001 c 26 s 35(1)(d), enabling the Governor in Council to make regulations implementing in whole or in part certain scheduled international conventions.

[21] Nothing in Canada's written constitution expressly accords treaty-making power to any of Canada's governments. This silence has permitted the government of Quebec to contend that the Crown prerogative of treaty-making is divided along the same lines as legislative jurisdiction under ss 91–92 of the Constitution Act 1867. As no court has ever squarely decided the point, the theoretical question survives. In practice, however, foreign States recognize the federal government in Ottawa as their proper interlocutor. This political fact—as much as, if not more than, any provision in the Canadian constitution—determines that treaty-making is a prerogative of the federal government. See generally

federal government, jurisdiction to implement Canadian treaty obligations is governed by the division of powers set out in ss 91–92 of the Constitution Act 1867.[22] Thus, where a treaty concerns subject matters falling within provincial jurisdiction, implementation is the responsibility of the country's ten provincial legislatures. In the case of far-reaching treaty regimes, implementing legislation may need to be enacted by both the federal and provincial legislatures. The complexity of this arrangement sometimes causes Canada to take longer than it (or other States) might like to ratify a treaty, but only rarely has it prevented Canada from ratifying a treaty at all.[23] Likewise, while federalism has the potential to be employed as a judicial avoidance technique,[24] it is very rare for a court to find both that Canada has a particular international obligation requiring domestic implementation and that no such implementation has occurred.

Much is made of the implementation requirement in the jurisprudence and commentary, and rightly so. But its importance can be overstated if considered in isolation from the principle of consistent interpretation. Though treaties have no direct legal effect in Canada without implementing legislation, the interpretive presumption of conformity with international law can give treaties an indirect, but still significant, legal effect in some cases.[25]

3. The Incorporation of Custom

While treaties are deemed as not having direct legal effect without legislative implementation, the same is not true of rules of customary international law. Again following English precedent, Canadian courts have affirmed that international customs are incorporated (or 'adopted') by Canadian common law (that is, by the judges) and therefore take direct effect in Canadian law without legislative implementation. This rule is described and applied in several decisions of the Supreme Court of Canada with reference to English authorities.

Stéphane Paquin (ed), *Les relations internationales du Québec depuis la Doctrine Gérin-Lajoie (1965-2005)* (Les Presses de l'Université Laval 2006). See also Côte (n 8) 284–88.

[22] See also Côté (n 8) 282.

[23] The most notorious example of a treaty that Canada could not ratify due to its inability to secure implementation by the provinces is the Convention on the Settlement of Investment Disputes between States and Nationals of Other States (adopted 18 March 1965, entered into force 14 October 1966) 575 UNTS 159 (ICSID Convention), to which Canada finally became a party on 1 November 2013 ([2013] Can TS No 24).

[24] ILA Final Report (n 1) paras 21, 41.

[25] See Section C(2).

Until the *Nevsun* case, the leading modern Canadian authority on the incorporation of customary international law was the decision of LeBel J for the majority of the Supreme Court of Canada in *Hape*.[26] The case's authority is somewhat lessened by the fact that LeBel J's discussion of incorporation was *obiter dictum* and sometimes at variance with the authorities he purported to rely upon. Despite these limitations, LeBel J's judgment affirms the existence and continuing vitality of the incorporation doctrine in Canadian law, citing leading Canadian[27] and English[28] cases approvingly and noting that while the Supreme Court of Canada had not, in recent cases, 'applied or discussed the doctrine . . . when it had the opportunity to do so', there was nevertheless 'a long line of cases in which the Court has either formally accepted it or at least applied it'.[29] LeBel J summarizes the incorporation doctrine as follows:

> In my view, following the common law tradition, it appears that the doctrine of adoption operates in Canada such that prohibitive rules of customary international law should be incorporated into domestic law in the absence of conflicting legislation. The automatic incorporation of such rules is justified on the basis that international custom, as the law of nations, is also the law of Canada unless, in a valid exercise of its sovereignty, Canada declares that its law is to the contrary. Parliamentary sovereignty dictates that a legislature may violate international law, but that it must do so expressly. Absent an express derogation, the courts may look to prohibitive rules of customary international law to aid in the interpretation of Canadian law and the development of the common law.[30]

Inasmuch as this passage suggests that courts have a discretion to incorporate customary norms or not, it is inconsistent with the 'common law tradition' LeBel J relies upon. *Trendtex Trading*, *Re Foreign Legations* and the other authorities that LeBel J approves clearly require courts, upon satisfying themselves that a customary rule exists in international law and is not ousted by

[26] See n 6.
[27] *The Ship 'North'* (n 5); *Reference as to Powers to Levy Rates on Foreign Legations and High Commissioners' Residences* [1943] SCR 208; *Reference as to Whether Members of the Military or Naval Forces of the United States of America are Exempt from Criminal Proceedings in Canadian Criminal Courts* [1943] SCR 483; *Saint John (Municipality of) v Fraser-Brace Overseas Corp* [1958] SCR 263; *Bouzari v Islamic Republic of Iran* (2004) CanLII (871) (ON CA) (*Bouzari*); *Mack v Canada (Attorney General)* (2002) CanLII 45062 (ON CA).
[28] *Trendtex Trading Corp v Central Bank of Nigeria* [1977] 1 QB 529 (EWCA).
[29] *Hape* (n 6) [38]–[39].
[30] *Hape* (n 6) [39].

domestic legislation, to give effect to that rule. Similarly, the incorporation doctrine has not previously been treated as an interpretive aid, as LeBel J suggests, but as determinative of the common law on the point in issue. One may wonder whether these statements were attempts by LeBel J to introduce new avoidance or 'blunting' techniques[31] into the Canadian incorporation doctrine.

While these aspects of LeBel J's depiction of incorporation may be criticized, his description of the doctrine as applying to 'prohibitive', as opposed to permissive, custom is admirably subtle. Where a customary international norm permits, without requiring States to take some course of action, the incorporation doctrine does not confide the decision-making power in the judge.[32] To do so would implicate the courts in foreign policy-making (the power of the executive) and law-making (the power of the legislature). LeBel J also rightly notes that customary international law may only be incorporated by the courts where it is not inconsistent with domestic legislation. Like other common law rules, custom may be curtailed, abolished or pre-empted by legislative enactment. LeBel J later applied this principle in *Kazemi Estate v Islamic Republic of Iran*, in which the appellant argued that customary international law had developed an exception to the State immunity doctrine permitting him to sue Iran before Canadian courts for the torture and killing of his mother. LeBel J disagreed that such an exception existed but added:

> Even if an exception to state immunity in civil proceedings for acts of torture had reached the status of a customary rule of international law … such an exception could not be adopted as a common law exception to s. 3(1) of the [*State Immunity Act*] as it would be in clear conflict with [that Act].[33]

The authority of *Hape* on the adoption of customary international law by the common law is at once affirmed and surpassed by the more recent decision of the Supreme Court of Canada in *Nevsun*, in which Abella J for the majority affirmed that 'Canada has long followed the conventional path of automatically incorporating customary international law into domestic law via the doctrine of adoption, making it part of the common law of Canada in the absence of conflicting legislation'.[34] The question in *Nevsun* was whether a pleading

[31] As described in the ILA Final Report (n 1) para 21.

[32] See, in English law, *R v Keyn* (1876) 2 Ex D 63 (Ct Crim Cas Res); *R v Jones* [2006] UKHL 16, (2007) 1 AC 136. See also *Kazemi* (n 6) [61].

[33] *Kazemi* (n 6) [61].

[34] *Nevsun* (n 5) [90].

should be struck for seeking damages for alleged breaches of customary international law norms against slavery, forced labour, cruelty, and crimes against humanity. The majority declined to do so, finding that it was not 'plain and obvious' that such claims had no reasonable likelihood of success given the incorporation doctrine. Notably, the Supreme Court split 5-4, with two sets of reasons expressing reservations about the breadth of the majority's affirmation of the incorporation doctrine.

Despite this, the existence of the incorporation doctrine must be regarded as settled in Canada today. The practical effect of the doctrine, however, is limited. For a Canadian court to have any cause to consider the incorporation question, a litigant must posit a rule of customary international law that is both relevant to the dispute and not already reflected in Canadian legislation or common law. Having identified such a norm, the litigant must satisfy the court that it has attained customary status in international law, and that its incorporation by Canadian common law is not prevented by inconsistent domestic legislation. Of these requirements, the first—identifying a customary norm of contemporary international law relevant to domestic adjudication and not already finding expression in Canadian law—may be the most difficult. So long as treaty-making continues to be the predominant mode of international law-making, particularly with regard to States' internal affairs, the opportunities for courts to give effect to the incorporation doctrine seem likely to diminish.[35]

4. The Presumption of Conformity with International Law

The last feature of Canadian law to be considered when discussing how the Canadian legal system engages with international law is the rule requiring domestic law to be interpreted, where possible, in conformity with the State's international obligations. The presumption is discussed in Section C(1)(b).

[35] If this prediction proves wrong, it may be due to the effect in Canadian law of the United Nations Declaration on the Rights of Indigenous Peoples, UNGA Res 61/295 (2 October 2007) A/RES/61/295. It very much remains to be seen whether the Declaration will be recognized as effective in Canadian law and, if so, whether that happens through implementing legislation, the incorporation doctrine, conforming interpretation, or a combination of such approaches.

C. Engagement with International Law in Canadian Practice

1. Canadian Alignment Techniques

The alignment of Canadian and international legal norms occurs both at the legislative level, through implementation by the federal and provincial legislatures of treaty obligations incurred by the federal executive, and at the judicial level, through incorporation of customary norms (rarely) and interpretation of domestic law in conformity with international legal requirements (much more frequently).

a. Legislative alignment

Canadian legislative bodies are charged with giving direct effect to treaty obligations incurred by the federal executive by means of implementing legislation.[36] The simplest case of legislative alignment of Canadian and international law is a federal or provincial enactment which expressly gives an international norm force of law domestically. As noted, other forms of implementation also exist and are frequently resorted to.

To describe this form of alignment as legislative is constitutionally and formally correct. But this description also simplifies the process by which Canadian treaty obligations are given legal effect domestically through legislation. In practice, the federal government will not incur treaty obligations before determining what implementing legislation, if any, will be required to ensure Canada's ability to perform its obligations.[37] Often no new legislation is required, either because the treaty operates purely on the State-to-State level with no consequences for Canada's domestic law (the usual case), or because Canada's existing legislation is deemed adequate to discharge the new obligations.[38] If, however, the federal executive considers that new legislation will be needed to harmonize Canadian law with the proposed treaty, this may inform its decision whether to incur the proposed obligation and, if so, when. Where the required implementing legislation is within federal jurisdiction, the federal executive can draft the legislation and sponsor it as a government bill in

[36] See Section B(2).

[37] Maurice Copithorne, 'National Treaty Law and Practice: Canada' in Duncan Hollis et al (eds), *National Treaty Law and Practice: Dedicated to the Memory of Monroe Leigh* (ASIL 2005) 96.

[38] See Elisabeth Eid and Hoori Hamboyan, 'Implementation by Canada of Its International Human Rights Treaty Obligations: Making Sense Out of the Nonsensical' in Oonagh Fitzgerald (ed), *The Globalized Rule of Law: Relationships between International and Domestic Law* (Irwin Law 2006), especially 455–59.

Parliament without consulting the provinces or other stakeholders. If, however, the necessary implementing legislation falls within provincial jurisdiction, the federal executive must convince the ten provincial executives of the merits of the proposed treaty and the desirability of their causing the provincial legislatures to enact new treaty-compliant laws in their jurisdictions. Thus while the task of aligning domestic laws with Canadian treaty obligations is in theory a legislative function, in practice it is led by the federal executive and will, in some cases, involve the provincial executives as well.

b. Judicial alignment

As we have seen, Canadian courts recognize the doctrine of incorporation, whereby customary international law is aligned with the common law through judicial, rather than legislative, action.[39] But the importance of this mechanism must not be overstated. Beyond the issues discussed in Section B(3), in certain cases where occasion has indeed arisen for application of the doctrine, Canadian courts have sometimes failed to see it.[40]

It is through the interpretive presumption of conformity with international law that Canadian courts have revealed themselves as powerful agents of alignment with international law. The Supreme Court of Canada has repeatedly endorsed and applied this principle of consistent interpretation in the last twenty-five years, in a variety of contexts.

The leading Canadian judicial statement about the presumption is found (again) in the judgment of LeBel J for the majority in *Hape*:

> The presumption of conformity is based on the rule of judicial policy that, as a matter of law, courts will strive to avoid constructions of domestic law pursuant to which the state would be in violation of its international obligations, unless the wording of the statute clearly compels that result. R. Sullivan, *Sullivan and Driedger on the Construction of Statutes* (4th ed. 2002), at p. 422, explains that the presumption has two aspects. First, the legislature is presumed to act in compliance with Canada's obligations as a signatory of international treaties and as a member of the international community. In deciding between possible interpretations, courts will avoid a construction that

[39] Section B(3).

[40] The *Hape* court (n 6) noted this itself at [38], citing *Gouvernement de la République démocratique du Congo v Venne* [1971] SCR 997, *Reference re Newfoundland Continental Shelf* [1984] 1 SCR 86, *Reference re Secession of Quebec* [1998] 2 SCR 217, and *Suresh v Canada (Minister of Citizenship and Immigration)* 2002 SCC 1, [2002] 1 SCR 3 (*Suresh*). Yet LaForest J for the majority of the court in *Re Canada Labour Code* [1992] 2 SCR 50 appears to have supported the doctrine, which was also applied in *Re Regina and Palacios* (1984) CanLII 1870 (ON CA) on a question of diplomatic immunity not covered by treaty.

> would place Canada in breach of those obligations. The second aspect is that the legislature is presumed to comply with the values and principles of customary and conventional international law. Those values and principles form part of the context in which statutes are enacted, and courts will therefore prefer a construction that reflects them. The presumption is rebuttable, however. Parliamentary sovereignty requires courts to give effect to a statute that demonstrates an unequivocal legislative intent to default on an international obligation.[41]

Notably, LeBel J describes the presumption as 'judicial policy'—a phrase that attempts to distance the doctrine from the older notion that this and other interpretive presumptions are founded on legislative intent. LeBel J also affirms that the presumption is rebuttable, yet he sets the bar very high and emphasizes that to find the presumption rebutted in a given case may result in a 'violation' or 'default' of Canada's international obligations.[42] In a subsequent case, *Németh*, the Court may have enunciated a slightly lower standard than 'unequivocal legislative intent to default on an international obligation', saying that where the provision to be interpreted is 'unambiguous', rather than 'unequivocal', it must be given effect.[43] Either way, it seems clear that the presumption is not easily rebutted.

Chief Justice McLachlin for the unanimous Supreme Court of Canada recently elaborated further on the place of the presumption of conformity in Canadian statutory interpretation. Repeating *Hape*'s statement that the values and principles of international law 'form part of the context in which Canadian laws are enacted', she added: 'This follows from the fact that to interpret a Canadian law in a way that conflicts with Canada's international obligations risks incursion by the courts in the executive's conduct of foreign affairs and censure under international law.' The Chief Justice continued:

> In keeping with the international context in which Canadian legislation is enacted, this Court has repeatedly endorsed and applied the interpretive presumption that legislation conforms with the state's international obligations.... This interpretive presumption is not peculiar to Canada. It is a feature of legal interpretation around the world.[44]

[41] *Hape* (n 6) [53].
[42] See ILA Final Report (n 1) para 23.
[43] *Németh* (n 6) [35].
[44] *B010 v Canada* (n 6) [47]–[48], citing André Nollkaemper, *National Courts and the International Rule of Law* (OUP 2011). See also ILA Final Report (n 1) para 23 with references

The role of international legal considerations as a potential constraint on administrative decision makers was affirmed in *Canada (Minister of Citizenship and Immigration) v Vavilov*. The majority of the Supreme Court of Canada set aside as unreasonable a decision of the Registrar of Citizenship to cancel Vavilov's certificate of citizenship on the basis that his parents were Russian spies when he was born in Toronto. The majority affirmed the presumption of conformity with international law and criticized the decision-maker's failure to refer to the relevant international law in interpreting the applicable legislative provisions.[45]

The potentially decisive impact of Canada's international obligations on domestic litigation, by means of the presumption of conformity, is particularly illustrated in three judgments of the Supreme Court of Canada.[46] In *GreCon Dimter*,[47] a procedural question arose under the Quebec Civil Code, which provided on the one hand that the Quebec court had jurisdiction to hear an action in warranty so long as it had jurisdiction over the principal action, and on the other hand that the Quebec court lacked jurisdiction where the parties had adopted a choice of forum or arbitration clause. In the case at bar, both statements were true: the principal action was between two Quebec companies over which the Quebec court undoubtedly had jurisdiction, and the action in warranty involved a German company whose contract with the Quebec company directed the parties to a German court in the event of a dispute. The courts below held that the Quebec courts had jurisdiction over the action in warranty despite the choice of forum clause. LeBel J for the Supreme Court of Canada reversed, finding that the Civil Code provision requiring the Quebec court to defer to foreign courts must take precedence. LeBel J reached this conclusion by invoking the presumption of conformity,[48] the international obligation at issue being Article II(3) of the New York Convention.[49]

The presumption of conformity was again decisive in *USA and Canada (Minister of Justice) v Anekwu*.[50] The US had requested Anekwu's extradition. He challenged the validity of Canada's committal and surrender orders on the basis that the Canadian-gathered evidence in support of his extradition request was hearsay. Anekwu contended that s 32(2) of the federal Extradition

[45] 2019 SCC 65 (*Vavilov*) [114], [178]–[182].

[46] See also, eg, *Ordon Estate v Grail* [1998] 3 SCR 437; *Baker* (n 10); *Canadian Foundation for Children, Youth and the Law v Canada (Attorney General)* 2004 SCC 4, [2004] 1 SCR 76.

[47] See n 5.

[48] *GreCon Dimter* (n 5) [39].

[49] While that provision is addressed to arbitration clauses rather than choice of forum clauses, the Quebec Civil Code (SQ 1991 c 64) provision (art 3148(2)) applied to both.

[50] *USA and Canada (Minister of Justice) v Anekwu* 2009 SCC 41, [2009] 3 SCR 3 (*Anekwu*).

Act required that Canadian-gathered evidence in support of an extradition request must satisfy the rules of evidence under Canadian law, including the rule against hearsay. Anekwu lost at first instance but succeeded on appeal. Charron J for the Supreme Court of Canada allowed the further appeal. While acknowledging that s 32(2), read in isolation, was unambiguous and therefore supported Anekwu's position (the rule against hearsay being undoubtedly a rule of evidence under Canadian law), the provision had to be interpreted in conformity with Canada's international extradition obligations. 'Adherence to the strictures of the hearsay rule in the extradition context ... would disable Canada from complying with its international obligations in a prompt and efficient manner...', observed Charron J. 'Hence, such an interpretation should be avoided.'[51]

The third case is *Thibodeau*.[52] French-speaking passengers of Air Canada complained to the Office of the Commissioner of Official Languages that the airline had failed to offer services in French in breach of Canada's Official Languages Act[53]. The trial judge awarded damages despite the limited liability established by the Montreal Convention, as implemented in federal law by the Carriage By Air Act.[54] The Federal Court of Appeal overturned, holding that the Montreal Convention precluded the award of damages. In dismissing the appeal, Cromwell J for the majority of the Supreme Court of Canada invoked the presumption of conformity with international law to find that the Official Languages Act's remedial provision 'cannot—and should not—be read as authorizing Canadian courts to depart from Canada's international legal obligations under the *Montreal Convention*'.[55]

The Supreme Court of Canada's determination to reach internationally-compliant results has gone so far as to even cause it to depart from its own precedent—an illustration of what the Final Report describes as overriding alignment.[56] In *Mugesera v Canada (Minister of Citizenship and Immigration)*,[57] a deportation case involving an alleged Rwandan *génocidaire*, the court considered the elements of a crime against humanity—a question it had first considered in the *Finta* case of 1994.[58] In the decade between *Finta* and *Mugesera*, the international Criminal Tribunals for the former Yugoslavia and Rwanda

[51] ibid [5]–[6].
[52] See n 5.
[53] RSC 1985 c 31 (4th Supp).
[54] RSC 1985 c C-26.
[55] *Thibodeau* (n 5) [6]; see also [113].
[56] ILA Final Report (n 1) paras 45–46.
[57] 2005 SCC 40, [2005] 2 SCR 100 (*Mugesera*).
[58] *R v Finta* [1994] 1 SCR 701 (*Finta*).

had developed what the court called 'a vast body of international jurisprudence'.[59] Having recalled the 'importance of interpreting domestic law in a manner that accords with the principles of customary international law and with Canada's treaty obligations',[60] the Court observed,

> These tribunals have generated a unique body of authority which cogently reviews the sources, evolution and application of customary international law. Though the decisions of the ICTY and the ICTR are not binding upon this Court, the expertise of these tribunals and the authority in respect of customary international law with which they are vested suggest that their findings should not be disregarded lightly by Canadian courts applying domestic legislative provisions, such as ss. 7(3.76) and 7(3.77) of the *Criminal Code*, which expressly incorporate customary international law. Therefore, to the extent that *Finta* is in need of clarification and does not accord with the jurisprudence of the ICTY and the ICTR, it warrants reconsideration.[61]

After considering *Prosecutor v Akayesu*[62] and other decisions on point, the Court declared:

> ... the judgment of our Court in *Finta* appears to be inconsistent with the recent jurisprudence of the ICTR and the ICTY. The close relationship between our domestic law and international law on this question mandates that the nature and definition of crimes against humanity should be closely aligned with the jurisprudence of the international criminal courts.
>
> We see no reason to depart from the well-reasoned and persuasive findings of the ICTY and the ICTR on the question of discriminatory intent. Insofar as *Finta* suggested that discriminatory intent was required for all crimes against humanity (see *Finta*, at p. 813), it should no longer be followed on this point.[63]

The Court concluded its judgment with this ringing endorsement of Canadian judicial compliance with international law:

> In the face of certain unspeakable tragedies, the community of nations must provide a unified response. Crimes against humanity fall within this category.

59 *Mugesera* (n 53) [126].
60 ibid [82].
61 ibid [126].
62 Case No ICTR-96-4-A (Appeals Chamber), 1 June 2001.
63 *Mugesera* (n 57) [143]–[44].

> The interpretation and application of Canadian provisions regarding crimes against humanity must therefore accord with international law. Our nation's deeply held commitment to individual human dignity, freedom and fundamental rights requires nothing less.[64]

In another instance of overriding alignment, *Ezokola,* the Supreme Court of Canada again recast Canadian jurisprudence in the light of international law.[65] Ezokola, a Congolese diplomat to the United Nations in New York, sought asylum in Canada for himself and his family in January 2008 claiming he could no longer work for the Kabila government and that he would be regarded as a traitor for having resigned. Canada's Refugee Protection Division found that Ezokola was excluded from refugee protection under Article 1F(a) of the Refugee Convention on the ground of his supposed complicity in crimes against humanity committed by the Congolese government he had served. The Federal Court allowed Ezokola's application for judicial review on the ground that criminal responsibility for crimes against humanity requires personal participation in the crime alleged or personal control over the events leading to the crime alleged. The Federal Court of Appeal disagreed and restored the Division's decision, holding that a senior government official could be complicit in the crimes of his or her government simply by remaining in his or her position without protest and by continuing to defend the government's interests despite knowledge of the government's crimes. The Supreme Court allowed the appeal. It called the Federal Court of Appeal's approach 'guilt by association' and expressly departed from a longstanding Federal Court of Appeal precedent.[66] It did so to 'rein in the Canadian approach to complicity under art. 1F(a)' and bring Canadian law in line with the Refugee Convention,[67] the international law to which Article 1F(a) expressly refers, and the approach to complicity taken by other States parties.[68] Lebel and Fish JJ, for the court, proceeded to review at length the applicable international legal norms, including the Vienna Convention on the Law of Treaties,[69] the Refugee Convention, and the Rome Statute.[70]

[64] ibid [173].
[65] See n 5.
[66] *Ramirez v Canada (Minister of Employment and Immigration)* [1992] 2 FC 306, (1992) CanLII 8540 (FCA).
[67] Convention relating to the Status of Refugees (adopted 28 July 1951, entered into force 22 April 1954) 189 UNTS 137.
[68] *Ezokola* (n 5) [30].
[69] (adopted 23 May 1969, entered into force 27 January 1980) 1155 UNTS 331.
[70] Rome Statute of the International Criminal Court (adopted 17 July 1998, entered into force 1 July 2002) 2187 UNTS 3. *Ezokola* (n 5) [31]–[36], [42]–[77].

A third instance of overriding alignment is *Office of the Children's Lawyer v Balev*, in which the Supreme Court of Canada departed from the prevailing Canadian approach to determining the habitual residence of children under the Hague Child Abduction Convention. It adopted the so-called hybrid approach instead of the parental intention approach employed to that point in Ontario and other Canadian jurisdictions. McLachin CJ explained that the hybrid approach is now favoured in European and Australasian jurisdictions, that the 'aim of treaties like the Hague Convention is to establish uniform practices in the adhering countries', and, therefore, the court 'should prefer the interpretation that has gained the most support in other courts and will therefore best ensure uniformity of state practice across Hague Convention jurisdictions, unless there are strong reasons not to do so'.[71]

Such corrective measures, revising Canadian jurisprudence to ensure alignment with international requirements, are not the sole prerogative of the Supreme Court of Canada. In *Strugarova v Air France*, a judge of the Ontario Superior Court of Justice re-opened his previous decision to review its correctness on a point of international aviation law.[72] Roberts J found that re-opening the defendants' motion was 'necessary to ensure that there is consistency and reliability in the decisions interpreting and applying the *Montreal Convention* and the *Warsaw Convention*' given the 'fundamental importance that there be consistency in interpreting the provisions of the Convention[s] from one country to another'.[73] Roberts J added that,

> As other jurisdictions may be relying on my February 2, 2009 Order, if that decision was incorrectly decided because the Montreal Convention should be applied to the present case, in order to preserve the integrity of the judicial process and as a matter of judicial principle, it is important that the Air France defendants' motion be re-opened and that all relevant principles be considered so that there is a reliable body of case law interpreting the *Warsaw Convention* and the *Montreal Convention*.[74]

c. Absence of other alignment techniques

A notable aspect of Canadian courts' engagement with international law is that certain alignment techniques known to other common law jurisdictions have

[71] *Office of the Children's Lawyer v Balev* 2018 SCC 16, [2018] 1 SCR 398 [49]; see also [33].
[72] 2009 CanLII 40552 (ON SC) (*Strugarova*).
[73] ibid [14].
[74] ibid [15].

gained no traction here. Canadian courts have generally not followed the High Court of Australia's decision in *Minister for Immigration and Ethnic Affairs v Teoh*,[75] or similar authorities,[76] in finding that ratification by the State of an international agreement gives rise to enforceable expectations that the government will act in conformity with it. This is not to say that international law has no place in controlling statutory discretions in Canadian law,[77] but the doctrine of legitimate expectations is not a recognized alignment technique in Canada. Similarly, the principle of legality, as enunciated in English case law in connection with human rights issues in particular, has not been taken up by Canadian courts.[78]

2. Canadian Avoidance Practices

a. Constitutional avoidance

Avoidance of international legal obligations is also, on occasion, a feature of the Canadian engagement with international law. Two general forms of avoidance can be observed: avoidance arising from the State's constitutional structure and avoidance practices adopted by the judiciary.

Two basic features of Canada's constitutional structure can serve as grounds to avoid performance of Canada's treaty-derived international obligations: the separation of treaty-making and law-making powers between the Crown and the legislatures, respectively, and the division of legislative powers between the federal and provincial legislatures. While the federal executive is recognized in Canadian law as competent to incur treaty obligations on behalf of the State, such obligations must be implemented by legislation before taking direct legal effect internally.[79] Hence, Canada may incur an obligation under an international convention that requires internal performance, and then find itself unable to secure such performance. While rare, such failures are not unheard of. The most notorious example is Canada's adhesion to, failure to perform and subsequent withdrawal from the Kyoto Protocol.[80] In that case a Liberal federal government signed the treaty in 1998 and ratified it in 2002. The

[75] (1995) 183 CLR 273 (HCA).

[76] Eg *Tavita v Minister of Immigration* [1994] 2 NZLR 257; *R v Secretary of State for the Home Department, ex p Ahemed* [1999] Imm LR 22 (EWCA); *Thomas v Baptiste* [1999] UKPC 13, [2000] 2 AC 1 (PC).

[77] See *Baker* (n 10) and *Vavilov* (n 45).

[78] See Shaheed Fatima in this volume, Section B(1).

[79] Section B(2).

[80] (1997) 37 ILM 32.

Liberals then lost the 2006 federal general election and were replaced by a minority Conservative government which opposed the Kyoto Protocol. In 2007 Parliament enacted legislation purporting to implement the protocol, over the governing party's opposition.[81] The Conservative government largely disregarded this legislation, and an effort to enforce it through the courts failed.[82] The Conservatives returned to power with a majority in 2011, and Parliament repealed the failed implementing legislation in 2012. Canada withdrew from the protocol later that year.

The Kyoto Protocol debacle is an outlier. More commonly, international law avoidance takes place judicially. Three examples are discussed below. Each is best described as evasive avoidance (in the helpful terminology of the Final Report).[83] Notably, in Canadian courts' engagement with international law, little trace of affirmative avoidance techniques, such as the act of State and political question doctrines, can be found. The act of State doctrine, in particular, was considered at length and rejected by the Supreme Court of Canada in *Nevsun*.[84] Instead of resorting to established techniques or doctrines, Canadian courts looking to avoid the application or consideration of an international legal point tend to do so in an ad hoc fashion.

b. Judicial avoidance

i. Charter obscurantism

The first avoidance practice will be called 'Charter obscurantism', meaning the long line of Supreme Court of Canada jurisprudence vacillating about whether the principle of consistent interpretation applies to Canada's constitutionally-entrenched human rights instrument, the Charter. In *Re Public Service Employee Relations Act (Alberta)*,[85] Dickson CJ (dissenting) enunciated two rather different approaches to the interpretive value of international human rights law in Charter cases. One approach depicted international norms as 'relevant and persuasive sources for interpretation of the *Charter*'s provisions',[86] comparable to the jurisprudence of United States courts under the American Bill of Rights. The second approach was notably stronger. Dickson CJ declared his belief that 'the *Charter* should generally be presumed to provide protection at least as great as that afforded by similar provisions in international human

[81] Kyoto Protocol Implementation Act SC 2007 c 30.
[82] See *Friends of the Earth v Canada (Governor in Council)* 2009 FCA 297 (CanLII).
[83] ILA Final Report (n 1) para 40.
[84] *Nevsun* (n 4) [27]–[59].
[85] [1987] 1 SCR 313 (*PSERA*).
[86] ibid 348.

rights documents which Canada has ratified'—an interpretive rule greatly resembling the presumption of conformity with international law.[87] As Dickson CJ was dissenting, neither of his two dicta resolved the question of what value, if any, international law had in Charter interpretation. Charter jurisprudence since has been, in the words of Stephen Toope, 'fluid, not to say unprincipled' on the point.[88] At the same time as the Supreme Court of Canada was clearly and consistently advancing the presumption of conformity with international law as a strong interpretive rule for every other aspect of Canadian law, it repeatedly declined to endorse it as a rule of Charter interpretation.

Recent Supreme Court of Canada decisions have seen it come round to adopting Dickson CJ's presumption-like approach. In two 2007 decisions,[89] the majority of the court approved Dickson CJ's dictum that the Charter should generally be presumed to provide protection at least as great as afforded by similar Canadian human rights obligations under international law. In *Divito v Canada (Public Safety and Emergency Preparedness)*[90] the court unanimously adopted Dickson CJ's dictum and observed that mobility rights under Charter s 6(1) should be 'interpreted in a way that is consistent with the broad protection under international law'.[91] Yet in 2014's *Kazemi* LeBel J appeared to backtrack from the presumptive approach, saying instead that 'the Charter will *often be understood* to provide protection at least as great as that afforded by similar provisions in international human rights documents to which Canada is a party'.[92] The majority of the court nevertheless endorsed Dickson CJ's presumption-like approach to Charter interpretation only three months later in *Saskatchewan Federation of Labour v Saskatchewan*,[93] without objection from the dissent. The court endorsed this approach in another two cases in 2017.[94]

Most recently, in *9147-0732 Québec inc*,[95] the majority of the Supreme Court of Canada at once affirmed the presumption-like approach to Charter interpretation and introduced what may prove to be a new form of obscurantism into Charter jurisprudence. Justice Brown and Rowe expressly approved

[87] ibid 349.

[88] Stephen J Toope, 'Keynote Address: Canada and International Law' in *The Impact of International Law on the Practice of Law in Canada: Proceedings of the 27th Annual Conference of the Canadian Council on International Law* (Kluwer 1999) 36. See also van Ert (n 6) 332–51.

[89] *Hape* (n 5) [55]–[56]; *Health Services and Support* (n 5) [70].

[90] 2013 SCC 47, [2013] 3 SCR 157 (*Divito v Canada*) [22]–[27].

[91] ibid.

[92] *Kazemi* (n 5) [150] (emphasis added).

[93] 2015 SCC 4, [2015] 1 SCR 245 [64]–[65].

[94] *India v Badesha* 2017 SCC 44, [2017] 2 SCR 127 [38]; *Ktunaxa Nation v British Columbia (Forests, Lands and Natural Resource Operations)* 2017 SCC 54, [2017] 2 SCR 386 [65].

[95] *Quebec (Attorney General) v 9147-0732 Québec inc* 2020 SCC 32 (*9147*).

Dickson CJ's dictum, equating it with the presumption of conformity that applies in non-Charter contexts.[96] Yet they also described the role of international law in Charter cases as 'to support or confirm an interpretation' of Charter rights arrived at through the applicable domestic interpretation principles and not 'to define the scope of Charter rights'.[97] This limitation on international law's application in Charter cases does not appear in prior cases.

ii. Wilful blindness or legal error

A second avoidance practice of Canadian courts in international law cases has been simply to disregard international law's requirements.[98] Whether this is done by accident or design is sometimes difficult to know. The most egregious instance of this is *Suresh*,[99] in which the Supreme Court of Canada effectively ignored Canada's obligation under Article 3(1) of the UN Convention against Torture not to return foreign nationals to their home States where they face a substantial risk of torture upon their return. Instead of giving effect to the clear international prohibition of non-refoulement, the court entered into futile speculations as to whether the prohibition of torture was *jus cogens*, found that torture was only 'an emerging peremptory norm of international law which cannot be easily derogated from', and concluded that Canada might therefore deport a refugee to torture without violating the Charter.[100]

iii. Ambiguity

The requirement articulated by English courts[101] that some ambiguity has to exist on the face of a legislative enactment before the principle of consistent interpretation is applied was effectively abandoned by the Supreme Court of Canada in *National Corn Growers v Canadian Import Tribunal*.[102] Gonthier J for the majority held that courts may resort to international agreements at the preliminary stage of the interpretive exercise to determine whether a latent ambiguity exists in the legislation despite its facial clarity.[103] The court was clearer still in *Crown Forest Industries Ltd v Canada*, stating that 'a court may refer to extrinsic materials which form part of the legal context (these include accepted model conventions and official commentaries thereon) without the need first

[96] ibid [31].
[97] ibid [22], [28].
[98] ILA Final Report (n 1) para 40.
[99] See n 40.
[100] *Suresh* (n 40) [59]–[79].
[101] Eg, *Salomon v Customs and Excise Commissioners* [1967] 2 QB 116, [1966] 3 All ER 871. See also Shaheed Fatima in this volume.
[102] [1990] 2 SCR 1324 (*National Corn Growers*).
[103] ibid 1372–73.

to find an ambiguity before turning to such materials.'[104] Despite these (and other)[105] pronouncements, lower courts do at times insist that they cannot properly have regard to international law because the legislation before them is unambiguous.[106] In some cases this practice appears to be an affirmative avoidance technique, or even an instance of negatory contestation.[107] In other cases, however, courts seem to be simply unaware of the controlling Supreme Court authorities.

The difficulty lies in distinguishing two similar-sounding, but quite different, propositions. The claim, '[a] statute that is unambiguously contrary to international law must be followed' is the unassailable conclusion to be drawn from the doctrine of parliamentary sovereignty. The claim, '[a] statute that is unambiguous must be given effect even if it is contrary to international law', is contrary to controlling Supreme Court precedents because it sets up ambiguity on the face of the statute as a prerequisite to considering the international law context of the enactment. The clear thrust of Supreme Court authority is that application of the presumption of conformity does not depend on an initial judicial determination that the statute, read without consideration of international law, is somehow ambiguous.

D. Conclusion

Canada's engagement with international law tends to favour an alignment posture over avoidance strategies. Contestation (in both the affirmative and negatory forms identified in the Final Report) is rare. Opportunities for international law avoidance are offered by Canada's generally dualist approach to treaties and the requirements of federalism. Yet, avoidance itself is not a prominent feature of Canadian jurisprudence, particularly when compared to the Supreme Court of Canada's strong espousal of the principle of consistent interpretation of domestic law with the State's international obligations. That said, the Supreme Court seems less committed to consistent interpretation in the context of constitutional protection of human rights under the Canadian

[104] [1995] 2 SCR 802 [44].

[105] Eg, *Hape* (n 5) [53]; *B010 v Canada* (n 5) [47]–[48]; *Society of Composers, Authors and Music Publishers of Canada v Entertainment Software Association* 2022 SCC 30 [45].

[106] This tendency is especially pronounced in the jurisprudence of the Federal Court and Federal Court of Appeal, eg, *Apotex Inc v Astrazeneca Canada Inc* 2012 FC 559 [116]; *Gitxaala Nation v Canada* 2015 FCA 73 [17]; *Tapambwa v Canada (Citizenship and Immigration)* 2019 FCA 34. For a correct appreciation of the ambiguity requirement since *National Corn Growers* from the Federal Court of Appeal, see *Canada v Seaboard Lumber Sales Co* [1995] 3 FC 113, (1995) CanLII 3604 (FCA).

[107] ILA Final Report (n 1) para 61.

Charter of Rights and Freedoms. Ironically, this is also where Canadian and international legal requirements are most likely to be consubstantial.[108] Even here, however, consideration of international sources is common, judicial departure from international requirements is rare, and consistent interpretation is gaining ground.

[108] ibid para 30.

9

Engagement of United States Courts with International Law

David Sloss

A. Introduction

This chapter addresses the engagement of United States (US) courts with international law. The first part (Part B) provides a brief overview of international law in the United States legal system. Part C then applies the analytical framework developed by the International Law Association (ILA) Study Group in its Final Report (ILA Final Report),[1] and examines cases in which United States domestic courts have engaged in various forms of avoidance, alignment, and contestation. The final part (Part D) offers some tentative conclusions.

B. International Law in the United States Legal System

1. Modes of Reception and Application

The United States Constitution divides power between one national government and fifty state governments. Consequently, judicial power is divided between one system of federal courts and fifty independent state judiciaries. Although the national government has primary responsibility for the conduct of international relations, state courts in the United States have applied international law for more than two centuries.

Originally written in 1787, the Constitution has been amended several times, but the textual provisions related to international law remain unchanged. The document mentions the law of nations only once. Article I §8, grants Congress

[1] ILA Study Group on Principles on the Engagement of Domestic Courts with International Law, 'Final Report: Mapping the Engagement of Domestic Courts with International Law' (Johannesburg, 2016) (ILA Final Report).

the power 'to define and punish … offenses against the Law of Nations'.[2] The Constitution does not specify whether courts should apply customary international law (CIL). However, United States courts applied CIL even before the Constitution was written and continued to do so after its adoption.[3]

In contrast to CIL, the text of the Constitution specifically directs courts to apply treaties. Article II grants the President the power to make treaties 'with the advice and consent of the Senate'.[4] Article I makes clear that the treaty power is a national power; states may not enter into 'any treaty' with a foreign government.[5] Article III grants federal courts jurisdiction over cases 'arising under' treaties.[6] Whereas Article III addresses federal courts, the Supremacy Clause in Article VI addresses state courts. It specifies that treaties are 'the supreme Law of the Land; and the judges in every State shall be bound thereby, any thing in the Constitution or Laws of any state to the contrary notwithstanding'.[7] The Supremacy Clause serves two important functions. First, it specifies that conflicts between treaties and state law should be resolved in favour of treaties. Second, as originally understood, it created a constitutional duty for state courts to apply treaties whenever they confronted a conflict between a treaty and state law.[8]

Judicial doctrine distinguishes between self-executing and non-self-executing treaties. For much of United States history, the self-execution doctrine did not affect the judicial application of the Constitution's treaty supremacy rule. The treaty supremacy rule, rooted in the text of the Supremacy Clause, governed the relationship between treaties and state law. The doctrine of self-execution operated at a federal separation-of-powers level to divide power over treaty implementation between Congress and the President.[9] In the early 1950s, though, in response to the advent of modern international

[2] Constitution of the United States of America (United States Constitution) art I (§8) cl 10.

[3] See generally David L Sloss et al (eds), *International Law in the U.S. Supreme Court: Continuity and Change* (CUP 2011) 23–36 (Sloss et al, *Continuity and Change*).

[4] United States Constitution art II (§2) cl 2. The President may bypass the art II requirement to obtain a two-thirds Senate majority for a treaty by concluding an international agreement in the form of a 'sole executive agreement' or a 'congressional-executive agreement'. See Louis Henkin, *Foreign Affairs and the U.S. Constitution* (2nd edn, Clarendon Press 1996) 215–24. For the different ways in which international agreements may be concluded in the United States legal system and how that affects their domestic implementation, see also Jean Galbraith, 'International Agreements and U.S. Foreign Relations Law: Complexity in Action' in Curtis A Bradley (ed), *The Oxford Handbook of Comparative Foreign Relations Law* (OUP 2019) 158–63.

[5] United States Constitution art I (§10) cl 1.

[6] United States Constitution art III (§2) cl 1.

[7] United States Constitution art VI, cl 2.

[8] See David L Sloss, *The Death of Treaty Supremacy: An Invisible Constitutional Change* (OUP 2016) 47–51 (Sloss, *Treaty Supremacy*).

[9] See ibid pts I and II.

human rights law, lawyers created an exception to the treaty supremacy rule for non-self-executing (NSE) treaties.[10] The NSE doctrine provides a rationale for courts to engage in affirmative avoidance—or, in some cases, negatory contestation—to avoid the application of international law.[11]

United States courts, additionally, often apply international law indirectly in the context of statutory interpretation. More than two centuries ago, in *Murray v Charming Betsy*, Chief Justice Marshall declared that 'an act of Congress ought never to be construed to violate the law of nations if any other possible construction remains'.[12] The principle that courts should interpret statutes in conformity with the nation's international legal obligations is known as the *Charming Betsy* canon. The canon can be a powerful tool for aligning domestic law with international law.[13] However, United States courts often engage in evasive avoidance by disregarding the *Charming Betsy* canon in cases where it is arguably applicable.

The *Charming Betsy* canon is broadly accepted in the US, at least in principle, but the use of international law in constitutional interpretation is more controversial. In the past two decades, the Supreme Court has cited foreign and international sources in decisions applying the Fourteenth Amendment Due Process Clause[14] and the Eighth Amendment ban on cruel and unusual punishments.[15] However, the Court's reliance on foreign and international sources in these cases provoked strident dissents from Justice Scalia and other conservative Justices.[16]

2. Broad Themes

The constitutional text related to international law has not changed in the past two centuries, but judicial attitudes towards international law have changed substantially. The United States in the eighteenth century was a weak, insecure nation eager to gain acceptance from older, established European

[10] See Sloss, *Treaty Supremacy* (n 8) pt III.

[11] See nn 119–24 and accompanying text (discussing application of the NSE doctrine in *Medellín v Texas*). See also, from a different perspective, Duncan B Hollis and Carlos M Vázquez, 'Treaty Self-Execution as "Foreign" Foreign Relations Law' in Bradley (n 4) 469–71.

[12] *Murray v The Charming Betsy* 6 US 64, 118 (1804).

[13] See also ILA Final Report (n 1) paras 23, 46.

[14] See, eg, *Lawrence v Texas* 539 US 558 (2003), 576–77.

[15] See, eg, *Roper v Simmons* 543 US 551 (2005), 575–78 (noting that 'the United States is the only country in the world that continues to give official sanction to the juvenile death penalty').

[16] See *Lawrence* (n 14) 598 (Scalia J, dissenting) ('this Court ... should not impose foreign moods, fads, or fashions on Americans'); *Roper* (n 15) 622–28 (Scalia J, dissenting).

powers.[17] Accordingly, during the eighteenth and nineteenth centuries, judicial engagement with international law was often characterized by alignment, rather than avoidance or contestation.[18] By the dawn of the twenty-first century, though, the United States was the world's preeminent superpower. (Of course, United States power has declined in the past decade, while China has emerged as a rising superpower.) Whereas an international law violation in the eighteenth century might have provoked a sharp response from a more powerful country that posed a threat to national survival, the consequences of most international law violations today are far less serious. Not surprisingly, then, judicial engagement today is more likely to involve avoidance or contestation. However, one must not overstate the point. One could cite examples of avoidance and contestation in the nineteenth century. Moreover, this chapter will identify several examples of alignment in contemporary practice.

Analysis of judicial engagement with international law in the United States must account for three broad factors that influence the behaviour of domestic courts: federalism, separation of powers, and individual rights. United States judges generally believe that they have an institutional responsibility to protect individual rights. However, in exercising that responsibility, courts are often constrained by considerations related to the division of power among the three branches of the federal government (separation of powers) and the division of power between the federal government and the states (federalism).[19] Federalism and the principle of separation of powers influence judicial decision-making in purely domestic cases, but those factors sometimes persuade courts to adopt a posture of avoidance or contestation with respect to international law. Two examples help illustrate this point.

In *Matar v Dichter*, Palestinian plaintiffs alleged 'that they were injured or lost family members in the 2002 aerial bombing of a Gaza apartment complex' and that the defendant 'Avraham Dichter, former head of the Israeli Security Agency, personally participated in the decision to bomb' the complex.[20] Plaintiffs alleged that Dichter committed war crimes in violation of international law. The court dismissed their claims against Dichter, without addressing the merits of the war crimes claim, holding that he was entitled

[17] See David M Golove and Daniel J Hulsebosch, 'A Civilized Nation: The Early American Constitution, the Law of Nations, and the Pursuit of International Recognition' (2010) 85 NYU Law Review 923.

[18] See Sloss et al, *Continuity and Change* (n 3) pts I and II. See also ILA Final Report (n 1) para 75 for similar remarks.

[19] On federalism and foreign affairs, see, eg, Jack L Goldsmith, 'Federal Courts, Foreign Affairs, and Federalism' (1997) 83 Virginia Law Review 1617.

[20] *Matar v Dichter* 563 F 3d 9 (2nd Cir 2009), 10.

to immunity. The court's immunity ruling relied heavily on a government 'Statement of Interest', in which the Executive Branch argued that Dichter was entitled to immunity under common law principles derived from international law.[21] The court invoked the 'traditional rule of deference to such Executive determinations' to support its immunity holding.[22] *Dichter* could be categorized as an example of 'avoidance', insofar as the court refused to address the merits of the war crimes claim. However, *Dichter* could also be classified as an example of 'consubstantial contestation',[23] because the court relied on immunity rules derived from international law to bar a decision on the war crimes claim. Regardless of how *Dichter* is classified, the transnational context of the case (both factually and legally) shifted the usual balance between the judiciary and the executive branch, leading the court to defer to the executive's view on the immunity defence.

In *Bond v United States*, the federal government charged Carol Anne Bond with violating the Chemical Weapons Convention Implementation Act (CWC Act), a federal statute designed to implement United States obligations under the Chemical Weapons Convention.[24] Bond argued that the federal government exceeded its authority by prosecuting her for conduct that, under the Constitution, fell within the exclusive regulatory authority of state governments. The Supreme Court avoided the constitutional question, deciding on statutory interpretation grounds that the CWC Act did not reach 'a purely local crime'.[25] (The Court did not explain why the crime at issue was 'a purely local crime', nor did it articulate any criteria for distinguishing between 'local crimes' and 'non-local crimes'.) The majority defended its interpretation of the statute—an interpretation that was arguably inconsistent with the text and purpose of the CWC Act[26]—by arguing that the statute 'must be read consistent with principles of federalism inherent in our constitutional structure'.[27] *Bond* provides an example of 'negatory contestation', which 'consists in the denial of the validity or applicability of an international law norm'.[28] The Court denied applicability of the CWC Act to Bond's criminal conduct. In doing so,

[21] ibid 14.
[22] ibid 15.
[23] For an explanation see ILA Final Report (n 1) para 63.
[24] *Bond v United States* 134 S Ct 2077 (2014). See Chemical Weapons Convention Implementation Act 22 USC §§6701–71; Convention on the Prohibition of the Development, Production, Stockpiling and Use of Chemical Weapons and on Their Destruction (adopted 3 September 1992, entered into force 29 April 1997) 1974 UNTS 45.
[25] *Bond* (n 24) 2083.
[26] For a critique of the Court's opinion in *Bond* (n 24), see David Sloss, 'Bond v United States: Choosing the Lesser of Two Evils' (2015) 90 Notre Dame Law Review 1583 (Sloss, 'Bond v United States').
[27] *Bond* (n 24) 2088.
[28] ILA Final Report (n 1) para 61.

the Court implicitly denied applicability of the treaty itself because the relevant statutory provisions were almost identical to the parallel treaty provisions.[29] The Court contested the applicability of the international norm because, in its view, application of the norm would have posed a threat to the Constitution's federal structure.

C. Practice of United States Courts

The ILA Final Report identifies three broad categories of engagement with international law: avoidance, alignment, and contestation. In accordance with that framework, this part analyses cases where United States courts have adopted these three strategies.

1. Avoidance

The ILA Final Report defines avoidance as 'the general posture or strategy of a domestic court avoiding the application of international law in circumstances where the latter may be applicable'.[30] It distinguishes between 'evasive avoidance' and 'affirmative avoidance'.

Evasive avoidance is 'where international law is not applied without any relevant argument being made and without any discussion by the court'.[31] United States courts routinely engage in evasive avoidance. For example, between 2010 and 2015, the Supreme Court decided three cases involving the Foreign Sovereign Immunities Act (FSIA) that involved evasive avoidance: *OBB Personenverkehr AG v Sachs*,[32] *Republic of Argentina v NML Capital, Ltd*,[33] and *Samantar v Yousuf*.[34] Congress enacted the FSIA to codify the international rules governing immunity of foreign sovereigns from the jurisdiction of domestic courts.[35] Even so, in these three FSIA cases the Court made virtually

[29] See Sloss, 'Bond v United States' (n 26) 1584–89.

[30] ILA Final Report (n 1) para 39.

[31] ibid para 40.

[32] *OBB Personenverkehr AG v Carol P Sachs* 577 US 27, 136 S Ct 390 (2015) (holding that Austria's State-owned railway company was immune from the jurisdiction of United States courts).

[33] *Republic of Argentina v NML Capital, Ltd* 573 US 134, 134 S Ct 2250 (2014) (holding that the FSIA did not preclude a United States court from issuing a subpoena to a private bank ordering disclosure of documents related to accounts belonging to Argentina).

[34] *Samantar v Yousuf* 560 US 305 (2010) (holding that an individual foreign official sued for conduct undertaken in his official capacity is not a 'foreign state' under the FSIA).

[35] See Foreign Sovereign Immunities Act 1976, 90 Stat 2891 (codified as amended at 28 USC §§1602–11).

no reference to international law. Instead, the Court's approach to interpreting the FSIA was similar to the approach it adopts when interpreting ordinary domestic statutes. Indeed, a casual reader who is not familiar with the FSIA would not know, based on the Court's opinions, that the cases implicated any international law issues.

In *OBB Personenverkehr*, the Court ruled that Austria's State-owned railway was entitled to immunity.[36] In terms of its substantive outcome, that decision yielded a result of consubstantial alignment as defined by the ILA Final Report: 'the application by the domestic court of domestic norms that are consubstantial with international norms.'[37] In contrast, it is debatable whether the outcome in *Argentina v NM Capital* or *Samantar* aligned with international law. Regardless, insofar as judicial application of the FSIA produced alignment with international norms in *OBB Personenverkehr*, this alignment resulted primarily from the congressional enactment of the statute, rather than a conscious judicial effort to harmonize interpretation of the FSIA with international norms.[38]

A court practices affirmative avoidance when it 'considers the application of international law but explicitly rejects it'.[39] Justice Scalia's dissenting opinion in *Thompson v Oklahoma* provides a classic example. In *Thompson*, the majority held that the Eighth Amendment to the Constitution bars the imposition of capital punishment for a crime committed by a 15-year-old defendant.[40] The Court noted that its conclusion was 'consistent with the views that have been expressed ... by other nations that share our Anglo-American heritage, and by the leading members of the Western European community', adopting a posture of alignment with international law.[41] Justice Scalia criticized the majority for relying on international sources. He asserted: 'We must never forget that it is a Constitution for the United States of America that we are expounding ... [T]he views of other nations, however enlightened the Justices of this Court may think them to be, cannot be imposed upon Americans through the Constitution.'[42]

The Ninth Circuit decision in *Republic of Marshall Islands v United States* is another example of affirmative avoidance.[43] Article VI of the Nuclear

[36] *OBB Personenverkehr AG* (n 32).
[37] ILA Final Report (n 1) para 49.
[38] See ibid: '[C]onsubstantial alignment can be independently adopted by a domestic court, but it can also be forced upon it by the executive or legislature producing consubstantial obligations' (footnotes omitted).
[39] ibid para 41.
[40] *Thompson v Oklahoma* 487 US 815 (1988).
[41] ibid 830. See ILA Final Report (n 1) para 49 (discussing consubstantial alignment).
[42] *Thompson* (n 40) 868 and fn 4 (Scalia J, dissenting).
[43] *Republic of Marshall Islands v United States* 865 F 3d 1187 (9th Cir 2017) (*Marshall Islands*).

Non-Proliferation Treaty (NPT) obligates the United States 'to pursue negotiations in good faith on effective measures relating to cessation of the nuclear arms race ... and to nuclear disarmament'.[44] The Marshall Islands sued the United States government in federal court, claiming that the United States is violating its obligations under the NPT. The Ninth Circuit dismissed the case. Judge McKeown's opinion avoided the question of whether the United States is violating its treaty obligations under the NPT, by reasoning that Article VI of the NPT is non-self-executing,[45] the Marshall Islands lacked standing to bring the claim,[46] and the case raised non-justiciable political questions.[47] The common thread linking all three rationales is that the case raised issues that 'fall quintessentially within the realm of the executive, not the judiciary'.[48]

Read together, Justice Scalia's dissenting opinion in *Thompson* and Judge McKeown's majority opinion in *Marshall Islands* suggest that judges often practice affirmative avoidance when presented with issues that they believe are 'too political' for judicial resolution.

2. Alignment

The ILA Final Report defines alignment as a posture where 'an attempt is made to align with international law or at least to harmonize domestic law or practice with international regulation'.[49] The Report distinguishes among four types of alignment: fair weather alignment, consubstantial alignment, overriding alignment, and hyper-alignment. This section addresses each category in turn.

Fair weather alignment is 'alignment with international law in run-of-the-mill, politically unproblematic situations'.[50] One could cite hundreds, perhaps thousands, of cases in which United States courts practice fair weather alignment. Many of those cases involve judicial application of multilateral, private international law treaties, such as the 1980 UN Convention on the International Sale of Goods (CISG), the 1980 Hague Convention on International Child

[44] Treaty on the Non-Proliferation of Nuclear Weapons (adopted 1 July 1968, entered into force 5 March 1970) 729 UNTS 161 art VI.
[45] *Marshall Islands* (n 43) 1192–99.
[46] ibid 1199.
[47] ibid 1200–01.
[48] ibid 1190. On how such arguments may be used to produce affirmative avoidance, see ILA Final Report (n 1) paras 21, 41.
[49] ILA Final Report (n 1) para 37.
[50] ibid para 44.

Abduction, and the 1999 Montreal Convention on International Carriage by Air.[51]

For example, in *Cohen v Cohen*,[52] an Israeli father filed a complaint in federal court, seeking a judicial order to return his child to him in Israel. The court applied the Hague Convention, as implemented by the International Child Abduction Remedies Act,[53] and determined that the United States was the child's 'habitual residence' under the treaty.[54] Accordingly, the court denied the request to order the child's return to Israel. Similarly, in *Baah v Virgin Atlantic Airways, Ltd*,[55] the plaintiff filed a tort claim against an airline, seeking compensation for personal injury sustained during air travel. The court noted that the Montreal Convention is a self-executing treaty.[56] It applied Article 33 of the Convention as the governing jurisdictional rule and concluded that it lacked jurisdiction because the treaty required the plaintiff to bring his claim in the United Kingdom.[57]

The Supreme Court's decision in *Bolivarian Republic of Venezuela v Helmerich & Payne Intern Drilling Co*[58] provides another example of fair weather alignment. This case involved judicial application of the FSIA. In contrast to the FSIA cases discussed in the previous section, where the Court practiced evasive avoidance by ignoring international law, Justice Breyer's opinion in *Venezuela v Helmerich & Payne Intern Drilling Co* explicitly addressed the international law implications of the statutory interpretation issue.[59] It bears emphasis that Justice Breyer is among the most 'international-law-friendly' members of the Supreme Court. Thus, in FSIA cases, the particular predilections of individual judges may well affect the choice between evasive avoidance and fair weather alignment.[60]

Consubstantial alignment is 'the application by the domestic court of domestic norms that are consubstantial with the international norms'.[61] The

[51] (adopted 11 April 1980, entered into force 1 January 1988) 1489 UNTS 3; (adopted 25 October 1980, entered into force 1 December 1983) 1343 UNTS 89; and (adopted 28 May 1999, entered into force 4 November 2003) 2242 UNTS 309, respectively. For analysis of judicial application of multilateral, private law treaties, see David L Sloss and Michael P Van Alstine, 'International Law in Domestic Courts' in Wayne Sandholtz and Christopher A Whytock (eds), *Research Handbook on the Politics of International Law* (Edward Elgar 2017) 92–102.

[52] *Cohen v Cohen* 858 F 3rd 1150 (8th Cir 2017).

[53] 22 USC §§9001–11.

[54] *Cohen* (n 52) 1153–54.

[55] *Baah v Virgin Atlantic Airways, Ltd* 473 F Supp 2d 591 (SDNY 2007).

[56] ibid 593.

[57] See ibid 593–97.

[58] *Bolivarian Republic of Venezuela v Helmerich & Payne Intern Drilling Co* 137 S Ct 1312 (2017).

[59] See ibid 1319–22.

[60] For similar observations, see ILA Final Report (n 1) para 78.

[61] ibid (n 1) para 49.

ILA Final Report notes that, in many cases, 'the distinction between evasive avoidance and consubstantial alignment is not easy to draw'.[62] In the US, this is especially true for international human rights because the United States has achieved a high degree of consubstantial alignment with international human rights norms through 'silent incorporation' of those norms into federal constitutional and statutory law. The fact that incorporation occurs silently—that is without explicit reference to international norms—means that silent incorporation may involve both consubstantial alignment and evasive avoidance.

Between 1948 and 1976, the United States aligned federal law with the norms of the Universal Declaration of Human Rights (UDHR) through a process of silent incorporation.[63] It employed three primary mechanisms to produce such alignment. First, in a series of decisions known as 'incorporation cases', the Supreme Court made most provisions of the Bill of Rights binding on state governments. The consensus view in 1791 was that the Bill of Rights bound the federal government, but not state governments. With minor exceptions, that consensus prevailed until 1948, when the UDHR was adopted. Between 1948 and 1971, the Supreme Court decided thirteen cases that 'incorporated' specific provisions of the Bill of Rights and made them binding on state governments.[64] For example, in *Robinson v California*, the Court held that the Eighth Amendment ban on cruel and unusual punishments binds state governments.[65] Before 1962, the states decided for themselves what types of punishment were 'cruel and unusual'. After 1962, the Supreme Court imposed a uniform federal standard. The Court's decision in *Robinson* did not mention international law, but *Robinson* and its progeny produced a high degree of alignment between United States constitutional law and the international prohibition on cruel, inhuman or degrading punishment.

Second, in addition to the incorporation cases, the Supreme Court decided numerous cases between 1948 and 1976 establishing federal constitutional protection for 'unenumerated rights'—namely, rights that are not specifically enumerated in the Constitution. For example, the Court decided in 1967 in *Loving v Virginia* that state laws prohibiting interracial marriage are unconstitutional.[66]

[62] ibid para 50.

[63] Universal Declaration of Human Rights, UNGA Res 217(III)(A) (10 December 1948) UN Doc A/RES/217(III)(A) (UDHR). This discussion of consubstantial alignment borrows liberally from David Sloss and Wayne Sandholtz, 'Universal Human Rights and Constitutional Change' (2019) 27 William & Mary Bill of Rights Journal 1183.

[64] See David Sloss, 'Incorporation, Federalism, and International Human Rights' in Austin Sarat (ed), *Human Rights and Legal Judgments: The American Story* (CUP 2017). The precise number of 'incorporation' cases during this period is contestable. Compare ibid (counting 13 express incorporation cases) with Sloss and Sandholtz (n 63) (counting 10 such cases during the same period).

[65] *Robinson v California* 370 US 660 (1962).

[66] *Loving v Virginia* 388 US 1 (1967).

The United States Constitution says nothing about marital rights, and many states prohibited interracial marriage before 1967. In *Loving*, though, the Court created a federal constitutional rule protecting an individual's right to marry the person of his or her choice. The Court's opinion did not reference international law, but *Loving* produced consubstantial alignment with Article 16 of the UDHR, which protects the right of 'men and women of full age' to marry 'without any limitation due to race, nationality, or religion'.[67]

Third, apart from Supreme Court decisions, Congress also promoted silent incorporation of human rights norms by enacting federal statutes that had the effect of aligning federal law with international norms. For example, Title II of the Civil Rights Act of 1964 guarantees 'all persons' equal access to 'any place of public accommodation ... without discrimination or segregation on the ground of race, color, religion, or national origin'.[68] The statute defines the term 'public accommodation' to include hotels, restaurants, theatres, and other similar establishments. Many such establishments are privately owned and operated. The Fourteenth Amendment Equal Protection Clause bars discrimination by governments, but does not regulate private conduct. Thus, the 1964 Act expanded the scope of federal anti-discrimination law by prohibiting discrimination by private actors. The statute helped promote alignment with the Convention on Racial Discrimination—still in draft form in 1964—which obligates states to prohibit 'racial discrimination by any persons, group, or organization'.[69] The legislative history of the 1964 Civil Rights Act shows that Cold War politics was a significant factor in generating political support for the legislation,[70] but it does not indicate that Congress had the conscious objective of aligning United States law with international human rights norms.

In sum, in this period—through a combination of federal legislation, judicial recognition of unenumerated rights, and the Supreme Court's incorporation decisions—the United States achieved a high degree of consubstantial alignment with international human rights norms. As of 1948, federal law in the United States provided significant protection for only 29 per cent of the rights articulated in the UDHR. In contrast, by 1976, federal law provided significant protection for about 74 per cent of the rights in the UDHR.[71] As of 2018, the

[67] UDHR (n 63) art 16. For other examples of Supreme Court decisions involving unenumerated rights, see Sloss and Sandholtz (n 63) 1220–24.

[68] Civil Rights Act of 1964, 78 Stat 241, 243.

[69] International Convention on the Elimination of All Forms of Racial Discrimination (adopted 21 December 1965, entered into force 4 January 1969) 660 UNTS 195 art 2(d).

[70] See Mary L Dudziak, *Cold War Civil Rights: Race and the Image of American Democracy* (Princeton University Press 2000).

[71] See Sloss and Sandholtz (n 63) 1185, 1205.

alignment between United States federal law and international human rights norms remained more or less the same as it was in 1976.[72]

International human rights aside, consubstantial alignment also characterizes judicial decisions in other areas of law. For example, the United States enacted the Refugee Act of 1980 to implement its obligations under the 1967 Protocol Relating to the Status of Refugees.[73] United States courts have applied the Refugee Act in thousands of cases; most of those decisions do not refer explicitly to the Protocol or other international law sources. Even so, straightforward application of the domestic statute on its own terms often promotes alignment with international norms because Congress incorporated those norms into the statute.[74]

Overriding alignment is 'the application of international law by the domestic court over conflicting domestic law'.[75] In the US, the 'later-in-time rule' provides that a later-enacted statute overrides a prior conflicting treaty and a later-ratified treaty overrides a prior conflicting statute. Thus, in principle, judicial application of a later-in-time treaty to override a prior conflicting statute would entail overriding alignment. The ILA Final Report notes that, in many cases, '"apparent" conflicts may be resolved' by interpreting the treaty and statute to be in harmony,[76] thus avoiding application of the later-in-time rule. In practice, US courts rarely apply a later-in-time treaty to override a prior statute because they avoid conflicts by interpreting the two instruments to be in harmony with each other. (In contrast, United States courts often apply later-in-time statutes to override prior conflicting treaties. At least some such cases involve 'negatory contestation'.[77])

Cook v United States is one of the few cases where the Supreme Court applied a treaty under the later-in-time rule to override a prior statute.[78] In *Cook*, United States Coast Guard officers boarded a British vessel that was allegedly engaged in illegal smuggling. Cook (the vessel's master) argued that the seizure was unlawful because it violated a 1924 treaty with Britain. The government argued that Section 581 of the Tariff Act of 1922 authorized the seizure. The Court held that the seizure was unlawful because the 1924 treaty superseded

[72] See ibid 1234–36.
[73] Refugee Act of 1980, 94 Stat 102; Protocol relating to the Status of Refugees (adopted 31 January 1967, entered into force 4 October 1967) 606 UNTS 267.
[74] See, eg, *In Re Fauziya Kasinga* 21 I&N Dec 357 (BIA 1996) (holding that the practice of female genital mutilation can be the basis for a grant of asylum under the statute).
[75] ILA Final Report (n 1) para 45.
[76] ibid.
[77] See nn 107–16 and accompanying text for discussion of negatory contestation.
[78] *Cook v United States* 288 US 102 (1933). This paragraph borrows liberally from Sloss, *Treaty Supremacy* (n 8) 138–40.

the 1922 statute under the later-in-time rule.[79] That was not the end of the matter, however, because Congress had re-enacted 'section 581 in the Tariff Act of 1930 in the identical terms of the act of 1922'.[80] The government argued that the 1930 statute superseded the 1924 treaty under the later-in-time rule. Justice Brandeis, writing for the Court, rejected that argument. He said: 'A treaty will not be deemed to have been abrogated or modified by a later statute, unless such purpose on the part of Congress has been clearly expressed';[81] he found no evidence that Congress had intended to abrogate or modify the treaty. Thus, the Court found a conflict between the 1924 treaty and the 1922 statute and applied the later-in-time rule to override the statute. However, it applied the presumption of consistency to support its holding that 1930 statute did not conflict with the 1924 treaty, even though the 1930 statute was virtually identical to the 1922 statute.

According to the ILA Final Report, 'in some instances a very strong presumption of consistency of domestic law with international obligations, even in the face of little or no ambiguity in domestic law, may produce overriding alignment'.[82] It is difficult to identify modern examples of this phenomenon in United States practice, but the Supreme Court decision in *Chew Heong v United States* provides an example from an earlier era.[83] An 1868 treaty between the United States and China promised 'free migration and emigration of their citizens and subjects, respectively, from the one country to the other'.[84] A decade later, with mounting political pressure to restrict Chinese immigration, an 1880 treaty permitted the United States to restrict immigration of Chinese labourers.[85] Then Congress enacted the Chinese Exclusion Act of 1882, suspending immigration of Chinese labourers for ten years.[86] Under the treaties and the statute, Chinese labourers who lived in the United States before the passage of the 1882 Act retained the right to exit and return. However, the government soon learned that courts were permitting entry of Chinese labourers who claimed falsely that they lived in the United States before 1882.[87] Accordingly, Congress enacted an amendment requiring Chinese labourers to produce a government-issued certificate establishing residence in the United

[79] See *Cook* (n 78) 111–19.
[80] ibid 119–20.
[81] ibid 120.
[82] ILA Final Report (n 1) para 46.
[83] *Chew Heong v United States* 112 US 536 (1884).
[84] Treaty of Trade, Consuls and Emigration (Burlingame-Seward Treaty) (China-US) 16 Stat 739.
[85] Treaty Concerning Immigration (China-US) 22 Stat 826 art I.
[86] Chinese Exclusion Act 1882, 22 Stat 58 (repealed).
[87] See David Sloss, 'Polymorphous Public Law Litigation: The Forgotten History of Nineteenth Century Public Law Litigation' (2014) 71 Washington and Lee Law Review 1757, 1814–18.

States before May 1882 as 'the only evidence permissible to establish this right of re-entry'.[88]

The Court held in *Chew Heong*, however, that a Chinese labourer was entitled to enter the country without the statutorily required certificate if he resided in the United States before enactment of the 1882 Act, left the country without a certificate before Congress passed the 1884 amendment, and sought re-entry after the amendment was passed:

> [Because] the purpose avowed in the act was to faithfully execute the treaty, any interpretation of its provisions would be rejected which imputes to Congress an intention to disregard the plighted faith of the government, and, consequently, the court ought, if possible, to adopt that construction [of the statute] which recognized and saved rights secured by the treaty.[89]

Thus, despite the unambiguous statutory language requiring a certificate to gain re-entry, and despite ample evidence that Congress probably did intend to abrogate treaty rights, the Court avoided a conflict between the statute and the treaties by applying a strong presumption of consistency and construing the statute in harmony with previously ratified treaties.

The ILA Final Report refers to the Supreme Court decision in *Roper v Simmons*[90] as an example of consubstantial alignment,[91] but this case might also be classified as an example of overriding alignment. *Roper* presented the question whether it is lawful to impose capital punishment on a person who was 17-years-old when he committed murder. The Court had held in *Stanford v Kentucky* in 1989 that the Constitution permits capital punishment for crimes committed by 16 and 17-year-olds.[92] The International Covenant on Civil and Political Rights (ICCPR) explicitly bars capital punishment 'for crimes committed by persons below eighteen years of age'.[93] When the United States ratified the ICCPR, it made a reservation to preserve its right to impose capital punishment in cases where it would be constitutionally permissible under *Stanford*.[94] Hence, when *Roper* came to the Supreme Court in 2005, *Stanford* provided the governing domestic rule. In *Roper*, however, the Court overruled

88 Chinese Exclusion Act 1884, 23 Stat 115 (repealed).
89 *Chew Heong* (n 83) 549.
90 *Roper* (n 15).
91 ILA Final Report (n 1) para 52.
92 *Stanford v Kentucky* 492 US 361 (1989).
93 International Covenant on Civil and Political Rights (adopted 16 December 1966, entered into force 23 March 1976) 999 UNTS 171 art 6(5).
94 See 138 Cong Rec S4783 (1992).

Stanford and created a new rule—barring capital punishment for crimes committed by 16 and 17-year-olds[95]—that aligned United States constitutional law with the international rule in the ICCPR. Formally, the Court in *Roper* simply reinterpreted the Eighth Amendment. In substance, though, the Court created a new rule of constitutional law that superseded the previous constitutional rule in *Stanford*. Thus, insofar as the Court in *Roper* relied partly on international sources to justify its decision to overrule *Stanford*,[96] *Roper* is a case of overriding alignment.

Finally, hyper-alignment occurs when a domestic court goes 'beyond what international law actually requires ... finding international obligations where none actually exist or are at least debatable'.[97] It is difficult to identify examples of hyper-alignment in recent United States judicial practice, but the DC Circuit decision in *Zuza v Office of the High Representative* may fit in this category.[98] The 1995 Dayton Peace Agreement, which ended the war in the former Yugoslavia, created the Office of the High Representative to oversee implementation of the agreement.[99] Before 2004, Zoran Zuza held a government position in the Republic of Srpska, a region within Bosnia and Herzegovina. In January 2004, Jeremy Ashdown exercised his authority as High Representative to remove Zuza from his government post.[100] Ten years later, Zuza sued Ashdown for wrongfully terminating his employment as a government official in the Republic of Srpska. At that time, Ashdown was no longer employed as High Representative. The court dismissed Zuza's claim against Ashdown, reasoning that Ashdown was entitled to immunity under the International Organizations Immunities Act, a federal statute.[101] From an international law perspective, it is debatable whether Ashdown—as a retired officer of an 'ad hoc international institution'[102]—was legally entitled to immunity from the jurisdiction of United States courts. Regardless, the court relied on a domestic statute that implements international rules to justify its ruling on the immunity issue.

[95] *Roper* (n 15).
[96] ibid 575–8.
[97] ILA Final Report (n 1) para 55.
[98] *Zuza v Office of the High Representative* 857 F 3d 935 (DC Cir 2017).
[99] See General Framework Agreement for Peace in Bosnia and Herzegovina (30 November 1995) UN Doc A/50/790-S/1995/999, Annex, art I annex 10.
[100] See *Zuza v Office of High Representative* 107 F Supp 3d 90 (DDC 2015), 91–92.
[101] See *Zuza* (n 98) 938–39. International Organizations Immunities Act of 1945, 59 Stat 669.
[102] See Office of the High Representative, 'General Information' available at <http://www.ohr.int/?page_id=1139> accessed 21 July 2023.

3. Contestation

The ILA Final Report distinguishes among three types of contestation: affirmative, negatory, and consubstantial contestation. This section addresses each of these categories.

Affirmative contestation occurs when a domestic court accepts 'the validity or applicability of the international law norm but giv[es] it a meaning different from that which is generally accepted'.[103] The Supreme Court decision in *United States v Alvarez-Machain* provides an example.[104] Humberto Alvarez-Machain was a citizen and resident of Mexico. Agents of the United States Drug Enforcement Administration (DEA) organized an operation to kidnap him from his home in Mexico and bring him to the United States for a criminal trial. At trial, Alvarez-Machain argued that his forcible abduction violated the bilateral extradition treaty between the United States and Mexico. The Court ruled that the treaty merely provided one permissible method for extradition, but did not prohibit other methods, such as transnational abduction.[105] Alvarez-Machain argued 'that the Treaty must be interpreted against the backdrop of customary international law, and that international abductions are so clearly prohibited in international law that there was no reason to include' a prohibition on forcible abductions in the treaty itself.[106] Most international law experts would presumably agree that the treaty, construed in light of customary international law, bars transnational forcible abductions. Even so, the Court applied its own, idiosyncratic approach to treaty interpretation and concluded that the treaty did not prohibit transnational kidnapping.

A special type of affirmative contestation occurs 'when a domestic court diverges from the interpretation of international law given by an international court'.[107] Here, *Sanchez-Llamas v Oregon* is on point.[108] The Supreme Court decided *Sanchez-Llamas* shortly after the International Court of Justice (ICJ) issued its decision in the *Avena* case.[109] In *Avena*, the ICJ ruled that the United States was obligated under the Vienna Convention on Consular Relations (VCCR)[110] to provide judicial hearings for individual prisoners who were sentenced to death or lengthy prison terms after their rights under Article 36 had

[103] ILA Final Report (n 1) para 58.
[104] *United States v Alvarez-Machain* 504 US 655 (1992).
[105] ibid 663–70.
[106] ibid 666.
[107] ILA Final Report (n 1) para 58.
[108] *Sanchez-Llamas v Oregon* 548 US 331 (2006).
[109] *Avena and Other Mexican Nationals (Mexico v United States of America)* (Judgment) [2004] ICJ Rep 12.
[110] (adopted 24 April 1961, entered into force 19 March 1967) 596 UNTS 261.

been violated. The ICJ held specifically that the United States may not invoke procedural default rules to prevent such individuals from obtaining a judicial hearing.[111] Mario Bustillo, one of the petitioners in *Sanchez-Llamas*, sought a judicial hearing to secure a remedy for a violation of VCCR Article 36. State courts in Virginia held that procedural default rules precluded him from obtaining a judicial hearing. On appeal to the Supreme Court, Bustillo argued that Virginia's decision to deny him a hearing violated the VCCR, as interpreted by the ICJ in *Avena*. The Supreme Court held, in essence, that the ICJ's interpretation of Article 36 was incorrect. Properly interpreted, Article 36 did not prohibit United States courts from applying procedural default rules to prevent individuals in Mr Bustillo's position from obtaining a judicial hearing.[112]

The ILA Final Report notes that affirmative contestation may sometimes 'be the result of the court explicitly or implicitly deferring to the position of the executive on the' particular interpretive question.[113] Judicial deference to the executive branch probably contributed to the outcomes in both *Alvarez-Machain* and *Sanchez-Llamas*. The United States Government submitted an amicus brief in *Sanchez-Llamas*, arguing that the VCCR does not preclude application of procedural default rules.[114] The Court did not explicitly rely on the government's brief to support its interpretation of Article 36, but it did note that 'the meaning given [to treaties] by the departments of government particularly charged with their negotiation and enforcement is given great weight'.[115] In *Alvarez-Machain*, the Court agreed with the government's construction of the treaty, but did not expressly defer to the government's interpretation. Justice Stevens, dissenting, argued that the government's 'wish to reinterpret the Treaty to allow for an action that the Treaty in no way authorizes should not influence this Court's interpretation'.[116] This passage suggests that Justice Stevens may have believed that the majority was unduly influenced by the government's interpretation of the treaty.

Negatory contestation involves 'the denial of the validity or applicability of an international law norm'.[117] *Breard v Greene* is one example of negatory contestation.[118] Angel Breard was a Paraguayan national on death row in Virginia. In state court proceedings, Virginia denied him his rights under the VCCR.

[111] *Avena* (n 109) [128]–[34].
[112] See *Sanchez-Llamas* (n 108) 350–60.
[113] ILA Final Report (n 1) para 58.
[114] *Sanchez-Llamas* (n 108), Brief for the United States as Amicus Curiae Supporting Respondents.
[115] *Sanchez-Llamas* (n 108) 355.
[116] *Alvarez-Machain* (n 104) 686–87 (Stevens J, dissenting).
[117] ILA Final Report (n 1) para 61.
[118] *Breard v Greene* 523 US 371 (1998).

Accordingly, he filed a habeas corpus petition in federal court to challenge the validity of his death sentence and to vindicate his treaty rights. Shortly before Breard filed his federal habeas petition, Congress enacted the Antiterrorism and Effective Death Penalty Act (AEDPA).[119] The Act limited the availability of federal habeas relief by requiring petitioners to 'develop the factual basis of [the] claim in State court proceedings'[120] before filing a federal habeas petition. The Supreme Court denied federal habeas relief because Breard failed to develop the factual basis of his VCCR claim in state court and because AEDPA superseded the VCCR under the later-in-time rule.[121] Thus, the Court denied the applicability of the VCCR because AEDPA superseded the VCCR as a matter of domestic law.

Breard differs from *Sanchez-Llamas* in two respects. First, the Supreme Court decided *Sanchez-Llamas* after the ICJ judgment in *Avena*, but the Court issued its judgment in *Breard* before *Avena* was decided, so the *Breard* Court was not contesting the ICJ's interpretation of the VCCR. Second, AEDPA was not applicable to Mr Bustillo's claim in *Sanchez-Llamas* because Bustillo sought habeas relief in state court and AEDPA applies only to federal habeas proceedings. Therefore, the later-in-time rule provided the basis for contestation in *Breard*, but not in *Sanchez-Llamas*.

The Supreme Court's decision in *Medellín v Texas* provides a different example of negatory contestation.[122] Like both *Breard* and *Sanchez-Llamas*, *Medellín* arose from a VCCR violation. However, in contrast to *Sanchez-Llamas*—where the claimants in United States courts were not included in the *Avena* case—Mr Medellín was one of the Mexican nationals specifically covered by the ICJ judgment in *Avena*. Therefore, *Medellín* implicated Article 94 of the Charter of the United Nations (UN Charter), which obligates the United States 'to comply with the decision of the International Court of Justice in any case to which it is a party'.[123] The ICJ judgment in *Avena* obligated the United States to provide a judicial hearing for Medellín, and Article 94 obligated it to comply with that judgment. Medellín argued that the Article 94 obligation was directly binding on Texas state courts under the Supremacy Clause, which stipulates that treaties (such as the UN Charter) are 'the supreme Law

[119] Antiterrorism and Effective Death Penalty Act of 1996, 110 Stat 1214.
[120] *Breard* (n 117) 376 (quoting 28 USC s 2254(a)).
[121] ibid 375–77.
[122] *Medellín v Texas* 552 US 491 (2008).
[123] Charter of the United Nations and Statute of the International Court of Justice (adopted on 26 June 1945, entered into force on 24 October 1945)1 UNTS XVI (UN Charter), art 94.

of the Land', and that 'judges in every State (including Texas) shall be bound thereby'.[124]

The Supreme Court rejected Medellín's claim on the ground that Article 94 is not self-executing.[125] The Court's rationale in *Medellín* is subject to conflicting interpretations. Ultimately, the Court failed to clarify the meaning of the term 'non-self-executing'; it failed to articulate useful criteria for distinguishing between self-executing and non-self-executing treaty provisions; and it failed to provide a coherent rationale to support its conclusion that Article 94 is non-self-executing.[126] Regardless, *Medellín* provides a good example of negatory contestation. The Court denied the applicability of Article 94 because, in the Court's view, Article 94 is not self-executing.[127]

Consubstantial contestation occurs when domestic courts contest 'the content of one rule of international law ... because of the application, even if indirect, of the substance of another rule of international law'.[128] *Owens v Republic of Sudan* provides an example.[129] *Owens* arose under the 'terrorism exception' to the FSIA. Congress first enacted the terrorism exception in 1996, then made major amendments in 2008.[130] The current version provides, in part:

> A foreign state shall not be immune from the jurisdiction of courts of the United States ... in any case ... in which money damages are sought against a foreign state for personal injury or death that was caused by an act of torture, extrajudicial killing, aircraft sabotage, hostage taking, or the provision of material support or resources for such an act if such act or provision of material support or resources is engaged in by an official, employee, or agent of such foreign state while acting within the scope of his or her office(...)[131]

The statute expressly creates a private right of action for claims against foreign states.[132] However, the statute authorizes claims against only a small number of foreign states designated by the government as 'state sponsor(s) of terrorism'.[133]

[124] US Constitution art VI, cl 2.
[125] See *Medellín* (n 121) at 504–14.
[126] For detailed critiques of *Medellín*, see David L Sloss, 'Taming Madison's Monster: How to Fix Self-Execution Doctrine' (2015) Brigham Young University Law Review 1691, 1721–36; David L Sloss, 'Executing Foster v. Neilson: The Two-Step Approach to Analyzing Self-Executing Treaties' (2012) 53 Harvard International Law Journal 135, 182–87.
[127] One could also classify *Medellín* as an example of affirmative avoidance (see ILA Final Report (n 1) para 41) because the Court considered the application of UN Charter art 94 but explicitly rejected it.
[128] ILA Final Report (n 1) para 63.
[129] *Owens v Republic of Sudan* 864 F 3d 751 (DC Cir 2017).
[130] See ibid 763–65 (summarizing the history of the terrorism exception).
[131] FSIA (n 34) §1605A(a)(1).
[132] ibid §1605A(c).
[133] ibid §1605A(a)(2).

The *Owens* plaintiffs were victims of terrorist bombings carried out by al Qaeda against United States embassies in Kenya and Tanzania. 'Starting in 2001 victims of the bombings began to bring suits against the Republic of Sudan and the Islamic Republic of Iran', alleging that Iran and Sudan provided material support to al Qaeda.[134] The DC Circuit largely affirmed the lower court judgments awarding damages against both Iran and Sudan. *Owens* clearly involves contestation: the damage awards against sovereign states are at odds with international rules protecting sovereign immunity. Even so, the decision in *Owens*—and the 'terrorism exception' that it applied—might be justified as an effort to implement other international law principles, such as Article 14 of the Convention Against Torture,[135] and the UN guidelines on the right to a remedy.[136]

D. Conclusion

This chapter has shown that United States courts routinely practice fair weather alignment and consubstantial alignment to harmonize domestic law with international law. In the past decade alone, United States courts have decided hundreds of cases involving fair weather alignment and thousands of cases involving consubstantial alignment. In contrast, cases involving overriding alignment or hyper-alignment are quite rare.

In the decade after the Supreme Court decision in *Breard v Greene*, cases implicating the VCCR yielded dozens, perhaps hundreds, of judicial decisions involving either affirmative or negatory contestation. Setting aside VCCR cases, however, judicial decisions involving affirmative or negatory contestation are relatively rare. Since Congress enacted the terrorism exception to the FSIA in 1996, federal courts have decided dozens of cases implicating the terrorism exception, many of which involve consubstantial contestation. Similarly, since enactment of the Torture Victim Protection Act (TVPA) in 1992,[137] federal courts have decided a few hundred cases under that statute. Insofar as the TVPA imposes civil liability for torture committed by foreign

[134] *Owens* (n 129) 762.

[135] Convention Against Torture and Other Cruel, Inhuman, or Degrading Treatment or Punishment (adopted 10 December 1984, entered into force 26 June 1987) 1465 UNTS 85. Article 14 grants torture victims 'an enforceable right to fair and adequate compensation'.

[136] Basic Principles and Guidelines on the Right to a Remedy and Reparation for Victims of Gross Violations of International Human Rights Law and Serious Violations of International Humanitarian Law, UNGA Res 60/147 (16 December 2005) UN Doc A/RES/60/147.

[137] Torture Victim Protection Act 1992, 106 Stat 73 (1992) (TVPR).

government officials who might be entitled to immunity under international law, some of those cases also involve consubstantial contestation.[138] Aside from these examples, though, decisions involving consubstantial contestation seldom arise.

United States courts also routinely engage in evasive avoidance by deciding cases without reference to international law, even though international law could potentially apply. In many cases, courts engage in evasive avoidance because the parties do not raise relevant international law arguments. When the parties do not invoke international law, courts are unlikely to do so on their own initiative. The failure of parties to present international law arguments is partially attributable to the fact that many United States lawyers are not familiar with international law.[139] However, to some extent, evasive avoidance may also be a product of tactical decisions by litigants. In cases where international human rights norms are potentially applicable, human rights claimants may have a better chance of winning by focusing on domestic law arguments to the exclusion of international law arguments.

Courts sometimes invoke the NSE doctrine to justify a posture of affirmative avoidance.[140] A prior empirical study, based on judicial decisions between 1970 and 2006, estimated that United States courts decided almost ninety percent of treaty cases without even mentioning the NSE doctrine. Courts specifically held that treaties were non-self-executing in only about five or six percent of treaty cases.[141] It is possible that lower courts have been applying the NSE doctrine to support affirmative avoidance with greater frequency since the Supreme Court's 2008 decision in *Medellín*. However, available scholarly analysis is inconclusive in this respect.[142] Aside from judicial decisions involving the NSE doctrine, cases where courts practice affirmative avoidance are relatively rare.

[138] See, eg, *Yousuf v Samantar*, 699 F 3d 763 (4th Cir 2012) (rejecting the defendant's immunity defense to a claim under the TVPA (n 137)).

[139] See ILA Final Report (n 1) para 78.

[140] See, eg, *Marshall Islands* (n 43).

[141] David Sloss, 'United States' in David Sloss (ed), *The Role of Domestic Courts in Treaty Enforcement: A Comparative Study* (CUP 2009).

[142] See Oona A Hathaway et al, 'International Law at Home: Enforcing Treaties in U.S. Courts' (2012) 37 Yale Journal International Law 51, 70–76; David Sloss, 'Medellin's Influence on the Judicial Application of Treaties' (*Opinio Juris*, 4 February 2012) <http://opiniojuris.org/2012/02/24/medellin%E2%80%99s-influence-on-the-judicial-application-of-treaties/>, accessed 21 July 2023.

10

Engagement of Albanian Courts with International Law

Gentian Zyberi and Semir Sali

A. Introduction

After the regime change in the early 1990s, Albania signed and ratified many international and regional treaties, especially in the field of human rights, including amongst others the two International Covenants, the Convention Relating to the Status of Refugees, the UN Convention Against Torture, and the European Convention for the Protection of Human Rights and Fundamental Freedoms (ECHR).[1] This broadened scope of international legal obligations incumbent upon Albania has increased the potential for its highest domestic courts, namely the Albanian Supreme Court and the Albanian Constitutional Court, to engage with international law in disputes brought before them. In general, these courts appear to follow a strategy of alignment—and even hyper-alignment—with international law, although one may also encounter, rarely, the adoption of strategies of avoidance or contestation. Usually, whenever a case has required these courts to engage with international law, the primacy of the international legal norm under consideration has not been disputed. Sometimes, the eagerness of Albanian courts to give effect to international norms goes even beyond Albania's actual treaty obligations. This is unsurprising within a national context where both the executive and the legislative

[1] International Covenant on Civil and Political Rights (adopted 16 December 1966, entered into force 23 March 1976) 999 UNTS 171; International Covenant on Economic, Social and Cultural Rights (adopted 16 December 1966, entered into force 3 January 1976) 993 UNTS 3; Convention relating to the Status of Refugees (adopted 28 July 1951, entered into force 22 April 1954) 189 UNTS 137; Convention against Torture and Other Cruel, Inhuman or Degrading Treatment or Punishment (adopted 10 December 1984, entered into force 26 June 1987) 1465 UNTS 85; European Convention for the Protection of Human Rights and Fundamental Freedoms (adopted 4 November 1950, entered into force 3 September 1953) ETS No 5 (ECHR). Albania acceded to the two Covenants in October 1991; to the Refugee Convention in August 1992; to the Convention Against Torture in May 1994; and to the ECHR in October 1996.

branch have been keen to expand the scope of Albania's international legal obligations. To some extent, this tendency towards alignment confirms the findings of the International Law Association (ILA) Study Group Final Report (ILA Final Report) based on observations from several countries that encourage 'their courts to adopt a strategy or posture of alignment, occasionally even going into hyper-alignment'.[2]

The first part of this chapter will briefly sketch out the status of international law in the Albanian legal system, based on the relevant provisions of the Albanian Constitution. The second part will then analyse selected relevant caselaw concerning human rights obligations under the ECHR, international criminal law (Albania's accession to the Statute of the International Criminal Court), the law of immunities, and the law of the sea, based on the typology developed in the ILA Final Report.[3] The reason for focusing on the practice of the Constitutional Court is that its mandate under Article 131 of the Constitution includes broad powers to check the compatibility of international agreements with the Constitution, domestic laws and other international law norms binding on Albania.[4] In fulfilling this function, the Constitutional Court has rendered several relevant decisions. The practice of the Supreme Court is also important given that this court engages more regularly with international law, whereas district and appeals courts tend to do so more rarely. More importantly, the Supreme Court's legal findings are binding on the lower courts.[5] The main cases from these courts, which are analysed below, fall primarily in the category of alignment (sometimes including hyper-alignment), with few occasions of avoidance and contestation. The final part of the chapter will try to discern whether there exists, in the practice of Albanian courts, a common pattern in approaching international law; and if so, identify it.

[2] ILA Study Group on Principles on the Engagement of Domestic Courts with International Law, 'Final Report: Mapping the Engagement of Domestic Courts with International Law' (Johannesburg, 2016) (ILA Final Report) para 75.

[3] ibid especially para 36.

[4] Constitution of the Republic of Albania, Law No 8417, 21 October 1998 (as modified by Law No 9675, 13 January 2007, Law No 9904, 21 April 2008, Law No 88/2012, 18 September 2012, and Law 137/2015, 17 December 2015) (Constitution). See especially art 131(a), (b), and (c).

[5] Constitution (n 4) art 141(2). This paragraph provides that, '[f]or the unification or amendment of judicial practice, the Supreme Court has the right to select particular judicial cases for review in the joint colleges'.

B. The Status of International Law in the Albanian Legal System

The Albanian Constitution regulates in considerable detail the place of international law in the Albanian legal system.[6] First, in Part 1 which is concerned with basic principles, Article 4(2) establishes the superior status of the Constitution as the highest law in the Republic of Albania.[7] Subsequently, Article 5 of the Constitution stipulates that 'the Republic of Albania applies international law that is binding upon it'.[8] While at first sight Article 5 appears to have only declaratory effect, it in fact functions as a singular and necessary link between two distinct legal systems. This article establishes the necessary connection between Albania's domestic legal system and international law which becomes an integral part of it. Based on the principle *pacta sunt servanda*, this constitutional provision is the basis upon which international law enjoys a special status in Albania's domestic legal system.

Part 7 of the Constitution deals specifically with normative acts and international agreements, establishing a hierarchy of legal sources applicable in Albania. Article 116(1) lists ratified international agreements immediately after the Constitution and before other domestic laws.[9] Although not explicitly sanctioned in the text of the Constitution, scholars have always maintained that such an order of precedence actually constitutes a formal hierarchy of the sources of law in Albania for two main reasons:[10] First, Article 4 establishes the Constitution as the supreme law of the land; second, according to Article 122(2), 'an international agreement that has been ratified by law has superiority over laws of the country that are not compatible with it'.

Similarly with other European Constitutions,[11] the Albanian Constitution provides that ratification by Parliament is mandatory for political treaties, such as those involving territory, peace, alliances, the military, freedoms and liberties, participation in international organizations, or those involving a financial

[6] For the place accorded to international law in 27 countries see, eg, Dinah Shelton (ed), *International Law and Domestic Legal Systems: Incorporation, Transformation, and Persuasion* (OUP 2011). More generally, see Malgosia Fitzmaurice and Cees Flinterman (eds), *Interactions between International and Municipal Law: A Comparative Case Law Study* (TMC Asser Instituut 1993).

[7] Constitution (n 4) art 4.

[8] Constitution (n 4) art 5.

[9] Constitution (n 4) art 116(1).

[10] Luan Omari and Aurela Anastasi, *E Drejta Kushtetuese* (ABC 2010) 47.

[11] Constitution of the Italian Republic, 22 December 1947 (as amended to 20 April 2012), Official Gazette No 298, art 80; Constitution of the French Republic, 28 September 1958 (as amended to 23 July 2008), art 53; Spanish Constitution, 6 December 1978 (as amended to 27 September 2011), ss 93–94. For other similar constitutions see <https://www.constituteproject.org> last accessed 24 July 2023.

contribution by the State.[12] However, the list is not exhaustive, since Parliament retains discretion to ratify other international agreements which do not involve the abovementioned subjects, but are considered important enough to require decision-making on its part.[13]

Ratification by Parliament is done by law, and serves a dual purpose.[14] First, it vests the treaty with the force and solemnity of an act approved by the elected representatives of the Albanian people. Second, it directly incorporates the (international) treaty into domestic legislation. A ratified international agreement becomes part of the domestic legal system after its publication in the Official Gazette.[15] Such an agreement is implemented directly, except where it is non-self-executing and its implementation requires the passing of new legislation.[16] It should be noted that a self-executing treaty does not necessarily entail the direct effect of that treaty.[17] As a general rule, any ratified treaty which would introduce an obligation, rather than a right for citizens, is to be considered a non-self-executing treaty, considering that Article 17(1) of the Constitution, which mandates that any limitation to rights and freedoms must be introduced by law[18] operates as *lex specialis* to any other norm introduced in the domestic legal system. The same rationale is valid for rules of customary international law (CIL). Therefore, while it normally falls upon Parliament to identify which binding international norms require implementation by (separate) law, it is up to the courts to apply the above test and decide, on a case-by-case basis, whether a particular ratified treaty, or rule of CIL, has direct effect or whether it needs specific legislation in order to be applied by courts.

[12] Constitution (n 4) art 121(1).

[13] Constitution (n 4) art 121(2).

[14] The issue of Parliamentary involvement in international treaty-making has been the subject of many discussions: See recently in Jenny S Martinez, 'The Constitutional Allocation of Executive and Legislative Power Over Foreign Relations: A Survey' in Curtis A Bradley (ed), *The Oxford Handbook of Comparative Foreign Relations Law* (OUP 2019) 104–6. For a study on Commonwealth African States see Ernest Yaw Ako and Richard Frimpong Oppong, 'Foreign Relations Law in the Constitutions and Courts of Commonwealth African Countries' in Curtis A Bradley (ed), *The Oxford Handbook of Comparative Foreign Relations Law* (OUP 2019) 585–94; for some other Commonwealth States, see Joanna Harrington, 'Scrutiny and Approval: The Role for Westminster-Style Parliaments in Treaty-Making' (2006) 55 ICLQ 121; for an earlier study focusing on Europe, the United States, Argentina, and Brazil, see Stefan Riesenfeld and Frederick Abbot (eds), 'Symposium on Parliamentary Participation in the Making and Operation of Treaties' (1991) 67 Chicago-Kent Law Review 293–704.

[15] Constitution (n 4) art 122(1).

[16] ibid. Exceptions concerning non-self-executing treaties are common where a legal system allows for direct application of international treaties through incorporation. See Pierre-Hugues Verdier and Mila Versteeg, 'International Law in National Legal Systems: An Empirical Investigation' in Anthea Roberts et al (eds), *Comparative International Law* (OUP 2018) 220.

[17] European Commission for Democracy Through Law (Venice Commission), 'Report on the Implementation of International Human Rights Treaties in Domestic Law and the Role of Courts' (8 December 2014) Doc No CDL-AD(2014)036 paras 29–30.

[18] Constitution (n 4) art 17(1).

C. The Practice of Albanian Courts

The Constitutional Court and the Supreme Court, the highest[19] courts in Albania, have dealt on several occasions with cases involving the application of international law. Although the Constitutional Court is not formally part of the Albanian judiciary,[20] under the Constitution it has been vested with a leading role in determining the compatibility of Albanian laws with international law agreements to which Albania is party.[21] The Supreme Court has a recognized role in the unification or amendment of judicial practice, with which lower courts have to comply.[22] Overall, these courts seem to have generally adopted a strategy of alignment when engaging with international law, although some examples of contestation (both local and internationally minded)[23] can also be encountered in their caselaw.

1. Cases of Hyper-alignment: Going the Extra Mile

By way of introduction, it must be noted that Albanian courts are generally positively inclined towards engaging with international law. On some occasions, such eagerness to apply international—in particular human rights[24]—norms has led the two highest courts to go beyond Albania's legal obligations under international law by deciding on the basis of, or by referring to, non-binding instruments or non-ratified treaties. This practice is illustrative of the posture of 'hyper-alignment' as discussed in the ILA Final Report.[25]

The first notable case concerns what is probably the Constitutional Court's most important decision following the approval of the new Albanian Constitution in 1998. This decision dealt with the prohibition of the death

[19] The authors refer to both courts as 'highest' in view of the fact that while the Supreme Court is the highest court in the judiciary system, its judgments may still be reviewed by the Constitutional Court on constitutional grounds.

[20] *See* Constitution (n 4) pts 8 and 9.

[21] Constitution (n 4) art 131.

[22] Constitution (n 4) art 141(2).

[23] For the distinction between local contestation and internationally minded contestation, see ILA Final Report (n 2) para 65.

[24] For a general discussion of enforcing international human rights norms in domestic courts see, among others, Benedetto Conforti and Francesco Francioni (eds), *Enforcing International Human Rights in Domestic Courts* (Martinus Nijhoff 1997); M Shah Alam, 'Enforcement of International Human Rights Law by Domestic Courts: A Theoretical and Practical Study' (2006) 53 Netherlands International Law Review 399; Michael Kirby, 'Domestic Courts and International Human Rights Law: The Ongoing Judicial Conversation' (2010) 6 Utrecht Law Review 168.

[25] ILA Final Report (n 2) para 55.

penalty during peacetime.[26] At the time, Albania had been a member of the Council of Europe (CoE) since 1995, had acceded to the ECHR, and had ratified this Convention's Protocols Nos 1, 2, 4, 7, and 11.[27] Despite having enacted a moratorium on the application of the death penalty and having declared its intention to ratify Protocol No 6 of the ECHR concerning the prohibition of death penalty during peacetime[28] within three years from the date of joining the CoE, Albania had not yet done so. In its judgment, the Constitutional Court criticized this failure, holding, among other things, that the signing and ratification of Protocol No 6 ECHR was not only a political, but also a (unilateral) legal obligation. According to the Court, the fulfilment of such an obligation on time, 'would affirm the credibility of the Republic of Albania in the international arena, as a state that shows seriousness and responsibility in fulfilling its unilateral obligations'.[29] Following this introductory statement, the Court engaged in an analysis of the relevant provisions of the Constitution and found that the death penalty violated the right to life, was a cruel and unusual punishment, and did not serve the main aim of any criminal punishment, which was the rehabilitation of the offender. While arguably these arguments could have been enough for the Court to persuasively render its judgment, it went further and claimed that the death penalty was incompatible with and in violation of the ECHR.[30] Despite the Constitutional Court's arguments in this respect, it is undisputed that the ECHR as such did not prohibit the death penalty, at least not at that time when not all contracting parties had ratified

[26] Constitutional Court, Judgment No 65/99, 10 December 1999.

[27] Protocol to the Convention for the Protection of Human Rights and Fundamental Freedoms (adopted 20 March 1953, entered into force 18 May 1954) ETS No 9; Protocol No 2 to the Convention for the Protection of Human Rights and Fundamental Freedoms, Conferring upon the European Court of Human Rights competence to give advisory opinions (adopted 6 May 1963, entered into force 21 September 1970) ETS No 44; Protocol No 4 to the Convention for the Protection of Human Rights and Fundamental Freedoms, securing certain rights and freedoms other than those already included in the Convention and in the first Protocol thereto (adopted 16 September 1963, entered into force 2 May 1968) ETS No 46; Protocol No 7 to the Convention for the Protection of Human Rights and Fundamental Freedoms (adopted 22 November 1984, entered into force 1 November 1988) ETS No 117; Protocol No 11 to the Convention for the Protection of Human Rights and Fundamental Freedoms, restructuring the control machinery established thereby (adopted 11 May 1994, entered into force 1 November 1998) ETS No 155. For a recent discussion of Albania's relationship with the CoE, see Irma Spahiu, 'The Impact of the Pan-European General Principles of Good Administration on Albanian Law: A Struggle between Law-Making and Implementation' in Ulrich Stelkens and Agné Andrijauskaité (eds), *Good Administration and the Council of Europe: Law, Principles and Effectiveness* (OUP 2020).

[28] Protocol No 6 to the Convention for the Protection of Human Rights and Fundamental Freedoms concerning the Abolition of the Death Penalty (adopted 28 April 1983, entered into force 1 March 1985) ETS No 114.

[29] Judgment No 65 (n 26) 3.

[30] ibid 8.

Protocol No 6. Otherwise, there would have been no need for the Protocol in the first place.[31]

A second and more direct case of hyper-alignment concerns the reopening of criminal proceedings following a judgment of the European Court of Human Rights (ECtHR) finding that the ECHR was violated in the original proceedings. In 2008, Albania introduced new legislation to allow for the reopening of civil cases following a judgment of the ECtHR.[32] Until 2017,[33] the reopening of criminal cases remained impossible, at least according to the Code of Criminal Procedure (CCP). While the Albanian government was in the process of working on a draft amendment to the CCP for this purpose, the Constitutional Court and the Supreme Court grew impatient and accepted this possibility through judicial activism. After the *Barberá, Messegué, and Jarabo* case,[34] the *Xheraj* case officially became the second time[35] a Constitutional Court had ever directed other courts to reopen criminal proceedings following a judgment of the ECtHR, despite the absence of such a provision in the CCP.[36]

In *Xheraj v Albania*,[37] the domestic proceedings were focused on whether the prosecution should have been granted leave to file an appeal out of time against a verdict of acquittal, despite the fact that it had submitted such a request almost a year after the proscribed time limit of ten days. After lengthy proceedings, the Supreme Court ultimately accepted the prosecution's appeal and quashed the judgment of acquittal, thereby confirming a previous guilty

[31] For a brief discussion of the legal developments on death penalty abolition in the European context, see Nigel Rodley and Matt Pollard, *The Treatment of Prisoners under International Law* (OUP 2011) 289–94; William A. Schabas, *The Abolition of the Death Penalty in International Law* 3rd ed. (OUP 2002) 259–309. See also more generally Roger Hood and Carolyn Hoyle (ed), *The Death Penalty: A Worldwide Perspective* (OUP 2015).

[32] Code of Civil Procedure of the Republic of Albania, Law No 8116, 29 March 1996 (as amended) art 494(2)(ë), added to by Law No 10052, 29 December 2008.

[33] Law No 35/2017 of 30 March 2017, art 258 (amending art 450 of the Code of Criminal Procedure) ('if the ground for the revision of the final decision results from a European Court of Human Rights judgment making the re-adjudication of the case indispensable').

[34] *Barberà, Messegué and Jabardo v Spain*, App No 10590/83, 6 December 1988; followed by Spanish Constitutional Court, Judgment 245/1991, 16 December 1991, BOE (Official State Gazette) No 13 of 15 January 1992, 39.

[35] With the exception of the *Van Mechelen* case (*Van Mechelen and Others v The Netherlands*, App Nos 55/1996/674/861-864, 23 April 1997), whereby in view of the impossibility of reopening criminal proceedings under Dutch law, it was the Minister of Justice who first ordered the applicants' provisional release and subsequently waived the remainder of their sentences.

[36] This classification does not include cases where constitutional courts have so-called positive annulment powers and can act as legislators to fill legal gaps, a case in point being the Italian Constitutional Court (see n 50). Moreover, it should be noted that the Spanish Constitutional Court did not base its decision on the direct applicability of the ECtHR judgment, but rather on a derived violation of the Spanish Constitution (see n 34). See also Matthias Hartwig, 'Much Ado about Human Rights: The Federal Constitutional Court Confronts the European Court of Human Rights' (2005) 6 German Law Journal 869, 882.

[37] *Xheraj v Albania*, App No 37959/02, 29 July 2008.

verdict of twenty years of imprisonment. After exhausting all local remedies, Mr Xheraj lodged an application with the ECtHR, which in turn, found an infringement of the principle of legal certainty, and consequently a violation of Article 6(1) ECHR on the right to a fair trial.[38] While the ECtHR did not order any non-pecuniary remedies in its *dispositif*, it still considered

> that the most appropriate form of redress for this continuing situation would be for the applicant's final acquittal of 14 December 1998 to be confirmed by the authorities and his conviction in breach of the Convention to be erased with effect from that date.[39]

Based on this passage, Mr Xheraj seized the Constitutional Court again, seeking the annulment of the Supreme Court's judgment of 20 June 2001 and the enforcement of the ECtHR's judgment instead. In its decision, while rejecting Mr Xheraj's application, the Constitutional Court noted that as Article 46 ECHR obliges States to abide by the ECtHR's final judgments, they are under an obligation to take all necessary measures to ensure the judgments' effective implementation. The Constitutional Court stressed the importance of reopening criminal proceedings in implementing the ECtHR's judgments as a possible tool towards achieving effective *restitutio in integrum* of the infringed right protected by the Convention.[40] It deplored the fact that Parliament had not yet amended the CCP with a provision similar to Article 494(2)(ë) of the Code of Civil Procedure, but added that the Supreme Court, as the authority responsible for the breach of the Convention, had to find a solution to the issue, even by way of analogy to the Code of Civil Procedure if necessary.[41]

Mr Xheraj then turned to the Supreme Court, which, however, rejected his request to reopen the proceedings, arguing that Article 450 of the CCP did not foresee final judgments of the ECtHR as a ground for reopening criminal proceedings.[42] Mr Xheraj did not agree and reverted back to the Constitutional

[38] ibid [61].
[39] ibid [82].
[40] Constitutional Court, Decision on Inadmissibility No 22/10, 9 March 2010, 6 [4].
[41] ibid [5].
[42] CCP (n 33) art 450 at the time envisioned only four grounds on which the reopening of criminal proceedings was possible: when

a) the facts on the merits conflict with those of another judgment which is final;
b) the judgment was based on a civil court judgment, which has later been quashed;
c) new evidence has arisen, which if considered separately or in conjunction with any other previously tendered evidence, indicates that the judgment was wrongly decided upon;
d) it has been proved that the judgment was tainted by falsified evidence or any other facts constituting a crime.

Court. On this occasion, the latter made plain its disagreement with the Supreme Court. The Constitutional Court first stated:

> The Parliament is under an obligation to take such measures as to ensure compliance with the ECHR's dispositions. If it fails to do so, domestic courts must remedy this legal vacuum, and directly apply the ECtHR's judgments in accordance with Articles 122 of the Constitution and Articles 19 and 46 of the ECHR.[43]

The Constitutional Court's approach required the accommodation of the ECtHR's judgments by direct reliance on constitutional provisions, despite the fact that the necessary domestic criminal law provisions were lacking. Indeed, Article 122 of the Constitution may serve as a basis for the direct application of the ECHR in the Albanian legal system. In addition, as mentioned above, according to Article 46(1) of the ECHR, Member States 'undertake to abide by the final judgment of the Court in any case to which they are parties'. That notwithstanding, it should be noted, that remedies ordered by the ECtHR are binding only when they are phrased in mandatory terms and included in the *dispositif*.[44] In *Xheraj*, the ECtHR *ordered* the payment of pecuniary damages, but only *recommended* that confirming the judgment of acquittal would be 'the most appropriate form of redress'.[45] This is because States enjoy a certain margin of appreciation as to how they enforce the obligation under Article 46 of the Convention.[46] The ECtHR itself has noted that 'the Convention does not give it jurisdiction to direct a state to open a new trial or to quash a conviction' and that 'it cannot find a state to be in breach of the Convention on account of its failure to take either of these courses of action when faced with the execution of one of its judgments'.[47] Thus, contrary to the Constitutional Court's assertion, domestic courts are not obliged to act, and do not bear responsibility if no legal remedy is available in their legal system to enforce the ECtHR's judgments.[48]

[43] Constitutional Court, Judgment No 20/11, 1 June 2011, 6–7.

[44] Laurence R Helfer, 'Redesigning the European Court of Human Rights: Embeddedness as a Deep Structural Principle of the European Human Rights Regime' (2008) 19 EJIL 125, 147 (and fn 131).

[45] *Xheraj v Albania* (n 37) [61].

[46] Council of Europe Committee of Ministers, 'Recommendation No R (2000) 2 of the Committee of Ministers to Member States on the Re-Examination or Reopening of Certain Cases at Domestic Level following Judgments of the European Court of Human Rights' (19 January 2000) Explanatory Memorandum, para 1.

[47] *Lyons and Others v The United Kingdom*, App No 15227/03, 8 July 2003 (Decision on Admissibility), 9.

[48] Hartwig (n 36) 886.

It should be noted that the Constitutional Court only has annulment powers.[49] The Court can strike down a law or a legal provision as unconstitutional, but cannot declare them unconstitutional for not including a right or a liberty protected by the Constitution. Consequently, it could not act like other constitutional courts, such as the Italian one, which, only about two months before had struck down Article 630 of the Italian Code of Criminal Procedure in the part where it did not provide other grounds for reopening criminal proceedings, 'when that is necessary ... to conform to a final judgment of the ECtHR'.[50] This might be the reason why the Constitutional Court decided instead to interpret Article 450(1)(a) of the CCP as widely as possible, so as to include the ECtHR's judgments.

Nevertheless, the Constitutional Court did not deal with a crucial element of Article 450(1)(a) of the CCP, which clearly provides that a reopening of proceedings may be granted only when '*the facts* on the merits conflict with *those* of another judgment which is final'.[51] Even accepting that an ECtHR judgment may be considered as 'another judgment which is final' for the purposes of Article 450(1)(a), it is still hard to accept that an ECtHR judgment is decided on a conflicting set of 'facts' which contradict those of the prior, domestic judgment. The ECtHR is certainly not a trier of new facts and, where criminal cases are concerned, does not decide on the guilt or innocence of a defendant, but rather only reviews the judgments of domestic courts vis-à-vis the rights and liberties guaranteed by the ECHR. It appears then that the Supreme Court was correct when it first denied the applicability of Article 450(1)(a) of the CCP to final judgments of the ECtHR.[52] Eventually, however, it had to give way to the interpretation of the Constitutional Court.[53] This case also illustrates the diverse dynamics that may develop within the domestic sphere due to differing approaches adopted by domestic courts towards the interpretation and enforcement of international obligations, with the Constitutional Court preferring hyper-alignment and the Supreme Court adopting what appears to be a strategy of affirmative avoidance.[54]

A third example of hyper-alignment can be found in a 2002 case of the Constitutional Court, when the Council of Ministers asked the Court whether

[49] Constitution (n 4) art 132(1).

[50] Italian Constitutional Court, Judgment No 113/2011, 4 April 2011, <www.cortecostituzionale.it/actionSchedaPronuncia.do?anno=2011&numero=113> last accessed 24 July 2023 (in Italian, with English translation).

[51] CCP (n 33) art 450(1)(a) (emphasis added).

[52] Although it should have probably followed another reasoning, namely the 'contradictory facts' requirement under CCP (n 33) art 450(1)(a).

[53] Supreme Court, Criminal Bench, Judgment No 52102-01226-00-2011, 7 March 2012.

[54] ILA Final Report (n 2) paras 39 and 41.

the Statute of the International Criminal Court (ICC Statute or Rome Statute)[55] was compatible with the Constitution.[56] Article 35 of the Constitution provides that '[n]o one may be sentenced more than once for the same criminal offense or be tried again, except for cases when the re-adjudication of the case is ordered by a higher court, in the manner specified by law'. When analysing the principle of *ne bis in idem* in the Rome Statute vis-à-vis the Albanian Constitution, the Court seemed to follow a rather peculiar reasoning. Considering that the Rome Statute is based on the principle of complementarity, the Court interpreted the assessment by the ICC of Article 20 of the Rome Statute (*ne bis in idem*) as constituting a review by a higher court, thus placing the International Criminal Court in the position of 'the highest court (in relation to the prosecution of [international] crimes).[57] While this interpretation is debatable, if not incorrect, it demonstrates the willingness of Albania's Constitutional Court to ascribe wide-ranging primacy to international law.

Finally, the *Grori v Albania* case provides an interesting instance of *apparent* hyper-alignment from the perspective of the ECtHR.[58] In that case, the applicant was tried *in absentia* in Italy, was sentenced there to life imprisonment, and was subsequently arrested by Albanian authorities in Albania. The central issue was whether the prison sentence imposed by Italian courts could be declared valid and enforceable in Albania. Article 514(e) of the CCP, the law applicable at the time of the applicant's detention, provided that a foreign sentence could be declared valid and enforceable by Albanian courts on the condition, among others, of the prior consent of the person concerned.[59] While that particular provision was certainly an absurdity—no rational person would give his or her consent to suffer a criminal sentence—and was quickly repealed by Parliament,[60] the district and appeal courts were hesitant to disregard the letter of the law, and denied as a result the enforceability of the Italian (foreign) judgment in view of the applicant's obvious lack of consent. On appeal, the case was relinquished to the Joint Benches of the Supreme Court,[61] which quashed

[55] Rome Statute of the International Criminal Court (adopted 17 July 1998, entered into force 1 July 2002) 2187 UNTS 3.

[56] Constitutional Court, Judgment No 186/02, 23 September 2002.

[57] ibid 8.

[58] *Grori v Albania*, App No 25336/04, 7 July 2009.

[59] Code of Criminal Procedure of the Republic of Albania, Law No 7905, 21 March 1995 (as amended) (CCP) art 514(e).

[60] Law No 8813, 13 June 2002 (amending the CCP).

[61] CCP (n 59) art 438. The Supreme Court may relinquish its jurisdiction in favour of the Joint Benches of the Supreme Court which are competent for the unification and amendment of court practice. See Mbaresa Veleshnja Gentry and Engjellushe (Angel) Kozeli Mozina, 'Update: Researching the Albanian Legal System' (*GlobaLex*, Hasuer Global Law School Program NYU, July/August 2019) <https://www.nyulawglobal.org/globalex/Albania1.html> last accessed 24 July 2023, s 3.3. In such cases, the Joint Benches issue a 'unifying judgment'.

the previous judgments and unanimously held that the prior consent of the convicted person was not required in proceedings concerning the recognition and enforcement of foreign judgments.[62] In support of their reasoning, the Joint Benches also made reference, as persuasive authority, to the Convention on the Transfer of Sentenced Persons[63] and the European Convention on the International Validity of Criminal Judgments,[64] acknowledging, however, that the latter was not ratified by Albania and did not form part of the domestic legal system. Responding to the second claim that there was no bilateral agreement with Italy on the recognition and enforcement of criminal judgments, the Joint Benches held that, first, Parliament had already introduced such concept in the domestic criminal procedural law, and, second, that even in the absence of ratified agreements, generally accepted rules of international law may be applied by recourse to the principle of good will and reciprocity.[65] According to the Joint Benches, the Ministry of Justice has full discretion on whether to trigger the conversion proceedings of a foreign judgment by forwarding the request to the Prosecution Service. Such discretion is derived from the political will of the Albanian State and as such is not justiciable by courts.[66] The same rationale was then confirmed by the Constitutional Court.[67]

According to the ECtHR, the reliance of both the Supreme Court and the Constitutional Court on 'the principle of good will and reciprocity' and the reference to international law instruments which were not yet in force between Albania and Italy could not meet the standard of 'lawfulness' under Article 5(1) of the ECHR.[68] The ECtHR concluded that 'the Supreme Court's search for a more adequate legal basis for the applicant's detention, led it to import into domestic law provisions of international law instruments which had not yet entered into force with respect to the Republic of Albania'.[69] It appears, however, that the ECtHR's reasoning was based on a grossly incorrect reading of the Supreme Court's unifying judgment. The ECtHR misquoted

[62] Supreme Court, Joint Benches, Unifying Penal Judgment No 1, 30 January 2003. Available at <https://www.gjykataelarte.gov.al/sq/vendime-unifikuese-ne-vite> accessed 6 January 2024.

[63] Convention on the Transfer of Sentenced Persons ETS No 112.

[64] European Convention on the International Validity of Criminal Judgments ETS No 70.

[65] Supreme Court, Unifying Penal Judgment (n 62) 8–9.

[66] ibid 9. Unlike extradition, which requires the existence of a corresponding bilateral or multilateral treaty between the requestor and requested State, art 512(1) of the CCP provides that, as a rule the proceedings to recognize a foreign criminal sentence are triggered when the Ministry of Justice transfers the request to the Prosecution Service. Article 512(2) provides that such proceedings can be triggered *also* when the Ministry of Justice transfers the request pursuant to an international agreement (emphasis added).

[67] Constitutional Court, Judgment No 13/04, 12 July 2004.

[68] *Grori v Albania* (n 58) [160].

[69] ibid [158].

the judgments by claiming that both the Constitutional and Supreme Court had considered the old provision of Article 514 of the CCP as 'inadequate' and that a legal basis could be provided by reference to international law norms.[70] Based on this incorrect assumption, the ECtHR found that one of these treaties (European Convention on the International Validity of Criminal Judgments and the Convention on the Transfer of Sentenced Persons) was not yet in force and could not have been properly relied on by the Albanian courts as a basis for the detention of the applicant.

The Joint Benches had made clear that the *ratio decidendi* of the case was based on a teleological and systemic interpretation of the CCP, and references to non-ratified international instruments were made only in support of the main argument, that is in order 'to help [them] understand, interpret and correctly apply the provisions of the Code of Criminal Procedure relevant to the case at bar'.[71] The Joint Benches went on to explain that in cases where the plain meaning of the text would lead to an absurd conclusion, whereby it would be left to the convicted person to decide whether the foreign judgment would be recognized at all, the teleological and systemic interpretation of the provision takes precedence.[72] According the Joint Benches, the concept of 'consent of the convict' should be construed as to include the consent regarding the country which the person should serve the sentence, and not include also the consent to the validity and enforcement of the sentence as such.[73] Such principle was 'recognised and accepted in international conventions' and also consistent with the 'object and purpose of the provisions of the Code of Criminal Procedure in its entirety'[74] Moreover, Article 512 of the CCP clearly provides for the recognition and enforcement of a foreign judgment upon a political decision of the Ministry of Justice, which can request it (through the Public Prosecution's Office) *also* on the basis of an international agreement.[75] Therefore, the legal basis relied upon by the Supreme Court was not 'the principle of good will and reciprocity' itself or the 'import into domestic law provisions of international law instruments which had not yet entered into force', but rather consisted of an extensive judicial interpretation of an inadvertent error included in a specific provision (corrected subsequently) in the context of the other relevant CCP provisions, coupled with references to relevant international law as persuasive

[70] ibid [157].
[71] Supreme Court, Unifying Penal Judgment No 1 (n 62) 6.
[72] ibid 7.
[73] ibid 7.
[74] ibid 8.
[75] CCP (n 59) art 512(2).

authority. While it is unclear how the ECtHR misinterpreted such a short and relatively straightforward reasoning,[76] this case provides an interesting instance where otherwise routine cases can be considered hyper-alignment in a false-positive fashion by external actors, probably due to mistranslation.

2. Cases of Affirmative Contestation

a. Law of immunities

The *Haxhiaj v Chemonics* case concerned an employment dispute between an individual and a private company which claimed immunity before Albanian courts.[77] The defendant, Chemonics International Inc., challenged the jurisdiction of the Tirana District Court, alleging that, on the basis of an international agreement between the Albanian and the United States Government, it enjoyed immunity from civil liability before Albanian courts.

In 1992, Albania and the United States had entered into a bilateral economic agreement concerning United States economic, technical, and related assistance to Albania.[78] Paragraph 3(d) of the agreement provided:

> Individuals, *public or private organizations*, and employees of public or private organizations, *under contract with or financed* by the Government of the United States of America, who are present in the Republic of Albania to perform work in connection with this agreement, shall be *immune from all civil liability directly related to the performance of such work.* (emphasis added)

As the Tirana District Court upheld its jurisdiction on the matter, Chemonics filed an interlocutory appeal with the Civil Bench of the Supreme Court. Considering the complexity of the issue, the case was relinquished to the Joint Benches of the Supreme Court. First, the Supreme Court noted that the defendant was in charge of implementing a project financed entirely by the United States Agency for International Development (USAID), an agency of the United States Government. Consequently, as a contractor of USAID in Albania, Chemonics was, according to paragraph 3(d) of the agreement, immune from all civil liability directly related to the performance of that project.[79]

[76] The Supreme Court judgment is only nine pages long.

[77] Supreme Court, Joint Benches, Unifying Civil Judgment No 8, 10 June 2011 (*Chemonics*).

[78] Agreement concerning Economic, Technical and Related Assistance (Albania-United States of America), TIAS 12456.

[79] ibid paras 12.1–12.2.

The Court then turned to the question of whether the granting of immunity would infringe the fundamental right of access to court under Article 42(2) of the Constitution and Article 6(1) ECHR. Applying the *Ashingdane* test developed by the ECtHR,[80] the Court quickly found that '[o]n the basis of the scope of the agreement and its legitimate aim, [we] find no unreasonable relation of proportionality between this limitation and the aim sought'.[81] Accordingly, the Court upheld the defendant's absolute immunity in civil cases, even with regard to employment related disputes.[82] It noted, however, that, according to Article 32(2) of the Vienna Convention on Diplomatic Relations (VCDR), the sending State may waive the immunity of those who enjoy diplomatic immunity from jurisdiction.[83]

According to the Joint Benches, although the United States-Albania agreement had not provided for such a possibility, this did not mean that a waiver was not possible. Indeed, the parties had waived their immunity by expressly mentioning the jurisdiction of Albanian courts in the employment contract. The Supreme Court also dismissed the claim that the 'waiver' was invalid because in view of Article 7(3) of the Labour Code, all '[a]rrangements on jurisdiction are valid only if they are concluded after the dispute has arisen'. According to the Court, this provision was not applicable in this case, as it related to a waiver of jurisdiction and not an agreement on changing it.[84] Thus, the waiver of immunity had been valid.

This notwithstanding, both findings are subject to criticism. Regarding the first question, namely whether *Chemonics* enjoyed immunity before Albanian courts in relation to employment disputes, it is very dubious whether the plain meaning of the term 'civil liability directly related to the performance of such work' supports such an expansive interpretation as to include 'employment contracts' in general, rather than simply tort actions directly related to the implementation of a certain project financed by the United States Government vis-à-vis third parties. Indeed, such an interpretation would even lead to an illogical conclusion, whereby *Chemonics*, a private contractor, would have enjoyed more immunity than the United States embassy in Tirana itself vis-à-vis employment disputes with local staff.[85] The ECtHR has found that States

[80] *Ashingdane v the United Kingdom*, App No 8225/78, 28 May 1985.
[81] *Chemonics* (n 77) [13]–[14].
[82] ibid [16].
[83] Vienna Convention on Diplomatic Relations (adopted 18 April 1961, entered into force 24 April 1964) 500 UNTS 95 art 32(1) and (2).
[84] *Chemonics* (n 77) [1]–[25].
[85] This is because the United States-Albania Agreement limits immunity to only such liability directly related to the performance of the United States-Albania Technical Agreement, whereas work done by an embassy is general in nature.

cannot invoke immunity in employment disputes, except for the cases listed in Article 11(2) of the United Nations Convention on Jurisdictional Immunities of States and Their Property (UNCJISP).[86] Although not yet in force, on several occasions the ECtHR has emphasized that Article 11 of the Convention has achieved the status of CIL.[87] Considering that Albania has not formally objected to the rule, it may be asserted that Article 11 of the Convention applies to Albania as a matter of CIL.[88]

Even if, *arguendo*, paragraph 3(d) of the United States-Albania Technical Agreement could be construed as waiving the labour jurisdiction of Albanian courts in favour of immunity under Article 11(1) UNCJISP, such a treaty obligation would violate another treaty obligation, namely Article 6 ECHR.[89] Indeed, the majority on the bench failed to explain why the granting of immunity to a private contractor for employment disputes would serve a legitimate aim in the first place. Most importantly, it further failed to explain how it was proportionate to the absolute limitation of the right of access to court.

In addition, Chemonics was not, unlike the referring Civil Bench incorrectly assumed, an intergovernmental organization.[90] It was simply a private organization that under the bilateral agreement was eligible to functional immunity with regard to the performance of its contract with USAID. While granting such functional immunity may well serve a legitimate aim, it still remains highly disproportionate to impose an absolute restriction of the right to access to court for employment disputes.[91]

[86] United National Convention on Jurisdictional Immunities of States and Their Property, UNGA Res 59/38 (2 December 2004) Annex (UNCJISP) art 11(2). See *Wallishauser v Austria*, App No 156/04, 19 November 2012; *Sabeh El Leil v France*, App No 34869/05, 29 June 2011; *Cudak v Lithuania* App No 15869/02, 23 March 2010.

[87] *Wallishauser* (n 86) [60]; *Sabeh El Leil* (n 86) [54]. For an analysis of UNCJISP (n 86) art 11, see Joanne Foakes and Roger O'Keefe, 'Article 11' in Roger O'Keefe et al (eds), *The United Nations Convention on Jurisdictional Immunities of States and Their Property: A Commentary* (OUP 2013).

[88] While Article 11(1) UNCJISP provides a saving clause (unless States decide otherwise) it is clear from the United States-Albania Technical Agreement has a narrow application, namely that the immunity would apply to only work done in relation to the performance of such Agreement.

[89] Although the agreement was probably intended to have a limited temporal effect, it is still a valid treaty today. The issue thus becomes more of a treaty conflict between the United States-Albania bilateral treaty and the Albania-ECHR treaty obligations. The VCLT does not provide a solution to this conflict. In practice, Albania would have to decide which treaty it will violate.

[90] It appears that the Civil Bench incorrectly assumed that Chemonics enjoyed immunity similar to international organizations and further complicated the case by asking the Joint Benches to also pronounce on a more general question, namely whether international organizations (such as the UN or its specialized agencies) enjoy immunity in relation to employment disputes before Albanian courts. The Joint Benches, however, decided to narrow its response to only those employment disputes which arose as a direct application of the 1992 Albania-United States agreement. *See*, *Chemonics* (77) [9].

[91] Moreover, is it highly doubtful whether employment disputes can be correctly categorized as 'civil liabilities directly related to the performance of its work' under the United States-Albania agreement (n 78).

As to the second question, the majority of the Joint Benches overlooked two important aspects of the concept of waiver under international law. Under the VCDR, a waiver should be a) express; and b) invoked by the sending State.[92] While the VCDR is not applicable in the present case (since the United States-Albania Technical Agreement did not accord diplomatic status to contractors) it is clear that *Chemonics* did not enjoy immunity on a personal capacity. At most, such immunity was functional in nature, and operated exclusively to liability work directly related to the performance of work in connection with the agreement. Thus, it was for the United States Government to either invoke, or eventually waive the immunity of any USAID contractor. The fact that neither happened further supports the argument that paragraph 3(d) of the United States-Albania Technical Agreement provided for a very narrow immunity, namely non-contractual liability in connection to work directly related to the implementation of such agreement.

The jurisprudence of the Supreme Court regarding State immunity in employment disputes has been, indeed, quite inconsistent. In *Brahimllari v Consulate General of Greece in Korçë*,[93] a case decided six months after *Chemonics*, a Civil Bench of the Supreme Court held that the defendant, the Greek Consulate General in Korçë, was entitled to immunity from legal process before Albanian courts despite the fact that the case concerned a former local employee who did not exercise any governmental function at the Consulate General.[94] This approach appeared to change two years later. In *Jatru v Consulate General of Greece in Korçë*,[95] a case very similar to *Brahimllari*, a different Civil Bench of the Supreme Court reversed a judgment of the Korçë District Court which had previously upheld the jurisdictional immunity of the Greek Consulate General. While still making reference to the VCDR, the Supreme Court was in this case highly influenced by the case law of the ECtHR. It first held that international law did not support any more the proposition that State immunity is absolute, and distinguished between acts performed by States in their sovereign capacity from those performed in their private capacity (acts *jure imperii*/acts *jure gestionis*). The Court then cited the ECtHR and the European Court of Justice (now Court of Justice of the European Union) in finding that States cannot claim immunity with regard to contracts of employment with persons who did not perform functions falling within the exercise

[92] Likewise, in the case of the immunities of international organizations, it is usually the organization which can legally invoke immunity on behalf of an official.
[93] Supreme Court, Civil Bench, Judgment No 00-2011-2304(569), 13 December 2011.
[94] Mr Brahimllari was employed as a driver at the General Consulate of Greece.
[95] Supreme Court, Civil Bench, Judgment No 00-2013-2586(679), 19 December 2013.

of public powers. Since the applicant had been employed as a guard and receptionist by the Consulate General, the Supreme Court concluded that Albanian courts had jurisdiction to hear the case.

Yet, in April 2015, the Supreme Court reverted to its previous jurisprudence and upheld the jurisdictional immunity of Qatar in *Nuraj v Embassy of the State of Qatar*.[96] The reasoning of the Court mirrored the one in *Brahimllari* and (rather unsurprisingly) did not explain the departure from the holding in *Jatru*. As expected, on 16 March 2016, the Constitutional Court confirmed the principle of limited State immunity in employment disputes with local staff of diplomatic missions by quashing *Nuraj* and sending the case back to the Supreme Court.[97] However, on the merits, the Constitutional Court requested the Supreme Court to specify whether the applicant, other than having worked as a secretary, had also exercised, as alleged by the Embassy of Qatar, duties 'directly connected' with the fulfilment of the mission according to the VCDR or Article 11 UNCJISP. After rehearing the case, the Supreme Court agreed with the legal reasoning of the Constitutional Court, but confirmed on the merits its previous judgment and upheld Qatar's plea of immunity.[98] The Supreme Court argued that as (former) secretary to the Ambassador and translator, the applicant Mrs Nuraj, had been privy to confidential information and that her functional tasks were directly connected to the diplomatic activity of the Embassy of Qatar, thus falling within the exception set out by Article 11(2) of the UNCJISP and CIL.[99] As this reasoning was consistent with the Constitutional Court's legal findings, an application for another constitutional review was later denied by the Constitutional Court.[100] It seems that both Courts correctly applied the law to the relevant facts, considering that the applicant's role, namely a private secretary to the Ambassador, was one of the specific examples cited by the ILC as falling within the exception set out in Article 11(2)(a) UNCJISP.[101]

b. Law of the sea

A final example of engagement with international can be found in the second case where the Constitutional Court was asked to assess the compatibility of an international agreement with the Constitution before its ratification. This

[96] Supreme Court, Civil Bench, Judgment No 00-2015-1245(187), 8 April 2015.
[97] Constitutional Court, Judgment No 18/16, 16 March 2016.
[98] Supreme Court, Civil Bench, Judgment No 00-2016-2159 (228), 29 June 2016.
[99] ibid [18]–[22].
[100] Constitutional Court, Judgment on Admissibility No 242/16, 21 December 2016. See also ibid, Dissenting Opinion of Judges Tusha and Kristo.
[101] (1991) II(2) ILC Yearbook 42 [9] ('Examples of such employees are private secretaries, code clerks, interpreters, translators and other persons entrusted with functions related to State security or basic interests of the State').

method of constitutional review is preferable to methods of constitutional review post ratification, since the review happens before the State contracts an international obligation. While, as discussed above, in the first case the Court found no obstacle for the ratification of the ICC Statute by the Albanian Parliament, in the second case the issue was more complex. This time, the Constitutional Court had to decide on the constitutionality of an agreement signed, between Albania and Greece, but not yet ratified, concerning the delimitation of their respective continental shelf areas and other maritime zones to which they are entitled under international law (Maritime Delimitation Agreement or Agreement).[102] In its judgment, the Constitutional Court found that the Agreement (i) was negotiated without the conferral of full powers by the President of the Republic; (ii) that, contrary to its title, the agreement in fact delimited internal and territorial waters; (iii) that it disregarded basic rules of international law on maritime delimitation in order to reach a fair and equitable result; and that (iv) it failed to recognize certain islands as constituting special circumstances for the purpose of maritime delimitation.

The Court strongly criticized the use of the 'strict equidistance' method instead of the 'equitable principles/relevant circumstances' method, stating that the latter was supported by decisions of international courts, by State practice and by the 1982 United Nations Convention on the Law of the Sea (UNCLOS).[103] The judgment acknowledged that the strict equidistance method may have been adopted in the past (as had been the case with the maritime delimitation agreement between Albania and Italy[104]), but that had occurred only in instances of delimitation between opposite coastal States, and only when such method had brought the expected result, that is an equitable solution.[105] It referred to Article 15 UNCLOS in mentioning that even in cases of delimitation of the territorial sea between States with opposite or adjacent coasts, equidistance is not applied where it is necessary by reason of

[102] Constitutional Court, Judgment No 15/10, 15 April 2010. See Agreement between the Hellenic Republic and the Republic of Albania on the Delimitation of their Respective Continental Shelf Area and Other Maritime Zones to which They Are Entitled under International Law (Albania-Greece), as reproduced in Giampiero Francalanci et al, 'Albania-Greece: Report Number 8–21' in David A Colson and Robert W Smith (eds), *International Maritime Boundaries* (ASIL/Brill 2011) 4462.

[103] ibid paras 88, 92, 94, 99. See United Nations Convention on the Law of the Sea (adopted 10 December 1982, entered into force 16 November 1994) 1833 UNTS 3 arts 15, 74(1), 83(1) for the delimitation of the territorial sea, exclusive economic zone, and continental shelf, respectively.

[104] Agreement between Albania and Italy for the Determination of the Continental Shelf of Each of the Two Countries (Albania-Italy) art I(1), available at <https://www.un.org/Depts/los/LEGISLATIONANDTREATIES/STATEFILES/ALB.htm> last accessed 24 July 2023 and as reproduced in Jonathan I Charney and Robert W Smith, 'Albania-Italy: Report Number 8–11' in Jonathan I Charney and L M Alexander (eds), *International Maritime Boundaries* (ASIL/Brill 1998) 2447 with short commentary.

[105] Judgment No 15 (n 102) [96]–[97].

historic title or other special circumstances to delimit the territorial seas of the two States applying a different method.[106] Thus, considering the coastal geography between Albania and Greece, the Court concluded that Article 1 of the Agreement, which prescribed the application of the strict equidistance method only and did not take into account possible special circumstances, was 'in violation of the 1982 Law of the Sea Convention, State practice and the relevant international jurisprudence'.[107] In the Court's view, the result of the Agreement was a *de facto* delimitation of maritime boundaries that had impermissibly changed the existing maritime borders between the two States. The Court found a violation of Article 3 of the Constitution, which provides that 'the independence of the state and the *integrity of its territory* [. . .] are the bases of this state, which has the duty to respect and protect them'.[108] While the Court may have over-reached somewhat in suggesting how the technical negotiations should have proceeded,[109] it was nevertheless correct in barring the ratification of the Agreement for failing to recognize the presence of special circumstances, in accordance with Article 15 UNCLOS, second sentence. It is uncertain whether this outcome may be seen as a clear instance of affirmative contestation[110] considering that the Constitutional Court did neither contest an *existing* international law obligation (there was no binding agreement under international law at that time) nor did it wish to change an *existing* international law of the sea rule. Indeed, the Court criticized the Government for applying international law in a manner inconsistent with the relevant UNCLOS provisions, rules of CIL, and international caselaw on the matter. Due to the Court's assessment of the proposed Agreement beyond its compatibility with the Constitution, this case may be classified, in the authors' view, as an example of internationally minded contestation or even an effort at alignment through development.

D. Conclusion

The caselaw of the Albanian Constitutional Court and the Supreme Court has clarified a number of issues concerning the place and applicability of international law in the Albanian legal system. In the limited number of cases

106 ibid [91], [99].
107 ibid [98] (emphasis added).
108 Constitution (n 4) art 3 (emphasis added).
109 Judgment No 15 (n 102) [95], [107].
110 ILA Final Report (n 2) para 59.

brought before them, these domestic courts have adopted a general strategy of alignment with international law. Occasionally, this has entailed going as far as practically legislating in order to fill the gaps of the domestic system, and to ensure that the State complies with its international law obligations, especially those enshrined in the ECHR, which enjoys constitutional status in Albania.[111] The eagerness of the highest Albanian courts to follow the ECtHR's jurisprudence and their commitment to human rights issues is understandable. At the same time, other important constitutional principles, namely the rule of law and the separation of powers need to be given proper attention, too. It is true that, following the ECtHR's judgment in the *Xheraj* case, Albania might have been committing a continuous breach of the Convention if the case were not reopened for consideration. However, it is questionable whether the judiciary is well placed to remedy this legal vacuum by implicitly assuming competences that the Constitution attributes exclusively to the legislative branch. Notably, with regard to the law of jurisdictional immunities, the Supreme Court seems to have erroneously upheld, in principle, a foreign company's absolute immunity in civil cases, including employment related disputes. In assessing the validity of the Maritime Delimitation Agreement between Albania and Greece, the Constitutional Court seems to have adopted a strategy of internationally minded contestation or even an effort at alignment through development by concluding that this Agreement violated not only the Albanian Constitution, but also the relevant rules of the international law of the sea as enshrined in UNCLOS.

The limited case law dealing with international law norms points towards a strong willingness on the part of Albanian courts to engage constructively with international law and give it effect. Reference to international norms and obligations may well involve an attempt of these courts to enhance their own confidence, and even the legitimacy of their arguments. Within this strong trend of alignment, one can, however, discern cases of international law being applied both correctly and incorrectly. As highlighted in the ILA Final Report, the inconsistent quality of engagement with international law by domestic courts reflects, to some extent, the quality of the parties' submissions, as well as the available expertise in a certain field of international law within any given court.[112] Also, similar to other jurisdictions, Albanian judges have limited time to decide and draft judgments on jurisdictional matters which, according to

[111] See also a brief discussion on the ECHR's status in the Albanian legal system, Spahiu (n 27) 674–75.

[112] ILA Final Report (n 2) para 78. See also on the engagement of Albanian judges with the ECHR and the ECtHR caselaw in particular, Spahiu (n 27) 678–79, 680–1.

law, have to be dealt with rather expediently. In turn, this makes it difficult, if not impossible, for judge-rapporteurs to provide thorough discussions on complex international law issues. For this reason, more critical analysis of these decisions by Albanian legal scholars and practitioners, legal interventions from the executive branch of the Government, and interventions from third parties in the form of *amici curiae* briefs, might assist domestic courts in improving their performance when engaging with international law in the Albanian legal order.

Acknowledgement and Note

This chapters draws from previous work in Gentian Zyberi and Semir Sali, 'The Place and Application of International Law in the Albanian Legal System' in Siniša Rodin and Tamara Perišin (eds), *Judicial Application of International Law in Southeast Europe* (Springer 2015) 81–108. All references to findings in the caselaw of Albanian courts are based on our own translations from the Albanian original.

11
Engagement of Belgian Courts with International Law

Frédéric Dopagne

A. General Features of the Constitutional Framework in Belgium

The Constitution of Belgium[1] can be distinguished from other, more recent, constitutional texts by the remarkably scant provisions it contains in relation to international law—or even EU law. Notwithstanding several attempts to incorporate various additional provisions in it,[2] Title IV of the Constitution, which is dedicated to the State's 'international relations', comprises currently only four Articles which mainly deal with specific, complicated issues arising out of the far-reaching powers enjoyed by the federated entities.[3] Furthermore, whilst Article 34 of the Constitution, according to which 'the exercise of specific powers may be conferred upon public international law institutions by a treaty or a law', is at times construed as ensuring the precedence of EU law over Belgian law (including the Constitution),[4] no further constitutional provision

[1] The Belgian Constitution of 1831 (as revised up to 17 March 2021) (Constitution). For the English translation of the Belgian Constitution, see 'The Belgian Constitution (English Translation)' Legal Affairs and Parliamentary Documentation Department of the Belgian House of Representatives (March 2021) D/2021/468/04, available at <https://www.dekamer.be/kvvcr/pdf_sections/publications/constitution/GrondwetUK.pdf> last accessed 23 July 2023.

All Constitutional Court judgments referenced in this chapter can be found at <www.const-court.be>, while judgments of the Council of State are available at <http://www.raadvst-consetat.be/?lang = fr&page = caselaw>. Where Court of Cassation judgments are available at <https://juportal.be/home/accueil>, this is indicated in the respective reference. All websites were last accessed 23 July 2023.

[2] See also Patricia Popelier and Catherine Van de Heyning, 'The Belgian Constitution: The Efficacy Approach to European and Global Governance' in Anneli Albi and Samo Bardutzky (eds), *National Constitutions in European and Global Governance: Democracy, Rights, the Rule of Law* (Springer 2019) 1261 and fn 192.

[3] Constitution (n 1) arts 167–69.

[4] See the opinion of the General Assembly of the Council of State on the draft law assenting to the Treaty of Lisbon, Council of State, Opinion No 44.028/AV, Parl Doc, Senate (2007–2008) 4-568/1, at 341.

can be found with respect to the hierarchical relationship between (non-EU) international law and domestic law.

As far as the reception of international law in the domestic legal order is concerned, Article 167(2) of the Constitution provides that international treaties, which are ratified by the King, namely the executive branch under Article 37 of the Constitution, 'produce effects only after having received the assent of the House of Representatives'. Such assent (*assentiment, instemming, Zustimmung*) is given in the form of a law, which normally merely states that the treaty at stake 'shall produce its full and complete effect'.[5] This somewhat obscure terminology means that the law of assent endows the treaty with binding force in the domestic legal order, and accordingly allows for its applicability in domestic courts.[6] Additionally, it is understood that the law itself enters into force only after its publication in the *Moniteur belge* (the Belgian Official Gazette), and that the treaty—even where it has duly received parliamentary assent—cannot in any event produce effects in the Belgian legal order, as long as it is not in force for Belgium in the international legal order.[7] In this sense, the Belgian constitutional system adopts a rather dualist approach as far as treaties are concerned, since treaties are not considered automatically incorporated in the domestic legal order. However, it is worth stressing that the law of assent does not exactly entail the transformation of the treaty into Belgian law: the nature of the substantive norms concerned remains that of international treaty law.[8]

It must also be pointed out that Article 167(3) of the Constitution mirrors Article 167(2), in respect of treaties concluded by the 'communities' and the 'regions' (the main categories of Belgian federated entities). On the occasion of the comprehensive constitutional revision in 1993, when Belgium became a federal State, communities and regions were granted the treaty-making power in respect of all matters falling within the scope of their (internal) competence. On the blueprint of Article 167(2), Article 167(3) provides that these treaties shall not produce effects until they have received the assent of 'the Parliament' (that is the Parliament of the community(ies) and/or region(s) involved).

[5] This approach is similar to the approach adopted by the Greek Constitution, as discussed in the ILA Study Group on Principles on the Engagement of Domestic Courts with International Law, 'Final Report: Mapping the Engagement of Domestic Courts with International Law' (Johannesburg, 2016) (ILA Final Report) para 18.

[6] Court of Cassation, *Ligue des États arabes v TM*, Case No S.99.0103.F/1 (12 March 2001), available at <https://juportal.be/home/accueil>; and casenote by Joe Verhoeven in (2002) Revue Critique de Jurisprudence Belge 377; Court of Cassation, *Leroy* (25 November 1955) Pasicrisie I 1955, 285.

[7] *Ligue des États arabes* (n 6).

[8] This non-rigid distinction between monism and dualism, incorporation and transformation, in the approach used by different domestic legal orders for different sources of international law is common as discussed in the ILA Final Report (n 5) para 18.

Along the same lines, 'mixed' treaties, namely treaties for which the respective competences of the federal State and the federated entities overlap, cannot be applicable in the Belgian legal order unless the assent has been given by all the parliamentary assemblies concerned.[9]

Given the limited number of constitutional provisions which are relevant to the question of the status of international law in the Belgian legal system, a series of specific issues have been determined over time in the caselaw of Belgian courts. Some of these judgments may appear as genuine 'political' decisions, in the sense that they take a stance on fundamental questions of principle which have been left unanswered by the constitutional text. The most striking example is probably, in this regard, the 1971 judgment of the Court of Cassation in the *Fromagerie Franco-Suisse 'Le Ski'* case affirming for the first time the supremacy of international treaties over Belgian legislation.[10] Such a particular 'choice' does not go without raising questions about the underlying conception of the separation of powers.[11] Nevertheless, it seems inevitable that, failing appropriate constitutional guidance, judges—and eminently the three Supreme Courts, namely the Court of Cassation, the Council of State, and the Constitutional Court—themselves determine essential questions concerning the relationship between Belgian law and international law.[12] By contrast, the fact that Belgian courts as a matter of standard practice decide, for example, on the self-executing character of a norm of international law (namely the ability of the norm to confer rights or obligations directly to individuals, in the absence of national implementing measures, and thus be directly applicable before domestic courts[13]) is something extremely mundane that can also be observed in other jurisdictions and that is not due to some lack of constitutional framework. Rather, it is simply because the self-executing nature is per

[9] Cooperation Agreement of 8 March 1994 between the Federal State, the Communities and the Regions on the further rules for the conclusion of mixed treaties, Moniteur belge (17 December 1996); *Ligue des États arabes* (n 6).

[10] Court of Cassation, *Fromagerie Franco-Suisse "Le Ski"* (27 May 1971) Pasicrisie I 1971(4), 959 (*Le Ski*). Although the case concerned European Community law, the rule of supremacy was established generally for international treaties. See Popelier and Van de Heyning (n 2) 1231.

[11] See on this issue Pierre d'Argent, 'Remarques sur le conflit entre normes de droit interne et de droit international' (2012) 45 Revue Belge de Droit International 355, 358–60. As observed by Verdier and Versteeg, issues of treaty supremacy over domestic legislation have usually been addressed through constitutional provisions. See Pierre-Hugues Verdier and Mila Versteeg, 'International Law in National Legal Systems: An Empirical Investigation' in Anthea Roberts et al (eds), *Comparative International Law* (OUP 2018) 222.

[12] On the persistent controversy between the three Supreme Courts (Court of Cassation, Council of State, and Constitutional Court) around the supremacy of international law over the Constitution, see Pierre d'Argent, 'Jurisprudence belge relative au droit international public (1993–2003)' (2003) 36 Revue Belge de Droit International 599–604; Pierre d'Argent, 'Jurisprudence belge relative au droit international public (2004–2007)' (2007) 40 Revue belge de droit international 164–70.

[13] See Verdier and Versteeg (n 11) 219.

se a question of interpretation of the rule of international law, and therefore a question which is ultimately for the judge to decide (while being in principle dependent on a common criterion, namely the intention of the creators of the rule).[14]

It is also worth stressing that the Belgian Constitution does not allude at all to customary international law. In this respect too, Belgian courts have, to some extent, filled the gap. For example, the Court of Cassation determined that customary international law is automatically applicable in the domestic legal order, without any formality being necessary for its reception[15]—in particular the Parliament's assent which is reserved for treaties. Likewise, it is in the caselaw of the Court of Cassation that the issue of the hierarchy of norms between customary international law and domestic legislation has been settled: in the jurisprudence to date, domestic legislation takes precedence over customary international law.[16]

Against this backdrop, the three sections hereafter aim at providing a brief overview of the jurisprudence of Belgian courts—with a focus on the three Supreme Courts—that tends to bespeak alignment techniques (B), avoidance techniques (C), and contestation techniques (D), respectively, in the terminology of the International Law Association (ILA) Study Group Final Report (ILA Final Report). Needless to say, these distinctions are however not straightforward in Belgian caselaw.

B. Alignment Techniques

In the practice of Belgian courts, alignment techniques may be discerned from the use of the principle of consistent interpretation (1), as well as the possibility to invoke non-self-executing rules of international law (2) in cases before them.

1. Consistent Interpretation

The principle of consistent interpretation, requiring that domestic law be interpreted as far as possible in a manner consistent with the international obligations binding upon the State, is well established in the caselaw of the Court

[14] *Jurisdiction of the Courts of Danzig* (Advisory Opinion) PCIJ Ser B No 15, 17–18.
[15] See inter alia Court of Cassation, 19 March 1842, Pasicrisie I 1842, 122.
[16] Court of Cassation, *Pittacos*, 26 May 1966, Pasicrisie I 1966(3), 1211.

of Cassation.[17] Although the principle was applied as early as 1925, in a case concerning international obligations stemming from the Versailles Treaty,[18] the most famous—and arguably far-reaching—precedent for its application is the *Sharon* case decided in 2003.[19] In this case, the Court of Cassation first held that, under customary international law, serving Heads of State and Heads of Government enjoy full immunity from jurisdiction in criminal matters. Turning to Article 5(3) of the Law of 16 June 1993 (the Belgian law on universal jurisdiction for grave breaches of international humanitarian law, in the version in force at the time of the judgment), which provided that 'the immunity linked to the official capacity of a person does not prevent the application of the Law',[20] the Court considered that this provision 'would contravene' the aforementioned principle of customary international law 'should it be interpreted as having the object of excluding the immunity established by that principle'.[21] Therefore, this provision 'cannot have such an object but must be construed as excluding only that the official capacity of a person may entail their exemption from criminal responsibility with respect to the crimes of international law listed in the Law'.[22]

It is noteworthy that the Court of Cassation preferred to rely on a particular interpretation of the Law of 16 June 1993 to reconcile the latter with the applicable international obligations, instead of acknowledging that the Law conflicts with these international obligations—and settling this conflict accordingly. In light of its wording, it can hardly be denied that Article 5(3) was effectively in conflict with the rule of immunity under customary international law as identified by the Court. However, such an approach would likely have led the Court to affirm the precedence of customary international law over domestic legislation, and thus to depart from its long-standing jurisprudence giving supremacy

[17] In the caselaw of the Council of State, see *ASBL Mouvement contre le racisme, l'antisémitisme et la xénophobie*, Judgment No 83.584 (23 November 1999), reprinted in (1999) Revue du Droit des Étrangers 715.

[18] Court of Cassation, *Compagnie Osram* (8 January 1925) Pasicrisie I 1925, 101.

[19] Court of Cassation, *HSA and others v SA and YA*, Case No P.02.1139.F/2 (12 February 2003) (*Sharon*), and Pierre d'Argent, 'Monsieur Sharon et ses juges belges' (2003/13) 6091 Journal des Tribunaux 243.

[20] Law of 16 June 1993 relating to the repression of grave breaches of violations of international humanitarian law (as amended by Law of 10 February 1999) art 5(3).

[21] See *Sharon* (n 19).

[22] See *Sharon* (n 19). It is notable that two months after the Court of Cassation judgment in *Sharon*, the domestic law under consideration was modified to reflect the customary law limitation of immunity with respect to such proceedings. See Law modifying the Law of 16 June 1993 relating to the repression of grave breaches of violations of international humanitarian law and article 144ter of the Judicial Code (23 April 2003) art 4: 'Article 5, paragraph 3, of the same law, modified by law of 10 February 1999, is replaced by the following provision: "(3). The international immunity attached to the official status of a person does not prevent the application of this law within the limits established by international law." ' (author's translation)

to domestic legislation in case of a conflict with customary international law.[23] It may be that the Court was not prepared to do so, and to explicitly extend to customary international law its settled caselaw on the supremacy of international treaty law.[24] It may also be that the Court simply sought to prevent the State from incurring international responsibility due to a breach of customary international law by Belgian legislation.[25] Be that as it may, the *Sharon* judgment highlights the great potential of the principle of consistent interpretation in the practice of the Court of Cassation. In this case, the principle of consistent interpretation led to overriding alignment with international law, as defined in the ILA Final Report.[26]

This potential of consistent interpretation is further illustrated by a 2008 case in which the principle resulted in the Court of Cassation going as far as changing its existing jurisprudence on a particular issue of criminal law.[27] In the wake of a judgment by the European Court of Human Rights (ECtHR) against Belgium, the Court of Cassation held that the interpretation of the Belgian legislation in its former jurisprudence was incompatible with Article 6 of the European Convention of Human Rights (ECHR) and Article 14 of the International Covenant on Civil and Political Rights (ICCPR) on fair trial, and accordingly favoured an alternative interpretation in line with these treaty provisions, as construed by the ECtHR.[28]

Moreover, the principle of consistent interpretation, which in the precedents discussed above was applied to ordinary legislation, seems to have been extended by the Constitutional Court to the provisions of the Constitution concerning the protection of fundamental rights, under which the Court has jurisdiction to review ordinary legislation. These are the provisions of Title II of the Constitution on the 'rights of Belgians', Article 170 setting forth the

[23] *Pittacos* (n 16).

[24] See *Le Ski* (n 10).

[25] It is worth recalling that the *Sharon* judgment came one year after the International Court of Justice (ICJ), in the *Arrest Warrant* case, found Belgium responsible of a breach of the immunity from criminal jurisdiction and inviolability of a foreign minister for foreign affairs: the breach was caused by Belgian authorities issuing and circulating an arrest warrant for alleged violations of international humanitarian law referred to in the Law of 16 June 1993 (*Arrest Warrant of 11 April 2000 (Democratic Republic of the Congo v Belgium)* (Judgment) [2002] ICJ Rep 3, 33 [78]. The Law in itself was not challenged by the ICJ in that case. However, the Court of Cassation, when giving its *Sharon* judgment, may have been sensitive to the possibility that the Belgian State would be found (again) in breach of its international obligations, due to the very existence of the Law, should the latter be construed as excluding immunity rules.

[26] ILA Final Report (n 5) para 46.

[27] Court of Cassation, *ÜG*, Case No P.08.0070.N (17 June 2008), available at <https://juportal.be>.

[28] According to the former jurisprudence of the Court of Cassation, in case of theft the personal implication of co-perpetrators or accomplices in the aggravating circumstances defined by legislation, is irrelevant for the application of these circumstances. Given that such an interpretation is contrary to the right to a fair trial, the Court of Cassation now considers that aggravating circumstances must be assessed for each co-perpetrator or accomplice individually.

principle of the legality of taxes, Article 172 containing the principle of non-discrimination in tax matters, and Article 191 on the protection of foreigners present on Belgian territory. Indeed, the Constitutional Court as a matter of standard practice holds that, where one of these constitutional provisions is alleged to have been breached by a legislative norm, and a provision of an international treaty binding upon Belgium has an 'analogous scope' to that of the constitutional provision invoked, the Court shall 'take into account' the treaty provision in its assessment of the constitutionality of the legislative norm. This is because, according to the Court, in such a case the constitutional provision and the treaty provision constitute an 'indissociable whole'.[29] Implicitly, this requirement to 'take into account' the treaty provision, in such situations of 'consubstantial norms',[30] means that the constitutional provision cannot be interpreted in a way that would prove at odds with the analogous treaty provision. It is likely that the Constitutional Court has adopted this conciliatory approach in order to avoid having to deal (again), should the interpretation of the constitutional provision reveal that it affords a lower protection of fundamental rights than the analogous treaty provision, with the thorny question of conflict between the Constitution and international (treaty) law.[31]

2. Invoking Non-Self-Executing International Law before Belgian Courts

While the previous section was devoted to a technique for reconciling domestic legal provisions with international law, this section relates to the broader harmonization or alignment of the conduct of the State, even beyond enacting legislation, with international law. The question raised in the caselaw discussed below is whether rules of international law which have been determined to be non-self-executing can be relied on by individuals before Belgian courts, to serve as an objective norm of reference to assess the legality of the acts of the State. Thus not for the individual to enjoy subjective rights pursuant to the rule of international law—as it is assumed that this rule is, precisely,

[29] One of the leading cases in this respect is Constitutional Court, Judgment No 147/2004 (15 September 2004). On the details of this approach, see Pierre d'Argent, Alexia de Vaucleroy, Frédéric Dopagne, and Esther Lanotte 'Jurisprudence belge relative au droit international public (2012–2017)' (2018) Revue belge de droit international 216–18.

[30] See ILA Final Report (n 5) para 30. This is an example of the use of the principle of consistent interpretation leading to consubstantial alignment, as discussed ibid para 53.

[31] In 1994, the Constitutional Court seems to have contended that the Constitution takes precedence over conflicting international treaties (Judgment No 12/94 (3 February 1994)).

non-self-executing. In other words, can the action of the State be controlled—and restricted—by the domestic judge based on the international obligations binding on the State, even where these international obligations are not meant to confer subjective rights directly on individuals? Based on existing Belgian caselaw, three scenarios are plausible here.

First, an individual—provided that they have the required legal standing under domestic law—may challenge the validity of a legal act of the State, which allegedly infringes international law obligations binding on the State. The Council of State, which has jurisdiction to review the conformity of administrative acts (whether of a regulatory or individual nature) with superior norms, used to consider in this respect that, where international law is the superior norm of reference, it does not have to be self-executing to be taken into account.[32] However, recent caselaw indicates that the Council of State has dismissed,[33] although not yet systematically,[34] grounds of annulment which are solely based on the violation of non-self-executing international norms.

For its part, the Constitutional Court, which has jurisdiction to annul legislative norms it finds incompatible with certain provisions of the Constitution, has explicitly held that, where the individual that seeks the annulment invokes a constitutional provision in conjunction with a treaty norm, the treaty norm is not required to have self-executing character for the Court to take it into consideration in its review.[35]

As a further example, in a case concerning the seizure, in the context of a criminal investigation, of some correspondence that had apparently been exchanged with the apostolic nunciature in Brussels, the Brussels Court of Appeal's Chamber of Indictments decided that the seizure must be annulled due to the inviolability of the official correspondence of diplomatic missions.[36] The rule of inviolability, reflected in Article 27(2) of the 1961 Vienna Convention,[37] is not self-executing. The Brussels Chamber of Indictments, however, did not hesitate to rely on it as a norm of reference for its review.

[32] Council of State, *Corveleyn v Etat belge, ministre de la Justice* (7 October 1968), reprinted in (1969/38) 4679 Journal des Tribunaux 694, with observations by Joe Verhoeven.

[33] Council of State, *ASBL Pétitions patrimoine*, Judgment No 192.641 (23 April 2009); *XXX*, Judgment No 196.388 (25 September 2009); *Ville d'Andenne*, Judgment No 216.815 (12 December 2011).

[34] See Council of State, *SA Mobistar*, Judgment No 214.183 (27 June 2011).

[35] Constitutional Court, Judgment No 106/2003 (22 July 2003); Judgment No 32/2015 (12 March 2015); Judgment No 162/2015 (19 November 2015).

[36] *Aartsbisdom Mechelen en Godfried Danneels*, Case No 4970 (22 December 2010) (unreported). The judgment was quashed by the Court of Cassation (5 April 2011) Pasicrisie 2011(4), but for reasons unrelated to the question of the inviolability of the diplomatic correspondence and the non-self-executing nature of the international law rules under consideration.

[37] Vienna Convention on Diplomatic Relations (adopted 18 April 1961, entered into force 24 April 1964) 500 UNTS 95.

The second scenario concerns the civil liability of the State under domestic law, and in particular Article 1382 of the Belgian Civil Code (tort liability), for a breach of international law. As a matter of principle, it is not disputed that the State can incur liability under Belgian tort law where its authorities—from whatever branch of government: legislative, executive, or judicial—have breached Belgium's international obligations.[38] However, the question here again is whether the rule of international law at stake needs to be self-executing for the court to use it as a norm of reference in this type of proceedings, or whether it suffices that the rule is simply binding on Belgium, thereby regulating the conduct of all State organs.

Until 2017, there was not much consistency on this issue in the decisions of the Court of Cassation. In some cases, the Court referred to rules of international treaties having 'effects' in the domestic legal order.[39] This was likely an implicit reference to Article 167(2) of the Constitution requiring that treaties obtain Parliamentary assent in order to be applicable in the domestic legal order,[40] which is a formality for the reception of international treaty law, and distinct from the issue of the possible self-executing nature of treaty provisions. In other cases, the Court referred instead to rules of international treaties having 'direct effects' in the domestic legal order.[41] This rather seemed to be a reference to self-executing provisions in treaties, as 'direct effect' (*effet direct*, *rechtstreekse werking*) is the French and Dutch terminology commonly used to depict specifically the self-executing character of an international norm.

In 2017, the Court of Cassation clarified its caselaw:[42] it explicitly required treaty provisions to be self-executing, for the violation of these provisions to constitute a potential basis for the State's tort liability under Article 1382 of the Civil Code. The dispute originated from the bombardment of bridges on the Danube during the NATO-led military intervention against Serbia in 1999. Two transport companies sued the Belgian State to claim compensation for the economic loss they suffered as a result. They alleged that the Belgian government took part in NATO's decision to use force, in breach of Article 2(4) of the UN Charter. The Brussels Court of Appeal, however, held that this treaty

[38] See Court of Cassation, *État belge v FJML*, Case No C.02.0570.F (28 September 2006), available at <https://juportal.be/home/accueil>.

[39] See, eg, Court of Cassation, *ONSS v LH and DP* (25 October 2004) Pasicrisie 2004, 1667; *Garage Herbosch-La Louvière*, Case No C.06.0457.F (21 December 2007), available at <https://juportal.be/home/accueil>; *État belge v CPAS de Wavre* (27 June 2008) Pasicrisie 2008(6–8), 1749.

[40] See Section A.

[41] See, eg, Court of Cassation, Case No C.98.0477.F (14 January 2000); *Vulstoffen Exploitatie*, Case No C.07.0073.N (5 June 2008); both available at <https://juportal.be/home/accueil>.

[42] Court of Cassation, *Touax, Touax Rom v État belge*, Case No C.13.0528.F (9 February 2017) (*Touax*), available at <https://juportal.be/home/accueil>.

provision is not self-executing, hence its violation cannot be invoked by individuals in the context of Article 1382 of the Civil Code. The Court of Cassation then confirmed that there can be a tort entailing the State's liability for breach of 'an international treaty' only if the latter has 'direct effects in the domestic order' ('*effets directs*', '*rechtstreekse werking*').[43] As a result of this particular interpretation of Article 1382 of the Civil Code, the potential scope of the Belgian State's tort liability for breach of international law rules[44] is therefore restricted to the violation of those rules which are self-executing.[45]

In the third scenario, the individual does not seek annulment of a legal act of the State, nor do they seek compensation based on the State's civil liability, but request that the court draws (other) appropriate consequences from the breach of international law allegedly committed by the State. In this regard, the Court of Cassation appears to have implicitly accepted in a number of criminal cases that, as a matter of principle, the individual could invoke the State's alleged violation of international law—in the cases at hand, treaty provisions—with a view to challenging the prosecution.[46] Interestingly enough, the international law provisions concerned were obviously non-self-executing.

From the foregoing, it appears that Belgian caselaw accepts, to a certain extent, that rules of international law can be used by individuals in the context of a judicial review of acts of the State, even though those rules are not self-executing. In that sense, the practice of Belgian courts reveals overriding alignment with international law. Nonetheless, a significant departure from this trend can be discerned from the 2017 *Touax* judgment of the Court of Cassation, in which the judges refused to endorse the view that the State's tort

[43] ibid.

[44] In *Touax*, the Court of Cassation addressed international treaties alone because it was a treaty provision (art 2(4) of the UN Charter) that was at stake, yet it may be argued that the Court's decision to require a self-executing character would likely be extended by the Court to rules of customary international law as well.

[45] This is in contrast to the regime of State responsibility under international law, for the purposes of which it is irrelevant whether the rule of international law breached is self-executing or not: see Articles on Responsibility of States for Internationally Wrongful Acts, UNGA Res 56/83 (12 December 2001) UN Doc A/RES/56/83, Annex, art 1.

[46] See, eg, concerning the Convention Relating to the Status of Refugees (adopted 28 July 1951, entered into force 22 April 1954) 189 UNTS 137 art 28, and Schedule, para 13(I), Court of Cassation, *Ertl* (16 February 1970) Pasicrisie 1970(I), 533; concerning various bilateral or multilateral treaties on extradition and/or mutual legal assistance in criminal matters, see (although in none of these cases the ground of cassation based on international law was eventually accepted, but not because of the non-self-executing character) Court of Cassation, *EHL*, Case No P.05.1594.F (15 February 2006); *NS*, Case No P.01.1765.F (13 March 2002); Case No P.98.0974.N (17 August 1998); Case No P.94.1005.N (23 August 1994); Case No 19900410.6 (10 April 1990); all available at <https://juportal.be/home/accueil>.

liability could arise in case of breach of a rule of international law that is not self-executing.[47]

C. Avoidance Techniques

From the outset it should be underlined that no consistent or systematic trend in the caselaw of Belgian courts clearly reflects the use of avoidance techniques when engaging in international law. In particular, Belgian courts are generally not inclined to resort to non-justiciability doctrines. For instance, the so-called theory of the '*actes de gouvernement*', a theory comparable to the political question doctrine, which is well-established in French jurisprudence, is virtually unknown to Belgian courts.[48] By the same token, the act of State doctrine has not been applied in Belgian caselaw. A number of specific features will nevertheless be mentioned in the three sub-sections that follow. They all tend to disclose underlying avoidance techniques, although it proves difficult to put very clear labels on the elements of existing practice.

1. Priority of Constitutionality Review

The first feature is to be ascribed to constitutional arrangements rather than an attitude of the courts themselves, although these arrangements were devised after informal talks between the respective presidents of the three Supreme Courts. Enacted in 2009, Article 26(4) of the Special Law on the Constitutional Court provides that, when it is alleged before a court that a norm having a legislative nature infringes 'a fundamental right guaranteed in a wholly or partly similar manner by a provision of Title II of the Constitution and by a provision of European or international law', the court shall, subject to certain exceptions, refer the question of compatibility with the provision of Title II of the Constitution to the Constitutional Court for a preliminary ruling.

[47] The Court of Cassation' s approach in *Touax* is an example of affirmative avoidance as discussed in ILA Final Report (n 5) para 41, with the non-self-execution argument acting as a blunting technique (ibid paras 21, 41). On avoidance see the discussion in Section C.

[48] See, however, Council of State, *XXX*, Judgment No 73.027 (9 April 1998), where the act whereby the receiving State (Belgium) informs the sending State that a diplomatic agent is declared *persona non grata*, was considered, 'by its nature', as falling outside the jurisdiction of the Council of State to review the legality of administrative acts. This reasoning seems to be an allusion to the theory of the '*actes de gouvernement*'.

In other words, lower courts are no longer allowed to immediately review the conformity of the legislative norm with European or international law, and to refuse to apply it in case of non-conformity, based on the principle of supremacy of EU or international law over domestic legislation. Nor are they allowed anymore, where the fundamental rights at stake are protected under EU law, to immediately refer the case to the Court of Justice of the European Union for a preliminary ruling on the interpretation of the relevant EU provisions. For these reasons, the compatibility of this mechanism with EU law has been questioned.[49]

Be that as it may, the priority of the constitutionality review may give the impression that European or international law is less 'trusted' as a potential, valid standard for appraising the human rights compliance of Belgian legislative norms. However, this impression of avoidance of international law should not be overstated. As pointed out above,[50] the Constitutional Court itself, within the framework of its constitutionality review (including upon reference for a preliminary ruling), 'takes into account' treaty provisions that have an 'analogous scope' to that of the constitutional provision invoked, applying the principle of consistent interpretation to the Constitution. Therefore, Article 26(4) of the Special Law on the Constitutional Court does not seem to entail that, in practice, the consideration of international law will necessarily be postponed, as it will in principle be included already in the constitutionality review. This does not mean, however, that, once the Constitutional Court has ruled that the legislative norm is compatible with the Constitution, with reasoning that rests on the Constitution alone even if the latter is construed in light of consubstantial norms of international law, the lower court having referred the question for a preliminary ruling (or any other court) should be precluded from carrying out its own assessment of the conformity with international law.[51] This further waters down the impression of avoidance of international law, that Article 26(4) might give at first sight.

[49] See, amongst others, Nicolas Cariat, 'Quelques réflexions quant à la compatibilité de la loi spéciale sur la Cour constitutionnelle avec le droit de l'Union européenne' (2011/28) 6446 Journal des Tribunaux 573. Upon reference by some Belgian courts, the Court of Justice of the European Union (CJEU) held that it manifestly lacks jurisdiction to give the requested preliminary ruling on the compatibility of the mechanism with EU law, as the dispute in the main proceedings could not be considered to be connected with EU law: see mainly Case C-457/09 *Claude Chartry v Belgian State* [2011] ECR I-00819.

[50] See Section A(1).

[51] In this sense, Council of State, *Orde van Vlaamse Balies*, Judgment No 206.397 (2 July 2010), and (2010–2011) 74 (19) Rechtskundig Weekblad 806.

2. Invoking Customary International Law before the Court of Cassation

It has never been disputed in Belgium that, as far as customary rules are concerned, 'international law is part of the law of the land'.[52] Unlike treaties, customary international law is not subject to parliamentary assent or any other formality to acquire binding force in the domestic legal order. On the contrary, its rules are automatically incorporated in the latter.[53]

It should be stressed, however, that this immediate applicability in the Belgian legal order does not involve, as such, that customary international law can constitute the legal basis of a ground of cassation before the Court of Cassation. According to Article 608 of the Code of Civil Proceedings, only breaches of the 'law' may give rise to an appeal before the Court of Cassation. While treaties may be included in the concept of 'law' within the meaning of Article 608 because of the existence of the law granting Parliamentary assent to each treaty ratified by Belgium, and which must be mentioned in the statement of the ground of cassation along with the reference to the treaty itself, the same reasoning cannot be followed for customary international law. Hence the refusal of the Court of Cassation, in older judgments, to regard the latter as a 'law' the violation of which it can sanction.[54] This approach can be regarded as an illustration of affirmative avoidance in respect of customary international law.[55]

That said, it seems that the Court may have recently changed its position. In the Belgian part of the multi-jurisdiction litigation between NML Capital Ltd and Argentina, the Court had to deal with the seizure of bank accounts belonging to the Argentinian embassy in Brussels. It found that the seizure infringes Articles 22(3) and 25 of the Vienna Convention on Diplomatic Relations, as well as 'the rule of customary international law *ne impediatur legatio*'.[56] The possibility of invocation of customary international law as a ground of cassation was not explicitly contested. Nevertheless, it remains uncertain whether this judgment amounts to a full and clear departure from previous jurisprudence, and the related affirmative avoidance of customary international law, for the Court also relied on the Vienna Convention. This

[52] See, eg, Verhoeven referring to the nineteenth century caselaw of the Court of Cassation: Joe Verhoeven, *Droit international public* (Larcier 2000) 454.

[53] As discussed in the ILA Final Report (n 5) para 18, it is common for a domestic legal system to treat different sources of international law differently with respect to their reception in the domestic order.

[54] See, eg, Court of Cassation, *Bindels v Administration des Finances* (16 June 1947) Pasicrisie I 1947, 268.

[55] See ILA Final Report (n 5) para 41.

[56] *République d'Argentine v NMC Capital Ltd*, Case No C.11.0688.F/1 (22 November 2012), reprinted in (2013/15) 6517 Journal des Tribunaux 290, with casenote by Pierre d'Argent.

dual reference, to both a treaty source and customary international law, might be explained indeed by the Court's hesitation to quash the appealed judgment based on the customary rule alone.[57] Likewise, there is some persistent ambiguity in a recent judgment of the Court upholding the immunity from jurisdiction of the Netherlands and the Dutch central bank,[58] as the Court's ruling was formally made under Articles 24(1) and 27 of the 1972 European Convention on State Immunity,[59] to which Belgium is party, without any explicit reference to customary international law.

3. Domestic Legislation on Immunity

Of possible relevance in terms of avoidance is also the recent trend of the Belgian legislature to pass laws regulating immunities, not always fully reflecting existing rules of international law.[60] Such an approach, whilst being quite common in common law systems, is much more unusual in civil law countries where immunity issues are traditionally decided by the courts on the basis of applicable international law directly. As far as Belgium is concerned, the legislature's justification of this practice has been that these laws aim to enhance legal certainty, judges and bailiffs being allegedly more familiar with municipal legislation than with (regularly unwritten) rules of international law. This phenomenon seems to reveal a preference for domestic legislation, upon which the courts are actively prompted to rely instead of international law, and may lead to instances of evasive avoidance.[61] Three elements, nevertheless, might be regarded as qualifying or counterbalancing the potential evasive avoidance of international law, which may be discerned from the enactment of a growing number of domestic legislative provisions on immunity matters.

First, it is true that the ultimate objective behind this recent trend might be to ensure respect for international law itself—through translating the latter into national legal provisions. After all, all provisions concerned were adopted

[57] See also for this point Eric De Brabandere, 'Belgian Courts and the Immunity of International Organizations' (2013) 10 International Organizations Law Review 464, 473.

[58] Court of Cassation, *J-P A v Royaume des Pays-Bas and De Nederlandsche Bank*, Case No C.14.0322.F (23 October 2015), available at <https://juportal.be/home/accueil>.

[59] European Convention on State Immunity (adopted 16 May 1972, entered into force 11 June 1976) ETS No 74.

[60] See art 1*bis*(1) of the Preliminary Title of the Code of Criminal Procedure (immunity from criminal jurisdiction of certain persons); and, in the Code of Civil Procedure: arts 1412*ter* (immunity from execution of cultural property of foreign States and international organizations), 1412*quater* (immunity from execution of assets of foreign central banks and international monetary institutions) and 1412*quinquies* (immunity from execution of property of foreign States and international organizations).

[61] As discussed in the ILA Final Report (n 5) para 50.

in a context of diplomatic tensions with certain foreign States or international organizations, against which court proceedings or enforcement action were instituted in Belgium, or which were under threat of being subjected to such proceedings or action.[62] Against this backdrop, it is understandable that the aim of the Belgian authorities was actually to safeguard Belgium's interests at the international law level, and resort to domestic norms was only a means to achieve this objective.

Second, it may well be that, in any event, international law will 'resist' the 'invasion' of domestic legislation, and will still have an important role to play before Belgian courts. Indeed, it is submitted that, despite the presence of a domestic law provision, relevant international law rules cannot be ignored by the domestic court:[63] as necessary, they may have to be taken into account in the framework of consistent interpretation,[64] or—in case of clear-cut conflict—through the application of the principle of supremacy of international treaty law.

Third, it must be stressed that another recent trend consists in the Belgian executive branch increasingly intervening before Belgian courts in order to defend the immunities of certain foreign States or of the North Atlantic Treaty Organization.[65] In existing practice, it is the applicable rule *of international law* that the Belgian government seeks to protect, and thus its attitude can be qualified as an alignment technique. However, it cannot be ruled out that, in future practice, the government—and the courts—in arguing such issues would rather refer to the domestic immunity legislation, thus pursuing again a strategy of evasive avoidance.

D. Contestation Techniques

Affirmative contestation of international law[66] can be found, in particular, in three 2009 judgments of the Court of Cassation, in which the immunity

[62] See, eg, the seizures performed on property belonging to the Russian Federation in an effort to enforce the arbitral award in the *Yukos* case, and which prompted the adoption of art 1412*quinquies* of the Code of Civil Procedure (see, in this respect, Frédéric Dopagne, 'L'immunité de saisie des biens de l'Etat étranger et de l'organisation internationale: notes sur l'article 1412*quinquies* du Code judiciaire' (2016/4) 6632 Journal des Tribunaux 57).

[63] See Frédéric Dopagne, 'L'immunité de saisie des biens de l'Etat étranger et de l'organisation internationale: notes sur l'article 1412*quinquies* du Code judiciaire' (n 62) esp 57–58.

[64] See Section B(1).

[65] See the cases concerned and the discussion in Frédéric Dopagne, 'L'État belge devant ses tribunaux en défense des immunités du droit international' in Pierre d'Argent et al (eds), *Les visages de l'État: Liber amicorum Yves Lejeune* (Bruylant 2017) 281–91.

[66] As discussed in the ILA Final Report (n 5) para 59.

from jurisdiction and from execution of international organizations was set aside.[67] In these cases, the Court of Cassation, building on the European Court of Human Rights' judgment in *Waite and Kennedy*,[68] determined that, where the individual has no reasonable alternative remedy available to them, the immunity entails a disproportionate limitation of the right of access to a court.[69] These decisions cannot be regarded as illustrating a principled, negatory contestation approach towards international law, since the immunity was actually excluded on the basis of another rule of international law, namely the individual's right of access to court, laid down in Article 6 of the ECHR.[70]

Turning to negatory contestation, a striking precedent is the *Yahoo!* case, which was determined in 2015 for the third and last time by the Court of Cassation.[71] In this criminal case, brought against Yahoo! for alleged non-compliance with the Belgian legislation requiring providers of electronic communications services to release data requested by the Public Prosecutor's Office in the framework of criminal investigations, the defendant consistently argued that the special procedure under the United States-Belgium Treaty on mutual legal assistance in criminal matters should have been used by the Belgian Public Prosecutor to channel his request to Yahoo!'s offices in California. Instead, the Public Prosecutor had sent the request by email and by ordinary letter. The applicability of the bilateral treaty in the case at hand was, indeed, fairly obvious, as unanimously confirmed by authors who commented on the case at various stages.[72] Throughout the proceedings, however, the various courts that heard the case, refrained from addressing this international law issue or held that it was irrelevant, in what appears to be an (implicit) endorsement of the Public Prosecutor's (express) argument that the mechanisms of the bilateral treaty do not allow for swift actions, and should therefore be disregarded.[73] This ruling,

[67] Court of Cassation, *Union de l'Europe occidentale v Siedler (SM)*, Case No S.04.0129.F (21 December 2009); *Secrétariat du Groupe ACP v BD*, Case No C.07.0407.F (21 December 2009); *Secrétariat du Groupe ACP v Lutchmaya (L M-A)*, Case No C.03.0328.F (21 December 2009); all available at <https://juportal.be/home/accueil>.

[68] ECtHR, *Waite and Kennedy v Germany*, App Nos 26083/94 and 28934/95 (Judgment of 18 February 1999).

[69] See for a discussion with some critical remarks De Brabandere (n 58) 476ff, especially 481–92.

[70] See also the discussion in the ILA Final Report (n 5) para 59. In that sense, this case can also be characterised as an example of consubstantial contestation (ibid para 63).

[71] Court of Cassation, *Yahoo! Inc*, Case No P.13.2082.N (1 December 2015), available at <https://juportal.be/home/accueil>.

[72] See inter alia Pierre d'Argent, 'Jurisprudence belge relative au droit international public (2008–2011)' (2012) 45 Revue belge de droit international 325; Ludivine Kerzmann, 'L'affaire Yahoo! ou à qui s'adresse l'obligation de collaboration instaurée par l'article 46bis du Code d'instruction criminelle?' (2011/44) Revue du droit des technologies de l'information 123.

[73] This was therefore a case where the domestic court 'ignor[ed] clearly applicable international law norms, perhaps due to the fact that [it found] their application objectionable in the circumstances', ILA Final Report (n 5) para 62.

however, proves isolated, and accordingly should probably be considered as a mere 'accident'.

E. Conclusion

It seems difficult to pinpoint 'techniques'—in the sense of strategies—that would illustrate a general principled approach of Belgian courts in their engagement with international law. Leaving aside the use of the principle of consistent interpretation, which by definition reflects the will of Belgian courts to secure some degree of alignment of domestic with international law, the brief survey above shows that the caselaw is, in many respects, not always clear-cut, and that several developments are under way. Among these ongoing developments, we can mention the possible invocation of non-self-executing international norms before domestic courts in order to assess the legality of the acts of the State, and the possible invocation of customary international law as a ground of cassation.

As a result, straightforward conclusions can hardly be drawn with regard to the engagement of Belgian courts with international law. This being said, it can probably be asserted that the Belgian judge normally has a posture of 'openness' to international law, thus an attitude of alignment. Indeed, there seem to be no genuine and across-the-board contestation mechanisms, in the sense of negatory contestation (aside from the likely 'accident' of the *Yahoo!* case). In addition, the techniques that have been put in the category of avoidance above, prove fairly 'soft' in comparison to, for example, the doctrines of non-justiciability that exist in other legal systems.

12

Engagement of English Courts with International Law

Shaheed Fatima KC

A. Increasing Engagement of English Courts with International Law

In 2005, Lord Bingham observed:

> To an extent almost unimaginable even thirty years ago, national courts in this and other countries are called upon to consider and resolve issues turning on the correct understanding and application of international law, not on an occasional basis, now and then, but routinely, and often in cases of great importance.[1]

In England,[2] that trend has continued, unabated. In October 2015, in a speech entitled 'The Importance of International Law for Government Lawyers', the Attorney-General commented: 'So just how important is international law? The short answer is, very. I have been struck in my first year as Attorney General just how central it is to the daily work of government.'[3] That central role is unlikely to diminish in the near future; unsurprisingly Brexit led to high profile litigation[4] and, as the post-Brexit relationship between the UK and the EU continues to develop there will be an ongoing need to consider the relationship between English law, EU law and international law. The relationship between English law, the European Convention on Human Rights (ECHR) and

[1] Foreword in Shaheed Fatima, *Using International Law in Domestic Courts* (Hart Publishing 2005).

[2] The analysis in this chapter focuses on English caselaw.

[3] UK Attorney-General, Jeremy Wright QC, 'The Importance of International Law for Government Lawyers' (Government Legal Service International Law Conference, 15 October 2015) <https://www.gov.uk/government/speeches/the-importance-of-international-law-for-government-lawyers> accessed 22 July 2023.

[4] See, eg, *R (Miller) v Secretary of State for Exiting the European Union* [2017] UKSC 5, [2018] AC 61 (*Miller* (2017)) and *R (Miller) v Prime Minister* [2019] UKSC 41, [2020] AC 373.

the European Court of Human Rights (ECtHR) will also continue to attract attention, and controversy: as illustrated by the widespread coverage of the recent challenge to the UK Government's policy to remove asylum seekers to Rwanda. Prior to the Supreme Court judgment in November 2023, the ECtHR granted an urgent interim measure under Rule 39 of the Rules of the Court. The ECtHR indicated to the UK Government that the applicant should not be removed to Rwanda until three weeks after the delivery of the final domestic decision in his ongoing judicial review proceedings.[5]

The increasing use and application of international law in English courts may be attributed to various developments—political and legal, domestic and international—but perhaps the key ones are (a) increasing treaty regulation, resulting in a trickle-down, or 'inward-looking'[6], effect as treaty provisions are given domestic legal effect, and (b) increasing, and increasingly visible, vertical international law obligations which the UK owes—or arguably owes—to individuals and which those individuals seek to enforce through litigation. These two developments, in particular, result in greater opportunities for engagement by English courts with international law.

Against this backdrop of increasing opportunities for engagement, this chapter summarizes the principal ways in which English courts have engaged with the primary sources of international law and does not, therefore, purport to give an exhaustive description of all the ways in which international law may arise for consideration before English courts. I consider, in turn, the status and use of incorporated treaties, unincorporated treaties, and customary international law (CIL) in English courts. I then consider, briefly, how English courts have approached issues concerning foreign relations, before making some final observations.

It is important, however, to start with some preliminary context. English law is a dualist legal system.[7] The primary underpinning of this dualism is the constitutional principle of Parliamentary sovereignty or supremacy and the corollary that an exercise of the Royal prerogative by the executive (which includes

[5] See the press release issued by the Registrar of the European Court of Human Rights (ECtHR), dated 15 June 2022 in relation to *KN v UK*, App No 28774/22. For the Supreme Court judgment see *R (on the application of AAA (Syria)) v Secretary of State for the Home Department* [2023] UKSC 42, [2023] 1 WLR 4433.

[6] For the term see ILA Study Group on Principles on the Engagement of Domestic Courts with International Law, 'Final Report: Mapping the Engagement of Domestic Courts with International Law' (Johannesburg, 2016) (ILA Final Report) para 12. This chapter uses other terminology from the ILA Final Report too: see below and (n 98) in particular.

[7] It was described as such by the Supreme Court in *R (Yam) v Central Criminal Court* [2015] UKSC 76, [2016] AC 771 [35]; in *Miller* (2017) (n 4) [55], [57], [79], and most recently in *R (SC) v Secretary of State for Work and Pensions* [2021] UKSC 26, [2022] AC 223.

the treaty-making power) does not enable the executive to change the law, unless this is expressly provided by statute.[8] It is, therefore, constitutional theory and practice and, less overtly, political reality that guide and shape English courts' engagement with international law, rather than a consistent response to either specific norms of, or the general idea of, international law (whether described by reference to attitudes of alignment, avoidance, contestation, or some other terminology).[9]

The underlying constitutional principles that explain the engagement of English courts with international law are settled and uncontroversial. However, the proper limits and application of those principles continue to be challenged and developed through caselaw. Given the number of cases and the diverse subject-matter that they cover, there are frequent opportunities to examine the relationship between English courts, English law, and international law. In addition to the Rwanda policy mentioned above: consider, for example, the restatement of dualism by the Supreme Court in the *SC* case, the *Miller* (2017) case, and the controversy (and litigation)[10] over the October 2015 amendment to the Ministerial Code. The possibility of ongoing development is also illustrated by Lord Bingham's extra-curial assertion that the rule of law requires compliance, by the State, with its obligations in international law as in national law,[11] and Lord Steyn's *obiter* comments on Parliamentary supremacy: that it is 'a construct of the common law' and that it is

> not unthinkable that circumstances could arise where the courts may have to qualify a principle established on a different hypothesis of constitutionalism. In exceptional circumstances involving an attempt to abolish judicial review or the ordinary role of the courts [the Supreme Court] may have to consider whether this is a constitutional fundamental which even a sovereign

[8] See also Paul Craig, 'Engagement and Disengagement with International Institutions: The U.K. Perspective' in Curtis A Bradley (ed), *The Oxford Handbook of Comparative Foreign Relations Law* (OUP 2019) 394: 'There is a proximate normative connection between [Parliamentary] sovereignty thus conceived, and the dualist perspective ... The latter is designed to protect the former.'

[9] This chapter uses the terminology in the ILA Final Report (n 6) and, in particular, the terminology of avoidance, alignment and contestation, see ibid para 37.

[10] The amendment involved the deletion of the underlined words: 'The Ministerial Code should be read alongside ... the background of the overarching duty on Ministers to comply with the law including international law and treaty obligations and to uphold the administration of justice and to protect the integrity of public life.' The Court of Appeal held that the deletion did not involve any change in substance and that, as indicated by public explanations made by Lord Faulks (then Minister of State at the Ministry of Justice), the 2015 Code did not change the duty to comply with the law which existed in the 2010 Code. See *R (Gulf Centre for Human Rights) v Prime Minister* [2018] EWCA Civ 1855 and *R (Gulf Centre for Human Rights) v Prime Minister* [2016] EWHC 1323 (Admin).

[11] Tom Bingham, *The Rule of Law* (Penguin Books 2011) ch 10.

Parliament acting at the behest of a complaisant House of Commons cannot abolish.[12]

B. Practice of English Courts

1. Treaties

As noted above, in the UK, treaty-making is part of the Royal prerogative and vests in the executive. Two related points arise from this fact; both of them are underpinned by the principle of non-justiciability, which could, itself, be regarded as an example of affirmative avoidance.[13]

The first point is that treaty-making is part of the traditional, non-justiciable, Royal prerogative. That means that a decision to sign or ratify a treaty would not be amenable to judicial review, nor would a decision that a particular treaty should not be signed or ratified.[14] This is because the 'nature and subject-matter are such as not to be amenable to the judicial process'.[15]

The second point is that, because treaties are entered into by the executive, the constitutional position, pursuant to the principle of Parliamentary sovereignty, is that they do not—without more (eg statutory incorporation)—form part of, or alter the content of, English law. As Leggatt J (as he then was) has explained, '[i]n a parliamentary democracy, Parliament and not the executive makes laws. If treaties entered into by the executive were to be recognized by the courts as part of English law without the need for legislation, that would effectively empower the executive to make law without the approval of Parliament'.[16]

In light of these two points, the starting point is that English courts lack the competence to interpret or apply unincorporated treaties[17] That starting point

[12] *R (Jackson) v Attorney General* [2005] UKHL 56, [2006] 1 AC 262, [102] (Lord Steyn).

[13] See ILA Final Report (n 6) paras 21, 41.

[14] *JH Rayner (Mincing Lane) v Department of Trade and Industry* [1990] 2 AC 418 (*Tin Council*), 499F-500C (Lord Oliver) and *Lewis v Attorney General of Jamaica* [2000] UKPC 35, [2001] 2 AC 50, 77B (Lord Slynn).

[15] *Council of Civil Service Unions v Minister for the Civil Service* [1985] AC 374, 418B-C (Lord Roskill).

[16] *R (Al-Saadoon) v Secretary of State for Defence* [2015] EWHC 715 (Admin), [2015] 3 WLR 503 [267]. See also, *Miller* (2017) (n 4) [55]–[56]. As the Supreme Court recently stated, citing Lord Oliver in *Tin Council* (n 14) and *Miller* (2017) (n 4), 'although treaties are agreements intended to be binding upon the parties to them, they are not contracts which domestic courts can enforce', and 'it is a fundamental principle of our constitutional law that an unincorporated treaty does not form part of the law of the United Kingdom' *SC* (n 7) [76]–[78] (Lord Reed). See also *R (Friends of the Earth) v Secretary of State for Transport* [2020] UKSC 52, [2021] PPTSR 190 (*FoE*) [108] (Lord Hodge and Lord Sales, with whom the other members of the Supreme Court agreed).

[17] See, eg, Lord Oliver in *Tin Council* (n 14) 499F-500C and *British Airways v Laker Airways* [1984] UKHL 7, [1985] AC 58 [28] (Lord Diplock).

as described in the *Tin Council* case has exceptions, as Lord Oliver recognized when he referred to incorporated treaties (see further below).[18] Generally stated, it is accepted that an English court may adjudicate on the interpretation of an unincorporated treaty in order to determine rights or obligations under domestic law.[19] However, even then, there are limits: English courts may be reluctant to interpret an unincorporated treaty 'where the contracting parties have embraced an alternative means of resolving differences' or where there is 'a live dispute on the meaning of an unincorporated provision on which there was no judicial authority'.[20]

As Lord Oliver recognized, where treaties are given force of law in the UK by statute, either directly or indirectly, then the judicial restraint described above is unnecessary. In these situations English courts may interpret and apply the incorporated treaty provisions. This is an example of alignment. Before embarking on treaty interpretation an English court will consider the mode of incorporation, that is the way in which, and the extent to which, the treaty or treaty provision has been incorporated into English law. As to this, '[t]here is no rule specifying the precise legislative method of incorporation'.[21] Parliament therefore has wide-ranging discretion regarding the mode by which, as well as the extent to which, it chooses to incorporate treaties into English law. There are, however, a few well-established, and favoured, modes of incorporation. Perhaps the most common one is for a statute to expressly state that all or part of a treaty, which is often scheduled to the statute, has force of law.[22]

The process of treaty interpretation itself will be undertaken by applying international law principles, namely those in the Vienna Convention on the Law of Treaties (VCLT).[23] This use of the VCLT is another example of alignment. English courts use the VCLT as a source of law, even though it is not an

[18] *Tin Council* (n 14), 500 (passage beginning 'These propositions do not, however, involve as a corollary that the court must never look at or construe a treaty.').

[19] *R (Campaign for Nuclear Disarmament) v Prime Minister* [2002] EWHC 2777 (Admin) [36] (Simon Brown LJ):

> Should the court declare the meaning of an international instrument operating purely on the plane of international law? In my judgment the answer is plainly no. All of the cases relied upon by the applicants in which the court has pronounced upon some issue of international law are cases where it has been necessary to do so in order to determine rights and obligations under domestic law'.

[20] *R (Cornerhouse) v Director of Serious Fraud Office* [2008] UKHL 60, [2009] 1 AC 756 (*Cornerhouse*) [45] and [44] (Lord Bingham).

[21] *R (European Roma Rights Centre) v Immigration Officer at Prague Airport* [2004] UKHL 55, [2005] 2 AC 1 (*European Roma Rights Centre*) [42] (Lord Steyn).

[22] See, eg, Diplomatic Privileges Act 1964, s 2(1) and Consular Relations Act 1968, s 1(1).

[23] (adopted 23 May 1969, entered into force 27 January 1980) 1155 UNTS 331. See, eg, *Al-Malki v Reyes* [2017] UKSC 61, [2019] AC 735 [10] (Lord Sumption): 'It is not in dispute that, so far as an English statute gives effect to an international treaty, it falls to be interpreted by an English court in accordance with the principles of interpretation applicable to treaties as a matter of international law.'

incorporated treaty itself. This is because the primary provisions concerning interpretation, Articles 31 and 32, are considered to have the status of CIL.[24]

By taking the step of statutory incorporation, Parliament has already made a—and probably *the* most important—decision about the method and extent to which English law is to be harmonized with the UK's international law obligations. However, that does not mean that the role of English courts in interpreting such treaties is always a purely mechanical one of alignment. The interpretative exercise, and the application of the incorporated treaty provision to the facts of a particular case, provide considerable opportunities for engagement with international law.

At one end of that spectrum of incorporated treaties are those provisions where Parliament's intent—as to the method and extent of incorporation—is clearly discernible from, and expressly set out in, the statute. The role of the court in these cases may be largely limited to identifying the scope of the particular incorporated treaty provision and applying it to the facts in that case. It is therefore directed towards alignment.[25] But even in this role, avoidance or contestation tendencies may manifest themselves in the interpretative analysis. The court may, for example, engage in avoidance by limiting the sources to which it has regard in interpreting the treaty provision or it may engage in contestation by limiting the role or influence of those sources in the interpretative analysis. See, eg, Lord Hoffmann's observation:

> Parliament may pass a law which mirrors the terms of the treaty and in that sense incorporates the treaty into English law. But, even then, the metaphor of incorporation may be misleading. It is not the treaty but the statute which forms part of English law. And English courts will not (unless the statute expressly so provides) be bound to give effect to interpretations of the treaty by an international court, even though the United Kingdom is bound by international law to do so.[26]

Indeed, statutory provisions may identify the sources which the English court may consider in the interpretative analysis, and their status. This may mean that alignment becomes a more complex exercise. For example, section 2 of

[24] See, eg, *European Roma Rights Centre* (n 21) [18] (Lord Bingham) and *Fothergill v Monarch Airlines* [1980] UKHL 6, [1981] AC 251, 282D (Lord Diplock).

[25] A recent example of simple or 'fair weather' alignment (for the terminology see ILA Final Report (n 6) para 44) is *Chief Constable of Sussex v Secretary of State for Transport* [2016] EWHC 2280 (QB).

[26] *R v Lyons* [2002] UKHL 44, [2003] 1 AC 976 [27] (emphasis added). This is an example of affirmative contestation, see ILA Final Report (n 6) para 58.

the Human Rights Act 1998 (HRA) gives an English court discretion as to the influence and weight which it decides to give to judgments of the ECtHR.[27] Following a number of cases involving the relationship between the ECHR, the HRA and unincorporated treaty provisions (primarily the United Nations Convention on the Rights of the Child),[28] in *SC*, the Supreme Court considered whether the HRA has given domestic legal effect to unincorporated treaties and concluded that it had not. Lord Reed, with whom the other members of the Court agreed, said that a 'misunderstanding appears to have arisen in this jurisdiction from the fact that the [ECtHR] frequently has regard to international law, and to its interpretation by competent institutions, when interpreting the [ECHR]'.[29] Lord Reed described the approach of the ECtHR in relation to the use of international law as 'eclectic'.[30] However, he went on to note that the ECtHR has not treated provisions of international treaties as if they were directly incorporated into the ECHR itself, so as to impose specific obligations on the contracting States via the ECHR. Nor does the ECtHR refer to international materials for the purpose of determining whether contracting States have complied with their obligations under unincorporated treaties. He explained that even where rules of international law are incorporated into domestic law, the ECtHR has described its role as being confined to ascertaining whether those rules are applicable and whether their interpretation is compatible with the ECHR. Lord Reed therefore concluded that there was no basis in the case law of the ECtHR, as taken into account under the HRA, 'for any departure from the rule that our domestic courts cannot determine whether this country has violated its obligations under unincorporated international treaties'.[31] He went on to identify, in that regard, a 'misunderstanding' that has appeared 'in some recent judgments of this court', and analysed the use of unincorporated treaties in those cases.[32]

[27] The Human Rights Act 1998 (HRA) is an example of indirect incorporation: the European Convention for the Protection of Human Rights and Fundamental Freedoms (adopted 4 November 1950, entered into force 3 September 1953) ETS No 5 (ECHR) was not made part of English law but HRA s 6 makes it unlawful for a public authority to act incompatibly with the ECHR rights set out in the Schedule to the HRA.

[28] (adopted 20 November 1989, entered into force 2 September 1990) 1557 UNTS 3

[29] *SC* (n 7) [80].

[30] He identified the following examples in this regard: '[T]he court has regard to international law in seeking to avoid a conflict between the [ECHR] and other treaties, so far as it can. It also sometimes takes account of international law where it is incorporated into the law of a contracting state, and is for that reason relevant to the issue before the court. International law also has a broader significance . . . as evidence of a European consensus . . . which can inform the interpretation of the [ECHR], the width of the national margin of appreciation, and the court's assessment of proportionality.' *SC* (n 7) [80]

[31] ibid [84].

[32] ibid [85]–[96].

Although, in English cases decided pursuant to the ECHR/HRA, it is often possible to identify which source of law is being applied, and in what way, this is not always clear. That is because the ECHR contains norms, such as freedom of expression, that also exist independently as a matter of English law, albeit with similar content (these are described, in the ILA Final Report, as 'consubstantial norms').[33] It can, therefore, sometimes be difficult to identify—from judicial interpretation of the norm in question—to what extent that interpretation is influenced by ECHR jurisprudence and/or English jurisprudence. This similarity of content may also lead to transfusions of substantive international law content into the (similar) English norm.

As *SC* demonstrates, what appears to be simple alignment may, on closer analysis, reveal multiple layers; not all of which may involve alignment. Thus, aligning domestic, English, law with the ECHR may involve interpretation by reference to other international law instruments[34] or the recognition of consubstantial alignment on the international plane,[35] or consideration of the inter-relationship between three different systems: (a) international law; (b) ECHR law; and (c) English law.[36] The diverse approach of English courts in such cases defies general characterization in the terminology of avoidance, alignment etc. That is because these are usually high fact-specific and therefore unique cases involving multiple levels of analyses; interpretations of different regimes of substantive law; and consideration of the relationships between these different legal regimes.

At the other end of the incorporated treaty spectrum are hybrid statutes—viz., statutes which do not directly or indirectly incorporate a treaty but which are intended to give effect to all or part of an unincorporated treaty as is

[33] ILA Final Report (n 6) para 30.

[34] Eg, in *R (Al-Saadoon) v Secretary of State for Defence* [2016] EWCA Civ 811, the Court of Appeal construed the scope of ECHR art 5 by reference to a range of instruments and, in particular, the International Convention for the Protection of All Persons from Enforced Disappearance (adopted 20 December 2006, entered into force 23 December 2010) 2716 UNTS 3 ([147]–[55]).

[35] Eg, in *Ibrahimi and Abasi v Secretary of State for the Home Department* [2016] EWHC 2049 (Admin), Green J ([41]) observed that ECHR art 3 'is a reflection or embodiment of the principle recognised in Article 33 of the Convention' relating to the Status of Refugees (adopted 28 July 1951, entered into force 22 April 1954) 189 UNTS 137.

[36] See, in particular, *Al-Jedda v United Kingdom*, App no 27021/08, 7 July 2011 and *R (Serdar Mohammed) v Ministry of Defence* [2017] UKSC 2, [2017] 2 WLR 327. Note also the similar difficulties in the context of EU law, eg in C-402/05P and C-415/05P *Yassin Abdullah Kadi and Al Barakaat International Foundation v Council of the European Union and Commission of the European Communities* [2008] ECLI: EU:2008:461. On how affirmative or consubstantial contestation may be produced in such cases, see ILA Final Report (n 6) paras 59, 63. For a more recent example of the interaction between English, EU, and international law see *R (Western Sahara Campaign UK) v HMRC* [2015] EWHC 2898 (Admin) (the preliminary ruling from the European Court of Justice (Grand Chamber) is at [2018] 3 CMLR 15).

apparent from either (a) the long title or preamble of the statute[37] or (b) from extrinsic evidence.[38] Although the proper approach to category (b) was historically debated, it is now well-established that in both categories (a) and (b) the statute should be interpreted by reference to the underlying, unincorporated, treaty.[39]

This form of engagement could be regarded as evidence of more ambitious alignment than the one in relation to incorporated treaties simpliciter, because the statute is interpreted by reference to the underlying treaty even though the substantive content of the statute does not directly incorporate the treaty. However, the alignment here is not materially different from that which exists in relation to incorporated treaties. This is because the interpretation of a hybrid statute (by reference to an unincorporated treaty) has the same constitutional rationale as the interpretation of an incorporated treaty, that is to construe the legislation so as to give effect to Parliament's intention. Like incorporated treaties simpliciter, hybrid statutes also give rise to judicial discretion regarding interpretative sources, their weight and how they are applied to the facts. That discretion gives rise to opportunities for different forms of engagement.

In conclusion, and taking into account hybrid statutes, it is difficult to characterize the approach of English courts to incorporated treaties as being solely or even primarily one of avoidance, alignment, or contestation. Whilst, on the most general level, the overall picture tends towards alignment there are opportunities for both avoidance and contestation.

Incorporated treaties are distinguishable from treaties which the UK has either signed or ratified as a matter of international law, but which have no formal status as a matter of English law (unincorporated treaties). With the *Tin Council* as a starting point, it may be thought that the approach of English courts to unincorporated treaties would be more enlightening, vis-à-vis the relationship of English courts, and their engagement with international law, than their approach to incorporated treaties. I turn now to consider that approach to unincorporated treaties.

English courts have developed two principal canons of interpretation in relation to unincorporated treaties. These canons evidence alignment, in

[37] Eg, see the long title of the Suppression of Terrorism Act 1978 which states: 'An Act to give effect to the European Convention on the Suppression of Terrorism' (the Convention is not given force of law).

[38] See, eg, Criminal Justice Act 1988, s 134(1) which gives effect to the UK's obligations under the United Nations Convention Against Torture and Other Cruel, Inhuman and Degrading Treatment or Punishment (adopted 10 December 1984, entered into force 26 June 1987) 1465 UNTS 85 (UNCAT).

[39] *Salomon v Commissioners of Customs and Excise* [1967] 2 QB 116 (CA), 144B-F (Diplock LJ).

theoretical purpose if not always in practical effect—provided that it is constitutionally permissible for the court to embark on interpretation in the first place. These two canons are (a) the presumption of compatibility (the POC) and (b) the principle of legality (the POL). They are addressed in turn below.

The premise underlying the POC is that Parliament cannot have intended to legislate contrary to the UK's international law obligations as contained in unincorporated treaties. The POC applies to ambiguous or obscure provisions in primary or subordinate legislation and enables recourse to unincorporated treaties for the resolution of the ambiguity or obscurity in a way that is compatible with the UK's unincorporated treaty obligations.[40]

The pre-condition of a statutory ambiguity or obscurity is a malleable aspect of the POC: it may be readily used to enable any of avoidance, alignment, or contestation. It may be said that Lord Bridge's broad definition, in *Brind*, of an ambiguous provision—as being, 'capable of a meaning which either conforms to or conflicts with the [ECHR]'[41]—is itself an example of a pro-alignment approach since it would tend to facilitate recourse to the unincorporated treaty. Examples of cases where courts have referred to the lack of statutory ambiguity in the context of the POC are *MacDonald v Advocate General for Scotland*[42] and *R v Kelly*.[43]

One notable pro-alignment step is the application of the POC outside the statutory context, to the common law: 'Of course there is a strong presumption in favour of interpreting English law (whether common law or statute) in a way which does not place the United Kingdom in breach of an international obligation.'[44] This enables the invocation of unincorporated treaty obligations where the common law is unclear or developing; in such cases courts may define or even develop the common law so as to be consistent with the UK's

[40] *R v Secretary of State for the Home Department, ex p Brind* [1991] UKHL 4, [1991] AC 696, 747H–48A (Lord Bridge) and 760G (Lord Ackner). A recent illustration (of the POC being invoked in the extradition context and by reference to the post-Brexit Trade and Co-operation Agreement) is *Badea v Romanian Judicial Authority* [2022] EWHC 1025 (Admin) [41], and note the reference to *Konecny v District Court in Brno-Venkov, Czech Republic* [2019] UKSC 8, [2019] 1 WLR 1586 (in which, at [16], the Supreme Court described Part 1 of the Extradition Act 2003 as giving effect in domestic law to the European Council Framework Decision: 'The choice of form and methods to achieve that result is left to member states. In this instance, the United Kingdom has departed significantly from a direct implementation of the scheme of the Framework Decision. The provisions of Part 1 ... must, nevertheless, be interpreted as intended to give effect to the Framework Decision, and, so far as possible, construed consistently with its terms and purpose.')

[41] *Brind* (n 40).

[42] *MacDonald v Advocate General for Scotland* [2003] UKHL 34, [2003] ICR 937 [54]. After referring to *Brind* (n 40) Lord Hope observed 'the precise way in which the [Sex Discrimination Act 1975] is framed leaves very little room for judicial reform and development.'

[43] *R v Kelly* [2000] QB 198 (CA), 210C ('we find no ambiguity at all in section 2 [of the Crime (Sentences) Act 1997])'.

[44] *Lyons* (n 26).

international law obligations. See, for example, *R v G* where Lord Steyn considered the common law of recklessness by reference to the United Nations Convention on the Rights of the Child.[45]

Although the POC is, prima facie, an example of alignment, it does, of course, conform to the requirements of the constitutional principle of Parliamentary supremacy. That is why the POC has no application where the relevant statutory provision is clear and unambiguous, even if that clarity results in an outcome which is contrary to the UK's unincorporated treaty obligations.[46] Nor will the POC be applied in the common law context where there is prior statutory regulation and/or incorporated treaty obligations.[47] This means that, in practice, there is a fairly circumscribed ambit within which the POC may operate. The pro-alignment aspects of this method of engagement may, therefore, be more theoretical than real.

By contrast with the POC, there is no pre-condition of statutory ambiguity or obscurity before the POL can be applied. The POL enables general words in primary and subordinate legislation to be construed compatibly with fundamental rights on the basis that Parliament cannot have intended, by using general words, to override such rights.[48] Whilst the right in question must already be a part of domestic law,[49] the nature and scope of the right may be affected by (a) CIL and/or (b) the content of unincorporated treaties. This means that the POL provides opportunities for consubstantial alignment but, like the POC, the POL is displaced where, 'the statute conferring the power makes it clear that such was the intention of Parliament'.[50] Once again this demonstrates the importance of Parliamentary supremacy. In *Al-Saadoon* the Court of Appeal rejected the submission that the UK's human rights obligations under Articles 10 and 11 of UNCAT are enforceable public law obligations owed by domestic public authorities in domestic law, provided that their violation has not been mandated or empowered by Parliament through clear primary legislation. The Court of Appeal rejected this submission on the bases that (a) the POL is a principle of statutory interpretation and not a broad principle as to how the

[45] *R v G* [2003] UKHL 50, [2004] 1 AC 1034 [53]: 'It is true that the Convention became binding on the United Kingdom after Caldwell was decided. But the House cannot ignore the norm created by the Convention. This factor on its own justified a reappraisal of [*R v Caldwell* [1982] AC 341].'

[46] *Salomon* (n 39) 143D-E (Diplock LJ). This may lead to affirmative avoidance or negatory contestation. See ILA Final Report (n 6) paras 41, 61.

[47] As recognized by both Lord Nicholls and Lord Hoffmann in *Re McKerr* [2004] UKHL 12, [2004] 1 WLR 807 [30], [71].

[48] *R v Secretary of State for the Home Department, ex p Simms* [1999] UKHL 33, [2000] 2 AC 115, 131E (Lord Hoffmann).

[49] *European Roma Rights Centre* (n 21) [29].

[50] *R v Secretary of State for the Home Department ex p Pierson* [1997] UKHL 37, [1998] AC 539, 575D (Lord Browne-Wilkinson).

courts should develop common law;[51] (b) the POL requires the fundamental rights in question to be part of the extant domestic law;[52] and (c) there is no room for the POL where Parliament has already entered the field to strike the appropriate balance.[53] *Al-Saadoon* may therefore be regarded as an illustration of affirmative avoidance.

Apart from these two specific interpretative mechanisms, English courts are often invited to consider unincorporated treaties and other international law materials in a range of other, softer ways. For example, unincorporated treaties have been used (a) as aids in construing legislation[54] and (b) as illuminating the purpose and object of domestic legislation.[55] Such usage is broadly one of alignment, in the limited sense that it evidences an awareness and interest by English courts in international law. But it would be misleading to regard such ad hoc, and often unexplained, usage, as evidencing some kind of systemic or widespread alignment. That there is no such systemic substantive alignment and, possibly, quite the contrary is illustrated by the following three points (in addition to the points already made above).

First, the fact that English courts have rejected attempts to apply the POC to statutory conferrals of executive power.[56] Thus, the rule is as follows: where Parliament gives an executive decision-maker a broad power, English courts will not apply the POC so as to *require* the decision-maker to exercise her discretion in a way that is compatible with the UK's unincorporated treaty obligations.[57] This has been recently affirmed by the Supreme Court.[58] This is distinct

[51] ibid [198].

[52] ibid [199].

[53] ibid [200].

[54] See, eg, *A v Secretary of State for the Home Department* [2004] UKHL 56, [2005] 2 AC 68 in which Lord Bingham used a range of international materials when determining the validity of a derogation from ECHR art 5.

[55] See, eg, *McIntosh v Lord Advocate* [2001] UKPC D1, [2003] 1 AC 1078 where Lord Bingham referred to the policy underlying the Misuse of Drugs Act 1971 and the Proceeds of Crime (Scotland) Act 1995 by reference to the Convention against Illicit Traffic in Narcotic Drugs and Psychotropic Substances (adopted 19 December 1988, entered into force 11November 1990) 1582 UNTS 95, and *ZH Tanzania v Secretary of State for the Home Department* [2011] UKSC 4, [2011] 2 AC 166 in which Lady Hale noted that '[i]n all actions concerning children the best interests of the child shall be a primary consideration. This is a binding obligation in international law, and the spirit, if not the precise language, has also been translated into our national law [section 11 of the Children Act 2004]' (ibid [23]). More recently, see *Crown Prosecution Service v Beaumont* [2022] EWHC 849 (Admin) in which the Divisional Court said, of the Extradition Act 2003, 'We are prepared to assume for present purposes that Parliament would not have intended the arrangements to operate in a way which would result in individuals being tried, or having to serve sentences, in circumstances which would breach accepted rules of international law governing extradition between states.' (at [26])

[56] Although there have been occasional judicial statements which are not easy to reconcile with this: see, eg, *R v Secretary of State for the Home Department, ex p Venables* [1997] UKHL 25, [1998] AC 407, 499.

[57] *Brind* (n 40) 748.

[58] In *Yam* (n 7) the Supreme Court held that a domestic decision-maker exercising a discretionary common law power was not bound to have regard or give effect to the UK's purely international

from the situations where, for example, the decision-maker *chooses* to take account of an unincorporated treaty obligation in making a particular decision or *chooses* to give effect to unincorporated treaty obligations in a policy. In those situations there may be justiciable errors of law. Thus, the decision-maker's self-direction as to the meaning of the treaty obligation may be challenged as being wrong and, similarly, the decision-maker's failure properly to give effect to the unincorporated treaty obligation in the policy may be challenged.[59]

Secondly, although such voluntary executive decisions may lead to justiciable errors of law in principle, (a) an English court may refuse to review the decision where it considers that there is inadequate judicial authority on the meaning of the provision in question, and (b) in certain contexts, an English court may apply a less rigorous standard of review than that which is typically applied to alleged errors of law, by simply asking whether the decision-maker took a 'tenable view' of the unincorporated treaty provision. As to the first point, the case of *R v Secretary of State for the Home Department, ex parte Launder*[60] is an example of a case where the English court held that the executive voluntary self-direction (as to the then unincorporated ECHR) was subject to judicial review. However, that case was distinguished in *Cornerhouse*. In *Cornerhouse*, Lord Bingham refused to review the decision of the Director of the Serious Fraud Office because of the lack of judicial authority regarding the provision in question (Article 5 of the OECD Convention on Combating Bribery of Foreign Public Officials in International Business Transactions)[61]

obligations, although she could have regard to those obligations if she considered it appropriate. See also *FoE* (n 16) [108] ('Ratification does not constitute a commitment operating on the plane of domestic law to perform obligations under the treaty. Moreover, it cannot be regarded in itself as a statement devoid of relevant qualification for the purposes of domestic law, since if treaty obligations are to be given effect in domestic law that will require law-making steps which are uncertain and unspecified at the time of ratification.'); *R (EOT and KTT) v Secretary of State for the Home Department* [2022] EWCA Civ 307 *(EOT and KTT)* [35] (Underhill LJ):

> In the first place, many of the obligations imposed by [the treaty] are in very general terms, and it is a matter for the Government (subject to general public law constraints) in what manner it chooses to implement them. Further, it is always open to the Government, since [the treaty] is unincorporated, to make it clear that it has chosen not to give effect to it, whether generally or in some particular respect. As a matter of constitutional principle such a decision could not be challenged in the domestic courts.

[59] See *EOT and KTT* (n 58) for a discussion of some of these issues, at [25]–[34] and the first instance judgment in *R (KTT) v Secretary of State for the Home Department* [2021] EWHC 2722 (Admin) [15]–[37] and [52]. The appeal considered the Government's policy regarding the grant of leave to remain to victims of trafficking, by which the UK Government chose to implement its obligations under the Council of Europe Convention on Action against Trafficking in Human Beings (adopted 3 May 2005, entered into force 1 February 2008) ETS No 197 (ECAT), and whether the policy complied with the relevant provisions of ECAT.

[60] *R v Secretary of State for the Home Department, ex p Launder* [1997] UKHL 20, [1997] 1 WLR 839.

[61] (adopted 21 November 1997, entered into force 15 February 1999) 2802 UNTS 225.

which the Director had, voluntarily, taken into account. As to the second point, in *Cornerhouse* Lord Brown said that when an executive decision-maker voluntarily self-directed herself in (unincorporated) international law and was challenged, then 'the "tenable view" approach is the furthest the court should go in examining the point of international law in question'.[62] The 'tenable view' was considered by the Supreme Court in *Benkharbouche v Embassy of the Republic of Sudan*.[63] Lord Sumption (with whom the other members of the Supreme Court agreed) accepted that there are circumstances in which an English court considering the international law obligations of the UK may properly limit itself to asking whether the UK has acted on a 'tenable view' of those obligations. He gave some examples where that might be so but he declined to treat those examples

> as pointing to a more general rule that the English courts should not determine points of customary international law but only the 'tenability' of some particular view about them. If it is necessary to decide a point of international law in order to resolve a justiciable issue and there is an ascertainable answer, then the court is bound to supply that answer.[64]

The standard of review was considered again recently in *R (Friends of the Earth) v Secretary of State for International Trade*: the Court of Appeal applied the 'tenable view' when considering the Paris Agreement.[65]

Thirdly, the extant position is that unincorporated treaties do not give rise to legitimate expectations. This area of the law is not free from ambiguity and it may not be settled. On the basis of Australian authority,[66] English courts have held, on two occasions, that the ratification of an unincorporated treaty could give rise to a representation on which members of the public could rely as creating a legitimate expectation that future executive decision-making would be compatible with the unincorporated treaty obligations.[67] Against these two cases there are three others which doubt the proposition that mere ratification

[62] *Cornerhouse* (n 20) [68]. The 'tenable view' was applied by Lloyd-Jones J in *R (ICO Satellite) v The Office of Communications* [2010] EWHC 2010 (Admin).

[63] *Benkharbouche v Embassy of the Republic of Sudan* [2017] UKSC 62, [2019] AC 777 (*Benkharbouche*).

[64] ibid [35].

[65] In arriving at this conclusion the Court of Appeal stated that the Paris Agreement was pre-eminently an unincorporated treaty; there was no jurisprudence as to the precise legal meaning of the Paris Agreement and it is for the executive to determine the interpretation of it. See *R (Friends of the Earth) v (1) Secretary of State for International Trade* [2023] EWCA Civ 4 [40], [50].

[66] *Minister for Immigration and Ethnic Affairs v Teoh* (1995) 183 CLR 273 (HC).

[67] See *R v Secretary of State for the Home Department, ex p Ahmed* [1999] Imm AR 22, 36 and *R v Uxbridge Magistrates' Court, ex p Adimi* [1999] EWHC 765 (Admin), [2001] QB 667 [57].

of a treaty can, without more, give rise to legitimate expectation.[68] These inconsistent decisions illustrate the tension at the fringes of the relationship between English law and international law.

The way in which English courts treat, and engage with, unincorporated treaties therefore varies considerably, ranging from alignment to contestation and avoidance. One general explanation for this varying mode of engagement is the overarching need to consider Parliamentary sovereignty. However, it is not always clear that Parliamentary sovereignty necessarily *requires* a particular approach to international law rather than, perhaps, permitting a range of possible outcomes. It may be that in some cases references to Parliamentary sovereignty reflect judicial conservatism or a perceived, or real, lack of 'relative institutional competence' (whether by reference to the distinct roles/competences of the executive/judiciary or domestic judiciary/international judiciary).

2. Customary International Law

It is sometimes said that CIL is automatically incorporated into English law.[69] However, it is more accurate to describe CIL as a source of English law.[70]

From a constitutional perspective, English courts are generally more receptive to the use of CIL than they are to the use of unincorporated treaties. This is because, as a matter of principle, the reception of CIL into English law does not give rise to the constitutional difficulties posed by unincorporated treaties.[71] Unlike treaties, save for those that codify CIL, CIL rules do not become binding on the UK as a sole consequence of the acts of the UK executive, although the executive may have contributed to the formation of the rule in question (since its acts or omissions are, by definition, examples of State practice and may evidence *opinio juris*).[72] This distinguishes CIL from treaties and means that CIL

[68] *R (European Roma Rights Centre) v Immigration Officer* [2003] EWCA Civ 666, [2004] QB 811 [51] and [100] (the House of Lords' judgment (n 21) does not address this issue); *Chundawadra v IAT* [1988] Imm AR 161, 173–74 and *Behluli v Secretary of State for the Home Department* [1998] EWCA Civ 788, [1998] Imm AR 407, 415.

[69] See, eg, the majority of the Court of Appeal in *Trendtex Trading Corp v Central Bank of Nigeria* [1977] 1 QB 529 and, in particular, the following comment by Lord Denning MR: 'rules of international law are incorporated into English law automatically and considered to be part of English law unless they are in conflict with an Act of Parliament'.

[70] *R v Jones* [2006] UKHL 16, [2007] 1 AC 136 [11].

[71] For similar considerations see also ILA Final Report (n 6) para 74.

[72] ILC, 'Second Report on Identification of Customary International Law by Michael Wood, Special Rapporteur' (22 May 2014) UN Doc A/CN.4/672, paras 41b, 76.

may be treated as a source of English common law without undermining the principle of Parliamentary sovereignty. Thus, as the Court of Appeal has stated:

> The presumption is that a rule of customary international law will be taken to shape the common law unless there is some positive reason based on constitutional principle, statute law or common law that it should not (for ease of reference, we refer to these together as reasons of constitutional principle). The presumption reflects the policy of the common law that it should be in alignment with the common customary law applicable between nations. The position is different from that in relation to unincorporated treaty obligations, which do not in general alter domestic law. In part, since the making of treaties is a matter for the executive, this reflects the principle that the Crown has no power to alter domestic law by its unilateral action ... The common law is more receptive to the adoption of rules of customary international law because of the very demanding nature of the test to establish whether a rule of customary international law exists ... That is not something that the Crown can achieve by its own unilateral action by simple agreement with one other state. Accordingly, in the case of a rule of customary international law the presumption is that it will be treated as incorporated into the common law unless there is some reason of constitutional principle why it should not be. In the case of an obligation in an unincorporated treaty the relevant rule is the opposite of this, namely that it will not be recognised in the common law.[73]

As the Court of Appeal has observed: this initial, threshold, engagement of English law with CIL is, therefore, one of alignment. As a source of law, CIL may be used in a number of ways: for example, it may assist with the interpretation of statutes[74] or it may assist with the development of the common law.[75] Whether CIL is able to be used as such a source of law in a particular case depends on whether (assuming that the rule contended for does exist as a matter of CIL) the particular use is consistent with the applicable constitutional constraints.

[73] *R (Freedom and Justice Party) v Secretary of State for the Foreign and Commonwealth Affairs* [2018] EWCA Civ 1719, [2019] QB 1075 [117].

[74] CIL principles regarding State immunity are often considered by English courts, including in the context of interpreting the State Immunity Act 1978: recent examples include *Benkharbouche* (n 63) and *General Dynamics United Kingdom Ltd v State of Libya* [2021] UKSC 22, [2022] AC 318.

[75] Eg, in *R (Freedom and Justice Party) v Secretary of State for the Foreign and Commonwealth Affairs* [2016] EWHC 2010 (Admin) the Divisional Court found that members of special missions visiting the UK with the approval of the Foreign Office enjoyed personal inviolability and/or immunity from criminal process as a matter of CIL and English common law. This conclusion was upheld by the Court of Appeal, see (n 73).

Thus, where a rule of CIL exists and is sought to be relied upon before an English court as a source of English law, it may only be applied by an English court if the application (a) does not conflict with, or undermine, an Act of Parliament, and (b) is otherwise permissible, as a matter of English law, constitutional principles, and judicial competence. One example of the first condition is *R (Keyu) v Secretary of State for Foreign and Commonwealth Affairs*, where Lord Neuberger PSC opined that 'it appears to be quite inappropriate' for courts to develop the common law by reference to CIL (if there was a rule of CIL requiring a State to investigate deaths) in light of the express provision made by Parliament for the investigation of deaths.[76] An example of the second condition is *R (Akarcay) v Chief Constable of the West Yorkshire Police*, where Burnett LJ commented,

> [e]ven if it could be shown that [CIL] imposed an obligation not to recognize Northern Cyprus, in my opinion it could not form part of the common law. To treat it as such would contravene the unequivocal constitutional principle that questions of recognition are for the executive. It is not for the courts to dictate to the executive whether they can, must, or cannot recognise a state.[77]

Finally, and in order to avoid overstating the alignment aspect of the engagement between CIL and English law: it is important to remember that, in practice, there are not many cases in which rules of CIL have been successfully invoked and applied in English cases.[78]

C. Blunting/Moderating Techniques and Foreign Relations

The preceding sections consider the engagement of English courts with international law by reference to the primary *sources* of international law and do not, therefore, purport to give an exhaustive description of all the ways in which international law may arise for consideration before English courts. However, there is an expanding number of related cases that are noteworthy—even

[76] *R (Keyu) v Secretary of State for Foreign and Commonwealth Affairs* [2015] UKSC 69, [2016] AC 1355 [117].

[77] *R (Akarcay) v Chief Constable of the West Yorkshire Police* [2017] EWHC 159 (Admin) [23].

[78] For recent unsuccessful attempts see *UK P&I Club NV v Republica Bolivariana de Venezuela* [2023] EWCA Civ 1497 (anti-suit injunctions/state immunity); *Al-Saadoon* (n 16) (torture) and *Al-Malki v Reyes* [2015] EWCA Civ 32, [2016] 1 WLR 1785 (trafficking) [57]–[60], [64] (Lord Dyson MR). The argument in the Court of Appeal was that the international prohibition on trafficking takes precedence over the international rule of diplomatic immunity. The argument did not succeed before the Court of Appeal and was not pursued on appeal: see *Reyes v Al-Malki* (n 22), [40]–[41].

though they do not readily fit into the source-based analysis—that engage foreign relations and international law.[79] This kind of case often involves the claimant challenging executive conduct but the challenge directly or, more often, indirectly impugns the conduct of a foreign State or foreign State officials. The alleged unlawfulness sometimes involves a breach of human rights. It is difficult to generalize about these cases because they are so highly fact-sensitive. However, one theme is that they often involve the principle of non-justiciability (already referred to above) or the foreign act of State doctrine, both of which have been considered by the Supreme Court in a number of recent cases, including *Belhaj v Straw* and *Maduro v Guaido*.[80]

Both of these concepts may be analysed by reference to relative institutional competence and, in that sense, both concepts link back to the constitutional tensions already addressed above. However, avoidance may be one consequence of these concepts since both of them operate as bars to adjudication and preclude English courts engaging with what are often difficult and highly sensitive questions of international law.[81]

D. Conclusion

In general, English courts are open to, and engage with, the potential use and application of international law. Whether international law will ultimately be applied in a particular case is likely to depend on several issues or layers of analysis. One of the most important initial issues is whether the engagement in question is constitutionally permissible and appropriate. Although the overall framework in this regard is relatively clear, the application in individual cases may give rise to sensitive questions, finely balanced analysis and, sometimes, unsatisfactory outcomes. Furthermore, even where there are no insuperable constitutional obstacles: there will often be a range of other legal and factual issues. Each of these layers, in each individual case, could be analysed as providing opportunities for avoidance, alignment and contestation but it is difficult to venture beyond this observation given the diverse range of situations in which international law may arise before English courts.

[79] For a recent discussion of this topic, see Eirik Bjorge and Cameron Miles, 'Crown and Foreign Acts of State Before British Courts: *Rahmatullah*, *Belhaj*, and the Separation of Powers' in Bradley (n 7).

[80] *Belhaj v Straw* [2017] UKSC 3, [2017] 2 WLR 456; *Maduro Board of the Central Bank of Venezuela v Guaido Board of the Central Bank of Venezuela* [2021] UKSC 57, [2022] 2 WLR 167. See also *Shergill v Khaira* [2014] UKSC 33, [2015] AC 359 in relation to non-justiciability.

[81] In that sense the act of State doctrine (and non-justiciability) would operate as blunting or moderating techniques, ILA Final Report (n 6) para 21.

13

Engagement of Kosovo's Domestic (Internationalized) Courts with International Law

Zane Ratniece

A. Introduction

Studying the engagement of 'domestic courts' with 'international law' usually implies an assessment of how domestic judges have engaged with a foreign source of law. This, however, is different in the case of Kosovo. For a considerable time, Kosovo courts were staffed also with international judges, and, for some time, Kosovo domestic law was essentially a *lex specialis* international law. In particular, following the 1999 NATO military campaign in the Federal Republic of Yugoslavia, the United Nations Security Council (UNSC) adopted Resolution 1244, establishing an 'international civil presence' for the 'interim administration' of Kosovo.[1] The United Nations Interim Administration in Kosovo (UNMIK), in coordination with the 'international security presence'[2] in the territory, the NATO-led Kosovo Force (KFOR), 'involv[ed] the assertion of plenary administration by the United Nations'.[3] Under UNSC Res 1244, UNMIK adopted regulations applicable in the territory of Kosovo. These regulations, according to the International Court of Justice (ICJ), 'possesse[d] an international legal character',[4] while, at the same time, extending to 'regulate ... matters which would ordinarily be the subject of internal, rather than international, law'.[5]

[1] UNSC Res 1244 (10 June 1999) UN Doc S/RES/1244, paras 5, 10.

[2] ibid paras 5, 9.

[3] Ralph Wilde, *International Territorial Administration: How Trusteeship and the Civilizing Mission Never Went Away* (OUP 2008) 2–3, and 144–46 for more detail.

[4] *Accordance with International Law of the Unilateral Declaration of Independence in respect of Kosovo* (Advisory Opinion) [2010] ICJ Rep 403, 439 [88] (*Kosovo Advisory Opinion*).

[5] ibid 440, para 89.

In February 2008, Kosovo declared independence,[6] and adopted its Constitution[7] and laws, which repealed and replaced UNMIK regulations in the Kosovo's domestic legal system. Around the same time, the EU Mission in Kosovo (EULEX) was established.[8] From this point onwards, Kosovo courts, including international judges, had to determine whether Kosovo law or UNMIK regulations were applicable given that UNMIK still formally remained in Kosovo. After outlining the process of internationalization of Kosovo's domestic courts (Section B), this contribution discusses the manner in which Kosovo courts sought to resolve the tension between international law, namely UNMIK regulations, and the newly created domestic constitutional order. This contribution depicts significant legal issues that emerged from the approach taken by the Kosovo courts in respect of UNMIK regulations concerning the normative primacy of the Kosovo Constitution (Section C(1)).

Section C(2) explores the active interaction between domestic and international law in the adjudication of war crimes cases pertaining to the 1998/1999 Kosovo conflict. Kosovo's domestic courts, while tackling some legal constraints as regards the applicability of customary international law in cases before them, engaged with this source of international law. Section C(3) explores the engagement by Kosovo courts with instruments adopted between Kosovo and the European Union (EU) in the context of setting up the Kosovo Specialist Chambers and identifies forms of Kosovo's commitment to align itself with international standards regarding the prosecution and adjudication of international crimes. Section D concludes.

B. Internationalization of Kosovo Domestic Courts

1. During UNMIK's Administration of Kosovo

In the course of UNMIK's administration of Kosovo, domestic courts were structurally and institutionally internationalized. In particular, on 25 July 1999, the Special Representative of the UN Secretary-General (SRSG), the head of UNMIK, issued Regulation 1999/1 regarding the authority of UNMIK in Kosovo. This Regulation provided that 'the administration of the judiciary

[6] Kosovo Declaration of Independence, Pristina, 17 February 2008, available at <http://old.kuvendikosoves.org/common/docs/Dek_Pav_e.pdf> last accessed 26 March 2022.

[7] Constitution of the Republic of Kosovo of 2008 (as amended) (Kosovo Constitution).

[8] Council Joint Action 2008/124/CFSP of 4 February 2008 on the European Union Rule of Law Mission in Kosovo, EULEX KOSOVO [2008] OJ L42/92.

[was] vested in UNMIK and [was] exercised by the' SRSG, who could appoint 'any person to ... the judiciary'.[9]

Subsequently, a series of regulations were adopted, 'which increasingly introduced international personnel into the legal system of Kosovo', culminating with Regulation 2000/64, which permitted the creation of three-judge panels within the District Courts and the Supreme Court of Kosovo that included 'at least two international judges' (Regulation 64 Panels).[10] The presence of international judges in Kosovo courts was further reinforced in Regulation 2001/9 on a Constitutional Framework for Provisional Self-Government in Kosovo, promulgated on 15 May 2001.[11] The Constitutional Framework aimed to develop self-government in Kosovo pending a final settlement and establish provisional institutions of self-government, including in the judicial field. It defined the responsibilities relating to the administration of Kosovo between the SRSG and the provisional institutions of self-government of Kosovo. As regards international judges, the Constitutional Framework provided that '[i]nternational judges ... shall serve within the judicial system according to the rules established by the SRSG' and reserved to the SRSG exclusive powers to decide upon requests regarding the assignment of international judges.[12]

The deployment of international judges and prosecutors in Kosovo courts 'was deemed necessary in order to preserve the independence and impartiality of the judiciary' in the adjudication of 'serious crimes, including cases of war and inter-ethnic crimes'.[13] International judicial staff thus handled such cases as war crimes, murder, the illegal possession of weapons, and drug trafficking.[14]

[9] UNMIK, Regulation 1999/1 On the Authority of the Interim Administration in Kosovo (25 July 1999) UNMIK/REG/1999/1 ss 1.1 and 1.2.

[10] Rosalyn Higgins et al, *Oppenheim's International Law: United Nations* (OUP 2017) 1410–11. See UNMIK, Regulation 2000/6 On the Appointment and Removal from Office of International Judges and International Prosecutors (15 February 2000) UNMIK/REG/2000/6 s 1; UNMIK, Regulation 2000/34, Amending UNMIK Regulation 2000/6 On the Appointment and Removal from Office of International Judges and International Prosecutors (27 May 2000) UNMIK/REG/2000/34 s 1; UNMIK, Regulation 2000/64 On Assignment of International Judges/Prosecutors and/or Change of Venue (15 December 2000) UNMIK/REG/2000/64 ss 1 and 2. See also OSCE Mission in Kosovo, 'Review 1: The Criminal Justice System in Kosovo (February–July 2000)' (10 August 2000), 13; Tom Perriello and Marieke Wierda, 'Lessons from the Deployment of International Judges and Prosecutors in Kosovo' (International Center for Transnational Justice, March 2006), 13–15, <https://www.ictj.org/sites/default/files/ICTJ-FormerYugoslavia-Courts-Study-2006-English_0.pdf> accessed 23 July 2023.

[11] UNMIK, Regulation 2001/9 On a Constitutional Framework for Provisional Self-Government in Kosovo (15 May 2001) UNMIK/REG/2001/9.

[12] ibid chs 8.1(h) and 9.4.7. See also Gentian Zyberi, 'Kosovo Special Courts' in Antonio Cassese (ed), *The Oxford Companion to International Criminal Justice* (OUP 2009) 403–4; Ingo Winkelmann, 'Mixed Courts, Other (National Courts with International Participation)' in MPEPIL (OUP, May 2006) paras 13–14.

[13] Higgins et al (n 10) 1412; cf the discussion in Wilde (n 3) 216–25, esp 221–22; Eyal Benvenisti, *The International Law of Occupation* (2nd edn, OUP 2012) 286–88.

[14] UNSC 'Report of the Secretary-General on the United Nations Interim Administration Mission in Kosovo' (2 October 2001) UN Doc S/2001/926, 11 para 49.

In the meantime, in November 2005, the UN Secretary-General appointed his Special Envoy Martti Ahtisaari to undertake the future status process of Kosovo envisioned in UNSC Resolution 1244.[15] After more than one year of UN-sponsored negotiations, it became clear to the Special Envoy that Serbia and Kosovo were unable to reach an agreement on Kosovo's future status. The Special Envoy prepared a Comprehensive Proposal for the Kosovo Status Settlement and recommended that Kosovo become an independent State. The proposal was endorsed by Kosovo but was not accepted by Serbia.[16]

2. After the Kosovo's Declaration of Independence

On 17 February 2008, the Kosovo Assembly held a session, during which it adopted[17] the Kosovo Declaration of Independence, declaring Kosovo an independent and sovereign State.[18] The Declaration also stated that Kosovo fully accepted the obligations of the Comprehensive Proposal for the Kosovo Status Settlement.[19] Further, on 9 April 2008, the Kosovo Assembly adopted the Kosovo Constitution, which came into force on 15 June 2008.[20]

As was reported by the UN Secretary-General, the Constitution was 'designed in such a way that it would effectively remove from UNMIK its . . . powers as an interim civil administration'.[21] Overall, the events in Kosovo had 'contributed to creating a profoundly new reality in which UNMIK [could] no longer perform as effectively as in the past the vast majority of its tasks as an interim administration'.[22] Hence, the UN Secretary-General intended to 'reconfigure UNMIK in order to allow for the European Union to take on an increasing role in the rule of law sector...'.[23]

[15] UNSC 'Letter dated 10 November 2005 from the President of the Security Council addressed to the Secretary-General' (10 November 2005) UN Doc S/ 2005/709.

[16] UNSC 'Report of the Special Envoy of the Secretary-General on Kosovo's future status' (26 March 2007), annexed to UN Doc S/2007/168; UNSC 'Comprehensive Proposal for the Kosovo Status Settlement' (26 March 2007) UN Doc S/2007/168/Add.1 (Comprehensive Proposal). See also UNSC 'Report of the European Union/United States/Russian Federation Troika on Kosovo' (4 December 2007), annexed to UN Doc S/2007/723.

[17] UNSC 'Report of the Secretary-General on the United Nations Interim Administration Mission in Kosovo' (28 March 2008) UN Doc S/2008/211 para 3.

[18] Kosovo Declaration of Independence (n 6).

[19] ibid paras 1, 3.

[20] Kosovo Constitution (n 7).

[21] UNSC 'Report of the Secretary-General on the United Nations Interim Administration Mission in Kosovo' (12 June 2008) UN Doc S/2008/354 para 7.

[22] UNSC 'Report of the Secretary-General on the United Nations Interim Administration Mission in Kosovo' (15 July 2008) UN Doc S/2008/458, para 3.

[23] ibid.

Around the same time, EULEX was established.[24] UNMIK had been established for 'an open-ended period of time under UNSC Resolution 1244', but EULEX 'was intended to substitute for the rule-of-law functions' of UNMIK.[25] EULEX's task was, amongst others, to ensure that cases of war crimes, terrorism, organized crime, corruption, inter-ethnic crimes, financial/economic crimes, and other serious crimes were properly adjudicated.[26] However, 'controversies pertaining to the (. . .) mandate' of EULEX prevented its deployment and functioning for several months.[27] Eventually, as discussed by de Wet, the UNSC 'explicitly endorsed the UNMIK reconfiguration . . . through the adoption of a Presidential Statement' on 26 November 2008.[28] The Statement 'welcomed the cooperation between the United Nations and other international actors within the framework of' UNSC Resolution 1244.[29] EULEX assumed full operational responsibility in the area of rule of law on 9 December 2008 within the framework of UNSC Resolution 1244. It assumed the responsibility for all but a few cases previously handled by UNMIK.[30]

Similar to UNMIK, EULEX appointed international judges to the Kosovo domestic courts to work with local judges.[31] However, unlike as it had been with UNMIK international judges, the role of EULEX judges was governed by a law adopted by the Kosovo Assembly on the basis of the Kosovo Constitution. In particular, the 'Law on Jurisdiction'[32] regulated their integration and

[24] Council Joint Action on EULEX (n 8).

[25] Erika de Wet, 'The Governance of Kosovo: Security Council Resolution 1244 and the Establishment and Functioning of Eulex' (2009) 103 AJIL 83.

[26] Council Joint Action on EULEX Kosovo (n 8) art 3(d).

[27] de Wet (n 25) 84–86.

[28] ibid 89.

[29] ibid. See also UNSC 'Statement by the President of the Security Council' (26 November 2008) UN Doc S/PRST/2008/44; UNSC 'Report of the Secretary-General on the United Nations Interim Administration Mission in Kosovo' (24 November 2008) UN Doc S/2008/692 para 50.

[30] UNSC 'Report of the Secretary-General on the United Nations Interim Administration Mission in Kosovo' (17 March 2009) UN Doc S/2009/149 paras 12 and 13.

[31] Kosovo Assembly, Law No 03/L-053 On the Jurisdiction, Case Selection and Case Allocation of EULEX Judges and Prosecutors in Kosovo (13 March 2008) (Law on Jurisdiction) arts 4(7), 5(2), (3), and (5). As regards the situation in north Kosovo, see OSCE Mission in Kosovo, 'The Mitrovicë/Mitrovica Justice System: Status Update and Continuing Human Rights Concerns' (LSMS Issue 1, January 2011), 2, <https://www.osce.org/files/f/documents/f/6/75526.pdf> accessed 24 July 2023.

[32] Law on Jurisdiction (n 31). This law was amended, restricting the competence of EULEX judges. See Kosovo Assembly, Law No 05/L-103 On Amending and Supplementing the Law Related to the Mandate of the European Union Rule of Law Mission in the Republic of Kosovo (17 June 2016); Law No 04/L-273 On Amending and Supplementing the Law Related to the Mandate of the European Union Rule of Law Mission in the Republic of Kosovo (23 April 2014). On 14 December 2018, EULEX finalized its reconfiguration. As part of finalizing the phasing out of EULEX's executive judicial competencies, it completed the handover of the police and prosecution case files to the Kosovo authorities. See UNSC 'Report of the European Union High Representative for Foreign Affairs and Security Policy to the Secretary-General on the activities of the European Union Rule of Law Mission in Kosovo from 16 October 2018 to 15 January 2019', annexed to UN Doc S/2019/102.

jurisdiction in the judicial system of Kosovo.[33] According to the Constitutional Court of Kosovo, EULEX-appointed international judges were part of the domestic judiciary bound to respect the domestic constitutional order,[34] irrespective of EULEX's legal basis under international law.

In addition to the courts of general jurisdiction, international judges were appointed to the Constitutional Court of Kosovo. Such initial composition of the Constitutional Court was based on transitory provisions of the Constitution, which provided that three out of nine judges must be international. The international judges were appointed by the International Civilian Representative (ICR), after consulting the President of the European Court of Human Rights (ECtHR).[35] The ICR was responsible for supervising the implementation of the Comprehensive Proposal for the Kosovo Status Settlement.[36] According to its author, the UN Special Envoy for Settling Kosovo's Status Martti Ahtisaari, the Comprehensive Proposal '[provided] the foundations for a future independent Kosovo'.[37] Unlike UNSC Res 1244, the Comprehensive Proposal was initially integrated in the Kosovo Constitution, which afforded superiority to the Comprehensive Proposal 'over all other legal provisions in Kosovo'.[38] Therefore, the mandate of the international judges in the Constitutional Court emanated from a framework receptive to Kosovo's independence. The international judges' mandate expired in 2018.[39]

[33] See also Robert Muharremi, 'The European Union Rule of Law Mission in Kosovo (EULEX) from the Perspective of Kosovo Constitutional Law' (2010) 70 ZaöRV 357, 374.

[34] *Constitutional Review of the Decision of the Special Chamber of the Supreme Court of Kosovo, ASC-09-089, dated 4 February 2010*, Case No KI 25/10, Judgment of 30 March 2011 (Constitutional Court) (*Kosovo Privatisation Agency Constitutional Review*) [61].

[35] See Dren Doli et al, 'Promising Early Years: The Transformative Role of the Constitutional Court of Kosovo' (2016) Working Paper 4/2016 (Analitika-Centre for Social Research), 17, <http://legalpoliticalstudies.org/wp-content/uploads/2016/09/Final-September-2016-Constitutional-Court-Kosovo-WP.pdf> accessed 24 July 2023, citing Kosovo Constitution (n 7) art 152 (repealed 7 September 2012).

[36] Comprehensive Proposal (n 16) arts 12.3, 12.4. Transitional provisions of the Kosovo Constitution provided for the mandate and powers of the International Civilian Representative (ICR) in accordance with the Comprehensive Proposal, and that the ICR was the final authority in Kosovo regarding interpretation of the civilian aspects of the Comprehensive Proposal. See Kosovo Constitution (n 7) arts 146, 147 (repealed 7 September 2012).

[37] As regards the appointment of international judges to the Constitutional Court at the time, see Kosovo Constitution (n 7) art 152(4). See also UNSC 'Report of the Special Envoy of the Secretary-General on Kosovo's future status' (26 March 2007), annexed to UN Doc S/2007/168.

[38] Kosovo Constitution (n 7) art 143 (repealed 7 September 2012). As held by the Kosovo Constitutional Court, with the amendment of the Kosovo Constitution in 2012, the Comprehensive Proposal 'has no legal effect in the constitutional order of the Republic of Kosovo'. See *Constitutional Review of Decree No 24/2020 of the President of the Republic of Kosovo of 30 April 2020*, Case No KO 72/20, Judgment of 28 May 2020 (Constitutional Court) [450] *in fine*.

[39] Constance Grewe, 'Constitutional and Supreme Court with International Participation' in Hélène Ruiz Fabri (ed), MPEiPro (OUP, March 2020), para 44.

Lastly, by a constitutional amendment and a law adopted by the Kosovo Assembly,[40] the Kosovo Specialist Chambers were established to conduct trials with regard to allegations stemming from a 2011 report of the Council of Europe on, amongst others, inhumane treatment of people and illicit trafficking in human organs in Kosovo.[41] The Specialist Chambers are attached to each level of the court system in Kosovo, including the Constitutional Court, and as regards the latter have 'introduce[d] a unique, bivariate model of constitutional review to Kosovo'.[42] The Specialist Chambers are staffed with international judges and have a seat in The Hague. At the time of writing, two cases are in trial phase.[43] The engagement by the Specialist Chambers with international law is not discussed here, but only briefly noted.

Given that Kosovo court panels with the participation of international judges handled most serious cases, such as war crimes, caselaw reveals various postures as regards their engagement with international law. At the same time, as the next section discusses, caselaw shows how different legal frameworks within which the panels operated affected their openness to international law. Furthermore, the initial legal framework applicable in Kosovo stemming from UNSC Res 1244 was itself subject to contestation by Kosovo courts.

C. Practice of Kosovo Domestic Courts

1. UNMIK Regulations

In the case of *Kosovo Privatisation Agency*, the domestic courts were confronted with the relationship between the law emanating from UNSC Res 1244 and the

[40] Kosovo Assembly, Amendment No 24 of the Constitution of the Republic of Kosovo, No 05-D-139 (3 August 2015); Kosovo Assembly, Law No 05/L-053 On Specialist Chambers and Specialist Prosecutor's Office (3 August 2015).

[41] Parliamentary Assembly of the Council of Europe (PACE), 'Inhumane Treatment of People and Illicit Trafficking in Human Organs in Kosovo: Report by Mr Dick Marty' (7 January 2011) Doc 12462 (PACE Report).

[42] Doli et al (n 35) 24 and the discussion at 23–24.

[43] Kosovo Specialist Chambers, Cases, available at <https://www.scp-ks.org/en/cases> last accessed 24 July 2023. On 26 April 2017 and 28 June 2017, the Specialist Chamber of the Constitutional Court of the Kosovo Specialist Chambers rendered judgments as to the compatibility of the Rules of Procedure and Evidence before the Kosovo Specialist Chambers (KSC-CC-PR-2017-01/F00001/A01/2 (27 March 2017), available at <https://www.scp-ks.org/sites/default/files/public/f00001-a01-kcs-cc-pr-2017-01-presidentdecisionreferralrpe_-_confidentiality_lifted.pdf> last accessed 24 July 20223) with the fundamental rights and freedoms enshrined in the Kosovo Constitution (n 7). The Constitutional Chamber extensively referred to the caselaw of the European Court of Human Rights (ECtHR). See *Referral of the Rules of Procedure and Evidence adopted by Plenary on 17 March 2017 to the Specialist Chamber of the Constitutional Court pursuant to Article 19(5) of Law no 05/L-053 on Specialist Chambers and Specialist Prosecutor's Office*, KSC-CC-PR-2017-01, Judgment of 26 April 2017.

laws adopted on the basis of the Constitution of Kosovo. The case concerned UNMIK Regulation 2002/12 on the Establishment of the Kosovo Trust Agency (KTA),[44] an agency set up to administer publicly owned and socially owned enterprises and related assets. After Kosovo's declaration of independence, the Kosovo Assembly adopted a Law on the Privatisation Agency of Kosovo (Law on PAK),[45] establishing the PAK as the 'successor' of the KTA and providing that Regulation 2002/12 would cease to have legal effect.[46] However, the KTA continued its operation and 'insisted that it remained the final authority on issues of privatization'.[47] The question therefore arose as to the relationship between these two competing sources of law.

a. The legal nature of UNMIK regulations

When faced with the question of the relationship between domestic legislation and UNMIK regulations, the Special Chamber of the Supreme Court, a specialized chamber with competence to examine privatization-related matters established under UNMIK Regulation 2002/13,[48] sought a clarification from the SRSG regarding the matter. The SRSG pointed to the international law nature of the regulations, stating that UNMIK Regulation 2002/12 on the KTA remained in force and was applicable in Kosovo under UNSC Res 1244. The Law on PAK could not abolish or repeal this Regulation. Furthermore, according to the SRSG, the PAK could 'at best be considered to act as an agent of the KTA operating without KTA/UNMIK approval and authority'.[49]

The international legal character of UNMIK regulations was, as discussed in the Introduction, also underlined by the ICJ in its *Kosovo Advisory Opinion*. As regards the question of whether UNMIK regulations formed part of the applicable international law, the ICJ held that they had been 'adopted by the [SRSG] on the basis of the authority derived from SC resolution 1244 … and thus ultimately from the United Nations Charter'.[50] The regulations 'derive[d] [their] binding force from the binding character of resolution 1244 (1999) and

[44] UNMIK, Regulation 2002/12 On the Establishment of the Kosovo Trust Agency (13 June 2002) UNMIK/REG/2002/12.

[45] Kosovo Assembly, Law No 03/L-067 On the Privatisation Agency of Kosovo (21 May 2008).

[46] ibid arts 1 and 31(2).

[47] Kushtrim Istrefi, 'Contestation of Kosovo's Statehood from Within: EULEX Judges Adjudicating Privatization Matters through "Status Neutrality"' (2020) 45 Review of Central and East European Law 432, 437.

[48] See UNMIK, Regulation 2002/13 On the Establishment of a Special Chamber of the Supreme Court of Kosovo on Kosovo Trust Agency Related Matters (13 June 2002) UNMIK/REG/2002/13.

[49] Clarification by Special Representative of the UN Secretary-General of Section 5.2 of Regulation 2008/4 (12 November 2009), cited in *Kosovo Privatisation Agency Constitutional Review* (n 34) [20] and [21].

[50] *Kosovo Advisory Opinion* (n 4) [88].

thus from international law'. They, therefore, '[possessed] an international legal character'.[51] This led to the peculiar situation that, as noted by the ICJ, a substantial body of law possessing international legal character extended to 'regulate matters which would ordinarily be the subject of internal, rather than international, law'.[52] The next section turns to the strategies adopted by the Kosovo courts in resolving the question of the relationship between UNMIK Regulation 2002/12 and the Law on PAK enacted by the Kosovo Assembly.

b. Their relationship with the domestic legal order

i. *Supreme Court*

The proceedings in the *Kosovo Privatisation Agency* case were brought by the KTA which sought to contest the competence of the PAK, which had started to exercise its authority under the Law on PAK.[53] By its decision of 4 February 2010, the Appellate Panel of the Special Chamber of the Supreme Court (composed of EULEX judges) refused to apply the Law on PAK, adopted by the Kosovo Assembly. According to the Appellate Panel of the Special Chamber, the Law on PAK was not the law applicable in Kosovo; instead, it had to be treated as internal rules of an organization within the privatization process.[54] By refusing to apply the Law on PAK over the conflicting UNMIK Regulation, the Appellate Panel seemed to adopt a posture of overriding alignment with international law.[55] This was challenged by the PAK before the Constitutional Court, whose response deserves closer scrutiny as regards its engagement with UNMIK regulations deriving their binding force from UNSC Resolution 1244.

ii. *Constitutional Court*

The Constitutional Court approached UNMIK regulations with reference to a provision of the Constitution different from the provisions governing the applicability of international law in the Kosovo legal order. It referred to Article 145(2) which provides that '[l]egislation applicable on the date of the entry into force of the Constitution shall continue to apply to the extent it is in conformity with [the] Constitution until repealed, superseded or amended in accordance

[51] ibid.
[52] ibid [89]. See also Michael Ioannidis, 'Kosovo's Declaration of Independence and the Creation of a New Legal Order: Can a Revolution against International Law Be Legal?' (2011) EUI Working Papers Law 2011/07, <http://hdl.handle.net/1814/17234> last accessed 24 July 2023.
[53] Istrefi (n 47) 437.
[54] Case No ASC-09-089, Appellate Decision of 4 February 2010 (Special Chamber of the Supreme Court), cited in *Kosovo Privatisation Agency Constitutional Review* (n 34) [24].
[55] ILA Study Group on Principles on the Engagement of Domestic Courts with International Law, 'Final Report: Mapping the Engagement of Domestic Courts with International Law' (Johannesburg, 2016) (ILA Final Report), para 45.

with [it]'.[56] According to the Constitutional Court, the 'legislation' applicable on the date of the entry into force of the Constitution included UNMIK regulations.[57]

Therefore, the Constitutional Court considered that, from the perspective of domestic constitutional law, UNMIK regulations were 'legislation', and not rules of international law as held by the ICJ. In doing so, the Court adopted a strategy of affirmative contestation, as 'it diverge[d] from the interpretation … given by' the ICJ.[58] While the Constitutional Court did not refer to the ICJ on this matter, it did so in relation to 'the existence of Kosovo as an independent State and [to] its legislation emanating from its Assembly'. It noted that, according to the ICJ, Kosovo's declaration of independence did not violate general international law.[59] The Constitutional Court therefore appears to have been selective in engaging with the ICJ *Kosovo Advisory Opinion*.

Having classified UNMIK regulations as 'legislation' under Article 145(2) of the Constitution, the Constitutional Court proceeded to say that under this provision regulations would only continue to apply to the extent that they were in conformity with the Constitution, and until they were repealed, superseded or amended in accordance with it, including by subsequent legislation.[60] It then held that, as UNMIK Regulation 2002/12 had been repealed by the Law on PAK, this Regulation was no longer applicable.[61]

The Constitutional Court's reasoning revealed a particular way of contesting international law emanating from the UN Charter, and dealing with matters normally regulated by internal law, in this special case of a territory previously administered by a UN mission. In particular, in the Court's view, such international legal rules could be repealed by the Kosovo Assembly and rendered inapplicable by virtue of Article 145(2) of the Constitution.

iii. Subsequent developments

Subsequently, in a different set of proceedings, the question returned to the Special Chamber of the Supreme Court. In *SOE v AA*, the KTA attempted to intervene on behalf of a socially owned enterprise, triggering a response by the

[56] *Kosovo Privatisation Agency Constitutional Review* (n 34) [58].
[57] ibid.
[58] ILA Final Report (n 55) para 58.
[59] *Kosovo Privatisation Agency Constitutional Review* (n 34) [53] and [54]; see for a comment Istrefi (n 47) 439.
[60] ibid [58]. The strategy employed by the Constitutional Court in this case could also be qualified as affirmative avoidance, given that the Court 'consider[ed] the application of international law but explicitly reject[ed] it, as this [was] … the appropriate position under domestic law', namely art 145(2) of the Constitution. See ILA Final Report (n 55) para 41.
[61] *Kosovo Privatisation Agency Constitutional Review* (n 34) [59].

Special Chamber of the Supreme Court to the judgment of the Constitutional Court.[62] While the Special Chamber accepted that the Law on PAK was valid Kosovo law, and that 'as a Kosovar Court' it was bound by the Constitutional Court's judgment,[63] it rejected the view that Kosovo's declaration of independence had had any effect on the applicability of the legal rules adopted under the authority of the UN. Referring to UNSC Resolution 1244 and UNMIK Regulation 2002/12, it stated that measures adopted by the UNSC under Chapter VII of the UN Charter were 'valid and enforceable' for Kosovo, and that the Constitutional Court was 'misunderstanding that UN law under Chapter VII does not depend on acceptance'.[64]

Additionally, the Special Chamber of the Supreme Court noted that the Constitutional Court was not the final authority on the interpretation of UN law,[65] and proceeded to interpret the relevant legal instruments itself. It held that UNSC Resolution 1244 did not settle 'the final status of Kosovo but only a preliminary status' and that it had been 'designed as [a] step in the direction of the final status'.[66] Furthermore, the Special Chamber considered that it had the authority to assess the implementation of UNSC Resolution 1244, in so far as UNMIK was concerned. It stated that the 'interim administration [had] ended' as it had not 'continu[e]d to administer Kosovo SOE's [socially owned enterprises] ... [and] there remained just occasional expression of concern and occasional appearance' before the Special Chamber.[67] Given that the UNSC had been unable to settle the status of Kosovo, and UNMIK had omitted to administer Kosovo, the Special Chamber found that 'the acts of Kosovo legislature [were] valid even if they [were in] conflict with UN Regulations formerly issued by UNMIK'.[68]

The Special Chamber of the Supreme Court therefore, like the Constitutional Court, adopted a strategy of contestation as regards the application of the relevant UNMIK Regulation. However, unlike the Constitutional Court, it sought to justify its decision by reference to UNMIK's mandate, and not plainly domestic law.[69]

[62] *SOE v AA*, Appeal No SCA-09-0042, Decision of 29 November 2012 (Special Chamber of the Supreme Court of Kosovo).
[63] ibid 4.
[64] ibid.
[65] ibid.
[66] ibid.
[67] ibid.
[68] ibid 5.
[69] This attitude of the Special Chamber of the Supreme Court may be qualified as a particular posture of negatory contestation, as it denied the applicabilty of UNMIK Regulations because of UNMIK's conduct in the discharge of its duties. See ILA Final Report (n 55) para 61.

2. Customary International Law

a. UNMIK Regulation 1999/24 on the law applicable in Kosovo

The current Constitution of Kosovo does not explicitly mention 'customary international law', although custom is arguably encompassed by the reference in Article 19(2) of the Constitution to 'legally binding norms of international law' (beyond ratified treaties).[70] Prior to the adoption of the 2008 Constitution, the law applicable in Kosovo was determined in accordance with UNMIK regulations. Thus, before outlining the postures adopted by Kosovo domestic courts in their engagement with customary international law, it is necessary to note that its applicability previously depended on how the courts interpreted this law stemming from UNSC Res 1244, in particular UNMIK Regulation 1999/24 which governed the law applicable in Kosovo.[71]

Regulation 1999/24 provided that the law applicable in Kosovo was UNMIK regulations and the law in force in Kosovo on 22 March 1989,[72] namely immediately before the autonomous status of Kosovo within the SFRY was rescinded. Additionally, pursuant to Section 1.2 of the Regulation, the courts could apply subsequent law, 'if a subject matter or a situation [was] not covered by' the law in force on 22 March 1989, and that subsequent law '[was] not discriminatory and [complied] with' relevant human rights standards.[73] Section 1.4 of the Regulation provided that in criminal proceedings, the defendant had 'the benefit of the most favourable provision in the criminal laws which were in force in Kosovo between 22 March 1989 and the date' of the Regulation.[74]

In this regard, the Constitution that was in force on 22 March 1989, namely the 1974 Constitution of the Socialist Federal Republic of Yugoslavia (the 1974 Constitution), did not provide for the direct applicability of customary international law in the domestic legal order, but only of promulgated treaties.[75] However, the subsequent Constitution, the 1992 Constitution of the Federal Republic of Yugoslavia (the 1992 Constitution), incorporated also 'generally accepted rules of international law' into the domestic legal system.[76]

[70] See n 157.

[71] UNMIK, Regulation 1999/24 On the Law Applicable in Kosovo (12 December 1999) UNMIK/REG/1999/24, as amended by Regulation 2000/59 Amending UNMIK Regulation 1999/24 On the Law Applicable in Kosovo (27 October 2000) UNMIK/REG/2000/59 (Regulation 1999/24).

[72] ibid s 1.1.

[73] ibid s 1.2, and s 1.3 for applicable human rights standards.

[74] ibid s 1.4.

[75] Constitution of the Socialist Federal Republic of Yugoslavia of 1974, Službeni List SFRJ No 9/74, art 210.

[76] Constitution of the Federal Republic of Yugoslavia of 1992, Službeni List SRS No 1/1992, art 16.

b. The *Llapi* case before UNMIK and EULEX judges

Difficulties in interpreting UNMIK Regulation 1999/24 and whether, as regards customary international law, it provided for the application of the 1974 Constitution or the 1992 Constitution emerged already in the first major war crimes trial in Kosovo, the *Gashi et al* case ('*Llapi* case').[77] In the course of these lengthy proceedings, which involved several retrials, the panels composed of UNMIK and then EULEX international judges took different approaches in engaging with customary international law.

i. Trial panel

The discussion relevant to the present contribution arose in the trial panel at the District Court of Pristina in relation to allegations of illegal detention by former members of the Kosovo Liberation Army (KLA). According to the indictment, the accused had also failed to prevent illegal detention and to take any steps to identify and punish the KLA members responsible for those offences, engaging issues of command responsibility under customary international law.[78] In assessing the engagement by the trial panel with customary international law, its interpretation of UNMIK Regulation 1999/24 and its reasoning on customary international law are both relevant.

First, in determining whether the 1974 or the 1992 Constitution was applicable under UNMIK Regulation 1999/24, the trial panel was guided by the purpose of the international civil presence in Kosovo, and noted that UNMIK regulations must be interpreted so as to give effect to 'their intent and purpose'.[79] Referring to UNSC Res 1244, it considered that the main responsibilities of the international civil presence included protection and promotion of human rights.[80] Further, the trial panel found that Article 16 of the 1992 Constitution, which provided for the applicability of 'generally accepted rules of international law', incorporated 'generally accepted rules of customary international law into the internal legal order...'.[81] The trial panel held that this provision was not discriminatory and complied with the relevant human rights standards. Thus, it was applicable pursuant to UNMIK Regulation 1999/24.[82]

[77] OSCE Mission in Kosovo, 'Case Report: The Public Prosecutor's Office vs Latif Gashi, Rrustem Mustafa, Naim Kadriu and Nazif Mehmeti—The "Llapi Case"' (17 December 2003), 2, available at <https://www.osce.org/files/f/documents/9/7/19312.pdf> last accessed 24 July 2023.

[78] *Prosecutor v Latif Gashi et al (Llapi)*, Case No 425/2001, Judgment of 16 July 2003 (District Court of Pristina).

[79] ibid 8.

[80] ibid 9.

[81] ibid 23.

[82] ibid 23, 26.

In this respect, the trial panel considered also the argument that Article 16 of the 1992 Constitution could be considered as less favourable to the accused, since, unlike the 1974 Constitution, it embraced customary international law. However, it held that such an argument would mean that 'regulations imposed by UNMIK ... prevented the enforcement in 2003 of humanitarian law in Kosovo which had already been recognised and specifically endorsed by Article 16' of the 1992 Constitution.[83] In this regard, the trial panel found that 'this was clearly not the intention of UNMIK [as] the entire contents of Regulation 1999/24 [was] directed towards ensuring that internationally recognised human rights standards ... were recognised and firmly established in Kosovo'.[84] Further, as explained by the SRSG, Section 1.4 of the Regulation 1999/24 on the most favourable criminal law[85] had been intended to reflect the principle under Article 15(1) of the International Covenant on Civil and Political Rights (ICCPR) that, 'if subsequent to the commission of the offence, a provision is made by law for the imposition of a lighter penalty, the offender shall benefit' from it.[86] In so far as the trial panel sought to determine the law applicable in Kosovo under UNMIK Regulation 1999/24, as a form of law governing domestic matters, in a manner consistent with internationally recognized human rights standards, its approach reveals the posture of alignment.[87]

Second, the trial panel's reasoning concerning the alleged illegal detention revealed an instance of a domestic court seeking to further international law. Having observed that 'illegal detention' was not mentioned in Common Article 3 of the Four Geneva Conventions or in Additional Protocol II relevant to non-international armed conflicts, it found that the 'treaty-based international legal obligations in internal armed conflict [had] failed to keep pace with reasonable human rights standards'.[88] Despite the reluctance on the part of States to include relevant obligations in treaties, the view of the panel was that domestic courts should not be hesitant to assert the existence of relevant obligations under customary international law.[89] The ICTY Appeals Chamber in *Tadić* had acknowledged that significant State and judicial authority had begun to support the view that the 'grave breaches' system applied regardless

[83] ibid 23.
[84] ibid.
[85] Regulation 1999/24 (n 71) s 1.4.
[86] *Gashi et al* (2003) (n 78) 23. See International Covenant on Civil and Political Rights (adopted 16 December 1966, entered into force 23 March 1976) 999 UNTS 171 art 15(1).
[87] ILA Final Report (n 55) para 44. In its further assessment, the trial panel in *Gashi et al* also referred to UNMIK regulations as 'a form of domestic law', over which international human rights standards had primacy. See *Gashi et al* (2003) (n 78) 25.
[88] ibid 18, 21.
[89] ibid 20–21.

of whether the armed conflict was international,[90] although it was not clear to the trial panel why the Appeals Chamber in that case had eventually rejected that view. Further, *Tadić* had concerned the events in 1992, whereas the *Gashi et al* case concerned atrocities allegedly committed in 1998 and 1999. This assessment was bolstered by the fact that the right to review of detention was 'a fundamental principle of international law' enshrined in Article 9(3) and (4) of the ICCPR.[91]

The trial panel then determined the existence of rules under customary international law similar to those found in Articles 42 and 43 of the Fourth Geneva Convention.[92] The parties to a non-international armed conflict were authorized to detain individuals provided that there was 'genuine suspicion that the person concerned [was] a threat to the security of the detaining authority or [to] those whom it represent[ed] in the conflict'.[93] Further, there had to be a form of review for the determination of the lawfulness of the detention. The review had to be independent and prompt.[94] In so far as the trial panel was thus prepared to further the approach taken by the ICTY Appeals Chamber in *Tadić* as regards the 'grave breaches' system, its approach may be seen as revealing a posture of hyper-alignment with international law.[95] The trial panel engaged with international law, while simultaneously contributing to its advancement.

As regards command responsibility in a non-international armed conflict, the trial panel held that such mode of responsibility was a rule of customary international law, and took the view that applying it in that case 'would not create a new criminal offence' under domestic law but would 'amount at most to an adaptation or better understanding of the criminal offence of war crime [under] Article 142 [of the SFRY Criminal Code] in connection with Article 30 (command responsibility as a criminal act by omission) ... '.[96] The trial panel therefore appeared to adopt a strategy of (perhaps consubstantial) alignment of domestic with customary international law through the use of the principle of consistent interpretation.[97]

[90] *Prosecutor v Dusko Tadić a/k/a 'Dule'* (Interlocutory Appeal on Jurisdiction) ICTY-94-I (2 October 1995) [83].
[91] *Gashi et al* (2003) (n 78) 18–19.
[92] Geneva Convention relative to the Protection of Civilian Persons in Time of War (adopted 11 August 1949, entered into force 21 October 1950) 75 UNTS 287, arts 42 and 43 on internment.
[93] *Gashi et al* (2003) (n 78) 38–39.
[94] ibid 19–22.
[95] ILA Final Report (n 55) para 55.
[96] *Gashi et al* (2003) (n 78) 24. For a critical view on the 'importing' of objective *mens rea* standard into the SFRY Criminal Code, see Roozbeh (Rudy) B Baker, 'Customary International Law in the 21st Century: Old Challenges and New Debates' (2010) 21 EJIL 173, 201–3.
[97] ILA Final Report (n 55) para 46.

ii. Appeals panel

The trial panel's judgment was appealed to the Supreme Court. In 2005, a Supreme Court panel, composed of UNMIK international judges, overturned the trial panel's findings as regards the applicability of customary international law. The Supreme Court panel held that the argument that Article 16 of the 1992 Constitution was applicable to the case was contrary to the 'express provisions of UNMIK Regulation 1999/24'.[98]

In particular, the Supreme Court held that, under UNMIK Regulation 1999/24, the law applicable in Kosovo, apart from UNMIK regulations, consisted in the laws in force in Kosovo on 22 March 1989.[99] In addition, the Supreme Court deemed that Section 4 of UNMIK Regulation 1999/24, which contained transitional provisions, determined the law applicable in Kosovo. Section 4 provided that '[a]ll legal acts, including judicial decisions...which occurred, during the period from 10 June 1999 up to the date of the present regulation... shall remain valid...'.[100] The Supreme Court thus opined that the laws applicable in Kosovo, in addition to those in force on 22 March 1989, were the laws 'passed between 10 June 1999 and 27 October 2000 [the date of the Regulation as amended] that [were] not discriminatory'.[101]

In that light, the Supreme Court considered that, to interpret UNMIK Regulation 1999/24 'to mean that the laws in effect in Kosovo includ[ed] [the] laws in force in Kosovo subsequent to 22 March 1989 would defeat the clear meaning of the words [as] used by the United Nations'.[102] Similarly, '[t]o interpret the meaning of Section 4 [of the Regulation] to include all laws passed between 10 June 1999 and the present time...(or any future date) would defeat the clear meaning of the words [as] used by the United Nations'.[103] The Supreme Court added that 'to interpret the words in [the Regulation] in any other fashion than to give them their plain meaning would create potential ambiguity in the intention of the United Nations'.[104]

The Supreme Court therefore concluded that the 1992 Constitution '[fell] outside the parameters of UNMIK Regulation 1999/24', as it had been 'adopted subsequent to 22 March 1989' and 'clearly [did] not fall within the ambit of [the] laws passed between 10 June 1999 and 27 October 2000'.[105] On the

[98] *Gashi et al*, AP-KZ No 139/2004, Decision of 21 July 2005 (Supreme Court), 8.
[99] ibid 5 and 8.
[100] Regulation 1999/24 (n 71) s 4.
[101] *Gashi et al* (2005) (n 98) 8.
[102] ibid.
[103] ibid.
[104] ibid.
[105] ibid.

other hand, the 1974 Constitution had been in effect in Kosovo on 22 March 1989, 'the date referred to in UNMIK regulation 1999/24'. Given that the 1974 Constitution provided for the direct applicability of promulgated treaties only and not of customary international law,[106] the Supreme Court concluded that the trial panel had erroneously relied on 'customary international law' or 'generally accepted rules of international law' in deciding the case.[107] The Supreme Court therefore overturned the charges of illegal detention. It also remitted the case to the first instance court for retrial.[108]

It is unclear why the Supreme Court deemed that Section 4 of UNMIK Regulation 1999/24 determined the law applicable in Kosovo, limiting its Section 1 on 'Applicable Law'. Section 4 clearly referred to transitional provisions as regards the validity of legal acts taken until the adoption of the Regulation.[109] Whereas Section 1 on 'Applicable Law' provided for a possibility to apply laws in force in Kosovo after 22 March 1989 if a court determined that 'a subject matter or situation [was] not covered' by UNMIK regulations or the laws in force in Kosovo on 22 March 1989, and the subsequent law was not discriminatory and complied with the respective international human rights standards.[110] The plain meaning of this provision was that also subsequent laws could be applied. The Supreme Court's refusal to consider this provision, despite its plain meaning, might be viewed as affirmative contestation.[111]

iii. Subsequent proceedings

The re-trial in the *Gashi et al* case took place before the District Court of Pristina in 2009.[112] This was after Kosovo's declaration of independence. UNMIK international judges no longer sat on the panels in Kosovo domestic courts. Instead, EULEX international judges had been deployed to adjudicate cases falling within their jurisdiction.[113] The *Gashi et al* case was one of the cases that had been handed over from UNMIK to EULEX, and thus was re-tried by a panel, composed of a majority of EULEX judges, whose judgment[114] was again appealed to the Supreme Court.

This time, the Supreme Court panel, composed of a majority of EULEX judges, endorsed the approach of the first trial panel that customary

[106] ibid 5–7.
[107] ibid 8.
[108] ibid 12–14, 19–20.
[109] Regulation 1999/24 (n 71) s 4.
[110] ibid s 1.2.
[111] ILA Final Report (n 55) para 58.
[112] *Gashi et al*, Case No 526/2005, Decision of 2 October 2009 (District Court of Pristina).
[113] See Section B(2) and Law on Jurisdiction (n 31).
[114] *Gashi et al* (2009) (n 112).

international law was applicable. It even considered that the Supreme Court, in its earlier decision rendered in 2005,[115] had upheld the first trial panel's findings in that regard.[116] In connection with the charges referring to joint criminal enterprise and command responsibility, the Supreme Court panel, composed of a majority of EULEX judges, hence referred to these modes of criminal liability as having been established under customary international law at the time when the respective offences had been committed.[117]

c. *Thaçi et al* case before the Kosovo Specialist Chambers

The question of applicability of customary international law has been raised also in recent proceedings before the Specialist Chambers. In particular, the accused in the *Thaçi et al* case argued that the Specialist Chambers could not exercise jurisdiction over crimes solely under customary international law, but only if they had been incorporated into domestic law applicable at the time the alleged crimes had been committed, notably the 1974 Constitution and the SFRY Criminal Code.[118] They also argued that the Kosovo Constitution did not provide for the direct applicability of customary international law.[119]

However, in interlocutory appeal proceedings, a Court of Appeals panel of the Specialist Chambers found that Article 19(2) of the Kosovo Constitution used the term 'legally binding norms of international law', which referred to customary international law.[120] Further, there was no legal basis 'for a requirement of a corresponding provision under domestic law applicable at the time of the alleged crimes', which was consistent with ECtHR jurisprudence on Article 7 of the European Convention on Human Rights.[121] As regards the 1974 Constitution, the appeals panel, referring to Article 145(2) of the Kosovo Constitution, held that the Kosovo Constitution had 'superseded any constitution previously applicable in the territory of Kosovo and that the Specialist Chambers [were] only bound to uphold the protections enshrined in it'.[122] The appeals panel therefore held that the 1974 SFRY Constitution did not apply.[123]

[115] See Section C(2)(b)(ii).

[116] *Gashi et al*, AP-KZ No 89/2010, Decision of 26 January 2011 (Supreme Court) [111]–[13].

[117] ibid [109]–[117]. As regards further proceedings, see *Gashi et al*, P No 448/2012, Decision of 7 June 2013 (Basic Court of Pristina); *Gashi et al*, PAKR 440/13, Judgment of 11 August 2015 (Court of Appeals); *Gashi et al*, Plm KZZ 18/2016, Judgment of 13 May 2016 (Supreme Court).

[118] See *Motions Challenging the Jurisdiction of the Specialist Chambers*, KSC-BC-2020-06/F00412, Decision of 22 July 2021 (Pre-Trial Judge) [15]–[16] and [21].

[119] See *Appeals Against 'Decision on Motions Challenging the Jurisdiction of the Specialist Chambers'*, KSC-BC-2020-06/IA009/F00030, Decision of 23 December 2021 (Panel of the Court of Appeals Chamber) [17]–[19] and [21].

[120] ibid [24] and [26] *in fine*.

[121] ibid.

[122] ibid [26]–[27], citing Kosovo Constitution (n 7) art 145(2).

[123] ibid [26]–[27].

It may be observed that the Court of Appeals panel of the Specialist Chambers tackled the laws previously in force in Kosovo in a manner similar to the Constitutional Court in the case of *Kosovo Privatisation Agency* discussed above. More specifically, like the Constitutional Court, the Court of Appeals panel referred to Article 145(2) of the Kosovo Constitution, recognizing the constitutional framework in place.

3. Other International Instruments

a. International relations

Subsequent to Kosovo's declaration of independence, the EU sought modalities of cooperation with the newly established institutions in Kosovo given its status-neutral position as to whether Kosovo was considered a State by reference to UNSC Res 1244. As it was more complex to formally conclude international treaties with Kosovo, co-operation was ensured, for example, through exchange of letters.

To implement these instruments in the domestic legal order, the institutions of Kosovo adopted them in accordance with the domestic procedure for the ratification of international agreements. Kosovo ratified in that manner the exchange of letters between the President of Kosovo and the High Representative of the EU for Foreign Affairs concerning the extension of the mandate of EULEX.[124] The same instruments were not adopted by the EU in accordance with similar procedures.[125]

The Constitutional Court of Kosovo had the opportunity to consider Kosovo's international obligations in relation to one of these agreements, notably relating to the establishment of the Kosovo Specialist Chambers for the adjudication of crimes allegedly committed during and in the aftermath of the 1998/1999 Kosovo conflict.[126]

[124] Kosovo Assembly, Law No 04/L-148 On Ratification of the International Agreement between the Republic of Kosovo and the European Union on the European Union Rule of Law Mission in Kosovo (7 September 2012). See also Kosovo Assembly, Law No 04/L-274 On Ratification of the International Agreement between the Republic of Kosovo and the European Union on the European Union Rule of Law Mission in Kosovo (23 April 2014).

[125] The agreement with the EU is not listed in the Treaties Office Database of the European External Action Service.

[126] See *Amendment to the Constitution proposed by the Government and referred by the President of the Assembly on 9 March 2015, by Letter No 05-433/DO-318*, Case No KO 26/15, Judgment of 14 April 2015 (Constitutional Court) (*Amendment to the Constitution*).

b. The Kosovo Specialist Chambers

i. Background

Following a request by the Parliamentary Assembly of the Council of Europe (PACE), Dick Marty submitted a report on inhumane treatment of people and illicit trafficking in human organs in Kosovo (PACE Report), containing allegations of, amongst others, inhuman treatment and killing of people during and in the aftermath of the armed conflict in Kosovo.[127] The PACE Report referred to several obstacles to discovering the truth as regards these events. It stated that witnesses were reluctant or too afraid to testify, or that they did not trust protective measures or had been eliminated.[128] There were also 'signs of collusion between the criminal class and high political and institutional office bearers'.[129] In the form of reflections, the PACE Report considered that, overall, there was a 'glass ceiling of accountability' in Kosovo.[130] At the same time, there was a need to ascertain the truth as regards the reported events.[131]

On 25 January 2011, the PACE, on the basis of the report, adopted a Resolution on the investigation of allegations of inhuman treatment of people and illicit trafficking in human organs in Kosovo.[132] The Resolution invited the administration of Kosovo to cooperate with EULEX and any other 'international judicial body mandated to conduct follow-up investigations and in the framework of any other procedures intended to find out the truth about crimes linked to the conflict in Kosovo'.[133] In September 2011, a special investigative task force was formed, deriving its jurisdiction from the EU Council Joint Action on EULEX, to conduct a criminal investigation into the allegations contained in the PACE Report.

On 14 April 2014, the President of Kosovo and the High Representative of the EU for Foreign Affairs exchanged letters regarding the work of the special investigative task force. The letter of the Kosovo President referred to the establishment of a specialist court within the domestic court system of Kosovo and a specialist prosecutor's office for any trial and appellate proceedings arising from that investigation.[134] Subsequently, the Kosovo Assembly approved Law

[127] PACE Report (n 41).
[128] ibid (B). Explanatory memorandum, paras 21, 25, 69.
[129] ibid (B). Explanatory memorandum, para 21.
[130] ibid (B). Explanatory memorandum, para 169.
[131] ibid (B). Explanatory memorandum, paras 6, 21, 176.
[132] Parliamentary Assembly of the Council of Europe (PACE), Resolution 1782 (2011) on Investigation of Allegations of Inhuman Treatment of People and Illicit Trafficking in Human Organs in Kosovo (25 January 2011).
[133] ibid para 19.6.
[134] Letter of the Kosovo President to the High Representative of the Union for Foreign Affairs and Security Policy, 14 April 2014, attached to Law No 04/L-274 (n 124).

No 04/L-274 on the ratification of the international agreement between Kosovo and the EU, by which it ratified and undertook to implement 'the international agreement achieved through the exchange of instruments between [Kosovo] and the European Union'.[135]

In July 2014, the chief prosecutor of the special investigative task force stated that the latter had found sufficient evidence to file an indictment against some former KLA senior officials.[136] The chief prosecutor claimed that [t]hese individuals [bore] responsibility for a campaign of persecution...directed against ethnic Serb, Roma, and other minority populations of Kosovo and...Kosovo Albanians...labelled either [as] collaborators with the Serbs or...political opponents of the KLA leadership'.[137] The information compiled indicated unlawful killings, abductions, enforced disappearances and illegal detentions in Kosovo and Albania.[138] As regards the allegations of organ trafficking contained in the PACE Report, the chief prosecutor stated that the special investigative task force had not secured the level of evidence so as to prosecute such offences.[139] The chief prosecutor urged the Kosovo Government and Assembly and the EU to finalize the establishment of a specialist court where charges could be filed.[140]

On 7 March 2015, the government proposed an amendment to the Kosovo Constitution concerning the Specialist Chambers and the Specialist Prosecutor's Office. The proposed amendment provided, *inter alia*, that '[t]o comply with its international obligations in relation to the [PACE Report], the Republic of Kosovo may establish the Specialist Chambers and the Specialist Prosecutor's Office within the justice system of Kosovo...'.[141] This amendment was referred to the Constitutional Court for a prior review as to whether it did not diminish any of the fundamental rights and freedoms guaranteed by the Constitution.[142]

ii. Constitutional Court

For the purposes of the present contribution, it is relevant to note that, under Article 103(7) of the Kosovo Constitution, one of the requirements for the

[135] Law No 04/L-274 (n 124).

[136] Statement of the Chief Prosecutor of the Special Investigative Task Force (29 July 2014), Annex II to UNSC 'Report of the Secretary-General on the United Nations Interim Administration Mission in Kosovo' (1 August 2014) UN Doc S/2014/558, 18.

[137] ibid.

[138] ibid.

[139] ibid 20.

[140] ibid 21.

[141] *Amendment to the Constitution* (n 126) [23].

[142] ibid [14].

establishment of a specialized court was that there was a 'necessity' for its establishment.[143] In relation to the 'necessity' of the Specialist Chambers and the Specialist Prosecutor's Office, the Constitutional Court noted that their establishment was a requirement for Kosovo 'to comply with its international obligations'.[144] The Constitutional Court stated that '[t]hese international obligations stemm[ed] from the [PACE Report]', which outlined criminal allegations and recommended them for investigation and prosecution. The Court also held that these international obligations had been incorporated into the legal framework of Kosovo through the adoption of Law No 04/L-274,[145] ratifying the exchange of letters between the Kosovo President and the High Representative of the EU for Foreign Affairs of 14 April 2014 as an international agreement.

The Constitutional Court did not specify why the PACE Report constituted a binding instrument on Kosovo. It appears that the Court focused on the content rather than the form and legal nature of the Report, as the Court found it relevant that the Report contained certain criminal allegations and called for their 'investigation and prosecution'.[146] The Constitutional Court's reference to 'investigation and prosecution' in particular could be read in a way that the Court implied that Kosovo had a procedural obligation under international law to investigate and prosecute alleged grave breaches of human rights stemming from the PACE Report.[147] This would be in line with the incorporation into the Kosovo Constitution of international human rights standards, which provide for the procedural obligation to investigate, including the European Convention on Human Rights and the International Covenant on Civil and Political Rights.[148]

Further, the Constitutional Court stated that the 'international obligations' as regards the establishment of the Specialist Chamber and the Specialist Prosecutor's Office had been incorporated into the legal framework of Kosovo through the adoption of Law No 04/L-274.[149] It thus appears that the Constitutional Court considered that an international obligation on Kosovo to establish specifically the Specialist Chambers and the Specialist Prosecutor's Office for the investigations and prosecutions in relation to the PACE Report

[143] ibid [45].
[144] ibid [50].
[145] ibid [51].
[146] ibid [51].
[147] As regards the obligation under customary international law to prosecute (or extradite) attaching to war crimes and crimes against humanity, see M Cherif Bassiouni and Edward M Wise, *Aut dedere aut judicare: The Duty to Extradite or Prosecute in International Law* (Brill 1995) 20–22.
[148] Kosovo Constitution (n 7) art 22. See, eg, *Jelić v Croatia* App No 57856/11 (Judgment of 12 June 2014) [52]; *M and Others v Croatia* App No 50175/12 (Judgment of 2 May 2017) [67]–[68].
[149] *Amendment to the Constitution* (n 126) [51].

was contained in the exchange of letters between the Kosovo President and the High Representative of the EU for Foreign Affairs of 14 April 2014. Indeed, in her letter to the High Representative of the EU for Foreign Affairs, the Kosovo President had stated that 'Kosovo will set up dedicated separate judicial chambers...for any criminal proceedings that arise out of the [special investigative task force's] work'.[150] The letter of the Kosovo President also referred to specific features of these judicial chambers.[151]

In relation to the legal character of the exchange of letters in international law, the Constitution Court endorsed the view that it constituted an international agreement between Kosovo and the EU. In characterizing the instrument as an international agreement, the Court appeared to have been referring to domestic law, as it noted that the Kosovo Assembly had adopted Law No 04/L-274, ratifying that international agreement.[152] In that vein, the Court did not examine whether the exchange of letters constituted a treaty between Kosovo and the EU under international law.[153]

In light of the above, the Constitutional Court appears to have adopted a particular strategy of alignment to enforce international obligations and demands, as regards the investigation and prosecution of international crimes in relation to the 1998/1999 Kosovo conflict and the period after the conflict.

D. Conclusion

Significant part of the Kosovo courts' engagement with international law discussed in this chapter was connected to UNSC Resolution 1244 and UNMIK regulations. Furthermore, Kosovo courts were highly internationalized until 2018. First UNMIK international judges and later EULEX international judges sat on Kosovo courts' panels. Their practice explored in this chapter reveals the employment of diverse postures or strategies of engagement with international law. The reasoning of the Constitutional Court in the case of *Kosovo Privatisation Agency* shows that the Court chose to examine the law stemming from UNSC Res 1244 from the perspective of the domestic constitutional order, established following Kosovo's declaration of independence. The Court

150 Letter of the Kosovo President (n 134), 3.
151 ibid.
152 ibid paras 37 and 38.
153 In that sense, the posture adopted by the Constitutional Court may be qualified as evasive avoidance, as discussed in ILA Final Report (n 55) para 40, in that the Court did not refer to the pertinent rules under international law for the determination of the existence of an international agreement but decided the point only on the basis of domestic law.

found that the relevant UNMIK Regulation could be repealed domestically under the Constitution. The strategy of contestation adopted by the Special Chamber of the Supreme Court of Kosovo in respect of the same UNMIK Regulation was, however, different. As the *SOE v AA* case shows, the Special Chamber appeared to recognize that there was a conflict between the UNMIK Regulation and the relevant domestic legislation, and it regarded the latter as applicable only after having found that the interim administration under UNSC Res 1244 had ended. Further, the caselaw originating from the adjudication of war crimes in relation to the 1998/1999 Kosovo conflict shows how different ways of interpreting the law stemming from UNSC Res 1244 could lead to different outcomes as regards the engagement with customary international law. Eventually, the Kosovo courts appeared to align domestic law with customary international law, including through the use of the principle of consistent interpretation.

These instances of engagement with international law emanated from panels composed of international judges. Thus, it remains to be seen how Kosovo domestic courts will shape their own (not UNMIK's or EULEX's) strategies of engagement with international law. The Kosovo Constitution provides for a strong commitment to international law and instructs the courts to align with it. As already noted, Article 19 provides that ratified treaties are part of the domestic legal system and, generally, directly applicable,[154] and accords supremacy over laws of Kosovo to ratified international treaties and (other) legally binding norms of international law.[155] Furthermore, Article 22 incorporates human rights of nine international instruments[156] on level of the Constitution.[157] Further, Article 53 requires that the Constitution's human rights provisions be interpreted consistent with ECtHR caselaw, an example of constitutionally

[154] Kosovo Constitution (n 7) art 19.

[155] On the discussion that this includes also customary international law, see Visar Morina et al, 'The Relationship between International Law and National Law in the Case of Kosovo: A Constitutional Perspective' (2011) 9 ICON 274, 291–93.

[156] As held by the Constitutional Court, these human rights instruments 'have direct applicability in Kosovo and … priority over provisions of laws and other acts of public institutions'. See *Ćemailj Kurtiši and the Municipal Assembly of Prizren*, Case No KO 01/09, Judgment of 30 November 2009 (Constitutional Court) [34], [40]. In 2020, the ninth instrument was added in Article 22 of the Constitution, the Council of Europe Convention on Preventing and Combating Violence against Women and Domestic Violence (adopted 11 May 2011, entered into force 1 August 2014) 3010 UNTS 107.

[157] As held by the Constitutional Court, the rights and freedoms guaranteed by the international instruments referred to in Article 22 of the Constitution 'have the status of norms of constitutional rank and are an integral part of the Constitution, in the same way as all other provisions contained in the Constitution'. See *Constitutional Review of Judgments [AAUZH No 20/2019 of 30 October 2019; and AAUZH No 21/2019, of 5 November 2019] of the Supreme Court of the Republic of Kosovo*, Case No KI 207/19, Judgment of 10 December 2020 (Constitutional Court) [111]. See also Morina et al (n 155) 293–95.

mandated principle of consistent interpretation potentially leading to consubstantial alignment.[158] So far the practice of the Kosovo Constitutional Court reveals a strong alignment with the ECHR and the ECtHR caselaw in interpretation of the Constitution's human rights provisions.[159] Also, the Constitutional Court has acknowledged the applicability of ratified international treaties in accordance with Article 19 of the Constitution.[160]

Given that the Constitution envisages a relatively easy reception of international law into the domestic legal system, establishing a primarily monist system,[161] it may be anticipated that Kosovo domestic courts will take approaches to international law in line with these constitutional principles. At the same time, as Kosovo continues to conclude more treaties and join international organizations, Kosovo courts will face new and more complex questions of international law. Hence, further strategies of engagement by Kosovo domestic courts with international law are yet to be seen.

Acknowledgement and Note

This contribution has been written in the author's personal capacity and does not necessarily represent the views of any of the institutions to which the author is affiliated. This contribution is based on research completed in 2017, which has been updated in 2022. The author is grateful to the editors of this volume and Eleni Methymaki for their helpful comments on an earlier draft of the contribution.

[158] ILA Final Report (n 55) paras 23–24, 46–48.

[159] The Constitutional Court has held that, 'in accordance with Article 53 of the Constitution, it is its constitutional obligation to conduct an interpretation of human rights and fundamental freedoms in accordance with the case-law of ECtHR'. See *Gezim and Makfire Kastrati against Municipal Court in Prishtina and Kosovo Judicial Council*, Case No KI 41/12, Judgment of 25 January 2012 (Constitutional Court) [58]. See also, eg, *Constitutional Review of Decision Pml No 313/2018 of the Supreme Court of 10 December 2018*, Case No KI 12/19, Resolution on inadmissibility of 10 April 2019 (Constitutional Court) [38].

[160] See *Constitutional Review of the Law No 04/L-199, on Ratification of the First International Agreement of Principles Governing the Normalization of Relations between the Republic of Kosovo and the Republic of Serbia and the Implementation Plan of this Agreement (Visar Ymeri and others)*, Case No KO 95/13, Judgment of 2 September 2013 (Constitutional Court) [52].

[161] Morina et al (n 155) 282.

14
Engagement of Swiss Courts with International Law

Eva Maria Belser and Rekha Oleschak-Pillai

A. Introduction

The way in which domestic courts in Switzerland engage with international law and how they choose between the strategies of avoidance, alignment, and contestation is often difficult to predict and sometimes hard to understand. The choice of one of the three strategies, which all exist in great variety, depends on a number of hard and soft factors, such as the temporal sequence of the norms involved (where the *lex posterior* principle applies), the legal matter at stake (eg, whether it is a rather technical or highly political issue), the types and characteristics of the norms involved (eg, whether the international norm is part of a multilateral or bilateral treaty, or whether the domestic norm is of national or subnational origin), the field of law (eg, whether it is family, banking, or migration law), the domestic court involved (eg, whether it is a court of first instance or one of the federal courts) and its composition (eg, whether a connoisseur of international law is delivering the judgment or not).[1]

The engagement of domestic courts with international law raises a number of important issues relating to the predictability of court decisions, the coherence of the overall legal system and the specific roles of parliaments, executives, and courts in developing law and resolving norm and policy conflicts. As a rule, Swiss courts refer to international law and apply international norms just as they refer to domestic law and apply federal, cantonal, or municipal norms. Conflicts between international and domestic norms are rare and typically solved by the method of consistent interpretation. While the general posture of the judiciary is one of positive engagement with international law, numerous

[1] These factors broadly align with the variables identified in the ILA Study Group on Principles on the Engagement of Domestic Courts with International Law, 'Final Report: Mapping the Engagement of Domestic Courts with International Law' (Johannesburg, 2016) (ILA Final Report) paras 74–78.

nuances and exceptions appear when domestic and international norms clash in a way that cannot easily be resolved by harmonious interpretation. This is particularly true when new constitutional or statutory domestic norms conflict with existing international obligations. In a country of direct democratic constitution- and lawmaking, the question of how to deal with such conflicts is particularly controversial. On the one hand, Switzerland and its Constitution have opted for an open and reliable engagement with international law and for the acceptance of its authority; on the other hand, domestic law is generally seen as enjoying higher democratic legitimacy, as it is often the result of popular referenda, while international law is considered as 'foreign' or even 'imposed' law with weak democratic legitimacy, as it is negotiated by government officials and—if at all—only rubber-stamped by the country's representative bodies. This perception of a confrontation between the two legal systems is, however, deceptive. Obviously, the relations between domestic and international law and democratic legitimacy are much more complex. The international law friendly Constitution itself enjoys high democratic legitimacy, numerous international treaties have been accepted in popular referenda (while many statutes have not), international norms can protect democratic processes and outcomes, while domestic norms can pervert democracy into blunt majoritarianism.

This chapter aims at contributing to a better understanding of the engagement of the Swiss judiciary with international law. It focuses on the highest court of the country, the Swiss Federal Supreme Court (FSC), and looks at ways in which the supreme court judges deal with conflicts between domestic law and international human rights guarantees. The human rights focus has been chosen because it allows for a study of the engagement of courts with international law in a wide variety of legal settings (eg, family law, migration law). In addition, the protection of human rights is particularly challenging as international guarantees evolve dynamically, especially in the field of the European Convention of Humans Rights (ECHR), where the European Court of Human Rights (ECtHR) issues binding decisions. Finally, international human rights raise specific questions in the Swiss context whenever they conflict with domestic norms sanctioned by recent popular votes. They therefore allow us to examine how Swiss courts engage with international norms 'at the edge',[2] in particular in situations where domestic courts are put under stress by the simultaneous obligation to apply human rights and strong democratic pressure to unduly limit these rights.

[2] ibid paras 35–36.

The focus on norms dealing with highly controversial issues and norms 'at the edge' should not obscure the fact that, in most cases, dealing with international law is common practice in Swiss courts and does not raise any particular concerns. International law is widely used by domestic courts to resolve disputes—occasionally even to find inspiration for the resolution of domestic conflicts outside the reach of international law.[3] Where it is useful for better understanding the Swiss courts' engagement with international law, we will also refer to cases not (or only indirectly) linked to international human rights guarantees.

We will first outline the constitutional rules on the relationship between international law and domestic law (Section B) and deal with strategies of avoiding judicial engagement with international law (Section C). We will then examine how the Federal Supreme Court handle conflicts between international law and domestic constitutional and statutory law (Sections D and E) and, in our conclusions, analyse the interlinkages between the judiciary's engagement with international law and its stance in the counter-majoritarian dilemma (Section F).

B. The Status of International Law in the Swiss Legal Order

While the Swiss Federal Constitution of 1999[4] makes it clear that international law is binding on all Swiss State authorities, the hierarchy of international and domestic norms remains controversial. In answering open questions, the role of the judiciary is affected by the fact that, in Switzerland, courts play a more limited role than in other countries.

1. The Duty of All State Actors to Respect International Law

In its general provision on the rule of law, the Constitution requires the Confederation and the Cantons to respect international law and implicitly confirms Switzerland's monist approach to international law.[5] The principle of

[3] In BGE 26 I 444, the Federal Supreme Court (FSC) used principles of international law to judge a dispute between the cantons of Solothurn and Aargau with respect to a firing range with effects across the cantonal border.

[4] Federal Constitution (Bundesverfassung) of the Swiss Confederation of 18 April 1999, SR 101 (Constitution).

[5] ibid art 5. See, eg, Helen Keller, *Rezeption des Völkerrechts* (Springer 2003) 317ff; Federal Council, 'Das Verhältnis von Völkerrecht und Landesrecht' (2010) BBl 2263 and 'Complementary Report' (2011) BBl 3613. On federalism in Switzerland and the role of Cantons in foreign affairs, see Roland

monism is confirmed by the duty of the judiciary to apply international law and the jurisdiction of the FSC to hear disputes concerning a violation of international law.[6]

In contrast, the Constitution determines the hierarchy between international and domestic law only in a fragmentary way: First, the Federal Constitution can be amended at any time and in any way the authorities or the people successfully propose. The possibility of partial or total amendment of the supreme law is, however, limited by one substantive requirement, namely that the mandatory provisions of international law must be respected.[7] *E contrario*, the Constitution does not prevent constitutional amendments from violating non-mandatory international law rules. Popular initiatives contradicting international law, including human rights law, are therefore valid and amend the Constitution if accepted in a referendum. While the Constitution does not define 'mandatory provisions of international law', and an autonomous interpretation of the term would have been possible, practice has opted for a narrow understanding, equating 'mandatory provisions' with international *jus cogens*.[8] As a consequence of this, popular initiatives—such as the one on the 'prohibition of minarets', the 'automatic expulsion of foreigners' or 'limits to mass immigration', violating the ECHR or the bilateral treaties with the EU, have been taken to the urns and been accepted. Although the Constitution clearly requires all State actors to respect international law, it does not prevent constitutional amendments violating international law from entering into force.

Second, while any norm violating international *jus cogens* law is null and void, the hierarchy of non-mandatory international norms and domestic law is a matter of dispute. The wording chosen in Article 5(4) of the Constitution ('shall respect international law') clearly differs from the formula used to resolve domestic norm conflicts ('Federal law takes precedence over any

Portmann 'Foreign Affairs Federalism in Switzerland' in Curtis A Bradley (ed), *The Oxford Handbook of Comparative Foreign Relations Law* (OUP 2019).

[6] Constitution (n 4) art 190 and art 189(1)(b).

[7] ibid art 139(3), art 193(4), art 194(2).

[8] *Jus cogens* (or a peremptory norm of international law) is understood here as 'a norm accepted and recognized by the international community of States as a whole as a norm from which no derogation is permitted and which can be modified only by a subsequent norm of general international law having the same character', see ILC, 'Peremptory Norms of General International Law (Jus Cogens): Text of the Draft Conclusions and Draft Annex Provisionally Adopted by the Drafting Committee on First Readings' (29 May 2019) UN Doc A/CN.4/l.936, draft conclusion 2, with a non-exhaustive list at draft conclusion 24 and Annex; in the Swiss context, examples of generally accepted *jus cogens* norms are the prohibition of genocide, and other war crimes and the prohibition of torture, slavery and slave trade, and refoulement. See 'Report of the Federal Council on the Relationship between International Law and Domestic Law' (5 March 2010) 21 ('Das Verhältnis von Völkerrecht und Landesrecht Bericht des Bundesrates' (5 March 2010) BBl 2010, 2263).

conflicting provision of cantonal law').[9] When the constitutional text underwent a comprehensive revision in 1999, some authors championed a clear statement in favour of international law, while others insisted on allowing the legislature to adapt overriding domestic law. As it proved impossible to reach an agreement, the final decision was to opt for strategic ambiguity and leave the hierarchical ranking of international law open. While the compromise of the time probably was to allow the courts to decide on a case-by-case basis, the controversial question which has arisen since is whether Parliament and the people can also, on a case-by-case basis, opt for the supremacy of domestic law. There has been extensive discussion on these topics in the last few years,[10] but some of the difficult questions are yet to be resolved.

2. The Limited Role of the Judiciary

The Swiss polity is marked by strong democratic traditions that generally are averse to power being vested in courts. First, the FSC has no say in the assessment of popular initiatives aiming at constitutional amendments at the federal level; the competence of evaluating whether an initiative respects mandatory international law is granted to the Federal Assembly which generally opts for the validity of popular initiatives. The rule of *in dubio pro populo* states that in cases of doubt a popular initiative should be subjected to popular opinion and not be ruled out as void. While the rule itself is not explicitly mentioned in the Constitution, it has been developed and used by the FSC in interpreting and upholding cantonal initiatives.[11]

[9] Constitution (n 4) art 49(1).

[10] See, eg, Giovanni Biaggini, 'Über die Auslegung der Bundesverfassung und ihr Verhältnis zur EMRK' (2013) 114 Schweizerisches Zentralblatt für Staats- und Verwaltungsrecht 316; Christophe Herzig, 'Völkerrecht versus Landesrecht im Lichte der bundesgerichtlichen Rechtsprechung' (Jusletter, 2013), available at <https://jusletter.weblaw.ch/juslissues/2013/705/_11188.html> last accessed 24 July 2023; Astrid Epiney, 'Das Verhältnis von Völkerrecht und Landesrecht aus der Sicht des Bundesgerichts' (Jusletter, 2013), available at <https://jusletter.weblaw.ch/juslissues/2013/702/_11102.html> last accessed 24 July 2023; Eva Maria Belser, 'Massnahmen zur besseren Vereinbarkeit von Völkerrecht und Initiativrecht, Vernehmlassung zum materiellen Vorprüfungsverfahren von Volksinitiativen und zur Erweiterung der materiellen Schranken von Verfassungsrevisionen' (*Schweizerisches Kompetenzzentrum für Menschenrechte*, 13 June 2013) (on file with the authors), each with further references; Thomas Stadelmann, 'Verfassung – Bundesgesetze – Völkerrecht: Besteht Bedarf auf Anpassung der Bundesverfassung?' (Jusletter, 7 October 2019) available at <https://jusletter.weblaw.ch/juslissues/2019/995/verfassung---bundesg_9e079beb65.html__ONCE&login=false> last accessed 24 July 2023; Matthias Goldmann, 'Völkerrechtliche Vereinbarungen und direkte Demokratie' (2018) 78 ZaöRV 281.

[11] The FSC has interpreted in favour of upholding direct democratic instruments, while ruling on cantonal cases challenging the conduct of voting or their content. See, eg, BGE 143 I 129 und BGE 138 I 131; See Dispatch of the Federal Council relating to the new Federal Constitution, 20.11.1996, BBl 1997 I 433, s 1.

Second, the Constitution obliges courts to apply federal acts and international law.[12] This rather obscure norm is one of the most unique in the Swiss Constitution. Its function is not to remind the judiciary of its duty to respect the law and to apply it but rather to limit the scope of judicial review and to immunize federal acts and international law. This norm does not overturn the hierarchy of norms as such (the Constitution is still considered to prevail over federal acts and probably also over international law) but judicial enforcement of this hierarchy is excluded by the Constitution: the judiciary is therefore bound to apply federal acts and international law even if these violate the Constitution. The underlying idea of this far-reaching restriction to constitutional review is that the federal lawmaker (Parliament and the people) is in a better position to judge the conformity of statutes and international law with the—often very open and indeterminate—norms of the Constitution, and that (indirectly elected) judges should not be allowed to correct the legislator's understanding of the Constitution, and of the appropriate ways to concretize it nationally and internationally. We will see in Section D that the simultaneous obligation to apply federal acts *and* international law has allowed the FSC in many cases to effectively protect human rights by embracing international law guarantees.

Third, not all cases raising questions of engagement with international law are subject to appeal to the highest court. While the Constitution provides that access to the FSC is guaranteed by law, it also allows the legislature to introduce limitations.[13] These do not only relate to internal and external security, neutrality, diplomatic protection, and other matters related to foreign affairs, but also to numerous decisions in the field of immigration and asylum law, international legal and administrative cooperation, and various other fields.[14] Given the wide scope of access limitation, the FSC has had no need to develop elaborate doctrines of self-constraint in the field of political questions.[15]

12 Constitution (n 4) art 190.

13 ibid art 191(1) and (3).

14 Federal Act on the Federal Supreme Court of 17 June 2005, SR 173.110, art 83(b).

15 The long access limitation catalogue is contained in Federal Act on the Federal Supreme Court ibid art 83. While some exceptions are made with the aim of discharging the highest court from (clone) cases, others are consistent with the idea that the judiciary has a limited role of review in some fields. In a sense, this 'access limitation' operates as a legislative 'blunting' or 'moderating technique' in the sense ILA Final Report (n 1) para 21.

C. Avoiding Engagement of Courts with International Law

In line with the broad understanding of politics and the limited role of the judiciary in Switzerland, resolving conflicts between international law and domestic law is generally not seen as being the role of courts. In light of this, parliament and government are therefore reluctant to accept international obligations that conflict with domestic law (1), and courts tend to deny their justiciability in situations of potential conflict (2).

1. The Reluctance to Accept International Obligations

As a rule, Switzerland does not ratify international treaties that conflict with domestic law, and this prevents courts from having to deal with conflicts in the first place. Avoiding domestic courts' engagement by evading international obligations altogether is a popular strategy, particularly with respect to inward-looking obligations. The general view being that, if the legal system needs to be amended to accept new international obligations, it is up to the federal or cantonal legislators and not up to the courts to do so, the country usually delays ratification until the necessary legislative changes have been made. The ECHR, for instance, was only ratified in 1974 after female suffrage was introduced at the federal level in 1971 and the prohibition of the Jesuit Order was abolished in 1973. For similar reasons, the two International Covenants of 1966[16] only entered into force in 1992 for Switzerland, and the ratification of the International Convention on the Elimination of All Forms of Racial Discrimination of 1965[17] was delayed until 1994 as Parliament first had to adopt a new norm criminalizing racial discrimination.[18]

Finally, the Government and Parliament opt for reservations when they are not willing or able to bring domestic law in line with international law, but consider refusal of ratification or further delays in the ratification process as

[16] International Covenant on Civil and Political Rights (adopted 16 December 1966, entered into force 23 March 1976) 999 UNTS 171; International Covenant on Economic, Social and Cultural Rights (adopted 16 December 1966, entered into force 3 January 1976) 993 UNTS 3.

[17] International Convention on the Elimination of All Forms of Racial Discrimination (adopted 21 December 1965, entered into force 4 January 1969) 660 UNTS 195 (CERD).

[18] With the aim of joining CERD, the Federal Assembly added Article 261*bis* criminalizing incitement of hatred to the Swiss Criminal Code. The ratification, however, was further delayed by an optional referendum against the law (which was defeated in 1994). See Marcel A Niggli, *Rassendiskriminierung: Ein Kommentar zu Art. 261bis StGB und Art. 171c MStG – mit Rücksicht auf das "Übereinkommen vom 21. Dezember 1965 zur Beseitigung jeder Form von Rassendiskriminierung" und die entsprechenden Regelungen anderer Unterzeichnerstaaten* (2nd edn, Schulthess 2007).

inappropriate. When Switzerland finally ratified the ECHR, it made three reservations and deposited two interpretative declarations.[19] When it accepted the International Covenant on Civil and Political Rights (ICCPR) it made as many as nine reservations.[20]

The conviction that it is up to Parliament, not courts, to align domestic law with international obligations leads to very careful prior analyses of legal compatibility. Before proposing new legislation or the ratification of treaties, the Federal Council is under a legal obligation to provide substantive information about 'the effects on fundamental rights, the conformity with prevailing law and the relation to European law'.[21] If compliance with a new international treaty requires an amendment to the federal Constitution or a federal law, Parliament can incorporate the requisite domestic legislation into the referendum on the ratification of the international treaty to prevent the acceptance of an international treaty in conflict with domestic law.[22] For these reasons, it is widely seen as a mishap when courts have to decide on conflicts between international and domestic law.

2. Hesitance to Accept the Justiciability of International Norms

International norms are only considered to fall in the realm of courts when they are considered justiciable, i.e. sufficiently precise to be applied by courts without further clarification by Parliament or the Government. Swiss courts are generally reluctant to accept justiciability and tend to deny that the conditions are met when international norms contradict domestic norms—in such cases political choices need to be made.[23] When the FSC qualifies an international

[19] See, eg, Federal Council, 'Report: 40 Jahre EMRK Beitritt der Schweiz: Erfahrungen und Perspektiven' (2015) BBl 357, 371ff. The ECtHR had the opportunity to reflect upon the meaning of the 'interpretative declarations' and considered these not to have the character of a reservation in the case of *Belilos v Switzerland*, App No 10328/83, 29 April 1988.

[20] See for effects of reservations on judicial scrutiny, eg, BGE 133 I 286 (2007) [3.2] and [3.3], where the FSC examined the reservations to the Convention on the Rights of the Child and found that until the reservations are withdrawn, the appellants could only avail of the limited rights under the Convention.

[21] The obligation to take into consideration the legal background, the consequences for constitutional rights, the compatibility with superior law and the relationship with European law is enshrined in the Federal Act on the Federal Assembly of 13 December 2002 (Parliament Act, ParlA), SR 171.10, art 141(2)(a). Accordingly, dispatches on bills are required to include the above. Regarding treaty ratification see Federal Chancellery, Leitfaden zum Verfassen von Botschaften des Bundesrates (2006, revised edn 2020) 78ff which outlines the procedure to be taken with respect to treaties requiring domestic implementation and ratification.

[22] Constitution (n 4) art 141(a).

[23] See, eg, BGE 106 Ib 182 (1980) c 3; BGE 138 II 42 (2012) c 3.1.

norm as programmatic, this decision typically has the consequence that the Court will not engage with it any further (the norm thus becoming non-justiciable), but that it considers Federal Parliament and Government to be the competent bodies to ensure compliance with the norm (an interesting exception to this rule will be presented below).[24]

When the Federal Council proposes the ratification of an international treaty, it usually takes a position on the legal character of the norms involved. Most prominently, the Federal Council has stated that—in contrast to most norms of the ICCPR—the International Covenant on Economic, Social and Cultural Rights (ICESCR) was of a programmatic nature and did not guarantee directly applicable rights in the domestic order. When the FSC in 1994 was first asked to take a position on the matter, it paid tribute to the Federal Council's stance and relevant parliamentary debates, and denied the justiciability of the rights guaranteed in the Covenant,[25] engaging in affirmative avoidance.[26] This position—although increasingly criticized in doctrine and by international bodies[27]—has since been confirmed in numerous cases.[28] In its country report on the implementation of the Covenant submitted under Article 16(1) of ICESCR, the Federal Council now points to court cases to explain its refusal to accept the justiciability of core economic, social and cultural rights.[29] As a result, the country is caught in a vicious circle of denying the justiciability of the ICESCR, in which the FSC has first passed the buck to the Federal Council who has given it back to the Court.[30]

[24] In that sense, non-justiciability operates as a 'blunting' or 'moderating' technique, in the terms of the ILA Final Report (n 1) para 21, in the monist Swiss legal system, leading to affirmative avoidance (para 41).

[25] BGE 120 Ia 1 (1994) c 5.

[26] ILA Final Report (n 1) para 41.

[27] CESCR 'General Comment No 9: The Domestic Application of the Covenant' (3 December 1998) UN Doc E/C.12/1998/24 [10]; Ben Saul et al, *The International Covenant on Economic, Social and Cultural Rights: Commentary, Cases, and Materials* (OUP 2014) 164–66.

[28] See, eg, BGE 136 I 290 (2010) c 2.3.

[29] CESCR 'Implementation of the International Covenant on Economic, Social and Cultural Rights, List of Issues, Switzerland' (4 December 2009) UN Doc E/C.12/CHE/Q/2–3; CESCR 'Consideration of Reports submitted by States Parties under Articles 16 and 17 of the Covenant: Concluding Observations of the Committee on Economic, Social and Cultural Rights, Switzerland' (26 November 2010) UN Doc E/C.12/CHE/CO/2–3.

[30] See, eg, BGE 130 I 113 (2003) c 3; BGE 126 I 240 (2000) 2c.

D. Aligning Statutory Law with International Law—or Refusing to Do So

The strategy of preventing conflicts between international and domestic law fails when unforeseen and unplanned tensions arise from the dynamic evolution of existing international obligations. Legislators are well-suited to bring domestic law in line with international law at a specific point in time but are ill-placed to catch up with new caselaw, as well as the development of soft law into binding international norms. If violations of international law are to be avoided—which is generally (but not always) the accepted premise—dynamic evolutions of international law have to be introduced by the judiciary (or by the administration). The most commonly accepted way to do so (albeit not always applied consistently) is by applying the method of consistent interpretation (1). While recognizing the primacy of international law as a principle, the Swiss judiciary has accepted violations of international law when they were clearly and intentionally provided for in statutory law (2). This so-called 'Schubert practice' is, however, not applied in the field of human rights (3).

1. The Method of Consistent Interpretation

When the FSC in 1968 had to decide whether to give preference to a bilateral treaty or a more recent domestic act on postal services, it interpreted the domestic act in light of the treaty and gave it a meaning compatible with international obligations.[31] This practice of consistent interpretation has since been confirmed on numerous occasions[32] and has allowed solving almost all issues of apparent conflict between international and domestic norms.[33] The method of consistent interpretation applies to all legal fields and norms, even to the federal Constitution itself. However, the FSC generally takes a position of fair weather alignment, very rarely has it taken, as we shall see later, a position of overriding alignment.

In the field of human rights, domestic norms have been very strongly influenced by international law. Through a very dynamic jurisprudence, the FSC has recognized unwritten constitutional guarantees largely in line with the international bill of rights. The domestic bill of rights that codified this

[31] BGE 94 I 669 (1968) c 6a.

[32] See, eg, BGE 126 IV 236 (2010) c 4b, and cases discussed below.

[33] See, eg, Astrid Epiney 'Article 5' in Bernhard Waldmann et al (eds), *Bundesverfassung Basler Kommentar* (Basel 2015) art 5 paras 76, 84 et seq. See also ILA Final Report (n 1) para 45.

caselaw in 1999 was therefore largely congruent with international norms, producing consubstantial alignment,[34] and was meant to evolve in harmony with international commitments. When adjudicating human rights cases, the FSC customarily refers to the ECHR and the ECtHR caselaw and strives towards a consubstantial evolution of the guarantees—sometimes to the extent of neglecting an autonomous, potentially more progressive, interpretation of human rights norms.

The Swiss system of direct democracy places pressure on courts to conform to the prevailing political ethos and thus (indirectly) restrict courts from effectively exercising their counter-majoritarian role where necessary.[35] Hence, it should not be overlooked that in fields where strong democratic pressure exists, the FSC finds it difficult to enforce international guarantees and fulfil its counter-majoritarian role. For instance, provisions of the Swiss Civil Code favouring the male member of the family, even though clearly in violation of the right to equality enshrined in the federal Constitution, as well as in international human rights conventions, remained in force for a very long time. This did not change when the ECtHR found that the existing regime was incompatible with the principle of non-discrimination in the field of family law.[36] The discriminatory regime (mitigated by an ordinance of the Federal Council) persisted until the Federal Parliament in 2013 finally reached an agreement on how to bring Swiss family law in compliance with international human rights law. The FSC had established a violation of the Federal Constitution and international law but refused to provide a remedy arguing that there were several ways to bring Swiss caselaw in line with the right to equality—and that is was up to the legislator, not the court, to decide on the way forward.

In the past, this reluctance to engage with international law has also been quite conspicuous in the field of free speech. When the FSC in 1999 dealt with a case filed by a business association against a controversial researcher who had published 'false' information on health risks associated with the use of the microwave, the Court took the position that the researcher's freedom of speech

[34] See ILA Final Report (n 1) para 49.

[35] See generally for the problematic relationship between direct democracy and human rights, Daniel Möckli, 'Of Minarets and Foreign Criminals: Swiss Direct Democracy and Human Rights' (2011) 11 Human Rights Law Review 774. In a recent decision, the FSC was called upon to interpret criminal law in alignment with a pending legislative proposal to revise the criminal law regarding sexual assault. The appellant argued that this would be in line with the caselaw of the ECtHR as well as the Istanbul Convention. Here the Court denied the applicability of the broader interpretation brought forward by the appellants on the grounds that this does not constitute current law. See FSC, 6B 894/2021, Decision of 28 March 2022.

[36] *Burghartz v Switzerland*, App No 16213/90, 22 February 1994; see also *Losonci Rose et Rose c Suisse*, App No 664/06, 9 November 2010.

was indeed limited by the Unfair Competition Act. The Court held that it indeed constituted an act of unfair competition to state that 'food prepared in microwave ovens is a danger to health and leads to changes in the blood of those who consume it that indicate a pathological disorder and present a pattern that could be seen as the beginning of a carcinogenic process'.[37] Even though the Act would have been amenable to a consistent interpretation with free speech guarantees under the Constitution and the ECHR (eg, by limiting its application only to competitors), the FSC opted for a broad application of the domestic competition norms and applied them to a controversial research statement not explicitly falling within the scope of the Act. The ECtHR found that this had resulted in a violation of Article 10 ECHR.[38] Similarly, the FSC applied the Swiss Federal Radio and Television Act without attempting to align the domestic law (namely the rules on television advertisements) with Switzerland's international obligations, when it decided that the Swiss Television company had been acting lawfully when it refused to broadcast a commercial produced by a non-governmental organization.[39] According to the Court, advocacy against consumption of meat was covered by statutory prohibition of political advertisement.[40] In *Verein gegen Tierfabriken v Switzerland*, this decision was also found to be in violation of Article 10 ECHR.[41] In all the above-mentioned cases, the applicants explicitly invoked the norms of the ECHR (mostly consubstantial with fundamental rights guarantees in the federal Constitution) but the FSC was unwilling to steadily apply the method of consistent interpretation or decided to give more weight to the historic method of interpretation and the legislator's will to limit human rights. The cases hence constitute examples of affirmative avoidance, rather than of contestation. As a rule, the FSC tends to interpret restrictions imposed as being aligned with ECHR guarantees. It, however, is willing to return to alignment if subsequently the decision is found by the ECtHR to be in violation of the ECHR. In the 2013 decision on a similar subject matter, the FSC—having been rebuked by the ECtHR previously—was willing to find the restrictions as being in violation of ECHR guarantees.[42]

[37] BGE 125 III 185, 191.
[38] *Hertel v Switzerland*, App No 59/1997/843/1049, 25 August 1998.
[39] BGI 134 II 120.
[40] ibid.
[41] *Verein gegen Tierfabriken v Switzerland*, App No 24699/94, 28 June 2001. Quite exceptionally, the claimant had to file a second claim and was successful in finally broadcasting the commercial, *Verein Gegen Tierfabriken Schweiz v Switzerland*, App No 32772/02, 30 June 2009. In the decision of 16 November 2013 ((BGE 139 I 306), the FSC found in favour of the same association and held that the restrictions were in violation of Art 10 ECHR.
[42] ibid BGE 139 I 306

The reluctance to engage with international human rights obligations is probably most blatant in the area of migration law.[43] As observed by Helen Keller, 'jurisprudence in the law concerning the legal status of foreigners is not characterized by a tenor friendly to international law'.[44] Given the large number of cases at the ECtHR that are related to the right to remain in the country, and the numerous constitutional and statutory amendments, migration law is one of the most discussed and controversial areas of law in Switzerland.[45]

Additionally, the FSC has, so far, rarely ventured to examine the conformity of federal acts with programmatic international duties, and has not insisted on the fact that progressive duties ask for immediate action, coherent planning, and non-regression. It has rather accepted that parliaments enjoy broad—in fact, unlimited—discretion as to how (and if) to honour programmatic and progressive international duties. By itself, the characterization that a certain international norm is programmatic may be evidence of affirmative avoidance.[46] Despite this, the Court has accepted the idea that programmatic obligations of the Convention on the Elimination of All Forms of Discrimination Against Women[47] on gender equality (and their consubstantial domestic counterparts) do not allow cantonal legislators to abolish gender equality offices without providing for an equally effective alternative.[48]

2. The Schubert Practice

In situations where federal acts unequivocally violate international obligations the method of consistent interpretation is doomed to fail. The FSC then finds itself in a dilemma: it is under a constitutional obligation to apply federal acts (even when in contradiction with constitutional law) and under the same obligation to apply international law. While in such a situation the FSC would generally uphold the primacy of international law, it adopts a strategy of contestation when sanctioned by democratic will.

In 1973, the FSC was confronted with a bilateral treaty and a more recent federal act irreconcilable with that treaty, and it decided that the federal act

[43] See, eg, BGE 109 Ib 183 (1983); BGE 138 I 246 (2012); BGE 139 I 330 (2013)

[44] See Keller (n 5) 745.

[45] See generally, Marc Spescha et al, *Kommentar Migrationsrecht* (Orell Füssli 2020); Jens Hainmueller and Dominik Hangartner, 'Does Direct Democracy Hurt Immigrant Minorities? Evidence from Naturalization Decisions in Switzerland' (2019) 63 American Journal of Political Science 530.

[46] ILA Final Report (n 1) para 41.

[47] (adopted 18 December 1979, entered into force 3 September 1981) 1249 UNTS 13.

[48] BGE 137 I 305 (2011).

should trump international law if the legislator had been aware of the conflict, and willingly chose to violate international law. This had indeed been the situation in the case before the Court. When the Federal Assembly decided to introduce a duty to obtain a permit for foreigners purchasing land or homes in Switzerland, it very well realized that this obligation would violate a longstanding bilateral treaty with Austria guaranteeing equal treatment to Austrian citizens. The conflict was discussed in Parliament when the federal act was passed and politicians seemed to accept the idea that the treaty would have to be renegotiated, and that Austria, until this was achieved, would have the right to retaliate and restrict land acquisitions of Swiss citizens in Austria. When an Austrian citizen called Schubert took action and brought the matter before the courts, the FSC argued that it was not for the judiciary to invalidate an explicit decision of Parliament and gave precedence to the more recent domestic norm, adopting a strategy of negatory contestation.[49]

The judicial approach of accepting explicit international law violations by Parliament, the so-called 'Schubert-Praxis', has been mentioned by the Court on various occasions[50] but has rarely been applied. However, its underlying idea of accepting democratically adopted explicit violations of international law obligations has deeply entered Swiss thinking about the relations between international and domestic law.

3. The Exception to the Schubert Practice

In 1991, the FSC decided that the Schubert-Praxis did not apply when international human rights obligations, most notably the ECHR, were at stake (this exception has become known as the 'PKK practice').[51] The FSC pointed to the fact that violations of the ECHR could be brought before the ECtHR which would investigate whether a violation of the Convention had taken place regardless of whether this violation originated from an immunized federal act or any other domestic norm or decision. Under these circumstances, the FSC decided it would review the conformity of federal acts with the ECHR and not apply federal statutes, even more recent ones, if they violated the Convention.[52]

[49] See ILA Final Report (n 1) para 61.
[50] See, eg, BGE 139 I 16 (2012).
[51] BGE 125 II 417 (1991).
[52] The observation of the ILA Final Report (n 1) para 79 that one of the variables influencing the engagement of domestic courts with international law is 'the certainty and frequency of supervision or monitoring, in particular by international courts' is apt here.

Thus, according to the PKK practice, the FSC accepts explicit contestations of international law by the legislator in all cases, except in the field of human rights.

This landmark decision of 1991 was the beginning of the phenomenon of so-called 'backdoor constitutional review'. The FSC refused to apply federal acts that violated the ECHR, but as the international guarantees contained therein are largely consubstantial with those of the Constitution, there is, as a result, a human rights review of federal acts in light of both the ECHR, and also *de facto* the Constitution guaranteeing the same rights. Not only has the adoption of this procedure improved respect for international human rights obligations, it has also significantly reduced the effects of Article 190 of the Constitution, which prevents courts from reviewing federal statutory law. It must be stated that the PKK practice, also confirmed by the FSC, is hardly ever applied. It is all the more interesting that the FSC has used it recently in a case in which human rights law more generally, not the ECHR, was at stake. The case involved a conflict between a domestic rule (denying a disability pension for refugee children) and the international refugee convention—and the FSC decided to apply the international (human rights) norm, not the Federal Act.[53]

E. Muddling through the Jungle of Non-Aligned Constitutional Law

The unclear hierarchical relation between constitutional and international law was not considered problematic as long as constitutional and international norms were viewed as largely consubstantial (in the field of human rights) or independent of each other (in the field of State organization, power separation, and federalism). In recent times, however, a number of new constitutional norms, introduced by popular initiatives, unduly limiting constitutional and international human rights guarantees have led to highly contentious debates regarding engagement with international law. As most of these amendments are rather recent, the courts have not yet had many opportunities to take a position.

In a landmark decision of 2012, the FSC has, however, clearly taken a position in favour of international law, in particular the ECHR.[54] The case concerned a person of North Macedonian origin whose residence permit in

[53] BGE 146 V 87 (2020).
[54] BGE 139 I 16 (2012).

Switzerland was revoked based on a criminal conviction. This revocation had been issued in line with a new constitutional norm introduced by the popular initiative 'expulsion of foreign criminals' requiring 'automatic' revocation of a residence permit in case of conviction for any of the offences pursuant to the constitutional provision.[55] Referring to international caselaw, the FSC insisted that automatic expulsion violated the principle of proportionality and could not be upheld in light of the ECHR.[56]

In the meantime, the Federal Parliament has implemented the constitutional provision by amending the Criminal Code.[57] The new legal provision is not formulated as strictly as the constitutional norm is and does allow for non-expulsion in cases of hardship. Most observers agree, however, that the criminal norm, immunized by the Constitution, and concretizing the constitutional rules on expulsion still conflicts with international law, which is equally immunized.[58] The matter to be decided by the FSC is whether it upholds the PKK practice and strictly applies international human rights law (including its recent evolutions), as well as the bilateral treaty on free movement and posterior statutes not conflicting with them, or whether it will rather come back to the Schubert practice and respect the will of the legislator to violate (or slightly 'scratch') international law—at least in situations in which the legislator's will is backed by a decision of the constitution-maker to automatically expel criminal foreigners—no matter what international law says. The recent case law of the FSC however leans towards a much stricter textual interpretation and is reluctant to overturn lower court's rulings on expulsion.[59]

The bilateral treaties with the European Union (EU) are extremely important for Switzerland and raise many legal questions. In a much-debated decision of 2015, the FSC confirmed many of the principles discussed above and decided that the exception to the Schubert practice also applied to the set of treaties with the EU.[60] The question at hand was whether—and how—the FSC should apply the Agreement on Free Movement of Persons (AFMP),[61] and was particularly

[55] Constitution (n 4) art 121(3)–(6).

[56] See, eg, Eva Maria Belser, 'Das Bundesgericht nimmt das Ruder in die Hand' *Neue Zürcher Zeitung* (12 February 2013) 19; Biaggini (n 10) 326ff; Yvo Hangartner, 'Bundesgerichtlicher Positionsbezug zum Verhältnis von Bundesverfassung und Völkerrecht' (2013) 22 Aktuelle Juristische Praxis 698.

[57] Swiss Criminal Code of 21 December 1937 (as amended to 1 July 2020), SR 311.0, art 66(a).

[58] See, eg, Gerhard Fiolka and Luzia Vetterli, 'Die Landesverweisung nach Art. 66a StGB als strafrechtliche Sanktion' (2016) 5 Plädoyer 77, 82ff.

[59] BGE 144 IV 332 (2018) and 145 IV 55, both discussed in Babak Fargahi et al, 'Die ersten Urteile des Bundesgerichts zur Landesverweisung (Art. 66a ff. StGB)' (Jusletter, 15 April 2019), available at <https://jusletter.weblaw.ch/fr/juslissues/2019/976/die-ersten-urteile-d_a2babd3b9d.html__ONCE&login=false> last accessed 24 July 2023.

[60] BGE 142 II 35 (2015).

[61] Agreement between the European Community and its Member States, of the one part, and the Swiss Confederation, of the other, on the free movement of persons [1999] OJ L114.

contentious as a new constitutional provision 'against mass immigration'[62] had been adopted shortly before the Court's decision. As a matter of fact, the Constitution offered a simple answer to the question: According to its Article 190, courts must apply international law even if it violates the Constitution. So, when the FSC was asked to solve the conflict between a subsequent constitutional norm (accepted in a recent popular vote by a qualified majority) and a bilateral international treaty (accepted in an earlier popular vote by a simple majority), it was faced more with political pressure than with a real legal dilemma. Two statements of the Court, however, raise questions. First, the Court stated that it would give precedence to the AFMP even if the legislature should decide not to do so in the implementation phase and, without further reasoning, placed the AFMP on a similar footing as the ECHR.[63] Second, it affirmed that it can only deviate from the dynamic interpretation of the treaty by the European Court of Justice (ECJ) in case of a substantial reason ('triftiger Grund')—and did not qualify the recent decision of the Constitution-maker as such.

By refusing to adopt an interpretation of the country's international obligation compatible with the Constitution[64] and by relying on subsequent evolutions in EU free movement policy, not binding on Switzerland as a third country, the FSC seems to have opted for a strategy of overriding alignment, or even hyper-alignment, with international law.[65] This judicial approach has provoked reactions—within the population and, later, within the court itself. Firstly, the hyper-alignment approach has been challenged in a direct democratic initiative that was aimed at enshrining the supremacy of domestic law over constitutional law (Selbstbestimmungsinitiative).[66] It was however rejected by the voters in 2018 to the relief of large parts of the legal community, who saw in the initiative a threat to the rule of law and independence of the judiciary.

[62] Constitution (n 4) art 121(a).

[63] See before BGE 133 V 367 (2007).

[64] The FSC, namely, did not engage in affirmative contestation as defined in ILA Final Report (n 1) para 58.

[65] See for comments and further references Astrid Epiney, 'Auslegung und Verhältnis des Freizügigkeitsabkommens zum nationalen Recht' (Jusletter, 14 March 2016), available at <https://jusletter.weblaw.ch/juslissues/2016/839/auslegung-und-verhal_0fb26b9e01.html> last accessed 24 July 2023; Samantha Besson and Odile Ammann, 'L'interprétation des accords bilatéraux Suisse-UE: Une lecture de droit international' (2013) Schweizerisches Jahrbuch für Europarecht 331.

[66] The initiative proposed a constitutional amendment to regulate the relationship between constitutional law and international law, especially in cases of constitutional amendments conflicting with international treaties. See <https://www.admin.ch/gov/de/start/dokumentation/abstimmungen/20181125/selbstbestimmungsinitiative.html>last accessed 24 July 2023.

Secondly, this hyper alignment has been an issue within the Court itself. Most recently, the criminal chamber of the FSC issued a decision profoundly questioning the established approach. In a case concerning the application of the newly incorporated provisions in the Criminal Code implementing the 'expulsion initiative' mentioned before,[67] the Criminal Chamber, ruling on the application and interpretation of the AFMP, found that the AFMP does not include guidance on 'norm hierarchy' and that domestic courts should first apply 'familiar' domestic law.[68] The appellants argued that based on past jurisprudence of the ECJ, restrictions on free movement accordingly can only be justified when the person presents an actual, genuine and sufficiently serious threat affecting fundamental interests of society and therefore must be applied restrictively.[69] The court rejected these arguments stating that the jurisprudence referred to by the appellants predate the newly introduced provisions (Article 121a Constitution and Article 66a*bis* Criminal Code). It held that expulsion is an 'independent' legal provision and the reference to earlier case law on migration law are not relevant, as the legislator clearly intended more stringent rules in the criminal code.[70] Most disturbingly, the FSC did not engage with its earlier stance whereby a break from ECJ jurisprudence would only be undertaken when there is a substantial reason ('triftiger Grund') thereby leaving a gap as to how the AFMP and ECJ jurisprudence stand today. This matter, however, is also far from being settled. It is to be expected that the debates will continue.

F. Conclusion

While Swiss courts customarily engage with international law and use consistent interpretation to ensure the harmonious application of norms from different origins, new constitutional norms and their implementation in statutory law, have led to highly controversial debates about the relationship between domestic and international law. These controversies have had a deep impact on the relationship between the different branches of Government and the role

[67] 6B 235/2018, 1 November 2018. The decision of the criminal chamber has been criticized for its failure to use the opportunity to clarify the application of art 66abis of the Criminal Code and at the same time for less-well thought interpretation of the relation between domestic and international law. See Fargahi et al (n 59).

[68] ibid [3.4].

[69] ibid [4.1], [4.2].

[70] ibid [4.2].

of the people (and the cantons) as constitution- and law-makers, affecting domestic understandings of democracy and the rule of law.

As in many countries, Switzerland's judicial practice is highly responsive to international law but jealous of safeguarding its constitutional values against international intrusion. There is a tendency (not limited to Switzerland) to protect the domestic Constitution from too much outside influence, either because of democratic concerns, nationalistic introversion, or constitutional sentiments awakened by the proliferation of international law norms and institutions, and the intensification of global governance. Proponents of international law have not always wisely reacted to these trends. By propagating a general and unconditional doctrine of primacy for all international law norms and by labelling international law scepticism as backwardness and populism, they have sometimes stood in the way of open discussions on how to balance the different norms and policies involved.

For a number of years, the FSC has relied on fine-tuned and widely accepted principles when handling the—highly emotional but also rather rare—clashes between international and domestic norms: the general rule of alignment with international law, the Schubert practice as an exception allowing the legislator to opt for (temporary) international law violations and, finally, the counter-exception of the PKK practice refusing to apply the Schubert practice in human rights cases. By doing so, the FSC has—at least in theory—ensured the compliance of Switzerland with international human rights law, in particular the ECHR, while accepting non-compliance with other norms of international law in case Parliament and people willingly accept the consequences thereof. This way of proceeding has allowed the FSC to balance alignment and contestation of international law and to rather elegantly deal with the counter-majoritarian dilemma: the judiciary accepts explicit violations of international law by the legislators but not when they affect internationally guaranteed human rights. This mechanism, unfortunately not always strictly applied by the judiciary, is crucial to prevent a democracy from turning into a tyranny of the majority. The decision to extend the PKK practice to the bilateral treaties with the EU has affected this balance and raised the question of whether the Schubert practice still applies. In addition, outsourcing the counter-majoritarian dilemma to international law and protecting the rule of law based on international law arguments has proved to be a risky strategy. A popular initiative on self-determination and 'against foreign judges' that aimed to curtail the power of foreign as well as domestic judges was rejected by the voters.[71] Unfortunately,

[71] Selbstbestimmungsinitiative (n 66) 67.

international and domestic norms restraining the choices of the majority—and the implementation of these norms by the judiciary—are no longer seen by many as essential elements of democratic constitutionalism but as undemocratic devices imposed on the country from the outside that can be given up by opting out of international obligations. It remains to be seen how the FSC caselaw will evolve in light of these challenges.

PART 3
CROSS-CUTTING THEMES

15

Engagement of Domestic Courts with the Findings of United Nations Human Rights Treaty Monitoring Bodies

Machiko Kanetake

A. Introduction

International human rights law is one of the core areas in which international obligations are predominantly 'inward-looking'.[1] As contrasted with some other areas of international law that predominantly address a State's horizontal relations with other States, human rights treaties extensively overlap with domestic law in terms of their subject-matter.[2] Namely, both human rights treaties and domestic constitutional and administrative law concern the regulation of governmental authority exercised over individuals within the State's jurisdiction. This overlap creates a basic platform on which international and domestic guardians of human rights may interact with each other through their legal reasoning.

United Nations (UN) human rights treaty monitoring bodies are part of the international actors charged with assisting States' implementation of the respective human rights treaties. Monitoring bodies publish their comments, observations, and views while attempting to encourage, or even oblige, States parties to take certain actions at the domestic level.[3] The Human Rights

[1] ILA Study Group on Principles on the Engagement of Domestic Courts with International Law, 'Final Report: Mapping the Engagement of Domestic Courts with International Law' (Johannesburg, 2016) (ILA Final Report) para 12.

[2] Machiko Kanetake, 'The Interfaces between the National and International Rule of Law: A Framework Paper' in Machiko Kanetake and André Nollkaemper (eds), *The Rule of Law at the National and International Levels: Contestations and Deference* (Hart Publishing 2016) 15–18.

[3] See Scott Davidson, 'Intention and Effect: The Legal Status of the Final Views of the Human Rights Committee' in Grant Huscroft and Paul Rishworth (eds), *Litigating Rights: Perspectives from Domestic and International Law* (Hart Publishing 2002) 305; Human Rights Committee 'Draft General Comment No 33 (Second Revised Version as of 18 August 2008): The Obligations of States Parties under the Optional Protocol to the International Covenant on Civil and Political Rights' (25 August 2008) UN Doc CCPR/C/GC/33/CRP.3.

Committee, whose practice influences the modus operandi of other treaty monitoring bodies, deems its Views as exhibiting 'some important characteristics of a judicial decision'.[4] At the same time, the fact remains that the practical significance of UN human rights treaty monitoring bodies is ultimately contingent on acceptance by domestic authorities, including national judges.

The present chapter examines domestic courts' engagement with the formally non-binding outputs of UN human rights treaty monitoring bodies. The chapter starts with an overview of the varied modes of judicial engagement with the comments, observations, and views (collectively termed 'findings' in this chapter) of human rights monitoring bodies (Section B). Due to space constraints, this chapter only includes a fraction of the cases surveyed[5] with respect to the ten UN human rights treaty monitoring bodies.[6] Building on the analysis of court decisions, I identify normative pathways that connect domestic judicial reasoning with the findings of monitoring bodies (Sections C and D). While domestic judges' engagement with the findings of monitoring bodies is selective, domestic courts' reasoning can serve as a venue in which judges approve, adjust, or contest treaty interpretation put forward by UN human rights monitoring bodies (Section E).

B. The Practice of Domestic Courts

According to the International Law Association (ILA) Committee on International Human Rights Law and Practice (IHRLP) (1997–2008), which assembled and analysed an extensive body of court decisions, 'most courts have recognised that ... the treaty bodies' interpretations deserve to be given

[4] Human Rights Committee 'General Comment No 33: The Obligations of States Parties under the Optional Protocol' (5 November 2008) UN Doc CCPR/C/GC/33, para 11.

[5] I have collected and analysed 190 domestic court decisions (decided from 1982 to 2018) based on my own research, existing literature, the Oxford Reports on International Law in Domestic Courts (ILDC), the International Law Reports (ILR), and the reports of the International Law Association (ILA) Committee on International Human Rights Law and Practice (IHRLP) (1997–2008): ILA Committee on International Human Rights Law and Practice, 'Final Report on the Impact of Findings of the United Nations Human Rights Treaty Bodies' (2004) (2004 ILA Report); and ILA Committee on International Human Rights Law and Practice, 'Interim Report on the Impact of the Work of the United Nations Human Rights Treaty Bodies on National Courts and Tribunals' (2002) (2002 ILA Report).

[6] The ten bodies I have studied are the following: (i) Human Rights Committee; (ii) Committee on Economic, Social and Cultural Rights (CESCR); (iii) Committee on the Elimination of Racial Discrimination (CERD); (iv) Committee on the Elimination of Discrimination against Women (CEDAW); (v) Committee against Torture (CAT); (vi) Subcommittee on Prevention of Torture (SPT); (vii) Committee on the Rights of the Child (CRC); (viii) Committee on Migrant Workers (CMW); (ix) Committee on the Rights of Persons with Disabilities (CRPD); and (x) Committee on Enforced Disappearances (CED).

considerable weight'.[7] While a number of domestic courts indeed accommodate the findings in their reasoning, the limited survey of court decisions I have conducted shed light on the varied modes of judicial engagement. Depending on sociological and legal contexts, domestic judges may not be familiar with the UN treaty bodies' findings. Even if judges decide to engage with such findings, courts occasionally avoid, discount, and contest the interpretation put forward by the treaty bodies.

1. Postures of Alignment

UN human rights treaty monitoring bodies adopt broadly three types of findings: (i) General Comments and Recommendations, which are addressed to all States parties; (ii) Concluding Observations and Concluding Comments, which are addressed to a particular State party; and (iii) Views (or Decisions) and Suggestions and Recommendations, which pertain to individual communications or petitions. These findings have been used by domestic courts to inform the meaning of relevant human rights treaties, which often ultimately inform constitutional or statutory human rights provisions.

Among the cases I have analysed,[8] there are abundant examples of judicial engagement with the Human Rights Committee's General Comments on the International Covenant on Civil and Political Rights (ICCPR) and its protocols.[9] For instance, General Comments Nos 15 and 29 were mentioned in *A and Others (No 1)* before the UK House of Lords on the detention of suspected foreign terrorists, in which Lord Bingham, for the majority, resorted to the ICCPR and General Comments.[10] General Comment No 18 concerning non-discrimination was relied upon in *Ts'epe* in 2005 by the Court of Appeal in Lesotho to interpret Article 26 of the ICCPR in the process of constitutional

[7] 2004 ILA Report (n 5) para 175.

[8] See (n 5) on the scope of the research on which the chapter is based.

[9] International Covenant on Civil and Political Rights (adopted 16 December 1966, entered into force 23 March 1976) 999 UNTS 171; Optional Protocol to the International Covenant on Civil and Political Rights (adopted 16 December 1966, entered into force 23 March 1976) 999 UNTS 302; Second Optional Protocol to the International Covenant on Civil and Political Rights (adopted 15 December 1989, entered 11 July 1991) 1642 UNTS 414. For further examples, see 2002 ILA Report (n 5); 2004 ILA Report (n 5).

[10] *A and others v Secretary of State for the Home Department (No 1)* [2004] UKHL 56 [59]–[61], and [63] (Lord Bingham); Human Rights Committee 'General Comment No 15: The Position of Aliens Under the Covenant (1986)' (27 May 2008) UN Doc HRI/GEN/1/Rev.9 (Vol I), 15; Human Rights Committee 'General Comment No 29: States of Emergency (Article 4)' (31 August 2001) UN Doc CCPR/C/21/Rev.1/Add.11.

interpretation.[11] The same General Comment was invoked by the Kenyan High Court in 2006 to construe the scope of the non-discrimination principle, as well as by the Swiss Federal Supreme Court ten years earlier in finding violations of Articles 2, 14, and 26 of the ICCPR.[12] General Comment No 18 further informed the content of the ICCPR in the 2002 Canadian *Suresh* case.[13]

With regard to the Committee on Economic, Social and Cultural Rights (CESCR), General Comment No 3 was resorted to by the Constitutional Court of Peru in *Cuzco Bar Association* in 2005 for the purpose of identifying and explaining the 'principle of progressivity' as the notion applicable to the achievement of economic and social rights.[14] General Comment No 4 was invoked by the Supreme Court of British Columbia in *Victoria (City) v Adams* in 2008 in connection to Article 11(1) of the International Covenant on Economic, Social and Cultural Rights (ICESCR).[15] General Comment No 13 on the right to education was referred to by the German Federal Constitutional Court in 2013 in the course of upholding the constitutionality of general tuition fees at universities.[16] General Comment No 14 was relied upon by the High Court of Delhi in the *Mandal* case in 2010 to construe the right to health under the ICESCR ratified by India.[17]

While probably not as frequent as General Comments prepared by the Human Rights Committee and the CESCR, the opinions of other monitoring bodies likewise guide domestic judicial reasoning. For instance, the observation of the Committee on the Elimination of Discrimination against Women (CEDAW) appeared in *Bangladesh Legal Aid* in 2010, where the Bangladesh

[11] *Tsépe v Independent Electoral Commission and ors*, C of A (Civ) No 11/05 CC 135/05 (Lesotho, Court of Appeal), 12–14.

[12] *RM v Attorney-General* (2006) AHRLR 256 (KeHC); *M and Mme D v X et Chambre supérieure du Tribunal des mineurs du canton de Vaud*, BGE 122 I 109, Swiss Federal Supreme Court, Judgment of 10 April 1996, cited in 2002 ILA Report (n 5) para 55.

[13] *Suresh v Canada (Minister of Citizenship and Immigration)* 2002 SCC 1, [2002] 1 SCR 3.

[14] CESCR 'General Comment No 3: The Nature of States Parties' Obligations (Article 2 (1) of the Covenant)' (14 December 1990) UN Doc E/1991/23; *Cuzco Bar Association and ors v Congress of the Republic*, Case Nos 050-2004-A1/TC, 051-2004A1/TC, 004-2005-P1/TC, 007-2005-P1/TC, 009-2005-P1/TC, Judgment of 3 June 2005, ILDC 679 (PE 2005) (Peru, Constitutional Court) [H4].

[15] CESCR 'General Comment No 4: The Right to Adequate Housing (Article 11 (1) of the ICESCR)' (13 December 1991) UN Doc E/1992/23; *Victoria (City) v Adams* 2008 BCSC 1363 (SC British Columbia) [85]–[89].

[16] CESCR 'General Comment No 13: The Right to Education (Article 13 of the Covenant)' (8 December 1999) UN Doc E/C.12/1999/10, para 19; German Federal Constitutional Court (BVerfG), Order of the First Senate of 8 May 2013, 1 BvL 1/08, para 43.

[17] CESCR 'General Comment No 14: The Right to the Highest Attainable Standard of Health (Article 12 of the Covenant)' (11 August 2000) UN Doc E/C.12/2000/4; *Laxmi Mandal v Deen Dayal Harinagar Hospital and ors*, WP(C) Nos 8853/2008, and 10700/2009, Judgment of 4 June 2010 (High Court of Delhi) [23].

High Court referred to the position of the CAT on the absolute and non-derogable nature of the prohibition of torture.[18]

Country-specific reports or observations have also been relied upon by domestic judges in order to construe international and domestic human rights provisions. The Argentine Supreme Court, in its 2012 landmark decision *FAL* on the scope of legal abortion, took into account the Concluding Observations of the Human Rights Committee and the Report of the Committee on the Rights of the Child (CRC), including both the observations addressed to Argentina, and to other States.[19] In reinterpreting Article 86 of the Criminal Code and extending the scope of legal abortion to all cases of rape victims, the Supreme Court referred to the fact that the Human Rights Committee had 'expressed its concern' over the restrictive interpretation of Article 86 of the Argentine Criminal Code.[20] As another illustration, the Belize Supreme Court in the *Cal* case in 2007 made reference, not only to General Recommendation of the Committee on the Elimination of Racial Discrimination (CERD), but also to the country-specific Correspondence from the Chairperson of CERD to Belize's Permanent Representative to the UN in which the CERD drew attention to land privation in Belize without prior consultation of the Mayan people.[21]

As with country-specific concluding observations, findings relating to individual complaints also have received accommodating responses. For instance, in *FAL* the Argentine Supreme Court supported its interpretation by referring to the Human Rights Committee's criticism, in its Views, of Argentina for failing to ensure timely access to non-punishable abortion.[22] Likewise, the Supreme Court of Norway in *Federation of Offshore Workers Trade Unions* considered the Human Rights Committee's Views, in conjunction with the jurisprudence of the European Court of Human Rights (ECtHR) and the bodies of the International Labour Organization.[23] The German Federal Constitutional

[18] *Bangladesh Legal Aid and Services Trust and ors v Government of Bangladesh*, Writ Petition Nos 5863 of 2009, 754 of 2010, 4275 of 2010, Judgment of 8 July 2010 (Supreme Court of Bangladesh, High Court Division) [45].

[19] *F, A L s/medida autosatisfactiva*, F 259 XLVI, Judgment of 13 March 2012 (Supreme Court of Argentina) [12], [13], [26]; Human Rights Committee 'Concluding Observations: Argentina' (31 March 2010) UN Doc CCPR/C/ARG/CO/4; Human Rights Committee 'Concluding Observations: Peru' (15 November 2000) UN Doc CCPR/CO/70/PER; Human Rights Committee 'Concluding Observations: The Gambia' (12 August 2004) UN Doc CCPR/CO/75/GMB; CRC 'Concluding Observations: Argentina' (21 June 2010) UN Doc CRC/C/ARG/CO/3–4.

[20] *FAL* (n 19) [12].

[21] *Aurelio Cal and ors v Attorney-General of Belize*, Claims Nos 171 and 172 of 2007, Judgment of 18 October 2007, (2007) 71 WIR 110 (Belize, Supreme Court) [124].

[22] *FAL* (n 19) [26]; Human Rights Committee 'Views: Communication No. 1608/2007' (28 April 2011) UN Doc CCPR/C/101/D/1608/2007.

[23] *Federation of Offshore Workers Trade Unions (Oljearbeidernes Fellessammenslutning, OFS)*, Supreme Court of Norway, Rt 1997-580, cited in 2004 ILA Report (n 5) para 66.

Court cited the Views of the Human Rights Committee in holding that criminal trials in absentia were inconsistent with international law.[24] The Nepal Supreme Court in *Pant and Others* referred to the observation of the Human Rights Committee, together with ECtHR jurisprudence, in order to stress that Article 26 of the ICCPR encompasses non-discrimination on the ground of sexual orientation.[25]

The actual weight that the findings of the monitoring bodies carry in judicial interpretation varies, however. Some documents are employed in such a way that they substantively alter the outcome of judicial interpretation, while others are employed in a confirmatory manner in order to simply affirm the particular construction of human rights provisions that the courts have reached elsewhere (more akin to fair weather alignment). In the majority of cases examined, domestic courts often attribute only confirmatory value to the treaty bodies' findings.[26] In some cases, however, the treaty bodies' findings have attributed new meanings to treaty provisions, constitutional provisions, and other domestic law and brought a material difference to the outcomes. To illustrate, in a 2013 Colombian case, the Constitutional Court substantively relied upon General Comment No 15 on the ICESCR in instructing the government to guarantee the core of the right to water.[27] The Human Rights Committee's General Comment No 18 seems to have had a material impact in *Ts'epe* before Lesotho's Court of Appeal.[28] Likewise, the Human Rights Committee's concluding observations appear to be one of the key factors that defined how the Argentine Supreme Court interpreted the ICCPR and relevant provision of the criminal code in *FAL*.[29]

Finally, it must be noted that I have only examined cases where there was explicit engagement with the monitoring bodies' findings. The lack of express engagement with treaty monitoring bodies does not necessarily mean that judges have not taken into account their findings.

[24] German Federal Constitutional Court (BVerfG), Order of the Third Chamber of the Second Senate of 24 January 1991, 2 BvR 1704/90, cited in 2004 ILA Report (n 5) para 57.

[25] *Sunil Babu Pant and others v Nepal Government and others* (2007) 138 ILR 500 (unofficial English translation prepared by the Supreme Court of Nepal) (Nepal, Supreme Court, 21 December 2007) 522–23.

[26] This is an expression of simple or fair weather alignment with international law as per the ILA Final Report (n 1) para 44.

[27] Colombian Constitutional Court, Sentencia T-077/13, 14 February 2013 .

[28] *Ts'epe* (n 11).

[29] *FAL* (n 19) paras 12, 26.

2. Postures of Contestation

At the same time, domestic courts have occasionally challenged or deliberately avoided the observations addressed to individual States. Illustrative in this regard is the disagreement of Canadian and British courts with the CAT's Concluding Observations as to whether civil remedies shall be available for victims of torture committed abroad. In *Bouzari v Iran*, the Canadian courts dismissed the civil action brought by the alleged victims of torture against Iran, upholding Iran's jurisdictional immunity before Canadian courts. The applicants argued that Article 14(1) (right to redress) of the Convention against Torture[30] obliged States to provide a civil remedy for all acts of torture, including those committed outside the forum State. In rejecting this interpretation, the Ontario Superior Court endorsed the observation of the Attorney-General's expert who pointed out that the CAT had made no negative comments about the lack of a civil remedy in Canada for victims of torture committed abroad.[31] In other words, in the 2002 *Bouzari* judgment, the CAT's country-specific observations were employed in favour of the government and cited approvingly by the Court.

Interestingly, the *Bouzari* case was followed by the CAT's 2005 Concluding Observations to Canada, in which the Committee voiced its disagreement with the restricted availability of civil remedies to torture victims.[32] The Committee reiterated its concern in its 2012 Concluding Observations in a more specific manner.[33] The CAT's Observations to Canada then received criticism from the British judges in *Jones v Saudi Arabia* in 2006,[34] in which the House of Lords apparently disagreed with the CAT's interpretation and upheld sovereign immunity in civil proceedings instituted by victims of torture committed abroad. Having noted the CAT's critical remark on Canada's State report, Lord Bingham dismissed the relevance of its Observations, noting that '[w]hatever its value in influencing the trend of international thinking, the legal authority of the Committee's recommendation is slight'.[35] Lord Hoffmann found 'no

[30] Convention against Torture and Other Cruel, Inhuman or Degrading Treatment or Punishment (adopted 10 December 1984, entered into force 26 June 1987) 1465 UNTS 85 art 14(1).

[31] *Bouzari v Islamic Republic of Iran* [2002] OJ No 1624, Ontario Superior Court of Justice (1 May 2002) [51]–[52] (regarding Mr Greenwood's submission). The Court of Appeal in 2004 upheld the conclusion of the lower court, but did not refer specifically to the Committee's findings: *Bouzari v Islamic Republic of Iran* 2004 CanLII 871 (ON CA).

[32] CAT 'Conclusions and Recommendations: Canada' (7 July 2005) UN Doc CAT/C/CR/34/CAN, para 5(f).

[33] CAT 'Concluding Observations: Canada' (25 June 2012) UN Doc CAT/C/CAN/CO/6, para 15 (civil remedies and state immunity).

[34] *Jones v Saudi Arabia* [2006] UKHL 26.

[35] ibid [23] (Lord Bingham).

value' in the Committee's position.[36] This attitude is a clear example of affirmative contestation.[37]

3. Postures of Avoidance (or Indifference)

Domestic courts might also adopt strategies of avoidance towards country-specific observations, although it is methodologically difficult to identify whether judges have purposely avoided reference to the findings and, if so, why. In *Canadian Foundation for Children*, Canadian courts upheld the constitutionality of Section 43 of the Criminal Code, which justified the use by parents of reasonable corrective force against a child. In the course of constitutional interpretation, the Ontario Superior Court of Justice and the Court of Appeal referred to the CRC Report to suggest that Canada was not obliged under the Convention on the Rights of the Child to apply criminal sanctions in case of corporal punishment of children.[38] By contrast, the CRC Reports did not appear in the majority's reasoning in the subsequent decision of the Canadian Supreme Court in 2004.[39] This lack of reference to the CRC may be contrasted with Judge Arbour's dissenting opinion who drew attention to the CRC's 2003 Concluding Observations. The CRC had expressed therein its deep concern about Canada which had taken 'no action to remove section 43 of the Criminal Code'.[40] The majority seems to have displayed evasive avoidance engaging towards the CRC's critical Observations.

Likewise, in the 2011 *Asociación Solcom*,[41] a Spanish court made no reference to the Concluding Observations of the Committee on the Rights of Persons with Disabilities (CRPD), issued one month before the judgment, and in which the CRPD had addressed the specific point disputed before the court: the lack of resources to guarantee the right of persons with disabilities to

[36] ibid [57] (Lord Hoffmann).

[37] ILA Final Report (n 1) para 59.

[38] See *Canadian Foundation for Children, Youth and the Law v Canada (Attorney General)* 2000 CanLII 22397 (ON SC) (Ontario Superior Court of Justice) [98]; *Canadian Foundation for Children, Youth and the Law v Canada (Attorney-General)* (2002) 57 OR (3d) 511, 207 DLR (4th) 632 (Ontario Court of Appeal) [22]; see CRC 'Report' (18 June 1996) UN Doc A/51/41 (Supp No 41).

[39] On the other hand, the Canadian Supreme Court still referred to the reports of the Human Rights Committee: *Canadian Foundation for Children, Youth and the Law v Canada (Attorney General)* 2004 SCC 4, [2004] 1 SCR 76 [33].

[40] CRC 'Concluding Observations: Canada' (27 October 2003) UN Doc CRC/C/15/Add.215, paras 32–3. See *Canadian Foundation for Children* (n 39) [188] (Arbour J, dissenting opinion).

[41] *Asociación Solcom para la solidaridad comunitaria de las personas con diversidad funcional y la inclusión social and Asociación Asistencia para a vida independente v Conselleria de Traballo e Benestar*, Judgment of 26 October 2011, No 1090/2011, ILDC 1899 (ES 2011).

live independently and to be included in the community.[42] If the judges were at the time aware of the Concluding Observations, they might have deliberately avoided any reference to them.

Such avoidance practices must also be understood in the context of States' different attitudes in terms of their general readiness to judicially engage with treaty monitoring bodies. Broadly speaking, Canada, the UK, New Zealand, and possibly some other common law States tend to be less hesitant to employ their findings in judicial reasoning.[43] On the other hand, the 2004 Report of the ILA Committee on IHRLP records that it was unable to identify judicial references to the findings in Francophone African States, the Arab region, and some other regions. There were no identifiable judicial practices in Bulgaria, Jordan, Egypt, Saudi Arabia, Colombia, Ecuador, Chile, Argentina, Malaysia, Singapore, and Brunei.[44]

It is plausible that domestic courts may not even be aware of the existence of findings of UN human rights treaty monitoring bodies. Contrariwise, where such findings are available in the local language, and the public and civil society are familiar with the work of human rights bodies, there is stronger incentive for litigant parties to invoke the findings to support their claims. The judges' education could also affect their familiarity with human rights treaties and the findings of monitoring bodies. Where there is no requirement to study international law and human rights law for judicial qualification, this may create a disincentive for national judges to consult international treaties, and much more so General Comments, Concluding Observations, and Views.

C. Bindingness as Normative Basis for Judicial Engagement

This selective engagement by domestic courts with the findings of monitoring bodies leads me to analyse the normative basis on which judicial engagement with UN human rights treaty monitoring bodies happens. Circumstances

[42] Rafael Marín Aís, 'Analysis: ILDC 1899 (ES 2011)' in André Nollkaemper and August Reinisch (eds), Oxford Reports on International Law: International Law in Domestic Courts (OUP, 25 July 2012), paras A5–6.

[43] The reliance on 'persuasive authority' can be seen in the caselaw of the Canadian Supreme Court, for instance. See Jutta Brunnée and Stephen J Toope, 'A Hesitant Embrace: The Application of International Law by Canadian Courts' (2002) 40 Canadian Yearbook of International Law 3; H Patrick Glenn, 'Persuasive Authority' (1986) 32 McGill Law Journal 261; Graham Hudson, 'Neither Here Nor There: The (Non-)Impact of International Law on Judicial Reasoning in Canada and South Africa' (2008) 21 Canadian Journal of Law and Jurisprudence 322; Karen Knop, 'Here and There: International Law in Domestic Courts' (2000) 32 NYU Journal of International Law and Politics 501.

[44] 2004 ILA Report (n 5) para 29, fn 28.

may exist in which courts are obligated to consider the Views issued by treaty bodies. In most cases, however, judges invoke the findings of treaty bodies not out of obligation under domestic or international law, but based on their (rather subjective) persuasiveness (Section D).

1. Obligations Under Domestic Law

Domestic executive organs may be obligated under domestic law to give effect to the Views of treaty monitoring bodies in cases of individual communications and petitions. For instance, Colombian Law 288 of 5 July 1996 enabled the enforcement of awards of compensation made by international bodies, including the Human Rights Committee, under domestic law.[45] In the Czech Republic, the Ministry of Justice is responsible for coordinating the implementation of the Views of the Human Rights Committee under Act No 517/2002 Coll.[46] These domestic legislations require or facilitate the implementation by the executive of the decisions of UN human rights monitoring bodies. However, they may have little relevance in committing or enabling judicial organs to give effect to the Views, and much less to General Comments and Concluding Observations.

Where domestic laws allow for the reopening of a case, courts may give effect to the Views issued by a treaty body.[47] For instance, in Norway, a case may be reopened when an international court or the Human Rights Committee has found that the State has committed a violation.[48] But there seem to be relatively few States that have specific domestic legislation that enables courts to enforce the Views. The principle of *res judicata* is often a hurdle in that regard. In Slovakia, under an amendment to the Act on the Constitutional Court, individual communications were to be treated as individual complaints; but as this procedure was deemed contrary to the principle of *res judicata*, the amendment was repealed.[49]

In view of a limited role that domestic courts play in the case-specific responses to the Views of UN treaty monitoring bodies, the Spanish Supreme

[45] 2004 ILA Report (n 5) para 29, fn 32.

[46] Act No 517/2002 Coll on Some Measures in the System of Central State Organs, cited in 2004 ILA Report (n 5) para 29, fn 32.

[47] For detailed analysis, see Rosanne van Alebeek and André Nollkaemper, 'The Legal Status of Decisions by Human Rights Treaty Bodies in National Law' in Helen Keller and Geir Ulfstein (eds), *UN Human Rights Treaty Bodies: Law and Legitimacy* (CUP 2012). In Finland, a finding of a violation by the Human Rights Committee may create the government's obligation to pay compensation: see ibid 368.

[48] ibid 366, and fnn 41–43.

[49] 2004 ILA Report (n 5) para 40.

Court's judgment of July 2018 occupies a rather exceptional place.[50] On the basis of both domestic and international laws, the Spanish Supreme Court identified the binding character of the Views of the CEDAW at the domestic level.[51] The Supreme Court regarded the lack of specific procedures for implementing the CEDAW's Views as a breach of a Spanish constitutional mandate.[52]

2. Obligations Under International Law

a. Bindingness of the findings in substance

Under international law, States, and indirectly their courts, may be obligated to give effect to General Comments, Concluding Observations, and Views, if their substance reflects established treaty interpretation. Under Article 31(3)(b) of the Vienna Convention on the Law of Treaties (VCLT), the meaning of a treaty may develop through 'subsequent practice in the application of the treaty which establishes the agreement of the parties regarding its interpretation'.[53] The practices of monitoring bodies themselves do not constitute 'subsequent practice' for the purpose of Article 31(3)(b) VCLT. However, if a finding receives positive or supportive responses by States, or the acquiescence of States, it might be regarded as a reflection of the interpretation accepted by States parties through subsequent practice.[54] This then justifies domestic courts' references to monitoring bodies' findings.[55] That said, not all Comments, Observations, and Views, mentioned in Section B of this chapter, can be regarded as accepted treaty interpretation.

b. Bindingness of the findings in form

Additionally, it is difficult to justify judicial references to treaty bodies' findings on the basis of these documents' bindingness under international law. At the international level, the Human Rights Committee's Views and interim measures are generally considered by States as non-binding.[56] This holds true also for General Comments and Recommendations, and Concluding Observations.

[50] Judgment No 1263/2018 of 17 July 2018, ROJ: STS 2747/2018, ECLI: ES:TS:2018:2747 (Tribunal Supremo [Supreme Court], Sala de lo Contencioso-Administrativo [Contentious-Administrative Chamber], Spain).
[51] For details, see Machiko Kanetake, 'María de los Ángeles González Carreño v. Ministry of Justice' (2019) 113 AJIL 586.
[52] Judgment No 1263/2018 of 17 July 2018 (n 50) 13.
[53] Vienna Convention on the Law of Treaties (adopted 23 May 1969, entered into force 27 January 1980) 1155 UNTS 311 art 31(3)(b).
[54] See 2004 ILA Report (n 5) para 21.
[55] Eg, *R v Sin Yau-ming* (1991) 1 HKPLR 88 (Hong Kong, Court of Appeal) 107.
[56] See van Alebeek and Nollkaemper (n 47) 372–73, 385–90.

This traditionally accepted position is, however, increasingly contrasted with the Human Rights Committee's own position which stresses the normative significance of its findings.[57] And, the Human Rights Committee is not alone in suggesting that the Views and other findings are authoritative and therefore ought to be respected. The Colombian Constitutional Court in 2004 characterized the CESCR, which adopts General Comments, as the 'authorized interpreter' of the ICESCR.[58] In the *Test Trial Fund Clara Wichmann* case in 2005, a Dutch court noted that the CEDAW's General Recommendations should be considered when interpreting the Convention.[59] In the 2007 *Cal* case before the Belize Supreme Court, the judge noted that, given Belize's commitments under the CERD, the government '*should take this communication* [country-specific Correspondence] *seriously* and respond accordingly'.[60] In the aforementioned *Canadian Foundation for Children*, the Ontario Superior Court of Justice noted that the CRC 'is an important source for the interpretation of its [the Convention's] principles and standards'.[61] Nevertheless, the general basis of these, possibly case-specific, statements is still unclear, and at any rate they do not appear to claim that the Views or other findings are themselves binding.

D. Persuasiveness as Normative Basis for Judicial Engagement

A supplementary perspective on the practice of judicial engagement is offered by the concept of persuasiveness of the formally non-binding findings. In some of the cases I have examined, domestic courts explicitly or implicitly employ the notion of 'persuasiveness' as a basis for importing the monitoring bodies' findings in their judicial reasoning.

57 Eg, Human Rights Committee 'Draft GC 33' (n 3) 33.

58 Colombian Constitutional Court, Sentencia T-025/04, 22 January 2004 (unofficial English translation <www.brookings.edu>) [8.3.2] ('como intérprete autorizado del Pacto sobre la materia...').

59 *Test Trial Fund Clara Wichmann (Stichting Proefprocessenfonds Clara Wichmann) and ors v Netherlands*, District Court Judgment of 7 September 2005, (2005) HA ZA 03/3395, LJN: AU2088, ILDC 221 (NL 2005), para 3.18.

60 *Cal* (n 21) [125] (emphasis added).

61 *Canadian Foundation for Children* (2000) (n 38) [97].

1. Concept of Persuasiveness

Persuasiveness—or, in more familiar terms, the concept of 'persuasive authority'—has developed to account for inter-judicial communications. Judicial engagement with the findings of monitoring bodies is part of domestic courts' wider engagement with international or foreign instruments which do not have formal effect in the domestic legal order.[62] The concept of persuasiveness is contrasted with bindingness—or 'binding authority'—which denotes that a document carries independent obligatory force. A binding document or statement is authoritative just by virtue of its pedigree, while 'persuasive authority' stems from a document's or statement's merit.[63] Persuasiveness may potentially attach to any norms (whether domestic or international, binding or not) that are helpful in constructing the meaning and purpose of a particular domestic obligation.[64] The fact that 'persuasive authority' is not determined merely by an instrument's pedigree generally allows the judges wide discretion in selecting which documents they find persuasive.

In the cases studied, persuasiveness explicitly or implicitly has served as the basis for judicial engagement with monitoring bodies' findings. The South African High Court observed, for example, that 'General Comments have authoritative status under international law'.[65] The New Zealand Court of Appeal has found that a decision of the Human Rights Committee must be of 'considerable persuasive authority'.[66] The Dutch Administrative High Court regarded the Human Rights Committee's Views as authoritative, and noted that domestic courts could only deviate from Views if justified by weighty reasons.[67] The Belize Supreme Court in *Cal* accepted that it may regard the findings of the Inter-American Commission on Human Rights 'where appropriate and cogent, to be persuasive',[68] inasmuch as Belize was a party to the treaties monitored by the Inter-American Commission.[69] Other cases which do not

[62] For the analysis of judicial engagement with wider 'informal' international instruments, see Machiko Kanetake and André Nollkaemper, 'The Application of Informal International Instruments Before Domestic Courts' (2014) 46 The George Washington International Law Review 765.

[63] Chad Flanders, 'Toward a Theory of Persuasive Authority' (2009) 62 Oklahoma Law Review 55, 62.

[64] ibid.

[65] *Residents of Bon Vista Mansions v Southern Metropolitan Local Council* (2002) 6 BCLR 625 (High Court Witwatersrand, Local Division), cited in 2004 ILA Report (n 5) para 11. The Court invoked General Comment No 12 of the ICESCR in accounting for the duty to respect rights of access: *Residents of Bon Vista* ibid paras 17–18.

[66] *R v Goodwin (No 2)* [1993] 2 NZLR 390, cited in 2002 ILA Report (n 5) para 41, fn 52.

[67] *Appellante v de Raad van Bestuur van de Sociale Verzekeringsbank*, The Netherlands Central Appeals Tribunal, 21 July 2006, LJN: AY5560 [4.36], cited in van Alebeek and Nollkaemper (n 47) at 402, fn 199.

[68] *Cal* (n 21) [21].

[69] ibid para 22.

explicitly acknowledge persuasiveness still appear to assume it as a ground for judicial engagement. The ILA's Committee on IHRLP observed that despite the lack of binding force, committee decisions under an individual complaint procedure may still have 'considerable persuasive force' on decision-makers in domestic legal systems.[70]

2. Factors Constituting Persuasiveness

What constitutes persuasiveness is by no means clear-cut, and this highlights the weakness of the notion in terms of its concept and political underpinnings. Judges are by no means unequivocal about what factors render a monitoring body's findings persuasive, transforming them to more than mere non-binding documents. The ILA's Committee on IHRLP observed that the persuasiveness of the findings emanates from the mandate of each committee to monitor the implementation of the treaty and receive complaints, the expertise and reputation of its experts, and the legitimacy of the committee and its findings.[71]

It would seem that one of the factors that render the findings persuasive is the systemic connection between the bodies' documents and the treaties (or substantively comparable domestic law) that judges try to interpret. Namely, General Comments issued by the Human Rights Committee are institutionally connected to the ICCPR, which entrusts the Committee with interpreting the treaty provisions.[72] Such institutional connection tends to sustain the persuasiveness of the findings.

In turn, formally non-binding documents will be less persuasive if they are employed for the construction of treaties and domestic law which are not systemically tied to the documents. In *Mansouri-Rad*, the New Zealand's Refugee Status Appeals Authority noted that 'it is only appropriate that regard be had to the interpretation of those [international human rights] instruments by the "treaty bodies" set up under the instruments'.[73] The Refugee Status Appeals Authority observed that '[t]he decisions of the Human Rights Committee can be at least of *persuasive authority*'.[74] The Appeals Authority then contrasted the decisions of the human rights treaty monitoring bodies with those of the UN

[70] 2002 ILA Report (n 5) para 31.

[71] ibid para 33. See also Yuji Iwasawa, 'Domestic Application of International Law' (2016) 378 Recueil des Cours 235.

[72] See ICCPR (n 9) art 40.

[73] *Mansouri-Rad v Department of Labour*, Refugee Status Appeals Authority (2004) Refugee Appeal No 74665/03, (2005) NZAR 60 [73].

[74] ibid [73] (emphasis added).

Human Rights Commission (now the Human Rights Council) established by the UN General Assembly. According to the Appeals Authority, '[i]t is almost unnecessary to add that we do not see the UN Human Rights Commission as an appropriate point of reference, lying as it does *outside the treaty framework* earlier described'.[75] Thus in *Mansouri-Rad*, the systemic tie between a treaty and its monitoring body made it appropriate to judicially engage with the body's findings.

Another variable sustaining the persuasiveness of the findings concerns the perceived impartiality of the bodies that adopt those formally non-binding instruments. Impartiality was one of the reasons that the Privy Council, in the New Zealand case of *Tangiora*, found the Human Rights Committee's Views hard to dismiss despite the lack of binding force.[76] The Privy Council affirmed 'that a State party may find it hard to reject such findings when they are based on orderly proceedings during which the state party has had a proper opportunity to present its case'.[77] In that sense, the Views 'acquire *authority from the standing of its members and their judicial qualities of impartiality, objectivity and restraint*'.[78] Moreover, the Privy Council suggested that the functions of the Committee are adjudicative, as it makes a definitive and final ruling which is determinative of an issue that has been referred to it.[79]

This does not mean that all documents adopted by the Human Rights Committee possess the 'judicial qualities' of impartiality and objectivity. As suggested in the *Tangiora* case, the Committee's function is akin to an adjudicative body when it adopts the 'Views' in response to individuals' communications. By contrast, it has a relatively wider discretion, and thereby operates in a less adjudicatory manner, when adopting General Comments to assist States parties more generally. The Human Rights Committee operates in a less adjudicatory manner when adopting General Comments, which are designed to assist Member States more generally. The method or procedure for adopting General Comments and Recommendations varies depending on the human rights treaty bodies, despite some progress in harmonizing working methods. More fundamentally, the impartiality of the Committees' members themselves is not free from criticism. While members in principle serve in their personal capacity,[80] their close ties with their governments, whose lobbying often

[75] ibid [78] (emphasis added).
[76] *Tangiora v Wellington District Legal Services Committee* [1999] UKPC 42 (NZ).
[77] ibid [14].
[78] ibid.
[79] ibid.
[80] ICCPR (n 9) art 28(2); International Convention on the Elimination of All Forms of Racial Discrimination (adopted 21 December 1965, entered into force 4 January 1969) 660 UNTS 195 art 8(1);

conditions the members' election, may make it difficult for experts to act independently in all occasions.[81]

Conversely, where the bodies are perceived as partial and non-objective domestic judges tend to reject the reference to formally non-binding documents, adopting a strategy of contestation. In the aforementioned *Mansouri-Rad* case, New Zealand's Refugee Status Appeals Authority negated the persuasiveness of the decisions of the UN Human Rights Commission on the basis of its non-judicial, political nature. According to the Appeals Authority, 'the 52-state Commission is *highly politicised*, as witness the circumstances in which Cuba and China were successful in having the United States lose its seat in 2001'.[82]

E. Conclusion

The limited analysis of judicial decisions performed in this chapter has revealed that domestic courts have incrementally responded to the expectation of UN human rights treaty monitoring bodies that domestic organs implement their findings. Domestic courts employ General Comments and Recommendations, Concluding Observations, and Views, in order to give meaning to relevant human rights treaties which can further inform constitutional or statutory human rights provisions. At the same time, the actual modes of judicial (non-) engagement significantly vary, as shown in Section B. Given this variance, we cannot be certain whether domestic courts are generally willing to follow the observation of the International Court of Justice (ICJ) in the *Diallo* case that it '*should ascribe great weight* to the interpretation adopted by this independent body [that is, the Human Rights Committee] that was established specifically

Convention on the Elimination of All Forms of Discrimination against Women (adopted 18 December 1979, entered into force 3 September 1981) 1249 UNTS 13 and its Optional Protocol (adopted 6 October 1999, entered into force 22 December 2000) 2131 UNTS 83 art 17(1); Convention against Torture (n 30) art 17(1); Convention on the Rights of the Child (adopted 20 November 1989, entered into force 2 September 1990) 1577 UNTS 3 art 43(2); International Convention on the Protection of the Rights of All Migrant Workers and Members of their Families (adopted 18 December 1990, entered into force 1 July 2003) 2220 UNTS 3 art 72(2)(b); Convention on the Rights of Persons with Disabilities (adopted 13 December 2006, entered into force 3 May 2008) 2515 UNTS 3 art 43(3); International Convention for the Protection of All Persons from Enforced Disappearance (adopted 20 December 2006, entered into force 23 December 2010) 2716 UNTS 3 art 26(1).

[81] Jane Connors, 'An Analysis and Evaluation of the System of State Reporting' in Anne F Bayefsky (ed), *The UN Human Rights Treaty System in the 21st Century* (Brill 2000) 12 (regarding the monitoring process of State reports).

[82] *Mansouri-Rad* (n 73) [78] (emphasis added).

to supervise the application of that treaty'.[83] The limited survey of judicial decisions rather suggests that domestic judges can be accommodating, confrontational, or simply disinterested.

Looking at the normative basis of judicial engagement with treaty monitoring bodies, bindingness cannot fully account for it. Whether or not judges actually mobilize specific Comments, Observations, and Views depends partly on the persuasiveness of these documents. While the judicial decisions surveyed suggest some of the factors sustaining persuasiveness, these by no means help us in distinguishing which findings are considered persuasive and which not. The varied amenability to human rights treaty bodies can also be ascribed to how strict the separation of powers at the domestic level is. Judicial engagement with the bodies' findings given their formally non-binding character may signify judicial encroachment of the authority of legislative and executive organs, which are endowed with democratic legitimacy. Additionally, the decision of judges to invoke specific findings in their reasoning is presumably influenced by case-specific and value-laden factors. Beyond this, there are a number of sociological factors, such as general awareness of the work of UN human rights bodies, as well as the type of judicial training received, that affect judges' engagement with the outputs of UN human rights treaty monitoring bodies.

In any event, the accommodation or contestation by domestic courts of the findings has normative effects at the international level. References to such findings by domestic courts strengthen their normativity at the international level and may encourage other courts to follow suit, despite the lack of formal legal binding force. When domestic courts adopt a strategy of alignment with the findings of human rights treaty bodies this may strengthen the latter's authority, too. But the contrary is also true: judicial avoidance and contestation may undermine the normative authority of such findings, discourage other courts from adhering to them, and attenuate the presence of UN human rights treaty monitoring bodies more generally.

[83] *Ahmadou Sadio Diallo (Republic of Guinea v Democratic Republic of the Congo)* (Merits) [2010] ICJ Rep 639, 663–4 [66] (emphasis added). Also, in the *Wall* advisory opinion, the ICJ took into account the 'constant practice of the Human Rights Committee' in deciding on the extraterritorial applicability of the ICCPR: *Legal Consequences of the Construction of a Wall in the Occupied Palestinian Territory* (Advisory Opinion) [2004] ICJ Rep 136, 179 [109].

Acknowledgement:

This chapter reproduces part of the following journal article of the author: Machiko Kanetake, 'UN Human Rights Treaty Monitoring Bodies Before Domestic Courts' (2018) 67 International and Comparative Law Quarterly 201. Reprinted with permission.

16

A Paradoxical Engagement

International Investment Law and Arbitration before Domestic Courts

Andreas Kulick and Joel Dahlquist

A. Introduction: Two Paradoxes

The engagement of domestic courts with international investment law (IIL) differs to some extent from the engagement of domestic courts with other fields of international law. This is because the large majority of domestic court decisions pertaining to IIL relate to a very specific aspect of engagement with international law. They do not just deal with IIL; rather they deal with decisions of international investment tribunals. This chapter focuses primarily on domestic court decisions reviewing decisions by investment tribunals. This particularity of IIL produces two paradoxes: (1) regarding the basis of the further inquiry (first paradox); and (2) regarding the categorization of the forms of engagement identified by the International Law Association (ILA) Study Group Final Report (ILA Final Report) (second paradox). The first paradox pertains to the fact that domestic courts, at least to some extent, are placed at the controlling end of investment awards, while at the same time IIL is aimed at curbing action of the domestic sovereign, through the establishment of an international adjudicatory system beyond its influence. As for the second paradox, this study will reveal that acceptance of an arbitral award does not necessarily entail alignment with international law and its annulment does not necessarily mean contestation of international law. While we will describe the first paradox in the following, the second paradox only becomes apparent after thorough analysis of the caselaw, and thus it will be elaborated in Sections E and F.

The ILA Final Report[1] views the various forms of 'engagement' of domestic courts with international law through the lens of international law.

[1] ILA Study Group on the Principles on the Engagement of Domestic Courts with International Law, 'Final Report: Mapping the Engagement of Domestic Courts with International Law' (Johannesburg, 2016) (ILA Final Report).

The framework it establishes asks to what extent the 'traditional position', treating domestic law and court decisions as facts, has changed, shifting from 'outward-looking' towards 'inward-looking obligations'.[2] It also identifies three 'ideal types' of engagement with international law: avoidance, alignment, and contestation.[3]

This perspective captures an important facet of IIL,[4] accurately described in the Final Report:[5] IIL as—public law-type—control of the exercise of domestic public authority by international adjudication[6] with 'inward-looking' features.[7] Investment awards exercising such 'inward-looking' control vis-à-vis domestic courts' review or enforcement of (commercial) arbitral awards have discussed, inter alia, whether or not the State had encroached upon the investor's rights when its courts have overturned or not (properly) enforced a favourable arbitral award.[8]

This is, however, only one side of the coin. It merely displays the impact of investment arbitration on domestic legal systems, and not the impact of domestic litigation on IIL. Looking at this other side, three aspects comprise the aforementioned first paradox. First, IIL displays some of the typical features of international commercial arbitration, where lie its procedural roots.[9] Commercial arbitration, however, ultimately places domestic law and courts at the controlling end by, among other things, affirming their competence to set aside an award and by relying on them vis-à-vis enforcement.[10] International investment law either fully draws on these same mechanisms, for example, where the dispute is arbitrated under arbitral rules of the United Nations Commission on International Trade Law (UNCITRAL), the International

[2] ibid paras 11–12.

[3] ibid para 36.

[4] We use this term interchangeably for both the procedural and the substantive aspects of international investment law and arbitration.

[5] ILA Final Report (n 1) para 12.

[6] See Andreas Kulick, *Global Public Interest in International Investment Law* (CUP 2012) 94–99 with references.

[7] ILA Final Report (n 1) para 12.

[8] See, eg, *ATA Construction, Industrial and Trading Company v Hashemite Kingdom of Jordan*, ICSID Case No ARB/08/2, Award (18 May 2010); *Frontier Petroleum Services Ltd v Czech Republic*, UNCITRAL, Final Award (12 November 2010); *Saipem SpA v Bangladesh*, ICSID Case No ARB/05/07, Decision on Jurisdiction and Recommendation on Provisional Measures (21 March 2007) and Award (30 June 2009); *GEA Group Aktiengesellschaft v Ukraine*, ICSID Case No ARB/08/16, Award (21 March 2011); *White Industries Australia Limited v India*, UNCITRAL, Final Award (31 November 2011). Also, on this topic, the Agora 'Enhancing Commercial Arbitration – International Law Remedies For Wrongful Conduct By Domestic Courts' (2013) 29 Arbitration International 153, featuring contributions by Gabrielle Kaufmann-Kohler, William W Park, and Stephen Fietta and James Upcher.

[9] See Rudolf Dolzer and Christoph Schreuer, *Principles of International Investment Law* (2nd edn, OUP 2012) 237.

[10] See Nigel Blackaby and Constantine Partasides with Alan Redfern and Martin Hunter, *Redfern and Hunter on International Arbitration* (5th edn, OUP 2009) 441–42.

Chamber of Commerce (ICC), the Stockholm Chamber of Commerce (SCC), or the ICSID Additional Facility,[11] or at least depends on domestic courts for enforcement in case of disputes under the Convention on the Settlement of Investment Disputes between States and Nationals of Other States (ICSID Convention).[12] In other words, IIL is aimed at the international control of the exercise of domestic public authority while simultaneously—to a greater or lesser extent, depending on the forum—being subject to domestic law and domestic courts. That said, usually such control is exercised by a country different from the host State.

Second, and relatedly, the driving rationale behind the creation of the field of IIL was precisely to prevent engagement of domestic courts with foreign investments and to lift the dispute to the international plane:[13] The intricate system of bilateral investment treaties (BITs) and dispute settlement by international arbitration intended to detach the investor-State dispute from the domestic realm, precisely in order to keep the domestic courts out of the equation.[14] Yet, as mentioned above, the system's strength stems partly from its reliance on domestic courts for the enforcement of investment arbitration awards,[15] while sometimes the ultimate validity of arbitral awards is also determined by domestic courts. The paradox that domestic courts retain a certain degree of control over the dispute is somewhat alleviated by the aforementioned fact that those are usually not the courts of the host State.[16] Nonetheless, this issue creates tension vis-à-vis the supposed 'internationalization'[17] that IIL pursues.

Third, the treaty granting access to investment arbitration sometimes contains a *renvoi* to domestic law. The *Russia v Yukos* 2016 judgment of the Hague District Court is a case in point.[18] The court, reviewing the competence of the

[11] These rules allow ICSID to administer certain disputes that fall outside the scope of the Convention on the Settlement of Investment Disputes between States and Nationals of Other States (adopted 18 March 1965, entered into force 14 October 1966) 575 UNTS 159 (ICSID Convention).

[12] Cf ibid art 54.

[13] See, eg, Andrew Newcombe and Lluís Paradell, *Law and Practice of Investment Treaties* (Wolters Kluwer 2009) 28.

[14] Gus Van Harten, *Investment Treaty Arbitration and Public Law* (OUP 2007) 54–58.

[15] R Doak Bishop, 'Introduction' in R Doak Bishop (ed), *Enforcement of Arbitral Awards Against Sovereigns* (JurisNet 2009) 3–4.

[16] However, cases exist where the parties chose the host State as the seat of arbitration: eg, *Binder v Czech Republic*, UNCITRAL (*IAReporter*, 7 September 2011 and 26 March 2012) available at <http://www.iareporter.com/articles/20110907_6> and <http://www.iareporter.com/articles/20120327_1> last accessed 24 July 2023. The same occurs in the context of the now terminated North America Free Trade Agreement (NAFTA), as the treaty provided that the seat of arbitration must be in a NAFTA State (its successor treaty, the United States-Mexico-Canada Agreement (USMCA), only refers to the legal seat having to be in a New York Convention State).

[17] Kulick (n 6) 46–48.

[18] *Russia Federation v Veteran Petroleum Ltd, Russian Federation v Yukos Universal Ltd, Russian Federation v Hulley Enterprises Ltd*, The Hague District Court, Joint Cases C/09/477160/HA ZA 15-1, C/09/477162/HA ZA 15-2, C/09/481619/HA ZA 15-112, Judgment of 20 April 2016 (*Yukos*, Judgment).

tribunal in *Yukos v Russia*,[19] had to pronounce also on the question of whether the tribunal correctly found it had jurisdiction based on the provisional application of the Energy Charter Treaty (ECT), which Russia never ratified. In the reading of the Hague District Court,[20] Article 45 ECT makes the provisional application of specific treaty provisions, among which is access to investment arbitration under Article 26, conditional upon their compatibility with the domestic law of the State concerned. In other words, in this reading of Article 45 concerning the specific issue of provisional application, the ECT—and by extension, any other investment agreement with a clause similar to Article 45—would refer to domestic law as the ultimate benchmark of whether it applies provisionally under international law.

This chapter will consider these specific characteristics and tensions of IIL vis-à-vis the engagement of domestic courts with it, against the three 'ideal types' of engagement, namely avoidance, alignment, and contestation. The two main avenues for engagement discussed here are enforcement and challenge of arbitral awards before domestic courts. Intuitively, this would place enforcement decisions alongside alignment, challenges to arbitral awards alongside contestation, and decisions interpreting investment agreements somewhere between the two. Avoidance would be mostly absent in this scheme, given the active role arbitration rules allocate to domestic courts to ensure the effectiveness of IIL. Such categorization may be questionable, however, considering that court decisions that deny enforcement would be better placed in the contestation category, whereas decisions dismissing challenges would be an expression of alignment. As a first step, due to the particularity of domestic courts' engagement with IIL as described above, Sections B and C take a functional approach. They focus on the instruments chosen by the parties to the dispute and thus on the functions these instruments serve in the review of investment arbitration awards, rather than on the outcome of the decisions themselves in the individual instance. Section D will, then, look at decisions of EU courts relating to investment law and arbitration. Section E will add another layer to the inquiry and introduce the second paradox (see above), which will thereupon be further discussed in the conclusion (Section F).

[19] *Hulley Enterprises Limited (Cyprus) v Russian Federation*, UNCITRAL, PCA Case No AA226, *Yukos Universal Limited (Isle of Man) v Russian Federation*, UNCITRAL, PCA Case No AA227, *Veteran Petroleum Limited (Cyprus) v Russian Federation*, UNCITRAL, PCA Case No AA228, Interim Award (30 November 2009) and Final Award (18 July 2016) (*Yukos*, Interim Award and Award).

[20] See *Yukos*, Judgment (n 18) [5.6] et seq, annulling the UNCITRAL tribunal decision in this regard.

B. Instruments of Alignment: Enforcement and Beyond

Decisions on the enforcement of investment awards are the bread and butter of domestic courts' interaction with IIL. The backbone of the entire system, effective enforcement has been key to its success story.[21] In the terminology of the ILA Final Report, enforcement, if indeed effective, translates into 'alignment'.

This would be particularly true of decisions enforcing ICSID awards, as the ICSID Convention makes it an obligation to recognize an award as if it were a domestic court judgment, barring generally the possibility to halt or review execution.[22] While in the vast majority of cases domestic courts indeed grant *exequatur*, respondent States have tried in some instances to prevent enforcement.[23] For example, in the *CMS v Argentina* enforcement proceedings,[24] Argentina argued that Blue Ridge, the assignee of the award, could not be considered 'a party' for the purposes of Article 54(2) of the ICSID Convention, as it was not party to the arbitration proceedings. The State argued thus that Blue Ridge was prevented from seeking recognition and enforcement of the award, an argument that the Court rejected, granting Blue Ridge's petition.[25] Other attempts by respondent States to bar enforcement of ICSID awards, such as pleas of *forum non conveniens*,[26] have proved equally unavailing. Notably, however, obstacles to enforcement often arise because of State immunity,[27] which is recognized even under the ICSID Convention as an exception to the general obligation under Article 54.[28]

[21] See Van Harten (n 14) 117–19; see also Bishop (n 21) 3–4.

[22] See ICSID Convention (n 11) art 54; see also Dolzer and Schreuer (n 9) 310–11.

[23] Note again that under the ICSID Convention (n 11) art 54(1) the investor may seek enforcement in any ICSID Member State, not merely within the respondent State.

[24] *CMS Gas Transmission Company v Argentine Republic*, ICSID Case No ARB/01/8, Award (12 May 2005).

[25] *Blue Ridge Investments LLC v Argentine Republic (ICSID)* 902 F Supp 2d 367 (SDNY 2012) at 380.

[26] *Sistem Mühendislik İnşaat Sanayi Ve Ticaret Anonim Sirketi v Kyrgyz Republic and Kyrgyzaltyn JSC (ICSID)* (2012) ONSC 4351, Order of 25 July 2012 (Ontario Superior Court of Justice) (*Sistem*, Superior Court Order).

[27] Eg, *Werner Schneider, acting in his capacity as insolvency administrator of Walter Bau AG (In Liquidation) v Kingdom of Thailand (formerly Walter Bau AG (In Liquidation) v Kingdom of Thailand) (UNCITRAL)*, Decision of 30 January 2013, BGH III ZB 40/12 (German Federal Supreme Court) (*Schneider*); *Mr Franz Sedelmayer v Russian Federation (SCC)*, Order of 4 September 2008 2, BvR 2162/07 and 2 BvR 227 (German Federal Constitutional Court); see also *Mr Franz Sedelmayer v Russian Federation (SCC)*, Decision of 1 October 2009, BGH VII ZB 37/08 (German Federal Supreme Court).

[28] See ICSID Convention (n 11) art 55; and, eg, *AIG Capital Partners Inc and CJSC Tema Real Estate Company v Republic of Kazakhstan (ICSID)* [2005] EWHC 2239 (Comm) (the Court rejected the Claimant's assertion that granting immunity from enforcement deprived it of 'possessions' for the purposes of Protocol I to the European Convention on Human Rights (adopted 20 March 1953, entered into force 18 May 1954) ETS No 9 art 1, referring to Article 55 of the ICSID Convention (n 11) art 55 which explicitly allows for State immunity). However, under United States law, ICSID Convention (n 11) art 54 constitutes an exception to foreign sovereign immunity, see, eg, *Continental Casualty Company v Argentine Republic (ICSID)* 893 F Supp 2d 747 (ED Va 2012) at 750–51.

Other mechanisms that could produce/support alignment are preliminary injunctions to prevent the respondent State from acting in a way that would render moot the dispute, or orders to honour the arbitration agreement.[29]

C. Instruments of Contestation: Challenge and Beyond

In certain situations, IIL offers a formal instrument of contestation: the challenge of an arbitral award. This means that the courts of the arbitration seat may be called upon to decide whether an award must be set aside. But this comes with two important caveats: First, the majority of investment arbitrations are conducted under the ICSID Convention,[30] which in Articles 52 and 53 excludes any form of formal review of ICSID awards by domestic courts. Second, the scope of domestic courts' review for non-ICSID arbitrations, such as under UNCITRAL Rules or the ICC Rules, where a challenge is possible, is limited.

Article 34 of the UNCITRAL Model Law on International Arbitration,[31] which several States that are important arbitration hubs have endorsed in their domestic legislations,[32] inspired by the 1958 New York Convention on the Recognition and Enforcement of Foreign Arbitral Awards,[33] subjects domestic courts' competence to set aside an award to strict conditions. The same

[29] See, eg, *Sky Petroleum, Inc v Republic of Albania (UNCITRAL)*, Case No A-12-CA-023-SS (District Court, WD Texas, Austin Div), Order and Preliminary Injunction of 20 January 2012 (however, the Tirana Court of Appeal subsequently refused to recognize the United States District Court's decision, see *Sky Petroleum, Inc v Republic of Albania (UNCITRAL)*, Case No 32/1010, Decision of 1 March 2012 (Tirana Court of Appeal)); *Societe Generale de Surveillance (SGS) SA v Pakistan*, Supreme Court, Civil Appeal Nos 459/2002 and 460/2002, Judgment of 3 July 2002. In addition, Belize unsuccessfully tried to halt two UNCITRAL arbitrations by petitioning its domestic courts, see Luke Eric Peterson, 'In Lifting Injunctions Against Two Investment Treaty Arbitrations, Beliza Court of Appeal Hews to Recent Caribbean Court of Justice Ruling' (*IAReporter*, 4 November 2013) available at <https://www.iareporter.com/articles/in-lifting-injunctions-against-two-investment-treaty-arbitrations-belize-court-of-appeal-hews-to-recent-caribbean-court-of-justice-ruling/> last accessed 24 July 2023. See also on India's similar efforts, Ridhi Kabra, 'Analysis: In Latest Ruling to weigh in on Propriety of Parallel BIT Claims, a Local Court affirms Power to enjoin a Parallel Case, but sees Reason why Parallel Claims by Vodafone are not an Abuse' (*IAReporter*, 10 May 2018) available at <https://www.iareporter.com/articles/analysis-in-latest-ruling-to-weigh-in-on-propriety-of-parallel-bit-claims-a-local-court-affirms-power-to-enjoin-a-parallel-case-but-sees-reasons-why-parallel-claims-by-vodafone-are-not-an-abuse/> last accessed 24 July 2023.

[30] See UNCTAD, *World Investment Report 2020: International Production beyond the Pandemic* (UN 2020) 21.

[31] UNCITRAL Model Law on International Commercial Arbitration (1985), with amendments as adopted in 2006.

[32] See Blackaby and Partasides (n 10) 75–76. England, France, Sweden, Switzerland, and the United States have not implemented the Model Law, but have in most regards—including the rules governing set-aside proceedings—adopted legislation that is very similar to it.

[33] New York Convention on the Recognition and Enforcement of Foreign Arbitral Awards (adopted 10 June 1958, entered into force 7 June 1959) 330 UNTS 3 art V.

is broadly true for most domestic arbitration acts, including those that are not expressly based on the UNCITRAL Model Law. At the drafting of the Model Law, there was 'very wide support' for the view that international commercial awards should not be reviewed by domestic courts on their merits,[34] a position adopted in most of the jurisdictions where treaty-based arbitral awards have been challenged. There are two exceptions to this: Article 69 of the English Arbitration Act allows for a limited court review of points of English law. Additionally, for arbitrations whose seat is in the United States, the extra-statutory ground of review of 'manifest disregard of the law' applies under federal law.[35] Few challenges have been entertained so far though under either of these grounds.[36]

Besides issues of formality, such as incorrect constitution of the tribunal or a party's inability to present its case, the only permissible grounds for setting aside an award are generally: invalidity of the arbitration agreement, lack of jurisdiction or of arbitrability, and conflicts with public policy.[37] Thus, unsurprisingly, most domestic court decisions stress that the 'standard of review [...] is high' and that 'it is only in exceptional circumstances that an arbitral decision will be set aside'.[38] As The Hague District Court explained in its judgment on the *Chevron v Ecuador* award,[39] 'the court must exercise restraint. Set-aside proceedings may not be used as a disguised appeal and the general importance of an effectively operating arbitration procedure means that the civil court may only intervene in arbitral awards in significant cases'.[40] Other domestic courts have made similar statements.[41]

[34] UNCITRAL 'Report of the Working Group on International Contract Practices on the Work of Its Third Session (New York, 16–26 February 1982)' (23 March 1982) UN Doc A/CN.9/216 [107].

[35] Noah Rubins, 'Judicial Review of Investment Arbitration Awards' in Todd Weiler (ed), *Investment Law and Arbitration: Past Issues, Current Practice, Future Prospects* (Brill 2004) 369–70.

[36] An exception is the (unsuccessful) challenge against the award in *Thunderbird v Mexico*, *International Thunderbird Gaming Operations v United Mexican States* 473 F Supp 2d 80 (DDC 2007) (*Thunderbird*).

[37] See UNCITRAL Model Law (n 31) art 34(2).

[38] *Bayview Irrigation District No 11 and Others v United Mexican States (ICSID(AF))* (2008) CanLII 22120 (ON SC) (*Bayview*) [13].

[39] *Chevron Corporation (USA) and Texaco Petroleum Company (USA) v Republic of Ecuador*, UNCITRAL, PCA Case No 34877, Award (31 August 2011) (*Chevron*, Award).

[40] *Republic of Ecuador v Chevron Corporation (USA) and Texaco Petroleum Company (USA) (UNCITRAL)*, The Hague District Court, Cases Nos 386934/HA ZA 11-402 and 408948/HA ZA 11-2813, Judgment of 2 May 2012 (*Chevron*, Judgment) [4.4] (upheld by the Dutch Supreme Court by Judgment of 26 September 2014, Hoge Raad, ECLI:NL:HR:2014:2837); see also *United Mexican States v Feldman Karpa* (2005) CanLII 249 (ON CA) (*Feldman*) [37]; *Thunderbird* (n 36) 83.

[41] *RECOFI SA v Vietnam*, Swiss Federal Supreme Court, Ruling No 4A_616/2015 of 20 September 2016 (*RECOFI*), [3.1.1]; *Bayview* (n 38) [63]; *Czech Republic v CME*, Case No T 8735-01, Svea Court of Appeal, Judgment of 15 May 2003, 85 (published in English at (2003) 42 ILM 919).

On the other hand, the judgment[42] of the Supreme Court of British Columbia on the NAFTA award in *Metalclad v Mexico*[43] marks an early but noteworthy exception in this caselaw, establishing a high standard of review. Despite Canada's adoption of the UNCITRAL Model Law, and despite advocating a restrictive view in theory,[44] Justice Tysoe, on behalf of the Court, engaged in a detailed discussion of the tribunal's finding on the merits,[45] rejecting in particular the tribunal's broad view that transparency formed a distinctive part of the fair and equitable treatment standard enshrined in Article 1105 NAFTA. In his opinion, this provision rather focused on the international minimum standard of treatment, and transparency formed part of Chapter 18 of the NAFTA instead, which was not subject to investor-State dispute settlement under Article 1116.[46] Consequently, he set aside those parts of the award he considered to be incorrect.[47]

The judgment met serious criticism. Judge Brower, for example, argued that such 'heightened judicial review' ran counter to the very purpose of NAFTA's Chapter 11, which intended to provide for '*binding* arbitration of investor-state disputes, (subject to revision or *annulment* but not *appeal*)'.[48] Additionally, subsequent Canadian decisions on challenges to NAFTA awards did not follow Justice Tysoe's approach, being cautious to underline the 'high degree of deference'[49] granted to arbitral tribunals and the limits of review under Article 34 of the UNCITRAL Model Law.[50] Nonetheless, the impact of the *Metalclad* judgment on the interpretation of Article 1105 NAFTA cannot be denied. Less than three months after the decision was delivered, the NAFTA Free Trade Commission issued a Note of Interpretation on Article 1105 NAFTA that

[42] *United Mexican States v Metalclad Corporation (ICSID(AF))* (2001) BCSC 664 (CanLII) (SC British Columbia) (*Metalclad*, Judgment).

[43] *Metalclad Corporation v United Mexican States*, ICSID Case No ARB(AF)/97/1, Award (30 August 2000) (*Metalclad*, Award).

[44] *Metalclad*, Judgment (n 42) [50]–[56].

[45] ibid [56]–[105]. This was due to a very expansive interpretation of the Canadian provision equivalent to the UNCITRAL Model Law (n 31) art 34(2)(iii). In Justice Tysoe's reading, every misapplication of a NAFTA provision referred to in the dispute settlement clause of Article 1116 NAFTA would pass such threshold, thereby entitling the Court to basically reconsider the vast majority of the tribunals' substantive findings.

[46] *Metalclad*, Judgment (n 42) [61]–[75].

[47] ibid [134]–[37].

[48] Charles H Brower II, 'Investor-State Disputes Under NAFTA: The Empire Strikes Back' (2001–2002) 40 Columbia Journal of Transnational Law 43, 47 and 76 (emphases in original).

[49] *Feldman* (n 40) [37].

[50] See, eg, *United Mexican States v Cargill Inc (ICSID (AF))* (2011) ONCA 622 (*Cargill*) [27]–[53]; *Bayview* (n 38) [13], [14]; *Canada (Attorney General) v SD Myers Inc* (2004) FC 38 (CanLII); [2004] 3 FCR 368 (*SD Myers*) [33]–[42].

echoes his reasoning on the international minimum standard to some extent.[51] Moreover, later NAFTA arbitral tribunals proved rather anxious not to stretch Article 1105 too far, and in fact none of them adopted the *Metalclad* tribunal's broad findings on transparency.[52]

According to the standard of review adopted by the vast majority of domestic courts, considerations of IIL proper are mostly limited to issues of jurisdiction and to discussions on whether the award was in conflict with *ordre public*. In most cases, the latter test focuses on whether the tribunal's decision was so 'patently unreasonable' or disregarded the due process of law as to amount to a denial of justice.[53] Attempts at expanding the restrictive substantive review have been rejected by domestic courts. For example, in *Saarpapier v Poland*, the Swiss Federal Tribunal dismissed Saarpapier's argument that, since the principle that every expropriation must entail compensation formed part of the 'universal' *ordre public*, the judges should reconsider the tribunal's interpretation of the expropriation clause in the Germany-Poland BIT.[54]

On jurisdictional matters, several courts have engaged in a more extensive review than when challenges are based on other grounds. These cases have often centred on issues familiar to investment tribunals, such as whether there had been a (legal) investment[55] of an investor[56] under the terms of the applicable BIT, on the scope of seemingly restrictive arbitration clauses,[57] jurisdiction *ratione temporis*[58] and the consequences of so-called 'cooling-off' clauses.[59] In general, courts have reviewed such issues '*de novo*', that is granting

[51] NAFTA Free Trade Commission, 'Notes of Interpretation of Certain Chapter 11 Provisions' (31 July 2001) available at <http://www.sice.oas.org/tpd/nafta/Commission/CH11understanding_e.asp> last accessed 24 July 2023.

[52] This, however, might be attributed to the FTC's Note of Interpretation (ibid), instead. See, eg, *ADF Group Incorporated v United States of America*, ICSID Case No ARB(AF)/00/1, Award (6 January 2003) (*ADF*, Award) [147]; *Mondev International Limited v United States of America*, ICSID Case No ARB(AF)/99/2, Award (11 October 2002) (*Mondev*, Award) [100]–[125]; *Cargill, Inc v United Mexican States*, ICISD Case No ARB(AF)/05/02, Award (18 September 2009) [290].

[53] See, eg, *SD Myers* (n 50) [55]–[56]; *Feldman* (n 40) [66]–[69].

[54] *Saar Papier Vertriebs GmbH v Republic of Poland*, Swiss Federal Tribunal, Judgment of 1 March 2002 (*Saar Papier*) pts 2(b), (c).

[55] *SD Myers* (n 50) [62]–[70]; *Energoalians SARL (Komstroy) v Moldova*, Cour de Cassation, Chambre civile 1, Case No 16-16568, Judgment of 28 March 2018 (*Energoalians*, Cour de Cassation); *RECOFI* (n 41); *Czech Republic v Mr Pren Nreka*, Paris Court of Appeal, Record No 07/04675, Judgment of 25 September 2008.

[56] *Cem Uzan v Turkey*, Case No T 6582-16, Svea Court of Appeal, Judgment of 26 February 2018 (*Cem Uzan*); *Ukraine v Tatneft*, Paris Court of Appeal, 14/17964, 29 November 2016.

[57] *Czech Republic v European Media Venture* [2007] EWHC 2851 (Comm) (*EMV*); *GPF GP Sàrl v The Republic of Poland* [2018] EWHC 409 (Comm) (*Griffin*).

[58] *Saluka v Czech Republic*, Swiss Federal Tribunal, Judgment of 7 September 2006, pt 6.

[59] *Republic of Kazakhstan v Ascom Stati et al*, Case No T 2675-14, Svea Court of Appeal, Judgment of 9 December 2016 (*Ascom Stati*); *BG Group v Argentina*, discussed below in Section E.

very limited deference to the tribunal's determination,[60] often leading to courts independently interpreting the underlying investment treaty, as discussed below in Section E. In a number of recent cases, this has led domestic courts to set aside,[61] or partially set aside,[62] the arbitral award.

Finally, some less obvious[63] instruments of contestation should be mentioned. In particular, decisions interpreting BITs or the ICSID Convention, often by way of constitutional review, may function as an instrument to contest IIL and arbitration. For example, in *Council of Canadians et al v Canada*, the applicants challenged Canada's consent to binding investor-State arbitration under Chapter 11 of the NAFTA, arguing that NAFTA investment arbitration violated the independence and uniformity of Canada's judiciary. In their opinion, the latter's independence is encroached by the separate and independent arbitral tribunals that have final and exclusive authority to decide on matters essentially identical to those otherwise falling within the jurisdiction of Canadian courts, namely the review of governmental and administrative action.[64] The Ontario Court of Appeal rejected all these arguments. To the court, the analogy the applicants attempted to establish between domestic administrative review and investor-State arbitration was destined to fail because the rights granted to foreign investors under NAFTA were different in substance and origin to those granted to individuals under Canadian domestic law.[65] Similar matters have been raised against the investor-State dispute settlement clauses of the Canada-EU Comprehensive Economic and Trade Agreement (CETA) in a provisional application before the German Federal Constitutional Court, which the Court however dismissed unanimously.[66]

[60] For examples of express articulation of this approach, see *Republic of Ecuador v Occidental Exploration Production Co* [2007] EWCA Civ 656, [7]; *Government of the Lao People's Democratic Republic v Sanum Investments* [2015] SGHC 15, [32]–[33]; *Moldova v Energoalians*, Paris Court of Appeal, Record No 13/22531, Judgment of 12 April 2016 (*Energoalians*, Court of Appeal) 5; *Cem Uzan* (n 56) 22.

[61] See, eg, *Kyrgyz Republic v Valerie Belokon*, Paris Court of Appeal, Record No 15/01650, Judgment of 21 February 2017; *Energoalians*, Court of Appeal (n 60) (this was subsequently overturned by the Cour de Cassation, see *Energoalians*, Cour de Cassation (n 55)); *Russian Federation v ALOS 34 et al*, Case No T 9294-12, Svea Court of Appeal, Judgment of 7 June 2018.

[62] *Griffin* (n 57).

[63] Note other common procedural instruments, such as motions to stay an award, which may serve as mechanisms of 'temporary contestation'. See, eg, *Chevron*, Judgment (n 40).

[64] *Council of Canadians et al v Canada (Attorney General)* (2006) CanLII 40222 (ON CA) (*Council of Canadians*) [18], [31], [44], [46], [48], [49], [53].

[65] See, eg, ibid [45], [53]. For another example of constitutional review of investment treaties see Ecuador Constitutional Court, Dictamen No 027-10-DTI-CC, 17 August 2010 (where the Constitutional Court found that the dispute resolution clause of the China-Ecuador BIT violated the Ecuadorian constitution).

[66] *B et al v Federal Republic of Germany*, Judgment of 13 October 2016, 2 BvR 1368/16 et al (German Federal Constitutional Court).

D. European Union Law and International Investment Law before Domestic and EU Courts

In recent years, the relationship of IIL and European Union (EU) law has been increasingly discussed both by arbitral tribunals, and EU courts and EU Member States' domestic courts. EU courts have become important players in the engagement with IIL and arbitration. Moreover, domestic courts more and more have to rule on challenges to arbitral awards or their enforcement based on EU law. There are several relevant issues in this regard,[67] but we focus here on the relationship between investment arbitration and the EU dispute settlement system—Article 344 TFEU[68] being the crucial provision.

The Frankfurt Higher Regional Court in *Slovak Republic v Eureko*,[69] subsequently heard by the Court of Justice of the European Union (CJEU) as the *Achmea* case,[70] discussed in detail the competitive relationship of investment arbitration and the EU dispute settlement system.[71] In the underlying arbitration, the tribunal in *Eureko BV v Slovak Republic* had accepted jurisdiction in a dispute involving a claim under the 1991 Czechoslovakia-Netherlands BIT, to which Slovakia had succeeded upon its independence.[72] Slovakia filed a motion to set aside the award on jurisdiction before the Higher Regional Court of Frankfurt, which was the arbitration seat.[73] It argued that the decision on jurisdiction was in conflict with Article 344 TFEU, which established the

[67] Eg with regard to the Vienna Convention on the Law of Treaties (adopted 23 May 1969, entered into force 27 January 1980) 1155 UNTS 331 (VCLT) arts 30 and 59, and the Treaty on the Functioning of the European Union (2012) OJ C326/47 (TFEU) art 351. See, inter alia, Case C-205/06 *Commission v Republic of Austria* [2009] ECR I-01301; Case C-249/06 *Commission v Kingdom of Sweden* [2009] ECR I-01335; Case C-264/09 *Commission v Slovak Republic* [2011] ECR I-08065.

[68] TFEU (n 67) art 344 provides: 'Member States undertake not to submit a dispute concerning the interpretation or application of the Treaties to any method of settlement other than those provided for therein.'

[69] *Slovak Republic v Eureko BV (UNCITRAL)*, Frankfurt Higher Regional Court, Case No 26 SchH 11/10, Decision of 10 May 2012 (*Eureko*, Frankfurt Higher Regional Court). See also Jan K Schäfer and John P Gaffney, 'Intra-EU BITs: Toothless Tigers or Do They Still Bite? The OLG Frankfurt Considers the Impact of EU Law on the Investor-State Dispute Resolution Mechanism' (2013) 11 SchiedsVZ – German Arbitration Journal 68.

[70] Case C-284/16 *Slovak Republic v Achmea BV* [2018] ECLI:EU:C:2018:158 (*Achmea*).

[71] It briefly discussed VCLT (n 67) art 30 as well, see *Slovakia v Eureko*, Frankfurt Higher Regional Court (n 69) 125. The ruling has been confirmed with regard to the final award in the *Achmea (Eureko)* case by the Frankfurt Higher Regional Court in Case No 26 Sch 3/13, Decision of 18 December 2014. The CJEU's Opinion 2/13 (2014) ECLI:EU:C:2014:2454 on the accession of the EU to the European Convention on Human Rights (ETS No 5) was rendered on the same date. Hence, the Frankfurt Higher Regional Court could not take it into account in its reasoning.

[72] *Eureko BV v Slovak Republic*, UNCITRAL, PCA Case No 2008-13, Award on Jurisdiction, Arbitrability and Suspension (26 October 2010) (*Eureko*, Award on Jurisdiction).

[73] Unlike other jurisdictions, setting aside proceedings against partial awards are admissible under German arbitration law, see German Code of Civil Procedure, promulgate 5 December 2005, BGBI I S 3202 (as amended) s 1040(3).

prevalence—if not monopoly—of EU courts, above all the CJEU, to rule on matters of EU law, such as the freedom of capital transactions under Article 63 TFEU.[74]

The court rejected Slovakia's arguments, as Article 344 TFEU did not relate to disputes involving private persons, even if the respondent party was an EU Member State, as the CJEU's own caselaw showed. The potential danger that arbitral awards would violate EU law was not a sufficient reason to set aside the award. According to the court, if such violation indeed occurred, domestic courts would be in a position to consider the matter and, if necessary, file a preliminary reference to the CJEU.[75] The Frankfurt Higher Regional Court's decision was appealed to the German Supreme Court (*Bundesgerichtshof*), which ultimately did file a preliminary reference to the CJEU. In its judgment, the CJEU found that investor-State arbitration in intra-EU BITs was not compatible with the TFEU, contrary to the findings of both the Frankfurt court and the Advocate-General, who in his opinion in *Achmea* had concluded that intra-EU investment arbitration was permitted under EU law.[76] In the view of the CJEU, a treaty-based arbitral tribunal seated in a Member State on the basis of an intra-EU BIT is not a 'court or tribunal' under Article 267 TFEU, and is therefore outside the scheme envisioned by Article 344 TFEU. In short, the primacy of EU law precluded EU investors from instituting arbitration proceedings against other EU Member States based on BITs such as the Czechoslovakia-Netherlands BIT.[77]

The *Achmea* judgment is in keeping with the CJEU's restrictive view in Opinion 2/13 of 18 December 2014[78] regarding dispute settlement by international courts and tribunals established under other treaty regimes that may touch upon EU law issues. Furthermore, in an earlier opinion concerning the EU Free Trade Agreement with Singapore,[79] the CJEU had already found that an investor-State arbitration clause similar to that in the 1991 Czechoslovak-Netherlands BIT removed disputes from the jurisdiction of Member States courts in an impermissible way.[80]

The German Supreme Court subsequently implemented the preliminary ruling and annulled the arbitral award.[81] However, several questions remain

[74] *Eureko*, Frankfurt Higher Regional Court (n 69) 122–23. cf the argumentation of the applicants in *Council of Canadians* (n 64).

[75] *Eureko*, Frankfurt Higher Regional Court (n 69) 123, 124.

[76] *Achmea* (n 70) Opinion of Advocate General Wathelet [2017] ECLI:EU:C:2017:699.

[77] *Achmea* (n 70) [60].

[78] See CJEU Opinion 2/13 [81]. Particularly with regard to the Court's finding as to compatibility with TFEU (n 67) art 344 see [201]–[14].

[79] Opinion 2/15 (2017) ECLI:EU:C:2017:376 on the EU-Singapore FTA ('Singapore Opinion').

[80] ibid [292].

[81] *Slovak Republic v Achmea BV*, Decision of 31 October 2018, BGH I ZB 2/15.

open, following the CJEU's judgment. Where does the multilateral Energy Charter Treaty (ECT) fit into this scheme? What is the difference between treaty-based tribunals and contract-based tribunals?[82] Is there a difference between ICSID tribunals (which do not have a domestic seat of arbitration)[83] and non-ICSID tribunals, such as the one in *Achmea* (which have a domestic arbitration seat)? On this latter question, there is circularity in the CJEU's reasoning: if there is no role for the CJEU in 'non-ICSID' investment arbitration, how come the CJEU was approached in *Achmea* in the first place?

The *Achmea* saga demonstrates the role of domestic courts in determining pertinent questions of IIL, including its relationship to EU law. It should be noted that, at the time of writing, courts in another EU Member State—Sweden—are faced with two different set-aside attempts, where the *Achmea* judgment was invoked by the challenging States to support the contention that the respective tribunals did not have jurisdiction.[84] In one of them, the Svea Court of Appeal has requested a preliminary ruling on the role of the ECT in the scheme envisaged by the CJEU in *Achmea*, which only expressly addressed BITs between EU Member States, and in the other the Swedish Supreme Court has requested a preliminary ruling from the CJEU on the extent to which EU investors and EU Member States may agree to arbitration separate from an investment treaty.[85]

[82] According to the CJEU, commercial arbitrations 'originate in the freely expressed wishes of the parties', whereas treaty-based arbitrations 'derive from a treaty by which Member States agree to remove from the jurisdiction of their own courts, and hence from the system of judicial remedies which the second subparagraph of Article 19(1) TEU requires them to establish in the fields covered by EU law […]', *Achmea* (n 70) [55]. This reasoning is not entirely convincing, as investor-state arbitration presumably also derives from the 'freely expressed wishes of the parties', while commercial arbitration might also remove certain questions from the jurisdiction of the courts of the disputing parties.

[83] See ICSID Convention (n 11) arts 53, 54 and Section B.

[84] *Poland v PL Holdings Sárl*, Svea Court of Appeal, Case No T 8538-17 (currently on appeal; *Spain v Novenergia II Energy & Environment (SCA), SICAR B 124550*, Svea Court of Appeal, Case No T 4658-18.

[85] See Damien Charlotin, 'Post-Achmea Developments' (*IAReporter*, 22 May 2018) available at <https://www.iareporter.com/articles/post-achmea-developments-spain-wants-court-to-ask-ecj-to-rule-on-compatibility-of-energy-charter-treaty-with-eu-law-achmea-ruling-also-touted-by-poland-as-reason-for-discontinued-bit-case/> last accessed 24 July 2023; Joel Dahlquist 'Swedish Supreme Court to Send Achmea-Related Question to European Court of Justice' (*IAReporter*, 14 Dec 2019), available at <https://www.iareporter.com/articles/swedish-supreme-court-sends-achmea-related-issue-to-european-court-of-justice/> last accessed 24 July 2023; Lisa Bohmer, 'Swedish Court to Ask CJEU to Rule on Compatibility of ECT Arbitration Clause with EU Law'(*IAReporter*, 1 March 2021), available at <https://www.iareporter.com/articles/swedish-court-asks-cjeu-to-rule-on-compatibility-of-ect-arbitration-clause-with-eu-law/> last accessed 24 July 2023.

E. International Investment Arbitration, Domestic Courts, and General International Law—Towards the Second Paradox

Domestic courts, when asked to scrutinize the decisions of investment tribunals, have to engage not only with the award itself but—depending on the standard and level of review—also with the underlying general international law regime that the investment treaty framework is embedded in. Sometimes such engagement is limited to a few words on the arbitration clause contained in the treaty. But there is also a broader spectrum of engagement. On the one end, there are examples of domestic courts treating issues of treaty-based arbitration essentially as if it were based on contract, interpreting the treaty solely through a domestic law lens.[86] On the other end of the spectrum, several domestic courts have engaged extensively with international law, often including by means of treaty interpretation by the application of Articles 31–33 of the VCLT.[87]

This engagement occasionally reveals the court's view on international law more generally. This section briefly discusses two decisions that shed light on the role domestic courts grant general international law within their domestic legal orders, when acting as review authorities for international arbitration. These illustrate two different approaches towards international law in domestic courts, one involving broader engagement with international law, while the other being an example of a more defensive or sceptical approach towards the role of general international law in IIL.

In *Laos v Sanum*,[88] the Singapore High Court was seized to review the award on jurisdiction in the *Sanum v Laos* arbitration.[89] The central issue the High Court addressed in its judgment was whether the applicable BIT between Laos and the People's Republic of China (PRC) applied to Macau, where the claimant-investor was incorporated.[90] The arbitral tribunal, noting that the available factual material was rather scarce, had concluded that the BIT

[86] In addition to the *BG Group* case discussed below, see, eg, *Pren Nreka* (n 65); *Republic of Latvia v SwemBalt Aktiebolag*, Maritime and Commercial Court of Copenhagen, Case No S-22-01, Decision of 7 January 2003; *Kyrgyz Republic v Petrobart*, Case No T-5208-05, Svea Court of Appeal, Judgment of 19 January 2007.

[87] See, eg, *Ascom Stati* (n 59); *Saluka* (n 58); *EMV* (n 57); *Hungary v EDF*, Swiss Federal Supreme Court, Ruling No 4A_34/2015 of 6 October 2015.

[88] *Government of the Lao People's Democratic Republic v Sanum Investments Ltd* [2015] SGHC 15 ('*Laos v Sanum*, High Court Judgment').

[89] *Sanum Investments Limited v Lao People's Democratic Republic*, UNCITRAL, PCA Case No 2013-13, Award on Jurisdiction (13 December 2013) (*Sanum*, Award on Jurisdiction').

[90] *Laos v Sanum*, High Court Judgment (n 88) [20].

extended to Macau, and therefore it had jurisdiction.[91] Following the award and only days before Laos filed an application to set it aside for lack of jurisdiction, the governments of Laos and the PCR exchanged letters agreeing that '[the PRC-Laos BIT] ... is not applicable to [Macau] unless both China and Laos make separate arrangements in the future.'[92]

The High Court concluded that these letters represented a subsequent agreement pursuant to Article 31(3)(a) VCLT, which requires that such agreement be taken 'into account' when interpreting a treaty. Additionally, it stressed that the investor would always have to anticipate the possibility of a subsequent agreement that may influence the interpretation of the BIT under Article 31(3)(a) VCLT:[93] 'If Art 31(3)(a) is of general application to most treaties, then parties relying on the provisions of BITs would be forewarned that subsequent agreements could potentially affect the interpretation of the treaty provisions.'[94] Reviewing additional material, including other Chinese BITs and BITs of Macau, as well as several agreements and notes exchanged between Portugal and the PRC relating to Macau's hand-over, the court eventually concluded that the PRC-Laos BIT did not extend to Macau. Therefore, the arbitral tribunal lacked jurisdiction. The court noted that, in reaching this conclusion, the governmental letters played a prominent role.[95]

The court's reference to certain rules and authorities—other than the factual material—appears, however, eclectic. The High Court did not refer to the general rule of treaty interpretation as enshrined in Article 31(1) VCLT, namely interpretation according to the ordinary meaning of the text in its context and in light of its object and purpose.[96] Furthermore, the Court merely asserted that the exchange of letters between the PRC and Laos constituted a 'subsequent agreement' under Article 31(3)(a) VCLT.[97] A more in-depth analysis would have been commendable, considering in particular the work of the International Law Commission (ILC) on the matter.[98]

[91] *Sanum*, Award on Jurisdiction (n 89) [232], [300].
[92] Reply of the PRC Embassy in Vientiane, quoted in *Laos v Sanum*, High Court Judgment (n 98) [40].
[93] ibid [75]–[77].
[94] ibid [76].
[95] ibid [111].
[96] Rather, at [57] et seq, the Court jumped right at the moving treaty frontiers rule and, from [64] et seq to VCLT art 31(3)(a). Again, this is not to say that the tribunal's conclusions are wrong. For example, with regard to the ordinary meaning of 'territory' in PRC-Laos BIT art 8(1), the text of the treaty is inconclusive as the treaty does not, as many others do, contain a definition of what comprises the 'territory' of each of the contracting parties.
[97] *Laos v Sanum*, High Court Judgment (n 88) [70].
[98] Eg, the International Law Commission (ILC) Special Rapporteur's 2014 Report specifies the requirements of an 'agreement' for the purposes of VCLT art 31(3), see ILC, 'Second Report on Subsequent Agreements and Subsequent Practice in relation to Interpretation of Treaties, by Georg Nolte, Special Rapporteur' (26 March 2014) UN Doc A/CN.4/671 paras 49 et seq.

The Singapore Court of Appeal reversed the finding of the High Court, engaging extensively with general international law in its judgment.[99] Concerning the treaty's extension to Macau, it rejected the argument that the governmental notes constituted a subsequent agreement or subsequent practice under the VCLT. It underlined that giving the notes such an effect would constitute a retroactive amendment of the BIT, since nothing in the notes referred to an agreement or understanding existing before the critical date when Sanum had requested arbitration.[100]

In contrast to the Singapore courts in the *Sanum* saga, in *BG Group PLC v Republic of Argentina*[101] before the United States Supreme Court, the Court upheld the challenged award but did so in a manner which arguably did not satisfactorily engage with international law. Argentina had challenged the final award of an UNICTRAL tribunal rendered in *BG v Argentina*.[102] The tribunal had found that it had jurisdiction to hear the case, despite the fact that the claimant had not fulfilled the requirement of Article 8(2)(a) of the UK-Argentina BIT,[103] which required the observance of a grace period of 18 months of domestic litigation before instituting arbitration proceedings.[104]

The main issue before the Supreme Court was what standard of review was applicable to Article 8(2)(a) of the BIT: *de novo* review, namely full review as to the correct interpretation and application of the clause, or a standard that grants considerable deference to the decision of the arbitral tribunal? Under United States doctrine, the guiding principle is whether the issue in question pertains to the 'arbitrability' of a dispute as such, which cannot be left to arbitral tribunals but must ultimately be decided by the courts (hence, *de novo* review), or whether it pertains to 'the meaning and application of particular procedural preconditions for the use of arbitration', which is primarily for arbitral tribunals to determine (hence, deference).[105] Every matter that relates to

[99] *Sanum Investments Ltd v Government of the Lao People's Democratic Republic* [2016] SGCA 57.
[100] ibid [116].
[101] *BG Group PLC v Argentine Republic* (2014) 134 S Ct 1198 (*BG Group*, Judgment). For full disclosure, although he was never involved directly in the case, at the time of the oral pleadings as well as the rendering of the Supreme Court decision, Andreas Kulick was an associate at Cleary Gottlieb Steen & Hamilton LLP, the firm that represented Argentina before the Court. He also advised Argentina on a range of public international law matters, unrelated to this case, until he left Cleary Gottlieb in September 2014.
[102] *BG Group PLC v Argentine Republic*, UNICTRAL, Final Award (24 December 2007) (*BG Group*, Final Award).
[103] Agreement between the Government of the United Kingdom of Great Britain and Northern Ireland and the Government of the Republic of Argentina for the Promotion and Protection of Investments of 11 December 1990 (UK-Argentina BIT).
[104] *BG Group*, Final Award (n 102) [140]–[57]. The tribunal regarded the UK-Argentina BIT art 8(2)(a) as a condition of admissibility rather than one of jurisdiction.
[105] *BG Group*, Judgment (n 101) 1207.

whether or not the parties to the dispute have given their consent to arbitrate is a question of 'arbitrability'. Therefore, courts have the final say: 'The logic is simple: Because an arbitrator's authority depends on the consent of the parties, the arbitrator should not as a rule be able to decide for herself/himself whether the parties have in fact consented.'[106]

In this case, the Supreme Court majority (7-2) regarded Article 8(2)(a) of the BIT as an issue pertaining to the 'procedural preconditions for the use of arbitration', rather than to consent, and accordingly granted deference to the tribunal's determinations, accepting them as lawful.[107] In deciding this, the starting point was not the BIT and its Article 8(2)(a). Rather, the Supreme Court drew on its earlier rulings on matters of contract arbitration, determining that a clause such as Article 8(2)(a), if it were part of an arbitration contract, would not be a matter of consent: '[The clause] determines *when* the contractual duty to arbitrate arises, not *whether* there is a contractual duty to arbitrate at all'.[108] Arguing that 'a treaty is a contract, though between nations', the majority concluded that Article 8(2)(a) of the UK-Argentina BIT must be interpreted like a contract containing the same clause, thus categorizing the clause as merely procedural to which the more lenient deference standard applied.[109]

This is remarkable for a number of reasons. First, it was striking how the Court recalled caselaw that is about 100 years old to support its findings. Why a treaty concluded in 1991 and applied by an investment tribunal in 2007 should, in 2014, be interpreted according to the rules that the Supreme Court had deemed applicable to treaties in the early 1900s is a question that the majority did not even consider addressing.[110] Without going into the details of the customary rules of interpretation, as enshrined in Articles 31–33 VCLT, it is obvious that 'the intention of the contracting parties' is but one of several elements to examine under international law.[111] Given the Supreme Court's differing approach to interpretation, it is unsurprising that the Court's actual interpretation of the UK-Argentina BIT turned out as quite apodictic, if not to say simplistic.[112] Indeed, it completely overlooked the procedural framework around Article 8(2)(a): the architecture of international investment arbitration

[106] ibid Dissenting Opinion of Chief Justice Roberts, at 1221.

[107] *BG Group*, Judgment (n 101) 1212–13.

[108] ibid 1207 (emphasis in original).

[109] ibid 1208–10.

[110] Nor do the concurring and dissenting opinions of Justice Sotomayor and Chief Justice Roberts.

[111] For an overview of the rules of treaty interpretation see Anthony Aust, *Modern Treaty Law and Practice* (3rd edn, CUP 2013) 205–26.

[112] See, eg, the majority's very curt determination that 'we cannot say that the arbitrators' conclusions are barred by the [UK-Argentina BIT]', which lacked any kind of interpretation or argumentation at all.

set up by the BIT, general international law, and the UNCITRAL Arbitration Rules. One might even see in the Supreme Court equating a treaty to a domestic law contract and thus applying domestic principles of interpretation an example of a 'reactive turn to domestic law' as identified in the ILA Final Report.[113]

The *BG v Argentina* case before the Supreme Court demonstrates the complexities of evaluating domestic courts' engagement with international law along the lines of the three 'ideal types' of alignment, avoidance, and contestation.[114] The Court exercised deference towards the tribunal's award, and thus dismissed the motion to vacate it. If we take the criteria and the functional approach employed in Sections B–D, we would then have to categorize the majority's opinion on its face as an example of alignment. By contrast, the Chief Justice's opinion, which was much more in line with public international law doctrine, although it did not expressly discuss the rules of treaty interpretation, would have led to the vacating of the award, and thus to contestation. Thus, the *BG v Argentina* judgment points to a second paradox in the relationship of IIL and domestic courts, which the ILA Final Report partly accounts for[115] and will be further explained in the concluding section: Formal judicial acts such as acceptance, enforcement, and challenge do not necessarily conform to the forms of engagement identified by the Study Group, in particular alignment and contestation.

F. Conclusion

Recalling the first paradox as identified in the introduction, the review of the caselaw offers at least four 'soothing factors'. To reiterate, the paradox lies in the fact that, while IIL aims at curbing action of the domestic sovereign through an international adjudicatory system beyond the former's influence, domestic courts are at the same time accorded, at least to some extent, control over investment awards.

The first 'soothing factor' has already been mentioned: The State whose conduct is to be checked usually differs from the one exercising control over the arbitral award, as the seat of arbitration usually is not in the host State. However, this alone is an unsatisfactory response to the first paradox, since replacing one

113 ILA Final Report (n 1) para 22.
114 See Section A.
115 See ILA Final Report (n 1) paras 59–60, 65.

domestic sovereign power with another is hardly a comforting solution for an adjudication system that claims to be international in character.

The second and third factors pertain to the influence international law exerts on the exercise of control by domestic courts. Even outside the ICSID system, where review is fully internationalized and execution is more or less automatic, enforcement and challenges before domestic courts are subject to rules with—usually—international pedigree (second factor). As discussed in Sections B and C, most important arbitration laws adopt or are at least rooted in the UNCITRAL Model Law on International Arbitration. The Model Law, in turn, closely follows the rules of the New York Convention, which 167 countries have ratified and incorporated in their domestic law. Thus, eventually, it is international law, by way of a treaty, that sets the standards according to which domestic courts decide on enforcement of and challenges to investment awards.

Moreover, the restrictive scope of review established by the New York Convention, so the caselaw reveals, is taken seriously by domestic courts: In the vast majority of cases, judges have refused to expand review beyond very limited confines (third factor). For a long time, a sole noteworthy exception to this was the *Metalclad* judgment, although more awards have been set aside in the last few years.

Finally, the fourth 'soothing factor' is the observation that in most cases courts fend off attempts of host States to hamper enforcement or to set aside an award.[116]

While these four factors soothe the first paradox, the analysis has unearthed a second paradox in the relationship of IIL and domestic courts, as identified at the end of Section E: The formal avenues of engagement of domestic courts with IIL and arbitration, in particular acceptance of awards and annulment do not necessarily conform to the substantive ways of engagement, namely alignment (avoidance), and contestation. In other words, acceptance of an arbitral award does not necessarily mean alignment with international law generally, and challenge of an award does not necessarily mean contestation. What does this entail? Due to the fact that in the vast majority of cases engagement of domestic courts with international investment law effectively means engagement of domestic courts with the decisions of investment arbitration tribunals, we thus have to make a distinction here. The United States Supreme Court's decision in *BG v Argentina* illustrates this quite well. The majority upheld the

[116] See Sections B to D.

arbitral decision, although based on a reasoning that mostly ignored, if not defied, international (treaty) law.[117]

This divergence between formal and substantive ways of engagement, while less visible for most other fields,[118] is particularly prominent vis-à-vis IIL: The categorization under the ideal types of engagement with international law (alignment, avoidance, and contestation) requires, when analysing a particular case, a certain understanding of what the content of 'international law' at stake actually is. In other words, in order to assess whether a court is contesting, avoiding, or aligning with international law we must determine a certain standard of 'correctness' of application of international law. Given that reasonable people may often disagree over the interpretation and contents of an international rule or principle, we should not consider 'international law' as a monolith[119]—which would usually just lead us to test whether the domestic court aligns, contests, or avoids what *we* deem the correct content or application of international law. Rather, we suggest using a standard that must exercise deference to domestic courts' engagement with international law. Such deference must be exercised if, pursuant to the *lege artis* application of the relevant rules and principles of international law and secondary sources such as judgments and scholarship, domestic courts arrive at a reasonable interpretation of international law.

What is a reasonable interpretation for present purposes, namely when domestic courts review arbitral awards? The experience so far shows that domestic courts have adopted considerably different approaches towards the role of international law when treaty-based awards have been challenged at the seat of arbitration.

When evaluating the engagement with international law of domestic courts reviewing arbitral awards, the analysis must be two-tiered: first, with respect to the engagement with the international arbitral award; second, with respect to the substantive international law issue. Therefore, first, it must be enquired whether the domestic court upholds or dismisses the award (formal form of engagement); second, and following, we must look at the manner in which the domestic court employs (or does not employ) international law in order to reach its decision (substantive form of engagement). In this second substantive form of engagement, we suggest using a 'three-dimensional' evaluation. Such evaluation looks at three factors: (1) *Length*, namely how long is the actual

[117] See Section E.

[118] However, the ILA Final Report (n 1) notes some further similar instances in its paras 60 and 65.

[119] See also ibid para 3.

analysis dealing with international law; (2) *breadth*, namely has the domestic court made serious effort to take into account the relevant rules and principles of international law; and (3) *depth*, namely has the domestic court applied the rules and principles of international law *de lege artis* and considered the relevant caselaw, scholarship and other pertinent material.[120] The importance of the three factors increases from length to depth, as length alone is hardly telling. A short judgment may be of much better quality than a long-winded one. Nonetheless, a short discussion of matters of international law may often also lack in breadth and depth. However, both length and breadth still look at formal aspects of a domestic court's engagement with international law. Therefore, depth, as the third factor, enquires whether the domestic court engages with the substance of the international law question at issue. If the court's reasoning is rooted in a reasonable argument developed from a *lege artis* application of the relevant rules and principles of international law, it must be granted deference. This means that the three factors are not necessarily cumulative. If depth is high, both length and breadth can be low. However, if it is doubtful that the depth requirement is fully met, the two other factors—high length and/or high breadth—may tip the balance towards deference to the domestic court's engagement with international law.

Acknowledgement and Note

Andreas Kulick would like to thank Sam Steinbock (J.D. '14 (NYU)) and Paula Lobeck, Esq. for their able assistance in preparing an earlier version of this study. This study was last updated in the summer of 2018 and thus does not take into account the developments in domestic court practice after this, including the additional decisions in the *Yukos* saga. The positions taken in this contribution do not represent those of the institutions that the authors are affiliated with, nor of their clients.

[120] Eventually, however, an overall assessment that will have to take the final outcome of the domestic court's decision into account will be unavoidable.

17

Engagement of Domestic Courts with International Humanitarian Law

Sharon Weill

A. Introduction

This chapter, which is based on a larger research project,[1] examines how domestic courts engage with international humanitarian law (IHL), and identifies the following strategies of engagement. First, domestic courts may misuse or even distort the law in order to legitimize an illegal action of the State. Second, for policy considerations, they may avoid exercising jurisdiction over a case. Third, domestic courts may defer for their decision back to the political branches of government. Fourth, they may normatively apply the law, namely having a (limited) margin of appreciation while interpreting the law or establishing the facts. Fifth, pursuing an activist application of the law, domestic courts may attempt to harmonize their own (contradicting) domestic law with international law, in cases in which they are not explicitly empowered to do so, adopting strategies of alignment with international law. And, finally, they may develop the law and deliver judgments that go beyond the positive requirements of IHL.

Before discussing these strategies of engagement, two preliminary remarks shall be made. First, IHL norms have been largely endorsed at a domestic level through the obligations contained in the Geneva Conventions[2] and the Rome Statute of the International Criminal Court (ICC Statute)[3]. The difficulty in

[1] Sharon Weill, *The Role of National Courts in Applying International Humanitarian Law* (OUP 2014).

[2] Geneva Convention (I) for the Amelioration of the Condition of the Wounded and Sick in Armed Forces in the Field (adopted 12 August 1949, entered into force 21 October 1950) 75 UNTS 31; Geneva Convention (II) for the Amelioration of the Wounded, Sick and Shipwrecked Members of Armed Forces at Sea (adopted 12 August 1949, entered into force 21 October 1950) 75 UNTS 85; Geneva Convention (III) Relative to the Treatment of Prisoners of War (adopted 12 August 1949, entered into force 21 October 1950) 75 UNTS 135; Geneva Convention (IV) Relative to the Protection of Civilian Persons in Time of War (adopted 12 August 1949, entered into force 21 October 1950) 75 UNTS 287 (Fourth Geneva Convention).

[3] (adopted on 17 July 1998, entered into force 1 July 2002) 2187 UNTS 3.

applying IHL in most cases relates to the political obstacles that courts may face while engaging with these laws. The conduct of war has been traditionally the exclusive prerogative of the executive and its professional agencies, which generally conceal information from the public domain. This prevents the effective crystallization of public opinion, impairs the public's ability to influence decision-making, and weakens public demand for judicial scrutiny over armed conflict issues. The combination of these and other socio-psychological factors that favour unity and support for the State, all of which typically emerge in times of conflict, lead to a weakening of the checks and balances of a democratic system, including the oversight of the government by the judiciary. Thus, the engagement of domestic courts with IHL is complex and depends on courts' institutional position within their own governance structure.

Second, the International Law Association (ILA) Study Group Final Report (ILA Final Report) refers to a distinction between what domestic courts 'say' and 'what they are actually doing' when engaging with international law.[4] As far as it concerns IHL, it seems that what courts 'do' and 'say' have both a major impact on the enforcement process.[5] The following sections address the engagement strategies in turn.

B. Misuse of the Law—the Apologist Role of Courts

One of the functions of domestic courts within a democratic system is the granting of legitimacy to the government and its policies. Studies from the fields of sociology of law and political science show that States need to rely on courts as a legitimizing agent.[6] According to Cotterrell, courts have been accorded competence to exercise judicial review over the political branches and the level of independence required to safeguard the judiciary's authority in the eyes of the public, precisely in order to provide this legitimating effect.[7] Shamir has shown that courts, in order to legitimize State policies, must first secure

[4] ILA Study Group on Principles on the Engagement of Domestic Courts with International Law, 'Final Report: Mapping the Engagement of Domestic Courts with International Law' (Johannesburg, 2016) (ILA Final Report) para 40.

[5] See, eg, the *Abassi* case discussed below: the fact that the British court said in 2002 that the situation in Guantanamo amounted to a 'legal black hole' was of major importance at that time, even if the court did not otherwise offer substantive relief to the claimant. See the discussion in Section D.

[6] Roger Cotterrell, *The Sociology of Law* (Butterworths 1984) 234, 245; Martin Shapiro, *Courts: A Comparative and Political Analysis* (University of Chicago Press 1981) 17–28, 297; David D Caron, 'Towards A Political Theory of International Courts and Tribunals' (2007) 24 Berkeley Journal of International Law 401, 407.

[7] Cotterrell (n 6).

their own legitimacy as being independent.[8] They do so through rare landmark cases in which they rule against the interests of the State. These exceptional decisions are usually not significant for their merits, as their impact on the ground is often negligible, but rather for the reinforcement of the legitimacy of courts, and the attribution of the necessary semblance of independence. After establishing their own legitimacy as an institution that is seen as independent from any political interests, they can then be used to legitimate State action in most of the other cases.

Against this background we can observe that domestic courts may misuse IHL or distort the law, in order to legitimize their executive's illegal acts and policies. A good illustration for this is the Israeli High Court of Justice (HCJ) and its interpretation of Article 43 of the 1907 Hague Regulations[9]. In 1972, the HCJ ruled that new laws and long-term changes can be introduced in occupied territories by the occupying power for two reasons: the security needs of the Occupying Power (security consideration), or the welfare of the local population (humanitarian consideration).[10] In the same year, it further ruled that the residents of Kiryat Arba [a settlement] should be regarded as having been added to the local population. The court ruled so despite the fact that the transfer of the occupier's own population into an occupied territory is illegal.[11] Consequently, the 'humanitarian consideration' of Article 43 became a mechanism to protect the interests of the occupiers and not just the interests of the occupied population, as it was originally designed and intended to do. This ruling, in which the HCJ followed a strategy of (local) affirmative

[8] Ronen Shamir, 'Landmark Cases and the Reproduction of Legitimacy: The Case of Israel's High Court of Justice' (1990) 24 Law and Society Review 781, 782–83. See, also, Shapiro (n 6) 124. According to Benvenisti, courts within a State's democratic system are required to balance these two conflicting vectors: the institutional necessity of any government to rely on the courts as a legitimizing agent, and the need for the courts to be seen as independent. Eyal Benvenisti, 'United We Stand: National Courts Reviewing Counterterrorism Measures' in Andrea Bianchi and Alexis Keller (eds), *Counterterrorism: Democracy's Challenge* (Hart Publishing 2008) 275.

[9] Regulations Respecting the Laws and Customs of War on Land, annex to Convention (IV) Respecting the Laws and Customs of War on Land (adopted 18 October 1907, entered into force 26 January 1910) 205 CTS 277 (Hague Regulations) art 43: 'The authority of the legitimate power having in fact passed into the hands of the occupant, the latter shall take all the measures in his power to restore, and ensure, as far as possible, public order and safety, while respecting, unless absolutely prevented, the laws in force in the country.'

[10] This interpretation is based on a famous quotation by Professor Dinstein, see Yoram Dinstein, 'The Legislative Power in Administered Territories' (1972) 2 Tel Aviv University Law Review 505, 509, cited in all cases, in which the High Court of Justice (HCJ) applied the Hague Regulations (n 9) art 43. See, eg, HCJ 256/72 *Electricity Company for Jerusalem District v Minister of Defense* (1972) 27(1) PD 124; HCJ 7957/04 *Mara'abe et al v Israel Prime Minister et al* (2005) 60(2) PD 477 [18]. With this interpretation, the HCJ substituted the actual wording of Article 43, which imposes the obligation 'to restore, and ensure, as far as possible, public order and safety [*l'ordre et la vie public*], while respecting, unless absolutely prevented,' the local law.

[11] Fourth Geneva Convention (n 2) art 49(6).

contestation of IHL,[12] provided for the first time a legal basis to administer the illegal presence of the settlers in the Occupied Palestinian Territories (OPT). Since then, in the extensive jurisprudence of the HCJ, the 'local population' or the 'population of the region' has been constantly referred to as including the Jewish settlers. This interpretation has two implications. First, the equilibrium of Article 43, which balances humanitarian needs (of the occupied people) with security considerations (of the occupying forces), shifts in favour of the occupier and its population. The interests of the original local population in the OPT are now restricted not only by the endless security concerns of the Israeli army and the State of Israel, but also for the well-being of the Jewish settlers. Second, and more far-reaching, in 1972 the HCJ provided, as mentioned above, the State with a legal tool to administer the settlers. The State was given the authority, through the arm of the military commander, to issue the legislation required to provide the settlers with an Israeli environment within the OPT, in the form of military orders. By ignoring the illegality of the settlements under international law, and in ruling that the settlers are part of the local population for the purposes of Article 43, the HCJ subjected them to the regime of Article 43, which authorizes the introduction of military legislation 'for the benefit of the local population'. This legislation could be implemented without any need to officially annex the territory (and, more critically, its native people) in order to facilitate the lives of Israeli settlers there. Instead, the HCJ has enabled this to be done through IHL, via military orders. Such enactments have been used to address the everyday needs of Israeli settlers over the following 40 years, to the present day.

Koskenniemi observed a structural bias within the international legal order.[13] This observation also seems to be valid for domestic courts that apply IHL. The inherent partiality of domestic judges is related to the combination of a number of factors that influence their willingness to serve their State's national interests while engaging with IHL. First, the subjective default orientation of the judge tends to be to defend and favour her State's national interest. This is especially true in times of armed conflict. Courts are State institutions—they consist of judges who are citizens of the State, and who therefore share the same sociological and psychological mindset.[14] Second, when two parties

[12] See ILA Final Report (n 4) paras 58, 65.

[13] 'Out of any number of equally "possible" choices, some choices – typically conservative or status quo oriented choices – are methodologically privileged in the relevant institutions.' Martti Koskenniemi, *From Apology to Utopia: The Structure of International Legal Argument* (CUP 2006) 607. See also Duncan Kennedy, *A Critique of Adjudication {fin de siècle}* (Harvard UP 1997) 59–60.

[14] Brian Leiter, 'American Legal Realism' in Dennis M Patterson (ed), *A Companion to Philosophy of Law and Legal Theory* (2nd edn, Blackwell 2010) 249. See, also, José J Toharia, 'Judges' in James D

fall into a conflict that they cannot resolve between themselves, it is natural for them to resort to a third party for its resolution. This is the prototype triadic structure of courts (namely, two disputing parties and a third-party acting as decision-maker). The condition for this structure to be legitimate is for the decision-maker to be perceived as independent and impartial vis-à-vis the two conflicting parties. As the judge is a State agent, in cases where the State is party to the proceedings (and to the armed conflict from which these stem), the triadic structure is necessarily weakened, as the other party may perceive the third party as an ally of its adversary. Presumptions, the burden of proof, and other general rules may serve as legal tools to mask this structural bias through factual determination. In many legal systems, despite the complexity of establishing the facts in IHL cases (in which the State usually possesses exclusive information, and has all the necessary resources to invest, already giving it an advantage over its adversary), additional presumptions are granted in favour of the State, further weakening the triadic structure. The general presumptions of honesty, good faith, and integrity afforded to State officials assume that the authorities' factual claims are true, resulting in their version of the facts being given special weight. Moreover, it becomes extremely difficult to prove that the authorities' decision was arbitrary, as the judges' position is that the judiciary does not have the required expertise on military matters, which prevents courts from intervening in military professionals' assessments. This means that where State authorities claim that they were guided by reasonable considerations, their rationale will generally be upheld by domestic courts. Finally, the complex political relations between the States involved in an IHL case often lead to a selective enforcement of the law that depends on the nationality of the victim and the identity of the responsible State or individual.[15]

C. The Use of Avoidance Doctrines

Given that political objectives may be in certain situations irresistible, like during ongoing hostilities, domestic judges have developed avoidance techniques when engaging with IHL.[16] These permit judges to refrain from

Wright (ed), *International Encyclopedia of the Social and Behavioral Sciences* (2nd edn, Elsevier 2015) 879–84.

[15] Weill (n 1) ch 1.

[16] Eyal Benvenisti, 'Judicial Misgivings Regarding the Application of International Norms: An Analysis of Attitudes of National Courts' (1993) 4 EJIL 183.

exercising competence despite jurisdiction being established, shielding States from judicial scrutiny before their own domestic courts.[17] By avoiding to adjudicate a case and engage with IHL, through the use of doctrines developed by judges such as the act of State doctrine, the principle of non-justiciability, or the political question doctrine, the legal question remains outside the realm of justice and is left to the political arena.[18] Recourse to avoidance doctrines may be justified in light of the difficulty to assess evidence in foreign affairs cases, and to apply legal standards on policy questions, as well as the question of judges' expertise in these matters, and the institutional fear of judges that a decision will be ignored by the executive.[19] However, these decisions usually serve political goals, which are not always made public. Courts avoid or adjudicate cases in a way that corresponds to their relations with the government, and the degree of their independence vis-à-vis the political branches. The willingness to exercise competence differs from jurisdiction to jurisdiction, and is often not related to the legal question itself; because, as shown by the following examples, while in one jurisdiction an issue is not considered justiciable, in another it is.[20]

1. The *United States Targeted Killings* Case

In *Al-Aulaqi v Obama* (2010), a case that challenged President Obama's decision to authorize the targeted killing of a United States citizen in Yemen, the United States District Court for the District of Columbia addressed the question of justiciability in the context of targeted killings. The United States District Court of Columbia dismissed the case on the grounds that the father of Al-Aulaqi lacked standing, and that the claims were political questions and therefore not justiciable. The court held that the questions posed required 'expertise beyond the capacity of the Judiciary', the need for 'unquestioning adherence to a political decision by the Executive', and an assessment of 'strategic choices directing the nation's foreign affairs [that] are constitutionally committed to the political branches'.[21] Ruling that it is a non-justiciable political

[17] Louis Henkin, 'Is There a 'Political Question' Doctrine?' (1976) 85 Yale Law Journal 599. These can also be conceptualized as 'blunting techniques', as discussed in the ILA Final Report (n 4) paras 21, 41.

[18] In such cases, avoidance can be considered affirmative or professed. See ILA Final Report (n 4) para 41.

[19] Thomas M Franck, *Political Questions/Judicial Answers: Does the Rule of Law Apply to Foreign Affairs?* (Princeton UP 1992) 45–60.

[20] For further analysis, see Sharon Weill, 'Reducing the Security Gap through National Courts: Targeted Killings as a Case Study' (2016) 21 Journal of Conflict and Security Law 1, 49–67.

[21] *Al-Aulaqi v Obama*, 727 F Supp 2d 1 (DDC 2010) 76–77 (*US Targeted Killing* case). See also ibid 80:

question, the court left outside the realm of judicial review the question of the legality of the targeted killing of an American citizen, whose family alleged a violation of his right to life protected by the constitution. Even the court itself felt uneasy with the result: '[I]t does not appear that any court has ever – on political question doctrine grounds – refused to hear a United States citizen's claim that his personal constitutional rights have been violated as a result of United States government action taken abroad.'[22] Perhaps, as this case involved politically sensitive and complex questions, institutionally a first instance court could not decide otherwise. While it was ready to acknowledge that it is a 'drastic measure' for the United States to employ lethal force against one of its own citizens abroad, even if that citizen is an active member of a terrorist group, it only expressed its discontentment with its own judgment:

> To be sure, this Court recognizes the somewhat unsettling nature of its conclusion – that there are circumstances in which the Executive's unilateral decision to kill a US citizen overseas is 'constitutionally committed to the political branches' and judicially unreviewable.[23]

2. The *Israeli Targeted Killings* Case

The Israeli HCJ has responded differently to the question of justiciability of targeted killings. In 2000, Israel made public a policy of 'targeted killings' of alleged terrorists in the OPT. The legality of this policy was then challenged before the HCJ in 2002. The petitioners submitted that close to 300 members of alleged terrorist organizations had been killed by targeted killings and approximately 150 civilians who were close to the location had also been killed during those acts. Hundreds of others had been wounded. The petitioners claimed that this policy was in violation of IHL, notably the principle of distinction and the requirement of direct participation in hostilities while targeting civilians.[24]

> Because decision-making in the realm of military and foreign affairs is textually committed to the political branches, and because courts are functionally ill-equipped to make the types of complex policy judgments that would be required to adjudicate the merits of plaintiff's claims, the Court finds that the political question doctrine bars judicial resolution of this case.

[22] ibid 74.
[23] ibid 78.
[24] HCJ 769/02 *The Public Committee against Torture in Israel v Government of Israel* (2006) 2006(4) Tak-El3958 [1].

In the *Targeted Killings* ruling, President Barak, in one of his last rulings, discussed in length the role of the non-justiciability doctrine in the Israeli legal system and rejected the corresponding claims. The first ground for rejection was that the Israeli HCJ tends not to apply the non-justiciability doctrine where it might prevent review over basic rights, such as the right to life.[25] Moreover, the court found that, although the judgment was likely to have political or military implications, the question concerning the lawfulness of the 'State policy of preventive strikes which cause the death of terrorists and at times of nearby innocent civilians' was a question of legal character.[26]

Interestingly, the reasoning of the courts in the Israeli and the United States decision respectively could have led to opposite results, as in the United States case the claim involved an allegation of a violation of a United States citizen's constitutional rights, whereas in Israel the case was challenging a policy of general nature, and did not concern a concrete case. Notably, in an earlier case, such a general policy was ruled to be non-justiciable, when the HCJ was dealing with the general nature of the illegality of settlements.[27] Yet, their decisions reflect their different attitudes in adjudicating conduct of hostilities cases and their internal institutional policy on this matter, leading to differences in their engagement with IHL.

D. Deference to the Executive

In recent years, a growing trend of exercise of judicial review over 'forbidden areas', traditionally avoided, can be observed. Domestic courts have developed a nuanced and gradual way to address such matters, in the form of an open dialogue with the legislative and executive branches, through the use of the deference technique.[28] Accordingly, while courts are increasingly willing to exercise their competence over questions of IHL, they are still reluctant to overturn a decision by the executive on the merits, and tend to show significant deference to the latter to determine appropriate remedies in case of violations. This trend is illustrated well by the Guantanamo cases before the United Kingdom, United

[25] ibid [48]–[49].

[26] ibid [51]. For a discussion of how the HCJ engaged with IHL in the merits see, Antonio Cassese, 'On Some Merits of the Israeli Judgment on Targeted Killings' (2007) 5 Journal of International Criminal Justice 339.

[27] HCJ 4481/91 *Bargil, CEO of the 'Peace Now' Movement v Government of Israel* (1993) 47(4) PD 210.

[28] Benvenisti (n 8) 257.

States, and Canadian Supreme courts.[29] The following example focuses on the United Kingdom.

Rendered in 2002, the *Abbasi* case was amongst the first 'war on terror' cases dealt with by a court of a United States ally State. Abbasi, a British national, was captured in January 2002 by United States forces in Afghanistan during the armed conflict there and was transferred to Guantanamo Bay. Abbasi claimed that his fundamental right not to be arbitrarily detained was being infringed, and that his State owed him a duty under English public law to take positive steps to redress this violation. He therefore sought judicial review over the United Kingdom's decision not to afford him diplomatic protection, and asked the courts to compel the United Kingdom foreign office to make representations on his behalf to the United States. At the time of the proceedings, he had been held captive for eight months without access to a court or any other form of tribunal, or even to a lawyer.

The first non-justiciability claim raised by the UK Government was that English courts should not examine the legality of action taken by a foreign sovereign State—in this case the legality of the detention of prisoners at Guantanamo. The claim was not justiciable as 'for the court to rule on that assertion would be contrary to comity and to the principle of State immunity'.[30] This argument was firmly rejected by the court:

> Albeit that caution must be exercised by this court when faced with an allegation that a foreign state is in breach of its international obligations, this court does not need the statutory context in order to be free to express a view in relation to what it conceives to be a clear breach of international law, particularly in the context of human rights.[31]

The second non-justiciability claim was that the decision not to grant diplomatic protection was based on foreign policy considerations entirely confined to the political branch.[32] This claim was also rejected by the court on the grounds that the law of judicial review had developed and included 'the invasion of areas previously immune from review, such as the exercise of the prerogative'. In this context, the court stated that the issue of justiciability depends, not on general principle, but on the subject-matter and suitability of a

[29] See, eg, *Hamdan v Rumsfeld* 548 US 557 (2006); *Canada (Justice) v Khadr* [2008] 2 SCR 125, 2008 SCC 28. For further examples and discussion, see Weill (n 1) 117–34.

[30] *R (Abbasi) v Secretary of State for Foreign and Commonwealth Affairs* [2002] EWCA Civ 1598 (CA).

[31] ibid [57].

[32] ibid [68]–[106].

particular case: 'It is not an answer to a claim for judicial review to say that the source of the power of the Foreign Office is the prerogative. It is the subject matter that is determinative.'[33] Here, the citizen's legitimate expectation that his request will be considered, and that in that consideration all relevant factors will be thrown into the balance, can be reviewed by the court.

On the merits, however, the court was less affirmative, deferring entirely to the executive's judgment: '[W]hether to make any representations in a particular case, and if so in what form, is left entirely to the discretion of the Secretary of State.'[34] And with regard to the right of *habeas corpus*, the court declared that it can offer no direct remedy as 'the United States Government is not before the court, and no order of this court would be binding upon it', and that the respondent in this case, the UK, 'ha[d] no direct responsibility for the detention.'[35] While the decision was entirely deferred to the State by granting the latter a very broad margin of discretion, at the same time, the court openly questioned the legality of the detention in Guantanamo in what was, at that time, an unprecedented manner:

> In apparent contravention of fundamental principles recognised by both jurisdictions and by international law, Mr Abbasi is at present arbitrarily detained in a 'legal black-hole' ... What appears to us to be objectionable is that Mr Abbasi should be subject to indefinite detention in territory over which the United States has exclusive control with no opportunity to challenge the legitimacy of his detention before any court or tribunal.[36]

Moreover, the court directly addressed United States courts, in a remarkable attempt to dialogue and guide the American judges, who were supposed to rule on the right of habeas corpus of British citizens detained in Guantanamo:

> On the face of it we find surprising the proposition that the writ of the United States courts does not run in respect of individuals held by the government ... It is important to record that the position may change when the appellate courts in the United States consider the matter.[37]

[33] ibid [106].
[34] ibid [32].
[35] ibid [67].
[36] ibid [64], [66].
[37] ibid [15], [66]. See also ibid [18]: 'There have been widespread expressions of concern, both within and outside the United States, in respect of the stand taken by the United States government in cases such as *Hamdi*.'

Even though the litigation did not succeed, one shall recognize that the UK Court of Appeal went far beyond a prudent line in declaring that Abbasi was arbitrarily detained and in labelling Guantanamo Bay a 'legal black-hole'.[38] Although the court proved to be still reluctant to intervene on the merits and overturn the decision of the executive branch, once it has decided to exercise its competence and reject the application of avoidance doctrines, the results on the merits in similar cases may differ in the future. Second, the decision not to avoid judicial review in this case allowed the English court, if not to render a remedy on the merits, to engage in an audacious judicial dialogue with United States courts on the policy of detention in Guantanamo Bay during the early days of the 'war on terror'. By January 2005, following diplomatic pressure, Mr Abbasi and the three other British citizens still detained at Guantanamo were transferred to UK custody. It can reasonably be assumed that the *Abbasi* case was among the factors that influenced that decision. Therefore, also indirect statements and *obiter dicta* may have an important influence on the executive.

E. Normative Application of the Law: Alignment with International Humanitarian Law

In their normative role, domestic courts take an assertive role, apply IHL and offer protection against governmental abuse of power in accordance with the principle of separation of powers, as empowered by domestic law. An interesting example of such attitude is the limiting role performed by United States courts when reviewing on appeal the cases prosecuted at the military commissions at Guantánamo Bay.[39]

According to United States federal jurisprudence, military courts have competence to try non-nationals for violations of the international law of war.[40] While a number of persons were charged for material support of terrorism before the military commissions, the United States Court of Appeals for the District of Columbia ruled in 2012 in *Hamdan v United States* (*Hamdan*) that material support of terrorism was not proscribed as a war crime by

[38] ibid [64].

[39] For an account of the criminal trials at Guantanamo Bay, based on field research see: Sharon Weill and Mitch Robinson, 'Military Courts and Terrorism: The 9/11 Trial before the Guantanamo Bay Military Jurisdiction' in Ben Saul (ed), *Research Handbook on International Law and Terrorism* (Edward Elgar 2020).

[40] See the United States Supreme Court jurisprudence in *Ex Parte Quirin*, where the Supreme Court determined the competence of the military commission and ruled that enemy belligerents may be tried for violations of the 'law of war', *Ex Parte Quirin* 317 US 1 (1942).

international law. Thus, the military commissions lacked competence to try this offence.[41] The significance of the *Hamdan* ruling is that if conduct only violates domestic United States law and not international law, then it can only be prosecuted in a civilian court, not a military tribunal. As a consequence, the charges and convictions for providing material support to terrorism against Noor Uthman Muhammed and David Hicks were also vacated—although at that time the defendants had all already been set free.[42] A similar case was decided by the same Court of Appeals in the *al-Bahlul* case in June 2015 in the context of the charge of 'conspiracy', another cornerstone offence used in most of the ongoing and past Guantánamo Bay prosecutions. Judge Tatel of the Court of Appeals explicitly expressed her position on the court's role as guardian of the rule of law:

> Despite the government's protestations this court's holding will not 'inappropriately restrict' the nation' s ability to ensure that those who conspire to commit terrorism are appropriately punished. After all, the government can always fall back on the apparatus it has used to try federal crimes for more than two centuries: the federal courts.[43]

Several criteria may reinforce the authority of courts and legitimate their normative role and produce alignment with international law while engaging with IHL. The duration of the conflict, the timing of the review and the length of time that has lapsed since the armed conflict took place are important factors for courts when determining their willingness to exercise their authority. An active and independent civil society and media, which could influence public opinion and increase the demand for judicial scrutiny during the period after the conflict, are equally important factors. The initial stages of armed conflicts are typically characterized by a strong sense of patriotism and unity of the State in support of the executive. As courts are State institutions, and judges are citizens of their States, they form an integral part of the state system. However, this sense is not necessarily as strong when judicial review is carried out months or years after the facts (which frequently happens when a case is heard on second or final instance). The time interval, and public opinion that has meanwhile

[41] *Hamdan v United States* 696 F 3d 1238 (DC Cir 2012).

[42] See decision of the United States Court of Military Commissions Review of 18 February 2015, which vacated the conviction of Hicks. See David M Hicks, Appellant v United States of America, CMCR 13-004 (18 February 2015), available at <https://ccrjustice.org/sites/default/files/attach/2015/05/Hicksv.United%20States_13-004%20Decision_%282015.02.18%29.pdf> accessed 23 July 2023.

[43] *Al-Bahlul v US* 792 F 3d 1 (DC Cir 2015) 9–10.

crystallized due to media, non-governmental organizations' and academic reports concerning IHL violations, may have an impact on the willingness of courts to exercise their authority and engage with IHL. Once the conflict becomes protracted, it becomes easier for a court to rule against the State, a situation that is barely imaginable during the initial stages of a full-scale military operation.

Another aspect to be taken into account is the fact that domestic courts are part of a global legal order. Domestic courts increasingly become aware of this development when adjudicating IHL cases. Thus, if international tribunals or leading domestic courts have already reviewed the same issue, it may be legally and politically easier for other courts to take a more active or assertive role.

F. Activism in Domestic Courts

Activist decisions are defined here as domestic courts' engagement to align with international law contradicting domestic law, when courts are not empowered to do so. The case of Judge Baltasar Garzón in Spain is an example of such an 'activist' decision. Following a petition filed by family members and associations representing victims of the Franco regime before the Audiencia Nacional on 14 December 2006, Judge Garzón opened a criminal investigation into allegations of crimes against humanity committed during the Spanish civil war by the Franco regime. He ordered that exhumations and other preliminary steps be taken to ascertain facts. On 16 October 2008, he delivered a decision assuming jurisdiction over the case. While jurisdiction was over specific crimes such as 'illegal detentions', as they also amounted to crimes against humanity, the judge found that they were not subject to prescription and that the Spanish 1977 Amnesty Law of 15 October 1977, which affords amnesty to Franco-era crimes, was not applicable.[44] The judge interpreted the Amnesty Law as not applying to serious crimes, such as crimes against humanity. The non-applicability of the Amnesty Law to crimes against humanity was based, amongst others, on the obligation to investigate such crimes under international law, as supported by international jurisprudence such as the Inter-American Court of

[44] Diligencias Previas (Proc Abreviado) 399/2006-V, Judgment of 16 October 2008, Juzgado Central de Instrucción No 5 Diligencias Previas Proc Abreviado 399/2006 V (Audiencia Nacional). Jurisdiction was assumed, amongst others, over crimes committed by Franco and his high command during the war and the post-war period in respect of 'crimes against the state', which under arts 23(2), 23(4), and 65(1) of the Ley Organica Judicial corresponds to the jurisdiction of the Audiencia Nacional, carried out in the context of and connected to crimes against humanity.

Human Rights cases of *Barrios Altos v Peru*, decided on 14 March 2001, and the *Masacre de Mapiripán v Colombia*, decided on 5 September 2005.[45] In other words, the judge's reasoning produced overriding alignment with international law.[46] The reasoning was also supported by the Spanish Constitution and jurisprudence of the Supreme Court, which had determined that international law shall provide the interpretation for the enforcement of crimes against humanity. This decision did not pass unnoticed: not only was jurisdiction denied on appeal, Judge Garzón was indicted under Spain's prevarication law which allows judges to be prosecuted for unjust judgments.[47] Garzón was in addition suspended from his judicial functions.[48] While Garzón's interpretation went against the purpose of the Spanish Amnesty Law, it was coherent with international law. This is why it is difficult to justify this far-reaching reaction, as it is to justify the Amnesty law itself, in light of the fact that Spanish courts have consistently affirmed, while adjudicating cases based on universal jurisdiction, that amnesties granted by third States in order to prevent accountability for international crimes are not binding on Spanish courts.[49] Ironically, Spain's practice suggests that Franco's crimes may be only prosecuted in third States on the basis of universal jurisdiction.[50]

[45] *Barrios Altos v Peru* (Merits) IACtHR Series C No 75 (14 March 2001); '*Masacre de Mapiripán' v Colombia* (Merits) IACtHR Series C No 134 (15 September 2005).

[46] ILA Final Report (n 4) para 46.

[47] The complaint against Judge Garzón was filed by 'Manos Limpias', a right-wing political organization, on 26 January 2009 before the Criminal Chamber of the Supreme Court of Spain. Judge Garzón was indicted in April 2010 for the crime of *prevaricación*, alleging the abuse of his judicial authority by opening the inquiry into the Franco-era crimes. The crime of *prevaricación* is defined in art 446 of the Spanish Criminal Code as follows: 'The judge or magistrate who, knowingly, dictates an unjust sentence or resolution'. On 24 March 2011, Judge Garzón brought a case to the European Court of Human Rights challenging the lawfulness of his criminal prosecution, alleging a violation of the European Convention of Human Rights and Fundamental Freedoms (adopted 4 November 1950, entered into force 3 September 1953) ETS No 5 arts 6, 7, 8, 10, and 18. A case was also brought before the UN Human Rights Committee on 31 January 2016. The Human Rights Committee issued its decision on 26 August 2021 finding that the trials of Judge Garzón 'were arbitrary and did not comply with the principles of judicial independence and impartiality'. See OHCHR, 'Baltasar Garzón trials were arbitrary and failed to comply with principles of judicial independence and impartiality – UN Committee', Press Release (26 August 2021), <https://www.ohchr.org/en/press-releases/2021/08/baltasar-garzon-trials-were-arbitrary-and-failed-comply-principles-judicial?LangID = E&NewsID = 27410> accessed 23 July 2023; and Human Rights Committee 'Views: Communication No 2844/2016' (25 August 2021) UN Doc CCPR/C/132/D/2844/2016.

[48] Unanimous Decision of the Spanish General Council of the Judiciary, 14 May 2010 (pending trial). See Daniel Makosky, 'Spain Judicial Panel Suspends Judge Garzon over Franco Probe' (*Jurist.org*, 14 May 2010) <http://jurist.org/paperchase/2010/05/spain-judicial-panel-suspends-judge-garzon-over-franco-probe.php> accessed 23 July 2023.

[49] See Decision No 5 of 1 September 2000, Central Investigative Court (Audiencia Nacional) (indictment of Miguel Angel Cavallo); Decision No 6 of 20 September 1998, Central Investigative Court (Audiencia Nacional) (*Pinochet*).

[50] See the discussion in Mónica Pinto and Nahuel Maisley in this volume.

G. Conclusion

As discussed in this chapter different strategies of engagements with IHL have been identified in the practice of domestic courts. Domestic judges are entrusted to apply the law, while making a solid distinction between politics and law (or, at the very least, they must be perceived as doing so). This task is particularly challenging when domestic courts are adjudicating cases that involve international law issues that are politically sensitive, such as in situations of armed conflict. Indeed, when domestic courts engage with IHL in such cases, this will inevitably involve political interest, as the law itself is indeterminate and inherently political. The nuanced way domestic courts reflect these relations, as illustrated in this chapter, is an expression of the broader ongoing struggle between different political visions, translated into legal norms and behaviours, where the relations between international law and politics are being constantly shaped.

18

'Amp Up and Amplify: Defy!'

Engagement of Domestic Courts with International Sanctions

Eleni Methymaki and Antonios Tzanakopoulos

A. Introduction

The engagement of domestic courts with international sanctions should be understood within the broader context of increased interaction between domestic legal orders and international law.[1] Increased engagement is, in part, also a result of the increased imposition of sanctions (especially sanctions against individuals) since the (late) 1990s, and their ensuing 'juridification', namely the growing role played by law, legal regulation, and remedies in the imposition and operation of sanctions regimes.[2] For more than two decades, a clear shift is observable in international law: from comprehensive, State-focused sanctions, through sanctions targeting specific goods or resources fuelling conflict, to sanctions against individuals and other non-State actors, including asset freezes and travel bans. This targeting and individualization of sanctions has 'challenged the state-centric character' of international law,[3] impacting its horizontal, outward-looking structure.[4] More importantly for

[1] See the introductory chapter in this volume, 'Engagement of Domestic Courts with International Law: Principled or Unprincipled?'.

[2] On the 'juridification' of sanctions, see generally Eva Nanopoulos, *The Juridification of Individual Sanctions and the Politics of EU Law* (Hart 2020).

[3] ibid 13. At the same time, comprehensive and state-focused sanctions are still employed especially in the unilateral practice of States, and in United States practice in particular. Their effects remain destructive and inhumane. See Aziz Rana and Asli Ü Bâli, 'Sanctions Are Inhumane – Now, and Always' (Boston Review, 26 March 2020), available at <https://www.bostonreview.net/articles/aziz-rana-asli-u-bali-sanctions-are-inhumane-now-and-always/> last accessed 23 July 2023.

[4] See ILA Study Group on Principles on the Engagement of Domestic Courts with International Law, 'Final Report: Mapping the Engagement of Domestic Courts with International Law' (Johannesburg, 2016) (ILA Final Report) paras 10–13.

the purposes of this chapter, it has also provided opportunities for domestic courts to become actively engaged in this field.[5]

Sanctions, considered the necessary trait of any legal order as a coercive order,[6] have a distinct place in the decentralized international legal system. But the term 'sanctions' itself is vague, and the adjective 'international' does little to make it more precise. The term can and has been used to refer to anything from measures imposed collectively against a State or designated non-State entities (including individuals) by the international community as represented by the United Nations (UN), to similar 'restrictive' measures[7] taken by other international organizations, including the European Union (EU), to measures taken independently by States. Some clarification on how the term is used in the present chapter is thus required, and it is provided in Section B. Section C then discusses the engagement of domestic courts with international sanctions in cases that show—in the language of the International Law Association Study Group Final Report (ILA Final Report)—alignment with international law. As discussed in that section, however, such alignment bears marks of both avoidance and contestation. Section D turns to those cases where domestic courts have engaged in contestation of international legal norms in dealing with international sanctions. Here again, however, contestation can be presented also as (consubstantial) alignment, at least in part. Section E concludes, highlighting that the combative stance of domestic courts with regard to international sanctions has had at least some effect on the structure and operation of UN Security Council (UNSC or the Council) sanctions regimes. Even if that effect is modest, it underlines how a pattern of alignment-*cum*-contestation and of

[5] At the same time, sanctions remain a tool at the hands of States to be employed against other States in pursuance of different agendas. This often creates disputes at the inter-state level, which has also led to a recent increase in the involvement of international courts in the adjudication of sanctions. See, eg, the cases brought by Iran against the United States before the International Court of Justice challenging sanctions imposed by the latter: *Certain Iranian Assets (Iran v USA)* (Judgment) [2023] ICJ Rep, available at <https://www.icj-cij.org/sites/default/files/case-related/164/164-20230330-JUD-01-00-EN.pdf> and *Alleged Violations of the 1955 Treaty of Amity, Economic Relations, and Consular Rights (Iran v USA)* (Preliminary Objections) [2021] ICJ Rep 9; and see also *Appeal relating to the Jurisdiction of the ICAO Council under Article 8, Section 2, of the 1944 International Air Services Transit Agreement (Bahrain, Egypt, and UAE v Qatar)* (Judgment) [2020] ICJ Rep 172 and *Appeal relating to the Jurisdiction of the ICAO Council under Article 84 of the Convention on International Civil Aviation (Bahrain, Egypt, Saudi Arabia and UAE v Qatar)* (Judgment) [2020] ICJ Rep 81, relating to restrictive measures imposed by Bahrain, Egypt, Saudi Arabia, and the United Arab Emirates against Qatar in 2017.

[6] Hans Kelsen, 'Sanctions in International Law under the Charter of the United Nations' (1946) 39 Iowa Law Review 499.

[7] In European Union parlance, sanctions are most commonly referred to as 'restrictive measures'. See Treaty on the Functioning of the European Union [2016] OJ C 202/144 (TFEU) art 215; and, eg, Council Regulation (EU) No 269/2014 of 17 March 2014 concerning restrictive measures in respect of actions undermining or threatening the territorial integrity, sovereignty and independence of Ukraine [2014] OJ L78/6 (as amended).

contestation-*cum*-alignment in domestic court practice can exert pressure to implement certain changes at the international level.

B. Terminological Clarifications and Legal Framework

When seeking to understand the term 'international sanctions', the entity taking the measures is of some significance: it has effects on the legal basis for resort to the measures, as well as on their domestic implementation. The entity resorting to the measures also affects how these measures are to be properly called, and legally characterized. These two aspects are interrelated, and the following few paragraphs are meant to shed some light both on the legal basis for the adoption of 'sanctioning' measures, and their proper characterization.

A State (or a group of States) may adopt restrictive—'sanctioning'—measures against another State (such as freezing its assets or blocking trade with it) and/or target entities of the nationality of another State (such as freezing their individual assets or imposing on them travel or visa restrictions) in reaction to the target State's conduct. Although it is common to refer to such measures generically as 'sanctions', they are to be properly characterized in a number of ways. First, they may constitute measures of retorsion. Measures (or acts) of retorsion are 'unfriendly' but not as such internationally unlawful.[8] This is the case when the measures do not involve the breach of an obligation of the reacting State owed to the target State. A clear example is the expulsion of diplomats or the breaking off of diplomatic relations. Second, they may be characterized as countermeasures. For restrictive measures to qualify as countermeasures, the measures will involve a breach of international obligations of the reacting ('sanctioning') State owed to the target ('sanctioned') State, but the breach will be justified as a temporary and proportionate reaction to a previous breach of obligations of the target State which are owed (at least among others) to the reacting State.[9] These measures, in order to be lawful under

[8] See ILC, 'Draft Articles on Responsibility of States for Internationally Wrongful Acts, with commentaries' [2001] II(2) YBILC 31 (ARSIWA Commentary) 128 [3]. A question that we do not address in this chapter is whether measures of retorsion, such as the interruption of economic aid, may constitute prohibited economic coercion (or 'economic warfare'). This has long been contested in international law, state practice, and legal scholarship. See Antonios Tzanakopoulos, 'The Right to be Free from Economic Coercion' (2015) 4 Cambridge International Law Journal 616; more recently, Jessica Whyte, 'The Opacity of Economic Coercion' (LPE Project, 21 June 2023), available at <https://lpeproject.org/blog/the-opacity-of-economic-coercion/> last accessed 22 July 2023; Asli Ü Bâli, 'Weapons Against the Weak' (LPE Project, 29 June 2023), available at <https://lpeproject.org/blog/weapons-against-the-weak/> last accessed 22 July 2023.

[9] ARSIWA Commentary (n 8) 128 [1], 129 [6].

international law, will have to fulfil certain conditions, and must only aim to induce the target State to comply with its international obligations and in no case to serve as punishment.[10] Third, any such measures that are in the first instance internationally unlawful, and that cannot be justified as countermeasures, will simply be considered breaches of the international obligations of the reacting State, which engage that State's international responsibility. What is common in all these cases is that the measures are adopted in a decentralized manner, namely unilaterally by each State, even where States are acting in concert.

An international organization, such as the EU, may also adopt measures against a non-Member State and/or designated entities (including individuals) connected to that State.[11] It may do so by imposing on its Member States an obligation to adopt these measures in their domestic legal orders, or by adopting these measures in its own name, to the extent that it has direct relations with the targeted State or where the measures it adopts have direct effect in the domestic legal order of its Member States.[12] In any event, these measures will still be properly characterized as retorsion, countermeasures, or breaches of obligations, according to the scheme presented in the previous paragraph, and will still be unilateral measures even if adopted by the organization as a collective.

Only in one case can measures adopted by an international organization find a legal basis other than the scheme presented above. This is when the United Nations is acting, through the Security Council, in order to maintain or restore international peace and security under Chapter VII of the United Nations Charter (UN Charter). In accordance with Article 41 of the UN Charter, when the UNSC determines the existence of a 'threat to the peace, breach of the

[10] Articles on Responsibility of States for Internationally Wrongful Acts, UNGA Res 56/83, Annex (12 December 2001) UN Doc A/RES/56/83 (ARSIWA) arts 22, 49–53; ARSIWA Commentary (n 8) 129 [6]. See, for more detailed discussion, Alina Miron and Antonios Tzanakopoulos, 'Unilateral Coercive Measures and International Law' (The Left in the European Parliament 2022) 16–18, available at <https://papers.ssrn.com/sol3/papers.cfm?abstract_id=4235572> last accessed 22 July 2023; but see Alexandra Hofer, 'The Efficacy of Targeted Sanctions in Enforcing Compliance with International Law' (2019) 113 AJIL Unbound 168, discussing the concept of punishment in unilateral sanctions, including countermeasures.

[11] The EU, for example, has competence to adopt restrictive measures (sanctions) under the Common Foreign and Security Policy (see Treaty on European Union [2016] OJ C202/1, Title V) and art 215 of the TFEU (n 7).

[12] See, eg, EU Regulation 833/2014 (Council Regulation (EU) No 833/2014 of 31 July 2014 concerning restrictive measures in view of Russia's actions destabilizing the situation in Ukraine [2014] OJ L229/1) which directly prohibits trade in securities and other money-market instruments (art 5) and enjoins EU Member States to adopt the necessary legislative measures to impose penalties in case of violations of the provisions of the Regulation and ensure their implementation (art 8). See generally Antonios Tzanakopoulos, 'Sanctions Imposed Unilaterally by the European Union: Implications for the European Union's International Responsibility' in Ali Z Marossi and Marisa R Bassett (eds), *Economic Sanctions under International Law: Unilateralism, Multilateralism, Legitimacy, and Consequences* (TMC Asser 2015) 145.

peace, or act of aggression' under Article 39 of the UN Charter, it may adopt '*measures not involving the use of armed force* ... includ[ing] complete or partial interruption of economic relations and of rail, sea, air, postal, telegraphic, radio, and other means of communication, and the severance of diplomatic relations'.[13] The International Law Commission (ILC) noted in its work on State responsibility that it is for these non-forcible measures adopted under Chapter VII of the UN Charter (and, more generally, for restrictive measures adopted by a competent international organization) that the term 'sanctions' is commonly used, opting thus to use the term 'countermeasures' to describe the restrictive measures taken by States in a decentralized manner in response to a prior wrongful act and in order to induce compliance with the law.[14]

It is in this manner that the term 'international sanctions' is used in this chapter, to refer to non-forcible measures adopted by the Security Council under Chapter VII of the UN Charter. Where the Council has adopted such non-forcible measures, these are mandatory for UN Member States in accordance with Articles 25 and 103 of the UN Charter.[15] To comply with such mandatory sanctions, States have to implement them in their domestic legal orders, including by exercising their prescriptive and enforcement jurisdiction. Although in certain cases and in some domestic legal orders domestic courts may apply UNSC resolutions (UNSC Res) imposing sanctions directly, generally such decisions of the Council are not considered self-executing, even though they are binding on States as a matter of international law.[16] Therefore, it is necessary for States to enact domestic implementing measures to effect compliance, which usually take the form of general enabling legislation and/or ad hoc acts intended to implement specific sanctions regimes.[17] Additionally, where sanctions are imposed against natural or legal persons (under domestic

[13] Charter of the United Nations (adopted 26 June 1945, entered into force 24 October 1945) 1 UNTS XVI (UN Charter) art 41 (emphasis added).

[14] ARSIWA Commentary (n 8) 75 [3]; see also for a discussion A Pellet and A Miron, 'Sanctions' in MPEPIL (OUP August 2013), MN 4–11; Miron and Tzanakopoulos (n 10) 4.

[15] UN Charter art 25: 'The Members of the United Nations agree to accept and carry out the decisions of the Security Council in accordance with the present Charter.' UN Charter art 103: 'In the event of a conflict between the obligations of the Members of the United Nations under the present Charter and their obligations under any other international agreement, their obligations under the present Charter shall prevail.'

[16] Vera Gowlland-Debbas, 'Implementing Sanctions Resolutions in Domestic Law' in Vera Gowlland-Debbas (ed), *National Implementation of United Nations Sanctions: A Comparative Study* (Brill 2004) 37–41.

[17] See for an informative discussion ibid 41–46. Sometimes, domestic implementing measures are also adopted on the basis of general (namely, unrelated to UN measures) pre-existing legislation (eg, criminal or customs legislation or acts regulating emergency powers of the executive) which can blur the lines between domestic measures that implement UN sanctions and those that are taken as autonomous, restrictive measures by the State (ibid).

law, that is other than States), such as asset freezes, the State will usually have to adopt personal administrative acts to effect this.

In turn, these domestic implementing measures may be brought before the State's domestic courts either incidentally (eg, in the context of a private dispute) or on the basis of a direct challenge by the affected persons, and on the basis of domestic or international law (or both). The latter scenario became even more probable with the increasing sanctioning activity of the Security Council, combined with originally the absence, and then the very limited existence, of avenues at the international level for individuals to challenge UNSC sanctions and their designation under relevant decisions of the UNSC and of the respective sanctions committees.[18] This gives domestic courts an opportunity to engage with international law, and in particular with the relevant UNSC resolutions, as well as with the decisions taken by the Council's subsidiary bodies.[19]

It is this engagement of domestic courts with international sanctions that this chapter aims to map. As the following sections will argue, in engaging with international sanctions, domestic courts have challenged the international legal framework of Security Council sanctions, and the authority of the Council itself, and have had an enduring impact on the relevant international law and institutions.

C. Alignment(-*cum*-Contestation)

As a posture or strategy, alignment of domestic courts with international law is observed where domestic courts 'attempt ... to align [their determinations] with international law or at least to harmonize domestic law or practice with international regulation'.[20] As mentioned in the previous section, domestic courts may engage with international sanctions in different contexts and cases. This chapter is concerned primarily with cases where affected individuals or legal entities challenge the domestic measures implementing international sanctions in the domestic legal order. However, instances of alignment,

[18] In particular, the focus is on UN sanctions regimes that involve designations by the Security Council itself (through the relevant Sanctions Committee), and thus impose 'strict' obligations on Member States: see further Antonios Tzanakopoulos, 'Domestic Court Reactions to UN Security Council Sanctions' in August Reinisch (ed), *Challenging Acts of International Organisations before National Courts* (OUP 2010) 54. The latter chapter, from which this chapter also borrows, should be read as a 'prequel' of this work.

[19] Vera Gowlland-Debbas, 'Sanctions Regimes under Article 41 of the UN Charter' in Gowlland-Debbas (n 16) 21–22.

[20] ILA Final Report (n 4) para 37.

especially simple or 'fair weather' alignment,[21] are often identifiable when international sanctions come before the domestic judge incidentally, that is not as a matter of direct challenge but, for example, in the context of a dispute between private parties. An example will make this clearer.

In *Palladyne v Upper Brook* a dispute arose between a Dutch company, Palladyne International Asset Management BV (PIAM), and three Cayman Islands-based investment funds, for which it was acting as manager and director. The dispute was brought before the courts of the Cayman Islands, an Overseas Territory of the UK. The assets managed by the three Cayman Islands-based investment funds belonged to three Libyan entities, the Libyan Africa Investment Portfolio (LAP), the Libyan Foreign Bank (LFB), and the Libyan Investment Authority (LIA), all of which had been made subject to an asset freeze in accordance with the Libya (Restrictive Measures) (Overseas Territories) Order 2011 (as amended),[22] implementing in the Cayman Islands UNSC resolutions imposing financial sanctions on certain Libyan State entities, as well as on persons within and associated with the Qaddafi regime.[23] In the course of considering whether certain decisions taken by the three investment funds concerning the removal of PIAM as manager and director constituted prohibited 'use' of the frozen assets under the Libya (Restrictive Measures) (Overseas Territories) Order (as amended), and therefore a breach of its Article 10 (as well as of other provisions),[24] both the Cayman Islands Grand Court and the Court of Appeal engaged with the 'international system of sanctions deriving from United Nations Security Council resolutions'.[25]

In particular, according to the Court of Appeal there was a 'hierarchy of legislative instruments' which made both the relevant UNSC resolutions and EU legislation[26] 'important parts of the context against which the Order must be interpreted',[27] while according to the Grand Court the domestic sanctions

[21] In the terms of the ILA Final Report (n 4) para 44, simple or 'fair weather' alignment is observed 'in run-of-the-mill politically unproblematic situations ... includ[ing] instances where international law is cited explicitly in support of relevant domestic law, as well as other cases where the perceived content of international and domestic law converges'. Although cases involving international sanctions are hardly ever 'politically unproblematic' (ibid), the stakes (politically) for the Government are substantially lower when sanctions are raised in the context of a private dispute.

[22] Libya (Restrictive Measures) (Overseas Territories) Order 2011 No 1080.

[23] In particular, UNSC Res 1970 (2011) (26 February 2011) UN Doc S/RES/1970(2011) and UNSC Res 1973 (2011) (17 March 2011) UN Doc S/RES/1973(2011) paras 19–21 and Annex II, as modified by UNSC Res 2009 (2011) (16 September 2011) UN Doc S/RES/2009(2011) paras 14–19.

[24] *Palladyne International Asset Management BV v Upper Brook (A) Ltd and others*, CICA Appeal No 5 of 2019, Judgment of 18 November 2019 (*PIAM v Upper Brook*) [8], [10]–[12].

[25] ibid [15].

[26] As the UK had implemented the relevant UNSC resolutions for itself and for UK overseas territories in 'substantially the same' manner, EU legislation was also relevant to the interpretation of the Libya (Restrictive Measures) (Overseas Territories) Order. See *PIAM v Upper Brook* (n 24) [16].

[27] ibid [17].

legislation and 'the UN and international sanctions regime … was to be read as *a single harmonious code*.[28] In light of this, and because 'the purpose of the Order is to implement the relevant United Nations Security Council resolutions', the Court of Appeal considered that the meaning of the relevant terms of the domestic legislation had to 'be construed so far as is possible compatibly with those resolutions'.[29] To do that, the Court of Appeal did not merely rely on the provisions of the UNSC resolutions and their preambles, which were considered relevant for discerning the purpose of the sanctions regime against Libya,[30] but took into account also documents and reports produced by the competent UN Sanctions Committee and the Panel of Experts.[31] In other words, in this case the domestic courts used the relevant international law, in particular the decisions of the UNSC and its subsidiary bodies, to construct the broader context within which domestic legislation had to be interpreted and as a way to 'understand domestic legislation',[32] resulting in alignment of domestic law with international sanctions.

In the context of a direct challenge of the domestic measures implementing international sanctions, *Hany Youssef*,[33] the latest in a series of complaints brought by the same claimant before UK courts,[34] provides an example of alignment with international sanctions (and, simultaneously, of affirmative contestation of international human rights law). The claimant argued that the legislation on the basis of which an asset freeze had been imposed on him as a person designated by the Sanctions Committee monitoring the UNSC sanctions against Al-Qaida (1267 Committee), namely the ISIL (Da'esh) and Al-Qaida (United Nations Sanctions) (EU Exit) Regulations 2019 (2019 Regulations) and the Sanctions and Anti-Money Laundering Act 2018 (2018 Act), was contrary to the right of fair trial and access to justice under Article 6 and the right to private and family life under Article 8 of the

[28] ibid [42] (emphasis added).

[29] ibid [63]. Another example of this approach can be found in *Libyan Investment Authority v Maud* [2016] EWCA Civ 788 [17]–[18] (on which *PIAM v Upper Brook* relied). According to the Court of Appeal, 'the [EU sanctions] Regulations must be read and understood as a coherent whole against the background of the Security Council Resolutions' (ibid [18]).

[30] See also *Libyan Investment Authority v Maud* (n 29) [19] See also Daley J Birkett and Dini Sejko, 'Challenging UN Security Council and International Criminal Court-Requested Asset Freezes in Domestic Courts: Views from the UK and Italy' (2022) 55 Israel Law Review 107, 121–22.

[31] *PIAM v Upper Brook* (n 24) [79]–[80].

[32] ILA Final Report (n 4) para 26.

[33] *R (Hany Youssef) v Secretary of State for Foreign, Commonwealth and Development Affairs* [2021] EWHC 3188 (Admin).

[34] See also the discussion in section C of *Ahmed v HM Treasury* [2010] UKSC 2.

European Convention on Human Rights (ECHR).[35] The 2018 Act and the 2019 Regulations implemented in the UK the 1267 sanctions regime following UK withdrawal from the EU. According to the High Court, the 2018 Act provided for a process through which a sanctioned individual could request the Secretary of State to pursue a de-listing application before the 1267 Committee on their behalf, and in case of the Secretary of State's refusal to do so, a basis for the individual to challenge such refusal before the High Court.[36] However, the claimant argued that, because the 2018 Act did not allow a sanctioned person to challenge their actual designation and the imposition of the asset freeze before a court, it violated his rights under Articles 6 and 8 of the ECHR.[37]

The High Court did not agree with the claimant, finding that the 2018 Act intended to place restrictions on the right of access to court under common law,[38] which were held to be in accordance with Articles 6 and 8 of the ECHR. In particular, the High Court held that, in accordance with the pronouncements of the European Court of Human Rights (ECtHR) in the *Al-Dulimi* case,[39] Article 6 only prescribed 'a modest level of scrutiny'[40] by the courts of the domestic measures implementing UNSC sanctions,[41] which did not have to entail a substantive review of the reasons and evidence for the individual's designation or a remedy in the form of quashing the implementing measures. Rather, it was enough that the 2018 Act provided a basis for the individual to request the Secretary of State to pursue their de-listing and the possibility to challenge their refusal to do so.[42] Although this decision aligned the position under domestic law with the UK's obligations under the UNSC sanctions regime, in doing so the High Court seems to have downplayed what the ECtHR held to be required by Article 6 in *Al-Dulimi*, engaging thus in affirmative contestation.[43] More specifically, the ECtHR found in *Al-Dulimi* that the judicial review required under Article 6 could be 'relatively minimal, ensuring that the

[35] *Hany Youssef* (n 33) [3]–[5]. European Convention for the Protection of Human Rights and Fundamental Freedoms (adopted 4 November 1950, entered into force 3 September 1953) ETS No 5 (ECHR).

[36] *Hany Youssef* (n 33) [39]–[40].

[37] ibid [42]–[43]. See also [44]: the claimant based his arguments partly on the findings of the UKSC in *Ahmed* (n 34). On *Ahmed*, see the discussion in section C.

[38] *Hany Youssef* (n 33) [62]. On this basis, the High Court distinguished this case from *Ahmed* (n 34). See the discussion in section C.

[39] *Al-Dulimi and Montana Management Inc v Switzerland* (GC), App No 5809/08 (Judgment of 21 June 2016).

[40] *Hany Youssef* (n 33) [89].

[41] ibid [81]–[82].

[42] ibid [90]–[93].

[43] ILA Final Report (n 4) para 58.

listing of the person in question was not arbitrary',[44] but this still appears to require that some measure of substantive review of the designation itself takes place, contrary to what the High Court said in *Hany Youssef*. In that sense, the High Court seems to have given to Article 6 and the *Al-Dulimi* judgment 'a meaning different from that' which the ECtHR itself intended.[45] The way the High Court engaged with the supranational law of the EU should also be highlighted: in a clear posture of affirmative avoidance,[46] the Court refused to consider the pronouncements of EU courts on similar issues in the *Kadi* cases, given that following the UK's withdrawal from the EU 'the position as a matter of EU law [was] irrelevant'.[47]

A different, more complex, posture of alignment (or rather alignment-*cum*-contestation) can be found in *Abdelrazik v Canada*,[48] where a sanctioned individual brought a human rights claim under the Canadian Charter of Rights and Freedoms[49] against the Canadian Government. Mr Abdelrazik, a dual Canadian-Sudanese national, claimed (among others) that Canada had violated his right to return to Canada and enter the country under subsection 6(1) of the Canadian Charter. Canada had failed to provide him with the necessary travel documents and to facilitate his return to Canada, leaving him stranded in Sudan where he faced unlawful detention and was subjected to torture. The government argued that the inability of Mr Abdelrazik to return to Canada was not due to government conduct but due to 'his listing by the 1267 Committee as an associate of Al-Qaida'.[50]

A key feature of this case was that the governmental actions that Mr Abdelrazik complained of had begun before his designation by the 1267 Committee and his application did not directly attack the UNSC decision or the domestic implementing measures. Its sole legal basis was domestic constitutional law. The reason that the domestic court had to engage with the international sanctions regime was because the government invoked it as a defence for 'a pattern of conduct' starting in 2003,[51] ie three years before Mr Abdelrazik's designation by the 1267 Committee in 2006. In light of this, and

[44] See Marko Milanovic, 'Grand Chamber Judgment in Al-Dulimi v Switzerland' (EJIL:*Talk!*, 23 June 2016), available at <https://www.ejiltalk.org/grand-chamber-judgment-in-al-dulimi-v-switzerland/> last accessed 22 July 2023. See further *Al-Dulimi* (n 39) [146]–[47].

[45] See in that sense ILA Final Report (n 4) para 58.

[46] ibid para 41.

[47] *Hany Youssef* (n 33) [64].

[48] See generally Antonios Tzanakopoulos, 'United Nations Sanctions in Domestic Courts: From Interpretation to Defiance in *Abdelrazik v Canada*' (2010) 8 Journal of International Criminal Justice 249.

[49] Enacted as Part I of Schedule B to the Canada Act 1982 (UK).

[50] *Abdelrazik v Canada (Minister of Foreign Affairs)* [2009] FC 580, [2010] 1 FCR 267 [44].

[51] ibid [62].

having identified 'a tension between Canada's international and national obligations',[52] the Federal Court engaged with the international legal framework established by the UN Charter, including the competence of the UNSC under Chapter VII, and the sanctions regime under UNSC Resolution 1267 as amended and modified.[53]

The main issue in the case was whether Mr Abdelrazik's right to return to and enter Canada had been interfered with without this being 'a reasonable limit prescribed by law that can be demonstrably justified in a free and democratic society'.[54] Per the government, given that following his designation Mr Abdelrazik was subject to a global asset freeze and travel ban,[55] the asset freeze 'prevent[ed] [it], or anyone within Canada, from paying for transportation to Canada or providing such transportation for Mr Abdelrazik',[56] while due to the travel ban he was not permitted to enter Canada (despite the existence of two exceptions under UNSC Res 1822 (2008)).[57] Therefore, if Canada were to facilitate his return, it would violate its international obligations.[58]

The Federal Court was not persuaded by this argument and sought to align the government's conduct with what it considered the correct interpretation of UNSC Res 1822. More specifically, and relying partly on Canada's own practice in implementing the travel ban,[59] it held that UNSC Res 1822 did not prohibit transit through third-country airspace and that such an interpretation would 'lead[] to a non-sensical result',[60] whereby a Canadian citizen would be allowed to enter Canada as per the exception in UNSC Res 1822, paragraph 1(b), but would not be allowed to do so if they had to transit through the airspace or land of a third State for the same purpose.[61] Additionally, according to the Federal Court, the 1267 Committee was 'unaware of [any] obligation' of States to report such transit as part of their obligations under the sanctions regime.[62] As a result, the Court interpreted the travel ban imposed under the resolution as not

[52] ibid [5].
[53] ibid [23], [45] et seq, [121] et seq.
[54] ibid [61]
[55] See paragraph 1 of UNSC Res 1822 (2008) (30 June 2008) UN Doc S/RES/1822 (2008), which was the resolution applicable to Mr Abdelrazik at the time of the judgment.
[56] *Abdelrazik* (n 50) [56]. The implementing domestic legislation, the United Nations Al-Qaida and Taliban Regulations, SOR/99-444 (as amended), was triggered as soon as the 1267 Committee designated an individual and also 'prohibit[ed] anyone in Canada and any Canadian outside of Canada from providing funds to be used by persons listed'.
[57] *Abdelrazik* (n 50) [57]–[58]. The exceptions to the travel ban are outlined in UNSC Res 1822 (2008) para 1(b).
[58] *Abdelrazik* (n 50) [122].
[59] ibid [125]–[26].
[60] ibid [127].
[61] ibid.
[62] ibid [128].

prohibiting Mr Abdelrazik's return to Canada, highlighting that this was also in accordance with the travel ban's purpose.[63]

The Court's interpretation on this point is persuasive, although other courts have not arrived to the same interpretation of the law.[64] But, the Federal Court's engagement with UNSC Res 1822 in *Abdelrazik* went beyond this point: having ordered that the government facilitate Mr Abdelrazik's return to Canada, including by providing the airfare if necessary, the Court anticipated that the government may argue that it was prohibited from doing so due to the asset freeze. To address this, the Court fashioned the following interpretation of UNSC Res 1822: first, it held that there was an exception to the travel ban *and* the asset freeze for the 'fulfilment of a "judicial process"'.[65] Second, it considered that the execution of its judgment and its orders was part of a 'judicial process' and therefore covered by the exception.[66]

There are, however, two potential issues with this interpretation: first, the judicial process exception in the resolution only exists as regards the travel ban and not the asset freeze. Hence, the Court's finding may be considered as a misreading of the resolution or as 'giving it a meaning different from that which is generally accepted',[67] in the terms of the ILA Final Report. In light of this, *Abdelrazik* can also be considered as a case of affirmative contestation, whereby the domestic court either 'wishes to change the content of the [international] norm or ... perceives it as different from what is generally accepted'.[68] Second, the interpretation of the term 'judicial process' itself, although 'persuasive ... and [arguably] a correct interpretation of the relevant sections of Resolution 1822', is not necessarily the same interpretation that the UNSC itself would arrive to (the latter's interpretation being determinative as a matter of international law).[69] Were the UNSC to interpret the term 'judicial process' otherwise, that would mean that the Court in *Abdelrazik* engaged in affirmative contestation,[70] resulting in placing Canada in breach of its international obligations.

[63] ibid [129].

[64] See, eg, the Swiss Federal Court in *Yousef Nada v State Secretariat for Economic Affairs and Federal Department of Economic Affairs* (CH 2007) ILDC 461, available at <https://opil.ouplaw.com/display/10.1093/law:ildc/461ch07.case.1/law-ildc-461ch07> last accessed 22 July 2023, as discussed in Tzanakopoulos (n 48) 254 (fn 32).

[65] *Abdelrazik* (n 50) [162].

[66] ibid [163]–[64].

[67] ILA Final Report (n 4) para 58.

[68] ibid.

[69] See Tzanakopoulos (n 48) 255.

[70] See ILA Final Report (n 4) para 58.

Effectively, the Federal Court in *Abdelrazik* 'interpreted away' any conflict between Canada's obligations under the UN sanctions regime and its domestic obligations under the Charter of Rights and Freedoms. In that, on the face of it, the Federal Court aligned with international law (which it interpreted as not being in conflict with domestic law, a sort of reverse 'consistent interpretation',[71] and as not requiring the government to act in a way that could be found in breach of domestic law). Another reading of the case, however, is that underneath that superficial alignment lies a posture of contestation of the content of international law (the sanctions regime): 'the intention of the drafters of the Resolution' (the Security Council) 'quite simply... could not have been' to prevent someone from travelling for the purpose of returning to their State of nationality;[72] except it could well have been so, and indeed was found to have been so by the Swiss Federal Court in *Nada*.[73]

If this superficial alignment is stealth contestation, then what kind of contestation is it? Could it be argued that this is some sort of 'parochial' contestation of international law on the basis of domestic rules peculiar to the Canadian legal order? Not really, in that the rights relied on by the Federal Court also exist under international law; in fact the Court itself draws the parallel to international law at the very outset of its own judgment, characterizing the sanctions regime as 'untenable under the principles of international human rights'.[74] What is more, when determining the appropriate remedy for Mr Abdelrazik, the Federal Court even makes reference to *Chorzów Factory* and the principle of full reparation,[75] noting that 'principles of international law are helpful where it is necessary to fashion a just and appropriate Charter remedy'.[76] It seems as if the Canadian Court is fashioning a remedy for a violation of international law. The superficial alignment with international law here is nothing but affirmative, consubstantial contestation.[77]

A similar argument (that apparent alignment is in reality affirmative, consubstantial contestation) can be made for the case of *Othman* before the High Court of England and Wales.[78] In that case, the High Court 'read into' the domestic and EU measures implementing UNSC Res 1333 (2000) an exemption to the freezing of assets if the latter would result in a situation where the

[71] On consistent interpretation see ibid, paras 23–24, and on 'reverse' consistent interpretation see para 58.
[72] *Abdelrazik* (n 50) [127].
[73] See n 64 above.
[74] *Abdelrazik* (n 50) [51].
[75] *Case concerning the Factory at Chorzów* (Merits) [1928] PCIJ Ser A No 17, 47.
[76] *Abdelrazik* (n 50) [159].
[77] See ILA Final Report (n 4) paras 59, 63. See further section D below.
[78] *R (Othman) v Secretary of State for Work and Pensions* [2001] EWHC 1022.

designated individual's life or health would be at risk.[79] Reasonable (and in line with international obligations to guarantee the right to life) as this interpretation may be, it does not constitute alignment with the international sanctions regime, even if it attempts to appear so. This is because at the time of the decision, there was no provision for exemptions along the lines suggested by the High Court. The Security Council only allowed an exemption to the asset freeze for the payment of basic expenses in December 2002 (the case was decided in 2001), and then again only with the consent of the Sanctions Committee.[80]

It is obvious then that the High Court's interpretation of UNSC Res 1333 as allowing an exemption was not in line with what the drafter (and authoritative interpreter) of the resolution thought. Otherwise, there would have been no need for the Security Council to *introduce* an exemption in 2002, two years after UNSC Res 1333 and more than a year after the decision in *Othman*. Even if the High Court appeared to align itself with the content of UNSC Res 1333, in reality it contested it, at the very least on a consubstantial basis. It may even be speculated that the adoption of exemptions by the Security Council in 2002 was in part in response to the very reasonable point made by the High Court in *Othman*: after all, if an asset freeze leads to a designated individual not having access to any funds (including own funds and funds provided by anybody else) to pay for basic subsistence, this clearly engages the right to life.

D. Contestation(-*cum*-Alignment)

At the other end of the spectrum, domestic courts may adopt a clear posture of contestation of international sanctions, and not even try to pass their judgments off as alignment, as the Canadian Federal Court did in *Abdelrazik*, or the High Court of England and Wales did in *Othman*. And yet, such contestation may still result in consubstantial alignment, namely alignment with some other international norm via a consubstantial domestic norm.

As identified in the ILA Final Report, contestation may result from reliance on a different international norm or from reliance on domestic law. In that sense, it can either be characterized as internationally minded or as local contestation.[81] Additionally, contestation can either take the form of the domestic court 'giving [an international law rule] a meaning different from that which

[79] ibid [57].

[80] UNSC Res 1452 (2002) (20 December 2002) UN Doc S/RES/1452 (2002) paras 1 and 3, respectively.

[81] ILA Final Report (n 4) para 65. It would be internationally minded contestation even where the court is relying on a domestic rule which however has an equivalent international law norm (ibid).

is generally accepted' (affirmative contestation)[82] or 'den[ying] ... the validity or applicability of an international law norm, perhaps due to its (perceived) content' (negatory contestation).[83] In either case, where contestation is internationally minded, namely where it is based on a different rule of international law (or its domestic equivalent), '[w]hat may look at first as ... contestation may in reality involve partial consubstantial alignment'.[84] This is the case, for instance, where domestic courts review and/or refuse to apply domestic acts implementing and imposing sanctions because another international law norm, usually stemming from international human rights law, or an equivalent domestic rule, requires them to do so (or, to be more precise, is interpreted as requiring them to do so).

To be sure, there are some examples of negatory contestation undertaken by domestic courts in circumstances where it is difficult to argue that the domestic norm is consubstantial to international rules. In *Al-Qadi*, the Tenth Division of the Turkish Council of State annulled the decree of the Council of Ministers of Turkey which froze the assets of Mr Kadi (yes, the same Mr Kadi of EU courts fame).[85] This was because under Turkish law an asset freeze could only be imposed by court decision, not by administrative act.[86] Perhaps it could be argued that the Tenth Division was making a subtle argument about access to judicial oversight for something as important as asset freezes, but given the limited reporting of the case this is difficult to make out. It appears that the contestation of the obligation to freeze the assets of Mr Kadi under the UN sanctions regime was based purely on the demands of domestic law.

Similar considerations apply to the *Bosphorus* case before the Irish High Court.[87] Bosphorus Hava Yoları Turizm ve Ticaret Anonim Şirketi was a Turkish company that had leased an aircraft from JAT, the national air carrier of Yugoslavia and later Serbia. While the aircraft was undergoing maintenance in Dublin, the Irish Ministry for Transport impounded it in implementation of European Community (EC) (as it then was) Council Regulation 990/93/EEC, which in turn had been adopted to implement UNSC Res 820 (1993).

[82] ILA Final Report (n 4) para 59.

[83] ibid para 61.

[84] ibid paras 63, 65.

[85] UNSC 'Sixth Report of the Analytical Support and Sanctions Monitoring Team appointed pursuant to Security Council Resolution 1526 (2004) and 1617 (2005) concerning Al-Qaida and the Taliban and Associated Individuals and Entities' (8 March 2007) UN Doc S/2007/132 at 39, para 8.

[86] ibid; the decision was eventually overturned by the Board of Administrative Appeals of the Council of State.

[87] *Bosphorus Hava v Minister for Transport* [1994] 2 ILRM 551. The case would (much) later end up before the European Court of Human Rights, a cause célèbre: *Bosphorus Hava Yoları Turizm ve Ticaret Anonim Şirketi v Ireland* (GC) App No 45036/98 (Judgment of 30 June 2005).

Bosphorus challenged the decision. The Irish High Court clearly acknowledge that interpreting the EC measure that implemented the UNSC measure would in effect also constitute an interpretation of UNSC Res 820.[88] Even so, the court summarily rejected the interpretation of UNSC Res 820 that had been offered by the President of the relevant Sanctions Committee on the basis that it was 'unexplained'.[89] It proceeded to interpret UNSC Res 820 independently, citing domestic rules of interpretation, arriving at the exact opposite result from that favoured by the Council.[90] This was an instance of negatory contestation, rejecting an existing interpretation of an international rule given by the drafter of the rule, and adopting a different interpretation based on domestic rules.

An even clearer example is provided by the High Court of the province of Sindh in Pakistan. In *Al-Rashid*, the court found in favour of the Al-Rashid Trust, which had been designated under the 1267 sanctions regime, purely on the basis of a procedural requirement under domestic law. The United Nations (Security Council) Act 1948 required that a statutory notification be made for every listed person or entity. Since this notification had not been issued in the instance, the freezing order under the Act was found lacking.[91] It is questionable (also due to limited reporting) whether this case even constitutes negatory contestation, as it is not clear whether the Pakistani court aimed to challenge the international rule or was simply holding the executive to account for its sloppy practice.[92] But it is conceivable that the court simply relied on the domestic rule to strike down a decision that it thought problematic.

A clear case of consubstantial contestation is *Ahmed v HM Treasury* in the UK Supreme Court.[93] In *Ahmed*, five individuals had been designated and subjected to an asset freeze in the UK through acts of the executive implementing the UN sanctions regime first established in UNSC Res 1267 (1999). The implementing acts had been made in the exercise of powers

[88] *Bosphorus* (n 87) 557.

[89] ibid.

[90] ibid 557–60.

[91] UNSC 'Fifth Report of the Analytical Support and Sanctions Monitoring Team appointed pursuant to Resolution 1526 (2004) and 1617 (2005) concerning Al-Qaida and the Taliban and Associated Individuals and Entities' (20 September 2006) UN Doc S/2006/750 at 48, para 6. This decision was also appealed to the Supreme Court of Pakistan: UNSC 'Ninth Report of the Analytical Support and Sanctions Monitoring Team appointed pursuant to Resolution 1822 (2008) concerning Al-Qaida and the Taliban and Associated Individuals and Entities' (13 May 2009) UN Doc S/2009/245 at 38, para 7.

[92] This can also be understood as a case of affirmative avoidance: the court can be seen as having rejected the application of international sanctions as this was 'the appropriate position under domestic [procedural] law' (ILA Final Report (n 4) para 41).

[93] *Ahmed* (n 34). For the procedural history and an overview see Antonios Tzanakopoulos, 'The UK Supreme Court Quashes Domestic Measures Implementing UN Sanctions' (EJIL:*Talk!*, 23 February 2010), available at <https://www.ejiltalk.org/the-uk-supreme-court-quashes-domestic-measures-implementing-un-sanctions/>.

allegedly granted to the executive by the United Nations Act 1946 and without any further Parliamentary scrutiny. These individuals challenged the domestic implementing acts before the UK Supreme Court, and were finally successful, with the court quashing the domestic measures in part for removing their right to access to an effective remedy.[94]

In order to highlight the importance of *Ahmed*, we must summarize the development of UN sanctions, especially under the 1267 regime, up to that point.[95] Asset freezes and travel bans on individuals or legal entities under this regime, first introduced in 1999, had been in place in some cases for almost two decades. Challenges before domestic courts had floundered left, right, and centre for many years. At first, domestic courts would simply avoid considering any challenge to UN measures, citing lack of jurisdiction over the UN or resorting to other avoidance techniques.[96] This makes sense to an extent, as any direct review of UN sanctions would be difficult to justify under domestic law, while any direct review of domestic implementing measures of 'strict' UNSC obligations would still constitute indirect review of the UN sanctions regime—raising the same problems.

As time went by and the challenges to the UN sanctions regime were being rejected in domestic courts, the plight of designated individuals was becoming quite stark. They had no possibility to challenge their designations directly before the Security Council—they depended at best on the intercession of their State of nationality before the Council in a purely political process. They were also given no access to domestic courts in order to challenge their designation or its effects directly or indirectly. Eventually, some domestic courts stopped avoiding the issue. These opted, instead, either to directly—if incidentally—review the UN sanctions on the basis of international law,[97] or to try and 'consistently' interpret the international measure and the domestic implementing measure or other government conduct, aligning-*cum*-contesting the international measure.[98]

The problem with the former approach was that any review of the international measures as against international law could only take place for compliance with *jus cogens* norms.[99] This is because of the operation of Article 103

[94] *Ahmed* (n 34) [81]–[82].
[95] See for more detail Tzanakopoulos (n 18).
[96] See ILA Final Report (n 4) paras 39 et seq.
[97] This was the approach of the Court of First Instance (as it then was, now the General Court of the EU) in the first *Kadi* case: Case T-315/01 *Yassin Abdullah Kadi v Council of the European Union and Commission of the European Communities* [2005] ECLI:EU:T:2005:332 [209]–[32]. This was followed by the Swiss Federal Court in *Nada* (n 64). Notably, the case also ended up before the Grand Chamber of the ECtHR in *Nada v Switzerland* (GC) App No 10593/08 (Judgment of 12 September 2012).
[98] See the cases in section C above.
[99] See (n 97).

of the UN Charter, which provides that the obligations of UN Member States under the Charter (including obligations under UNSC resolutions in accordance with Article 25 of the UN Charter) shall prevail over conflicting obligations of Member States under 'any other international agreement'—including treaties for the protection of human rights. Therefore, such review could only be relatively lax, and in the cases where it was undertaken it invariably led to the confirmation of legality of the impugned measure.[100]

The problem with the latter approach is that it is only by so much that one can stretch interpretation before all pretence of alignment with the international rule collapses. As such, this strategy of alignment-cum-(stealth) contestation is not always available. It is here where the UK Supreme Court in *Ahmed* drops any pretence and flat out contests the international rule. The road had been paved of course by the EU Court of Justice in *Kadi I*, which disassociated the domestic (EU) implementing act from the UN regime, and proceeded to review the EU implementing act for compliance with EU (for our purposes 'domestic') law.[101] But let us return to the UK Supreme Court in *Ahmed*.

In that case, even though the Supreme Court (implicitly) accepted that it would be forcing the UK to breach its international obligations if it were to review and quash the relevant domestic act implementing the UN measures, it proceeded to do so. The court was able to avoid the overriding effect of Article 103 of the UN Charter, confirmed by the House of Lords in *Al-Jedda*,[102] by stating that the rights sought to be protected by the applicants in the case were invoked on the basis of UK domestic, rather than international, law. Counsel for the applicants had clearly adopted from the beginning a strategy of basing their arguments on domestic law only, in order to pre-empt the government's reliance on Article 103. In fact, this was made clear when the only counsel that argued (in the alternative) under the ECHR before the Supreme Court openly conceded that *Al-Jedda* was against that position, but invited the Court to reconsider its decision in *Al-Jedda*.[103]

The Court confirmed *Al-Jedda*, but went on to state that this did not clarify the position with respect to rights enjoyed under domestic law.[104] Lord Rodger made it clear that he was concerned with domestic law rights because rights

[100] ibid.

[101] See Joined Cases C-402/05P and C-415/05P *Yassin Abdullah Kadi and Al Barakaat International Foundation v Council of the European Union and Commission of the European Communities* [2008] ECLI: EU:2008:461; and see generally Antonios Tzanakopoulos, 'The *Solange* Argument as a Justification for Disobeying the Security Council in the *Kadi* Judgments' in Matej Avbelj et al (eds), *Kadi on Trial: A Multifaceted Analysis of the* Kadi *Judgment* (Routledge 2014) 121.

[102] *R (Al-Jedda) v Secretary of State for Defence* [2007] UKHL 58.

[103] *Ahmed* (n 34) [66] et seq.

[104] ibid [75].

under the ECHR would be caught by Article 103.[105] It was indeed by relying on the domestic (common) law right of access to a court that the Court finally quashed (in relevant part) the UK domestic implementing measure. This was done because of the exasperation of the court with the 1267 sanctions regime,[106] and its concern to guarantee the right to a remedy without coming up against Article 103 of the UN Charter. Its reliance may have been on the fact that domestic common law guarantees the right to a remedy (which could not be removed without Parliamentary authority; the Parliament is after all sovereign in the UK), but it is clear that the same right exists in international law.[107] Therefore, the contestation that the UK Supreme Court engaged in in *Ahmed* was not negatory, but in fact consubstantial.

E. Conclusion

The attitude of domestic courts towards international sanctions, including their progressively bolder approach to questions of judicial review, can be justified by the fact that international sanctions regimes, as the Canadian Federal Court observed in *Abdelrazik*, are characterized by 'a denial of basic legal remedies and … [are] untenable under the principles of international human rights'.[108] As the discussion in the previous sections illustrates, by engaging with international sanctions, be it through alignment-*cum*-contestation or through contestation-*cum*-alignment, domestic courts can challenge such international measures. And these challenges affect both the relevant international norms and the structure of the international legal system more generally. Two types of effects, one substantive and one procedural, can be identified.

First, by insisting either that UNSC decisions and implementing domestic measures must be interpreted in a way that conforms with fundamental (domestic and/or international) human rights, including the right of access to justice and the right to a remedy, or that implementing domestic measures have to be quashed to the extent that they are contrary to such rights, domestic courts are engaging in practice that may eventually elevate certain human

[105] ibid [174].

[106] Which can be gleaned in ibid [45].

[107] The precarity of this approach became evident in the subsequent *Hany Youssef* case (n 33): having found that in that case the Parliament had acted to restrict the common law right of access to court, the Court found such restriction to be compatible with the ECHR rights, refusing therefore to review the domestic measures implementing the international sanctions against the plaintiff.

[108] *Abdelrazik v Canada* (n 50) [51].

rights norms to the hierarchical status of *jus cogens*.[109] In doing so, they have sometimes adopted 'an unusually expansive reading of *jus cogens*'.[110] In any event, domestic courts have carved out a space for the application of human rights where international sanctions measures are concerned through a pattern of resistance and contestation.

Second, and from a procedural perspective, this attitude of domestic courts has forced States to push for reform of the UN sanctions system. This is because States are otherwise put in an impossible position, where they have to either disobey the Security Council, or their own courts. The pressure put on States has led to at least some avenues being established at UN level for designated entities to challenge their designations, factoring in certain human rights considerations into the process. In many ways, it was the engagement of domestic courts with international sanctions, including at the EU level,[111] that led to the establishment of the Focal Point,[112] and in the special case of the 1267 regime also of the Office of the Ombudsperson, which establishes a process for delisting that essentially renders the report of the Ombudsperson binding on the Security Council.[113] This is evident from the terms of UNSC Res 1904 establishing the Office of the Ombudsperson. According to the resolution's preamble, the UNSC '[took] note of challenges, both legal and otherwise, to the measures implemented by Member States ... and express[ed] its intent to continue efforts to ensure that procedures are fair and clear'.[114]

Whether these developments are in reality beneficial to designated individuals and help safeguard human rights is a complicated question.[115] On the one hand, '[o]n the surface at least ... human rights', and domestic courts, 'seemingly demand a legal ethos and rationality to be incorporated into the practice of blacklisting' individuals under international sanctions.[116] At the same time, however, the introduction of such procedural safeguards and a 'modest level of scrutiny'[117] in international sanctions, has also contributed to their

109 For this argument, see Tzanakopoulos (n 48) 262–64. This trend may have stalled more recently due to the decision of the ECtHR in *Al-Dulimi* (n 39) [8.2], where the court expressly stated that the rights of access to justice and to an effective remedy under Articles 6 and 13 ECHR did not have the status of *jus cogens*, and the approach of the English High Court in *Hany Youssef* (discussed in section C) that further watered down what Article 6 ECHR requires.

110 Devika Hovell, 'Due Process in the United Nations' (2016) 110 AJIL 1, 12, discussing specifically the approach of the EU CFI in *Kadi I* (n 97).

111 See Nanopoulos (n 2) 56–57.

112 See UNSC Res 1730 (2006). The Focal Point allowed designated entities to directly petition the Security Council for delisting, without having to go through their State of nationality.

113 See UNSC Res 1904 (2009); UNSC Res 1989 (2011).

114 UNSC Res 1904 (2009), preamble para 9.

115 See for a discussion Hovell (n 110).

116 Nanopoulos (n 2) 57.

117 As per the English High Court in *Hany Youssef* (n 33).

normalization, 'elid[ing] any real contestation of the emerging blacklisting machinery'.[118] Without making any claims of progress,[119] what this chapter has shown is that the field of international sanctions is rich in practice that demonstrates the different types of engagement of domestic courts with international law, and their potential for operating as 'agents of development'[120] of international law. In what direction the development takes us is of course always up for grabs.

Note: This chapter should be read as a sequel to Antonios Tzanakopoulos, 'Domestic Court Reactions to UN Security Council Sanctions' in August Reinisch (ed), *Challenging Acts of International Organisations before National Courts* (OUP 2010) 54.[121]

[118] See Nanopoulos (n 2) 159 and ch 6 generally.

[119] But see for a thoughtful discussion of the effects of the individualization and juridification of sanctions at the UN and EU level, Nanopoulos (n 2) ch 6 and generally.

[120] On domestic courts as agents of development of international law see the contributions in the 'Symposium on Domestic Courts as Agents of Development of International Law' (2013) 26 Leiden Journal of International Law 531.

[121] The title of the chapter ('Amp Up and Amplify: Defy!') is a quotation that finishes by saying 'We don't need the key—we'll break in': Zack de la Rocha, 'Know your Enemy' in Rage Against the Machine, *Rage Against the Machine* (Epic 1992).

ANNEX

INTERNATIONAL LAW ASSOCIATION JOHANNESBURG CONFERENCE (2016)

(STUDY GROUP ON) PRINCIPLES ON THE ENGAGEMENT OF DOMESTIC COURTS WITH INTERNATIONAL LAW

Members of the Study Group
Professor André Nollkaemper (Netherlands): *Chair*
Professor Yuval Shany (Israel): *Co-Rapporteur*
Professor Antonios Tzanakopoulos (UK): *Co-Rapporteur*

Professor Curtis A Bradley (US)
Professor BS Chimni (HQ)
Dr Frédéric Dopagne (Belgium)
Ms Shaheed Fatima QC (UK)
Professor James T Gathii (US)
Professor Yuji Iwasawa (Japan)
Professor Bing Bing Jia (HQ)
Professor Karen Knop (Canada)
Professor Ralf Michaels (US)
Justice Andreas Paulus (Germany)
Professor Anne Peters (Switzerland)
Justice Ariranga Pillay (HQ)
Professor Mónica Pinto (Argentina)
Professor August Reinisch (Austria)
Professor Anthea Roberts (Australia)

FINAL REPORT

Mapping the Engagement of Domestic Courts with International Law

by Antonios Tzanakopoulos*
Co-Rapporteur of the Study Group

Introduction

1. This Final Report is the outcome of the work of the Study Group on *Principles on the Engagement of Domestic Courts with International Law*. It draws on previously

* Associate Professor of Public International Law, University of Oxford; and Fellow of St Anne's College, Oxford. Apart from thanking the Chair of the Study Group, André Nollkaemper, its Co-Rapporteur, Yuval Shany, and all the members and researchers who submitted work, views, comments, and participated in the open and closed meetings of the Study Group, the author would like to acknowledge the excellent research assistance of Eleni Methymaki and Anna Ventouratou. Responsibility for all errors and omissions in this Final Report, however, rests with the author.

published work by the officers of the Study Group,[1] as well as from the Preliminary Report of the Study Group.[2] It mainly draws, however, on the discussions that took place during a number of both open and closed Study Group meetings since 2011, including in Amsterdam, London, Sofia,[3] Washington DC,[4] and Heidelberg, as well as from a number of thematic and national reports solicited from Study Group members and from scholars from around the world.[5]

2. After introducing the underlying reason for the work of the Study Group, namely the increased relevance of domestic[6] courts for international law (Part A, section I), the Final Report sets out the challenges presented by the different constitutional settings, the different methods and techniques of domestic court engagement with international law, and its different outcomes (Part A, section II). Part B of the Final Report seeks to map the postures or strategies of domestic court engagement with international law by drawing on the work submitted to the Discussion Group by its members and other scholars. Part C then discusses the grounds or reasons that emerge as justifying different strategies or postures of engagement, with a view to laying the groundwork for the normative exercise of compiling a set of principles or guidelines for the engagement of domestic courts with international law. This latter work, however, is one properly mandated to a Committee of the International Law Association, rather than the Study Group, whose work prepared the ground for such a normative exercise.
3. Before launching into the substantive discussion, the term 'engagement', chosen for the title of the Study Group's work, needs to be explained. The driving principle for the choice of the term was to avoid a binary approach (enforcement/application versus non-enforcement/breach) in favour of a functional approach: the term 'engagement' captures, in the Study Group's view, the richness of approaches of domestic courts to international law. The Study Group's aim is to try and extract some general categories of engagement from this diversity.
4. The courts of the European Union are included in the Study Group's understanding of 'domestic courts', at least to the extent that these, as functionally hybrid courts, engage in judicial/constitutional review that is akin to that normally undertaken by domestic courts.[7] This is not to question that EU courts do also operate in 'normal international law mode'.

[1] See generally the work of A Nollkaemper, and especially his *National Courts and the International Rule of Law* (OUP, Oxford 2011); the work of Y Shany, and especially his *Regulating Jurisdictional Relations between National and International Courts* (OUP, Oxford 2007); and A Tzanakopoulos, mainly 'Domestic Courts as the "Natural Judge" of International Law: A Change in Physiognomy' in J Crawford and S Nouwen (eds), *Select Proceedings of the European Society of International Law* (vol 3, Hart, Oxford 2012) 155–68; and 'Domestic Courts in International Law: The International Judicial Function of National Courts' (2011) 34 Loyola of LA Int'l & Comp L Rev 133–68.

[2] See International Law Association, *Report of the Seventy-Fifth Conference held in Sofia* (ILA, London 2012) 971–83.

[3] See ibid, 984–93.

[4] See International Law Association, *Report of the Seventy-Sixth Conference held in Washington, DC* (ILA, London 2014) 900–15.

[5] These reports will be made available on the Study Group's website at <http://www.ila-hq.org/en/study-groups/index.cfm/cid/1039> and a forthcoming publication. A list can be found at the end of this Final Report.

[6] The term 'domestic' is considered as interchangeable with 'national' and 'municipal' in this Final Report.

[7] See further paragraph 13 below.

PART A: THE CHALLENGES OF MAPPING DOMESTIC COURT ENGAGEMENT

I. The Increased Relevance of Domestic Courts for International Law

a. The traditional position

5. International law traditionally treats domestic law, including domestic court decisions, as facts.[8] As a fact, a domestic court decision construing international law may be seen either as being in harmony with the international obligations of the State or as being in breach of them.[9] In the latter case the domestic court decision may create an international dispute (or allow a dispute to 'mature' so as to become internationally justiciable, as for example is the case when the rule of exhaustion of local remedies applies), or it may engage the international responsibility of the State.[10] Furthermore, domestic court decisions are to be considered elements of the practice of States, or ways through which States may express their *opinio juris* or views on the proper interpretation of their international obligations. As such, they may contribute to the formation of customary international law or to the understanding of the scope and content of treaties. This is different from domestic court decisions potentially constituting 'material sources' of international law in the sense of Article 38(1)(d) of the ICJ Statute.
6. There is little doubt that significant areas of public international law have been shaped by domestic court jurisprudence, which provided the requisite state practice and *opinio juris* for the creation of custom—the law of immunity being but one such example.[11] Furthermore, since domestic courts are organs of the State, their decisions

[8] *Certain German Interests in Polish Upper Silesia* (Merits) [1926] PCIJ Ser A No 7 at 19. CW Jenks, *The Prospects of International Adjudication* (Stevens, London 1964) 552, already noted however that the general proposition that national laws are to be treated before international tribunals only as facts is 'at most, a debatable proposition the validity and wisdom of which are subject to, and call for, further discussion and review'.

[9] International courts commonly treat domestic laws, and domestic court decisions, as evidence of the breach by a State of its obligations under an international treaty or under customary law. See J Crawford, *Brownlie's Principles of Public International Law* (8th edn, OUP, Oxford 2012) 52; WTO, India: *Patent Protection for Pharmaceutical and Agricultural Chemical Products* (*India-Patents*)—Report of the Appellate Body (19 December 1997) WT/DS50/AB/R [65]. See however further Article 38(1)(d) ICJ Statute and paragraph 6 below.

[10] See Article 4 of the Articles on the Responsibility of States for Internationally Wrongful Acts (2001), Annex to UN General Assembly resolution 56/83 (12 December 2001), UN Doc A/RES/56/83 and Commentary (2001) II(2) YBILC ('ARSIWA'); and cf generally C Eustathiadès, *La responsabilité internationale de l'État pour les actes des organes judiciaires et le problème du déni de justice en droit international* (vol 1, Pedone, Paris 1936).

[11] See the collection of essays in A Tzanakopoulos and CJ Tams (eds), *Symposium on Domestic Courts as Agents of Development of International Law* (2013) 26 Leiden Journal of International Law 531–665, with contributions by R O'Keefe, R van Alebeek, D Hovell, Y Ronen, S Olleson, and S Wittich. Another area of international law which has been shaped to some extent by the jurisprudence of domestic courts is that of international environmental law. Important cases include the *Minors Oposa* case (*Minors Oposa v Secretary of the Department of Environmental and Natural Resources*, Supreme Court of Philippines, Judgment of 30 July 1993, 33 ILM 173 [1994]) and the *Vellore Citizens Welfare Forum* case (*Vellore Citizens Welfare Forum v Union of India and Ors*, Supreme Court of India, Judgment

may constitute subsequent practice affecting the content of international law norms, within the meaning of Article 31(3)(b) VCLT.[12] Finally, given that domestic courts could be seen as included in the term 'judicial decisions' in Article 38(1)(d) of the ICJ Statute, they may constitute subsidiary means for the determination of rules of international law.[13]

7. The potential for conflict between the courts and the executive in the area of formation of customary international law should be highlighted at this juncture. In principle, it is only when decisions of domestic courts are *not* 'rejected' by the State's executive (in the sense of being considered and outwardly presented as *not* representing the State's practice on the relevant issue) that they are capable of contributing towards the formation or development of customary law.[14] This is because the formation or development of custom arguably requires consistent practice of all branches of government.[15] The requirement of consistency could be seen as a projection of the domestic constitutional principle of separation of powers at the international level. It guarantees that the executive or legislative branch can adopt different approaches than those taken by courts in the course of formation of international law, and thereby they may limit the impact of domestic courts on the formation of that law.[16] Conflicting practice of different branches of government could not constitute the consistent practice required for the emergence of a customary norm. In any event, it also may be that a decision by the executive is annulled or declared to be incompatible with international law by a domestic court, in which case the executive action would not necessarily be considered to express the State's *opinio juris*. As such, the discussion above does not necessarily

of 28 August 1996, Air 1996 Sc 2715). See further D Bodansky and J Brunnée, 'The Role of National Courts in the Field of International Environmental Law' (1998) 7 Review of European Comparative and International Environmental Law 11; and M Anderson and P Galizzi (eds), *International Environmental Law in National Courts* (BIICL 2002).

[12] See *Prosecutor v Goran Jelisić*, ICTY Trial Chamber Judgment, Case No IT-95-10-T (14 December 1999) [61]; Second Report of Special Rapporteur Georg Nolte on 'Subsequent Agreements and Subsequent Practice in relation to the Interpretation of Treaties', UN Doc A/CN.4/671 (26 March 2014) [42].

[13] But see M Mendelson, 'The International Court of Justice and the Sources of International Law' in V Lowe and M Fitzmaurice (eds), *Fifty Years of the International Court of Justice: Essays in Honour of Sir Robert Jennings* (CUP, Cambridge 1996) 63, 69 and 82; A Pellet, 'Article 38' in A Zimmerman et al (eds), *The Statute of the International Court of Justice: A Commentary* (2nd edn, OUP, Oxford 2012) 862 [321]; cf A Roberts, 'Comparative International Law? The Role of National Courts in Creating and Enforcing International Law' (2011) 60 International and Comparative Law Quarterly 57.

[14] See Sir R Jennings and Sir A Watts (eds), *Oppenheim's International Law: Volume I Peace* (9th edn, Longman, London 1996): '[C]ourts are not organs of the state for expressing in a binding manner its views on foreign affairs'; E Benvenisti, 'Reclaiming Democracy: The Strategic Uses of Foreign and International Law by National Courts' (2008) 102 American Journal of International Law 241, 248; Roberts (n 13) 62.

[15] See International Law Commission, 'Identification of Customary International Law', UN Doc A/CN.4/L.869 (2015), draft conclusions 6–8; B Simma and A Paulus, 'The Responsibility of Individuals for Human Rights Abuses in Internal Conflicts: A Positivist View' (1999) 93 American Journal of International Law 306; see generally also I Wuerth, 'International Law in Domestic Courts and the *Jurisdictional Immunities of the State* Case' (2012) 13 Melbourne Journal of International Law 1, 5 citing this Study Group's Preliminary Report (n 2), as well as M Akehurst, 'Custom as a Source of International Law' (1975) 47 British Year Book of International Law 1, 21–22 and Roberts (n 13) 61.

[16] See *North Sea Continental Shelf Cases (The Netherlands/Germany; Denmark/Germany)* [1969] ICJ Reports 3, 44 [74].

imply priority of one branch of government over another in the formation of customary law.[17]

8. Even if not contradicted by the State's executive or other State organs, a domestic court's decision may still be of little or even negligible impact in the formation of customary law. States other than the forum state may also challenge the decision of the domestic court, thereby leading to contradictory State practice or *opinio juris*. Of course, this is in no way peculiar for domestic courts and simply reflects the normal process of the formation of customary international law.
9. The historically limited role of domestic courts in international law is further confirmed by the traditionally bilateralist performance structure of international obligations (*traité-contrat*). International obligations usually demand(ed) performance by one State towards another on the international plane—eg omission from intervention in its domestic affairs, abstention from the threat or use of force, default permission to innocently pass through the territorial sea, etc. Domestic courts would have little to say with respect to the performance of such obligations: the doctrine of immunity or 'act of State' would preclude them from pronouncing on another State's (sovereign) acts, while they would also traditionally avoid pronouncing on the conduct of international relations or foreign affairs of their own State, having developed a number of relevant 'avoidance techniques' to that effect.[18]

b. The reasons for increased engagement

10. The traditionally bilateralist performance structure of international law has been put under constant and significant strain in the last decades.[19] At the danger of stating the trite, more and more regulation is taking place today at the international plane, ie at a level beyond the State. The development of various areas of international law regulated by multilateral instruments, otherwise called 'sectoral regimes', do not fit within this bilateral scheme. The international law on the protection of human rights is the most obvious example of the bilateralist structure breaking down and being replaced by a multilateral framework of protection (*traité-loi*). International environmental law, aspects of the law of the sea, and other areas of international law, including international investment law, international economic law, international criminal law, international humanitarian law, and so forth, also reflect this development. The attempts then to protect general interests through the assumption of international obligations lead, in the event of a violation, to a lack of any identifiable 'specifically'

[17] But see the position of the ILA Committee on Formation of Customary (General) International Law, 'Final Report: Statement of Principles Applicable to the Formation of General Customary International Law' in International Law Association, *Report of the Sixty-Ninth Conference held in London* (ILA, London 2000) 712, 729. In discussing principle 9, the Committee notes in paragraph (e) of its commentary that 'since it is the executive which has primary responsibility for the conduct of foreign relations, that organ's formal position ought usually to be accorded more weight than conflicting positions of the legislature or the national courts'. The Committee does however go on to note the point on consistency made just above: 'But it should also be noted that, in such a case, the internal uniformity or consistency which is needed for a State's practice to count towards the formation of a customary rule may anyway be prejudiced'.

[18] See further Part A, section II, below.

[19] See generally B Simma, 'From Bilateralism to Community Interest in International Law' (1994) 250 Recueil des cours de l'Académie de droit international de La Haye 217.

injured State,[20] and make it more difficult to demonstrate any specific or quantifiable damage—on which all forms of reparation for internationally wrongful acts are predicated under the law of State responsibility.[21]

11. But even in traditionally bilateralist areas of international law, the latter has developed so as to remove the clearly inter-state slant in the implementation of international obligations. Indeed, traditional international law was primarily concerned with the establishment of State-to-State obligations that were to be implemented through conduct on the international plane, that is *outward-looking* obligations. States were then by-and-large free to determine what measures were required within the domestic legal order to implement these obligations, if any were required at all.
12. Today, however, international obligations are increasingly *inward-looking*. This means that they specifically enjoin States to undertake certain conduct *within their own domestic legal order*: to adopt a specific legal framework, to accord individual rights, to abstain from taking specific actions, etc. International human rights law (protection of specific rights) or international environmental law (eg curbing of emissions,[22] or obligations to grant access to information, justice, or obligations to allow participation in decision-making[23]) may be invoked as the obvious example. Still, one may also think of analogous examples from diverse fields, such as WTO law (obligations to regulate subsidies, curb dumping, adopt technical regulations within the domestic legal order in accordance with prescribed processes and on prescribed grounds, and so forth),[24] international investment law (curbing State regulatory power, even in areas of human rights, or environmental protection, in order to grant 'fair and equitable treatment' to investors—or, more simply, being bound to follow particular internationally accepted procedures in order to exercise regulatory power affecting, if only incidentally, foreign investments/investors, and so forth), international criminal law (obligations to criminalise within the domestic legal order certain behaviour defined in international treaties),[25] the international law of the sea, and even diplomatic and consular law, which traditionally required States to adopt certain conduct within their domestic legal order.[26]
13. Penetrating the façade of the unitary State, looking at these obligations from within it, ie from the perspective of the individuals within the jurisdiction of the State, these

[20] Cf Article 48 ARSIWA.

[21] See Article 31 ARSIWA and commentary.

[22] For example under the Kyoto Protocol to the United Nations Framework Convention on Climate Change (11 December 1997, entered into force 16 February 2005) 2303 UNTS 1.

[23] For example under the Aarhus Convention (Convention on Access to Information, Public Participation in Decision-Making and Access to Justice in Environmental Matters (25 June 1998, entered into force 30 October 2002) 2161 UNTS 447).

[24] cf E-U Petersman, 'Multi-Level Judicial Trade Governance Without Justice? On the Role of Domestic Courts in the WTO Legal and Political Settlement System' (2006) EUI Working Papers Law No2006/44.

[25] For example under the United Nations Convention against Corruption (31 October 2003, entered into force 14 December 2005) 2349 UNTS 41 and the United Nations Convention against Organized Crime (15 November 2002, entered into force 29 September 2003) 2225 UNTS 209.

[26] See eg the ICJ decisions in *LaGrand* [2001] ICJ Reports 466 and *Avena and other Mexican Nationals* [2004] ICJ Reports 12, where the US was required to bring its domestic law and process into compliance with its international obligations to allow consular assistance under the 1963 VCCR. See also the flare-up between the UK and Ecuador regarding the UK's ability to withdraw the qualification of Ecuador's Embassy in London as diplomatic premises under a relevant UK Statute of 1987: see the contributions of 16 and 17 August 2012 by R O'Keefe and D Akande, available at <http://www.ejiltalk.org>.

international obligations look merely as constraints on State power: executive or legislative action needs to take place within the limits set by the State's obligations. It is domestic law that in some way enables the 'reception' of international law in the domestic legal system (and it does so in virtually all domestic legal systems, even if with significant differences[27]). Individuals (and legal entities) within the State's jurisdiction will thus regularly challenge executive action for compliance with the limits imposed on such action (challenges against legislative action are, however, more unusual) without necessarily distinguishing whether these limits have their source in domestic or international law (especially in legal contexts where international law can be relied upon before domestic courts). It is also normal for domestic courts to be called upon to police executive compliance with the limits posed on State action—this, in the final analysis, is part of their mandate. As such, individuals will turn to domestic courts employing international legal arguments, and domestic courts will thus be forced to engage with these arguments.

14. The analysis above aims to account for the increased significance of domestic courts in the interpretation, application, but also development, of international law. This significance is mainly asserted rather than proven empirically, as is the increased engagement of domestic courts with international law. It makes sense to assert that this is so, given the high visibility of domestic decisions in the last couple of decades, be it—among others—with respect to sovereign immunity, or with respect to compliance with or disobedience of Security Council sanctions, and given further the increasing interdependence of States and concurrent 'blurring of the dividing line' between international and domestic law due to the new 'directionality' of international obligations described above.[28] While empirical research needs to be undertaken to prove in specific terms this increased engagement, to delineate its scope and impact, as well as to assess the increased significance for international law of domestic court decisions, this is not the mandate of this Study Group.[29]
15. One final note of caution is necessary, however. Even if there is increased engagement of domestic courts with international law in recent years, this may be more the case in some States than in others. A recent study by a member of this Study Group demonstrates that citations to domestic case law in international law textbooks and in judgments of many international courts and tribunals come overwhelmingly from Western liberal democratic States in general and from a handful of those States in particular.[30] Focusing on domestic case law as evidence of the content, or even as a

[27] See further Part A, section II.a, below.

[28] Benvenisti (n 14) 241–242, argues that the increased engagement of domestic courts with international law 'is part of a reaction to the forces of globalization, which are placing increasing pressure on the different branches of government to conform to global standards . . . Stated differently, most national courts, seeking to maintain the vitality of their national political institutions and to safeguard their one domestic status vis-à-vis the political branches, cannot afford to ignore foreign and international law'; cf Y Shany, 'National Courts as International Actors: Jurisdictional Implications' (2008) Hebrew University International Law Research Paper No. 22-08, available at <http://dx.doi.org/10.2139/ssrn.1292056>.

[29] But see for a classic statement of the assertion JG Collier and V Lowe, *The Settlement of Disputes in International Law* (OUP, Oxford 1999) 5.

[30] A Roberts, *Is International Law* International? (forthcoming: OUP, Oxford 2017). References were overwhelmingly made to US and UK case law, followed by French, Canadian, Australian, German and Israeli case law, and to a lesser extent Italian, South African, Dutch, and Belgian case law.

source, of international law may have the effect of rendering the practice of some significant States less visible to the extent that it rarely occurs in their domestic courts, or to the extent that the relevant decisions are rarely reported or not easily accessible (including because of linguistic barriers). It could also result in a disproportionate focus on accessible decisions in the domestic courts of influential, English-speaking, common law States, like the United States and the United Kingdom. A number of points could be made in this respect, drawing parallels to the relative weight to be accorded to practice coming from different States in the process of determining the emergence of customary law, noting the practice of some courts, notably the German and Israeli highest courts, of circulating (partial) translations of important judgments, and so forth. This Final Report is not the place to further discuss these issues, but they should be noted and it should also be highlighted that both the members of the Study Group and the author of the Final Report are acutely aware of such considerations.

II. The Infinite Variety of Engagement

16. The previous section aimed at laying the groundwork which potentially explains—if it does not prove—the increased significance of domestic courts for international law. But how domestic courts actually engage with international law is a perennial question that has yet to be mapped out satisfactorily. One reason for this is the 'infinite variety' of constitutional set-ups regulating the reception of international law within the domestic legal order of any given State, and the subsequent infinite variety of domestic court engagement with these rules of international law. This in part explains, if it does not justify, the application of (and thus arguably also compliance with) international law by the domestic court, as well as the denial of application of (and thus potential breach of) international law. These issues are taken up in turn.

a. Variations in the Reception of international law

17. The traditional distinction between **monism** and **dualism** leads to the two traditional methods of reception of international law into domestic law, thus corresponding roughly to **incorporation** and **transformation** respectively. If the domestic constitution adopts a monist approach, international law is (ideally) 'automatically' considered part of domestic law and thus incorporated in the legal order of the State. If, by contrast, the domestic constitution takes a dualist stance, then international law remains an external body of law that must be transformed into domestic law through the adoption of some domestic (usually legislative) act in order to lay claim to application in the domestic jurisdiction and before domestic courts.
18. This picture is already rather simplified.[31] In reality domestic law, even if it adopts a 'monist' stance, sets a number of prerequisites before 'incorporating' international

[31] See eg A Paulus, 'The Emergence of the International Community and the Divide between International and Domestic Law', in J Nijman and A Nollkaemper (ed), *New Perspectives on the Divide*

law, or distinguishes between different sources of international law—eg, treaties ratified by the US explicitly form part of the law of the land, while there is no specific provision for customary law;[32] by contrast, the UK arguably 'incorporates' customary law into the common law, or rather treats it as a source of the common law,[33] but requires transformation of treaties before there can be any domestic application.[34] The position is similar in Canadian law,[35] while a similar position has also been judicially developed in Israel.[36] The Greek constitution provides for the 'incorporation' of treaties ratified by Greece, which however takes place through the adoption of a formal law to that effect each and every time, while it makes little relevant provision for customary law, although it states in general terms that 'generally accepted rules of international law' constitute an 'inalienable part' of Greek law.[37] The South African Constitution determines that both treaties and custom are directly applicable in the South African legal order, but requires transformation of treaties unless they are self-executing, while custom is considered as automatically incorporated only if it is not in conflict with the Constitution or legislative acts.[38] In Germany, general international law is automatically incorporated with precedence over contrary legislation, whereas treaties of a political or legislative nature are incorporated by a law of parliament and share, in principle, their rank.[39] Constitutional orders may introduce distinctions even within the same source of international law: the German,[40] South African and Turkish constitutions distinguish between human rights treaties and other treaties as regards their legal effects in the domestic legal order; the legal position in the Argentinean legal order has nowadays evolved into prioritizing a 'constitutional bloc' consisting of the Constitution and human rights obligations, followed by international treaties and finally ordinary law;[41] the Austrian constitution grants a specific treaty (the ECHR) constitutional rank; the Swiss constitution grants quasi supra-constitutional status to *jus cogens* norms.[42] Notably, the Sri Lankan

between National and International Law (OUP, Oxford 2007) 228 – 234 for an argument that the juxtaposition between monism and dualism masks the pluralism of legal orders.

32 The position in Israel is similar: see the *Report on Israel* (2013) [1]–[2].

33 See in detail for the complex position of customary international law under UK law R O'Keefe, 'The Doctrine of Incorporation Revisited' (2008) 79 British Year Book of International Law 7–85 and cf the *Report on England* (2015) [35]–[39].

34 See also the *Report on England* (2015) [35]–[39]. See further the *Report on South Africa* (2013) (2)–(3) for the similar position that State.

35 *See the Report on Canada* (2013) 3–4.

36 See the *Report on Israel* (2013) [1]–[2].

37 See Article 28(1) of the Constitution of Greece (2008), available at <http://www.hellenicparliament.gr/UserFiles/f3c70a23-7696-49db-9148-f24dce6a27c8/001-156%20aggliko.pdf>.

38 See the *Report on South Africa* (2013) (2)–(3).

39 Cf Articles 25 and 59 of the German Basic Law; and BVerfG, Beschluss des Zweiten Senats vom 15. Dezember 2015 - 2 BvL 1/12 [35]ff, available at <http://www.bverfg.de/e/ls20151215_2bvl000112.html> (partial transl in Press Release No 9/2016 of 12 February 2016, available at <www.bverfg.de>); cf A Paulus, 'Germany' in D Sloss (ed), *The Role of Domestic Courts in Treaty Enforcement* (CUP, Cambridge 2009) 217–219.

40 Article 1(2) of the German Basic Law provides for a special status of core human rights treaties: see Beschluss des Zweiten Senats vom 15. Dezember 2015 (n 39) [76] with further references.

41 See generally the *Report on Argentina* (2015).

42 It should be noted that the 'Swiss' notion of *jus cogens* is broader than that currently acceptable under international law, but Swiss courts will not consider a treaty void for conflicting with the broader notion of *jus cogens*. See generally the *Report on Switzerland* (2013).

Constitution subjects all of international law to the Constitution and to ordinary law, but provides that investment treaties are only subject to the Constitution.[43]

19. Within this great variety, many further variations are possible. These relate to the hierarchical standing of international law, or of particular sources of international law, in the domestic hierarchical pyramid, some of which have been incidentally mentioned in the preceding paragraph. International law (or particular sources, or particular elements within sources, such as human rights treaties) may be given a standing equal to that of ordinary law, superior to that of ordinary law, or even superior to that of the domestic constitution. Further, even 'automatic' incorporation does not guarantee the applicability of international law in the domestic legal order, as domestic law may allow 'direct effect' of certain sources of international law only, or of some elements within such sources only (eg self-executing treaties), or may permit the local constitution or even subsequent or more special ordinary law to override international law. This brief sketch demonstrates that the distinction between monism and dualism is simplistic and often unhelpful: not only may both approaches be adopted within a given domestic legal order, but it can be further argued that there is no such thing as 'monism' properly so-called: in all circumstances, and as far as domestic courts are concerned, the reception of international law into the domestic legal order is regulated by domestic law itself, whether more or less stringently.
20. On the other hand, the position of international law on legal hierarchy and relevance is clear, and quite indifferent to any variations in its reception by domestic law. Domestic law (of any importance or hierarchical standing) may never constitute justification for the non-compliance by a State with its international obligations.[44]

b. Variations in the Application of International Law

21. Depending on the relevant domestic constitutional ordering, to which domestic courts are of course bound, the latter may proceed to give effect to international law, relying on relevant constitutional principles, or they may be able to refuse its application for a variety of reasons. Domestic courts have devised[45] a wide range of **blunting rules** or **moderating techniques** that moderate the effects of both **monism/incorporation** and **dualism/transformation.** To start with incorporation, there is no guarantee that this will lead to direct application of international law by the domestic court. Domestic courts have devised a variety of avoidance techniques, which allow them to blunt the otherwise sharp edge of constitutional requirements to apply international legal provisions: these include the doctrine of **non-justiciability** (wherein one might include the **political question** doctrine), the **act-of-State** doctrine, denials of **standing,** and the doctrine of **non-self-execution** of treaties, among others. Even the avoidance of substantive international law questions through **according immunity** (whether to a foreign State under international law or to the forum State under domestic law) may be seen as such a blunting technique, even though of course

[43] See the *Report on Sri Lanka* (2013) 6.

[44] See Article 3 ARSIWA and cf Article 27 of the Vienna Convention on the Law of Treaties (23 May 1969, entered into force27 January 1980) 1155 UNTS 331.

[45] Though the position may be taken that the blunting or moderating techniques 'stem' from domestic law and its provision as to the position of international law in the domestic legal system, and thus domestic courts merely apply, rather than devise, these techniques.

we have to recognize that respecting immunity itself may be a form of application of international obligations.

22. The increase in inward-looking norms of international law creates a larger contact area between domestic and international law, which in turn has the potential of leading to greater conflict between the two sets of rules. The importance of this development is illustrated in recent domestic cases which might be taken as signaling a '**reactive turn** (of domestic courts) **to domestic law**' in the face of 'inconvenient' international law. This 'reactive turn' might be considered another blunting technique, similar in function to the ones described above. The difference here is that the domestic court does not refuse to pronounce on a matter involving international law (as for example in cases of non-justiciability or act-of-State), but rather may accept that international law is implicated but deliberately—if sometimes implicitly—reject its application. A number of recent cases can be seen as falling in this category: reactions to Security Council sanctions, such as *Kadi*[46] in the EU courts and *Ahmed*[47] in the UK courts, form one such group; while cases like *Medellín*[48] in the US Supreme Court form another, to the extent that the latter court refuses to apply the binding decision of an international court. The constitutional acceptance of 'treaty override' by contrary domestic legislation provides another example of the 'reactive turn to domestic law'.[49] Whether these groups of cases do indeed form separate categories, or belong in the same category, is something that requires further study.[50] We may be dealing here with a type of constitutional review where fundamental values are invoked against (other) international law rules as part of a process of normative contestation. Such an approach would seem to conceive the legal order as unitary and attempt to hierarchically order various rules and principles within the unitary legal system. Or we may be dealing with a claim of hierarchical structuring of separate legal orders, whereby the international legal order is subjected to the court's domestic legal order (which from the perspective of the international legal order would be a clear breach of international law as indicated in paragraph 20 above).

23. Conversely, there are ways in which domestic courts may give indirect effect to international law even if the latter has not been **transformed** through a domestic act as required by the relevant constitutional framework. This is mainly done through the principle of **consistent interpretation**, which has been introduced through judicial practice,[51] or even through constitutional

[46] Joined Cases C-402/05 P and C-415/05 P [2008] ECR I-6351; cf Case T-85/09 *Kadi II* [2010] ECR II-5177; and Joined Cases C-584/10 P, 593/10 P and C-595/10 P *Kadi II* [2013] ECLI:EU:C:2013:518.

[47] [2010] UKSC 2.

[48] 552 US 491 (2008).

[49] BVerfG, Beschluss des Zweiten Senats vom 15. Dezember 2015 (n 39).

[50] Some views are set out in Part B below.

[51] For reasons of space, only a brief overview will be given here. The *locus classicus* is the US Supreme Court's *Charming Betsy* principle: *Murray v The Charming Betsy* 6 US 64, 118 (1804); see also *MacLeod v US* 229 US 416, 434 (1913); *F Hoffmann-La Roche Ltd v Empagran SA* 542 US 155, 163 (2004). See further on this C Bradley, *International Law in the US Legal System* (2nd edn, OUP, New York 2015) 15–18. In Germany the rule of consistent interpretation is seen as flowing from the *Völkerrechtsfreundlichkeit* of the Basic Law, and has been reiterated by the Federal Constitutional Court in 74 BVerfGE 358, 370; see also 128 BVerfGE 326, 367–372. In Switzerland the principle of consistent interpretation is called '*Schubert-Praxis*' and flows from the relevant practice of the Federal Supreme Court. A principle of consistent interpretation exists in Australia, as enunciated by the High Court in *Kruger and ors v Commonwealth of Australia* reported in 118 ILR 371, 374, 377–379. In New Zealand there exists a very strong presumption of conformity with international law: see P Sales and J Clement, 'International Law in Domestic Courts: the Developing Framework' (2008) 124 LQR 388, 393–394; as it does in Canada,

entrenchment,[52] in a significant number of domestic legal orders. Taking a fairly broad-brush approach to the principle, it effectively institutes a presumption in favour of harmony of domestic law with international law. The domestic court will presume that the domestic legislator did not mean to introduce legislation in breach of the State's international obligations, and will thus seek to interpret domestic law 'in the light of' or 'in accordance with' the State's international obligations, ie with international law. The presumption is of course rebuttable, but the difficulty of rebutting it fluctuates between different legal orders, some making the presumption virtually irrebuttable, others allowing its rebuttal even by necessary implication, as discussed below.

24. Consistent interpretation typically requires at least some ambiguity in domestic law, which needs to be construed, in order to invite the application of international law. However, different domestic courts have taken a variety of positions on the degree of ambiguity required to initiate the interpretative process, some requiring none at all.[53] Further, consistent interpretation in some cases refers merely to treaties, or it excludes from application constitutional texts, and so forth. A field of domestic law where the interpretative application of international law may be of particular interest is administrative law. If statutes authorizing administrative actions are subject to a presumption of consistency with international law, then so is the relevant administrative action, which may be challenged and brought under judicial scrutiny.

25. Domestic courts have also sought to apply other interpretative principles which are similar to the principle of consistent interpretation. One such principle is that of **legitimate expectations**, which has been used by Australian and Scottish courts and by the Privy Council.[54] It effectively construes treaty ratification (among others, possibly) as a promise on which it allows basing some doctrine of promissory estoppel. Finally, what may be seen as a most potent principle of interpretation is that of **legality**. It holds that the domestic legislature may not be considered as derogating from or abrogating an international right or duty save when it does so explicitly. In

both with respect to treaty obligations and obligations under general international law: *R v Hape* [2007] 2 SCR 292; 2007 SCC 26 [53]; *B010 v Canada (Citizenship and Immigration)* 2015 SCC 58 [47]–[48]; cf K Knop, 'Here and There: International Law in Domestic Courts' (1999-2000) 32 New York University Journal of International Law and Policy 501. South African courts also employ the principle of consistent interpretation: *AZAPO and ors v South Africa and ors* [1996] ZACC 16 [26]. Italian courts engage in a rather peculiar construction with results similar to those when adopting a principle of consistent interpretation: they consider international law rules as special norms who are not superseded by later (domestic) general norms. See B Conforti, 'National Courts and the International Law of Human Rights' in idem and F Francioni (eds), *Enforcing International Human Rights in Domestic Courts* (Martinus Nijhoff, The Hague 1997) 3, 11–12. As to the United Kingdom, there is (a) a presumption of compatibility in the common law regarding unincorporated treaty obligations; and (b) a statutory provision in the Human Rights Act 1998, which transforms the ECHR, which imposes a similar presumption. Finally, the ECJ has adopted a principle of consistent interpretation of EU law with international obligations of the EU: see Cases C-286/90 *Poulsen* [1992] ECR I-6019 [9]; and C-308/06 *Intertanko* ECR I-4057 [51].

[52] See the *Report on South Africa* (2013) (3)–(4).

[53] See for example the *Report on England* (2015) [27]–[31]; the *Report on South Africa* (2013) (5); and the *Report on Canada* (2013) 20.

[54] See for example *Minister for Immigration and Ethnic Affairs v Teoh* (1995) 183 CLR 273. There have been contradictory decisions in English courts regarding the doctrine of legitimate expectations deriving from the signature and ratification of an unincorporated treaty, see *Report on England* (2015) [33.3].

effect, this principle may lead to an almost irrebuttable presumption of conformity with international law, though in practice the strength of the presumption again varies.[55]

26. Finally, domestic courts may use international law as a way to '**understand**' the world, and thus domestic legislation, and not just as a method to interpret domestic law in order to avoid a breach of the State's international obligations.[56] In this conception of interaction between international and domestic law, international law provides a set of definitions which help the domestic court *understand* domestic legislation rather than *override* it. Examples could include the (controversial) use of international materials to understand the content of 'cruel and unusual punishment' in domestic law[57] and to interpret a presidential authorization to use force.[58] Another such example is the use of the Alien Tort Claims Act, a one-sentence long statute almost two centuries old, as a vehicle for examining the human rights-related practice of other States in US courts.[59]
27. All of the techniques described in paragraphs 23–26 above (which can also be positioned on a spectrum ranging from more to less rigid techniques) we may still call **blunting techniques**, as we did with the techniques described in paragraphs 21–22 (which we also called 'avoidance' techniques). This is because both sets of techniques each blunt the sharp edges of incorporation and transformation respectively.
28. To summarize, the main scheme so far positions the two **main techniques**, that of **incorporation** and that of **transformation**, at the opposite ends of a spectrum; but a number of **blunting rules** or **moderating techniques** immediately come into play and position the various legal orders all along the spectrum: **a first set of blunting rules** mainly moderate the impact of **incorporation**, pushing towards the transformation end of the spectrum, while **a second set of blunting rules** moderate the impact of the requirement for **transformation**, and pull towards the incorporation end of the spectrum.
29. An observation is called for with respect to the paradoxical counter-move indicated in paragraph 28 above: it refers precisely to the seemingly paradoxical moderation of the opposing main positions of incorporation and transformation, so that irrespective of the local constitutional set-up, blunting or moderating may lead to similar outcomes in differently internationally inclined domestic legal orders. This paradoxical counter-move is revealing, and perhaps points towards blunting or moderating as dependent not on the local constitutional set-up, but rather on the substance of the relevant domestic and international rules at stake in each instance of engagement. Once again then, the substance of the rules at stake seems to be decisive as regards the engagement of the domestic court with international law. This is not meant to ignore that, in some cases, other factors, such as the individual preferences of specific judges, may also explain some of the inclination or disinclination to apply international law. An attempt to discuss such factors is made in Part C, after the engagement of domestic courts with international law has been mapped in Part B.

[55] See the *Report on England* (2015) [27]ff, [33.3].

[56] See for example ibid, [33.2] citing *McIntosh v HM Advocate* [2003] 1 AC 1078, in which an unincorporated international treaty was used to 'illuminate' the object and purpose of the relevant domestic legislation.

[57] See *Roper v Simmons* 543 US 551 (2005).

[58] See *Hamdi v Rumsfeld* 542 US 507 (2004). See further Bradley (n 51) 309–311.

[59] See the litigation under the *Alien Tort Claims Act* 28 USC §1350 (1789); cf Roberts (n 13) 76–77.

30. To the operation of these main and moderating techniques we should add another interesting variation which also heavily depends on the substance of the rule at stake and is currently understudied: this is the use of '**consubstantial norms**'. Consubstantial norms are norms which happen to exist both at the international and at the domestic level, and provide for the same substantive regulation (ie, they have the same substance).[60] One example of such a norm could be the right to an effective remedy for violation of a vested right; or other fundamental human rights[61] which are guaranteed at both the international and most domestic levels.[62] In that sense 'consubstantial norms' could be likened to 'multi-sourced equivalent norms', which have been argued to exist at the international level.[63] The commitment of domestic constitutions to international law and human rights[64] as well as the references by domestic courts to their domestic and international counterparts[65] can be relevant to the concept of consubstantial norms. The reason for including the impact of such consubstantial norms in the Study Group's consideration of the various methods of engagement of domestic courts with international law is that they may serve to both align with and to contest international rules—as will be demonstrated in Part B, below. Before turning to this point, however, the variations in the outcome of domestic court engagement with international law must be briefly mentioned.

c. Variations in Outcome

31. A crucial aspect of the engagement of domestic courts with international law is whether, in the final analysis, the domestic court's 'intervention', as it were, leads to alignment with, or rather to breach of, international law. This is also a most difficult field of study. Not only does such an enquiry assume that international law always has fixed and objectively ascertainable contents;[66] it also ignores the fact that every

[60] The term 'consubstantial' is originally a theological term which seeks to describe the Holy Trinity as being 'of the same substance', ie 'consubstantial' (ομοούσιος). See further Tzanakopoulos, 'Domestic Courts in International Law', 142–4. The reference to 'same' substantive regulation need not (and probably should not) be understood as implying identical regulation—sometimes the domestic norm may be more protective of a particular right or value, but in order to be considered 'consubstantial' with an international norm it may not be *less* protective or may not strike a *different balance* from the one struck by the international norm. International law thus serves as the minimum standard of protection.

[61] For a discussion of the term 'fundamental rights' and its relationship to 'human rights' from an international-domestic comparative law perspective, see A Tzanakopoulos, 'Judicial Dialogue in Multilevel Governance: The Impact of the *Solange* Argument' in OK Fouchald and A Nollkaemper (eds), *The Practice of International and National Courts and the (De-Fragmentation) of International Law* (Hart, Oxford 2012) 185, 210–15.

[62] Indeed there is a feedback loop in the protection of fundamental human rights, with the American and French declarations of the eighteenth century influencing both the Universal Declaration of Human Rights and the first international treaties for the protection of human rights. These international documents then influenced the adoption of human rights protections in constitutions of States emerging from colonial rule or dictatorships. See ibid, and for examples see the *Report on Anglophone Africa* (2015) 10: many Anglophone African constitutions contain human rights protections influenced by international human rights instruments. See also the *Report on Sri Lanka* (2013) 2–3.

[63] See generally for the concept T Broude and Y Shany, 'The International Law and Policy of Multi-Sourced Equivalent Norms' in eidem (eds), *Multi-Sourced Equivalent Norms in International Law* (Hart, Oxford 2011) 1–15.

[64] Cf Article 6(3) TEU; Article 1(2) German Basic Law; Preamble and Article 1(a) South African Constitution.

[65] Cf PM Huber and A Paulus, 'Cooperation of Constitutional Courts in Europe' in M Andenas and D Fairgrieve (eds), *Courts and Comparative Law* (OUP, Oxford 2015) 281.

[66] On this see further paragraphs 50 and 73 below.

purported violation of international law has within it the seeds of a potential change in the law. In customary law, a 'violation' by a domestic court may lead to the emergence of a new customary rule, or to the modification of an existing one. In treaty law, a 'violation' could evolve into a 'subsequent practice' which establishes the agreement of the parties regarding the interpretation of the treaty (in the sense of Article 31(3)(b) VCLT respectively) or causes the treaty to fall into desuetude or obsolescence.[67] This creates an interesting feedback loop, where domestic court engagement may both violate and develop international law. One crucial question then is how to distinguish between breach of the law and its development, or the emergence of new law. In addition, to the extent that rules of international law are invoked to challenge other rules of international law, a breach of one set of norms may promote compliance with another set of norms, and may even have implications for their hierarchical standing.

32. There are examples of instances that can be cited as substantiating the feedback loop referred to in paragraph 31 above: the Greek and Italian courts' jurisprudence on sovereign immunity could (and perhaps sought to) effect a change in the customary law of immunity, and it may have been successful were it not for conflicting practice of other domestic courts and finally for the intervention of the International Court of Justice, which put an end to the discussion for the foreseeable future.[68] Similarly, Greek court jurisprudence on the definition of 'ship' under the 1992 CLC/FUND Conventions has caused the States parties to consider adopting the Greek courts' interpretation over the one they preferred earlier (and on the basis of which the Greek court decisions were in clear violation of the relevant instruments).[69] The jurisprudence of UK courts has led the European Court of Human Rights to change its interpretation of provisions in the ECHR in some instances.[70]

33. It thus appears that in a number of cases it will be very hard to determine with any certainty whether a particular domestic court decision is in alignment with or in breach of international law—much will depend on other States' reactions (or lack thereof) to the decision, as well as to the possibility of 'corrective intervention' or 'monitoring' by an international judicial organ, such as the International Court of Justice (but also the European Court of Human Rights, or the WTO dispute settlement organs, or an ad hoc or ICSID arbitral tribunal, among other possibilities).

PART B: MAPPING ENGAGEMENT

34. The difficulty in discerning any single principled approach to the engagement of domestic courts with international law is obviously the result of the great variety of domestic constitutional treatment of international law as to its position within the domestic legal framework, and the subsequent variations in the engagement of

[67] MG Kohen, 'Desuetude and Obsolescence of Treaties' in E Cannizzaro (ed), *The Law of Treaties Beyond the Vienna Convention* (OUP, Oxford 2011) 350.

[68] *Jurisdictional Immunities of the State (Germany v Italy: Greece Intervening)* [2012] ICJ Reports 99.

[69] *Marine Env'l Services MC and anor v 1992 IOPC Fund* (6 July 2006) ILDC 856 (GR 2006); cf Record of Decisions of the October 2012 Sessions of the IOPC Funds' Governing Bodies Doc IOPC/OCT12/11/1 (2012) [4.6.3]–[4.6.6]; see further Record of Decisions of the October 2015 Sessions of the IOPC Funds' Governing Bodies Doc IOPC/OCT15/11/WP.1 (2015) [2.1.5].

[70] Eg with respect to the admissibility of hearsay evidence under Article 6 ECHR: *R v Horncastle* [2009] UKSC 14 and cf *Al-Khawaja and Tahery v UK* (App Nos 26766/05 and 22228/06) (ECtHR Grand Chamber 2011) [146]–[147].

domestic courts with international law and in the outcome of such engagement, as described in Part A above. The most crucial part of the Study Group's work was to map the practices and methods of engagement and their potential outcomes. The main part, Part B, of this Final Report is concerned with mapping the relevant variety in domestic court engagement with international law, rather than seeking to explain what might be made of that variety. Part C then proceeds to identify the possible grounds behind domestic courts opting for one or the other strategy of engagement described in this part. But before moving on the mapping exercise, some preliminary comments are in order.

35. In the first phase of the work, members of the Study Group agreed that, in the interest of making the project manageable, the Study Group should focus on norms 'at the edge', that is to say on norms of international law that seem to suffer from 'legitimacy' deficits and are thus likely to provoke and encounter the resistance of domestic courts. While the term 'legitimacy' is itself contested, what is meant here is norms of international law that may be seen as problematic in three aspects: (a) **source legitimacy concerns**—such as those created by norms emerging from a vague law-making process, such as that of customary international law, or decreed by non-elected international organs, such as the secondary law of international organizations; (b) **procedural legitimacy concerns**—such as those created by norms produced in some manner which is procedurally incompatible with national traditions or otherwise problematic; and (c) **outcome/content legitimacy concerns**—such as those created by the potential or perceived conflict of international norms with deeply rooted local constitutional sensitivities.

36. The focus on norms 'at the edge' pulls with it the focus of the elaboration of principles of engagement of domestic courts with international law: problematic rules make for problematic responses by the organs charged with their interpretation and application, and thus the Study Group sought to focus on instances of domestic court resistance to, contestation of, but also development of international law. However, it became clear, in view also of the work submitted to the Study Group in the course of its operation by its members and by other scholars, that an exclusive focus on problematic norms 'at the edge' might present a skewed picture of the engagement of domestic courts with international law, overemphasizing resistance and contestation as a form of engagement. As such, the following three sections of this Part B generally map the engagement of domestic courts with all possible norms of international law, viewed statically (section I), dynamically (section II), and finally from the perspective of monitoring (section III). The concept of norms 'at the edge', however, continues to play a role in this analysis, as indeed it does in the context of identifying reasons for particular strategies or postures of engagement discussed in Part C.

I. Engagement Viewed Statically: Postures or Strategies

37. Whatever the contents of any norm of international law may be, there are broadly three **ideal types** of **strategy** or **posture**[71] of domestic court engagement with international law, qualified by the outcome of such engagement. These are: the **posture** or **strategy of avoidance** (where the question of international law is altogether dodged);

[71] The difference between 'strategy' and 'posture' is that the former term conveys a sense of genuineness in the approach, whatever the underlying purpose, while the latter term may convey a more

the **posture** or **strategy of alignment** (where—irrespective of the prescription of the constitutional framework, or even on the basis of an interpretation of such prescription which, on its face, seems to point towards avoidance—an attempt is made to align with international law or at least to harmonize domestic law or practice with international regulation); and the **posture** or **strategy of contestation** (where domestic law is ostensibly used as a method to contest the generally accepted content of existing international law, such as in cases like *Kadi* and possibly *Medellín*).

38. The three ideal types described above and elaborated on further below match Hirschmann's three categories of **exit** (avoidance), **voice** (contestation), **loyalty** (alignment).[72] However, further differentiation is required within each ideal type, and this is the purpose of the subsections that follow.

a. Avoidance

39. **Avoidance** is the general posture or strategy of a domestic court avoiding the application of international law in circumstances where the latter may be applicable. Such avoidance can be **evasive** or **affirmative**. It should be noted at the outset that the legislature or executive may also adopt a practice of avoidance by delaying ratification of treaties which would require changes in domestic law, or by allowing ratification/ratifying only with broad reservations which aim to shield domestic law from change.[73] In any event, the term avoidance should not be considered as being necessarily negative. The court may be forced by its own domestic law to avoid or refuse the application of international law, as described below. And delays in ratification or the making of reservations may be designed to ensure full compliance with all applicable international obligations.

40. **Evasive avoidance** is where international law is not applied without any relevant argument being made and without any discussion by the court. The court simply remains silent where the application of international law is plainly called for (and may even have been pleaded by the parties),[74] in a sort of 'willful blindness'.[75] An instance where this might be the case is where the legislature has passed a relevant law which may not fully reflect or may diverge from applicable international law. The domestic court may be bound to apply the relevant domestic law and may thus choose to silently ignore relevant international norms. An example is where States have passed immunity legislation, such as for example the UK, the US, Argentina, Japan, India, and so forth, with the expected result of prompting reliance on the domestic rather than the relevant international norms.[76] A countervailing trend which has been noted in some jurisdictions is for the executive to (be allowed to) intervene

rhetorical, rather than genuine, position. The two terms however are used interchangeably in this Final Report.

[72] See generally AO Hirschman, *Exit, Voice, and Loyalty: Responses to Decline in Firms, Organizations, and States* (Harvard University Press 1970).

[73] See the *Report on Switzerland* (2013) 6.

[74] For examples see the *Report on Israel* (2013) [31]–[32]; the *Report on Belgium* (2014) 9–10; the *Report on Canada* (2013) 19; the *Report on International Human Rights Law* (2015) 10; and the *Onondaga* litigation, reported in ILA Committee on the Implementation of the Rights of Indigenous Peoples, *Johannesburg Conference Draft Report* (2016) 18–19, available at <http://www.ila-hq.org/download.cfm/docid/22EA2347-3AC2-41A0-849732487DA9A7C4>.

[75] For the expression see the *Report on Canada* (2013) 19.

[76] See the *Report on Belgium* (2014) 4–5; and the *Report on India* (2013) 23 [53] and 25ff [57]ff.

in order to prompt the domestic court to comply with international obligations on immunity.[77]

41. Avoidance can also be **affirmative** (or **professed**). This is the case when the court considers the application of international law but explicitly rejects it, as this is, in the court's view, the appropriate position under domestic law. Some of the blunting or moderating mechanisms described above, such as non-justiciability or non-self-execution, may well lead to affirmative avoidance.[78] For example, the finding by a domestic court that internationally binding norms protecting social rights are programmatic and non-executable norms will lead it to determine that it is not up to it to apply these norms and to ensure compliance with them.[79] Similarly, the adoption of a dualist position with respect to treaties will allow (or impose on) courts to disregard international law, as compliance with it is seen as the responsibility of other State organs.[80] This will essentially leave it to the executive to comply with these norms uncontrolled by the domestic court, or to the legislature to produce consubstantial obligations which will allow the domestic court to weigh in. This can also be the outcome of the application of the principle of consistent interpretation, another moderating or blunting mechanism, when the presumption that the principle establishes is relatively weak and can be readily resisted by an argument that the law being interpreted is not ambiguous (or, for common law jurisdictions dealing with customary international law, that the common law does not require development).[81]
42. Affirmative is also the avoidance that ostensibly relies on international law to argue, though clearly wrongly, that on its own terms the latter is not applicable. A historical example of such affirmative avoidance is apartheid South Africa, where the application of customary law was rejected through the denial of its customary status: domestic courts would require 'universal' acceptance for a rule to be considered customary international law.[82] By setting the bar so high, it was virtually guaranteed that almost no norm would be granted customary international law status by a South African court.

b. Alignment

43. **Alignment** can come in a number of variations: **simple** or **'fair weather'** alignment; **overriding** alignment; **consubstantial** alignment; and **'hyper'**-alignment (or alignment 'on steroids'). Alignment, and in particular hyper-alignment is a strategy or posture particularly favoured by newer or smaller States that may wish to not appear parochial.[83] It is instructive in this connection that the US in the eighteenth century could be considered as 'bending over backwards' to (be seen as) align(ing) with

[77] See ibid and cf *Tachiona v US* 386 F.3d 2005 (2d Cir. 2004).

[78] See the *Report on South Africa* (2013) (14); the *Report on Israel* (2013) [26]–[30]; the *Report on Canada* (2013) 16ff; and the *Report on International Humanitarian Law* (2013) 3–5. See further ILA Committee on the Implementation of the Rights of Indigenous Peoples, *Johannesburg Conference Draft Report* (2016) 6, referring to instances where lawsuits by indigenous peoples in the domestic courts of Bolivia where found inadmissible even despite the fact that Bolivia has transformed relevant international law into domestic law.

[79] See the *Report on Switzerland* (2013) 7.

[80] See the *Report on Argentina* (2015) 2–3; the *Report on Anglophone Africa* (2015) 8; and the *Report on India* (2013) 5–6 [11]–[12] and 7ff [16]ff.

[81] See the *Report on England* (2015) [27]; and the *Report on Canada* (2013) 20.

[82] See the *Report on South Africa* (2013) (11)–(13).

[83] See the *Report on Albania* (2013) 1. See further Part C below.

international law. But it is by no means exclusively so, and much will depend on the particular variation of alignment in each case. The variations outlined above are now examined in turn.

44. **Fair weather alignment** is basically alignment with international law in run-of-the-mill, politically unproblematic situations. It is difficult to report on such alignment as examples abound in day-to-day life but, having no 'special' characteristics, they do not necessarily constitute 'newsworthy' instances. These may include instances where international law is cited explicitly in support of relevant domestic law, as well as other cases where the perceived content of the international and domestic law converge. Fair weather alignment becomes meaningful only when seen against the background of other types of alignment, and most crucially against the light of avoidance or contestation in politically charged circumstances. This is much like an omission, which becomes evident and meaningful only against the light of an obligation to act.[84] By contrast, the need to engage with politically charged rules, such as for example the rules of international humanitarian law in the context of an armed conflict in which the State whose courts are called upon to apply it is engaged, may well lead to (affirmative) avoidance or contestation.[85]
45. **Overriding alignment** consists in the application of international law by the domestic court over conflicting domestic law. Determining the existence of normative conflict is in itself a very difficult matter, as 'apparent' conflicts may be resolved through interpretation, leading some to only consider irresolvable conflicts as 'genuine'.[86] However, interpretation being an art rather than a science, it is difficult to draw a bright line between 'apparent' and 'genuine' conflicts. A rather large area could be said to be gray between the two extremes.
46. Consistent interpretation can be seen as a technique for producing consubstantial alignment, when a domestic court interprets domestic law in conformity with international obligations of the State (generally if a statute or domestic law is at least somewhat ambiguous). But in some instances a very strong presumption of consistency of domestic law with international obligations, even in the face of little or no ambiguity in domestic law, may produce overriding alignment. This is for example the case in Belgium, where domestic courts have resorted in consistent interpretation in circumstances where the domestic norm being interpreted did not at all seem ambiguous,[87] as well as in South American States where international human rights law has been relied upon even to change a given Constitution (or its up to that point predominant interpretation).[88] It is also the case in South Africa where the Constitutional Court has taken the position that the only reasonable interpretation of domestic legislation is an interpretation that is consistent with international law.[89]

[84] Cf V Lowe, *International Law* (OUP, Oxford 2007) 41, 92, on *opinio juris* shedding light on the practice of 'not doing something' in the context of customary international law formation.

[85] See the *Report on International Humanitarian Law* (2013) 2–9. See further paragraphs 41 above and 58 below respectively.

[86] See generally E Roucounas, 'Engagements parallèles et contradictoires' (1987) 206 Recueil des cours de l'Académie de droit international de La Haye 9; and M Milanovic, 'Norm Conflict in International Law: Wither Human Rights?' (2009) 20 Duke Journal of Comparative and International Law 69.

[87] See the *Report on Belgium* (2014) 4–5.

[88] See the *Report on South America* (2015) 18ff.

[89] See the *Report on South Africa* (2013) (5)–(6).

47. Further, it can be argued that allowing challenge of domestic law or domestic normative acts on the basis of international law despite the availability of blunting rules which could lead to avoidance (and so would not avoid the challenge to domestic law) also produces overriding alignment. This is again the case in Belgium, where non-self-executing international law norms have been relied on in order to seek annulment of domestic normative acts, to seek compensation, and even to challenge criminal charges.[90] Similar examples can be found in the area of international investment law, where certain domestic courts have applied the provisions of an international investment agreement in order to reverse conversion of contracts from one currency to another (though there is practice on the part of domestic courts for either evasively avoiding these issues, or affirmatively avoiding them by reference to blunting techniques).[91]
48. Both consistent interpretation and the non-invocation of blunting techniques leading to avoidance have also shaped the position in Argentina, which may be seen as having transitioned from a period of affirmative avoidance to one of overriding alignment.[92]
49. **Consubstantial alignment** is the application by the domestic court of domestic norms that are consubstantial with the international norms. As already mentioned above, the strategy or posture of consubstantial alignment can be independently adopted by a domestic court,[93] but it can also be forced upon it by the executive or legislature producing consubstantial obligations (ie ratifying a treaty only once they have changed domestic law to reflect the relevant international obligations, producing consubstantiality, in particular leading to *preemptive* consubstantial alignment).[94]
50. The question that emerges is *when* the action of the legislature or executive in producing domestic norms leads to (evasive) avoidance (see paragraph 40 above) rather than consubstantial alignment. One could easily argue that the passing of domestic law is a method for applying international law in the domestic legal order rather than for avoiding it (or for contesting its content). No easy answer can be given to this question, ie the distinction between evasive avoidance and consubstantial alignment is not easy to draw in these circumstances. Much will depend on what we consider the *content* of the specific international norm to be, and on whether we consider that the relevant domestic norm is consistent with that content. This highlights the potential for all categories to collapse into another or to alternate depending on context and perhaps also on the particular reader's viewpoint. It is however no reason not to undertake the mapping exercise, and to argue whether a particular domestic court engagement falls within one or the other category. Any such argument is essentially

[90] See the *Report on Belgium* (2014) 6ff.
[91] See the *Report on International Investment Law* (2013) [Kjos].
[92] See generally the *Report on Argentina* (2015), esp 5ff.
[93] See the *Report on India* (2013) 15–17 [34]–[37].
[94] See the *Report on Switzerland* (2013) 6 and consider the practice of Eastern European States in bringing their domestic law in conformity with the ECHR prior to joining the Council of Europe and having the obligation to do so. See also the practice of the UK where some statutes do not directly incorporate a treaty but are meant to give effect in whole or in part to the provisions of an unincorporated treaty. (Note that here the term 'incorporation' is meant to signify transformation into domestic law in the terminology used in Part A of this Report.) These statutes are meant to be interpreted with reference to the unincorporated treaty, producing consubstantial alignment. See the *Report on England* (2015) [21]–[23] and cf the *Report on Canada* (2013) where a similar approach of both full transformation and consubstantial transformation is used.

an argument as to the content of the relevant norms or (which amounts to the same thing) their interpretation, and this will always be an issue on which views will occasionally diverge, sometimes widely.[95]

51. Consubstantial alignment primarily takes place when the domestic court applies domestic law in a way that is aligned with what is required of the relevant State under relevant international law, even without any reference to such international law. The domestic law applied is consubstantial with the State's international obligations, and so the outcome is one of alignment with these international obligations. It should be noted that international law does not require that it be either incorporated or transformed into domestic law, and generally makes no provision on the way in which States will elect to comply. What is required is simply that compliance ensues, by whatever means. This is evident, for example, in the way the European Court of Human Rights has treated exhaustion of local remedies: the Court does not require that specific ECHR rights be explicitly pleaded before domestic courts. It only requires that the *substance* of these rights has been pleaded, even if solely under domestic law.[96]

52. However, because of this peculiar characteristic of consubstantial alignment, ie that no explicit reference to international law is required for consubstantial alignment to take place, showcasing examples may be difficult at times. Much will depend on the analysis of the specific case, of its result, and of the requirements of international law, by each scholar or commentator.[97] An example, however, could be the *Tsilhqot'in* case in the Supreme Court of Canada: while the domestic court did not refer to international law, its analysis of the concept of indigenous rights over land was seen as being substantively in line with relevant international law.[98] Another example could be the approach of some Russian courts to indigenous peoples' rights.[99] Similarly, the US Supreme Court's approach in *Roper v Simmons* on the application of the death penalty to minors could be seen in this light.[100] Further examples can be seen essentially in many cases in which an international court, say the ECtHR, has reviewed the action of domestic courts and has found no violation of an international obligation, say the ECHR, even if these courts did not explicitly refer to international law in the context of the relevant case. In many cases the domestic law that was applied will be considered consubstantial with the international obligations of the State under the ECHR, or the domestic court will have interpreted that law in consubstantial alignment with the ECHR, so as for alignment to ensue.

53. The principle or technique of consistent interpretation may also produce consubstantiality and thus consubstantial alignment. This will be the case where the domestic courts see no reason to depart from the plain meaning of legislation if it is consistent with international law, or where they engage in broad interpretation of

[95] See further paragraphs 31 above and 73 below.

[96] See *Castells v Spain* (App No 11798/85) Judgment of 23 April 1992 [32]; *Ahmet Sadik v Greece* (App No18877/91) Judgment 15 November 1996 [33]; *Azinas v Cyprus* (App No56679/00) Judgment of 28 April 2004 (Grand Chamber) [40]–[41]; *Gäfgen v Germany* (App No 22978/05) Judgment of 1 June 2010 (Grand Chamber) [142]–[146].

[97] See again paragraphs 31 and 50 above, and 73 below.

[98] See ILA Committee on the Implementation of the Rights of Indigenous Peoples, *Johannesburg Conference Draft Report* (2016) 17–18.

[99] See ibid, 26.

[100] See *Roper v Simmons* (n 57).

domestic legislation by relying on relevant (not directly applicable or unincorporated) international law.[101]

54. Domestic courts have on occasion confirmed the 'consubstantiality' of domestic and international norms, in particular in the area of fundamental human rights: examples include the Swiss Federal Tribunal in *Nada*,[102] as well as the Canadian Federal Court in *Abdelrazik*,[103] and the German Federal Constitutional Court in the 'student fees' and 'forced treatment' cases.[104] In other cases, domestic courts will often give preference to 'consubstantial' domestic law over applicable international law, but will clearly indicate that applicable international norms will be taken into consideration in the construction of the consubstantial domestic norms.[105] This is likely to produce consubstantial alignment; but when it deviates from or challenges the generally accepted content of an international norm it will constitute affirmative or consubstantial contestation, on which see further in the next subsection.

55. **Hyper-alignment** is a particular category of alignment where the domestic court may go beyond what international law actually requires (even though relying explicitly on international law), finding international obligations where none actually exist or are at least debatable.[106] An example of such alignment 'on steroids' can be seen in the case of Albania, where the domestic criminal law did not provide for a reopening of proceedings in the case that a violation of ECHR has been found by the ECtHR. This occasioned a split between the Albanian Constitutional Court and the Albanian Supreme Court (of Cassation), with the former ordering the latter to 'legislate' into existence such grounds for reopening proceedings, going beyond what was at the time the accepted interpretation of the ECHR.[107] In similar circumstances the Polish courts adopted the position that the lack of such grounds for reopening proceedings was regrettable, but also that it was not up to the domestic court to create such grounds.[108] Albanian courts have also relied on treaties not binding on Albania or on soft law in order to disregard domestic law in other instances of hyper-alignment,[109]

[101] See for example the *Report on Sri Lanka* (2013) 6, 8; the *Report on Canada* (2013) 11–15; and the *Report on England* (2015) [24]ff with respect to fully unincorporated treaties. See also ILA Committee on the Implementation of the Rights of Indigenous Peoples, *Johannesburg Conference Draft Report* (2016) 7–8, for examples of Chilean courts 'completing' the understanding of indigenous peoples' rights under domestic law by reference to international treaties, to some of which Chile had not even become a party; see further at 11–12 for the similar position adopted by the Supreme Court of Belize.

[102] *Youssef Nada v State Secretariat for Economic Affairs and Federal Department of Economic Affairs*, Administrative Appeal Judgment, Case No 1A 45/2007, Switzerland, Federal Tribunal (14 November 2007) 133 BGE II 450; ILDC 461 (CH 2007) [6.2].

[103] *Abdelrazik v Canada (Minister of Foreign Affairs)* [2010] 1 FCR 267; 2009 FC 580 [50]–[52].

[104] 128 BVerfGE 306 – Forced Treatment I; 134 BVerfGE 1, 34 [16] – Student Fees.

[105] See the *Report on Belgium* (2014) 6; see also the decision of the German Federal Constitutional Court on remuneration for translators, 134 BVerfGE 229 [88]; see further the discussion of international human rights law being used as a guide for the interpretation of Canadian law in ILA Committee on International Human Rights Law, *Johannesburg Conference Draft Report* (2016) 17–18, available at <http://www.ila-hq.org/download.cfm/docid/0375EBFB-FC78-4B52-8A9930EF64098049>. Cf the practice of EU courts of relying on both the ECHR and the ICCPR (and relevant jurisprudence thereunder) in analyzing fundamental rights under primary EU law, as for example in *Kadi II*: Case T-85/09 *Kadi II* [2010] ECR II-5177 [176]-[177].

[106] See the *Report on Albania* (2013) 1; and the *Report on India* (2013) 18ff [41]ff.

[107] See the *Report on Albania* (2013) 4.

[108] Ibid.

[109] See G Zyberi and S Sali, 'The Place and Application of International Law in the Albanian Legal System' in S Rodin and T Perišin (eds), *Judicial Application of International Law in Southeast Europe* (Springer, Berlin 2015) 86, 99–102.

while the Kosovo courts have also taken similar positions.[110] Sri Lankan courts also refer to regional instruments that are not binding on Sri Lanka, such as the ECHR.[111] Sri Lankan courts also can be considered as engaging in hyper-alignment in those cases where they have determined that soft environmental principles establish binding obligations on governmental authorities and become part of the common law.[112] Chilean courts and the Supreme Court of Belize have relied on international instruments not binding on the relevant States in the construction of indigenous peoples' rights under domestic law.[113] Other relevant examples of hyper-alignment are provided by African courts,[114] in particular Kenyan courts since the adoption of the 2010 Constitution.

56. One final such instance, which goes clearly beyond even consubstantial alignment to alignment on steroids is provided by Albanian courts in the context of the question whether the Rome Statute of the International Criminal Court is compatible with the Albanian Constitution. In responding to the question, the Albanian courts not only found the Rome Statute to be so compatible, and protecting human rights as the Albanian Constitution does, but went so far as to consider the ICC as the highest criminal court in the *Albanian* legal order.[115]

c. Contestation

57. Contestation also comes in a fair number of variations: **affirmative**; **negatory**; and **consubstantial**. Notably, contestation can refer to applicability or to content (interpretation): as such, affirmative contestation refers clearly to content; negatory contestation refers clearly to applicability (but this may be so due to the perceived content of the norm); and consubstantial contestation requires going beyond the posture of the court to determine whether what may seem as negatory contestation is in reality partial consubstantial alignment, using the contestation of the rule as a means for affecting its content. These are dealt with in turn below.

58. **Affirmative contestation** consists primarily in the domestic court accepting the validity or applicability of the international law norm but giving it a meaning different from that which is generally accepted, indicating thus that it wishes to change the content of the norm or that it perceives it as different from what is generally accepted. An example of such practice could be that of Israeli and Indian courts formally accepting the applicability of international law in a number of instances, but effectively rejecting its full application by diverging from the perceived as generally accepted meaning.[116] This may well be the result of the court explicitly or implicitly deferring to the position of the executive on the matter (of the interpretation of the international rule).[117] A special type of such affirmative contestation can appear when a domestic court diverges from the interpretation of international law given by an international court in a judgment, even when that is binding on the State, as sometimes happens

[110] See the *Report on Kosovo* (2015) 14–15.
[111] See the *Report on Sri Lanka* (2013) 6.
[112] Ibid.
[113] See n 101 above.
[114] See the *Report on Anglophone Africa* (2015) 8.
[115] See the *Report on Albania* (2013) 10.
[116] See the *Report on International Humanitarian Law* (2013) 2–4; the *Report on Israel* (2013) [21]ff; and the *Report on India* (2013) 26–27 [58]–[60].
[117] See the *Report on International Humanitarian Law* (2013) 2–4.

in UK[118] and US practice.[119] Finally, attempts at consistent or harmonious interpretation may result in affirmative contestation as described here, when the court can be seen as diverging from the generally accepted content of an international norm in order to avoid conflict with a domestic norm.[120] This could be seen as 'reverse' consistent interpretation in that domestic courts tend to interpret international law in a manner consistent with the provisions of domestic law (and even sometimes policy) rather than the other way around.

59. Another instance of affirmative contestation could be the one where a domestic court contests the content of an international rule by relying on another international rule. This is the case for example in the practice of Belgian courts that challenges the content of the rules of immunity of international organisations in cases where their application would result in breach of the international obligation to respect the right to a fair trial and / or to an effective remedy.[121] Similar (though far more isolated) examples can be found in the practice of UK courts,[122] which may have been influenced by the practice of the Belgian courts. The decision of South African courts to find a decision of the Tribunal of the Southern African Development Community directly applicable domestically, and to ignore the immunity of Zimbabwe in the process,[123] is also a potential example of affirmative contestation pitting one international rule against another, as are the South African cases regarding the arrest of Bashir on the basis of an arrest warrant issued by the International Criminal Court.[124] The debate between Human Rights Monitoring Bodies, such as the HRC or the CAT as to the proper interpretation of international human rights norms (and their relationship to rules of immunity) can also be seen in the light of affirmative contestation.[125] A rare example of affirmative contestation of this sort could be the decision of the Albanian Constitutional Court to review an international agreement for the delimitation of maritime zones between Albania and Greece not only against the Albanian Constitution (which would properly come under the preceding paragraph), but also against the general international law of the sea.[126]

60. Finally, domestic courts called upon to recognize and enforce foreign arbitral awards may engage in such types of contestation when reviewing international law application in the award, in accordance with rules of international law such as those under the 1958 New York Convention.[127] Notably, when review takes place not on the basis

[118] See *R v Lyons* [2003] 1 AC 976 [27] (Lord Hofmann) and see further the *Report on England* (2015) [17].

[119] See *Medellín v Texas* 552 US 491 (2008).

[120] What Judge Nussberger has called 'fake harmonious interpretation' in her dissent in *Al-Dulimi v Switzerland* (App No 5809/08) (ECtHR Grand Chamber 2016).

[121] See the *Report on Belgium* (2014) 9.

[122] See *Entico Corp Ltd v United Nations Educational Scientific and Cultural Association (UNESCO)* [2008] 531 EWHC (Comm).

[123] See the *Report on South Africa* (2013) (10)–(11). Cf the *Report on Anglophone Africa* (2015) 10, for the avoidance of enforcement of the same decision by the courts of Zimbabwe, which relied on relevant constitutional law.

[124] *Southern Africa Litigation Centre v Minister of Justice and Constitutional Development and Ors* (27740/2015) [2015] ZAGPPHC 402 (High Court) (24 June 2015); and *Minister of Justice and Constitutional Development and Ors v Southern African Litigation Centre and Ors* (867/15) [2016] ZASCA 17 (Supreme Court of Appeal) (15 March 2016).

[125] See the *Report on International Human Rights Law* (2015) 9.

[126] *See the Report on Albania* (2013) 10.

[127] See the *Report on International Investment Law [Kulick]* (2015) 6–7; for an example see the decision of The Hague District Court in the *Yukos* case, where as the court of the seat of the arbitration it quashed a US$ 50bn arbitral award for lack of jurisdiction: *The Russian Federation v Veteran Petroleum*

of the New York Convention but on the basis of domestic law which reflects, for example, the relevant UNCITRAL Model Law (which in turn reflects the New York Convention to a large extent), the type of contestation produced is consubstantial contestation,[128] on which see further below.

61. **Negatory contestation** consists in the denial of the validity or applicability of an international law norm, perhaps due to its (perceived) content. The principle of consistent interpretation may lead to negatory contestation of international law. As explained above, the strength of the interpretative presumption that the legislature did not mean to violate international law in making domestic law varies. For example in Switzerland, while consistent interpretation is used successfully in order to achieve alignment, occasionally it may be hard to apply in the context of federal acts (whether stemming from the legislature or the people through referenda) which clearly meant to disregard or violate applicable international obligations of the State.[129] In particular, if the legislator was aware of the conflict between international law and a proposed domestic law, and chose to legislate in breach, consistent interpretation will not be able to produce alignment, but the court will have to adopt a position of negatory contestation.[130] The position is similar in the UK, as well as other States.[131]
62. Further – and clearer – examples of negatory contestation can be seen in the practice of domestic courts ignoring clearly applicable international law norms, perhaps due to the fact that they find their application objectionable in the circumstances. An example is the *Yahoo* case in Belgian courts, where the bilateral US-Belgium treaty on mutual assistance in criminal matters is systematically ignored, despite being clearly applicable.[132] An even clearer example can be seen in the area of international investment law where the application of an international investment agreement would result in the breach of state aid rules also applicable in the host state under EU law (which in this connection can be seen as domestic law).[133]
63. **Consubstantial contestation:** What may look at first as negatory contestation may in reality involve partial consubstantial alignment with one rule of international law, thereby seeking to affect the content of another rule of international law, namely the rule whose application or content is contested. An example of such consubstantial contestation is provided in the reactions of some domestic courts and the EU courts to targeted anti-terrorist sanctions imposed by the UN Security Council under Chapter VII of the UN Charter. These sanctions obligate UN member States to, among others, freeze the assets and ban the travel of individuals and legal entities designated by the Security Council through the relevant Sanctions Committee.[134]

Ltd (Case No C/09/477160 / HA ZA 15-1); *The Russian Federation v Yukos Universal Ltd* (Case No C/09/477162 / HA ZA 15-2); and *The Russian Federation v Hulley Enterprises Ltd* (Case No C/09/481619 / HA ZA 15-112), Hague District Court, Judgment of 20 April 2016, available at < http://deeplink.rechtspraak.nl/uitspraak?id=ECLI:NL:RBDHA:2016:4230>.

128 Cf the *Report on India* (2013) 14–15 [33].
129 See the *Report on Switzerland* (2013) 11ff.
130 Ibid.
131 But see *Report on Canada* (2013) 11, noting the Supreme Court of Canada's requirement in *R v Hape* (n 51) [53] of 'unequivocal legislative intent to default on an international obligation' to support an argument that the presumption of conformity is rebutted.
132 See the *Report on Belgium* (2014) 10.
133 See *Ioan Micula and ors v Romania*, ICSID Case No ARB/05/20, Award of 11 December 2013 and the *Report on International Investment Law [Kjos]* (2013) 12.
134 See for example the regime imposed by Security Council Resolution 1267 (1999) and kept continuously in force ever since, with most significant updates coming in Security Council Resolutions

However, there was at first, and for some significant period of time, no way for those subjected to the sanctions to challenge their designation. Attempts to challenge the sanctions in domestic courts were normally bound to fail for lack of jurisdiction of domestic courts over the UN, or because of UN immunity, and so forth. At some point, nonetheless, domestic courts started considering the challenges, directed as they were against the domestic acts implementing the sanctions rather than directly against the UN act. In cases like *Kadi* in the Court of Justice of the European Union[135] (as well as *Kadi II*)[136] and *Ahmed* in the UK Supreme Court,[137] these courts reviewed the impugned domestic acts for compliance with the courts' domestic law (EU primary law and UK law respectively), and annulled them for violating fundamental human rights guaranteed under that law. This effectively forced the relevant States into an impossible situation: deprived of the domestic legal basis for implementing the UN measures, they had to either disregard their own courts or disobey the Security Council. From the perspective of international law this is clearly a problematic result: domestic law cannot serve to justify the breach of an international obligation.[138] However, the domestic law relied on in these cases, the protection of the fundamental human right to a fair trial and to an effective remedy, also constitutes international law. The contestation mounted by the domestic courts thus can be seen as consubstantial contestation: contesting the content of one rule of international law (the obligation imposed by the Security Council) because of the application, even if indirect, of the substance of another rule of international law (the right to a fair trial and to an effective remedy).[139]

64. A similar analysis can be made of the decision of the Italian Constitutional Court that found the ICJ Judgment in *Jurisdictional Immunities of the State* contrary to the Italian Constitution.[140] It is beyond question that the Italian Constitutional Court's decision constitutes a challenge to the ICJ's determination of the content of the international law of immunity on the basis of domestic constitutional law.[141] The contestation was founded, however, on the substance of the universally protected right of access to a court, even if by reference to its protection under the Italian Constitution. Essentially the Italian court can be seen as attempting to re-open the debate regarding the relationship between the international rule of sovereign immunity and internationally protected human rights, offering an alternative reading based on consubstantial

1333 (2000); 1730 (2006); 1904 (2009); 1988 (2011) and 1989 (2011), the latter two splitting the regime up for persons or entities associated with the Taliban and Al-Qaeda respectively; and 2252 (2015) extending the 1267/1989 regime to persons or entities associated with ISIS (or ISIL, or IS, or Da'esh).

[135] Joined Cases C-402/05 P and C-415/05 P [2008] ECR I-6351.

[136] Case T-85/09 *Kadi II* [2010] ECR II-5177; Joined Cases C-584/10 P, 593/10 P and C-595/10 P [2013] ECLI:EU:C:2013:518.

[137] [2010] UKSC 2.

[138] See paragraph 20 above.

[139] See generally A Tzanakopoulos, 'Collective Security and Human Rights' in E de Wet and J Vidmar (eds), *Hierarchy in International Law: The Place of Human Rights* (OUP, Oxford 2012) 42–70, for the argument that in relying on the right to a fair trial and to an effective remedy, cases like *Kadi* and *Ahmed* are effectively resolving a conflict between international norms (Chapter VII UN Security Council decisions and fundamental human rights) or alternatively reinterpreting Article 103 of the UN Charter.

[140] See Decision 238/2014 of the Italian Constitutional Court, available at <http://www.diritticomparati.it/2014/10/sentenza-n-238-anno-2014-repubblica-italiana-in-nome-del-popolo-italiano-la-corte-costituzionale-composta-dai-signori.html> [in Italian].

[141] See M Lando, 'Intimations of Unconstitutionality: The Supremacy of International Law and Judgment 238/2014 of the Italian Constitutional Court' (2015) 78 Modern Law Review 1028, 1038–9.

domestic law. By contrast, the decision of the US Supreme Court in *Medellín* cannot be likened to the examples above, and does not constitute consubstantial contestation, based as it is on the peculiarly American 'procedural default' rule, which finds no corresponding rule (in substance) in international law.[142]

65. Following the discussion on consubstantial contestation above, it can be argued that all types of contestation here examined may be also distinguished on the basis of whether they constitute **local contestation** or **internationally-minded contestation.** In the former case the domestic court is contesting the international rule by reliance on a domestic law principle which finds no corresponding principle in international law (thus 'local' contestation).[143] In the latter case the domestic court contests the content of an international rule by reliance on another international rule (affirmative contestation as described in paragraphs 59–60 above). Or it contests the content of an international norm by reliance on domestic law, but in cases where a parallel can be drawn between the domestic law relied on and international rules which are 'consubstantial' with that domestic law (consubstantial contestation).[144] Or, finally, the contestation may focus on the question of who is the authoritative interpreter of rules of international law, with the domestic court claiming—even if implicitly—a privileged role in this connection.[145] This final example could also be deemed as constituting affirmative contestation as described in paragraphs 58–60 above.

II. Engagement Viewed Dynamically: Development

66. Courts, as organs of the State, necessarily affect the content of norms of international law whenever they engage with them. They serve as agents of development (or harbingers of corrosion and decay) of international law norms. This is the dynamic aspect of their engagement with international law. All the strategies or postures discussed in section I above may also reflect a **strategy or posture of development** of international law, as they may either seek or achieve to set in motion the process of adjustment or change of the relevant international rules. Domestic courts do not single-handedly develop international law: they merely may set that process in motion, or continue it and consolidate change. But this they can do, and it is then up to other actors to weigh in (on which see paragraph 68 below).
67. One question that immediately comes up in the context of discussing domestic courts as agents of development of international law is whether the domestic court should be cognizant of its role as such an agent of development. This question cannot be answered with a high degree of certainty, however: it is difficult enough to determine what the domestic court is doing, and how it is engaging with international

[142] *Medellín* (n 119) could be seen as an example of local contestation.
[143] Which could also be regarded as a form of avoidance, the difference being however that contestation indicates some discomfort with the content of the international rule while avoidance merely ignores the international law rule.
[144] Eg in *Kadi* and *Ahmed* discussed above (see text at nn 135–137) domestic courts relied on constitutional rules protecting the right of access to a court and to an effective remedy, ie recognized aspects of the internationally protected right to a fair trial.
[145] The example here could be *Sanchez Llamas v Oregon* 548 US 331 (2006), where the domestic court claimed that it was the ICJ that read a provision in an international treaty wrongly, whereas the domestic court was reading it correctly (in the instance reference was to Article 36 VCCR).

law, let alone to determine what it thinks it is doing (except on rare occasions where courts explicitly articulate their views on their role in developing international law[146]). Further, it cannot be excluded that for a number of reasons domestic courts may not wish to engage in brazen statements as to their role and purpose. And even if they make statements as to what they think they are doing, these may well be geared towards shielding them from criticism or appeasing the various direct and indirect addressees of the decision. Thus, when called upon to choose between **what domestic courts are saying they are doing** and between **what they are actually doing**, the approach of this Final Report has generally been to assess what the court was actually doing. For example, there are instances where the domestic court may be paying lip service to an international legal rule, but then proceed to merely apply domestic law, or to avoid the relevant question altogether, thereby resulting in a violation of international law. Conversely, there are arguably instances where the domestic court, even though it makes no reference to international law, and even explicitly rejects its application, may be actually applying an international norm in deciding a case, even if only in its 'consubstantial' incarnation.

68. Even when domestic courts do not consciously engage in development as a strategy or posture, development of the law may still ensue. This is because domestic courts engaging with international law rules may set in motion a process which will call for and perhaps lead to the reaction of (a) **other domestic courts**, so as for practice to accumulate either for or against the position taken by the domestic court (also: *horizontal dialogue*, ie between courts in different domestic legal orders); (b) **international courts**, which may be seen as 'monitoring' the engagement of domestic courts with international norms (also: *vertical dialogue*, see further section III below); and finally (c) **States**, who are the principal lawmakers and the ultimate monitors of the engagement of both domestic and international courts with international norms that they (the States) have made (on which see also further section III below).

III. Informal 'Monitoring' of Engagement

69. The engagement of domestic courts with international norms, and the consequent impact on the content of such norms, is subject to an informal process of '**monitoring**', ie to decentralised **control** and **corrective intervention**. Domestic courts are accustomed, when acting within the domestic legal order, to functioning under the corrective control of the legislature. This sort of corrective intervention is far less ubiquitous in the decentralised legal system that is international law. Informal processes of monitoring domestic court engagement with international law are varied and diffuse, but such informal monitoring may be undertaken by international courts. An example is the *Jurisdictional Immunities of the State* case before the ICJ:[147] here the actions of Greek and Italian courts led to a dispute which was submitted to the ICJ. The ICJ reversed an attempt at the development—or erosion—of the international law of immunity that had been initiated by the domestic courts or by States (eg through

[146] See for example the Israeli Supreme Court in *Ajuri* [40], available at <http://elyon1.court.gov.il/Files_ENG/02/150/070/A15/02070150.A15.pdf>.

[147] *Jurisdictional Immunities of the State (Germany v Italy; Greece Intervening)* [2012] ICJ Reports 99.

reaction to and protest against the decision of a domestic court of another State).[148] But this may still not be the final word, as further reaction on the part of domestic courts has followed, with the Italian Constitutional Court engaging in (consubstantial) contestation.[149]

70. Given the paucity of international judicial settlement of disputes, judicial law-making by domestic courts that impacts on international law, while subject to informal and diffuse international monitoring, requires much more vigilance in order to be kept within acceptable limits, and in order to have a **developing** rather than a merely **corrosive effect** on international regulation (which could be cast as a form of fragmentation).[150] In the final analysis, the ultimate guardians will be the actual law-makers, the States, which also 'monitor' the engagement of domestic courts with international law. The State can seek to influence (by intervening in a case) or finally reject the position of its own domestic courts (by legislating to overrule it) or of the domestic courts of other States (by making protests or presenting claims to their States for violation of international law).

PART C: PRINCIPLES OF ENGAGEMENT?

71. Elaborating a set of principles of engagement would require, in addition to several other considerations, a determination of the **reasons** behind the choices of domestic courts with regard to their techniques and strategies of engagement with international law. Establishing the reasons for domestic courts opting to avoid or to contest or to align with international law in given circumstances, evaluating them as positive or negative from an international law perspective, and considering the costs of each strategic choice, would allow the elaboration of guidelines and practice directions for domestic courts. Significant work needs to be done in order for such guidelines, principles or practice directions to be elaborated, and this is beyond the remit or capacity of the Study Group.
72. As a contribution to the mapping exercise as to the engagement of domestic courts with international law, this Final Report presents some thoughts on the reasons for the adoption of the various strategies or postures of engagement, and the role of the various techniques developed by domestic courts in this respect. This is meant to assist further work in the direction of setting out a set of principles on the engagement of domestic courts with international law, possibly by a Committee to be established by the International Law Association.
73. Before giving some thoughts on the reasons, it should be mentioned (as it already has been in the other parts of the Final Report)[151] that the mapping of strategies or postures in Part B is not open and shut, as it depends on consensus regarding the content of the various rules of international law. The various categories may even collapse into one another depending on the observer's viewpoint and in particular her conception of the content of the international rule at stake. Just as it was highlighted in paragraph 50 above that the passing of domestic law could be seen as both a method for applying

[148] cf Roberts (n 13) 64ff.
[149] See paragraph 64 above.
[150] cf Knop (n 51) 506; and Shany (n 28) 27ff.
[151] See paragraphs 31 and 50 above.

international law in the domestic legal order and as a method for avoiding it (or for contesting its content), it could equally be argued that deference by the domestic court to the executive's interpretation of a particular treaty can be cast as avoidance (avoiding to engage with applicable international law) as easily as it can be cast as alignment (it is the executive that negotiated and concluded the treaty and thus has a better understanding of its content). Much will depend on one's evaluation of the content of the relevant law and the decision of the domestic courts. Some of these considerations may be imposed by virtue of constitutional provisions or principles in the domestic legal order, but they also constitute reasons why the domestic court has opted for a particular strategy or posture. But it is difficult to determine whether a court is 'hiding behind' constitutional constraints in order to avoid engagement with international law, or whether it is convinced that this is the correct position under its domestic law. What remains clear, from the perspective of international law, is that domestic courts can take widely diverging positions on the same issue. In the context of the exercise of discretion given to the State under international law, for example, some domestic courts may refuse to exercise that discretion, as they do not see themselves as the appropriate organ for this;[152] other courts may step up to the plate to obligate the State to exercise its discretion under international law in the particular manner decided by the court.[153] But this does not mean that the mapping exercise is pointless, nor does it mean that one should not attempt to set out the potential reasons for the adoption of the various strategies or postures adopted by domestic courts.

74. The strategy or posture adopted by domestic courts will depend to some degree a number of variables, partly identified in Part A of this Report as the challenges for mapping domestic court engagement with international law. The first such variable, as evident also from the preceding paragraph, is the domestic constitutional provision on the relationship of international and domestic law, and the various blunting mechanisms developed by and available to the courts for moderating the effects of these provisions. These can be used by domestic courts to shift the posture more towards avoidance or more towards alignment than a plain reading of the constitutional instrument or rules would suggest.

75. Another variable is the relative position of the State concerned in the international community or its strategic choice about approach to international law. Newer, smaller, or developing States (and their courts), as well as States that place a high premium on their reputation as supporters of the international 'rule of law' and international cooperation, may wish to promote or consolidate their position as well respected members of that community by adopting and encouraging their courts to adopt a strategy or posture of alignment, occasionally even going into hyper-alignment. The same goes for States emerging from the status of pariah States, such as South Africa post-Apartheid. By contrast, powerful States, who are long-standing members of the international community may engage in contestation in its various guises, whether mounting local (constitutional) resistance and turning away from international law, or seeking to influence its content and development (occasionally

[152] See *R v Keyn* (The *Franconia* case) (1876) 2 Ex D 63.

[153] See the *Korean 'Comfort Women'* case, Korean Constitutional Court (Judgment of 30 August 2011) 2006Hun-Ma788: Korean courts force Korea to pursue dispute settlement with Japan on the matter: this is because the discretion given to the Korean State under international law has to be structured in accordance with the Korean constitutional provisions on human rights. Cf the decisions of the Canadian courts in *Canada (Prime Minister) v Khadr* [2010] 1 SCR 44; 2010 SCC 3; and *Abdelrazik* (n 103).

also through consubstantial alignment rather than open contestation). Further, domestic courts in States undergoing radical (if still constitutional) change may look to international law as a way to protect themselves against themselves—ie to resist or to calm down constitutional but radical change. This may occasion a strategy or posture of alignment, perhaps even hyper-alignment.

76. A further variable, also identified as a challenge in Part A, is the type of rules involved in the adjudication. It has become apparent in Part B of the Report that the domestic courts of particular State do not exclusively conform to one particular strategy or posture, but may shift between them. These shifts can be explained in various ways, including by determining how politically or otherwise problematic the international rule and compliance with it is. It may be relatively easy to adopt a strategy or posture of alignment to politically unproblematic rules (or in circumstances which make alignment with the rules unproblematic) (fair weather alignment). In more problematic cases of politically- or value-laden rules, such as human rights or international humanitarian law rules, domestic courts may be more inclined to engage in avoidance or contestation.[154] It should be noted however that there are examples of domestic courts engaging with politically problematic international rules, such as those on the rights of indigenous peoples, in a manner which produces consubstantial alignment.[155]

77. Occasionally, strategies or postures of engagement may also roughly map on to the type of rule involved in terms of its 'directionality' (see Part A section I.b above). It is easy to surmise that avoidance will be the preferred strategy of engagement with outward-looking, horizontal rules of international law.[156] But within inward-looking norms things are less clear: whereas rules that obligate the state to regulate cross-border private relations[157] may occasion a larger degree of alignment (and development), vertical inward-looking norms which regulate the relationship between the State and those within its jurisdiction may occasion all types of engagement depending on their (perceived) specific content and the interests at stake. This is so in part because transnational rules are rather laxly supervised by either international courts or States. Domestic courts are in fact the main agents applying treaties including such rules, and indeed the treaties themselves envision domestic courts as the main agents of enforcement. As such, domestic courts are relatively comfortable interpreting the sometimes vague language of these rules (eg child 'in intolerable situation'), which in a purely horizontal or vertical context they might have found simply too vague, and opted to defer to the executive.

78. A number of other variables may play a role in this respect, and they have been identified by the Study Group, but may be too difficult to study in any exhaustive manner.

154 See generally the *Report on Israel* (2013) and cf the Swiss courts' position that the ICESCR is not directly effective, in contrast to most other human rights instruments in the domestic legal order, in the *Report on Switzerland* (2013) 8.

155 See n 101 above.

156 Note however that some seemingly outward-looking, horizontal rules are actually also inward-looking, and indeed specifically addressed to domestic courts (at least in part). The rules of immunity are such an example, and they occasion both alignment and contestation in their various incarnations.

157 Sometimes called 'transnational rules', these inward-looking rules are found in numerous international treaties such as the Convention on the International Sale of Goods, the Hague Convention on the Civil Aspects of International Child Abduction, the Montreal Convention for the Unification of Certain Rules for International Carriage by Air, or the New York Convention on the Recognition and Enforcement of Foreign Arbitral Awards, among others. Countless domestic court decisions refer to the rules in these treaties, while in dualist States they always get transformed into domestic law, even if simply by scheduling.

These include whether and to what extent counsel have pleaded international law before the domestic court, and the quality of these pleadings. Anecdotal evidence suggests that domestic courts rely heavily on good argument on the part of counsel, and this would make sense: domestic court judges are not international law scholars and good argument will assist them in properly dealing with the international law issues in the case (and vice versa). A related factor is the way that international law is employed by counsel before the court: it may be used by the claimant or applicant as a sword to attack a normative act or government position; but it may also be used by the government as a shield to defend against an attack by the claimant or applicant. The way that international law is used, against the background of the relative merits of the case, may affect the disposition of the domestic court towards it. A further factor is the general disposition of the domestic court or judge towards international law in general. A most important factor relates also to the independence of the judiciary in the relevant State. The problem with all these factors, however, is that they are all to some extent subjective. Hence the difficulty in studying them in an exhaustive manner.

79. A final variable is the certainty and frequency of supervision or monitoring, in particular by international courts. While in general international law there is the possibility of supervision or monitoring being exercised very occasionally, in the context of regional human rights treaties, especially those establishing courts with quasi-compulsory jurisdiction as their monitoring organs, supervision is much more certain and frequent. This, in large part, will occasion more alignment (as avoidance will not be appreciated by the monitoring court), though it also has the potential of leading to contestation.

List of Reports by Study Group members and invited scholars referred to in the Final Report

1 *Thematic Reports*
- 1.1 M Kanetake, *Report on International Human Rights Law* (2015)
- 1.2 HE Kjos, *Report on International Investment Law* (2013)
- 1.3 A Kulick, *Report on International Investment Law* (2015)
- 1.4 S Weill, *Report on International Humanitarian Law* (2013)

2 *National Reports*
- 2.5 EM Belser and R Oleschak, *Report on Switzerland* (2013)
- 2.6 F Dopagne, *Report on Belgium* (2014)
- 2.7 G van Ert, *Report on Canada* (2013)
- 2.8 S Fatima, *Report on England* (2015)
- 2.9 M Freitas Mohallem, *Report on South America* (2015)
- 2.10 R Gunaratne, *Report on Sri Lanka* (2013)
- 2.11 M Killander, *Report on Anglophone Africa* (2015)
- 2.12 M Pinto and N Maisley, *Report on Argentina* (2015)
- 2.13 Z Ratniece, *Report on Kosovo* (2015)
- 2.14 OG Schwartz, *Report on Israel* (2013)
- 2.15 H Woolaver, *Report on South Africa* (2013)
- 2.16 R Yadava and SP Kumar, *Report on India* (2013)
- 2.17 G Zyberi and S Sali, *Report on Albania* (2013)

Index

For the benefit of digital users, indexed terms that span two pages (e.g., 52–53) may, on occasion, appear on only one of those pages.

act of State doctrine
avoidance of IHL 337–38
Belgium 219
Canada 160
English courts 243–44
affirmative avoidance
Anglophone African approach to customary law 32
Argentina
constitutional law 118
customary international law 119
dualist approach to treaties 118–19
Canada 163–64
Israel's Supreme Court
judicial techniques employed 82
recent cases 92–94
practice of Chinese courts
foreign affairs 74–75
non-justiciability 75
self-executive treaties 75–76
unregulated subjects 76–77
Sri Lanka's Supreme Court 114
US courts 171–72, 185
affirmative contestation
Albania's court practice
law of immunities 200–4
law of the sea 204–6
Anglophone African approach to ratified treaties 26
Argentina's Supreme Court 134–40
Belgium 223–24
international human rights law 356–58
international sanctions
alignment-*cum* contestation 358–61
apparent alignment 361–62
Israel's Supreme Court 84–85
US courts 180–81, 184–85
Albania
acknowledgement and note 208
court practice
affirmative contestation 200–6
'hyper'-alignment 191–200
leading role of Constitutional Court 191
new approach after 1990 187–88
general strategy of alignment 206–7
international human rights law
general strategy of alignment 206–7
'hyper'-alignment 191–200
new approach after 1990 187–88
overview of key points 188
scope of international legal obligations after 1990 187–88
status of international law
constitutional law 189
hierarchical status 189
ratification of treaties 189–90
alignment techniques and strategies
Albania
general strategy of alignment 206–7
'hyper'-alignment 191–200
Argentina
constitutional reform 121
growing deference to international courts and tribunals 127–33
incorporation of customary international law 123–27
international treaties 122–23
Belgium
consistent interpretation 212–15
self-executing treaties 215–18
Canada
absence of other techniques 158–59
attitude of openness to international law 143–44
judicial alignment 152–58
legislative alignment 151–52
overview of key points 151
preferred approach 163–64

alignment techniques and strategies (*cont.*)
China
consistent interpretation 62
consubstantial alignment 68–70
'fair weather' alignment 62–65
'hyper'-alignment 70–72
international treaties 61
overriding alignment 65–67
consubstantial alignment
Anglophone African approach to ratified treaties 24–25, 27
ILA Final Report 27
practice of Chinese courts 68–70
use in Anglophone Africa 35
enforcement of IIL and beyond
backbone of the entire system 315
ICSID awards 315
mechanisms that could produce/ support alignment 316
English law
application of POC 236–37
customary international law 242, 243
hybrid statutes 235
incorporated treaties 235
opportunities for avoidance, alignment and contestation 244
treaty interpretation 231
unincorporated treaties 235–36
'fair weather' alignment
patterns of engagement identified by ILA 12–13
practice of Chinese courts 62–65
prevalence in Africa 35
prevalence in Anglophone Africa 35
findings of UN human rights treaty monitoring bodies 295–98
'hyper'-alignment
Anglophone African approach to ratified treaties 23
Anglophone African approach to unratified treaties 31
ILA Final Report 13
practice of Chinese courts 70–72
IHL norms 343–45
international sanctions
alignment-*cum* contestation 358–61
apparent alignment 361–62
claim before before UK court 356–58
contestation-*cum* alignment 362–67
different contexts and cases 354–55
Palladyne v Upper Brook 355–56
'over-riding' alignment
patterns of engagement identified by ILA 12–13
prevalence in Africa 35
practice of Chinese courts 65–67
practice of Israeli Supreme Court
IHL 84–87
IHRL 87–90
judicial techniques employed 82
relevance to IHL and IHRL 84
South African approach
consistent interpretation 41–47
'moral imperative' technique 47–49
overview of key points 40–41
Sri Lanka's Supreme Court
to ensure consistency 106–8
to fill lacunae in domestic law 110–11
other considerations 111–12
to understand and extend scope of domestic rights 108–10
Switzerland
consistent interpretation 280–83
exception to Schubert Practice 284–85
muddled approach to non-aligned constitutional law 285–88
overview 280
Schubert Practice 283–84, 289–90
US courts
consubstantial alignment 173–76
'fair weather' alignment 172–73
historical approach 167–68
hyper-alignment 179
overriding alignment 176–79
overview of general practices 184
Anglophone Africa
see also **South Africa**
case law 31
customary international law
case law 32–33
part of the law of the land 32
developments since independence 19
findings of UN human rights treaty monitoring bodies 295–96, 298
general absence of evasive avoidance 35
importance of case law 35–36

international human rights law 30
legal hierarchy 33–35
overview of key points 20
prevalence of fair weather alignment 35
ratified treaties
absence of case law 27
affirmative contestation 26
constitutional law 20–24
consubstantial alignment 27
contestation approach 29
incorporated international law 24–26
interpretation of domestic law provision 29–30
prima facie presumption of relevance 30
unincorporated international law 28–29
variance in approaches 20
relevant states 19
soft law 31
unratified treaties 31

apparent conflict 280

Argentina
affirmative avoidance (1853-1992)
constitutional law 118
customary international law 119
dualist approach to treaties 118–19
affirmative contestation (2017)
Fontevecchia decision 134–38
Muiña decision 138–40
era of overriding alignment (1994-2017)
constitutional reform 121
growing deference to international courts and tribunals 127–33
incorporation of customary international law 123–27
international treaties 122–23
era of transition (1992-1994) 120–21
findings of UN human rights treaty monitoring bodies
postures of alignment 297–98
postures of avoidance 301
new attitude to international law 140–41
overview of key points 117–18

avoidance techniques and strategies
Argentina
constitutional law 118
customary international law 119
dualist approach to treaties 118–19
Belgium
absence of consistent or systematic trend 219
customary international law 221–22
immunities 222–23
priority of constitutional review 219–20
Canada
constitutional avoidance 159–60
judicial avoidance 160–63
China
affirmative avoidance 73–77
evasive avoidance 72–73
international treaties 61
occasional practice 72
English law
incorporated treaties 235
opportunities for avoidance, alignment and contestation 244
findings of UN human rights treaty monitoring bodies 300–1
ILA Final Report 10–11
international humanitarian law
deference to executive 340–42
doctrines to avoid adjudication 337–38
Israeli Targeted Killings Case 339–40
United States Targeted Killings Case 338–39
one of three main patterns of engagement identified by ILA 12–14
practice of Israeli Supreme Court
affirmative avoidance 92–94
evasive avoidance 94–95
judicial techniques employed 82
relevance to IHL and IHRL 84
South African approach
to customary international law 39–40
denial of self-executing treaties 53–55
domestic and international contexts distinguished 52–53
overview of key points 49
rejection of customary international law 50–52
Sri Lanka's Supreme Court
difficulties of identification 112–13
IHRL 113–14

avoidance techniques and strategies (*cont.*)
Switzerland
justiciability of international norms 278–79
reluctance to accept international obligations 277–78
US courts
affirmative avoidance 171–72
evasive avoidance 170–71
historical approach 167–68
overview of general practices 185

Belgium
alignment techniques
consistent interpretation 212–15
self-executing treaties 215–18
avoidance techniques
absence of consistent or systematic trend 219
customary international law 221–22
immunities 222–23
priority of constitutional review 219–20
Constitutional framework
customary international law 212
ratification of treaties 210–11
scant provisions in relation to international law 209–10
status of international law 211–12
contestation
affirmative contestation 223–24
negatory contestation 224–25
court practice
alignment techniques 212–19
avoidance techniques 219–23
international law
general principled approach 225
posture of 'openness' 225
overview of key points 212
blunting/moderating techniques
English law 243–44
ILA Final Report 10–11

Canada
alignment techniques
absence of other techniques 158–59
court practice 151–59
judicial alignment 152–58
legislative alignment 151–52
overview of key points 151
preferred approach 163–64
attitude of openness to international law 143–44
avoidance practices
constitutional avoidance 159–60
IHL 340–41
judicial avoidance 160–63
findings of UN human rights treaty monitoring bodies
postures of alignment 296
postures of avoidance 300, 301
postures of contestation 299–300
international sanctions 358–61
overview of key points 144
status of international law
customary international law 147–50
international treaties 145–47
judicial notice of international law 144–45
presumption of conformity 150
case law
see also **court practice; judiciary**
Anglophone African approach
to customary international law 32–33
importance 35–36
to international case law 31
to ratified treaties 27
avoidance techniques in South Africa 52–53
Canada's respect for rule of law 148–49
China
international treaties 60–61
small numbers 78
growing Argentina's deference to international courts and tribunals 127–33
Human Rights Committee Communications 113–14
influence on Albania 203–4, 207–8
Israel's Supreme Court
affirmative avoidance 92–94
alignment with IHL 8–87
alignment with IHRL 87–90
contestation 90–92
evasive avoidance 94–95
South Africa 44
Sri Lanka's Supreme Court

impact of judicial precedent 103–200
limited engagement with international law 115
status of international law 101–2
China
alignment techniques and strategies
consistent interpretation 62
consubstantial alignment 68–70
'fair weather' alignment 62–65
'hyper'-alignment 70–72
overriding alignment 65–67
avoidance techniques and strategies
affirmative avoidance 73–77
evasive avoidance 72–73
occasional practice 72
case law 78
'inward-looking' character of international human rights law 77
participation in international law 57
practice of Chinese courts
alignment postures 62–72
avoidance techniques and strategies 72–77
varied approaches 78
significance of statutory law 77
status of international treaties
absence of constitutional provisions 57–58
case law 60–61
general practice of alignment or at worst contestation 61
hierarchical status 58–60
consistent interpretation
Anglophone African approach to ratified treaties 29, 30
Argentina's Supreme Court 122–23
Belgium 212–15
Canada's Supreme Court
ambiguity 162–63
Charter obscurantism 160–61
constitutional protection of human rights 163–64
Chinese courts 62, 69
ILA Final Report 27
South African approach
Bill of Rights interpretation 43–47
constitutional provisions 41
legislative interpretation 41–43
Sri Lanka's Supreme Court 99–100, 104–5, 106–8
Switzerland 280–83
use in Anglophone Africa 35
constitutional avoidance 159–60
constitutional law
Albania 189
Anglophone Africa
to legal hierarchy 33–35
to ratified treaties 20–24
Argentina
affirmative avoidance (1853-1992) 118
constitutional reform 121
incorporation of customary international law 123–27
Belgium
consistent interpretation 214–15
customary international law 212
priority of constitutional review 219–20
ratification of treaties 210–11
scant provisions in relation to international law 209–10
status of international law 211–12
Kosovo
easy reception of international law 269
Kosovo's international obligations 263–67
as special case 246
South Africa
Bill of Rights interpretation 43–47
controversy surrounding heavy use of international law 55–56
denial of self-executing treaties by South Africa 53–55
directly enforceable international law 38–40
indirect effect of international law 40
'moral imperative' technique of alignment 47–49
new Final South African Constitution 37
prominence 37–38
Sri Lanka
reception of international law in domestic legal order 102–3
status of international law 98–100

constitutional law (*cont.*)
Switzerland
application of federal acts and international law 276
determination of legal hierarchy 274
limitations on rights of appeal 276
muddled approach to non-aligned constitutional law 285–88
consubstantial alignment
Anglophone African approach to ratified treaties 24–25
ILA Final Report 27
practice of Chinese courts 68–70
US courts 173–76, 184
use in Anglophone Africa 35
consubstantial contestation
defined 14
international sanctions
Ahmed v HM Treasury 364–65
alignment-*cum* contestation 358–61
apparent alignment 361–62
US courts 183–84
consubstantial norms
China 68
defined 13
England and Wales 234
Israel 82–83
contestation
Albania's court practice
law of immunities 200–4
law of the sea 204–6
Anglophone African approach to ratified treaties
affirmative contestation 26
Botswana Court of Appeal 29
Argentina's Supreme Court
Fontevecchia decision 134–38
Muiña decision 138–40
Belgium
affirmative contestation 223–24
negatory contestation 224–25
China 61
defined 14
English law
incorporated treaties 235
opportunities for avoidance, alignment and contestation 244
findings of UN human rights treaty monitoring bodies 299–300, 309
ILL awards
establishment of high standard of review 318–19
formal instrument of contestation 316
generally adopted standard of review 319
interpretation of BITs and ICSID Convention 320
jurisdictional review 319–20
permissible grounds for setting aside an award 317
UNCITRAL Model Law 316–17
international sanctions
affirmative contestation 356–58
alignment-*cum* contestation 358–61
contestation-*cum* alignment 362–67
Israel's Supreme Court
IHL 84–85
judicial techniques employed 82
negatory contestation 90–92
prioritisation of domestic norms and national interests 90
UNMIK Regulations 255
US courts
affirmative contestation 180–81
applicability of international norm 169–70
consubstantial contestation 183–84
historical approach 167–68
negatory contestation 181–83
overview of general practices 184–85
court practice
see also **engagement with international law**
Albania
affirmative contestation 200–6
'hyper'-alignment 191–200
leading role of Constitutional Court 191
new approach after 1990 187–88
Argentina's Supreme Court
affirmative avoidance (1853-1992) 118–19
affirmative contestation (2017) 134–40
era of overriding alignment (1994-2017) 121–33
era of transition (1992–1994) 120–21

Belgium
alignment techniques 212–19
avoidance techniques 219–23
Canada
alignment techniques 151–59
judicial notice of international law 144–45
China
alignment postures 62–72
avoidance techniques and strategies 72–77
varied approaches 78
England and Wales
opportunities for avoidance, alignment and contestation 244
treaty-making 230
English law
customary international law 241–43
interpretation and incorporation of treaties 230–41
findings of UN human rights treaty monitoring bodies
ILA overview 294–95
postures of alignment 295–98
postures of avoidance 300–1
postures of contestation 299–300
international humanitarian law
activist decisions 345–46
avoidance 337–42
deference to executive 340–42
inherent partiality of domestic judges 336–37
legitimization of executive's illegal acts 335–36
legitimization of State policies 334–35
normative alignment 343–45
Israel's Supreme Court
alignment with IHL 8–87
alignment with IHRL 87–90
avoidance 92–95
contestation 90–92
engagement with IHRL and IHL norms 82–83
judicial techniques employed 82
relevance of avoidance 83
shifting attitude towards international law 95
Kosovo
customary international law 256–63
other international instruments 263–67
UNMIK Regulations 251–55
during UNMIK's administration of Kosovo 246–48
Sri Lanka's Supreme Court
determination of fundamental rights 97
impact of judicial precedent 97–98, 103–200
limited engagement with international law 115–16
Switzerland
alignment techniques and strategies 280–85
avoidance techniques and strategies 277–79
key issue of predictability 271–72
muddled approach to non-aligned constitutional law 285–88
United States
alignment 172–79
avoidance 170–72
contestation 180–84
overview of general practices 184–85
courts *see* **engagement of domestic courts**
customary international law *see also* **state practice**
Albania 190
Anglophone African approach 19
case law 32–33
part of the law of the land 32
Argentina 119, 123–27
Belgium 212, 221–22
Canada 147–50
English law 241–43
importance of domestic courts 3
Israel 80
Kosovo
Llapi Case before UNMIK and EULEX Judges 257–62
Thaçi et al Case before Kosovo Specialist Chambers 262–63
UNMIK Regulation 1999/24 256
source-specific patterns of engagement 9–10
South African approach
avoidance techniques 50–52

customary international law (*cont.*)
directly enforceable international law 39–40
'moral imperative' technique of alignment 47
Sri Lanka's Supreme Court 101

domestic courts *see* **engagement of domestic courts**
domestic law
see also **court practice**
Anglophone African approach to ratified treaties 29–30
disruption created by 'background noise' 4–5
international court judges distinguished 5
relationship with UNMIK Regulations 29–30
Sri Lanka's Supreme Court alignment techniques 110–11
dualism
Anglophone African approach 19
Argentina's approach to international treaties 118–19
English law 228–29
formal obstacle to engagement 12–13
ILA Final Report
blunting moves and moderating techniques 11
limited relevance of monism and dualism 9
Israel's approach to treaties 80
theory of *dédoublement fonctionnel* 3

engagement of domestic courts
see also **court practice**
Albania *see* **Albania**
Anglophone Africa *see* **Anglophone Africa**
Argentina *see* **Argentina**
'background noise' of domestic law 4–5
Belgium *see* **Belgium**
Canada *see* **Canada**
China *see* **China**
England and Wales *see* **England and Wales**
establishing 'principles of engagement' 6
findings of UN human rights treaty monitoring bodies *see* **UN human rights treaty monitoring bodies**
ILA study
difficulty of identifying clear pattern 11–12
diverse approaches to legal hierarchy and interpretation 10
Final Report 2016 6–7
gap between doctrine and actual practice of engagement 11
interaction between domestic and international courts 8–9
inward- and outward-looking norms 7–8
limited relevance of monism and dualism 9
source-specific patterns of engagement 9–10
status of international law 10–11
transition towards a more pragmatic approach 7
impact of loose connection between doctrine and practice 15
importance 3
international court judges distinguished 5
international humanitarian law *see* **international humanitarian law**
international investment law and arbitration *see* **international investment law and arbtration**
international sanctions *see* **international sanctions**
Israel *see* **Israel**
Kosovo *see* **Kosovo**
main patterns identified by ILA Final Report 12–14
normative expectations 4
South Africa *see* **South Africa**
Sri Lanka *see* **Sri Lanka**
Switzerland *see* **Switzerland**
United States *see* **United States**
England and Wales
avoidance of IHL 340–43
blunting/moderating techniques 243–44
court practice
customary international law 241–43
interpretation and incorporation of treaties 230–41
opportunities for avoidance, alignment and contestation 244
treaty-making 230

findings of UN human rights treaty monitoring bodies
postures of alignment 295–96
postures of avoidance 301
international law
blunting/moderating techniques 243–44
increasing engagement 227–30
international sanctions
alignment 356–58
apparent alignment 361–62
consubstantial contestation 364–65
EU law
Belgium 209–10
English law post-Brexit 227–28
ILA Final Report 10
international sanctions
contestation-*cum* alignment 362–67
legal basis for adoption 352
legal hierarchy 355–56
Kosovo 248
relationship with IIL
competitive relationship of investment arbitration and EU dispute settlement system 321–22
importance 321
open questions following CJEU's judgment 322–23
evasive avoidance
general absence in Anglophone Africa 35
Israel's Supreme Court
judicial techniques employed 82
recent cases 94–95
practice of Chinese courts 72–73
US courts 170–71, 185

'fair weather' alignment
patterns of engagement identified by ILA 12–13
practice of Chinese courts 62–65
prevalence in Anglophone Africa 35
US courts 172–73, 184

hierarchy *see* **legal hierarchy**
humanitarian law *see* **international humanitarian law**
'hyper'-alignment
Albania 191–200
Anglophone African approach
to ratified treaties 23
to unratified treaties 31
Argentina's Supreme Court 137–38
ILA Final Report 13
Switzerland 287–88
US courts 179

immunities
Albania 200–4
Anglophone African approach 32–33
Argentina 119
Belgium 222–23
Canada 149
China 59–60, 65–66
South Africa 47–48, 55
United States 168–69, 170–71, 179, 184–85
incorporated international law
Anglophone African approach to ratified treaties
countries where international law unincorporated 28–29
countries with incorporation 24–26
Argentina's approach to customary international law 123–27
Canada's approach to customary law 147–50
English law 230–41
ILA Final Report 10
Sri Lanka 105
international human rights law
Albania
general strategy of alignment 206–7
'hyper'-alignment 191–200
new approach after 1990 187–88
Anglophone African approach
jurisprudence 30
legal hierarchy 33–35
Argentina
affirmative contestation (2017) 134–38
growing deference to international courts and tribunals 127–29
Belgium
consistent interpretation 214
Canada
Charter obscurantism 160–62
consistent interpretation 163–64

international human rights law (*cont.*)
China 77
English law
continuing attention and controversy 227–28
relevance of ECtHR judgments 232–34
findings of UN human rights treaty monitoring bodies
acknowledgement 310
court practice 294–301
incremental response to UN expectations 308–9
normative basis of judicial engagement 301–4
overview of key points 293–94
persuasiveness as normative basis for judicial engagement 304–8
ILA Final Report 10
international sanctions
affirmative contestation 356–58
alignment-*cum* contestation 358–61
Israel
practice of Israeli Supreme Court 82–83
relevance to geopolitical reality 80–81
practice of Israeli Supreme Court
relevance of avoidance 83
South African approach
indirect effect of international law 40
'moral imperative' technique of alignment 47–48, 49
Sri Lanka's Supreme Court
affirmative avoidance 114
avoidance 113–14
filling lacunae in domestic law 110–11
introduction of international law norms 100
understanding and extending scope of domestic rights 108–10
Switzerland
consistent interpretation 280–83
Constitutionally determined hierarchy 274
exception to Schubert Practice 284–85
muddled approach to non-aligned constitutional law 285–88
reluctance to accept international obligations 277–78
US courts
consubstantial alignment 174–76

international humanitarian law
Argentina
affirmative contestation (2017) 138–40
incorporation of customary international law 124–25
avoidance
deference to executive 340–42
doctrines to avoid adjudication 337–38
Israeli Targeted Killings Case 339–40
United States Targeted Killings Case 338–39
court practice
activist decisions 345–46
avoidance 337–42
deference to executive 340–42
normative alignment 343–45
distinction between what domestic courts 'say' and 'do' 334
Israel
Israeli Targeted Killings Case 339–40
legitimization of executive's illegal acts 335–36
practice of Israeli Supreme Court 82–83
relevance of avoidance 83
relevance to geopolitical reality 80–81
misuse of law by courts
inherent partiality of domestic judges 336–37
legitimization of executive's illegal acts 335–36
legitimization of State policies 334–35
norms
endorsement at domestic level 333–34
overview of key points 333
politically sensitive issues 347
US deference of judiciary to executive 168–70

international investment law and arbitration
acknowledgement and note 331
alignment of enforcement and beyond

backbone of the entire system 315
ICSID awards 315
mechanisms that could produce/support alignment 316
contestation - challenge and beyond
establishment of high standard of review 318–19
formal instrument of contestation 316
generally adopted standard of review 319
interpretation of BITs and ICSID Convention 320
jurisdictional review 319–20
permissible grounds for setting aside an award 317
UNCITRAL Model Law 316–17
overview of key points 314
relationship with EU law
competitive relationship of investment arbitration and EU dispute settlement system 321–22
importance 321
open questions following CJEU's judgment 322–23
role of international law in domestic legal orders
application of BIT to Macau 324–26
broad spectrum of engagement 324
standard of review applicable to BIT 326–28
underlying complexities 328
'soothing factors' 328–31
underlying paradoxes 311–14

international law
see also **international treaties; status of international law**
Albania's new approach after 1990 187–88
Belgium
general principled approach 225
posture of 'openness' 225
scant provisions in Constitutional framework 209–10
Chinese participation 57
England and Wales
blunting/moderating techniques 243–44
increasing engagement 227–30
ILA Final Report
diverse approaches to legal hierarchy and interpretation 10
source-specific patterns of engagement 9–10
importance of domestic courts 3
modes of reception and application in US
constitutional interpretation 167
constitutional law 165–66
judicial doctrine 166–67
statutory interpretation 167
three broad factors 167–70
normative basis of judicial engagement with UN treaty monitoring 303–4
reception in Sri Lank's domestic legal order
impact of judicial precedent 103–200
international law in the Constitution 102–3

International Law Association (ILA)
difficulty of identifying clear pattern of engagement 11–12
distinction between what domestic courts 'say' and 'do' about IHL 334
diverse approaches to legal hierarchy and interpretation 10
Final Report 2016 6–7
findings of UN human rights treaty monitoring bodies 294–95
gap between doctrine and actual practice of engagement 10–11
inward- and outward-looking norms 7–8
limited relevance of monism and dualism 9
main patterns of engagement 12–14
source-specific patterns of engagement 9–10
status of international law 10–11
transition towards a more pragmatic approach 7

international sanctions
alignment
alignment-*cum* contestation 358–61
claim before before UK court 356–58
contestation-*cum* alignment 362–67
different contexts and cases 354–55
Palladyne v Upper Brook 355–56
bolder approach of domestic courts 367–68

international sanctions (*cont.*)
legal basis for adoption 351–54
meaning and scope 350–51
necessary trait of any legal order 350–51
note 369
overview of key points 354
safeguarding of human rights 368–69
shift in international law 349–50
international treaties
see also **dualism; international law; monism; status of international law**
Albanian approach 189–90
Anglophone African approach to ratified treaties
absence of case law 27
affirmative contestation 26
constitutional law 20–24
consubstantial alignment 27
contestation approach 29
incorporated international law 24–26
interpretation of domestic law provision 29–30
prima facie presumption of relevance 30
unincorporated international law 28–29
variance in approaches 20
Anglophone African approach to unratified treaties 31
Argentina
affirmative avoidance (1853-1992) 118–19
era of transition (1992-1994) 120–21
overriding alignment (1994-2017) 122–23
Belgium 210–11
Canada
domestic legal effect 146
federal and provincial competence 146–47
implementation requirement 145–46, 147
legislative alignment 151–52
Westminster model 145
English treaty-making 230
findings of UN human rights treaty monitoring bodies
acknowledgement 310
court practice 294–301
incremental response to UN expectations 308–9
normative basis of judicial engagement 301–4
overview of key points 293–94
persuasiveness as normative basis for judicial engagement 304–8
Israel 80
role in domestic ILL dispute settlement
application of BIT to Macau 324–26
broad spectrum of engagement 324
standard of review applicable to BIT 326–28
underlying complexities 328
source-specific patterns of engagement 9–10
South African approach
consistent interpretation 42–43
denial of self-executing treaties 53–55
directly enforceable international law 38–39
status in China
absence of constitutional provisions 57–58
case law 60–61
general practice of alignment or at worst contestation 61
hierarchical status 58–60
Switzerland
importance of EU treaties 286–87
muddled approach to non-aligned constitutional law 286
United States
constitutional requirements 166
judicial doctrine 166–67
overriding alignment 176–79
internationally minded contestation
ILA Final Report 362–63
local contestation distinguished 191
interpretation *see* **consistent interpretation**
investment law and arbitration *see* **international investment law and arbitration**
inward-looking norms
China 77
ILA Final Report 73
Israel
factors determining engagement with international law

judicial preferences and conceptions 81–82
overview of key points 80
relevance to geopolitical reality 80–81
international humanitarian law
Israeli Targeted Killings Case 339–40
legitimization of executive's illegal acts 335–36
practice of Israeli Supreme Court
alignment with IHL 8–87
alignment with IHRL 87–90
avoidance 92–95
contestation 90–92
engagement with IHRL and IHL norms 82–83
judicial techniques employed 82
relevance of avoidance 83
shifting attitude towards international law 95
status of international law
customary international law 79
greater openness under Barak 80

judiciary
see also **court practice**
Canadian alignment techniques 152–58
Canadian avoidance practices
ambiguity 162–63
Charter obscurantism 160–62
wilful blindness or legal error 162
distinguishing role of international judges 5
engagement with findings of UN human rights treaty monitoring bodies
normative basis of judicial engagement 301–4
persuasiveness as normative basis for judicial engagement 304–8
factor determining Israel's engagement with international law 81–82
inherent partiality of domestic judges in applying IHL 336–37
Kosovo
after Kosovo's declaration of independence 249–51
as special case 245
during UNMIK's administration of Kosovo 246–47
role in international courts 5
Switzerland
application of federal acts and international law 276
limitations on rights of appeal 276
rule of *in dubio pro populo* 275
safeguarding of constitutional value 289
United States
deference of judiciary to executive 168–70
self-executing and non-self-executing treaties distinguished 166–67
jus cogens *see* **norms**
justiciability *see* **non-justiciability**

Kosovo
acknowledgement and note 269
court practice
customary international law 256–63
other international instruments 263–67
UNMIK Regulations 251–55
domestic courts yet to be shaped 268–69
internationalization of domestic Courts
after Kosovo's declaration of independence 248–51
during UNMIK's administration of Kosovo 246–48
overview of key points 245–46
significance of UNSC Resolution 1244 and UNMIK Regulations 267–68
UNMIK Regulations
legal nature 252–53
relationship between competing sources of law 251–52
relationship with domestic law 253–55

law of the sea
Albania
affirmative contestation 204–6
internationally minded contestation 206–7
Albania's court practice 204–6
legal hierarchy
see also **status of international law**
Albania 189
Anglophone African approach 33–35
Belgium 212

legal hierarchy (*cont.*)
China 58–60
ILA Final Report 10
international sanctions 355–56
Sri Lanka 100
Switzerland
Constitutionally determined 274
highly controversial issue 273
non-mandatory international norms 274–75
local contestation
Anglophone Africa 29
ILA Final Report 362–63
internationally minded contestation distinguished 191
Israel 90

moderating techniques
English law 243–44
ILA Final Report 10–11
monism
Anglophone African approach to ratified treaties 20–21
ILA Final Report
blunting moves and moderating techniques 11
limited relevance of monism and dualism 9
Israel's approach to customary international law 79
Switzerland 273–74
'moral imperative' technique of alignment 47–49, 55

negatory contestation
Belgium 224–25
Canada 163–64
Israel's Supreme Court 90–92
US courts 181–83, 184–85
non-justiciability
avoidance of IHL
doctrines to avoid adjudication 337–38
Israeli Targeted Killings Case 339–40
England and Wales
court practice 243–44
treaty-making 230
formal obstacle to engagement 12–13
practice of Chinese courts 75
Sri Lanka's Supreme Court 105
Switzerland
international norms 278–79
reluctance to accept international obligations 277
normative conflict 271–73
norms
Albania
approach to human rights 191
willingness to engage with international law 207–8
Anglophone African approach 31
'background noise' of domestic law 4–5
Belgium
legal hierarchy 212
priority of constitutional review 219–20
self-executing character 211–12
transformation of treaty into Belgian law 210
consubstantial norms
China 68
defined 13
England and Wales 234
Israel 82–83
domestic alignment with IHL norms 343–45
findings of UN human rights treaty monitoring bodies
bindingness not fully accounted for 309
normative basis of judicial engagement 301–4
formal obstacles to engagement 12–13
ILA Final Report
blunting moves and moderating techniques 11
diverse approaches to legal hierarchy and interpretation 10
inward- and outward-looking norms 7–8
transition towards a more pragmatic approach 7
importance of domestic courts 3
international humanitarian law
application to politically sensitive issues 347
US courts 174
inward-looking norms
China 77
ILA Final Report 73

'moral imperative' technique of alignment in South Africa 47–49, 55
practice of Israeli Supreme Court
engagement generally 82–83
IHL 84–86
IHRL 87
prioritisation of domestic norms and national interests 90
role of domestic courts 4
source-specific patterns of engagement 9–10
Sri Lanka
alignment techniques and strategies 108–10
introduction of IHRL norms 100
Switzerland
application of federal acts and international law 276
consistent interpretation 280
difficulties with new constitutional norms and their implementation 288–89
hierarchy of non-mandatory international norms 274–75
highly controversial issues 273
justiciability of international norms 278–79
muddled approach to non-aligned constitutional law 285–88
US courts
consubstantial alignment 174–76
contested applicability 169–70
international human rights law 174

opinio juris
England and Wales 241–42
ICJ as source of law 7–8
South Africa 50–52
Sri Lanka 105
overriding alignment
Argentina
constitutional reform 121
growing deference to international courts and tribunals 127–33
incorporation of customary international law 123–27
international treaties 122–23
Canadian Supreme Court 155–57
patterns of engagement identified by ILA 12–13
practice of Chinese courts 65–67
Switzerland 287
US courts 176–79

political question doctrine
avoidance of IHL 338–39
Belgium 219
Canada 160
United States Targeted Killings Case 338–39
presumption of compatibility (POC) 235–39
principle of legality (the POL) 235–38

rule of law
Albania 206–7
Anglophone Africa 29
basic principle of governance 4
England and Wales 229
IHL 343–44
Kosovo 249
normative expectations 4
South Africa 48, 49
Switzerland 273–74, 287, 288–90

sanctions *see* **international sanctions**
Schubert Practice
human rights obligations excepted 284–85
Swiss alignment strategy 283–84
self-executing treaties
Belgium 215–18
China 75–76
South Africa 53–55
United States 166–67
soft law
Anglophone African approach 31
Switzerland 271
source-specificity 9–10
South Africa
see also **Anglophone Africa**
alignment techniques and strategies
consistent interpretation 41–47
'moral imperative' technique 47–49
overview of key points 40–41
avoidance techniques and strategies
denial of self-executing treaties 53–55

South Africa (*cont.*)
domestic and international contexts distinguished 52–53
overview of key points 49
rejection of customary international law 50–52
constitutional law
Bill of Rights interpretation 43–47
controversy surrounding heavy use of international law 55–56
denial of self-executing treaties by South Africa 53–55
directly enforceable international law 38–40
indirect effect of international law 40
'moral imperative' technique of alignment 47–49
new Final South African Constitution 37
prominence 37–38
findings of UN human rights treaty monitoring bodies 305–6
generally receptive to international law 55
overview of key points 38
Sri Lanka
alignment techniques and strategies
to ensure consistency 106–8
to fill lacunae in domestic law 110–11
other considerations 111–12
to understand and extend scope of domestic rights 108–10
avoidance techniques and strategies
difficulties of identification 112–13
IHRL 113–14
overview of key points 98
reception of international law in domestic legal order
impact of judicial precedent 103–200
international law in the Constitution 102–3
status of international law
absence of hierarchy 100
case law 101–2
constitutional law 98–100
customary international law 101
human rights 100
Supreme Court practice
determination of fundamental rights 97
impact of judicial precedent 97–98, 103–200
limited engagement with international law 115–16
State practice
see also **customary international law; subsequent practice**
Albania 204–5
Canada 158
England and Wales 241–42
ICJ as source of law 7–8
South Africa 50–52
Sri Lanka 101, 105, 115
status of international law
see also **international treaties**
Albania
constitutional law 189
hierarchical status 189
ratification of treaties 189–90
Belgium 211–12
Canada
customary international law 147–50
international treaties 145–47
judicial notice of international law 144–45
presumption of conformity 150
domestic and international judges compared 5–6
ILA Final Report 10–11
Israel
customary international law 79
greater openness under Barak 80
Sri Lanka
absence of hierarchy 100
case law 101–2
constitutional law 98–100
customary international law 101
human rights 100
Switzerland
Constitutionally determined hierarchy 274
hierarchy of non-mandatory international norms 274–75
highly controversial issues 273
monist approach 273–74
UNMIK Regulations
legal nature 252–53
relationship with domestic law 253–55

subsequent practice 303, 326
Switzerland
alignment techniques and strategies
consistent interpretation 280–83
exception to Schubert Practice 284–85
muddled approach to non-aligned constitutional law 285–88
overview 280
Schubert Practice 283–84, 289–90
avoidance techniques and strategies
justiciability of international norms 278–79
reluctance to accept international obligations 277–78
court practice
alignment techniques and strategies 280–85
avoidance techniques and strategies 277–79
key issue of predictability 271–72
muddled approach to non-aligned constitutional law 285–88
difficulties with new constitutional norms and their implementation 288–89
focus on norms 273
muddled approach to non-aligned constitutional law 285–88
overview of key points 272–73
role of judiciary
application of federal acts and international law 276
limitations on rights of appeal 276
rule of *in dubio pro populo* 275
safeguarding of constitutional value 289
status of international law
Constitutionally determined hierarchy 274
hierarchy of non-mandatory international norms 274–75
highly controversial issues 273
monist approach 273–74
strategies determined by variety of hard and soft factors 271

transformation *see* **dualism**
treaties *see* **international treaties**

UN human rights treaty monitoring bodies
acknowledgement 310
court practice
ILA overview 294–95
postures of alignment 295–98
postures of avoidance 300–1
postures of contestation 299–300
incremental response to UN expectations 308–9
normative basis of judicial engagement
obligations under domestic law 302–3
obligations under international law law 303–4
overview 301–2
overview of key points 293–94
persuasiveness as normative basis for judicial engagement
concept of persuasiveness 305–6
factors constituting persuasiveness 306–8
overview 304
UN sanctions
alignment-*cum* contestation 358–61
apparent alignment 361–62
importance of *Ahmed* 365–67
legal basis for adoption 352–54
legal hierarchy 355–56
United States
avoidance of IHL
deference to executive 340–42
United States Targeted Killings Case 338–39
court practice
alignment 172–79
avoidance 170–72
contestation 180–84
overview of general practices 184–85
domestic alignment with IHL norms 343–45
modes of reception and application of international law
constitutional interpretation 167
constitutional law 165–66
judicial doctrine 166–67
statutory interpretation 167
three broad factors 167–70